The IDG Books Bible Advantage

The *UNIX Webmaster Bible* is part of the Bible series brought to you by IDG Books Worldwide. We designed Bibles to meet your growing need for quick access to the most complete and accurate computer information available.

Bibles work the way you do: They focus on accomplishing specific tasks — not learning random functions. These books are not long-winded manuals or dry reference tomes. In Bibles, expert authors tell you exactly what you can do with your software and how to do it. Easy to follow, step-by-step sections; comprehensive coverage; and convenient access in language and design — it's all here.

The authors of Bibles are uniquely qualified to give you expert advice as well as insightful tips and techniques not found anywhere else. Our authors maintain close contact with end users through feedback from articles, training sessions, e-mail exchanges, user group participation, and consulting work. Because our authors know the realities of daily computer use and are directly tied to the reader, our Bibles have a strategic advantage.

Bible authors have the experience to approach a topic in the most efficient manner, and we know that you, the reader, will benefit from a "one-on-one" relationship with the author. Our research shows that readers make computer book purchases because they want expert advice on a product. Readers want to benefit from the author's experience, so the author's voice is always present in a Bible series book.

In addition, the author is free to include or recommend useful software in a Bible. The software that accompanies a Bible is not intended to be casual filler but is linked to the content, theme, or procedures of the book. We know that you will benefit from the included software.

You will find what you need in this book whether you read it from cover to cover, section by section, or simply one topic at a time. As a computer user, you deserve a comprehensive resource of answers. We at IDG Books Worldwide are proud to deliver that resource with the *UNIX Webmaster Bible*.

Brenda McLaughlin
Vice President and Group Publisher
Internet: YouTellUs@IDGBooks.com

UNIX®
WEBMASTER
BIBLE

UNIX®
WEBMASTER
BIBLE

by Naba Barkakati

IDG Books Worldwide, Inc.
An International Data Group Company

Foster City, CA ◆ Chicago, IL ◆ Indianapolis, IN ◆ Southlake, TX

UNIX® Webmaster Bible

Published by
IDG Books Worldwide, Inc.
An International Data Group Company
919 E. Hillsdale Blvd.
Suite 400
Foster City, CA 94404
www.idgbooks.com (IDG Books Worldwide Web Site)

Library of Congress Catalog Card No.: 96-78310

ISBN: 0-7645-3016-X

Printed in the United States of America

10 9 8 7 6 5 4 3 2 1

1B/RV/RQ/ZW/IN

Distributed in the United States by IDG Books Worldwide, Inc.

Distributed by Macmillan Canada for Canada; by Contemporanea de Ediciones for Venezuela; by Distribuidora Cuspide for Argentina; by CITEC for Brazil; by Ediciones ZETA S.C.R. Ltda. for Peru; by Editorial Limusa SA for Mexico; by Transworld Publishers Limited in the United Kingdom and Europe; by Academic Bookshop for Egypt; by Levant Distributors S.A.R.L. for Lebanon; by Al Jassim for Saudi Arabia; by Simron Pty. Ltd. for South Africa; by Pustak Mahal for India; by The Computer Bookshop for India; by Toppan Company Ltd. for Japan; by Addison Wesley Publishing Company for Korea; by Longman Singapore Publishers Ltd. for Singapore, Malaysia, Thailand, and Indonesia; by Unalis Corporation for Taiwan; by WS Computer Publishing Company, Inc. for the Philippines; by WoodsLane Pty. Ltd. for Australia; by WoodsLane Enterprises Ltd. for New Zealand. Authorized Sales Agent: Anthony Rudkin Associates for the Middle East and North Africa.

For general information on IDG Books Worldwide's books in the U.S., please call our Consumer Customer Service department at 800-762-2974. For reseller information, including discounts and premium sales, please call our Reseller Customer Service department at 800-434-3422.

For information on where to purchase IDG Books Worldwide's books outside the U.S., please contact our International Sales department at 415-655-3172 or fax 415-655-3295.

For information on foreign language translations, please contact our Foreign & Subsidiary Rights department at 415-655-3021 or fax 415-655-3281.

For sales inquiries and special prices for bulk quantities, please contact our Sales department at 415-655-3200 or write to the address above.

For information on using IDG Books Worldwide's books in the classroom or for ordering examination copies, please contact our Educational Sales department at 800-434-2086 or fax 817-251-8174.

For authorization to photocopy items for corporate, personal, or educational use, please contact Copyright Clearance Center, 222 Rosewood Drive, Danvers, MA 01923, or fax 508-750-4470.

 is a trademark under exclusive license to IDG Books Worldwide, Inc., from International Data Group, Inc.

About the Author

Naba Barkakati is an expert programmer and successful computer book author with experience in a wide variety of systems from MS-DOS and Windows to UNIX and the X Window System. He bought his first personal computer — an IBM PC-AT — in 1984 after graduating with a Ph.D. degree in electrical engineering from University of Maryland at College Park, Maryland. While pursuing a full-time career in engineering, Naba dreamed of writing software for the emerging PC software market. As luck would have it, instead of building a software empire like Microsoft, he ended up writing *The Waite Group's Microsoft C Bible* — one of the first 1,000-page tutorial-reference books that set a new trend in the computer book publishing industry.

Over the past eight years, Naba has written 20 computer books on a number of topics ranging from Windows programming with Visual C++ to Linux. He is the author of several best-selling titles such as *The Waite Group's Turbo C++ Bible*, *Object-Oriented Programming in C++*, *X Window System Programming*, *Visual C++ Developer's Guide*, and *Borland C++ 4 Developer's Guide*. His books have been translated into French, Dutch, Polish, Greek, Japanese, Chinese, and Korean. Naba's latest book is *Linux SECRETS* published by IDG Books in February 1996.

Naba lives in North Potomac, Maryland, with his wife, Leha, and their children, Ivy, Emily, and Ashley.

Welcome to the world of IDG Books Worldwide.

IDG Books Worldwide, Inc., is a subsidiary of International Data Group, the world's largest publisher of computer-related information and the leading global provider of information services on information technology. IDG was founded more than 25 years ago and now employs more than 8,500 people worldwide. IDG publishes more than 270 computer publications in over 75 countries (see listing below). More than 90 million people read one or more IDG publications each month.

Launched in 1990, IDG Books Worldwide is today the #1 publisher of best-selling computer books in the United States. We are proud to have received eight awards from the Computer Press Association in recognition of editorial excellence and three from *Computer Currents'* First Annual Readers' Choice Awards. Our best-selling ...For Dummies® series has more than 25 million copies in print with translations in 30 languages. IDG Books Worldwide, through a joint venture with IDG's Hi-Tech Beijing, became the first U.S. publisher to publish a computer book in the People's Republic of China. In record time, IDG Books Worldwide has become the first choice for millions of readers around the world who want to learn how to better manage their businesses.

Our mission is simple: Every one of our books is designed to bring extra value and skill-building instructions to the reader. Our books are written by experts who understand and care about our readers. The knowledge base of our editorial staff comes from years of experience in publishing, education, and journalism — experience which we use to produce books for the '90s. In short, we care about books, so we attract the best people. We devote special attention to details such as audience, interior design, use of icons, and illustrations. And because we use an efficient process of authoring, editing, and desktop publishing our books electronically, we can spend more time ensuring superior content and spend less time on the technicalities of making books.

You can count on our commitment to deliver high-quality books at competitive prices on topics you want to read about. At IDG Books Worldwide, we continue in the IDG tradition of delivering quality for more than 25 years. You'll find no better book on a subject than one from IDG Books Worldwide.

John J. Kilcullen

John Kilcullen
President and CEO
IDG Books Worldwide, Inc.

IDG Books Worldwide, Inc., is a subsidiary of International Data Group, the world's largest publisher of computer-related information and the leading global provider of information services on information technology. International Data Group publishes over 276 computer publications in over 75 countries. Ninety million people read one or more International Data Group publications each month. International Data Group's publications include: **ARGENTINA:** Annuario de Informatica, Computerworld Argentina, PC World Argentina; **AUSTRALIA:** Australian Macworld, Client/Server Journal, Computer Living, Computerworld, Computerworld 100, Digital News, IT Casebook, Network World Australia, PC World, Publishing Essentials, Reseller, WebMaster; **AUSTRIA:** Computerwelt Osterreich, Networks Austria, PC Tip; **BELARUS:** PC World Belarus; **BELGIUM:** Data News; **BRAZIL:** Annuário de Informática, Computerworld Brazil, Connections, Super Game Power, Macworld, PC Player, PC World Brazil, Publish Brazil, Reseller News; **BULGARIA:** Computerworld Bulgaria, Networkworld/Bulgaria, PC & MacWorld Bulgaria; **CANADA:** CIO Canada, Client/Server World, ComputerWorld Canada, InfoCanada, Network World Canada; **CHILE:** Computerworld Chile, PC World Chile; **COLOMBIA:** Computerworld Colombia, PC World Colombia; **COSTA RICA:** PC World Centro America; **THE CZECH AND SLOVAK REPUBLICS:** Computerworld Czechoslovakia, Elektronika Czechoslovakia, Macworld Czech Republic, PC World Czechoslovakia; **DENMARK:** Communications World, Computerworld Danmark, Macworld Danmark, PC Privat Danmark, PC World Danmark, PC World Danmark Supplements, TECH World; **DOMINICAN REPUBLIC:** PC World Republica Dominicana; **ECUADOR:** PC World Ecuador; **EGYPT:** Computerworld Middle East, PC World Middle East; **EL SALVADOR:** PC World Centro America; **FINLAND:** MikroPC, Tietoverkko, Tietoviikko; **FRANCE:** Distributique, Golden, Hebdo-Distributique, Info PC, Le Guide du Monde Informatique, Le Monde Informatique, Reseaux & Telecoms; **GERMANY:** Computer Partner, Computerwoche, Computerwoche Extra, Computerwoche Focus, I/M Information Management, Macwelt, PC Welt; **GREECE:** GamePro, Multimedia World; **GUATEMALA:** PC World Centro America; **HONDURAS:** PC World Centro America; **HONG KONG:** Computerworld Hong Kong, PCWorld Hong Kong, Publish in Asia; **HUNGARY:** ABCD CD-ROM, Computerworld Szamitastechnika, PC & Mac World Hungary, PC-X Magazine; **ICELAND:** Tolvuheimur/PC World Island; **INDIA:** Information Systems Computerworld, PC World India, Publish in Asia; **INDONESIA:** InfoKomputer PC World, Komputek Computerworld, Publish in Asia; **IRELAND:** ComputerScope, PC Live!; **ISRAEL:** People & Computers; **ITALY:** Computerworld Italia, Computerworld Italia Special Editions, Macworld Italia, Networking Italia, PC Shopping, PC World Italia, PC World/Walt Disney; **JAPAN:** DTP World, HP Open World Japan, Macworld Japan, Nikkei Personal Computing, Open World Japan, OS/2 World Japan, SunWorld Japan, Windows World Japan; **KENYA:** East African Computer News; **KOREA:** Hi-Tech Information/Computerworld, Macworld Korea, PC World Korea; **MACEDONIA:** PC World Macedonia; **MALAYSIA:** Computerworld Malaysia, PC World Malaysia, Publish in Asia; **MEXICO:** Computerworld Mexico, Macworld, PC World Mexico; **MYANMAR:** PC World Myanmar; **NETHERLANDS:** Computer! Totaal, LAN Magazine, LanWorld Buyers Guide, Macworld, Net Magazine, Totaal! Beurskrant; **NEW ZEALAND:** Absolute Beginner's Guide, Computer Buyer, Computer Industry Directory, Computerworld New Zealand, MTB, Network World, PC World New Zealand; **NICARAGUA:** PC World Centro America; **NIGERIA:** PC World Nigeria; **NORWAY:** Computerworld Norge, Computerworld Privat (Datamagasinet), CW Rapport Norge, IDG's KURSGUIDE, Macworld Norge, Multimediaworld, PC World Ekspress, PC World Nettverk, PC World Norge, PC World's Produktguide, Windows World Spesial; **PAKISTAN:** Computerworld Pakistan, PC World Pakistan; **PANAMA:** PC World Panama; **P. R. OF CHINA:** China Computer Users, China Computerworld, China Infoworld, China Telecom World Weekly, Computer & Communication, Electronic Design China, Electronics Today, Electronics Weekly, Game Camp, Game Soft, Network World China, PC World China, Popular Computer Weekly, Software Weekly, Software World, Telecom World; **PERU:** Computerworld Peru, PC World Profesional Peru, PC World Peru; **PHILIPPINES:** Computerworld Philippines, PC World Philippines, Publish in Asia; **POLAND:** Computerworld Poland, Computerworld Special Report, Macworld, Networld, PC World Komputer; **PORTUGAL:** Cerebro/PC World, Computerworld/Correio Informático, Dealer World Portugal, MacIn/PCIn, Multimedia World Portugal; **PUERTO RICO:** PC World Puerto Rico; **ROMANIA:** Computerworld Romania, PC World Romania, Telecom Romania; **RUSSIA:** Computerworld Russia, Mir PK, Sety; **SINGAPORE:** Computerworld Singapore, PC World Singapore, Publish in Asia; **SLOVENIA:** MONITOR; **SOUTH AFRICA:** Computing S.A., InfoWorld S.A., Network World S.A., Software World; **SPAIN:** Computerworld España, COMUNICACIONES WORLD, Dealer World, Macworld España, PC World España; **SWEDEN:** CAP&Design, Computer Sweden, Corporate Computing, MacWorld, Maxi Data, MikroDatorn, Natverk & Kommunikation, PC/Aktiv, PC World, Windows World; **SWITZERLAND:** Computerworld Schweiz, Macworld Schweiz, PCtip; **TAIWAN:** Computerworld Taiwan, Macworld Taiwan, PC World Taiwan, Publish Taiwan, Windows World; **THAILAND:** Thai Computerworld, PC World Thailand; **TURKEY:** Computerworld Turkiye, MACWORLD Turkiye, PC WORLD Turkiye; **UKRAINE:** Computerworld Kiev, Computers & Software, Multimedia World Ukraine, PC World Ukraine; **UNITED KINGDOM:** Acorn User, Amiga Action, Amiga Computing, Appletalk, Computing, GamePro, Macworld, Network News, Parents and Computers, PC Advisor, PC Home, PSX Pro UK, The WEB; **UNITED STATES:** Cable in the Classroom, CD Review, CIO Magazine, Computerworld, Computerworld Client/Server Journal, Digital Video Magazine, DOS World, Federal Computer Week, GamePro, InfoWorld, I-Way, JavaWorld, Macworld, Multimedia World, Netscape World Online, Network World, PC Entertainment, PC World, Publish, SunWorld Online, SWATPro Magazine, Video Event, WebMaster; **URUGUAY:** PC World Uruguay; **VENEZUELA:** Computerworld Venezuela, PC World Venezuela; and **VIETNAM:** PC World Vietnam.   7/16/96

Dedication

This book is dedicated to my wife Leha, and daughters Ivy, Emily, and Ashley.

Acknowledgments

I am grateful to Greg Croy for providing me this opportunity to write a tutorial guide for the Webmaster. Erik Dafforn guided me through the manuscript submission process and kept everything moving. Gary Garcia took care of the development editing and ensured the consistency of the book's content. I appreciate the guidance and support all three of you have given me during this project.

I would like to thank Dennis Cox for reviewing the manuscript for technical accuracy and for providing many useful suggestions to improve the book's content.

Thanks to everyone at IDG Books who worked behind the scenes to transform my raw manuscript into this well-edited and beautifully packaged book. In particular, thanks to Nancy Albright, Judy Brunetti, Mary Ann Faughnan, Hank Moran, and Faithe Wempen for the thorough copy editing and Tracy Cramer for making the necessary arrangements for the book's companion CD-ROM.

I would like to thank Jonathan Gross (editor, WEBsmith magazine) for creating a copy of SSC's CD for use in this book. Thanks to SSC's Belinda Frazier for facilitating the provision of the CD.

Finally, my greatest thanks go to my wife Leha for her patience and understanding and for taking care of everything while I stayed glued to my PCs the last few months. As I wrap up the book, my daughters Ivy, Emily, and Ashley are tracking my progress and counting the days to the deadline. Thanks for being there!

(The Publisher would like to give special thanks to Patrick J. McGovern, without whom this book would not have been possible.)

Credits

Senior Vice President and Group Publisher
Brenda McLaughlin

Acquisitions Manager
Gregory S. Croy

Acquisitions Editor
Ellen L. Camm

Software Acquisitions Editor
Tracy Lehman Cramer

Marketing Manager
Melisa M. Duffy

Managing Editor
Andy Cummings

Administrative Assistant
Laura J. Moss

Editorial Assistant
Timothy J. Borek

Production Director
Beth Jenkins

Supervisor of Project Coordination
Cindy L. Phipps

Supervisor of Page Layout
Kathie S. Schutte

Supervisor of Graphics and Design
Shelley Lea

Production Systems Specialist
Debbie J. Gates

Project Coordinator
Valery Bourke

Senior Development Editor
Erik Dafforn

Associate Development Editor
Gary Garcia

Copy Edit Coordinator
Barry Childs-Helton

Copy Editors
Nancy Albright
Judy Brunetti
Mary Ann Faughnan
Hank Moran
Faithe Wempen

Technical Editor
Dennis Cox

CD-ROM Contractor
Specialized Systems Consultants, Inc.

Layout and Graphics
E. Shawn Aylsworth
Brett Black
Linda M. Boyer
J. Tyler Connor
Angela F. Hunckler
Drew R. Moore
Mark Owens
Anna Rohrer
Theresa Sánchez-Baker
Brent Savage
Kate Snell

Proofreaders
Nancy L. Reinhardt
Rachel Garvey
Dwight Ramsey
Robert Springer
Carrie Voorhis

Indexer
David Heiret

Production Administration
Tony Augsburger
Todd Klemme
Jason Marcuson
Jacalyn L. Pennywell
Leslie Popplewell
Patricia R. Reynolds
Theresa Sánchez-Baker
Melissa Stauffer
Bryan Stephenson

Contents at a Glance

Table of Contents

Introduction

The recent popularity of the Internet is primarily due to the World Wide Web, which makes it easy to access information residing on computers throughout the Internet. All that a user needs is a Web Browser — an application that downloads and displays Web documents — to begin enjoying the benefits of the Web. Of course, the magic of the Web is possible because of the Web sites around the world — these are computers running Web servers that make Web documents (or Web pages, as they are commonly called) available on demand.

The Web sites are set up and managed by a new breed of computer professionals — the *Webmasters*. The Webmaster is the person responsible for the care and feeding of a Web site. To do the job properly, a Webmaster has to be something of a cross between a system administrator, software developer, graphics designer, and salesperson. Most of all, the Webmaster has to learn the new world of the Internet, Web servers, Hypertext Transfer Protocol (HTTP), and Hypertext Markup Language (HTML).

When writing Web server applications, the Webmaster is a software developer. To help prepare the Web pages, the Webmaster has to be a graphics designer with a knack for the Hypertext Markup Language (HTML). Last, but not the least, the Webmaster has to be good at marketing because a Web site is of no use without users visiting it (and to get the users, the Webmaster has to promote the site).

Each Web site has at least one Webmaster and the number is growing fast. A significant factor contributing to the growth of Web sites is their use to publish information inside an enterprise. Businesses are using such internal Web sites to distribute information to the employees. Information published on a typical internal Web site includes employee information, company policies and procedures, upcoming events, job openings, and much more. Such internal Web sites are accessible only to users on a company's local area network (commonly referred to as an *intranet*).

When it comes to resources for the Webmaster, the Internet itself happens to be the biggest resource. Unfortunately, only an experienced Webmaster can easily locate the right information on the Net. There are books on individual topics such as HTML authoring or how to set up a Web server, but no single book addresses the needs of the Webmaster in a balanced manner. What the Webmaster needs is a guide that covers all major aspects of a Webmaster's job from setting up a Web server to writing Web applications in Java.

UNIX Webmaster Bible is a technical guide designed to address the Webmaster's needs. With its focus on security and database connectivity, this book is particularly useful to Intranet Webmasters. Because most of the Web sites run on UNIX systems using the NCSA or Apache HTTP server, the book showcases UNIX Internet tools. The unique aspects of *UNIX Webmaster Bible* are the tips, techniques, and shortcuts for using UNIX Internet tools to successfully publish information on the Web. In addition to providing tips and shortcuts for the Webmaster, the book includes a custom version of SSC's CD-ROM packed with freeware and shareware tools for the Webmaster.

By reading *UNIX Webmaster Bible*, you get the following benefits:

+ Receive a CD-ROM containing a plethora of UNIX utilities and files for the Webmaster
+ Learn the Webmaster's role
+ Get an overview of various Internet Information Services including FTP, GOPHER, WAIS, and Mail Servers
+ Learn about the World Wide Web
+ Learn how to install and set up NCSA, Apache, and CERN HTTP servers
+ Become familiar with system security and Internet firewalls
+ Get an overview of the Web publishing process from design to implementation
+ Learn HTML including HTML extensions supported by Netscape Navigator and Microsoft Internet Explorer
+ Learn to use Web authoring tools
+ Receive a tutorial introduction to the Common Gateway Interface (CGI)
+ Learn to write CGI programs in Perl, C, C++, and Tcl
+ Learn how to access relational databases through the Web
+ Understand the basics of Java programming
+ Learn JavaScript

Notational Style

UNIX Webmaster Bible uses a simple notational style. All listings are typeset in a monospace font for ease of reading. All file names, function names, variable names, and keywords appearing in text are are also in the same monospace font. The first occurrence of new terms and concepts are in *italic*. In listings with both user input and system output, text you are directed to type is in **boldface**.

Each chapter starts with a short list of all the neat things you learn in that chapter. The summary at the end of the chapter tells you a bit more about what the chapter covers.

Following the time-honored tradition of the IDG Books Bible series, I have used a number of icons to help you pinpoint useful information quickly:

Note   The Note icon marks a general interesting fact — something I thought you'd like to know.

Tip   This Tip icon marks things you can do to make your job simpler — hints that you can try.

Caution   The Caution icon marks warning messages. With this icon, I'm telling you: Watch out! This could hurt your system!

Webmaster   The Webmaster icon marks facts that are not well-documented but important for a Webmaster to know. It's not that no one knows this fact — it's just hard to find, and knowing this fact clears up many other questions you might have.

Cross Ref   The Cross Reference icon points out paragraphs that lead you to other chapters in the book for a deeper discussion of a topic.

URL   The URL icon points to one or more URLs that you can access on the Web for further information about a topic or to download interesting software. Although the book often mentions version numbers for software, you should visit the Web sites indicated by these URL icons to learn about the latest versions of various software.

Organization of the Book

UNIX Webmaster Bible has 24 chapters, organized into five parts, and four appendixes:

+ Part I: **Webmaster in Training** includes five chapters that cover the basics of the Internet and describe the various Internet information services such as FTP, GOPHER, WAIS, and USENET News typically found on any Internet host. The World Wide Web is introduced as the gateway to the Internet information services and Hypertext Transfer Protocol (HTTP) is briefly described. Part I also describes the role of a Webmaster.

+ Part II: **Getting Your Web Site Up and Running** has four chapters that provide step-by-step instructions on how to set up several popular Web servers for UNIX. Security and Internet firewalls are discussed in this part.

+ Part III: **Publishing on the Web** has nine chapters that show how to design Web pages and implement them using Hypertext Markup Language (HTML). This part also covers various Web authoring tools such as Internet Assistant for Microsoft Word and provides suggestions for promoting the Web site.

+ Part IV: **Developing Web Applications** includes four chapters that focus on the software development aspect of a Webmaster's job. This part shows how to use the Common Gateway Interface (CGI) to create interactive Web pages. Perl programming and use of other programming languages such as C, C++, and Tcl are also covered in this part. The last chapter in this part shows how to provide access to databases through the Web.

+ Part V: **Extending Web Applications** has two chapters. The first chapter provides an introduction to Java programming with some simple examples. The second chapter is devoted to JavaScript programming.

+ PartVI: **Appendixes**: The Appendixes summarize the Webmaster resources on the accompanying CD-ROM and provide a list of Webmaster resources on the Internet. Additionally, the Appendixes include a quick reference guide to HTML.

If you are a new Webmaster, you should proceed sequentially through the book. Those who are already knowledgeable about the Internet information services and the Web may begin with Part II where you learn how to install the Web server. Webmasters with specific Web authoring questions should go directly to a relevant chapter in Part III. Parts IV and V are meant for Webmasters who want to get started with developing Web applications using Perl, C, C++, and Java. For information about the companion CD-ROM, you should consult Appendix A.

It's time to get started on your Web adventure. Take out the companion CD-ROM and install Linux, if you need a UNIX system. Then, turn to a relevant chapter, and let the fun begin. Before you know it, you'll become an expert Webmaster!

I hope you enjoy reading this book as much as I enjoyed writing it!

Webmaster in Training

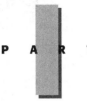

Internet Basics

The recent popularity of the Internet is primarily due to the World Wide Web (also called *Web* or *WWW*), which makes it easy to access information that resides on computers throughout the Internet. Although the Internet — a set of interconnected computer networks that spans the globe — has been around for quite a while, its benefits did not reach the masses until the Web came along in 1993.

Before the Web, you had to use arcane UNIX commands to access and use information available on the Internet. Now that you have the Web, you can enjoy the benefits of the Internet by using a Web browser — a graphical application that retrieves and displays Web documents. A click of the mouse is all it takes to go from reading a document to downloading a file through the File Transfer Protocol (FTP) — one of many Internet services. You can read news and even send mail from the Web browser.

The magic of the Web is possible because of the Web sites around the world. *Web sites* are the computers that run the Web servers that make Web pages (also called *Web documents*) available on demand.

Note *Webmasters* (a new breed of computer professionals) set up and manage the Web sites. The Webmaster is the person responsible for the care and feeding of a Web site. To do the job properly, a Webmaster must be a cross between a system administrator, software developer, graphics designer, and salesperson. Most of all, the Webmaster must learn about the new world of the Internet, Web servers, Hypertext Transfer Protocol (HTTP), and Hypertext Markup language (HTML).

Each Web site has at least one Webmaster and the number of Web sites is growing fast. A significant factor contributing to the growth of Web sites is the use of the Web to publish information inside an enterprise. Businesses are using such internal Web sites (called *intranets*) to distribute information to their employees. Information published on a typical internal Web site includes employee information, company policies and procedures, upcoming events, job openings, and much more.

This book's goal is to serve as a comprehensive source of technical information for the major aspects of a Webmaster's duties. Besides providing tips and shortcuts for the Webmaster, the book includes a CD-ROM packed with tools for the Webmaster. These tools include everything from the Linux operating system to a selection of Web servers that run under various UNIX systems.

Before you try to set up and configure a Web server, you need to understand the basics of the Internet and how various Internet services work. You don't have to become an expert on internetworking or UNIX, but you do have to understand the basics. The first part of this book includes five chapters that describe various Internet information services with an emphasis on the Web.

Cross Ref This chapter starts with an overview of the Internet. Then it explains the Transmission Control Protocol/Internet Protocol (TCP/IP) and how names and IP addresses identify computers. Chapter 2 introduces the Internet services such as FTP, Gopher, and the Wide Area Information Server (WAIS). Chapter 3 explains how the Web acts as a gateway to various Internet services. Chapter 4 provides a user's view of the Web — how the user accesses the Web through a Web browser. The last chapter of this part, Chapter 5, explains the multiple roles of the Webmaster.

Understanding the Internet

How you view the Internet depends on your perspective. As a user, you may see the Internet as a service provider. For example, you may already be familiar with electronic mail (or e-mail) and newsgroups — the mainstay of the Internet. E-mail enables you to exchange messages and documents with anyone on the Internet. The newsgroups provide a bulletin-board system that spans the globe.

Technically speaking, the Internet is a worldwide network of networks. The term *internet* (without capitalization) is a short form of *internetworking* — the interconnection of networks. The Internet Protocol (IP) was designed with the idea of connecting networks.

Physically, the Internet is similar to a network of highways and roads. This similarity has prompted the popular press to call the Internet the *Information Superhighway*. Just as the network of highways and roads includes some interstate highways, many state roads, and many more residential streets, the Internet has some very high-bandwidth networks (45-Mbps T3 backbones) and many lower-capacity networks (ranging from 28,800-bps dial-up connections to 1.5-Mbps T1 links). The high-bandwidth network constitutes the backbone of the Internet.

Unlike commercial online services (such as CompuServe and America Online), the Internet is neither run by a single organization, nor is it managed by any central computer. You can view the physical Internet as a network of networks managed collectively by hundreds of cooperating organizations. I know that a collection of networks managed by hundreds of organizations sounds amazing, but it works!

Note

Users view the Internet as a collection of common services such as:

✦ **Electronic mail (e-mail):** You can send e-mail to any other user on the Internet by using addresses such as president@whitehouse.gov.

✦ **Newsgroups:** You can read newsgroups and post news items to newsgroups with names such as `comp.os.linux.networking` or `comp.os.linux.setup`.

✦ **Information retrieval:** You can search for information with tools, such as `archie` and `gopher`, and browse information with a Web browser. You also can download files with File Transfer Protocol (FTP). Reciprocally, users on other systems also can download files from your system, typically through a feature called *anonymous FTP*.

✦ **Remote access:** You can use `telnet` to log into another computer (the remote computer) on the Internet, if you have access to that remote computer.

Chapter 2 further describes these Internet services and explains how they run on a UNIX system. The next few sections briefly describe how you typically use the Internet.

Exchanging e-mail

Most people use the Internet to keep in touch with friends, acquaintances, loved ones, and strangers through e-mail. If you have not used e-mail much, you may wonder why it is such a big deal. Even if you have used your company's internal e-mail system, you may not appreciate the convenience of Internet e-mail until you try it.

You can send a message to a friend on the other coast and get back a reply within a couple of minutes. Essentially, you can send a message anywhere in the world from an Internet host, and that message typically makes its way to the destination within minutes — something you cannot do with regular paper mail.

Because you can store and forward e-mail, you can arrange to send and receive e-mail without making your UNIX system a full-time host on the Internet. If your system is not a full-time Internet host, you won't get the benefits of immediate message delivery.

Participating in newsgroups

The Internet helps you communicate in many ways. With e-mail, you can exchange messages with people you already know. Sometimes, however, you may want to participate in group discussions. For example, if you need help in setting up an X Window System on a PC running Linux (Linux is a UNIX clone for 486 and Pentium PCs), you may want to ask anyone who knows about this subject. To speak with a knowledgeable source, you can post a message on the appropriate Internet newsgroup; someone is likely to give you an answer.

The Internet newsgroups are like the bulletin boards or forums on other online systems (such as CompuServe and America Online). You'll find a wide variety of newsgroups that cover subjects ranging from politics to computers. Think of the Internet newsgroups as gathering places — virtual meeting places where you can ask questions and discuss various issues.

Locating and browsing information

You may already have experienced sharing files among computers on a LAN (local area network). Typically, a LAN has a server, and any user on the LAN can access and use the information in the files stored on that server.

The Internet (a collection of interconnected networks) also allows the Internet hosts (the computers on the Internet) to share information by using a variety of protocols. For example, the File Transfer Protocol (FTP) specifies how to select and download files from another computer on the Internet. You use FTP to download software from the Internet.

Note   Another, more recent information-sharing protocol is the Hypertext Transfer Protocol (HTTP). It allows computers to exchange documents formatted in the Hypertext Markup Language (HTML). HTML and HTTP form the foundation of the World Wide Web, where you can look at documents maintained on other computers on the Internet. You learn more about World Wide Web in Chapters 3 and 4.

Networking Basics

To understand the Internet, you need to understand networking. Like any other technical subject, networking is full of terminology and jargon that a newcomer may find daunting. This section introduces some basic concepts of networking, starting with a layered model of networking and proceeding to details of TCP/IP network protocols.

The OSI seven-layer model

A commonly used conceptual model of networking is the seven-layer Open Systems Interconnection (OSI) reference model, developed by the International Standards Organization (ISO). The OSI reference model describes the flow of data between the physical connection to the network and the end-user application. Each layer is responsible for providing particular functionality, as shown in Figure 1-1.

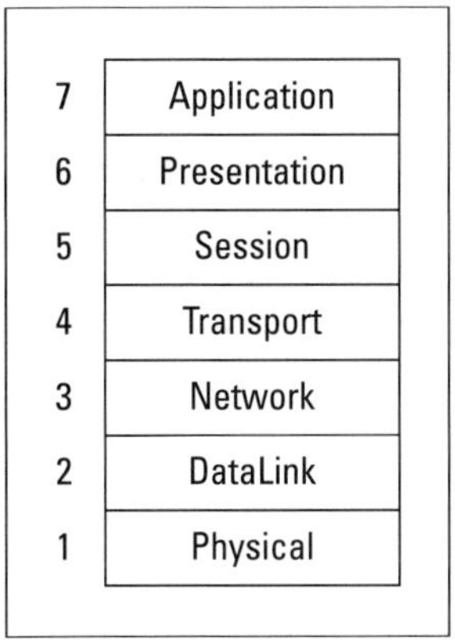

7	Application
6	Presentation
5	Session
4	Transport
3	Network
2	DataLink
1	Physical

Figure 1-1: An OSI seven-layer reference model of networking.

As Figure 1-1 shows, the OSI layers are numbered from bottom to top. Basic functions (such as physically sending data bits through the network cable) are at the bottom, and functions that deal with higher-level abstractions of the data are at the top. The purpose of each layer is to provide services to the next-higher layer in a manner such that the higher layer does not have to know how the services are actually implemented.

The purposes of the seven layers in the OSI reference model are as follows:

✦ The *physical layer* transmits raw bits of data across the physical medium (the networking cable or electromagnetic waves, in case of wireless networks). This layer carries the data generated by all the higher layers. The physical layer deals with the following three physical components:

- *Network topology* (such as bus or star), which specifies how various nodes of a network are physically connected

- *Transmission medium* (such as RG-58 coaxial cable, shielded or unshielded twisted pair, fiber-optic cable, and microwave), which carries the actual signals representing data

- *Transmission technique* (such as Carrier Sense Multiple Access with Collision Detection [CSMA/CD], used by Ethernet; and token-based techniques, used by Token-Ring and Fiber Distributed Data Interface [FDDI]), which defines the hardware protocols for data transfer

✦ The *data-link layer* deals with logical packets (or *frames*) of data. This layer packages raw bits from the physical layer into frames, the exact format of which depends on the type of network (such as Ethernet or Token Ring). The frames used by the data-link layer contain the physical addresses of the sender and the receiver of data.

✦ The *network layer* knows about the logical network addresses and how to translate logical addresses to physical ones. At the sending end, the network layer converts larger logical packets to smaller physical data frames. At the receiving end, the network layer reassembles the data frames into their original logical packet structure.

✦ The *transport layer* is responsible for the reliable delivery of messages that originate at the application layer. At the sending end, this layer divides long messages into several packets. At the receiving end, the transport layer reassembles the original messages and sends an acknowledgment of receipt. The transport layer also checks to make sure that it has received data in correct order and on time. In case of errors, the transport layer requests retransmission of data.

✦ The *session layer* allows applications on different computers to initiate, use, and terminate a connection (or *session*). The session layer translates the names of systems to appropriate addresses (for example, IP addresses in TCP/IP networks).

✦ The *presentation layer* manages the format used to exchange data between networked computers. Data encryption and decryption, for example, would be in this layer. Most network protocols do not have a presentation layer.

✦ The *application layer* is the gateway through which application processes access network services. This layer represents services (such as file transfers, database access, and electronic mail) that directly support applications.

The OSI model is not specific to any hardware or software; it simply provides an architectural framework and gives us a common terminology for discussing various networking capabilities.

A simplified four-layer network model

The OSI seven-layer model is not a specification; it provides guidelines for organizing all network services. Most implementations adopt a layered model for networking services, and you can map these layered models to the OSI reference model. A simplified model, for example, can adequately represent the TCP/IP networking model.

Network-aware applications usually deal with the top three layers (session, presentation, and application) of the OSI seven-layer reference model. Thus, you can combine these three layers into a single layer called the *application layer*.

You also can combine the bottom two layers of the OSI model — physical and data link — into a single physical layer. These combinations result in a simplified four-layer model, as shown in Figure 1-2.

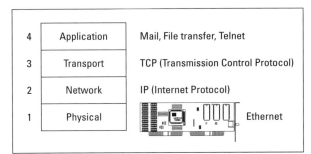

Figure 1-2: A simplified four-layer networking model.

At each of these layers, information is exchanged through one of many network protocols.

Network protocols

Note A *network protocol* refers to a detailed process agreed upon by the sender and receiver for exchanging data at a specific layer of the networking model. Thus, you can see the following protocols in the simplified four-layer network model of Figure 1-2:

✦ Physical-layer protocols such as Ethernet, Token Ring, and FDDI

✦ Network-layer protocols such as the Internet Protocol (IP), which is part of the TCP/IP protocol suite

✦ Transport-layer protocols such as the Transmission Control Protocol (TCP) and User Datagram Protocol (UDP), which are part of the TCP/IP protocol suite

✦ Application-layer protocols such as File Transfer Protocol (FTP), Simple Mail Transfer Protocol (SMTP), Domain Name Service (DNS), `telnet`, and Simple Network Management Protocol (SNMP) that also are part of the TCP/IP protocol suite

Note The term *protocol suite* refers to a collection of two or more protocols from these layers that form the basis of a network. Some of the well-known protocol suites are as follows:

✦ IPX/SPX (Internet Packet Exchange/Sequenced Packet Exchange) protocol suite, used by Novell NetWare

✦ NetBIOS and NetBEUI (Network BIOS Extended User Interface)

✦ TCP/IP protocol suite

Note Of these protocol suites, you want the TCP/IP protocol suite, because that's what UNIX systems support well. TCP/IP networking is practically synonymous with UNIX.

TCP/IP and the Internet

TCP/IP has become the protocol of choice on the Internet — the "network of networks." TCP/IP evolved from ARPAnet — a packet-switching network that evolved from research initiated by the U.S. Government's Advanced Research Projects Agency (ARPA) in the 1970s. Subsequently, ARPA acquired a *Defense* prefix and became DARPA. Under the auspices of DARPA, the TCP/IP protocols emerged as a popular collection of protocols for *internetworking* — a term used to describe communication among networks.

 Note TCP/IP has flourished for several reasons. A significant reason is that the protocol is an *open protocol,* which means that the technical descriptions of the protocol appear in public documents, so anyone can implement TCP/IP software.

Another, more important reason for TCP/IP's success is the availability of sample implementation. Rather than describe network architecture and protocols on paper, each component of the TCP/IP protocol suite begins life as a specification with a sample implementation.

RFCs

 Tip Documents known as Request for Comments (RFCs) describe the details of each TCP/IP protocol. You can acquire these documents from the Internet. You can get the RFCs from `ftp://rs.internic.net/rfc`.

More on TCP/IP

Although this chapter gives you a detailed overview of TCP/IP networking, a single chapter simply isn't enough to provide all available information about TCP/IP. For more information on how to set up, configure, and use TCP/IP, consult one of the following books:

✦ Douglas E. Comer, *Internetworking with TCP/IP: Principles, Protocols, and Architecture,* Prentice Hall, 1988

✦ Evi Nemeth, Garth Snyder, Scott Seebass, and Trent R. Hein, *UNIX System Administration Handbook, Second Edition,* Prentice Hall, 1995

✦ W. Richard Stevens, *UNIX Network Programming,* Prentice Hall, 1990

✦ Matthew Naugle, *Network Protocol Handbook,* McGraw-Hill, 1994

In fact, this notation of uniformly naming Internet resources is itself documented in an RFC. The notation, called the *Uniform Resource Locator (URL),* is described in RFC 1630, "Universal Resource Identifiers in WWW," written by T. Berners-Lee, the originator of the World Wide Web (WWW).

Think of RFCs as being the working papers of the Internet research-and-development community. All Internet standards are published as RFCs. Many RFCs do not specify any standards, however; they are informational documents only.

Important RFCs

Following are some of the RFCs that you may find interesting:

RFC 768, "User Datagram Protocol (UDP)"

RFC 791, "Internet Protocol (IP)"

RFC 792, "Internet Control Message Protocol (ICMP)"

RFC 793, "Transmission Control Protocol (TCP)"

RFC 821, "Simple Mail Transfer Protocol (SMTP)"

RFC 822, "Format for Electronic Mail Messages"

RFC 950, "IP Subnet Extension"

RFC 959, "File Transfer Protocol (FTP)"

RFC 1034, "Domain Names: Concepts and Facilities"

RFC 1058, "Routing Information Protocol (RIP)"

RFC 1112, "Internet Group Multicast Protocol (IGMP)"

RFC 1155, "Structure of Management Information (SMI)"

RFC 1157, "Simple Network Management Protocol (SNMP)"

RFC 1310, "The Internet Standards Process"

RFC 1519, "Classless Inter-Domain Routing (CIDR) Assignment and Aggregation Strategy"

RFC 1521, "Multipurpose Internet Mail Extensions (MIME)"

RFC 1583, "Open Shortest Path First Routing V2 (OSPF2)"

RFC 1597, "Address Allocation for Private Internets"

RFC 1625, "WAIS over Z39.50-1988"

RFC 1661, "Point-to-Point Protocol (PPP)"

RFC 1725, "Post Office Protocol, Version 3 (POP3)"

RFC 1738, "Uniform Resource Locators (URL)"

RFC 1739, "A Primer on Internet and TCP/IP Tools"

RFC 1796, "Not All RFCs Are Standards"

RFC 1855, "Netiquette Guidelines"

(continued)

(continued)

RFC 1866, "Hypertext Markup Language — 2.0"

RFC 1886, "DNS Extensions to support IP Version 6"

RFC 1883, "Internet Protocol, Version 6 (IPv6) Specification"

RFC 1880, "Internet Official Protocol Standards"

RFC 1884, "IP Version 6 Addressing Architecture"

RFC 1918, "Address Allocation for Private Internets"

Tip   The RFCs continue to evolve as new technology and techniques emerge. As a Webmaster, you should keep an eye on the RFCs to monitor emerging networking protocols.

IP addresses

When you have many computers on a network, you need a way to identify each one uniquely. In TCP/IP networking, the *IP address* is the computer address. Because TCP/IP deals with internetworking, the address is based on the concept of a network address and a host address. Think of a network address and a host address as two addresses that uniquely identify a computer:

✦ The *network address* indicates the network on which the computer is located.

✦ The *host address* identifies the computer on that network.

Thus, the complete IP address uniquely identifies any computer on any network that's part of the Internet.

Dotted-decimal addresses

The IP address is a 4-byte (32-bit) value (although the next-generation IP addresses will be 16-byte values). The convention is to write each byte as a decimal value and to put a dot (.) after each number. Thus, you see network addresses such as 140.90.23.100. This way of writing IP addresses is called *dotted-decimal* notation.

Address classes

You can interpret the bits in an IP address as follows:

```
<Network Address, Host Address>
```

In other words, a specified number of bits of the 32-bit IP address is a network address; the rest of the bits are a host address. The host address identifies a computer, whereas the network address identifies the LAN to which that computer is connected.

To accommodate networks of various sizes (the network size is the number of computers in that network), the IP address includes the concept of several classes of network. Figure 1-3 shows the five classes of IP addresses (named Class A through Class E).

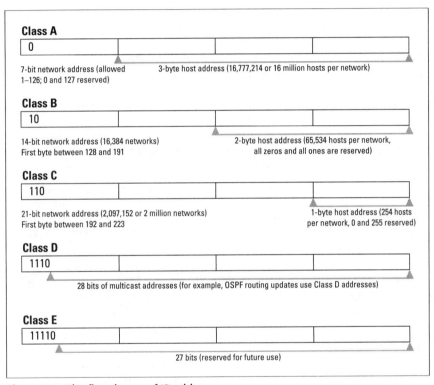

Figure 1-3: The five classes of IP addresses.

Of the five address classes, only Classes A, B, and C are used for addressing networks and hosts; Class D and E addresses are reserved for special use.

Note Class A addresses support 126 networks, each with up to 16 million hosts. Although the network address is 7-bit, two values (0 and 127) have special meaning; therefore, you can have only 1 through 126 as Class A network addresses.

Note Class B addresses are for networks with up to 65,534 hosts. You can have, at most, 16,384 Class B networks.

Note Class C addresses are for small organizations. Each Class C address allows up to 254 hosts, and approximately 2 million Class C networks can exist. If you are in a small company, you may have one of the Class C addresses.

You can tell the class of an IP address by the first number in the dotted-decimal notation, as follows:

✦ Class A addresses: 1.xxx.xxx.xxx through 126.xxx.xxx.xxx

✦ Class B addresses: 128.xxx.xxx.xxx through 191.xxx.xxx.xxx

✦ Class C addresses: 192.xxx.xxx.xxx through 223.xxx.xxx.xxx

Even within the five address classes, the following IP addresses have special meaning:

✦ An address with all zeros in the network portion of the address signifies the local network — the network where the message with this IP address originated. Thus, the address 0.0.0.200 means host number 200 on this Class C network.

✦ The Class A address 127.xxx.xxx.xxx is used for *loopback* — communications within the same host. Conventionally, 127.0.0.1 is used as the loopback address. Processes that need to communicate through TCP with other processes on the same host use the loopback address to avoid having to send packets out on the network.

✦ Turning on all the bits in any part of the address means a broadcast message. The address 128.18.255.255, for example, includes all hosts on the Class B network 128.18. The address 255.255.255.255 is known as a limited broadcast; all workstations on the current network will receive the packet.

IP address requests

If you want to set up your own independent network that will provide access to the Internet, you will need unique IP addresses for your network. IP addresses are administered through the Network Information Center (NIC), at the following address:

Network Solutions
InterNIC Registration Services
505 Huntmar Park Drive
Herndon, VA 22070
Phone: (703) 742-4777
Fax: (703) 742-4811

If you get Internet access through an Internet Service Provider (ISP), do not worry about getting IP addresses for your systems; your ISP will provide the necessary IP addresses.

Tip If you already have Internet access, you can get the application forms (for IP address) from `ftp://rs.internic.net/templates`.

Download the appropriate application form (the form depends on whether your network is in the United States, Europe, or Asia), fill it in, and mail it to `netreg@internic.net`.

If you have Internet access and a Web browser, you can browse more information about InterNIC at the address `http://rs.internic.net/`.

Cross Ref The Internet has grown explosively. IP addresses are in great demand, and now you must explain to the NIC why you need a network address (even if it's only a Class C address). Today, acquiring IP addresses is nearly impossible. The NIC encourages you to get the necessary IP addresses from the ISP at the same time you connect your network to the Internet. Chapter 6 tells you more about connecting your network to the Internet through an ISP.

Until recently, anyone could get an IP address for free. Due to a recent change, however, you must pay a yearly fee of $50 (U.S.) for your network's IP address.

Tip If you do not plan to connect your network to the Internet, you do not need a unique IP address. RFC 1597 ("Address Allocation for Private Networks") provides guidance on what IP addresses you can use within *private networks* (any network that's not connected to the Internet). Three blocks of IP addresses are reserved for private networks:

 ✦ 10.0.0.0 to 10.255.255.255

 ✦ 172.16.0.0 to 172.16.255.255

 ✦ 192.168.0.0 to 192.168.255.255

You can use addresses from these blocks for your private network without having to coordinate with any organization.

Next-generation IP (IPv6)

When the 4-byte IP address was created, the total number of addresses supported by a 4-byte address seemed to be adequate. By now, however, Class A and Class B addresses are running out, and Class C addresses are depleting at a fast rate. In addition, the proliferation of Class C addresses has introduced a unique problem. Each Class C network needs an entry in the *network routing tables* — the tables that contain information on how to locate any network in the Internet. (Class A and B networks also need entries in routing tables, but only 126 Class A and 16,384 Class B networks exist, compared to approximately 2 million possible Class C networks.) Too many Class C addresses means too many entries in the routing tables. The Internet Engineering Task Force (IETF) recognized this problem in 1991, at which time work began on the next-generation IP addressing scheme (called *IPng*) which was to eventually replace the old 4-byte addressing scheme (called *IPv4,* for IP Version 4).

Note The IETF proposed and debated several alternative addressing schemes. The final contender, with a 128-bit (16-byte) address, was called *IPv6* (for IP Version 6). The latest news is that the IETF declared the core set of IPv6 addressing protocols to be an IETF Proposed Standard on September 18, 1995.

The IPv6 is designed to be an evolutionary step from IPv4. The proposed standard provides direct interoperability between hosts by using the older IPv4 addresses and any new IPv6 hosts. The idea is that users can upgrade their systems to use IPv6 when they want and that network operators are free to upgrade their network hardware to use IPv6 without affecting current users of IPv4.

Network mask

The *network mask* is an IP address that has 1s in the bits that correspond to the network address and 0s in all other bit positions. The class of your network address determines the network mask.

 Note If you have a Class C address, for example, the network mask is 255.255.255.0. Thus, Class B networks have a network mask of 255.255.0.0, and Class A networks have 255.0.0.0 as the network mask.

Network address

The *network address* is the bitwise-AND of the network mask with any IP address in your network. If the IP address of a system on your network is 206.197.168.200, and the network mask is 255.255.255.0, the network address is 206.197.168.0. As you may have noticed, the network address has a zero in the host-address area. When you request an IP address from NIC, you get a network address.

Subnets

If your site has a Class B address, you get one network number, and that network can have up to 65,534 hosts. Even if you work for a large corporation that has thousands of hosts, you may want to divide your network into smaller subnetworks (or *subnets*). If your organization has offices in several locations, for example, you may want each office to be on a separate network. You can do this by taking some bits from the host-address portion of the IP address and assigning those bits to the network address. This procedure is known as *defining a subnet mask*.

Essentially, you add more bits to the network mask. If you have a Class B network, for example, the network mask would be 255.255.0.0. Then, if you decide to divide your network into 128 subnetworks (each of which has 512 hosts), you would designate 7 bits from the host address space as the subnet address. Thus, the subnet mask becomes 255.255.254.0.

TCP/IP routing

Routing refers to the task of forwarding information from one network to another. Consider the two Class C networks 206.197.168.0 and 164.109.10.0. You need a routing device to send packets from one of these networks to the other.

Webmaster Because a routing device facilitates data exchange between two networks, it has two physical network connections, one on each network. Each network interface has its own IP address, and the routing device essentially passes packets back and forth between the two network interfaces. Figure 1-4 illustrates how a routing device has a physical presence in two networks and how each network interface has its own IP address.

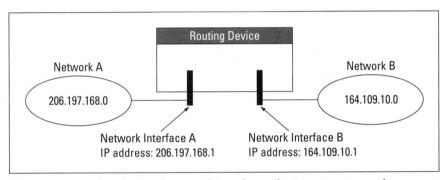

Figure 1-4: A routing device allows packet exchange between two networks.

The *routing device* could be a general-purpose computer with two network interfaces or a dedicated device designed specifically for routing. Such dedicated routing devices are called *routers*.

Note The generic term *gateway* also refers to any routing device. For good performance (high packet transfer rate), you want a dedicated router, whose sole purpose is to route packets of data in a network.

The term *gateway* refers to a routing device regardless of whether the device is another PC or a router. When you configure TCP/IP networking on a system, you must specify the IP address of your network's gateway to other networks.

A single routing device, of course, does not connect all the networks in the world; packets get around in the Internet from one gateway to another. Any network connected to another network has a designated gateway. You can even have specific gateways for specific networks. In TCP/IP networking, a routing table keeps track of the gateway associated with an external network and the type of physical interface (such as Ethernet or Point-to-Point Protocol over serial line) for that network. A default gateway gets packets that are addressed to unknown networks.

In your LAN, all packets addressed to another network go to your network's default gateway. If that gateway is physically connected to the destination network, the gateway can physically send the packets to the destination host. If that gateway does not know the destination network, however, it sends the packets to the next default gateway (the gateway for the other network on which your gateway also "lives"). This way, packets travel from one gateway to the next until they reach the destination network (or you get an error message saying that the destination network is unreachable).

Note To efficiently send packets around in the network, routers exchange information (as routing tables) so that each router can have a "map" of the network in its vicinity. Routers exchange information by using a routing protocol from a family of protocols called Interior Gateway Protocol (IGP). A commonly used IGP is the Routing Information Protocol (RIP).

Note In TCP/IP routing, any time a packet passes through a router, it's considered to have made a *hop*. In RIP, the maximum size of the Internet is 15 hops. A network is considered to be unreachable from your network if a packet does not reach the destination network within 15 hops — that is, if any network is more than 15 routers away.

Within a single network, you don't need a router as long as you do not use any subnet mask to break the single IP network into several subnets. In that case, however, you have to set up routers to send packets from one subnet to another.

Domain Name System (DNS)

You can access any host computer in a TCP/IP network with an IP address. Remembering the IP addresses of even a few hosts of interest, however, is tedious. This fact was recognized from the beginning of TCP/IP, and the association between a host name and IP address was used. The concept is similar to that of a phone book, in which you can look up a telephone number by searching for a person's name.

The Network Information Center (NIC), which was located in the Stanford Research Institute (SRI), maintained the association between names and IP addresses in a text file named HOSTS.TXT. This file contained the names and corresponding IP addresses of networks, hosts, and routers on the Internet. All hosts on the Internet transferred that file by FTP. (Can you imagine all hosts getting a file from a single source in today's Internet?) As the number of Internet hosts increased, the single-file idea became intractable. The hosts file was becoming difficult to maintain, and it was hard for all the hosts to update their hosts file on time. To alleviate the problem, RFCs 881, 882, and 883 introduced the concept and plans for Domain Name in November 1983. Eventually, this introduction led to the Domain Name System (DNS) as you know it today (documented in RFCs 1032, 1033, 1034, and 1035).

Domain-name hierarchy

DNS provides a hierarchical naming system similar to your postal address, which you can read as "your name" at "your street address" in "your city" in "your state" in "your country." If I know your full postal address, I would locate you by starting with your city in your country. Then I would locate the street address to find your home, ring the doorbell, and ask for you by name.

Note DNS essentially provides an addressing scheme for an Internet host that is similar to the postal address. The entire Internet is subdivided into several domains (such as gov, edu, com, mil, and net). Each domain is further subdivided into subdomains. Finally, within a subdomain, each host is given a symbolic name. To write a host's *fully qualified domain name (FQDN),* string together the host name, subdomain names, and domain name with dots (.) as separators. Following is the full domain name of a host named addlab in the subdomain nws within another subdomain noaa in the gov domain: addlab.nws.noaa.gov.

Figure 1-5 illustrates part of the Internet DNS, showing the location of the host addlab.nws.noaa.gov.

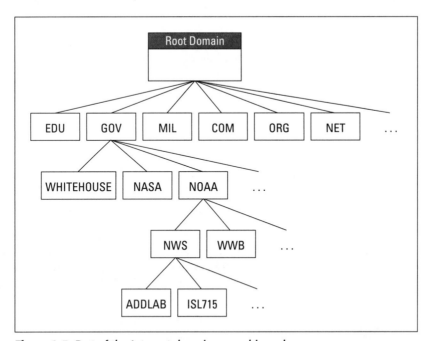

Figure 1-5: Part of the Internet domain-name hierarchy.

For a commercial system in the com domain, the name of a host may be as simple as idgbooks.com.

Tip You can refer to a user on a system by appending an At sign (@), followed by the host's domain name, to the user name (the name under which the user logs in). Thus, you would refer to the user named naba at the host lnbsoft.com as naba@lnbsoft.com.

That's how you refer to users when you send electronic mail.

Name servers

TCP/IP network applications resolve a host name to an IP address by consulting a *name server* (another host you can access from your network). If you decide to use DNS on your network, you must set up a name server in your network or indicate a name server (by an IP address).

Later sections of this chapter discuss the configuration files /etc/host.conf and /etc/resolv.conf; in these files you specify how host names convert to IP addresses. In particular, you specify the IP addresses of a name server in the /etc/resolv.conf file.

Tip If you do not use DNS, you still can have host-name-to-IP-address mapping through a text file named /etc/hosts. The entries in a typical /etc/hosts file may look like the following example:

```
# This is a comment
127.0.0.1      localhost
206.197.168.2     lnbsun
206.197.168.50    lnb386
206.197.168.100   lnb486
206.197.168.150   lnbmac
206.197.168.200   lnbsoft
```

As the example shows, the file lists a host name for each IP address. The IP address and host names will be different for your system, of course.

Webmaster When you rely on the /etc/hosts file for name lookup, however, you must replicate this file on each system on your network. This procedure can become a nuisance even in a network that has five or six systems.

TCP/IP Setup

As a Webmaster, you may not have to set up TCP/IP networking on UNIX workstations. However, you should know how to configure TCP/IP; knowledge of the configuration files helps you track down problems. You also should know how to reconfigure TCP/IP if some network information (such as the nameserver's IP address) changes.

Like almost everything else in UNIX, TCP/IP setup is a matter of preparing a group of configuration files (text files that you can edit with any text editor). Most of these configuration files are in the /etc directory. The next few sections describe the important aspects of TCP/IP setup.

TCP/IP configuration files

Many UNIX systems include utility programs (sometimes with a graphical interface) that let you configure TCP/IP network. Such utility programs help you by hiding the details of the configuration files. Nevertheless, you should know the names of the files and their purposes so that you can edit the files manually, if necessary. For example, Linux includes the netconfig script, which lets you specify one name server. However, you may want to add an alternative name server. To do so, you need to know about the /etc/resolv.conf file, which stores the IP addresses of name servers.

The following sections describe the basic TCP/IP configuration files.

The /etc/hosts file

The /etc/hosts text file contains a list of IP addresses and host names for your local network. Without a name server, any network program on your system consults this file to determine the IP address that corresponds to a host name.

Following is the /etc/hosts file from my system (a PC running Linux 1.2.13), showing the IP addresses and names of other hosts on my LAN:

```
#
# hosts     This file describes several host-name-to-address
#           mappings for the TCP/IP subsystem. It is mostly
#           used at boot time, when no name servers are running.
#           On small systems, this file can be used instead of a
#           "named" name server. Just add the names, addresses,
#           and any aliases to this file...
#

# For loopback
127.0.0.1     localhost

# Other hosts on the LAN
206.197.168.200    lnbsoft.com lnbsoft
206.197.168.50     lnb386
206.197.168.100    lnb486
206.197.168.150    lnbmac
206.197.168.2      lnbsun

# End of hosts.
```

As the example shows, each line in the file starts with an IP address, followed by the host name for that IP address. You can have more than one host name for a given IP address.

The /etc/networks file

The /etc/networks file is another text file that contains the names and IP addresses of networks. These network names are commonly used in the route command to specify a network by name instead of its IP address. The following is a sample /etc/networks file from my system:

```
#
# networks   This file describes several net-name-to-address
#         mappings for the TCP/IP subsystem. It is mostly
#         used at boot time, when no name servers are running.
#

loopback    127.0.0.0
localnet    206.197.168.0

# End of networks.
```

Name resolution configuration file

By now you have seen two mechanisms for converting a host name to an IP address — the /etc/hosts file and DNS. The /etc/hosts file is a text file on your system that associates an IP addresses with a host name. DNS is an Internet service where a name server translates a host name to one or more IP addresses (yes, one name can actually translate to multiple IP addresses).

When any networking application runs, the application uses a library called the *resolver library* to look up the IP address corresponding to a host name. A configuration file specifies the order in which the resolver library uses /etc/hosts file and the DNS to look up host names. The name of this configuration file depends on the type of your UNIX system.

In Linux, the /etc/host.conf file specifies how to resolve names. A typical /etc/host.conf file may contain the following lines:

```
order hosts, bind
multi on
```

The entries in the /etc/host.conf file tell the resolver library what services to use, in which order, to resolve names.

The order option indicates the order of services. The sample entry specifies that the resolver library should first consult the /etc/hosts file and then check the name server to resolve a name.

Note The `multi` option determines whether a host in the `/etc/hosts` file can have multiple IP addresses. Hosts that have more than one IP address are called *multihomed,* because the presence of multiple IP addresses implies that the host has several network interfaces (the host "lives" in several networks simultaneously).

 Webmaster In Solaris and HP-UX, the `/etc/nsswitch.conf` file specifies the lookup order for name service — the file is named `nsswitch` because it controls the name service switch. For example, here's a sample `/etc/nsswitch.conf` file:

```
# File: /etc/nsswitch.conf
# Controls the search order for many system services
hosts: files [NOTFOUND=continue TRYAGAIN=continue] dns
```

The `hosts:` line in this file specifies that the resolver should first look up names in the `/etc/hosts` file and consult DNS only if `/etc/hosts` does not resolve the name.

The `/etc/resolv.conf` file

The `/etc/resolv.conf` file is another configuration file used by the resolver — a library that determines the IP address for a host name. Following is a sample `/etc/resolv.conf` file:

```
domain digex.net
order local,bind
nameserver 164.109.1.3
nameserver 164.109.10.23
```

The first line specifies your system's domain name. The `nameserver` line provides the IP addresses of name servers for your domain. If you have multiple name servers, you should list them on separate lines.

Initializing TCP/IP at boot time

You should start your network automatically every time you boot the system. For this to happen, you must put the appropriate commands in one or more startup scripts. The `init` process runs immediately after UNIX boots. The process consults the `/etc/inittab` file and then executes various commands (typically, shell scripts), depending on the current run level. The names of these scripts vary from one UNIX system to another. The scripts, however, are usually in the `/etc` directory and the name typically starts with an `rc`.

One of these startup scripts performs the basic network setup; the script sets up the network and starts several persistent network programs (called *daemons*). Typically, the network startup script runs the `ifconfig` and `route` commands:

✦ `ifconfig` configures any network interface on your system. The configuration associates an IP address with a physical network interface. At minimum, the loopback device (`lo`) must be configured. If you have an Ethernet card, that device (the device name depends on your UNIX system — on Sun workstations the name is `le0`, on Linux it is `eth0`) also is configured by a separate `ifconfig` command.

✦ `route` sets up the routing tables for the network. The routing table controls how network packets are delivered to specific IP addresses.

In Linux you may use the following commands to configure the loopback device using `ifconfig` and `route`:

```
/sbin/ifconfig lo 127.0.0.1
/sbin/route add -net 127.0.0.0
```

The Linux command to configure an Ethernet card is a bit more complex. Here is an example that sets up an Ethernet card with the IP address 206.197.168.200:

```
/sbin/ifconfig eth0 206.197.168.200 netmask 255.255.255.0 broadcast
        206.197.168.255
```

In Linux, the binary files for the `ifconfig` and `route` commands reside in the `/sbin` directory. On other UNIX systems, the location may be different. Also, you should consult your system's online help for more information on the syntax of `ifconfig` and `route` commands. For example, to find out more about `ifconfig`, type the following command:

```
man ifconfig
```

The startup scripts also start several other networking services (daemons or programs that run persistently). Two common services are `inetd` and `nfsd`:

✦ `inetd` launches specific server programs upon request from clients. (You learn more about `inetd` in "The `inetd` super server" section later in this chapter.)

✦ `nfsd` shares one or more directories with other systems on the network using the Network File System (NFS). On some systems this daemon is called `rpc.nfsd`.

At a Web site, the startup script may also start an HTTP daemon (`httpd`), which is the Web server program. You learn about Web server setup in Chapters 7 and 8.

TCP/IP Diagnostics

A working network connection is necessary for any Web site. As a Webmaster, you must be able to diagnose problems with TCP/IP networking. The TCP/IP protocol suite includes several tools that help you monitor and diagnose problems. The next few sections describe a few of these tools.

Checking connectivity to a host

To check for a network path to a specific host, use the `ping` command. Ping is a widely used TCP/IP tool that uses a series of Internet Control Message Protocol (ICMP, often pronounced *eye-comp*) messages. (ICMP provides for an Echo message to which every host responds.) When Ping uses the ICMP messages and replies, it can determine whether the other system is alive; it also can compute the round-trip delay in communicating with that system.

The following example shows how I run `ping` to see whether one of the systems on my network is alive:

```
ping 206.197.168.50
PING 206.197.168.50 (206.197.168.50): 56 data bytes
64 bytes from 206.197.168.50: icmp_seq=0 ttl=32 time=3.4 ms
64 bytes from 206.197.168.50: icmp_seq=1 ttl=32 time=1.8 ms
64 bytes from 206.197.168.50: icmp_seq=2 ttl=32 time=1.8 ms
64 bytes from 206.197.168.50: icmp_seq=3 ttl=32 time=1.9 ms
        (press Ctrl-C here)
--- 206.197.168.50 ping statistic ---
4 packets transmitted, 4 packets received, 0% packet loss
round-trip min/avg/max = 1.8/2.2/3.4 ms
```

Tip   On some systems, `ping` simply reports that a remote host is alive. You can still get the timing information with the command `ping -s`.

`ping` continues to run until you press Ctrl+C to stop it; then it displays summary statistics, showing the typical time it takes to send a packet between the two systems. In this example, the host being `ping`-ed is on an Ethernet LAN and the round-trip travel time is between 2 and 4 milliseconds.

Note   For a typical dial-up TCP/IP connection, the round-trip travel time is in hundreds of milliseconds. For example, here's a typical output from `ping` when you are on a system connected to the Internet through a 28.8 Kbps modem:

```
ping 140.90.23.100
PING 140.90.23.100 (140.90.23.100): 56 data bytes
64 bytes from 140.90.23.100: icmp_seq=0 ttl=244 time=336.0 ms
64 bytes from 140.90.23.100: icmp_seq=1 ttl=244 time=290.2 ms
```

(continued)

```
64 bytes from 140.90.23.100: icmp_seq=2 ttl=244 time=350.2 ms
64 bytes from 140.90.23.100: icmp_seq=3 ttl=244 time=300.2 ms
64 bytes from 140.90.23.100: icmp_seq=4 ttl=244 time=340.2 ms
64 bytes from 140.90.23.100: icmp_seq=5 ttl=244 time=290.2 ms

--- 140.90.23.100 ping statistic ---
6 packets transmitted, 6 packets received, 0% packet loss
round-trip min/avg/max = 290.2/317.8/350.2 ms
```

The time at the end of each line shows the round-trip time for a packet originating at your system to reach the designated IP address (140.90.23.100, in this case) and back to your system again.

Incidentally, you do not have to have an account on a system to ping its IP address. Although a system may disable the automatic response to the ICMP messages that ping uses, most systems respond to ping.

Checking network status

To check the status of the network, use the netstat command. This command displays the status of network connections of various types (such as TCP and UDP connections). You can get many different types of network information from netstat. For example, you can view the status of the interfaces with the -i option, as follows:

```
netstat -i
Name Mtu   Net/Dest     Address     Ipkts  Ierrs Opkts Oerrs Collis Queue
le0  1500  206.197.168.0 lnbsun      1778   0     1165  0     0      0
lo0  1536  loopback     localhost   789    0     789   0     0      0
```

In this case, the output shows the current status of the loopback (lo0) and Ethernet (le0) interfaces on a Sun workstation. For each interface, you can see the IP address, as well as statistics on packets transmitted. Here, Ipkts and Ierrs are the number of good and erroneous incoming packets, respectively. Opkts and Oerrs provide the respective counts for outgoing packets. The Collis column lists the number of collisions that occur when two or more systems begin to transmit simultaneously in an Ethernet network. The Queue column is the number of packets in queue.

Tip   Another useful netstat option is -r, which shows the routing table. If you are having trouble ping-ing a host (that you specify with an IP address), check the IP routing table to see whether a default gateway is specified. Then check the gateway's routing table to ensure that paths to an outside network appear in that routing table.

Following is a typical result of `netstat -rn` (the n option shows all destinations and gateways as IP addresses) on a Sun workstation:

```
netstat -rn
Routing tables
Destination         Gateway            Flags   Refcnt Use       Interface
127.0.0.1           127.0.0.1          UH      1      787       lo0
206.197.168.0       206.197.168.2      U       3      1476      le0
```

Each line in the routing table indicates how packets are transmitted to a specific destination and which physical network interface carries the packets. For example, the local network (whose network address is 206.197.168.0) uses the le0 (Ethernet) interface, and the default gateway happens to be this workstation (whose IP address is 206.197.168.2).

The Flags column further qualifies the route: U means the route is up (that is, it is active), G is a gateway (one that transfers packets between two networks), and H means a host route (thus, UH means the host route is up). The remaining columns provide other information about the route such as the number of TCP connections (shown in the Refcnt column) and the number of packets transmitted (in the Use column).

You can use a few other options with the `netstat` command. For example, `netstat -s` shows packet statistics for each type of protocol: IP, ICMP, TCP, and UDP.

TCP/IP Services and Client/Server Architecture

By design, a typical Internet service is implemented in two parts — a server that provides information and one or more clients that request information. Such client/server architecture has been gaining popularity as an approach for implementing distributed information systems. The client/server architecture typically consists of a collection of computers connected by a communication network. The functions of the information system are performed by processes (computer programs) that run on these computers and communicate through the network.

In recent years, the client/server architecture has become commonplace as the mechanism that brings the centralized corporate databases to desktop PCs on a network. In a client/server environment, one or more servers manage the centralized database and clients gain access to the data through the server.

Like a database server, an Internet service (such as FTP or Web) also provides a service using the client/server model. A user who wants to access information uses a client (for example, a Web browser) to connect to a server and download information (for example, Web pages from a Web server). In this case, the Web server acts as a database manager — the data are the HTML files (Web pages).

> **Note** Client/server architecture requires clients to communicate with the servers. TCP/IP provides a standard way for clients and servers to exchange packets of data. The next few sections explain how TCP/IP-based services communicate. From this discussion, you learn about the port numbers associated with many well-known Internet services.

TCP/IP and sockets

Client/server applications (such as Web servers and browsers) use TCP/IP to communicate. These Internet applications perform TCP/IP communications by using the Berkeley Sockets interface (so named because the socket interface was introduced in Berkeley UNIX around 1982). The sockets interface consists of a library of routines that an application developer can use to create applications that can communicate with other applications on the Internet. There is even a Windows Sockets API (Application Programming Interface — a fancy name for the library of functions) that's modeled after the Berkeley Sockets interface. The Winsock interface, as it's known, provides a standard API that Windows programmers can use to write network applications.

> **Note** Although you may not write network applications using sockets, you do have to use many network applications in your job as a Webmaster. Knowledge of sockets can help you understand how network-based applications work, which, in turn, helps you find and correct any problems with these applications.

Socket definition

Network applications use sockets to communicate over a TCP/IP network. A *socket* is an abstraction that represents a bidirectional end-point of a connection. Because a socket is bidirectional, you can send data as well as receive it through a socket. A socket has the following three attributes:

✦ The network address (the IP address) of the system

✦ The port number identifying the process (a process is a computer program running on a computer) that exchanges data through the socket

✦ The type of socket (such as stream or datagram) identifying the protocol for data exchange

Essentially, the IP address identifies a network node, the port number identifies a process on the node, and the socket type determines the manner in which data is exchanged — through a connection-oriented or a connectionless protocol.

Connection-oriented protocol

The socket type indicates the protocol being used to communicate through the socket. A connection-oriented protocol works like a normal phone conversation. When you want to talk to your friend, you have to first dial your friend's phone number and establish a connection before you can have a conversation. In the same way, connection-oriented data exchange requires both the sending and the receiving processes to establish a connection before data exchange can begin.

Note In the TCP/IP protocol suite, TCP — Transmission Control Protocol — supports a connection-oriented data transfer between two processes running on two computers on the Internet. TCP provides a reliable two-way data exchange between processes.

As the name TCP/IP suggests (and as the "Networking protocols" section indicates), TCP relies on IP — Internet Protocol — for delivery of packets. IP does not guarantee delivery of packets; nor does it deliver packets in any particular sequence. IP does, however, efficiently deliver packets from one network to another. TCP is responsible for arranging the packets in the proper sequence, detecting whether errors occurred, and requesting retransmission of packets in case of any error.

TCP is useful for applications that plan to exchange large amounts of data at a time. Also, applications that need reliable data exchange use TCP. For example, FTP uses TCP to transfer files.

In the sockets model, a socket that uses TCP is referred to as a *stream socket*.

Connectionless protocol

A connectionless data-exchange protocol does not require the sender and receiver to explicitly establish a connection. Using a connectionless protocol is like shouting to a friend in a crowded room — you cannot be sure your friend actually heard you.

Note In the TCP/IP protocol suite, the User Datagram Protocol (UDP) provides connectionless service for sending and receiving packets called *datagrams*. Unlike TCP, UDP does not guarantee that datagrams ever reached their intended destination; nor does UDP ensure that the datagrams are delivered in the order they were sent.

UDP is used either by applications that exchange small amounts of data at a time or by applications that do not need the reliability and sequencing of data delivery. For example, Simple Network Management Protocol (SNMP) uses UDP to transfer data.

In the sockets model, a socket that uses UDP is referred to as a *datagram socket*.

Sockets and the client/server model

It takes two sockets to complete a communication path. When two processes communicate, they use the client/server model to establish the connection. The server application listens on a specific port on the system — the server is completely identified by the IP address of the system where it runs and the port number where it listens for connections. The client initiates connection from any available port and tries to connect to the server (identified by the IP address and port number). When the client makes the connection, the client and the server can exchange data according to their own protocol.

The sequence of events in sockets-based data exchanges depends on whether the transfer is connection-oriented (TCP) or connectionless (UDP). Figure 1-6 shows the typical sequence of events for a connection-oriented data transfer using sockets.

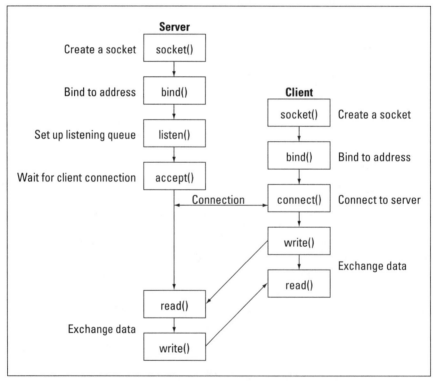

Figure 1-6: Connection-oriented data transfer with sockets.

Each step in Figure 1-6 shows the names of sockets functions that the client and the server call. As Figure 1-6 shows, the server "listens" on a specific port, waiting for clients to request connection. Data transfer begins only after a connection is established.

For connectionless data transfers, the server waits for a datagram to arrive at a specified port. The client does not wait to establish a connection; it simply sends a datagram to the server. Figure 1-7 shows the events that occur during connectionless data transfers.

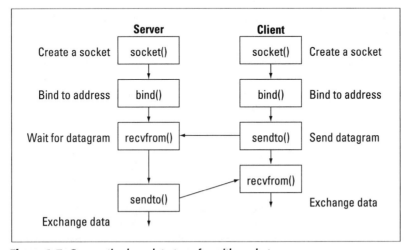

Figure 1-7: Connectionless data transfer with sockets.

As Figure 1-7 shows, the client and the server use the socket calls `sendto` and `recvfrom` to send and receive data. When the server reads a datagram by calling `recvfrom`, the `recvfrom` function returns the datagram as well as the network address of the client that sent the datagram. This return enables the server to send a response to the correct client process.

Client/Server communications with TCP/IP

The basic event sequence shown in Figures 1-6 and 1-7 indicate the Berkeley Sockets API functions that a client or server typically calls. Although the exact set of function calls depend on the type of socket (stream or datagram) and whether the application is a server or a client, the basic steps are as follows:

1. Create a socket.
2. Bind an IP address and port to the socket.
3. Listen for connections if the application is a server using a stream socket.
4. Establish connection if the application is a client using a stream socket.
5. Exchange data.
6. Close the socket when done.

Connectionless sockets that implement data transfer using UDP do not require Steps 3 and 4.

Regardless of whether the application is a server or a client, each application first creates a socket. Then the application associates (binds) the socket with the local computer's IP address and a port number. The IP address identifies the machine on which the application is running, and the port number identifies the application that's using the socket.

Note Servers typically listen to a well-known port number so that clients can connect to that port to access the server. For a client application, the process of binding a socket to the IP address and port is the same as that for a server, but the client can use zero as the port number — the sockets library automatically uses an unused port number for the client.

For a connection-oriented stream socket, the communicating client and server applications have to establish a connection. The exact steps for establishing a connection depend on whether the application is a server or a client.

Note In the client-server model, the server must be up and running before the client can run. After the server application creates a socket and binds the socket to a port, it calls the `listen` function to set up a queue of connections, which determines how many clients can connect to the server. Typically, a server listens to anywhere from 1 to 5 connections. The size of the listen queue, however, is one of the parameters you can adjust (especially for a Web server) to ensure that the server responds to as many clients as possible.

After the server sets up the listen queue, it calls the `accept` function to wait for a connection from a client.

Establishing the connection from the client side is somewhat simpler. After the client creates a socket and binds the socket to a network address, it must call the `connect` function to establish connection with the server. To call `connect`, the client must know the network name or IP address of the server, as well as the port on which the server accepts connection. As the next section shows, all Internet services have well-known standard port numbers.

Note After a client establishes connection to a server using a connection-oriented stream socket, the client and server can exchange data by calling the `send` and `recv` functions. Like a conversation between two persons, the server and client alternately send and receive data — the meaning of the data depends on the message protocol used by the server and the clients. Usually, a server is designed for a specific task and inherent in that design is a message protocol that the server and clients use to exchange the necessary data. For example, the Web server and the Web browser (client) communicate by using the Hypertext Transfer Protocol (HTTP).

Internet services and port numbers

The TCP/IP protocol suite has become the common language of the Internet, because many standard services are available on all systems that support TCP/IP. These services make the Internet tick by enabling the transfer of mail, news, and Web pages:

✦ FTP (File Transfer Protocol) allows transfer of files between computers on the Internet. FTP uses two ports — data is transferred on port 20 while control information is exchanged on port 21.

✦ HTTP (Hypertext Transfer Protocol) is a recent protocol for sending HTML documents from one system to another. HTTP is the underlying protocol of the Web. By default, the Web server and client communicate on port 80.

✦ SMTP (Simple Mail Transfer Protocol) is a protocol for exchanging e-mail messages between systems. SMTP uses port 25 for information exchange.

✦ NNTP (Network News Transfer Protocol) is a protocol for distribution (in a store-and-forward fashion) of news articles across the Internet. NNTP uses port 119.

✦ TELNET allows a user on one system to log into another system on the Internet (the user must provide a valid user ID and password to successfully log into the remote system). TELNET uses port 23 by default. The TELNET client, however, can connect to any specified port.

✦ SNMP (Simple Network Management Protocol) is a protocol for managing all types of network devices on the Internet. Like FTP, SNMP uses two ports: 161 and 162.

✦ TFTP (Trivial File Transfer Protocol) is a protocol for transferring files from one system to another (typically used by X terminals and diskless workstations to download boot files from another host on the network). TFTP data transfer takes place on port 69.

✦ NFS (Network File System) is a system for sharing files among computers. NFS uses Sun's Remote Procedure Call (RPC) facility, which exchanges information through port 111.

✦ WAIS (Wide Area Information Service) is a service for searching data on distributed systems. WAIS uses port 210. (In the /etc/services file, you find information about WAIS under the service named z3950 because WAIS uses the ANSI standard Z39.50 protocol.)

A well-known port is associated with each of these services. The TCP protocol uses this port to locate a service on any system. (A server *process* — a computer program running on a system — implements each service.)

Note Like the /etc/hosts file, which stores the association between host names and IP addresses, the association between a service name and a port number (as well as a protocol) is stored in another text file, named /etc/services. Following are some of the entries in the /etc/services file on a UNIX system:

```
#
# Network services, Internet style
#
# Notice that it is currently the policy of IANA to assign a single well-known
# port number for both TCP and UDP; hence, most entries here have two entries
# even if the protocol doesn't support UDP operations.
# Updated from RFC 1340, ''Assigned Numbers'' (July 1992). Not all ports
# are included, only the more common ones.
#
#                 from: @(#)services     5.8 (Berkeley) 5/9/91
#                 $Id: services,v 1.9 1993/11/08 19:49:15 cgd Exp $
#
tcpmux          1/tcp       # TCP port service multiplexer
echo            7/tcp
echo            7/udp
discard         9/tcp       sink null
discard         9/udp       sink null
systat          11/tcp      users
daytime         13/tcp
daytime         13/udp
netstat         15/tcp
qotd            17/tcp      quote
msp             18/tcp      # message send protocol
msp             18/udp      # message send protocol
chargen         19/tcp      ttytst source
chargen         19/udp      ttytst source
ftp             21/tcp
# 22 - unassigned
telnet          23/tcp
# 24 - private
smtp            25/tcp      mail
# 26 - unassigned
time            37/tcp      timserver
time            37/udp      timserver
rlp             39/udp      resource       # resource location
nameserver      42/tcp      name           # IEN 116
whois           43/tcp      nicname
domain          53/tcp      nameserver     # name-domain server
domain          53/udp      nameserver
mtp             57/tcp                     # deprecated
bootps          67/tcp      # BOOTP server
bootps          67/udp
bootpc          68/tcp      # BOOTP client
bootpc          68/udp
```

```
tftp             69/udp
gopher           70/tcp        # Internet Gopher
gopher           70/udp
rje              77/tcp        netrjs
finger           79/tcp
www              80/tcp        http    # World Wide Web HTTP
www              80/udp                # HyperText Transfer Protocol
link             87/tcp        ttylink
kerberos         88/tcp        krb5    # Kerberos v5
kerberos         88/udp
supdup           95/tcp
# 100 - reserved
hostnames       101/tcp        hostname      # usually from sri-nic
iso-tsap        102/tcp        tsap          # part of ISODE.
csnet-ns        105/tcp        cso-ns  # also used by CSO name server
csnet-ns        105/udp        cso-ns
rtelnet         107/tcp               # Remote Telnet
rtelnet         107/udp
pop2            109/tcp               postoffice      # POP version 2
pop2            109/udp
pop3            110/tcp               # POP version 3
pop3            110/udp
sunrpc          111/tcp
sunrpc          111/udp
auth            113/tcp               tap ident authentication
sftp            115/tcp
uucp-path       117/tcp
nntp            119/tcp        readnews untp  # USENET News Transfer Protocol
ntp             123/tcp
ntp             123/udp               # Network Time Protocol
netbios-ns      137/tcp               # NETBIOS Name Service
netbios-ns      137/udp
netbios-dgm     138/tcp               # NETBIOS Datagram Service
netbios-dgm     138/udp
netbios-ssn     139/tcp               # NETBIOS session service
netbios-ssn     139/udp
imap2           143/tcp               # Interim Mail Access Proto v2
imap2           143/udp
snmp            161/udp                      # Simple Net Mgmt Proto
snmp-trap       162/udp        snmptrap  # Traps for SNMP
cmip-man        163/tcp               # ISO mgmt over IP (CMOT)
cmip-man        163/udp
cmip-agent      164/tcp
cmip-agent      164/udp
xdmcp           177/tcp               # X Display Mgr. Control Proto
xdmcp           177/udp
# Rest of the file not shown...
```

You may find that browsing through the entries in the /etc/services file is instructive, because they show the breadth of Internet services available under TCP/IP.

Note As a Webmaster, you need to know that port number 80 is designated for World Wide Web service. That is, the Web server listens to port 80 on your system.

The inetd **super server**

The client/server model requires that the server be up and running before a client makes a request for service. A simplistic idea would be to run all the servers all the time. This idea is not practical, however, because each server process would use up system resources as memory and processor time. Besides, you don't need all the services up and ready at all times. To solve this problem, run a single server (inetd) that listens to all the ports and then starts the appropriate server when a client request comes in.

For example, when a client tries to connect to the FTP port, inetd starts the FTP server and lets it communicate directly with the client (and the FTP server exits when the client disconnects).

Note Because it starts various servers on demand, inetd is called the *Internet super server*. Typically, a UNIX system starts inetd when the system boots. The inetd server reads a configuration file named /etc/inetd.conf at startup. This file tells inetd which ports to listen to and what server to start for each port. For example, on a Linux system the entry in the /etc/inetd.conf file that starts the FTP server looks like this:

```
ftp      stream  tcp    nowait  root    /usr/sbin/tcpd  /usr/sbin/wu.ftpd
```

The first item on this line, ftp, tells inetd the name of the service. inetd uses this name to look up the port number from the /etc/services file. If you use the grep command to look for ftp in the /etc/services file, here's what you find:

```
grep ftp /etc/services
ftp       21/tcp
tftp      69/udp
sftp      115/tcp
```

You can see that the port number of the FTP service is 21. This information tells inetd to listen to port 21 for FTP service requests.

The rest of the fields on the FTP entry have the following meanings:

✦ The second and third fields of the entry, stream tcp, tell inetd that the FTP service uses a connection-oriented TCP socket to communicate with the client. For services that use the connectionless UDP sockets, these two fields say dgram udp.

✦ The fourth field, nowait, tells inetd to start a new server for each request. If this field says wait, inetd waits until the server exits before starting the server again.

✦ The fifth field provides the user ID that inetd uses to run the server. In this case, the server runs the FTP server as root.

✦ The sixth field specifies the program to run for this service and the last field is the argument that inetd passes to the server program.

Tip Browse through the /etc/inetd.conf file on your system to find out the kinds of services that inetd can start. Some of these services (such as finger, systat, and netstat) provide information that intruders can use to break into your system. You may want to turn off these services by placing a comment character (#) at the beginning of the lines that start these services. When you make such a change to the /etc/inetd.conf file, you must restart the inetd server by following these steps:

1. Use the ps command with appropriate options and determine the process identifier (ID) of inetd. For example, on Linux, type ps -x | grep inetd and note the first number on the resulting line. That would be the process ID of inetd.

2. Type kill -HUP pid where pid is the process ID (a number) of inetd. This restarts inetd and it again reads the /etc/inetd.conf file.

Stand-alone servers

Although starting servers through inetd is a smart approach, inetd is not efficient if a service must start frequently. The Web server must start frequently if many users click on a Web-page link with the result that many requests arrive at the Web server. For such high-demand services, it's best to start the server in a stand-alone manner. Such stand-alone servers run as daemons — processes that run continuously. That is, the server listens on the assigned port and whenever a request arrives, the server handles the request by making a copy of itself. This way, the server keeps running forever.

Cross Ref You learn more about running stand-alone Web servers in Chapter 7.

Physical Networking

The previous sections focus on the TCP/IP networking protocol and TCP/IP-based Internet services. You must, however, have a physical connection to Internet before you can use the Internet services. Two common choices for a physical network connection are the following:

✦ Ethernet connection to a local area network (LAN) that's already connected to the Internet. This connection is a common occurrence in large organizations that have their own high-bandwidth connection to the Internet.

✦ Dial-up network connection to an Internet Service Provider (ISP). Typically, individuals and small businesses rely on dial-up networking to connect to the Internet.

The next few sections briefly describe these two physical network connections.

Ethernet networking

Ethernet is a popular choice for the physical data-transport mechanism, for the following reasons:

✦ Ethernet is proven technology (it has been around since the early 1980s).

✦ Ethernet provides good data-transfer rates: a maximum rate of 10 million bits per second (10 Mbps).

✦ Ethernet hardware is relatively low-cost. For example, PC Ethernet cards are approximately $100 (U.S.).

✦ Most UNIX workstations (such as those from Sun, HP, and IBM) typically come with built-in Ethernet hardware.

The following sections provide an overview of Ethernet networks.

Ethernet basics

Ethernet is a standard way to move packets of data between two or more computers connected to a single cable. (Larger networks are constructed by connecting multiple Ethernet segments with gateways.) Because you use a single wire, you must use a protocol for sending and receiving data, because only one data packet can exist on the cable at any time. An Ethernet LAN uses a data-transmission protocol known as *Carrier Sense Multiple Access/Collision Detection* (CSMA/CD) to ensure that multiple computers can share the single transmission cable. Ethernet controllers embedded in the computers follow the CSMA/CD protocol to transmit and receive Ethernet packets.

The idea behind the CSMA/CD protocol is similar to the way that you may have a conversation in a party. You listen for a pause (*carrier sense*) and talk when no one else is speaking. If you and another person begin talking at the same time, both of you realize the problem (*collision detection*) and pause for a moment; then one of you starts speaking again. As you know from experience, everything works out.

In an Ethernet LAN, each Ethernet controller checks the cable for presence of signals — that's the carrier-sense part. If the signal level is low, a controller sends its packets on the cable; the packet contains information about the sender and the intended recipient. All Ethernet controllers on the LAN listen to the signal, and the recipient receives the packet. If, somehow, two controllers send out a packet simultaneously, the signal level in the cable rises above a threshold, and the controllers know that a collision occurred (that is, two packets were sent out at the same time). Both controllers wait for a random amount of time and then send their packets again.

Ethernet was invented in the early 1970s at the Xerox Palo Alto Research Center (PARC) by Robert M. Metcalfe. In the 1980s, Ethernet was standardized by a cooperative effort of three companies: Digital Equipment Corporation (DEC), Intel, and Xerox. Using the first initials of the company names, that Ethernet standard became known as the *DIX standard*. Later, the 802-series standards (developed by the Institute of Electrical and Electronics Engineers [IEEE]) included the DIX standard. The formal Ethernet specification is formally known as IEEE 802.3 CSMA/CD, but people continue to call it Ethernet.

Note

Ethernet sends data in packets (also known as *frames*) with a standard format that consists of the following sequence of components:

- ✦ 8-byte preamble
- ✦ 6-byte destination address
- ✦ 6-byte source address
- ✦ 2-byte length of the data field
- ✦ 46- to 1,500-byte data field
- ✦ 4-byte frame-check sequence (used for error-checking)

You don't need to know much about the innards of Ethernet packets except to note the 6-byte source and destination addresses. Each Ethernet controller has a unique 6-byte (48-bit) address. At the physical level, packets must be addressed with these 6-byte addresses.

Address Resolution Protocol (ARP)

Note   In an Ethernet LAN, two Ethernet controllers can communicate only if they know each other's 6-byte physical Ethernet address. You may wonder how IP addresses are mapped to physical addresses. The Address Resolution Protocol (ARP), which specifies how to obtain the physical address that corresponds to an IP address, solves this problem. Essentially, when a packet has to be sent to an IP address, the TCP/IP protocol uses ARP to find the physical address of the destination.

When the packet is meant for an IP address outside your network, that packet is sent to the gateway that has a physical presence on your network. This gateway can respond to an ARP request for a physical address.

Ethernet cables

The original Ethernet standard used a thick coaxial cable (nearly half an inch in diameter) called *thickwire* or *thick Ethernet.* (The IEEE 802.3 standard, however, calls this wire *10BASE5.*) This designation means the following:

- ✦ The data-transmission rate is 10 megabits per second (10 Mbps).
- ✦ The transmission is baseband (that is, the cable's signal-carrying capacity is devoted to transmitting Ethernet packets only).
- ✦ The total length of the cable can be no more than 500 meters.

Thickwire was expensive, and the cable was rather unwieldy.

Note   Presently, two other forms of Ethernet cabling are more popular. The first alternative to thick Ethernet cable is *thinwire* (or *10BASE2*), which uses a thin, flexible coaxial cable. A thinwire Ethernet segment can be, at most, 185 meters long. The other, more recent alternative is Ethernet over unshielded twisted-pair cable (UTP), known as *10BASET.*

To set up a 10BASET Ethernet, you need an Ethernet *hub* — a hardware box with phone jacks. You build the network by running twisted-pair wires from each PC's Ethernet card to this hub.

Tip   Thinwire has a feature that makes it attractive for small offices or home offices that have more than one PC. You can daisy-chain the thinwire cable from one PC to another and construct a small Ethernet LAN, as shown in Figure 1-8.

As Figure 1-8 shows, you need Ethernet cards in the PCs. The cards should have thinwire connectors, called *BNC connectors.* You also need segments of thinwire cable (technically known as *RG-58 thin coaxial cables with 50-ohm impedance*). For each Ethernet card's BNC connector, you need a BNC T connector (so called because the connector looks like a *T*). You also need two 50-ohm terminators for the two end points of the Ethernet network. Then, to complete your own Ethernet LAN, connect the parts in the manner shown in Figure 1-8. I used this approach to connect several PCs and a workstation in my home office.

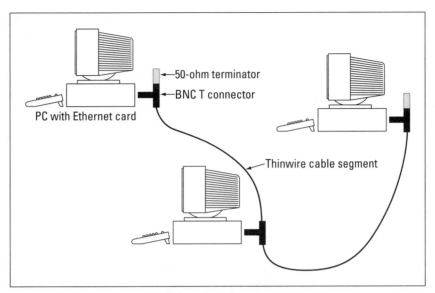

Figure 1-8: Constructing a small thinwire Ethernet LAN.

Caution Remember that you have to use the BNC T connectors and 50-ohm terminators even if you are connecting only two workstations on a LAN; you can't simply connect the two Ethernet cards with a cable.

Dial-up network

If you have a UNIX system (such as a PC running Linux) at home or in a small office, you may want to use a modem to connect to the Internet. At the other end of the modem, you need a system that's already on the Internet. This system could be a system at your office, your university, or a commercial Internet Service Provider (ISP). *Dial-up networking* is what you do when you establish a network connection between your UNIX system and a remote computer through a dial-up modem.

Note A significant difference exists between dial-up networking and plain old serial communication. Both approaches use a modem to dial up another computer and establish a communication path, but the serial communication software makes your computer act like a terminal connected to the remote computer. The dial-up connection is used exclusively by the serial communication software. You could not run another copy of the communication software and use the same modem connection, for example.

In dial-up networking, you run TCP/IP or other network-protocol software on your PC as well as on the remote system with which your PC has a dial-up communication path. That communication path simply forms the physical layer in the OSI seven-layer network model. The network protocols exchange data packets over the dial-up connection. You can use any number of network applications to communicate over the single dial-up connection. With dial-up networking, your PC truly becomes part of the network to which the remote computer belongs. (If the remote computer is not on a network, the dial-up networking creates a network that consists of the remote computer and your PC.) Thus, you can have any number of network applications, ranging from a Web browser to a `telnet` session, running at the same time, with all applications sharing the physical data-transport capabilities of the dial-up connection.

The next few sections describe TCP/IP over a dial-up connection, because TCP/IP is the dominant protocol of the Internet and UNIX systems have built-in support for TCP/IP. To be more accurate, I should say that the discussion in these sections applies to TCP/IP over any point-to-point communication link. The dial-up part simply reflects the fact that most of us will use a modem to establish the point-to-point communication link to a remote computer.

Like TCP/IP networking over Ethernet, TCP/IP networking over a dial-up link is a matter of specifying the *protocol* — the convention — for packaging a network packet over the communication link. Two popular protocols exist for TCP/IP networking over point-to-point serial communication links:

✦ Serial Line Internet Protocol (SLIP) is a simple protocol that specifies how to frame an IP packet on a serial line. RFC 1055 describes SLIP.

✦ Point-to-Point Protocol (PPP) is a more advanced protocol for establishing a TCP/IP connection over any point-to-point link, including dial-up serial links. RFC 1661 describes PPP.

Serial Line Internet Protocol (SLIP)

SLIP originated as a simple protocol for framing an *IP packet* — an Internet Protocol packet that consists of an IP header (which includes the source and destination IP addresses) followed by data (the data being sent from source to destination). RFC 1055, "A Nonstandard for Transmission of IP Datagrams over Serial Lines: SLIP," Ronkey, 1988, describes SLIP. As the title of RFC 1055 suggests, SLIP is not an official Internet standard; it's a defacto standard.

Note   SLIP defines two special characters for framing IP packets:

✦ SLIP-END is octal 300 (decimal 192), and it marks the end of an IP packet.

✦ SLIP-ESC is octal 333 (decimal 219), and it is used to "escape" any SLIP-END or SLIP-ESC characters that are embedded in the packet (to ensure, for example, that a packet does not end prematurely, because the IP packet happens to include a byte with decimal 192).

Note The protocol involves sending out the bytes of the IP packet one by one and marking the end of the packet with a SLIP-END character. The following convention is used to handle any SLIP-END and SLIP ESC characters that happen to be in the IP packet:

✦ Replace a SLIP-END character with SLIP-ESC, followed by octal 334 (decimal 220).

✦ Replace a SLIP-ESC character with SLIP-ESC, followed by octal 335 (decimal 221).

That's it! Based on the most popular implementation of SLIP from Berkeley UNIX, SLIP uses a few more conventions:

✦ Packets start and end with the SLIP-END character to ensure that each IP packet starts anew.

✦ The total size of the IP packet (including the IP header and data, but without the SLIP framing characters) is 1,006 bytes.

SLIP's simplicity has led to its popularity. SLIP has several shortcomings, however:

✦ Both ends of the SLIP connection have to know their IP addresses; you cannot change the IP address of either end without having to reconfigure software, but different computers (at different times) can use one end of a dial-up connection. Although some schemes have been worked out to allow dynamic assignment of IP addresses, the protocol does not have any provisions for address negotiation.

✦ Both ends of SLIP must use the same packet size, because the protocol does not allow the two ends to negotiate the packet size.

✦ SLIP has no support for data compression. (As you will learn later in this section, Compressed SLIP, or CSLIP, introduces compression in SLIP.)

✦ SLIP cannot identify the packet type. Accordingly, SLIP can carry only one protocol — the one that both ends of SLIP are hard-wired to use. A transport mechanism (such as SLIP) should carry packets of any protocol type.

Note The lack of data compression in SLIP was addressed by Compressed SLIP (CSLIP), which is described in RFC 1144, "Compressing TCP/IP Headers for Low-Speed Serial Links," Jacobson, 1990. CSLIP compresses TCP/IP header information, which tends to be repetitive in packets exchanged between the two ends of a SLIP connection. CSLIP does not compress the packet's data.

CSLIP is often referred to as the *Van Jacobson compression,* in recognition of CSLIP's author. Incidentally, PPP also supports the Van Jacobson TCP/IP header compression.

Point-to-Point Protocol (PPP)

Point-to-Point (PPP) fixes the shortcomings of SLIP and defines a more complex protocol. Unlike SLIP, PPP is an official Internet standard; it is documented in RFC 1661, "The Point-to-Point Protocol," Simpson, 1994.

Note

PPP includes the following main components:

✦ A packet-framing mechanism that uses a modified version of the well-known High-Level Data Link Control (HDLC) protocol

✦ A Link Control Protocol (LCP) to establish, configure, and test the data link

✦ A Network Control Protocol (NCP) that allows PPP to carry more than one type of network packet — such as IP, IPX, and NetBEUI (Network BIOS Extended User Interface) — over the same connection

PPP is gradually replacing SLIP as the protocol of choice for transporting packets over point-to-point links. Along with the ubiquitous serial link, some versions of PPP work over several other types of point-to-point links. Some of the point-to-point links where PPP works include Synchronous Optical Network (SONET), X.25, and Integrated Services Digital Network, (ISDN).

Understanding PPP frames

The PPP frame has a more complex structure than SLIP does. The PPP frame structure is based on International Standards Organization (ISO) standard 3309, "Data Communications — High-Level Data Link Control Procedures — Frame Structure," 1979. The HDLC protocol uses a special flag character to mark the beginning and the end of a frame. Figure 1-9 shows the structure of a complete PPP frame.

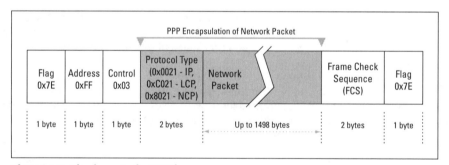

Figure 1-9: The format of a PPP frame.

As Figure 1-9 shows, the PPP frames begin and end with a flag character whose value is always 0x7E (that's 7E in hexadecimal notation). The Address and Control fields come from HDLC; they have the fixed values of 0xFF and 0x03, respectively. The PPP data consists of a 2-byte protocol field. (This field can be only 1 byte; the length of this protocol field is negotiated with the LCP before the exchange of any PPP frames.)

Note Within the encapsulated network packet, PPP uses 0x7D as the escape character. To send a byte that has a special meaning (such as 0x7E, which marks the beginning and end of a frame), PPP uses the following steps:

1. Embeds 0x7D in the data

2. Places the data byte being escaped

3. Toggles the sixth bit of that data byte

Thus, if the PPP data includes 0x7E, that byte is replaced by the 2-byte sequence 0x7D, followed by 0x5E. (If you toggle the sixth bit of 0x7E or 0111 1110 in binary, you get 0x5E or 0101 1110 in binary.)

Tip When you use PPP to set up a link between your UNIX system and a remote computer, your PC first sends LCP packets to set up the data link. After your PC establishes the physical data link and negotiates any optional parameters, it sends NCP packets to select one or more network protocols to be used over that link. Thereafter, any of those network protocols can send packets over the PPP link.

You don't need to know the complete details of PPP to use it effectively; just set up the PPP connection. The exact steps required to establish a PPP connection, however, vary from one version of UNIX to another.

Routing through the PPP connection

A common use of a PPP connection is to connect two geographically separated networks or, more commonly, to connect a small local area network (LAN) to the Internet. In a typical scenario, you have a small Ethernet LAN that you want to connect to the Internet. You can do this with a UNIX system that has both an Ethernet card and a modem (or you can settle for a router that accomplishes the task). The UNIX system has a presence on your Ethernet LAN through its Ethernet-card inter- face. If you can establish a PPP connection to a system on the Internet, you can use the UNIX system as the gateway between your LAN and the remote system (which, presumably, you have already connected to the Internet). Figure 1-10 illustrates such a scenario.

In this case, you have a small Ethernet LAN with a few PCs and a Class C IP address of 206.197.168.0. You have assigned 206.197.168.200 as the IP address of your UNIX system's Ethernet-card interface (you should do this with the `ifconfig` command in the system startup scripts — the ones that run when the system boots).

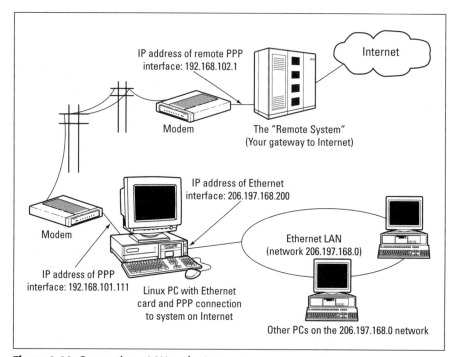

Figure 1-10: Connecting a LAN to the Internet.

The UNIX system also has a modem through which you establish a PPP connection to a remote system on the Internet. Both ends of the PPP connection have unique IP addresses. Make sure that the systems on your Ethernet LAN can access the Internet. Use your UNIX system as a gateway to route network packets between the Ethernet LAN and the remote system; the UNIX system is the only one that has both PPP and Ethernet interfaces. To accomplish this goal, you must perform the following steps:

✦ The UNIX system must have IP forwarding capability. Many UNIX systems have this ability enabled by default. When IP forwarding is enabled, the UNIX kernel automatically forwards packets from one interface to another. (*Kernel* refers to the core operating system, as opposed to all the supporting programs in an operating system.) If IP forwarding is not enabled on your version of UNIX, you must rebuild the kernel to enable the IP forwarding capability.

✦ Use the `route` command on the UNIX system to set up a route to the remote system. A *route* specifies a path between two network nodes. A typical specification says something like this: "All packets for the 206.197.168.0 network should be sent to the Ethernet interface named `eth0`." The *gateway* IP address is used as the destination for any network address without an explicit route. If you do have a PPP link, you may want to say, "Send any packet with an unresolved address to the remote IP address of the PPP link." You should use the remote end of the PPP connection as the gateway on the UNIX system.

✦ Make sure that all workstations on your LAN use the UNIX system as the gateway.

✦ Make sure that the remote gateway has a properly routed IP address for your UNIX system. Without this step, TCP/IP packets from the Internet cannot reach your LAN. If you get your Internet connection from an ISP, the ISP will (for a fee, of course) provide you properly routed IP addresses for all your LAN workstations.

Note Although a UNIX system with a PPP connection can act as a gateway between a LAN and the Internet, a more economical solution may be to use a dial-up router that's specifically designed to connect your LAN to the Internet. In both cases you need an ISP to provide you access to a remote system that's already connected to the Internet.

Summary

The Internet is presently very popular, as Internet Service Providers (ISPs) are springing up all over the United States and in much of the world. Online services (such as America Online and CompuServe) now offer Internet mail and Web browsing, which brings even more people to the Internet. To be a Webmaster, you must understand the basics of Internet and TCP/IP networking — the universal language of the Internet. This chapter provided an overview of Internet, TCP/IP networking, and how Internet services use TCP/IP. The next chapter describes some common Internet information services — Internet services designed to deliver information.

Where to go next . . .

✦ As a Webmaster, you have to be familiar with all Internet information services (World Wide Web is one of such information service). Chapters 2 and 3 cover the important Internet information services.

✦ If you want an overview of what is expected of a Webmaster, see Chapter 5.

✦ If you want to start setting up a Web site, see Chapter 6 for a summary of your options for a Web site.

✦ If you already have a Web site up and you want to get into authoring HTML documents, see Chapter 10.

✦ ✦ ✦

Internet Information Services

In Chapter 1, you learn that computers on the Internet use TCP/IP to communicate with one another. The computers communicate to exchange information. For example, a user on one computer may want to transfer a file from another computer. In this case, the two computers use the File Transfer Protocol (FTP) to transfer the file. One system acts as the FTP client and requests the file. The other system is the FTP server and sends the file. FTP is an example of an *information service* because the FTP server offers information upon request. FTP is layered on top of TCP/IP — that is, FTP uses TCP/IP to send and receive packets (including the packets that transfer the contents of a file from one system to another).

Besides FTP, you have several other important information services such as Gopher, Wide Area Information Servers (WAIS), and Web. As a Webmaster, you need to know about these services because each service provides a unique way of distributing information. Along with the Web server, you may also want to implement these information services on your system.

This chapter provides an overview of the important Internet information services. Because the Web is the main focus of this book, I describe the Web in detail in Chapter 3.

An Overview of Internet Information Services

Note The term *Internet service* refers to many network applications that employ client/ server models to perform specific tasks. These network applications employ TCP/IP to communicate with each other. On UNIX systems, TCP/IP-based Internet services provide a wide spectrum of capabilities from the ability to log on a remote system to transferring files between systems.

Many Internet services are specifically designed to deliver information from one system to another. The information may be in the form of mail messages, news items, or data files. FTP and World Wide Web are examples of Internet services that deliver information to the user. FTP lets a user download a file from any system on the Internet while the Web lets a user download and view documents that reside on another system. This book uses the term *Internet information service* for such information delivery services.

Note As a Webmaster and, therefore, an information provider, you'll be interested in one or more of the following Internet information services:

✦ Mailing Lists

✦ File Transfer Protocol (FTP)

✦ Gopher

✦ Wide Area Information Servers (WAIS)

✦ World Wide Web

The next sections briefly describe these services from a Webmaster's perspective — as an information provider. The subsequent sections show how to set up a few important services. Chapter 3 explains how a user accesses these Internet information services from the Web browser and, consequently, views the Web as the gateway to all information services.

Cross Ref For detailed information about all aspects of the Web, see Chapters 6 through 25.

Mailing lists

A *mailing list* is a simple form of information service. You set up a list of e-mail addresses so that when you send a message to the list, it goes out to every address on the list.

A mailing list is a convenient way to keep a discussion going among a group of people with similar interests. For example, as a salesperson, you can use a mailing list to allow the users of your product to share their experiences and report any problems. The technical support staff can monitor the list and respond to problems. Additionally, users can solve problems by helping each other.

Note Mailing lists may not be as exciting as a Web site, but they have a distinct advantage over other Internet information services such as FTP or Web. With e-mail, you can reach nearly everyone with any type of online access, even people who occasionally dial into a system and read mail. On the other hand, to use FTP or Web, your system must be directly connected to the Internet as opposed to dialing into a system and logging in as a user with your PC acting as a remote terminal.

Many corporations use internal e-mail systems (such as Microsoft Mail or Lotus cc:Mail). Typically, a corporation's internal mail system is connected to the Internet through a mail gateway that uses the Simple Mail Transfer Protocol (SMTP) to exchange mail with Internet hosts. The use of an SMTP gateway allows the corporation's internal users to exchange e-mail with anyone on the Internet (even though these users may not be able to use FTP or Web). With a mailing list, you can reach these users whose only access to the Internet is through e-mail.

Online services, such as America Online (AOL) and CompuServe, also have Internet mail gateways, which means that AOL and CompuServe users can also join mailing lists. The biggest benefit of a mailing list service is that you can reach a large population of users.

Note You can implement a small mailing list through the basic facilities of the standard UNIX e-mail software such as `sendmail`, which sends and receives mail by using SMTP over a TCP/IP network connection. To set up and maintain a large mailing list, however, you need to use a mailing list manager (such as Majordomo). You learn more about mailing lists in the "Sharing Information through Mailing Lists" section of this chapter.

File Transfer Protocol (FTP)

As the name implies, the File Transfer Protocol (FTP) allows users to transfer files between systems on the Internet. On any system that has a TCP/IP connection to the Internet, a user can use the `ftp` command to connect to the FTP server on another system and then use a set of commands to locate and download files.

Because FTP requires that the user log in before downloading files, the user must have an account on the system before using FTP. You can, however, set up FTP so that it allows anyone to log in with the user name `anonymous` and transfer one or more files from a selected set. The term *anonymous FTP* refers to an FTP server that allows users to log in with the user name `anonymous`.

Tip Anonymous FTP is useful when you want to provide files that users can download and use. In particular, to offer binary files (such as shareware programs or patches) of the software you sell, provide these files through anonymous FTP.

You can also use anonymous FTP extensively to download software from the Internet for use in administering your Web site. Typically, when you set up an Internet information service (such as Web or Gopher), you start by downloading the appropriate server software from an Internet host. Then, you unpack compressed files and install files according to the instructions. In this book, you see many examples of how to download files with anonymous FTP. From these examples, you learn the important FTP commands.

Although it may be difficult for novice users to learn to use the FTP commands, the Web browser makes downloading files easier by using anonymous FTP. When you define a hypertext link with the appropriate format, users can click on the link on a Web page and view a listing of files available for downloading. To download a file, the user simply clicks on the filename. Because Web makes it simple to use anonymous FTP, many Web sites provide files for downloading through anonymous FTP.

Note   FTP is an integral part of UNIX. Typically, the FTP server is already set up on your UNIX system, but you have to perform some steps to set up anonymous FTP.

Anonymous FTP has one drawback — it creates a potential for someone to break into your system and do something that harms it. This vandalism can happen because anonymous FTP allows anyone on the Internet to log into your system, and an intelligent user can access sensitive files on your system. However, with proper care you can set up anonymous FTP so that all that any user can do is download a designated set of files from your system (see the "Make anonymous FTP secure" section for more information).

Gopher

Until 1991, you couldn't easily locate information on the Internet. If, however, you knew the location of a file, you could use anonymous FTP to download that file.

Around 1991, a program named *Archie* was developed at McGill University. Like the Web search tools of today, Archie is a search tool that can locate files in anonymous FTP sites. Archie accesses anonymous FTP sites and creates a database of files that are available through anonymous FTP. A user runs an Archie client, connects to an Archie server, and then searches for a file by name. This provides the location of files with matching names. Then FTP is used to download the file. Still, Archie was a big step forward in locating information on the Internet.

As Archie gained popularity, a team at the University of Minnesota developed a simple menu-based system called *Gopher* for distributing information throughout the campus. To use Gopher, you must run a Gopher client program. The Gopher client connects to a Gopher server and displays a menu based on information sent by the server. Figure 2-1 shows a typical text-based menu displayed by a Gopher client.

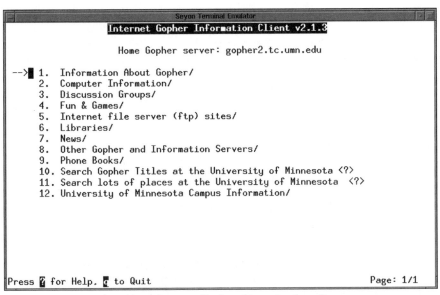

```
                        Seyon Terminal Emulator
              Internet Gopher Information Client v2.1.3

                  Home Gopher server: gopher2.tc.umn.edu

  -->█ 1.    Information About Gopher/
        2.    Computer Information/
        3.    Discussion Groups/
        4.    Fun & Games/
        5.    Internet file server (ftp) sites/
        6.    Libraries/
        7.    News/
        8.    Other Gopher and Information Servers/
        9.    Phone Books/
       10.    Search Gopher Titles at the University of Minnesota <?>
       11.    Search lots of places at the University of Minnesota  <?>
       12.    University of Minnesota Campus Information/




Press ? for Help. ? to Quit                            Page: 1/1
```

Figure 2-1: A typical text-based menu displayed by a Gopher client.

The user browses and downloads information by selecting menu items. The Gopher client can also display text data downloaded from the server.

URL To set up a Gopher server on your UNIX system, you need the server software. This software is available by anonymous FTP from the system `boombox.micro.umn.edu` in the `/pub/gopher/Unix` directory. You learn how to download, unpack, and set up a Gopher server in the "Running a Gopher service" section of this chapter.

Wide Area Information Servers (WAIS)

WAIS (pronounced *"ways"*) was developed by Thinking Machines, Inc. (in collaboration with Dow Jones, Apple Computer, and KPMG Peat Marwick LLP) as a general-purpose information retrieval system for distributed data. Brewster Kahle, the leader of the WAIS development team at Thinking Machines, formed WAIS, Inc., to develop a commercial version of WAIS. In 1991, however, Thinking Machines released the original version of WAIS on the Internet for free use by anyone. A new organization (funded by the National Science Foundation, a U.S. government agency) called Clearinghouse for Networked Information Discovery and Retrieval (CNIDR) maintains the public domain version of WAIS. This version of WAIS goes by the name `freeWAIS`.

WAIS is a tool designed for searching data (stored in files). WAIS sets up an index of all data beforehand so that when a search request comes in, the server can locate the information quickly. The WAIS indexing software can handle many types of files including text, GIF, TIFF, PostScript, mail, and news (from Internet newsgroups).

A drawback of WAIS is the size of the index file. The indexing software treats each word in a text file as a keyword. Thus, the size of the index may be as large as or larger than the data itself.

Although Gopher and Web allow you to browse data (view data downloaded from a server), WAIS allows you to search for data. Thus, WAIS complements Gopher and the Web. If your Web site maintains a large volume of data and you want users to search through the data files using keywords, you may want to set up WAIS on your system. You can set up a Web-to-WAIS gateway so that users can search and view data directly from a Web browser.

URL If you decide to set up WAIS, you must download the `freeWAIS` software from an Internet site. You can download `freeWAIS` at the same time you download Gopher; `freeWAIS` is also in the `/pub/gopher/Unix` directory (which is where you can find the Gopher software) on the `boombox.micro.umn.edu` system.

Note Although this book does not cover WAIS in detail, you can find more information about WAIS in the *Internet SECRETS* by John R. Levine and Carol Baroudi (published by IDG Books Worldwide, Inc., 1995).

World Wide Web

The World Wide Web is the newest and most exciting of all Internet services. Users find the Web helpful because a graphical browser lets them easily view various types of documents from any server on the Internet. In fact, most Web browsers let the user access all types of Internet information services (FTP, Gopher, WAIS, and more). For example, you can use `telnet` to log into a system directly from the Web browser.

The native *Web documents* (also called *Web pages*) are text files with embedded formatting commands. The document formatting language is known as *Hypertext Markup Language (HTML)*. The Web browser interprets HTML and displays the Web page with appropriate formatting. The Web browser is the client in World Wide Web. The Web server and Web browser exchange information by using a standard protocol called *Hypertext Transfer Protocol (HTTP)*. Thus, the combination of HTTP and HTML form the basis of the Web.

Cross Ref Each Web document is specified by a naming convention called *Uniform Resource Locator (URL)*. As you learn in Chapter 3 (which describes the format of URL in detail), a URL can specify many different types of Internet resources. For example, you can specify FTP and Gopher servers by using a URL.

The URL of a Web page includes the name of the system where that document resides, as well as the name of the document. When the user clicks on a link, the Web browser connects to the Web server on the system where the document resides and requests the document by name. The server sends the document; the Web browser client interprets and displays that document. In this manner, the user can move from one link to another browsing Web pages stored on systems across the Internet.

Cross Ref This book is all about the Web, so I won't describe the Web anymore in this chapter. You find a more detailed overview of the Web in Chapter 3. Chapter 4 presents the Web from the user's point of view. Subsequent chapters cover all other aspects of the Web — from preparing HTML documents to developing Java applications — to present your Web site's information in a unique way.

Sharing Information through Mailing Lists

Electronic mail — e-mail — is one of the most popular services on the Internet. Everyone likes the convenience of being able to send a message without having to play the game of "phone tag," in which you leave phone messages for each other without ever successfully making a contact by phone. When you send an e-mail message, it waits in the recipient's mailbox until the recipient is ready to read it.

E-mail started as a simple mechanism in which messages were copied to a user's mailbox file, and that simple mechanism is still used today. In most UNIX systems, your mail messages are stored in the /usr/spool/mail directory in a text file with the same name as your user name.

Messages are still addressed to a user name. If John Doe logs in with the user name jdoe, all of his e-mail is addressed to jdoe. The only other piece of information needed to uniquely identify the recipient is the fully qualified domain name (FQDN) of the recipient's system. Thus, if John Doe's system is named someplace.net, his complete e-mail address becomes jdoe@someplace.net. Given that address, anyone on the Internet can send e-mail to John Doe.

Most UNIX systems come with ready-to-use e-mail software. To set up and use e-mail on a UNIX system, you need two types of mail software:

Note ✦ *Mail user agent* software allows you to read your mail messages, write replies, and compose new messages.

Note ✦ *Mail transport agent* software sends and receives mail message text. The exact method used for mail transport depends on the underlying network. In TCP/IP networks, the mail transport agent delivers mail by using the Simple Mail Transfer Protocol (SMTP). Most UNIX systems use sendmail, a powerful and popular mail transport agent for TCP/IP networks.

Most mail transport agents run as *daemons* — background processes that run as long as your system is up. The reason is that you or another user on the system may send mail at any time, and the transport agent has to be there to deliver the mail to its destination. The mail user agent runs only when the user wants to check mail.

Webmaster Typically, the startup scripts automatically start a mail transport agent after the system boots. Most UNIX systems use the `sendmail` mail transport agent. Because the system is usually set up to start `sendmail` at boot time, you just have to use an appropriate `sendmail` configuration file to start e-mail on your UNIX system.

The `sendmail` configuration file

You cannot use e-mail until the `sendmail` mail transport agent is configured properly; mail cannot be sent or received if `sendmail` is not configured properly. `sendmail` has the reputation of being a complex but complete mail-delivery system. If you look at `sendmail`'s configuration file (`/etc/sendmail.cf`), you see that `sendmail` is indeed complex. Luckily, you do not have to become an expert on the `sendmail` configuration file (a whole book has been written on that subject; see the sidebar "More on `sendmail`"). All you need is a predefined configuration file from another system and you're all set. Often your UNIX system comes with a `sendmail` configuration file that should work as is.

The `sendmail` alias file

Along with the `sendmail.cf` file, `sendmail` also consults an alias file named `/etc/aliases` (on some systems, this file is `/usr/lib/aliases`) to convert a name into an address. The location of the alias file appears in the `sendmail` configuration file.

Each alias is typically a shorter name for an e-mail address. The system administrator uses the `sendmail` alias file to forward mail, to create mailing lists (a single alias that means several users), or to refer to a user by several different names. For example, here are some typical aliases:

```
barkakati: naba
naba: naba@lnbsoft
all: naba, leha, ivy, emily, ashley
```

More on `sendmail`

This chapter shows you how to use a `sendmail` configuration file to implement a simple mailing list on your system. `sendmail`, however, is a complex mail system. *sendmail,* by Bryan Costales with Eric Allman and Neil Rickert (O'Reilly & Associates, 1993), can help you learn how to configure `sendmail`.

The first line says mail sent to barkakati should be delivered to the user named naba on the local system. The second line indicates that mail for naba should be sent to the user name naba on the lnbsoft system. The last line defines all as the alias for the five users naba, leha, ivy, emily, and ashley.

As you see in the "A sendmail alias mailing list" section, you can set up a mailing list simply by defining an alias in the /etc/aliases file. Before you learn how to define a mailing list, however, you must learn about the underlying mechanism used by sendmail to deliver mail, which is explained in the next section.

Mail-delivery mechanism

On an Internet host, the sendmail mail transport agent delivers mail by using the Simple Mail Transfer Protocol (SMTP). For documentation on SMTP, see RFC 821, "Simple Mail Transfer Protocol," Jonathan Postel, 1982.

Webmaster SMTP-based mail transport agents listen to the TCP port 25 and use a small set of text commands to interact with other mail transport agents. In fact, the commands are simple enough for you to use them directly to send a mail message. The following example shows how I use SMTP commands to send a mail message to my account on a Linux system from a telnet session running on another system on the LAN:

```
telnet lnbsoft.com 25
220-lnbsoft.com Sendmail 8.6.12/8.6.9 ready at Sun, 3 Mar 1996 22:46:11 -0500
220 ESMTP spoken here
HELO
250 lnbsoft.com Hello lnb486 [206.197.168.100], pleased to meet you
MAIL FROM: naba@lnb486.lnbsoft.com
250 lnb486... Sender ok
RCPT TO: naba
250 naba... Recipient ok
DATA
354 Enter mail, end with "." on a line by itself
Testing ...1 2 3
Sending mail by telnet to port 25
.
250 WAA00951 Message accepted for delivery
QUIT
221 lnbsoft.com closing connection
Connection closed by foreign host.
```

In this listing, my input (the commands I typed) appears in boldface. The other text is displayed by the system. The strings HELO, MAIL FROM, RCPT TO, DATA, and QUIT are SMTP commands.

I begin the session with the `telnet` command that opens a `telnet` session to port 25 — the port where `sendmail` expects SMTP commands. The `sendmail` process on the Linux system immediately replies with an announcement.

I type HELO to introduce myself. The `sendmail` process replies with a greeting. To send the mail message, I start with the `MAIL FROM:` command that specifies the sender of the message (I enter the user name on the system from which I am sending the message).

Next, I use the `RCPT TO:` command to specify the recipient of the message. If I want to send the message to several recipients, I just provide each recipient's address with the `RCPT TO:` command.

To enter the mail message, I use the `DATA` command. In response to the `DATA` command, `sendmail` displays an instruction that tells me to end the message with a period on a line by itself. I enter the message and end it with a single period on a separate line. The `sendmail` process displays a message indicating that the message has been accepted for delivery. Finally, I quit the session with `sendmail` by using the `QUIT` command.

Afterward, I log into my Linux system and check mail with the `mail` command. The following is what I see when I display the mail message that I sent through the sample SMTP session with `sendmail`:

```
Message 6:
From naba@lnb486.lnbsoft.com Sun Mar  3 22:47:08 1996
Date: Sun, 3 Mar 1996 22:46:36 -0500
From: naba@lnb486.lnbsoft.com
Apparently-To: naba@lnbsoft.com

Testing ...1 2 3
Sending mail by telnet to port 25
```

As this example shows, the SMTP commands are simple enough to understand. This example should help you understand how a mail transfer agent uses SMTP to transfer mail on the Internet.

Note This SMTP example also illustrates how a typical TCP/IP-based Internet information service works. Services (such as FTP and Web) use protocols of similar form for information exchange between clients and servers.

A `sendmail` **alias mailing list**

You can implement a simple mailing list through a `sendmail` alias. In the list's simplest form, all you have to do is define an alias for the addresses in the `/etc/aliases` file. For example, suppose a large company has several Web sites (one in each major department) and the Webmasters decide to keep in touch through a mailing list. One of the Webmasters, Emily, volunteers to set up a mailing list for the group. To set up the mailing list, Emily (who logs in with the user name `emily`) adds the following alias to the `/etc/aliases` file:

```
webmasters: emily, webmaster@sales, webmaster@mktg, webmaster@appdev,...,
    ...,
    webmaster@admin
```

In this case, the address list includes Emily and the Webmasters at all Web sites in the company (typically, mail to the Webmaster is addressed to the user name `webmaster`). If the list of addresses gets too long to fit in a line, end a line with a comma and then indent the next line with a tab character.

Webmaster After defining an alias in the `/etc/aliases` file, you must log in as `root` and make the new alias active by running the command:

```
/usr/lib/sendmail -bi
```

Along with the `webmasters` alias, you can define two other aliases:

✦ The alias `listname-request` is where users send mail to subscribe to (or "unsubscribe" from) the list.

✦ The alias `owner-listname` is where errors (such as bounced messages) are sent.

In this case, because Emily sets up the `webmasters` list, she may define the two aliases as follows:

```
webmasters-request: emily
owner-webmasters: emily
```

For a simple mailing list, one person is usually responsible for everything.

Storing the address list in a separate file

Although defining an alias with all the addresses works, the drawback is that you must edit the `/etc/aliases` file whenever you want to add a new name to the list. You need to log in as `root` to edit the `/etc/aliases` file (or ask the system administrator to edit the file for you). For ordinary users without the `root` privilege, a better solution is to store the address list in a separate file in your home directory and make `sendmail` read that file with the `:include:` directive in the alias definition.

For example, Emily may put the address list for the `webmasters` list in the `/home/emily/mlist/webms` file (assuming that `/home/emily` is the login directory of user `emily`). If so, the `/etc/aliases` file would reference the address list like this:

```
webmasters: :include:/home/emily/mlist/webms
```

In the `/home/emily/mlist/webms` file, each address appears on a separate line as follows:

```
emily (Emily B. -- list owner)
webmaster@appdev (Webmaster, Application Development Group)
webmaster@mktg (Webmaster, Marketing Department)
```

As you can see, you can put helpful comments in parentheses.

Every time `sendmail` sends a message to the `webmasters` alias, it reads the `/home/emily/mlist/webms` file. Thus, you can add a new user by simply editing this file.

If you use an address file, make sure that only the owner can modify the file. Use the command `chmod 644 filename` to make the file read-only for everyone but the owner (that's what the 644 permission means).

Ensuring that replies go to the list

Tip When you set up a mailing list, you want any replies to go back to everyone in the list so that discussions can take place among the group. When you use a `sendmail` alias to define a mailing list, however, the reply goes back to the person who sent the message instead of the entire list. To correct this problem, make the alias start a new `sendmail` process and change the sender's address through the `-f` option of `sendmail`.

The following approach shows you how to define the `webmasters` list:

```
webmasters: "|/usr/lib/sendmail -fwebmasters -oi dist-webmasters"
dist-webmasters: :include:/home/emily/mlist/webms
```

This definition of `webmasters` runs `sendmail` with the `-f` option (this option sets the From address of the message) and sends mail to another alias (`dist-webmasters`) that points to the file containing the actual addresses. The `-f` option works only when mail is sent by a trusted user such as `root` (you can specify the trusted users in the `sendmail.cf` configuration file).

Note When mail for the list arrives from another system, `sendmail` runs under a trusted user name. So, the mail goes with `webmasters` as the return address. Unfortunately, when a user on the local system sends mail, the `-f` option does not work because `sendmail` runs under that user's name (and the user probably is not considered a trusted user). A solution to this problem is to set up the mailing list on a system where none of the list members have an account; this ensures that mail to the list always comes from a remote system.

Using Majordomo to automate mailing lists

Majordomo is a set of Perl scripts (written by Brent Chapman) that automate the task of managing mailing lists. The following sections show you how to download Majordomo from the Internet (you have to use anonymous FTP) and set it up on your system.

Note As you learn from the following sections, to install Majordomo on your system, you need a C compiler (for a program called `wrapper`) and Perl Version 4.036 (also known as Perl 4.0 Patch level 36). If your system does not have Perl, you can get it through anonymous FTP from many Internet sites such as `ftp.uu.net`.

Getting the files

URL You can get the Majordomo files as a compressed `tar` archive (`tar` is a UNIX archiving format) through anonymous FTP from the `ftp.greatcircle.com` site. The following is a sequence of commands that I used to download the Majordomo files (my input appears in boldface and comments appear in italic):

```
ftp ftp.greatcircle.com
Connected to miles.GreatCircle.COM.
220 miles FTP server (Version 5.60auth/mjr) ready.
Name (ftp.greatcircle.com:naba): anonymous
331 Guest login ok, send ident as password.
Password:   (Enter your e-mail address)
230 Guest login ok, access restrictions apply.
Remote system type is UNIX.
Using binary mode to transfer files.
ftp> cd /pub/majordomo
250 CWD command successful.
ftp> get majordomo-1.93.README
200 PORT command successful.
150 Opening BINARY mode data connection for majordomo-1.93.README (54569 bytes).
226 Transfer complete.
54569 bytes received in 9.86 seconds (5.41 Kbytes/s)
ftp> get majordomo-1.93.tar.Z
200 PORT command successful.
150 Opening BINARY mode data connection for majordomo-1.93.tar.Z (243507 bytes).
226 Transfer complete.
243507 bytes received in 50.99 seconds (4.66 Kbytes/s)
ftp> get majordomo-faq.txt
200 PORT command successful.
150 Opening BINARY mode data connection for majordomo-faq.txt (43954 bytes).
226 Transfer complete.
43954 bytes received in 10.88 seconds (3.95 Kbytes/s)
ftp> bye
221 Goodbye.
```

The `majordomo-1.93.tar.Z` file is the main Majordomo distribution; the other files are Majordomo documentation. In particular, you should read the `majordomo-1.93.README` file for information on installing and configuring Majordomo. The next few sections summarize the steps.

Installing and configuring Majordomo

After you download the Majordomo files, you have to first unpack the archive, and then install and configure Majordomo. The following steps show you how to install and configure Majordomo:

1. Log in as `root` and add a new user named `majordom`. Specify 54 as both user ID and group ID (Majordomo Makefile uses these values). Specify `/usr/local/majordomo` as the home directory.

2. Use the `mv` command to move the `majordomo-1.93.tar.Z` file to the `/usr/local/majordomo` directory.

3. Uncompress the file with the following command:

   ```
   uncompress majordomo-1.93.tar.Z
   ```

   This creates the file `majordomo-1.93.tar`.

4. Extract files from the `tar` archive with the following command:

   ```
   tar xvf majordomo-1.93.tar
   ```

   This creates a `majordomo-1.93` directory in `/usr/local/majordomo` and puts a number of files in that directory.

5. Change directory to `/usr/local/majordomo/majordomo-1.93` and edit the Makefile. Make sure that the variable `W_BIN` is set as follows:

   ```
   W_BIN=/usr/local/majordomo
   ```

6. Type `make` to build the `wrapper` program.

7. Type `make install` to copy Perl scripts to the `/usr/local/majordomo` directory.

8. Type `make install-wrapper` to install the `wrapper` program (the `wrapper` program provides a security layer; the Perl scripts execute through the `wrapper`).

9. Set up `/etc/majordomo.cf` as a link to the Majordomo configuration file `/usr/local/majordomo/majordomo.cf` as follows:

   ```
   ln -s /usr/local/majordomo/majordomo.cf /etc/majordomo.cf
   ```

10. If your system does not have Perl installed in `/usr/local/bin`, add a symbolic link from `/usr/local/bin/perl` to wherever you have Perl installed on your system. For example, if the Perl executable is `/usr/bin/perl`, use the following command to set up the symbolic link:

    ```
    ln -s /usr/bin/perl /usr/local/bin/perl
    ```

11. Edit the Majordomo configuration file, `/usr/local/majordomo/majordomo.cf`, and set the following Perl variables:

> `$whereami` to the name of the host where Majordomo is set up
>
> `$homedir` to location of Majordomo files (`/usr/local/majordomo`)
>
> `$listdir` to the directory where Majordomo lists reside

12. Edit the `sendmail` aliases file (`/etc/aliases` or `/usr/lib/aliases` depending on the version of UNIX), and then add the following lines:

```
# Majordomo
owner-majordomo: list-owner-name
majordomo:"|/usr/local/majordomo/wrapper majordomo"
majordom: owner-majordomo
```

Replace `list-owner-name` with the name of the user who manages the Majordomo lists.

This completes the basic installation and configuration of Majordomo. Now, you can add mailing lists.

Creating a Majordomo mailing list

To create a new Majordomo mailing list, you have to add a number of aliases to the `sendmail` aliases file. For example, suppose I want to set up and manage a mailing list called `webms` (for Webmasters). Then, I would add the following lines to the `/usr/lib/aliases` file. (Note that my login ID is `naba`.):

```
# A list
owner-webms: naba
webms: "|/usr/local/majordomo/wrapper resend -l webms -h lnbsoft.com webms-
    outgoing"
webms-approval: owner-webms
webms-outgoing: :include:/usr/local/majordomo/lists/webms
owner-webms-outgoing: owner-webms

webms-archive: "|/usr/local/majordomo/wrapper archive -f /usr/local/majordomo/
    archives/webms -m -a"
owner-webms-archive: owner-webms

webms-request: "|/usr/local/majordomo/wrapper request-answer webms"
owner-webms-request: owner-webms
```

Next, I must add the names of the recipients to the file named `webms` in the `/usr/local/majordomo/lists` directory (the directory specified by the variable named `$listdir` in the Majordomo configuration file). For example, I may add:

```
naba (Naba B. -- list owner)
webmaster@appdev (Webmaster, Application Development Group)
webmaster@mktg (Webmaster, Marketing Department)
```

This creates a Majordomo list. Now, I can send mail to `webms` and have Majordomo send the mail to everyone on the list.

Webmaster Before you can use the new aliases, you must log in as `root` and make `sendmail` read the aliases. Type the following command to reload the aliases:

```
/usr/lib/sendmail -bi
```

Tip If the mailing list does not work, you may have permission settings on the directories and files. Also, Majordomo can automatically add or delete names from the mailing list — all this can be done by sending mail to Majordomo. To learn more about this and to troubleshoot any problems, please read the `majordomo-1.93.README` file in the `/usr/local/majordomo` directory.

Serving Files with Anonymous FTP

Anonymous FTP is a common service on the Internet. When you use FTP to transfer files to or from a remote system, you must log into the remote system before you can use the `ftp` command.

Note Anonymous FTP refers to the use of the user name `anonymous`, which anyone can use with the `ftp` command to transfer files from a system. Anonymous FTP is a common way to share files on the Internet. In this chapter's previous section called "Using Majordomo to automate mailing lists," you saw an example of how to download software by using anonymous FTP. Throughout this book, you see many other examples of how to use anonymous FTP to download software from the Internet.

If you have used anonymous FTP to download files from various Internet sites, you already know the convenience of that service. With anonymous FTP, you can make information available to anyone on Internet. If you have software that you want to share with the world, set up anonymous FTP on your system and place the software in an appropriate directory. After that, all you need to do is announce to the world (probably through a posting in a newsgroup) that you have a new program available. Now anyone can get the software from your system at his or her convenience.

Tip Even if you run a for-profit business, you can use anonymous FTP to support your customers. If you sell some hardware or software product, you may want to provide technical information or software "fixes" through anonymous FTP.

Unfortunately, the convenience of anonymous FTP comes at a price. If you do not configure the anonymous FTP service properly, intruders and pranksters may gain access to your system. Some intruders may simply use your system's disk as a temporary holding place for various files; others may fill your disk with junk files, effectively making your system inoperable. At the other extreme, an intruder may gain user-level (or, worse, `root`-level) access to your system and do much more damage.

Note You may already have anonymous FTP available on your system. The default setup, however, may not employ all possible security precautions.

The following sections show you how to try out and secure an anonymous FTP server on your UNIX system.

Try existing anonymous `ftp` service

You can try the existing anonymous `ftp` service from any Internet site or a system on your LAN — even from your UNIX system.

The following is a sample anonymous FTP session from an Internet host to my UNIX system (my input appears in boldface):

```
access5% ftp dcc05211.slip.digex.net
Connected to dcc05211.slip.digex.net.
220 dcc05211 FTP server (Version wu-2.4(1) Wed May 10 21:00:32 CDT 1995) ready.
Name (dcc05211.slip.digex.net:naba): anonymous
331 Guest login ok, send your complete e-mail address as password.
Password:              (I typed xx)
230-The response 'xx' is not valid
230-Next time please use your e-mail address as your password
230-     for example: joe@access5.digex.net
230-Welcome, archive user! This is an experimental FTP server. If have any
230-unusual problems, please report them via e-mail to root@dcc05211
230-If you do have problems, please try using a dash (-) as the first character
230-of your password -- this will turn off the continuation messages that may
230-be confusing your ftp client.
230-
230 Guest login ok, access restrictions apply.
ftp> ls -l
200 PORT command successful.
150 Opening ASCII mode data connection for /bin/ls.
total 7
drwxrwxr-x  2 root    wheel    1024 Sep 28 20:44 bin
drwxrwxr-x  2 root    wheel    1024 Sep 28 20:44 etc
drwxrwxr-x  2 root    wheel    1024 Dec 3 1993 incoming
drwxrwxr-x  2 root    wheel    1024 Nov 17 1993 lib
drwxrwxr-x  2 root    wheel    1024 Sep 28 20:44 pub
drwxrwxr-x  3 root    wheel    1024 Sep 28 20:44 usr
-rw-r--r--  1 root    root      312 Aug 1 1994 welcome.msg
226 Transfer complete.
remote: -l
442 bytes received in 0.18 seconds (2.4 Kbytes/s)
ftp> cd pub
250 CWD command successful.
ftp> ls -l
200 PORT command successful.
150 Opening ASCII mode data connection for /bin/ls.
```

(continued)

```
total 0
-rwxrwxr-x  1 root    wheel      0 Jul 10 1993 dummy_test_file
226 Transfer complete.
remote: -l
81 bytes received in 0.059 seconds (1.3 Kbytes/s)
ftp> bye
221 Goodbye.
access5%
```

Why worry about anonymous ftp?

To understand why there are worries about the use of anonymous FTP, you must know how FTP works. The FTP server listens to TCP port 21. An FTP client program communicates with the server by using a set of text commands. Additionally, anyone also can communicate with the FTP server by running the telnet program and connecting to port 21. The following is a sample session with the default anonymous ftp setup on my UNIX system (my input appears in boldface):

```
telnet dcc05211.slip.digex.net 21
Trying 204.192.70.170 ...
Connected to dcc05211.slip.digex.net.
Escape character is '^]'.
220 dcc05211 FTP server (Version wu-2.4(1) Wed May 10 21:00:32 CDT 1995) ready.
help
214-The following commands are recognized (* =>'s unimplemented).
  USER  PORT  STOR  MSAM*  RNTO  NLST  MKD   CDUP
  PASS  PASV  APPE  MRSQ*  ABOR  SITE  XMKD  XCUP
  ACCT* TYPE  MLFL* MRCP*  DELE  SYST  RMD   STOU
  SMNT* STRU  MAIL* ALLO   CWD   STAT  XRMD  SIZE
  REIN* MODE  MSND* REST   XCWD  HELP  PWD   MDTM
  QUIT  RETR  MSOM* RNFR   LIST  NOOP  XPWD
214 Direct comments to ftp-bugs@dcc05211.
help site
214-The following SITE commands are recognized (* =>'s unimplemented).
  UMASK  CHMOD  GROUP  NEWER  INDEX  ALIAS  GROUPS
  IDLE   HELP   GPASS  MINFO  EXEC   CDPATH
214 Direct comments to ftp-bugs@dcc05211.
USER anonymous
331 Guest login ok, send your complete e-mail address as password.
PASS xx
230-The response 'xx' is not valid
230-Next time please use your e-mail address as your password
230-    for example: joe@access5.digex.net
230-Welcome, archive user! This is an experimental FTP server. If have any
230-unusual problems, please report them via e-mail to root@dcc05211
230-If you do have problems, please try using a dash (-) as the first character
230-of your password -- this will turn off the continuation messages that may
230-be confusing your ftp client.
```

```
230-
230 Guest login ok, access restrictions apply.
site exec ls -1
200-ls -1
200-total 7
200-drwxrwxr-x  2 root    wheel    1024 Sep 28 20:44 bin
200-drwxrwxr-x  2 root    wheel    1024 Sep 28 20:44 etc
200-drwxrwxr-x  2 root    wheel    1024 Dec 3 1993 incoming
200-drwxrwxr-x  2 root    wheel    1024 Nov 17 1993 lib
200-drwxrwxr-x  2 root    wheel    1024 Sep 28 20:44 pub
200-drwxrwxr-x  3 root    wheel    1024 Sep 28 20:44 usr
200--rw-r--r--  1 root    root      312 Aug 1 1994 welcome.msg
200 (end of 'ls -1')
quit
221 Goodbye.
Connection closed by foreign host.
```

Webmaster This listing shows the FTP commands, including some potentially troublesome commands, such as SITE EXEC. In some older versions of FTP, you can use this command to gain shell access. Luckily, however, all known security holes have been fixed in this example's version of the FTP server.

Webmaster Another typical problem with anonymous FTP is the permission settings of the home directory of the user named ftp — the user name for anyone who logs into ftp as anonymous. If /home/ftp — the home directory of the anonymous ftp user — is owned by ftp, anyone could use one of the SITE commands and create new files. The permission setting of the /home/ftp directory tree is something that you must change so that you can fix any potential security problems with anonymous FTP.

Make anonymous FTP secure

To avoid any potential security problems with anonymous FTP, you should follow a specified set of guidelines. The following basic steps show you how to make anonymous FTP secure:

1. Log in as root, and use the following commands:

   ```
   cd /home
   ls -1R ftp | more
   ```

2. Look through the resulting directory listing, and verify that all files are owned by root. If not, use the chown root * command to change the file's ownership to root.

3. Change the `ftp` user's shell to `/bin/false`, because the `ftp` user does not need a shell to log in. Here's how to change the shell for the `ftp` user:

```
chsh ftp
Changing shell for ftp.
New shell [/bin/true]: /bin/false
warning: "/bin/false" is not listed as a valid shell.
Shell changed.
Ignore the warning from chsh.
```

4. Change the permission setting of the `ftp` user's home directory, denoted by `~ftp`, to 555 (read and execute only), as follows:

```
chmod 555 ~ftp
```

5. Change the permission setting of `~ftp/bin` and `~ftp/etc` to 111 (execute only). Also change the permission of the contents of `~ftp/bin` to 111, as follows:

```
chmod 111 ~ftp/etc
chmod 111 ~ftp/bin
chmod 111 ~ftp/bin/*
```

6. Make sure that the `~ftp/etc/passwd` file does not contain any encrypted passwords; replace all password fields with an asterisk. In particular, make sure that the `root` user does not have a blank password field (as indicated by two adjacent colons), like this one:

```
root::0:0:root:/:/bin/sh
```

Use a text editor, and put an asterisk between the first pair of colons, as follows:

```
root:*:0:0:root:/:/bin/sh
```

7. Change the permission setting of all files in the `~ftp/etc` directory to 444 (read only), as follows:

```
chmod 444 ~ftp/etc/*
```

8. Change the permission settings of `~ftp/pub`, `~ftp/usr`, and `~ftp/lib` to 555, as follows:

```
chmod 555 ~ftp/pub
chmod 555 ~ftp/usr
chmod 555 ~ftp/lib
```

9. The `~ftp/incoming` directory is used to allow anonymous `ftp` users to leave files on your system. You can make this directory somewhat secure by changing the permission settings of the `~ftp/incoming` directory to 1733, as follows:

```
chmod 1733 ~ftp/incoming
```

This permission setting allows anonymous users to copy files into the `incoming` directory, but does not allow them to view the contents of the directory or delete any existing files.

10. Just to be safe, create zero-length `.rhosts` and `.forward` files in `~ftp`, and make them read-only, as follows:

```
touch ~ftp/.rhosts
touch ~ftp/.forward
chmod 400 ~ftp/.rhosts
chmod 400 ~ftp/.forward
```

Cross Ref Chapter 9 provides more information on how to secure your Web site. In that chapter, you'll also find more details on securing the Washington University FTP server (called the *WU FTP daemon*) — one of the common FTP servers used on UNIX systems.

Running a Gopher Service

As a Webmaster, you can set up a Gopher server to provide menu-based access to information stored in files on your Web site. To set up the Gopher server, you have to perform the following general steps:

✦ Use anonymous FTP to download the Gopher software from the University of Minnesota.

✦ Extract the files from the downloaded compressed archive.

✦ Edit the Makefile and build the Gopher server and client programs.

✦ Install the Gopher software in appropriate directories.

✦ Prepare the information to be served by the Gopher server.

✦ Start the Gopher server.

The following sections walk you through the basic steps.

Gopher protocol

Before you download and set up the Gopher software, you should see the Gopher protocol in action. Like most other Internet services (such as FTP and SMTP), Gopher clients and servers use simple text messages to communicate with each other.

A Gopher client first connects to port 70 of the system where the Gopher server is running. Then, it sends a *selector string* — a string that describes the document that the client wants. The server responds by sending the document. Then, it ends the transfer with a single period and closes the connection. If the client sends a single carriage return, the Gopher server returns a directory listing.

URL   You can test the Gopher protocol by using the `telnet` program. Here's a sample session with the Gopher server at the University of Minnesota (the system is `gopher.tc.umn.edu`):

```
telnet gopher.tc.umn.edu 70
Trying 134.84.132.3...
Connected to gopher.tc.umn.edu.
Escape character is '^]'.
(Press Enter)
1Information About Gopher  <t> 1/Information About Gopher <t> gopher.tc.umn.edu
    <t> 70 <t> +
1Computer Information <t> 1/computer <t> spinaltap.micro.umn.edu <t> 70
1Discussion Groups <t> 1/Mailing Lists <t> gopher.tc.umn.edu <t> 70 <t> +
1Fun & Games <t> 1/fun <t> spinaltap.micro.umn.edu <t> 70
1Internet file server (ftp) sites <t> 1/FTP Searches <t> gopher.tc.umn.edu <t>
    70 <t> +
1Libraries <t> 1/Libraries <t> gopher.tc.umn.edu <t> 70 <t> +
1News <t> 1/News <t> gopher.tc.umn.edu <t> 70 <t> +
1Other Gopher and Information Servers <t> 1/Other Gopher and Information Servers
    <t> gopher.tc.umn.edu <t> 70 <t> +
1Phone Books <t> 1/Phone Books <t> gopher.tc.umn.edu <t> 70 <t> +
7Search Gopher Titles at the University of Minnesota <t> mudhoney.micro.umn.edu
    <t> 4325
7Search lots of places at the University of Minnesota <t> mindex:/lotsoplaces
    spinaltap.micro.umn.edu <t> 70
1University of Minnesota Campus Information <t> 1/uofm <t> gopher.tc.umn.edu <t>
    70 <t> +
.
Connection closed by foreign host.
```

This listing shows the raw text that the server sends. Each line has anywhere from three to five columns — tab characters separate the columns. In the listing, the tab character is shown as <t>. The Gopher client typically presents this as a menu. Figure 2-1 shows the Gopher menu corresponding to the text in the listing.

The first column of each line starts with a character that indicates the type of item followed by the item's full name. The second column is the selector string that the client must send to retrieve that item. The third and fourth items provide the Gopher server's name and port number, respectively. Some items have a fifth column with a plus sign (+) — these items have a Gopher+ attribute (Gopher+ is an extended version of the Gopher protocol that allows the server to provide additional blocks of information).

Note   You may be interested in the item type code — the single character at the beginning of each line. Knowledge of the type code tells you about the kind of information that a Gopher server can provide to clients. The following table describes the type code:

Type	Denotes
0	Text file
1	Directory
2	CSO phone book server
3	Error
4	Macintosh file in BinHex format (a format for encoding binary data)
5	DOS binary archive
6	UNIX uuencoded file
7	Index-search server
8	`telnet` session
9	Binary file
g	GIF image
h	HTML data
I	Image data
i	Inline text
M	Multipurpose Internet Mail Extension (MIME) data
s	Sound file
T	3270 terminal connection

Download Gopher software

URL The latest version of Gopher software is available from the University of Minnesota. You should download it through anonymous FTP from `boombox.micro.umn.edu`. The following listing shows the anonymous FTP session used to download Version 2.3 of Gopher (user input appears in boldface):

```
ftp boombox.micro.umn.edu
Connected to boombox.micro.umn.edu.
220 boombox.micro.umn.edu FTP server (Version wu-2.4(1) Wed Nov 22 12:32:08 PST
    1995) ready.
Name (boombox.micro.umn.edu:root): anonymous
331 Guest login ok, send your complete e-mail address as password.
Password:  (Enter your e-mail address here)
230-
230-Welcome to the University of Minnesota Academic & Distributed
230-Computing Services FTP site.
230-
230-
```

(continued)

```
230 Guest login ok, access restrictions apply.
Remote system type is UNIX.
Using binary mode to transfer files.
ftp> cd /pub/gopher/Unix
250 CWD command successful.
ftp> binary
200 Type set to I.
ftp> get gopher2_3.tar.gz
200 PORT command successful.
150 Opening BINARY mode data connection for gopher2_3.tar.gz (457136 bytes).
226 Transfer complete.
457136 bytes received in 229 secs (1.9 Kbytes/sec)
ftp> bye
221 Goodbye.
```

I used a 28.8 Kbps dial-up TCP/IP connection for this FTP transfer; that's why it took 229 seconds to transfer 457,136 bytes. On a higher bandwidth network connection, you may be able to transfer the file in 10 to 15 seconds.

The downloaded file is a UNIX `tar` archive that has been compressed with the GNU ZIP (GZIP) file compression program. I can tell all these from the file's name: `gopher2_3.tar.gz`. Many users provide files in compressed form to minimize the time needed to download the file. You have to uncompress and extract the files before you can set up the Gopher software.

Extract the Gopher source files

To extract the files from the downloaded compressed archive, copy the file to a suitable directory. (A good location is `/usr/local/src`.) Assuming that the `gopher2_3.tar.gz` file is already in `/usr/local/src`, use the following commands to uncompress the file (if you have downloaded a different version of Gopher, use that file's name in the `gunzip` command):

```
cd /usr/local/src
gunzip gopher2_3.tar.gz
```

This creates the file `gopher2_3.tar`. You may want to use the `ls -l` command to look at the file's size. You see a listing similar to this:

```
ls -l gopher*.tar
-rw-r--r--  1 naba      users     1835008 Mar  2 16:25 gopher2_3.tar
```

Note The compressed file was 457,136 bytes in size — roughly a fourth of the original file's size (1,835,008 bytes). Now you see why files are usually distributed in compressed form; downloading a compressed file saves a lot of time.

To extract the files from the `tar` file (`gopher2_3.tar`), use the `tar` command with the `xvf` option as follows:

```
tar xvf gopher2_3.tar
```

The `tar` command creates a directory named `gopher2_3` and places in it all the extracted files. The name of the directory may be different if you download a more recent version of Gopher than Version 2.3 (which is why the directory name is `gopher2_3`).

Build the Gopher programs

After unpacking the source code, you must build the Gopher software. Typically, you have to edit a Makefile and run the `make` command to build any software package you download from the Internet. The steps to build the Gopher software are even easier than usual; Gopher 2.3 comes with a utility program named `config` that automatically configures all the files used to build the Gopher server and client programs.

Perform the following steps to build and install the Gopher programs:

1. In the `/usr/local/src/gopher2_3` directory, type `config`. The `config` program checks for various header files and features of your system and generates new Makefiles to build the Gopher software on your system.

2. Type `make` to build the Gopher server and client programs.

3. Type `make install` to install the Gopher server and client, as well as the manual pages. By default, the Gopher client (`gopher`) is installed in the `/usr/local/bin` directory and the Gopher server program (`gopherd`) is installed in the `/usr/local/etc` directory.

That's it! You're done building and installing the Gopher software on your system.

Try out the Gopher client

After you install the Gopher software, you may want to try out the Gopher client program (called `gopher`). If your PATH environment variable includes the `/usr/local/bin` directory, you can run the Gopher client with the following command:

```
gopher
```

By default, the Gopher client connects to the Gopher server `gopher.tc.umn.edu` (the default home Gopher server), downloads the directory, and displays the directory as a menu (similar to the one in Figure 2-1). Your system's Internet connection must be up for this to work.

If the Gopher client starts up properly and displays the contents of the default home server, then the client works properly.

Configure the Gopher server

Now that you installed the Gopher software and tried the client program, you must configure the Gopher server (called `gopherd` for Gopher daemon). To configure the Gopher server, you have to edit the `gopherd.conf` configuration file.

Note The `gopherd.conf` configuration file controls how the Gopher server works. By default, both the Gopher server and its configuration file are installed in the `/usr/local/etc` directory. In this directory, you find an existing `gopherd.conf` file that you can edit to suit your needs. Each line in the configuration file has the following syntax:

```
Attribute: Value
```

This specifies the value for an attribute. For example, the `Org` attribute — the name of the organization that runs the site — may be defined as follows:

```
Org: LNB Software, Inc.
```

You can set many attributes in the configuration file. At a minimum, you must set the following attributes:

- ✦ `Site`: name of the site
- ✦ `Org`: name of the organization
- ✦ `Loc`: address of the site
- ✦ `Abstract`: summary of what the site offers
- ✦ `Admin`: name of the site administrator
- ✦ `AdminEmail`: e-mail address of the administrator

Tip You can find more information about the `gopherd.conf` file from the manual pages — just type:

```
man gopherd.conf
```

You should also create a directory named `/tmp/groups` for the Gopher server's use. Finally, you should create a data directory (for example, `/usr/local/gopher-data`) and provide that directory's name on the command-line that starts the Gopher server.

Start the Gopher server

You can start the Gopher server in two ways:

✦ Add an entry for the server in the `/etc/inetd.conf` and let `inetd` start the Gopher server whenever a client attempts to connect at port 70 of your system.

✦ Run the server as a daemon (a process that runs continuously).

Although it takes some system resources (memory and processor time) to keep the Gopher server running as a daemon, the server's response is better when it's already running. Therefore, you may want to run the Gopher server as a daemon.

To start the Gopher server, run the `gopherd` program with appropriate command-line options. (You may want to view the online manual for `gopherd` with the command `man gopherd`.)

```
cd /usr/local/etc
gopherd -u nobody -o /usr/local/etc/gopherd.conf /usr/local/gopher-data 70
```

This command causes the Gopher server to run under the user name `nobody` and serve data from the `/usr/local/gopher-data` directory on port 70 (the `-o` option specifies the Gopher configuration file).

Tip   You can run the Gopher client (type `gopher your-host-name`) to verify that your system's Gopher server is up and running.

Summary

Internet information services are the lifeblood of the Internet. Services (such as e-mail, FTP, Gopher, and Web) make it possible for the users to access information through client applications (such as a Web browser). This chapter provides an overview of Internet information services with a focus on e-mail, FTP, and Gopher. The next chapter introduces World Wide Web — the information service that has fueled the explosive growth of the Internet.

Where to go next . . .

✦ As a Webmaster, you must know a lot about the World Wide Web. If you are somewhat new to the Web, you should start with Chapter 3, which provides an overview of the Web.

✦ To get a user's view of the Web, see Chapter 4.

✦ If you had enough of an overview and want to set up your Web site, see Chapter 6 for a summary of your Web site options.

✦ If you are joining as a Webmaster at an existing Web site, and you want to author HTML documents, proceed to Chapter 10.

✦   ✦   ✦

Introduction to the World Wide Web

Chapter 2 describes many Internet services such as FTP, Gopher, and WAIS. The World Wide Web (WWW, W3, or simply the Web) is another Internet service.

An interesting characteristic of the Web is that the Web browser — the client side of the Web — can also access other Internet information services (such as FTP and Gopher). Thus, the user views the Web as the gateway to various information services.

Along with the Web browser's ability to access many different Internet information services, the Web server can also act as a gateway to information repositories such as traditional relational databases.

Cross Ref As a Webmaster, you must know about the Web. This chapter begins with an overview of the Web. Then Chapter 4 takes you to the client side of the Web and shows how the user uses a Web browser to access information on the Internet. Chapter 5 wraps up the first part of the book by explaining what it means to be a Webmaster.

What Is the World Wide Web?

If you have used a network file server of any kind, you know the convenience of being able to access files that reside at a shared location. By using a word processing application that runs on your computer, you can easily open a document that physically resides on the file server.

Now imagine a word processor that allows you to open and view a document that resides on any computer on the Internet. You can view the document in its full glory, with formatted text and graphics. If the document makes a reference to another document (possibly residing on yet another computer), you can open that linked document by clicking the reference. That kind of easy access to distributed documents is essentially what the World Wide Web provides.

Of course, the documents have to be in a standard format, so that any computer (with the appropriate Web browser software) can access and interpret the document. Additionally, a standard protocol is necessary for transferring Web documents from one system to another.

Note   The standard Web document format is Hypertext Markup Language (HTML), and the standard protocol for exchanging Web documents is Hypertext Transfer Protocol (HTTP).

Note   A *Web server* is the software that provides HTML documents to any client that makes the appropriate HTTP requests. A *Web browser* is the client software that downloads an HTML document from a Web server and graphically displays the contents.

Like a giant spider's web

The World Wide Web is the combination of the Web servers and the HTML documents that contain the information. In this view, the Web is like a giant book whose pages are scattered throughout the Internet. You use a Web browser to view the pages, as illustrated in Figure 3-1.

As Figure 3-1 shows, Web pages — the HTML documents — are linked by network connections that resemble a giant spider's web, so you can see why the Web is called the Web. The "World Wide" part comes from the fact that the Web pages are scattered around the world.

Links and URLs

Like the pages of real books, Web pages contain text and graphics. Unlike real books, however, Web pages can contain multimedia information (such as video clips, digitized sound, and links) to other Web pages that can take the user to the referenced Web page.

The *links* in a Web page are references to other Web pages that you can follow to go from one page to another. The Web browser displays these links as underlined text (in a different color) or images. Each link is like an instruction to the reader — as in "for more information, please consult Chapter 20," which you can find in a real book. In a Web page, just click the link; then the Web browser brings up the referenced page, even if it's on a different computer.

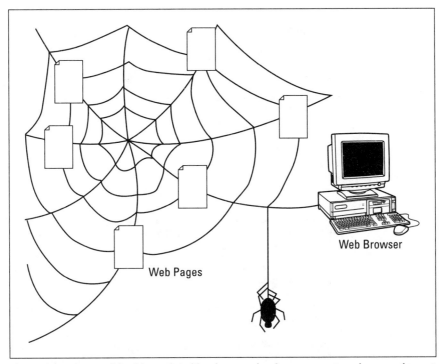

Figure 3-1: The World Wide Web is like thousands of pages, scattered across the network, that you can read from your computer by using a Web browser.

Note The links in a Web page are referred to as *hypertext* links; when you click a link, the Web browser jumps to the Web page referenced by that link.

This arrangement brings up a question. In a real book, you may ask the reader to go to a specific chapter or page in the book. How does a hypertext link indicate the location of the referenced Web page? In the World Wide Web, each Web page has a special name, called a *Uniform Resource Locator (URL)*. A URL uniquely specifies the location of a file on a computer.

As Figure 3-2 illustrates, a URL has the following sequence of components:

1. **Protocol:** The first field in the URL is the name of the protocol you must use to access the data that resides in the file specified by the URL. In Figure 3-2, the protocol is `http://`, which means that the URL specifies the location of a Web page. Listed here are the common protocol types and their meanings:

   ✦ `file://` specifies the name of a local file that is to be opened and displayed. You can use this file to view HTML files without having to connect to the Internet.

   ✦ `ftp://` specifies a file that is accessible through File Transfer Protocol (FTP).

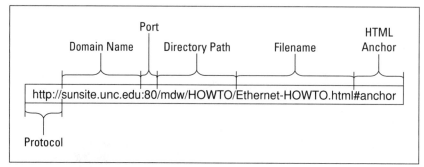

Figure 3-2: Various parts of a Uniform Resource Locator (URL).

- ✦ `gopher://` specifies a document and the name of a host system that runs the Gopher server from which the document is to be retrieved. (Gopher servers provide information by using a simple protocol.)

- ✦ `http://` specifies an HTML document that is accessible through Hypertext Transfer Protocol (HTTP).

- ✦ `mailto://` specifies an e-mail address that can be used to send an e-mail message.

- ✦ `news://` specifies a newsgroup that is to be read by means of Network News Transfer Protocol (NNTP).

- ✦ `telnet://` specifies a user name and a system name for remote login.

- ✦ `wais://` specifies the name of a Wide Area Information Server (WAIS) from which information is to be retrieved.

2. **Domain name:** This part of the URL contains the fully qualified domain name (FQDN) of the computer on which the file specified by this URL resides. You also can specify an IP address (see Chapter 1 for more information on IP addresses) in this field.

3. **Port address:** This field is the port address of the server that implements the protocol listed in the first part of the URL. This part of the URL is optional because you have default ports for all protocols. The default port for HTTP, for example, is 80. Some sites, however, may configure the Web server to listen to a different port. In such a case, the URL must include the port address.

4. **Directory path:** This field is the directory path of the file that is being referenced in the URL. For Web pages, this field is the directory path of the HTML file.

5. **Filename:** This field is the name of the file. For Web pages, the filename typically ends with `.html`. If you omit the filename, the Web server returns a default file (often named `index.html`).

6. HTML anchor: You use this optional part of the URL to make the Web browser jump to a specific location in the file. If this part starts with a question mark (?) instead of a pound sign (#), assume that the text following the question mark is query. The Web server returns information based on such queries.

When you learn more about HTML in Chapter 10, you'll see how to associate a URL with a hypertext link.

Hypertext Transfer Protocol (HTTP)

Hypertext Transfer Protocol (HTTP) — the protocol that underlies the World Wide Web — is called *Hypertext* because Web pages include hypertext links. The *Transfer Protocol* part refers to the standard conventions for transferring a Web page across the network from one computer to another. Although you really do not have to understand HTTP to set up a Web server or use a Web browser, you'll find it instructive to know how the Web works.

Webmaster Before you learn any more about HTTP, you must get a firsthand taste of it. On most systems, the Web server listens to port 80 and responds to any HTTP requests sent to that port. You can, therefore, use the `telnet` program to connect to port 80 of a system that has a Web server, and then try out some HTTP commands.

To see an example of HTTP at work, follow these steps:

1. Make sure that your UNIX system's connection to the Internet is up and running. (If you use SLIP or PPP, for example, make sure that you have established the connection.)

2. Type the following command:

    ```
    telnet www.idgbooks.com 80
    ```

3. After you see the `Connected...` message, type the following HTTP command:

    ```
    GET /
    ```

    In response to this HTTP command, the Web server returns a default HTML file (usually named `index.html`).

This example uses the old form of the `GET` command. In HTTP 1.0, the command lines are in the following form:

```
GET / HTTP/1.0
Accept: (List the types of formats that you accept)
From: (Provide your e-mail address)
(A blank line to indicate that you're done with your request)
```

The following is what I got when I tried the HTTP 1.0 form of the GET command on a well-known Web site (my input appears in boldface; comments are in italics):

```
telnet www.idgbooks.com 80
Trying 204.94.129.95...
Connected to www.idgbooks.com.
Escape character is '^]'.
GET / HTTP/1.0
... (Press Enter once more to send a blank line)
HTTP/1.0 200 OK
Date: Sat, 09 Mar 1996 03:40:38 GMT
Server: Apache/0.8.17
Content-type: text/html
Content-length: 2582
Last-modified: Mon, 12 Feb 1996 16:07:26 GMT

<TITLE>Welcome to IDG Books Worldwide, Inc.</TITLE>
<HTML>
<BODY BGCOLOR="#000000" TEXT="#FFFFFF" link="0099ff" vlink="#00ff99">

<P>
<FONT SIZE=2>Slow connection? Scroll down right now to the text-only navigation
links!</FONT>

<CENTER><A HREF="/cgi-bin/imagemap/maps/home.map"><IMG ISMAP SRC="/home.gif"
    BORDER=0 ALIGN=bottom></A></CENTER><P>
<P>

<CENTER>
<TABLE BORDER=0 VALIGN=CENTER CELLPADDING=0>
<TR><TD width=50% VALIGN=TOP><PRE>
</PRE><TD width=50% VALIGN=TOP><PRE>
</PRE></TR>
<TR ALIGN=left>
<TD><CODE><A HREF="/whats_hot/"><FONT SIZE=4><B>What's Hot</B><FONT SIZE=1></
    A><BR>Our hottest titles,<BR>with free excerpts and extras
<TD><CODE><A HREF="/online_bookshelf/"><FONT SIZE=4><B>Online Bookshelf</B><FONT
    SIZE=1></A><BR>Search the complete IDG Books catalog</TR>
<TR><TD></TR>

... (Lines deleted)

<A HREF="/cgi-bin/imagemap/maps/homebar.map"><IMG ISMAP BORDER=0 SRC="/pics/home
bar.gif" ALIGN=bottom></A></CENTER>
<P>
<font size=1>&copy; 1995 IDG Books Worldwide, Inc. All Rights Reserved.</font>
</BODY>
</HTML>
Connection closed by foreign host.
```

Webmaster When you try this example with `telnet`, you see exactly what the Web server sends back to the Web browser. The first few lines are administrative information for the browser. In HTTP 1.0, the server returns the following information:

✦ The current date and time. A sample date and time string looks like this:

```
Date: Sat, 09 Mar 1996 03:40:38 GMT
```

✦ The name and version of the Web server software. For example, for a site running the NCSA HTTPD Version 1.4.2, the server returns the following string:

```
Server: NCSA/1.4.2
```

✦ The type of document being returned by the Web server. For HTML documents, the content type is reported as follows:

```
Content-type: text/html
```

✦ The length of the document in number of bytes like this:

```
Content-length: 2582
```

✦ The data when the document was last modified. A sample string looks like this:

```
Last-modified: Mon, 12 Feb 1996 16:07:26 GMT
```

The document itself follows the administrative information. An HTML document has the following general layout:

```
<TITLE>Document's title goes here</TITLE>
<HTML>
<BODY optional attributes go here >
... (The rest of the document goes here)
</BODY>
</HTML>
```

You can identify this layout by looking through the listing that shows what the Web server returns in response to the `GET` command. Because the example uses a `telnet` command to get the document, you see the HTML content as lines of text. If you were to access the same URL (`http://www.idgbooks.com`) with a Web browser (such as Netscape Navigator), you would see the page in its graphical form, as shown in Figure 3-3.

Now that you know how the document appears in the browser, you may want to go through the HTML text returned by the `GET` command and try to correlate that text with what appears in Figure 3-3. Note that you don't see the entire document in Figure 3-3; you have to scroll down to view the rest.

Figure 3-3: The home page from www.idgbooks.com viewed with the Netscape Navigator 2.0 Web browser.

Note If you don't have a Web browser, you learn how to download and set up a Web browser in the next chapter.

This section's example of HTTP focuses on the GET command. GET is the most common HTTP command because it causes the server to return a specified HTML document.

Note The other two HTTP commands are HEAD and POST. The HEAD command is similar to GET; it causes the server to return everything in the document except the body. You use the POST command to send information to the server; it's up to the server to decide how to act on the information.

Is HTTP an Internet standard?

Despite its widespread use in the World Wide Web since 1990, Hypertext Transfer Protocol (HTTP) is not yet an Internet standard. All Internet standards are distributed as Request for Comment (RFC); no RFC for HTTP exists yet. At this writing, an Internet Draft — a working document of the Internet Engineering Task Force (IETF) — is available. That Internet Draft ("Hypertext Transfer Protocol — HTTP/1.1," Roy T. Fielding, Henrik Frystyk Nielsen, and Tim Berners-Lee, January 19, 1996) is presently in circulation. To learn more about HTTP/1.1 and the latest news about HTTP-related standards, use a Web browser to access the following URL: `http://www.w3.org/pub/WWW/Protocols/`.

Hypertext Markup Language (HTML)

Each Web document is a text file that contains special tags that define the structure of the document. The tags are from a document markup language called Hypertext Markup Language (HTML).

Note HTML includes tags to denote parts of a document (such as headers, bulleted lists, and parts that should be emphasized). The Web browser interprets these tags and displays a formatted document. Along with tags that control the document's layout, HTML also includes tags to embed images and even applications (such as a Java applet) in a document. You can also ask the user for input and have the Web browser send the user's response back to the Web server.

To give you a feel for HTML, here's a complete HTML document (this example shows only a few HTML tags):

```
<TITLE>A Sample HTML Document</TITLE>
<HTML>
<BODY>
<H1>Sample Document</H1>
This is a sample HTML document. It shows a
few HTML tags to give you a feel for what
the tags do.
<P>
This is a new paragraph and here's a bulleted
list.
<H2>Web servers for UNIX</H2>
<UL>
<LI> NCSA Web server is a popular <EM>public-domain</EM>
Web server.
<LI> CERN Web server is another public-domain server.
</UL>
</BODY>
</HTML>
```

Note For such a small file, you would type this into a file using your favorite text editor. On UNIX systems, HTML files usually have the .html file extension. On Windows 95 and Windows NT, you would use an .HTM extension for HTML files.

Cross Ref In HTML, angle brackets (⟨...⟩) enclose the tags. You learn all about these HTML tags in Chapters 10 through 14, but you can see how the document title appears within a pair of tags (⟨TITLE⟩ and ⟨/TITLE⟩). The ⟨H1⟩ and ⟨H2⟩ tags denote first and second level headers. ⟨P⟩ means a paragraph break. Bulleted lists use the ⟨UL⟩ and ⟨LI⟩ tags. The ⟨EM⟩ and ⟨/EM⟩ tags enclose text to be emphasized.

By the way, you do not have to enter the HTML tags in uppercase. I have shown the tags in uppercase so that they stand out in the document.

Note These HTML tags identify the parts of the document (such as header and bulleted list), but the tags do not specify the font size or style. The Web browser decides how to display these document parts. For example, Figure 3-4 shows how the popular Netscape Navigator 2.0 Web browser displays the sample HTML file.

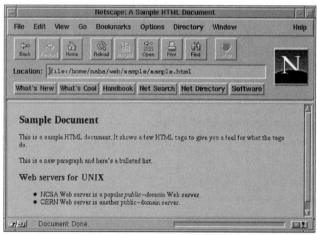

Figure 3-4: Sample HTML file displayed by a popular Web browser.

Web Servers and Clients

The Web server and client use HTTP to communicate with each other. The Web client (commonly known as a Web browser) connects to a Web server at port 80 of the system where the server is running. Then, the Web browser sends HTTP commands (such as GET) to request a document from the server. The Web server sends the document (usually in HTML format) and ends the connection.

HTML versions

The last official version of HTML is HTML 2.0. The September 22, 1995 draft of the HTML 2.0 specification (written by T. Berners-Lee and D. Connolly of MIT's World Wide Web Consortium — also known as the W3 Consortium) has been approved as a Proposed Standard (RFC 1866) by the Internet Engineering Task Force (IETF). You can view this document at the URL `http://www.w3.org/pub/WWW/MarkUp/html-spec/html-spec_toc.html`. A proposed HTML Version 3.0 existed, but that version did not evolve towards a standard. In May 1996, the W3 Consortium released the specification for HTML Version 3.2, which was developed with input from vendors such as IBM, Microsoft, Netscape Communications Corporation, Novell, SoftQuad, and Sun Microsystems. HTML 3.2 provides additional capabilities (such as tables, applets, text flow around images, and support for superscripts and subscripts) over HTML 2.0. HTML 3.2 is backward-compatible with HTML 2.0.

To learn more about the latest HTML standards, use a Web browser to access the URL `http://www.w3.org/pub/WWW/MarkUp/`. You find information about HTML 3.2 at the URL `http://www.w3.org/pub/WWW/MarkUp/Wilbur`.

Note that the features specified in HTML 3.2 already exist in the form of Netscape Mozilla extensions to HTML — Chapter 14 describes these extensions.

The Web browser interprets and displays the HTML document with text and graphics. Web browsers such as Lynx can display only the text part of an HTML document; most popular Web browsers, however, are graphical in nature. In fact, the nice graphics display is one of the reasons why the Web became so popular — Web browsers present information in a very attractive and easy-to-use manner. With a graphical Web browser, even a beginner can start using the Web in a matter of minutes.

The Web browser's connection to the Web server ends after the server sends the document. When the user browses through the downloaded document and clicks on another hypertext link, the Web browser again establishes a connection with the Web server named in the hypertext link. Then, the browser downloads the document, ends the connection, and displays the new document. Now the user can move from one document to another with ease.

Note A Web browser can do more than simply "talk" HTTP with the Web server — in fact, most Web browsers can also access FTP and Gopher.

Web browser and Internet information services

Along with accessing documents from the Web server, Web browsers can access any Internet service expressed in URL form. For example, if you open the URL `ftp://ftp.netscape.com`, the Web browser initiates an anonymous FTP session with the host `ftp.netscape.com` (see Chapter 2 for a description of anonymous FTP). The browser displays the contents of the FTP site. From the contents, you can select files to download. Similarly, you can use a Gopher URL (such as `gopher://gopher.tc.umn.edu/`) to browse and download files from a Gopher server.

Figure 3-5 illustrates the relationship between the Web browser and the Internet information services such as Web, Gopher, and FTP.

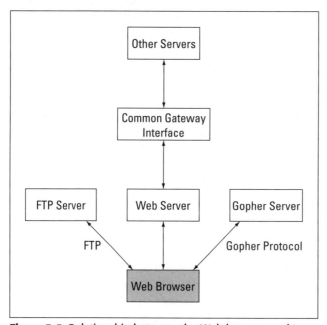

Figure 3-5: Relationship between the Web browser and Internet information services.

Note   As Figure 3-5 shows, the Web browser essentially has multiple personalities. When it interacts with a Web server, the Web browser is a Web client that "talks" HTTP to download documents. When it interacts with a Gopher server, the Web server behaves like a Gopher client. When the URL specifies an FTP server, the Web server acts like an FTP client. Some Web browsers can even directly access WAIS servers. This aspect of the Web browser — that is, the ability to access all Internet information services — is what makes the Web appear as a unified information service to the user. This is why users commonly think of the Web as the gateway to all Internet information services.

Web browser software

Web browsers exist for a wide variety of systems — from PCs and Apple Macintoshes to UNIX workstations. All Web browsers are categorized as follows:

✦ Text browsers that show the documents in plain text form without any formatting. Some text browsers (such as Lynx) provide a full-screen text interface.

✦ Graphical browsers that provide a point-and-click interface and that display Web documents in their full glory with formatted text and embedded images.

Chapter 4 shows you examples of several popular Web browsers. This section ("Web browser software") highlights the major Web browsers for a variety of systems. Although this book is about running a Web site on a UNIX platform, you must realize that your Web documents may be viewed with a wide variety of Web browsers by people around the world. Most of these Web browsers run on non-UNIX systems (such as PCs running Windows 95, Apple Macintoshes, or even text terminals).

As a Webmaster, your goal is to ensure that all users can access the information you offer at your Web site. Achieving this goal is especially important if you are promoting products through your Web site — you must be sure that the user gets to see your message regardless of the browser he or she uses to access your Web server.

URL

For a complete list of all available Web browsers, consult the following URL:

```
http://www.w3.org/hypertext/WWW/Clients.html
```

URL

Also consult the Web browser list in YAHOO! at the URL:

```
http://www.yahoo.com/Computers_and_Internet/Internet/World_Wide_Web/
        Browsers/
```

URL

Table 3-1 lists a sampling of browsers. The most popular graphical browsers are Netscape Navigator, NCSA Mosaic, and Microsoft Internet Explorer.

Table 3-1 **A Sampling of Currently Available Web Browsers**	
Browser	*Description*
E-Mail-Based Browser	
Agora	Provides Web access through e-mail. To try Agora, send e-mail to agora@mail.w3.org, with the single word *WWW* in the message body. To obtain and install Agora server software, send e-mail to agora-request@mail.w3.org.

(continued)

Table 3-1 *(continued)*

Browser	Description
Text-Based Browsers	
Emacs W3 mode	Developed by William Perry to provide a Web browser mode for Emacs. You can download the text files from the URL `ftp://ftp.cs.indiana.edu/pub/elisp/w3/`.
Line Mode Browser	Provides a line-oriented text interface through which users can access a Web server. Developed by Henrik Frystyk Nielsen, Tim Berners-Lee, and Nicola Pellow for use on text terminals. Runs on a wide variety of systems. You can download a `gzip`-ed `tar` archive of the browser from the URL `ftp://ftp.w3.org/pub/linemode/www_src.tar.gz`.
Lynx	Developed by Lou Montulli, University of Kansas, Lynx is a popular text-based Web browser with a full-screen text interface. You can download source files and precompiled binaries for Linux, BSDI, IBM AIX, Solaris, DEC Ultrix, and DEC OSF systems from the URL `ftp://ftp2.cc.ukans.edu/pub/lynx`. You can also download source code so you can build Lynx on most other UNIX systems.
Tom Fine's perlWWW	A text-mode browser written in Perl (you need Perl to run the browser). You can download the software from the URL `ftp://archive.cis.ohio-state.edu`, in `pub/w3browser/w3browser-0.1.shar`.
Browsers for Microsoft Windows	
Cello	Developed by Thomas R. Bruce of the Legal Information Institute at Cornell Law School, Cello is a Web browser that runs under Windows 3.1 (you need Winsock to run Cello). You can download Cello 1.01a from the URL `ftp://ftp.law.cornell.edu/pub/LII/Cello`.
Galahad for BIX	Designed as an off-line access tool for the Byte Information eXchange (BIX) online service, Galahad is a graphical Web browser for Windows 3.1. For more information on Galahad and to download a trial copy, visit the URL `http://www.mcs.com/~jvwater/main.html`.
GWHIS	A commercial Windows Web browser from Quadralay Corporation. GWHIS is based on Mosaic. For information, access the URL `http://www.quadralay.com/products/products.html`.

Browser	Description
Browsers for Microsoft Windows	
Internet Explorer	A graphical Web browser from Microsoft that runs on Windows 95, Windows NT, and Macintosh. For Windows 3.1, you need Internet Explorer Version 1.5. You can download Microsoft Internet Explorer 2.0 (for Windows 95) for free from the URL `http://www.microsoft.com/windows/download/msie20ms.exe`.
Mosaic for Windows	A Windows-based graphical Web browser developed by Briand Sanderson, Carl Samos, Judd Weeks, and Rick Vestal, at the National Center for Supercomputing Applications (NCSA), located at the University of Illinois at Urbana-Champaign (UIUC), USA. You can download Mosaic from the URL `ftp://ftp.ncsa.uiuc.edu/PC/Windows/Mosaic/` (look in the `Win31x` directory for the Windows 3.1 version, the `Win95` directory for the Windows 95 version, and the `WinNT` directory for the Windows NT version of the software).
Mosaic In A Box for Windows 95	Commercial version of NCSA Mosaic for Windows 95, sold by SPRY (CompuServe's Internet Division). For more information on this product, visit the URL `http://www.spry.com/about/products/mosaic.html`.
Netscape Navigator	A popular Web browser from Netscape Communications Corporation. As of this writing, you can download Netscape Navigator 2.0 from the URL `ftp://ftp.netscape.com/` (look in the `2.0` directory).
SlipKnot	A Windows-based graphical Web browser. Developed by MicroMind, Inc. for users of UNIX shell accounts (SlipKnot does not require any TCP/IP connection between the user's system and the Internet). SlipKnot is released as shareware. The URL `ftp.netcom.com/pub/pb/pbrooks/slipknot/slnot150.zip` lets you use SlipKnot Version 1.5 for a 30-60 day trial period.
WinWeb	A graphical Web browser for Windows 3.1 and Windows 95. You can download WinWeb from the Tradewave Corporation (for more information, visit URL `http://galaxy.einet.net/EINet/WinWeb/WinWebHome.html`).
Browsers for Macintosh	
MacWeb	A graphical Web browser for Macintosh. You can download MacWeb from the Tradewave Corporation (for more information, visit the URL `http://galaxy.einet.net/EINet/MacWeb/MacWebHome.html`).

(continued)

Table 3-1 *(continued)*

Browser	Description
Mosaic for Macintosh	A graphical Web browser for the Macintosh. You can download Mosaic for Macintosh (for both the older Motorola 680x0 Macintosh and the newer Power Macintosh) from the URL `http://www.ncsa.uiuc.edu/SDG/Software/MacMosaic/News/download.html`.
Netscape Navigator	Macintosh version of the popular Web browser from Netscape Communications Corporation. As of this writing, you can download Netscape Navigator 2.0 from the URL `ftp://ftp.netscape.com/` (look in the `2.0` directory).
Samba	A graphical Web browser for the Macintosh, developed by R. Cailliau and N. Pellow at CERN (the European Laboratory for Particle Physics where World Wide Web originated). You can download the software from the URL `ftp://info.cern.ch/ftp/pub/www/bin/mac`, but you need to check the terms under which the software is distributed.
Browsers for OS/2	
WebExplorer for OS/2	A graphical Web browser for IBM OS/2 operating system. You can download the software from the URL `ftp://ftp.ibm.net/pub/WebExplorer/`.
Browsers for UNIX (Based on the X Window System)	
Arena	The World Wide Web Consortium uses Arena (developed by Dave Raggett, Håkon W. Lie, Henrik Frystyk, and Yves Lafon, Arena) as a testbed browser for HTML 3.0. (In May 1996, the World Wide Web Consortium introduced HTML 3.2.) Arena runs on UNIX systems with the X Window System. You can download binaries for Linux, SunOS, Solaris, SGI IRIX, and DEC OSF from the URL `http://www.w3.org/pub/WWW/Arena/Dist-beta-2`.
Chimera	An X-based Web browser that does not require Motif. You can download Chimera from the URL `ftp://ftp.isri.unlv.edu/pub/chimera/`.
Grail	An experimental Web browser written in a free object-oriented programming language named Python. For the graphical interface, Grail uses Tk, a free user-interface toolkit by John Ousterhout. Grail runs on any UNIX system that has Python and Tk available. For more information on GRAIL visit the URL `http://monty.cnri.reston.va.us/grail/`.

Browser	Description
Browsers for UNIX (Based on the X Window System)	
MidasWWW Browser	Written by Tony Johnson, Midas WWW Browser is an X-based graphical Web browser (the name Midas comes from the name of the graphical user-interface toolkit used to build the browser). You can download Midas WWW for Linux from the URL `ftp://ftp.slac.stanford.edu/software/midaswww/`.
Mosaic for X	Motif-based graphical Web browser that runs on a variety of UNIX systems. Mosaic for X was the original Web browser that started the World Wide Web craze. The original development included Marc Andreessen, Eric Bina, and others at the National Center for Supercomputing Applications (NCSA), located at the University of Illinois at Urbana-Champaign (UIUC), USA. Subsequently, Marc Andreessen started Netscape Communications Corporation. You can download binaries for a wide variety of UNIX systems (including Linux, HP, DEC, IBM, and Sun) from the URL `ftp://ftp.ncsa.uiuc.edu/Mosaic/Unix/binaries/` (look under the current version number — as of this writing, the version number is 2.7b).
Netscape Navigator	UNIX version of the popular Web browser from Netscape Communications Corporation. As of this writing, you can download Netscape Navigator 2.0 for a variety of UNIX systems (including Linux, SunOS, Solaris, HP-UX, IBM AIX, DEC OSF, and SGI IRIX) from the URL `ftp://ftp.netscape.com/` (look in the `2.0/unix` directory).
tkWWW	A Tk-based Web browser developed by Joseph Wang. You can also edit HTML files with tkWWW. As of this writing, you can download tkWWW Version 0.7 from the URL `ftp://export.lcs.mit.edu:/contrib/tkWWW-0.7.tar.Z`. tkWWW should run on any UNIX system that has the Tk toolkit installed.
ViolaWWW	A graphical Web browser written by Pei Wei using the Viola scripting language and toolkit. You can download ViolaWWW source code (and binaries for Sun workstations) from the URL `ftp://ftp.ora.com/pub/www/viola`. Two versions are available: one uses plain X Window System, and the other one uses Motif.

Web server software

You need Web server software to set up your Web site. Typically, you would keep a Web server running continuously on your Web site. The server listens to incoming connections on port 80 and responds to any HTTP commands (such as GET) sent by a Web browser.

As a Webmaster responsible for running a Web site on a UNIX system, you have to install and run a UNIX Web server. There are Web servers available for other systems such as Macintosh, Windows 95, and Windows NT. Although you had to worry about browsers running on on-UNIX systems (because they could access your Web site), you do not have to worry about Web servers running on non-UNIX operating systems.

There are quite a few Web servers available for UNIX systems. Of these, the most popular Web servers are the freely available NCSA httpd, CERN httpd, and Apache servers.

Note Many corporations use the commercially available Netscape Web servers for their internal networks (often called *Intranets* for *intra-corporation network*). Commercial Web servers typically include the ability to exchange encrypted information. This feature is necessary for conducting business on the Web because users can securely send sensitive information (such as credit card numbers)

URL For a current list of Web servers, visit the following URL:

```
http://www.w3.org/hypertext/WWW/Servers.html
```

URL Table 3-2 lists a sampling of the currently available Web servers that run on one or more UNIX systems. Chapters 7 and 8 describe the installation and setup of several of these Web servers.

Table 3-2
A Sampling of Currently Available UNIX Web Servers

Web Server	Description
Apache	A freely available Web server that evolved from the well-known NCSA server. You can download the source code for Apache Version 1.03 from the URL http://www.apache.org/dist/. You can also download the binaries for Linux, BSDI, FreeBSD, NetBSD, HP-UX, IRIX, Solaris, SunOS, and UnixWare from the URL http://www.apache.org/dist/binaries/.
CERN httpd	Also known as W3C httpd, this freely available program is a well-regarded Web server. You can set up this server as a proxy — a Web server on a firewall machine — through which people inside the firewall can access the outside world. You can download the latest source code in gzip-ed tar format from the URL http://www.w3.org/hypertext/Dist/httpd/httpd_src.tar.gz.

Web Server	Description
GN	A server that provides both Gopher and HTTP access to data in a specified directory. GN is distributed under the GNU General Public License (GPL). (This distribution means that you get all the source code; if you modify anything, though, you must distribute all source code as well.) You can download the latest version of GN from the URL `ftp://ftp.acns.nwu.edu/pub/gn/gn.tar.gz`.
NCSA httpd	A popular and freely available Web server. You can download the software from the URL `http://hoohoo.ncsa.uiuc.edu/docs/setup/OneStep.html`. This URL displays a form on which you fill in some information to customize the server. After you submit the information (by clicking on a button on the form), you'll get back the server software. As of this writing, the version of NCSA httpd is 1.5a.
Netscape FastTrack Server	An entry-level, commercial Web server that Netscape Communications Corporation announced in March, 1996. Priced at $295 (U.S.), this server is available for major UNIX systems (HP-UX, SunOS, Solaris, IBM AIX, DEC OSF, and SGI IRIX). For more information, visit the URL `http://home.netscape.com/`.
Netscape SuiteSpot	A commercial Web server and associated toolset from Netscape Communications Corporation priced at $3,995 (U.S.). Visit the URL `http://home.netscape.com/` for more information about SuiteSpot.
Plexus	A public domain HTTP server written in Perl (you need Perl 4.0 patch level 36 or later) by Tony Sander and based on Marc VanHeyningen's original Perl server. For more information on Plexus (and to download the software) visit the URL `http://www.earth.com/server/doc/plexus.html`.
Spinner	An object-oriented HTTP 0.9 and HTTP 1.0 server distributed under the GNU General Public License. For information on Spinner (and how to download it), visit the URL `http://spinner.infovav.se/`.
WN	WN is a freely available Web server that is distributed under the GNU General Public License (GPL). WN uses the concept of a logical HTML file that's made up of many files. To download the source files for WN, visit the URL `http://hopf.math.nwu.edu/src.html`, where you'll find instructions on how to download the WN source code.

Summary

World Wide Web (WWW or Web) is the Internet information service that has propelled the Internet to the mainstream because the Web browser makes it easy for a user to browse documents stored in various Internet hosts. Businesses (small and large) are setting up Web servers on the Internet as well as on internal networks (Intranet). As a Webmaster, your primary job is to set up and maintain a Web server (and the information that the Web server provides). You must understand the basic principles on which the Web is built. Although this book concentrates on various aspects of the Web, this chapter provides an overview of it. The next chapter presents a user's view of the Web.

Where to go next . . .

✦ Much of a Webmaster's work involves preparing HTML documents. To learn about HTML, see Chapter 10.

✦ If you want to know about the duties of a Webmaster, see Chapter 5.

✦ One of the first tasks of a Webmaster is to set up the Web site. Chapter 6 describes your options for setting up a Web site.

✦   ✦   ✦

A User's View of the Web

Chapter 3 summarizes the Web and gives you a feel for how the Web works using the Hypertext Transfer Protocol (HTTP) and Hypertext Markup Language (HTML). Like any other Internet service, the Web uses the client/server model; the client side of the Web is the Web browser — the application that displays Web pages and lets the user follow links that are embedded in Web pages.

As a Webmaster, you must be as familiar with the client side of the Web as you are with the Web server. After all, the client end of the Web is where the user sits and your job is to make sure the user can easily use the information that your Web site provides. So, you need to know what type of Web browsers exist and how they display HTML documents.

You'll find that the Web browser is a useful testing tool for HTML documents. The Web browser lets you check your HTML documents and verify that all the hypertext links are working properly.

This chapter provides a user's view of the Web. The chapter starts with a discussion of popular Web browsers and their capabilities. Then you learn how to download a Web browser, set up the browser, and use it. (I'll cover both the Netscape Navigator and Mosaic browsers.)

Note Although Web browsers are available for many different computer systems, this chapter focuses on the Web browsers for UNIX systems only. The examples show how to download and use the Web browsers on Linux, a full-featured UNIX clone for PCs that is freely available from the Internet.

Gearing Up to Surf the Net

Like anything else, the World Wide Web is easier to understand after you have seen how it works. One of the best ways to learn about the Web is to "surf the Net" with a Web browser. Browsing Web pages is fun because the typical Web page contains both text and images. Also, browsing has an element of surprise; you can click the links and end up in unexpected Web pages. The links are the most curious aspect of the Web. You can start by looking at a page that shows today's weather; a click later, you can be reading that week's issue of *Time* magazine online.

Note   Before you can try anything, of course, you need a Web browser. (You also must have an Internet connection for your UNIX system, but I am assuming that you have already taken care of that part.)

Web browser choices

As described in the "Web browser software" section of Chapter 3, Web browsers are available for most major operating systems. For UNIX systems, you can choose from a number of graphical Web browsers that require the X Window System (also referred to as X) as the graphical environment. If you do not have X, you can use one of the text-only browsers. The following sections summarize the UNIX Web browsers.

Lynx

Lynx is a text-mode Web browser with a full-screen interface. Lynx is most useful when you have a dial-up shell account on a system on the Internet (which means your system acts as a terminal to the remote system). In this case, you can log into the remote system and run Lynx on that system. This ability lets you have access to the Web albeit in a text mode (you don't see any of the graphics).

For example, you may have a shell account with an Internet Service Provider (ISP) that allows you to log into the ISP's system and work at the UNIX shell prompt (or work through some menu system that the ISP provides). In such cases, Lynx can be very useful because you can still use the Web to find and view information.

 URL   **Using Lynx**

Figure 4-1 shows the full-screen text interface of Lynx with the White House home page (at the URL `http://www.whitehouse.gov`).

If you want to know how this page looks in a graphical Web browser, see Figure 4-17. None of the images show up in Lynx. In place of the image, you typically see a brief text label (in Chapter 12 you'll learn how to place labels in HTML documents so text-mode browsers show something meaningful in place of the image).

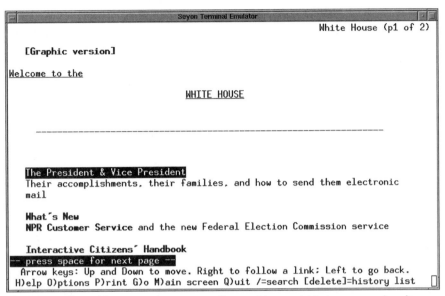

Figure 4-1: The White House home page (`http://www.whitehouse.gov`) as it appears in Lynx.

Lynx displays the links in boldface and the currently selected link in reverse-video. In Figure 4-1, the link labeled "The President & Vice President" is currently selected.

You can use the up- and down-arrow keys to move from one link to another. Press the right arrow to follow a link — Lynx downloads the new document referenced by the link. (Lynx also follows the link if you press Enter.) Press the left arrow to go back to the previous document (the behavior is similar to that of the Back button on many graphical Web browsers).

Underneath a page full of the Web document's text, Lynx displays instructions to the user. For example, if a Web page does not fit in a single page, Lynx shows a message that tells you to press the spacebar to move to the next page. In the status area at the bottom of the screen, Lynx also displays a short list of commands to help you navigate Web pages. For example, if you press g, Lynx prompts you for a URL.

Because Lynx works with text only, it quickly loads the Web pages. (I have to admit that sometimes when I want to locate information in a hurry, I fire up Lynx instead of the graphical Web browsers such as Netscape Navigator or Mosaic, even though I have a TCP/IP connection to the Internet.)

Tip You can also use Lynx as a tool to check out how your site's Web pages look on a text-only Web browser.

Downloading and installing Lynx

If you want to get Lynx for your UNIX system, you can get the software from the URL:

```
ftp://ftp2.cc.ukans.edu/pub/lynx
```

If you don't have any Web browser set up yet (but you have an Internet connection), use anonymous FTP to the download the Lynx files with these steps:

1. Start an FTP session with the following command:

   ```
   ftp ftp2.cc.ukans.edu
   ```

2. When prompted for a name, type `anonymous` and provide your e-mail address as your password.

3. Type the following command at the `ftp>` prompt to change to the Lynx directory:

   ```
   ftp> cd /pub/lynx
   ```

4. Use the `ls` command to view the directory listing. In the listing, you'll see a directory with a name that looks like `lynx2-5` (the name depends on the version and may be different when you try the `ls` command). Change to that directory with the following command:

   ```
   ftp> cd lynx2-5
   ```

5. List the contents again with an `ls` command. You'll see ready-to-run binaries for Linux, BSDI, IBM AIX, Solaris, DEC Ultrix, and DEC OSF operating systems. The files have names that begin with lynx2-5 followed by the operating system name. Choose the Linux binary that uses the `ncurses` library because the ncurses library provides a set of functions that programmers use to build full-screen text interfaces. This file is named `lynx2-5.linux-ncurses.exe.Z`. To download this file, I use the following command:

   ```
   ftp> get lynx2-5.linux-ncurses.exe.Z
   ```

6. After downloading the binary, you must also download the Lynx configuration file with the following command:

   ```
   ftp> get lynx.cfg
   ```

7. Download the `mime.types`, `mailcap`, and `lynx.man` files with the following commands:

   ```
   ftp> get mime.types
   ftp> get mailcap
   ftp> get lynx.man
   ```

8. Type `bye` to end the anonymous FTP session.

After downloading the files, copy the `lynx.cfg` file to the `/usr/local/lib` directory on your system as follows:

```
cp lynx.cfg /usr/local/lib
```

Then, uncompress the executable file with the following command:

```
uncompress lynx2-5.linux-ncurses.exe.Z
```

This step creates the file `lynx2-5.linux-ncurses.exe`, which is what you have to run when you want to use Lynx. You may want to copy the `lynx2-5.linux-ncurses.exe` file to a common directory such as `/usr/local/bin` and rename it to `lynx`, like this:

```
mv lynx2-5.linux-ncurses.exe /usr/local/bin/lynx
```

Next, copy the `mime.types` and `mailcap` files to the `/usr/local/lib/mosaic` directory (if this directory does not exist, create it) with the following commands:

```
cp mime.types /usr/local/lib/mosaic/mime.types
cp mailcap /usr/local/lib/mosaic/mailcap
```

Change the permission settings of these files to 644 (so that everyone can read the files, but only the owner can alter the files) with the following commands:

```
cd /usr/local/lib/mosaic
chmod 644 mime.types mailcap
```

Copy the lynx.man file (the online manual page for `lynx`) to the `/usr/man/man1` directory with the following command:

```
cp lynx.man /usr/man/man1/lynx.1
```

and change that file's permission to 644 with the following command:

```
chmod 644 / usr/man/man1/lynx.1
```

You can now run Lynx by typing `lynx` at the UNIX shell prompt.

Netscape Navigator for the X Window System

Netscape Navigator is the most popular Web browser around. You can get Navigator for a variety of systems including Windows 3.1, Windows 95, Macintosh, and many versions of UNIX. The UNIX versions of Netscape Navigator use the X Window System and Motif (but you do not need to have Motif on your system because the Motif libraries are statically linked into the Navigator program).

Note Although Netscape Navigator is a commercial product, Netscape Communications Corporation allows anyone to download the software for evaluation purposes. Commercial organizations are limited to an evaluation period of 90 days; others can take longer to evaluate. Many other users — most notably those from educational institutions, libraries, and charitable organizations — can download and use Netscape Navigator for free. The details are explained in a LICENSE file that accompanies the downloaded copy of the software.

Cross Ref Netscape continues to enhance Navigator with new features. For example, Navigator 2.0 (the latest version as of this writing) includes support for Java applets and JavaScript. Navigator 2.0 includes a built-in Java virtual machine that can execute Java code downloaded from a Web server. Support for JavaScript means Navigator 2.0 can interpret and act on JavaScript code in an HTML document. Chapter 23 covers Java programming and Chapter 24 covers JavaScript scripting.

Cross Ref The "Download Netscape Navigator" section in this chapter shows you in detail how to download, unpack, and install Netscape Navigator on your system.

NCSA Mosaic for the X Window System

NCSA Mosaic for the X Window System, from the National Center for Supercomputing Applications (NCSA) at the University of Illinois in Urbana-Champaign, is the original Web browser that started the Web revolution. Many popular graphical Web browsers are either based on or inspired by NCSA Mosaic. In fact, many members of the original NCSA Mosaic team eventually created Netscape Navigator.

NCSA Mosaic continues to evolve, with the latest version available through anonymous FTP from `ftp.ncsa.uiuc.edu`. At this FTP site, in the `/Mosaic/Unix/binaries/ 2.6` directory (2.6 refers to the current version of Mosaic — Version 2.7 is now in beta testing), you'll find a number of ready-to-run binaries as shown in the following list:

File Name	Test System
Mosaic-alpha30-2.6.Z	DEC Alpha, OSF1 3.0
Mosaic-dec-2.6.Z	DEC 3100, Ultrix 4.0
Mosaic-hp-2.6.Z	HP 9000/735, HP-UX 9.01
Mosaic-ibm-2.6.Z	IBM RS/6000, AIX 3.2
Mosaic-indy-2.6.Z	SGI Indy, IRIX 5.2
Mosaic-sgi-2.6.Z	SGI Indigo, IRIX 4.0.5
Mosaic-linux-2.6.Z	Pentium, Linux 1.1.94
Mosaic-solaris23-2.6.Z	Sun, Solaris 2.3
Mosaic-solaris24-2.6.Z	Sun, Solaris 2.4
Mosaic-sun-2.6.Z	Sun, SunOS 4.1.3
Mosaic-sun-lresolv-2.6.Z	Sun, SunOS 4.1.3 (linked to `libresolv.a`)

The Test System column lists the Mosaic developers that were used to test that specific binary file. You should be able to run the binary file on other compatible versions of that operating system. For example, `Mosaic-linux-2.6.Z` runs on Linux 1.2.13, the current stable version of Linux.

Tip

If your system is not on this list, you can get the source files from the `/Mosaic/Unix/source` directory located at the same FTP site (`ftp.ncsa.uiuc.edu`). The source file is a single compressed tar file (for Version 2.6, the filename is `Mosaic-src-2.6.tar.Z`).

Cross Ref

The "Download NCSA Mosaic" section in this chapter provides detailed instructions on how to download a copy of NCSA Mosaic.

Arena

Arena is an interesting Web browser to have; the World Wide Web Consortium uses it as a testbed for HTML 3.0. In other words, Arena has many new (but experimental) features that other Web browsers may not have.

URL

You can get Arena binaries through anonymous FTP from `ftp.w3.org`. The latest version is 0.97g, and the binaries for this version are in the `/pub/arena/0.97g` directory. In this directory, you'll find binaries for several UNIX systems including FreeBSD, Linux 1.2.8, IBM AIX 3.2, SGI IRIX 5.2, Solaris x86 Version 2.4, SunOS 4.1.3, and DEC Ultrix 4.3.

To download Version 0.97g of Arena for Linux, use the following steps:

1. Start an anonymous FTP session with `ftp.w3.org` (use the `anonymous` user name and your e-mail address as the password).

2. Change the directory with the following command at the `ftp>` prompt:

```
ftp> cd /pub/arena/0.97g
```

3. Set file type to binary and get the Linux binary with the following commands:

```
ftp> bin
200 Type set to I.
ftp> mget *linux*
mget arena-linux-1.2.8.gz? y
200 PORT command successful.
150 Opening BINARY mode data connection for arena-linux-1.2.8.gz
        (570727 bytes).
226 Transfer complete.
```

4. After you complete the file transfer, type `bye` to quit FTP.

Unpack the file with the following command:

```
gunzip arena-linux-1.2.8.gz
```

This command creates the file `arena-linux-1.2.8`. Type `chmod +x arena-linux-1.2.8` to make the file executable. Then, move it to a common location (such as `/usr/local/bin`) with the following command:

```
mv arena-linux-1.2.8 /usr/local/bin/arena
```

To run Arena, type `arena` at the shell prompt. Figure 4-2 shows the start-up screen of Arena (before it loads any URL).

As the message in Figure 4-2 indicates, if you wait a bit longer, Arena loads its release notes from the URL `http://www.w3.org/hypertext/WWW/Arena/0.97` (you can check out this page from your favorite Web browser). I decided to show Arena's built-in startup page because it shows off some new features of HTML 3.0 (for example, the ability to format math equations).

URL Arena is not particularly stable and it does not support many new features that popular Web browsers (such as Netscape Navigator) support. The only reason to keep a copy of Arena is to keep tabs on HTML 3.0 development at the World Wide Web Consortium (where you can see new features of HTML 3.0 by using Arena).

Downloading graphical browsers for X Window System

Of all the Web browsers for X Window System, the following are the most popular:

✦ Netscape Navigator, from Netscape Communications Corporation

✦ NCSA Mosaic for the X Window System, from the National Center for Supercomputing Applications (NCSA) at the University of Illinois in Urbana-Champaign

Webmaster Both Web browsers are copyrighted by their respective owners. Both products are available for free (at least for evaluation), but some constraints apply. Read the respective licenses (which you can view online after you download and install the browsers) for details. Essentially, a commercial organization can use NCSA Mosaic for internal use without paying a fee. If you plan to use Netscape Navigator beyond a 90-day evaluation period, however, you need to buy a licensed copy of the browser.

Here I show you how to download both of these browsers. You can try them and then decide which one you like best. The following examples show you how to download the Linux version of the browsers. As described in the "Web browser choices" section, these browsers are available for many different versions of UNIX.

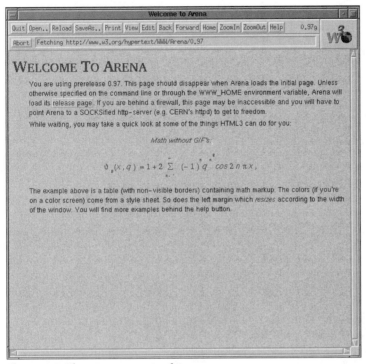

Figure 4-2: The startup screen of Arena.

Download Netscape Navigator

To download Netscape Navigator, follow these steps:

1. Make sure that your system's Internet connection is up and running.

2. Type the following command (shown in boldface):

```
ftp ftp.netscape.com
Connected to ftp20.netscape.com.
220 ftp20 FTP server (Version wu-2.4(17) Tue Feb 20 09:08:35 PST 1996) ready.
Name (ftp.netscape.com:naba): anonymous
331 Guest login ok, send your complete e-mail address as password.
Password: (Enter your e-mail address)
230-Welcome to the Netscape Communications Corporation FTP server.
230-
230-If you have any odd problems, try logging in with a minus sign (-)
230-as the first character of your password.  This will turn off a feature
230-that may be confusing your ftp client program.
230-
230-Please send any questions, comments, or problem reports about
230-this server to ftp@netscape.com.
230-
```

(continued)

```
230-*********** October 13, 1995 **********
230-Private ftp is now only on ftp1.netscape.com. Anonymous is supported on
230-ftp 2 through 8. If you are accessing a named account please use ftp1.
230-
230 Guest login ok, access restrictions apply.
Remote system type is UNIX.
Using binary mode to transfer files.
```

3. At the ftp> prompt, type the following command (shown in boldface):

```
ftp> cd pub/navigator
250 CWD command successful.
```

4. Type the ls command to view the file listing, as follows:

```
ftp> ls
200 PORT command successful.
150 Opening ASCII mode data connection for /bin/ls.
total 10
total 2
drwxr-xr-x    7 888       995             85 Jul 24 23:29 .
drwxr-xr-x   14 888       995           1024 May 23 22:44 ..
drwxr-xr-x    3 888       995             23 May 15 01:43 2.01
drwxr-xr-x    6 888       999             66 May  7 22:03 2.02
drwxr-xr-x    3 888       999             40 Jul 24 23:29 3.0
drwxr-xr-x    4 888       999             34 May 23 02:54 gold
drwxr-xr-x    5 888       999             53 Jun 13 00:01 intl
lrwxr-xr-x    1 888       999             13 May 23 23:15 sdk -> ../sdk/plugin
226 Transfer complete.
```

These directories refer to Netscape Navigator version numbers. As of this writing, the released version is Netscape Navigator 2.02, which should be in the 2.02 directory. The 3.0 directory contains the 3.0 beta software.

5. Change the directory to the UNIX version of Netscape Navigator 2.02 with the following command:

```
ftp> cd 2.02/unix
250-This software is subject to a license agreement. Be sure to read and
250-agree to the license BEFORE you use the software.
250-
250-EXPORT
250-You may not download or otherwise export or re-export Netscape Software or
250-any underlying information or technology except in full compliance with
250-all United States and other applicable laws and regulations. In particular,
250-but without limitation, none of the Software or underlying information or
250-technology may be downloaded or otherwise exported or re-exported (i) into
250-(or to a national or resident of) Cuba, Haiti, Iraq, Libya, Yugoslavia,
250-North Korea, Iran, or Syria or (ii) to anyone on the US Treasury
250-Department's list of Specially Designated Nationals or the US Commerce
250-Department's Table of Deny Orders. By downloading the Software, you are
250-agreeing to the foregoing and you are representing and warranting that you
```

```
250-are not located in, under control of, or a national or resident of any
250-such country or on any such list.
250-
250-REDISTRIBUTION and MIRRORING
250-Redistribution Not Permitted --
250-unless you are an educational institution and want to mirror for your
250-faculty, staff and students.  If you want to mirror, or are uncertain
250-about what to do, please see http://home.netscape.com/comprod/mirror/
     mirror_application.html
250-or send email to mirror@netscape.com.
250-
250-Please read the file README
250-  it was last modified on Thu May  2 01:37:48 1996 - 84 days ago
250 CWD command successful.
```

The message indicates that the version of Netscape Navigator is not for export to certain countries — the export control is due to the use of encryption software in Netscape Navigator.

6. Type the ls command to view the file listing, as follows:

```
ftp> ls
200 PORT command successful.
150 Opening ASCII mode data connection for /bin/ls.

total 92742
drwxr-xr-x   2 888      999           3072 May 13 23:32 .
drwxr-xr-x   6 888      999             66 May  7 22:03 ..
-rw-r--r--   1 888      999           1298 May 10 23:16 .message
-rw-r--r--   1 888      999          12905 May  2 01:37 LICENSE
-rw-r--r--   1 888      999           8879 May  2 01:37 README
-rw-r--r--   1 888      999        3005523 May  2 01:37 netscape-v202-
     export.alpha-dec-osf2.0.tar.Z
-rw-r--r--   1 888      999        2192957 May  2 01:37 netscape-v202-
     export.alpha-dec-osf2.0.tar.gz
-rw-r--r--   1 888      999        3826825 May  2 01:36 netscape-v202-
     export.hppa1.1-hp-hpux.tar.Z
-rw-r--r--   1 888      999        2858629 May  2 01:36 netscape-v202-
     export.hppa1.1-hp-hpux.tar.gz
-rw-r--r--   1 888      999        2344153 May  2 01:36 netscape-v202-
     export.i386-unknown-bsd.tar.Z
-rw-r--r--   1 888      999        1652010 May  2 01:36 netscape-v202-
     export.i386-unknown-bsd.tar.gz
-rw-r--r--   1 888      999        2818969 May  2 01:35 netscape-v202-
     export.i486-unknown-linux.tar.Z
-rw-r--r--   1 888      999        2030169 May  2 01:35 netscape-v202-
     export.i486-unknown-linux.tar.gz
-rw-r--r--   1 888      999        2608308 May  2 01:37 netscape-v202-
     export.mips-sgi-irix5.2.tar.Z
-rw-r--r--   1 888      999        1894334 May  2 01:37 netscape-v202-
     export.mips-sgi-irix5.2.tar.gz
```

(continued)

```
-rw-r--r--    1 888       999      1976909 May  2 01:37 netscape-v202-
     export.rs6000-ibm-aix3.2.tar.Z
-rw-r--r--    1 888       999      1385674 May  2 01:37 netscape-v202-
     export.rs6000-ibm-aix3.2.tar.gz
-rw-r--r--    1 888       999      2869999 May  2 01:36 netscape-v202-
     export.sparc-sun-solaris2.3.tar.Z
-rw-r--r--    1 888       999      2157901 May  2 01:36 netscape-v202-
     export.sparc-sun-solaris2.3.tar.gz
-rw-r--r--    1 888       999      2061495 May  2 01:35 netscape-v202-
     export.sparc-sun-solaris2.4.tar.Z
-rw-r--r--    1 888       999      1510135 May  2 01:35 netscape-v202-
     export.sparc-sun-solaris2.4.tar.gz
-rw-r--r--    1 888       999      5875123 May  2 01:36 netscape-v202-
     export.sparc-sun-sunos4.1.3_U1.tar.Z
-rw-r--r--    1 888       999      4377123 May  2 01:36 netscape-v202-
     export.sparc-sun-sunos4.1.3_U1.tar.gz226 Transfer complete.
```

This listing shows you the different versions of UNIX for which Netscape Navigator 2.02 is available. You can see the name of the system and the version of UNIX in the filename. All files appear in two forms — the version with a .Z extension is compressed with the UNIX compress command, the other one with .gz extension is compressed with the gzip command. The .gz files are smaller than the .Z files, so you can download the .gz files (assuming, of course, that you have the gzip software to uncompress the file).

7. Get the Linux version of Netscape Navigator with the following command:

```
ftp> mget *linux*
mget netscape-v202-export.i486-unknown-linux.tar.gz? y
```

If you have a SLIP or PPP connection over a modem, this step will take a while, because that command downloads 2,030,169 bytes. (The file size may be different by the time you download Netscape Navigator.)

8. Type bye to quit ftp.

After completing the download, use the gunzip command to uncompress the file. Use the following command to uncompress the file:

```
gunzip netscape-v202-export.i486-unknown-linux.tar.gz
```

This command creates the tar file netscape-v202-export.i486-unknown-linux.tar. Next, unpack that tar file with the following command:

```
tar xvf netscape-v202-export.i486-unknown-linux.tar
```

Note This command extracts the netscape program, as well as several support files. The README file is one support file, in particular, that you need to read for any last minute instructions. For example, the README file for Navigator 2.02 indicates that on Linux systems (as well as on SunOS 4.1 and BSDI), you must move the nls directory to the /usr/X11R6/lib/X11 directory. Use the following command from the directory where you unpacked the Netscape Navigator files to accomplish this task:

```
mv nls /usr/X11R6/lib/X11
```

 Note To support Java, Netscape Navigator 2.02 includes a file named moz2_02.zip (the Java class library). You must move this file to any one of the following locations:

```
/usr/local/netscape/java/classes
/usr/local/lib/netscape
$HOME/.netscape
```

The $HOME in the last line refers to your home directory — that is, the last line refers to a directory named .netscape in your home directory.

Finally, move the netscape program to a common directory, such as /usr/local/bin, so that any user can access it. (If you move the moz2_02.zip file to $HOME/netscape then other users won't have access to that file.) From the directory where you unpacked Netscape Navigator, type this command:

```
mv netscape /usr/local/bin
```

That's it! You can start Netscape Navigator by typing netscape in an xterm window. (Remember, you must start X before running netscape because Netscape Navigator uses the X Window System.)

Download NCSA Mosaic

To download NCSA Mosaic, follow these steps:

1. Make sure that your system's Internet connection is up and running.

2. Type the following command (shown in boldface):

```
ftp ftp.ncsa.uiuc.edu
Connected to ftp.ncsa.uiuc.edu.
220 larry FTP server (Version wu-2.4(25) Thu Aug 25 13:14:21 CDT 1994) ready.
Name (ftp.ncsa.uiuc.edu:naba): anonymous
331 Guest login ok, send your complete e-mail address as password.
Password: (Enter your e-mail address)
230-
230-Welcome to NCSA's new anonymous FTP server! I hope you find what you are
230-  looking for. If you have any technical problems with the server,
230-  please e-mail to ftpadmin@ncsa.uiuc.edu. For other questions regarding
230-  NCSA software tools, please e-mail softdev@ncsa.uiuc.edu.
230-
230-The mail archive-server is no longer supported. Of course, if
230-  you can read this, you don't need it anyway.
```

(continued)

```
230-
230-
230-Note to HyperFTP users: If you log in, and cannot list directories
230-  other than the top-level ones, enter a - as the first character of your
230-  password (e-mail address).
230-
230-If your ftp client has problems with receiving files from this server, send
230-  a - as the first character of your password (e-mail address).
230-
230-If you're ftp'ing from Delphi, please remember that the Delphi FTP client
230-  requires you to enclose case-sensitive directory and file names in double
230-  quote (") characters.
230-
230-You are user # 62 of an allowed 130 users.
230-
230-Please read the file README
230-  it was last modified on Tue Jan  3 18:54:35 1995 - 432 days ago
230-Please read the file README.FIRST
230-  it was last modified on Thu Jan 12 17:53:58 1995 - 423 days ago
230 Guest login ok, access restrictions apply.
Remote system type is UNIX.
Using binary mode to transfer files.
```

3. At the `ftp>` prompt, type the following command (shown in boldface):

```
ftp> cd Mosaic/Unix/binaries
250 CWD command successful.
```

4. Type the `ls` command to view the file listing, as follows:

```
ftp> ls
200 PORT command successful.
150 Opening ASCII mode data connection for /bin/ls.
total 30
drwxr-xr-x   6 12873    wheel        2048 Oct 25 17:51 .
drwxr-xr-x   6 12873    wheel        2048 Dec 23  1994 ..
-rw-r--r--   1 12873    other         169 Oct 10  1994 .index
drwx------   2 101      10           2048 Jul  7  1995 2.6
drwx------   2 18381    202          4096 Mar  6 13:06 2.7b
drwxr-xr-x   2 12873    wheel        2048 Aug 22  1994 app-defaults
drwxr-xr-x   7 15220    202          2048 Mar  6 13:04 old
226 Transfer complete.
```

Notice that there are two directories, named `2.6` and `2.7b`. These names refer to the version numbers of Mosaic at this writing. Version 2.7b is a beta version. If you want to get Version 2.6, type the following:

```
ftp> cd 2.6
250-Please read the file README-2.6
250-  it was last modified on Fri Jul  7 14:31:14 1995 - 247 days ago
```

```
250-Please read the file README.solaris
250-  it was last modified on Fri Jul  7 14:35:46 1995 - 247 days ago
250 CWD command successful.
```

5. View the file listing with the `ls` command, as follows:

```
ftp> ls
200 PORT command successful.
150 Opening ASCII mode data connection for /bin/ls.
total 22596
drwx------  2 101    10       2048 Jul 7 14:35 .
drwxr-xr-x  6 12873  wheel    2048 Oct 25 17:51 ..
-rw-r--r--  1 101    10     936964 Jul 7 11:41 Mosaic-alpha-2.6.Z
-rw-r--r--  1 101    10    1111311 Jul 7 11:41 Mosaic-dec-2.6.Z
-rw-r--r--  1 101    10     853351 Jul 7 11:42 Mosaic-hp-2.6.Z
-rw-r--r--  1 101    10     797705 Jul 7 11:43 Mosaic-ibm-2.6.Z
-rw-r--r--  1 101    10     915718 Jul 7 11:44 Mosaic-indy-2.6.Z
-rw-r--r--  1 101    10     903973 Jul 7 11:59 Mosaic-linux-2.6.Z
-rw-r--r--  1 101    10     648431 Jul 7 11:44 Mosaic-sgi-2.6.Z
-rw-r--r--  1 101    10    1708074 Jul 7 11:45 Mosaic-solaris-23-2.6.Z
-rw-r--r--  1 101    10     809343 Jul 7 11:45 Mosaic-solaris-24-2.6.Z
-rw-r--r--  1 101    10    1427238 Jul 7 11:46 Mosaic-sun-2.6.Z
-rw-r--r--  1 101    10    1442713 Jul 7 11:47 Mosaic-sun-lresolv-
        2.6.Z
-rw-r--r--  1 101    10       1835 Jul 7 14:31 README-2.6
-rw------- 1 101    10        845 Jul 7 14:35 README.solaris
226 Transfer complete.
```

This listing tells you the names of the systems for which Mosaic 2.6 is available.

6. Download the Linux version of Mosaic with the following commands:

```
ftp> mget *linux*
mget Mosaic-linux-2.6.Z? y
```

7. When the file transfer is complete (which could take a while over a dial-up SLIP or PPP connection), type `bye` to quit the `ftp` program.

Next, uncompress the `Mosaic-linux-2.6.Z` file with the following command:

```
uncompress Mosaic-linux-2.6.Z
```

Then you are left with the Mosaic 2.6 executable in the file named `Mosaic-linux-2.6`. Move this file to the `/usr/local/bin` directory under the name `mosaic`, as follows:

```
mv Mosaic-linux-2.6 /usr/local/bin/mosaic
```

Now you can run Mosaic by typing the `mosaic` command.

A quick look at NCSA Mosaic

Although Mosaic is not as popular as Netscape Navigator, it does require a brief description, which is what this section provides. Because of the popularity of Netscape Navigator, I will discuss it more extensively than Mosaic in subsequent sections.

URL To run Mosaic on a Linux system, start X (with the `startx` command) and then type `mosaic` in an `xterm` window. After Mosaic starts, it displays the NCSA Mosaic Home Page from URL `http://www.ncsa.uiuc.edu/SDG/Software/Mosaic/NCSAMosaicHome.html`. You can, however, easily open any URL in Mosaic.

Mosaic is the original Web browser that started all the current hoopla over the Internet. Before Mosaic, the Internet had the reputation of being hard to use. You had to know UNIX commands to use the Internet. Downloading an image or a document meant learning to use Internet applications such as `ftp`, which has its own command set. Then you had to unpack the files with the `tar` command (files were often archived with the `tar` command) and find an appropriate viewer program to see the image or document. All this changed when Mosaic came along in the spring of 1993.

With Mosaic, a single mouse click is all it takes to download and view a document with images. It was fortuitous that HTTP and HTML — the underpinnings of the World Wide Web — came together just as Mosaic 1.0 for the X Window System was developed and released to the Internet community in April 1993.

Note Mosaic development continues at NCSA, with versions available for Microsoft Windows as well as the Macintosh. At this writing, the current version of Mosaic is 2.6; 2.7 is in beta testing.

Mosaic is easy to use. The Mosaic window has a Motif user interface, as shown in Figure 4-3. Also shown are the major elements of the Mosaic interface. Like most Motif applications, Mosaic has a menu bar. The File pull-down menu includes an option to open a document specified by a URL.

The most important part of Mosaic's user interface is the document window, where Mosaic displays the Web page — the HTML document — with the embedded images and text. The hypertext links appear as underlined blue text.

Webmaster Above the document window, Mosaic displays the document title and URL — Web page address. A globe appears in the top-right corner, below the menu bar. When Mosaic connects to a Web server, the globe spins to indicate ongoing network activity. You can interrupt the download by clicking this spinning globe.

Below the document window, Mosaic displays a one-line status message. As it loads a Web page, Mosaic displays the size of each data item being downloaded. Each embedded image counts as a separate data item to be downloaded from the server.

Document window   Document title   Activity indicator (the "Spinning Globe")

Menu bar   Title bar with document title   Address of Web page

Status message   Button bar

Figure 4-3: Elements of the Mosaic window.

A row of buttons in the button bar at the bottom of the Mosaic window provides quick access to commonly used menu items. After you browse a few Web pages, you can use the Back and Forward buttons to move around among those pages.

Taking Netscape Navigator for a spin

Netscape Navigator is a successor to Mosaic in many ways. First, one of Mosaic's primary developers, Marc Andreessen, happens to be the force behind Netscape Navigator as well. Netscape Navigator improves on Mosaic in several ways; the most significant improvement, however, is how Netscape Navigator loads a Web page.

Webmaster When a Web page includes embedded images, the browser has to download each image separately. Mosaic displays a Web page only after everything on that page has been downloaded. Netscape Navigator, on the other hand, begins displaying the page when parts of it are available.

Netscape Navigator also finishes downloading a page faster, because it makes multiple connections with the Web server to download separate parts of the page in parallel. (This process puts more load on the Web server, but it's beneficial to the user.)

Netscape Navigator 2.0 includes the ability to send and receive e-mail messages. And, if you have access to a news server, you can read newsgroups directly. Advanced features in Netscape Navigator 2.0 include the support for JavaScript and the ability to run Java applets. You'll learn more about Java in Chapter 23.

Start Netscape Navigator

To run Netscape Navigator, type `netscape` at the command line in an `xterm` window (you must start X before running Netscape Navigator). When Netscape Navigator starts, it automatically loads the Web page identified by the URL `http://home.netscape.com/`, as shown in Figure 4-4.

Webmaster If you compare this syntax with the URL syntax shown in Chapter 3, you'll notice that this URL does not appear to have a filename. When a URL does not have a filename, the Web browser loads a default HTML file named `index.html`.

Note Typically, Web servers contain many Web pages that are organized in such a way that you can start at a main page and jump to the other pages. The main Web page on a Web server is known as the *home page*.

The URL `http://home.netscape.com/` represents the home page of Netscape Communications Corporation — the company that sells Netscape Navigator. Without a Web page, a Web browser cannot show anything. Netscape Communications provides a default Web page so that Netscape Navigator has something to show you when it first runs: Netscape's main home page on the Web.

Document window

Directory buttons   Title bar with document title   Activity indicator

Toolbar   Menubar   Document location

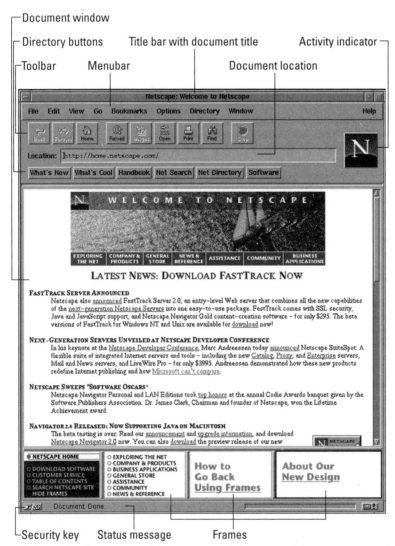

Security key   Status message   Frames

Figure 4-4: The Netscape home page and elements of the Netscape Navigator window. (Copyright © 1996 Netscape Communications Corporation.)

Netscape Navigator's user interface

If you compare the Netscape Navigator window shown in Figure 4-4 with the Mosaic window shown in Figure 4-3, you'll see many similarities. Like Mosaic, Netscape Navigator sports a Motif interface. The Netscape Navigator window also has a title bar that shows the current document title, as well as a menu bar that contains all the standard menus (such as File and Edit).

As in the Mosaic window, the most important part of the Netscape Navigator window is the document window — the large area where Netscape Navigator displays the Web page with its text and images.

Webmaster Below the document window, you see one of the new features of Netscape Navigator — frames. Frames are small windows where the Web page designer can display information that always stays visible (for example, a table of contents). The document window's right edge has a scrollbar that scrolls the document window only. The frames along the bottom edge of the document window always remain visible.

Immediately above the document window, you see three items that you can turn on or off from the Options menu:

✦ The *toolbar* (immediately under the menubar) gives you quick access to some common menu items:

• The Back and Forward buttons are for moving between Web pages that you've already seen.

• The Home button takes you to the Netscape home page.

• Reload forces the browser to download the current page again.

• Open allows you to open a new document specified by a URL.

• The Print button prints the current page.

• Find enables you to search the current document.

• The Stop button allows you to stop loading a Web page.

✦ The *document location* displays the location of the current Web page as a URL.

✦ *Directory buttons* are shortcuts to items in the Directory menu. These buttons allow you to access specific Web pages quickly. The Net Search button, for example, brings up a Web page from which you can search for specific topics (by entering keywords in a text-entry area) whereas the Net Directory button takes you to the Internet Directory.

Webmaster In the top-right corner of the Netscape Navigator window is the Activity Indicator button (with a large *N*). Netscape Navigator animates the Activity Indicator while it downloads a Web page. You can interrupt the download by clicking this button.

Webmaster In the bottom-left corner of the Netscape Navigator window is a gold key — the security key. When the security key appears whole, Netscape Navigator communicates with the remote Web server using a secure version of the HTTP protocol. The security key broken in two signifies an insecure connection.

Tip Fill in forms with private information such as social security number, or credit card number ONLY when Netscape Navigator's security key is solid.

Netscape Navigator displays status messages in the area to the right of the security key. When Netscape Navigator is busy downloading a Web page, it displays the percentage of the document that it has downloaded.

Surfing the Net

Where you go from the Netscape home page depends on you. All you do is click and see where you end up. Move your mouse pointer around. You'll know when you are on a link; the mouse pointer changes to a hand with an extended index finger. Click the link, and Netscape Navigator downloads the Web page referenced by that link.

How you use the Web depends on your need. When you begin, you may explore — browsing through Web sites and following links without any specific goal in mind. You may call this Web window shopping.

The other, more purposeful use of the Web is to find specific information from the Net. For example, you may want to locate all the Web sites that contain documents with a specified keyword. For such searches, you can use one of many Web search tools that are available on the Net.

A third type of use occurs when you want to visit a Web site with a known URL. For example, when you read about a specific topic in this book, you may come across a specific URL. In that case, go directly to that Web page.

Just browsing

If you want to just explore the Web, click on the Exploring the Net item in the second frame of Netscape's home page (see Figure 4-4). A new page appears with links to various Web search engines (Web sites that let you search for information on the Web). The new Web page also includes a clickable image — an image whose parts act as links to other Web pages — that can take you to a list of interesting Web sites. (Hint: Click on the part of the image that says WHAT'S COOL?.)

Note   Because the path that you take depends on what you click, and because the links may be different by the time you are ready to try Netscape Navigator, I'll present the same brief Web tour as I took. The beauty of the Web is that you can decide what path you want to take; there is no right or wrong path when you browse. After all, the point of surfing the Net is to satisfy your curiosity and meet your specific information needs.

On Netscape's WHAT'S COOL? page, I see the Virtually Hawaii link. This link offers views of Hawaii as seen through space and aircraft images (the site is funded by NASA, the U.S. Government's Space agency). When I click the Virtually Hawaii link, Netscape Navigator brings up the Virtually Hawaii home page, shown in Figure 4-5.

This page offers a virtual trip of Hawaii, with space and aircraft images of various locations in Hawaii. As I read the Virtually Hawaii page, I see a link that offers a Virtual Field Trip of Hawaii. When I click that link, Netscape Navigator displays another page, with links that offer virtual field trips to any of the Hawaiian islands. I click the link to visit Maui. Netscape Navigator brings up the appropriate page, as shown in Figure 4-6.

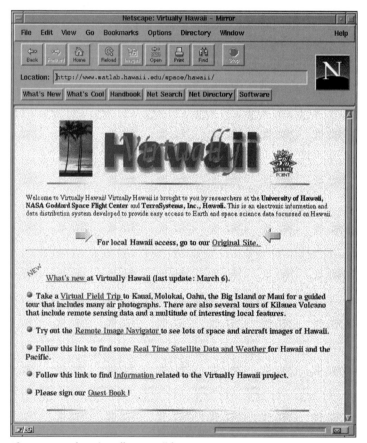

Figure 4-5: The Virtually Hawaii home page.

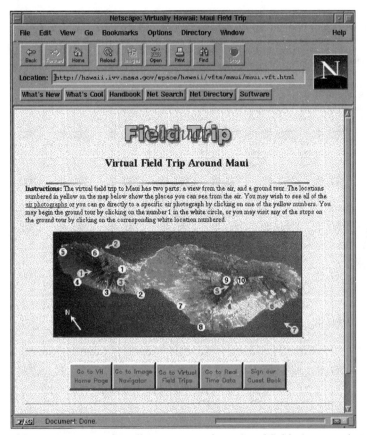

Figure 4-6: A page that allows you to take a virtual field trip around Maui.

The page shows an aerial view of Maui, with some locations marked by numbered circles. I click Location 4, in the northwest part of Maui. Netscape Navigator displays a page with information about Stop 4 of the virtual tour of Maui, as shown in Figure 4-7.

This stop happens to be Lahaina. The page describes Lahaina and includes some photographs of the area. The photographs appear as thumbnail images, so that you can tell what a photograph shows, but it does not take too long to download these small images from the Web server.

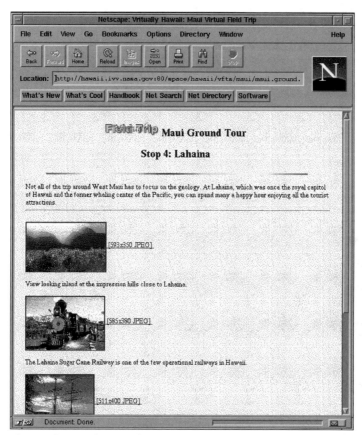

Figure 4-7: A Web page showing Stop 4 (Lahaina) on a virtual tour of Maui.

On the Lahaina page, I see a thumbnail image of the Lahaina Sugar Cane Railway. From an earlier trip to Hawaii, I recall the Sugar Cane train in Lahaina. Out of curiosity, I click that thumbnail. Netscape Navigator downloads and displays the full image, as shown in Figure 4-8.

Note This photograph is in JPEG (Joint Photographic Experts Group) format — a format for storing photographic images in compressed format. Because of the compressed format, Netscape Navigator can quickly download the image (compared with downloading an uncompressed image). The photograph looks quite good. I look at it some and then click Netscape Navigator's Back button several times to return to Netscape's WHAT'S COOL? page.

Figure 4-8: A Web page showing the Lahaina Sugar Cane train in Lahaina, Maui.

Next, on the WHAT'S COOL? page, I notice the THOMAS link. I had heard that the THOMAS page (named after Thomas Jefferson) provides information about bills passed by the U.S. Congress. I click the THOMAS link. Netscape Navigator downloads and displays the THOMAS page, as shown in Figure 4-9.

Turns out that from THOMAS you can perform keyword search on the full text of all versions of House and Senate bills. Obviously, THOMAS can be a very useful tool if your job requires you to stay current on any specific legislation. You can also learn a lot about how laws are made in the United States.

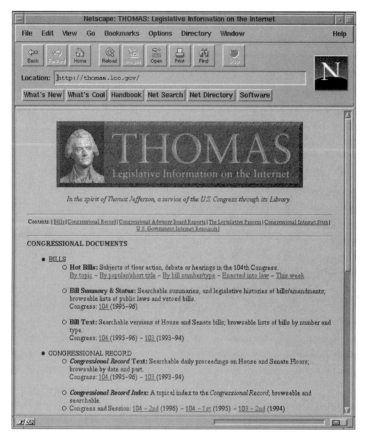

Figure 4-9: The THOMAS page, which provides information on bills in the U.S. Congress.

With a couple of clicks on the Back button, I go back to the WHAT'S COOL? page again. I am writing this chapter in the spring with tax season fast approaching, so I decide to check out the Internal Revenue Service (IRS), which also appears on the WHAT's COOL? page. When I click on the IRS link, I get a 404 Not Found error message, which means the link is probably old. Looking at the URL, however, I see that the first part looks like the U.S. Department of Treasury. I quickly edit the URL a bit (you can do this in the Location text field of Netscape Navigator) and try again. This time, Netscape Navigator displays the home page of the U.S. Department of Treasury that has a picture of the Secretary of the Treasury in the middle of the page. It seems that most government agencies feel the need to put up a picture of the Agency's head honcho on the home page, but private companies almost never display the likeness of the Chief Executive Officer on a Web page. (I wonder why.)

On the Treasury Department's page, I notice a link that says: `Visit the new IRS Server`. A click on that link brings up a Web page that asks me to click again for information on new ways to contact the IRS. When I click as instructed, Netscape Navigator downloads the IRS home page, as shown in Figure 4-10.

I am surprised by the look of the IRS Web page — it looks almost like an online magazine rather than the home page of a U.S. Government agency. The IRS page is laid out like a newspaper and even has a spinning globe on the masthead. When I explored the IRS page, I found many interesting links — all about taxes, of course. One of the links provided a plain language explanation of significant tax regulations.

Figure 4-10: The IRS home page.

After browsing the IRS pages, I return to Netscape's WHAT'S COOL? page. In the list of links, I notice the Internet Shopping Network (ISN). A while ago, I had joined ISN as a member (by providing my name, mailing address, and a credit card number). I click on the ISN link; Netscape Navigator displays the ISN home page, as shown in Figure 4-11.

In browsing through the product lists, I see a good price on a 1.6GB hard disk drive — I notice a Buy button next to the hard drive's description and price. When I click on the Buy button, Netscape Navigator, in turn, displays a new page, as shown in Figure 4-12.

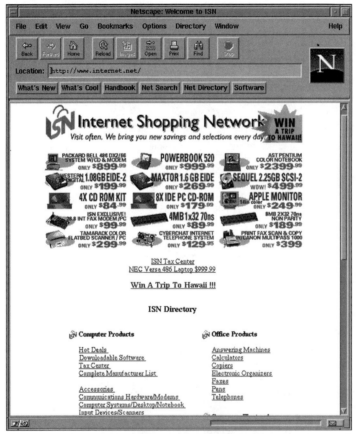

Figure 4-11: The Internet Shopping Network's home page. (Copyright © 1994, 1995, Internet Shopping Network.)

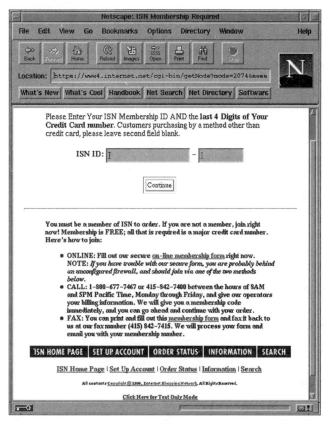

Figure 4-12: Secure ISN page that prompts for a membership ID. (Copyright © 1994, 1995, Internet Shopping Network.)

Just before the page appeared, Netscape Navigator displayed a message saying that the communications between my computer and the ISN computer will be secure. For more information on the document's security, the message also suggested that I select Document Info from Netscape Navigator's View menu. When I do, Netscape Navigator displays a new window with information about the document, as shown in Figure 4-13.

Webmaster The lower half of the Document Information window tells me a lot about the security feature of the document. If I provide my personal information and credit card number, Netscape Navigator will encrypt that information before sending it to the ISN computer. Of course, this implies that the protocol for exchanging Web pages is now different (because both sides must be able to encrypt and decrypt messages). I see that the URL (see Figure 4-12) now has https as the protocol instead of the usual

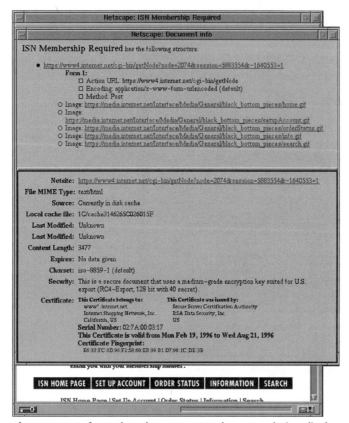

Figure 4-13: Information about a secure document being displayed by Netscape Navigator.

http — the extra s indicates that this is a secure protocol. Another indication of the secure protocol is the solid security key at the lower-left corner of the Netscape window. Until now, that security key appeared broken in two, but now the key appears whole.

I suddenly realize that I don't remember my ISN membership, so I decide not to buy the hard disk after all. I click on Netscape Navigator's Back button. Netscape Navigator's security key immediately appears broken because Netscape is no longer communicating using a secure protocol.

At this point, I notice that I spent nearly three hours browsing these Web sites (it really didn't seem that long!). It is past midnight, so I decide to end my Web tour by choosing Exit from the File menu. Netscape Navigator closes the window and exits.

Although you cannot repeat this Web tour exactly, I hope that you now have an idea of what it is like to surf the Net.

Searching for information

Sometimes a user may turn to the Web for specific information as opposed to casually browsing. To locate information on the Web, users turn to one of many Web indexes — sites that maintain a catalog of Web pages, usually searchable by keyword.

Tip   As a Webmaster, you need to hone your Web search skills and stay current on other Web sites that offer products and services similar to your site's. The best way to keep tabs on competing sites is to use the Web indexes to look for new sites. Additionally, your Web search skill can be valuable when someone in your organization must locate information. Because of your experience with the Web, you may be the person everyone turns to when someone needs information in a hurry.

Some Web directories are in print, but the ever-changing nature of the Web makes such print directories obsolete in no time. Your best bet for the latest information on Web sites is one of the online Web indexes.

URL   Here are some of the popular Web indexes:

- ✦ YAHOO! at `http://www.yahoo.com/` is a well-established Web index that you can search as well as browse; it's organized by categories and subcategories.

- ✦ AltaVista at `http://www.altavista.digital.com/` is an automated Web indexer that compiles a huge list of Web pages and Internet newsgroups that you can search by using keywords. Since it went online in December 1995, AltaVista has attracted a lot of attention due to its fast response time. When I want to search for something online, I usually turn to AltaVista first.

- ✦ Open Text at `http://search.opentext.com/` specializes in Intranet Web applications with a focus on applications that let users easily find information. You can see an example of Open Text's full-text search capability at the Open Text Web site.

- ✦ Lycos at `http://www.lycos.com/` indexes Web pages by using the title, heading, and words in the first 20 lines of the document as keywords.

- ✦ WebCrawler at `http://www.webcrawler.com/` is a Web index service owned by America Online. WebCrawler searches the Web and creates a database of documents.

- ✦ Deja News at `http://www.dejanews.com/` allows you to search the Internet newsgroups using one or more keywords.

Note   Although AltaVista beats all Web indexes in the speed and volume of searched material, YAHOO! remains a respectable source of information. Unlike many automated Web indexes (where a search engine routinely goes through the Web, one site at a time, and collects information on the documents at that site), YAHOO! uses a manual editing process. Some users say that this process improves the quality of information returned by YAHOO!. In other words, YAHOO! typically gives you a shorter, but more relevant, list of links. Additionally, the YAHOO! index is organized by category, which makes it amenable to browsing.

Another good point about YAHOO! is that the YAHOO! search results are returned on a page that contains links to other indexes such as Open Text, AltaVista, Lycos, WebCawler, Deja News, and many more. When you search YAHOO! using a keyword, and you do not like what YAHOO! returns, you can click on one of these links; YAHOO! submits a search request (with your original keyword) to the selected index, which can get you more results.

To begin a typical YAHOO! search, type the following URL (in the text field that shows a document's location in Netscape Navigator):

```
http://www.yahoo.com/
```

Netscape Navigator loads the YAHOO! home page, as shown in Figure 4-14.

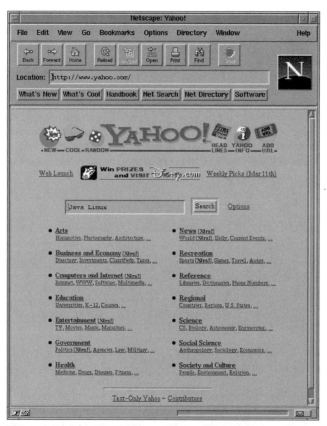

Figure 4-14: The YAHOO! home page. (Text and artwork copyright © 1996 by YAHOO!, Inc. All rights reserved. YAHOO! and the YAHOO! logo are trademarks of YAHOO!, Inc.)

The YAHOO! page shows a text-entry field in which you can type one or more keywords. I was looking for some information on Java for Linux; Figure 4-14 shows the keywords *Java* and *Linux* in the text field. To initiate a search, press Enter or click on the Search button. YAHOO!, in turn, performs the search and returns a new Web page with the search results. Figure 4-15 shows the results of the search, with Java and Linux as the keywords. As Figure 4-15 shows, YAHOO! provided quite a few relevant links that I could follow for further information on finding Java for Linux.

Figure 4-15: Results of searching for Java and Linux on YAHOO!

How to visit a specific site

URL In my Web tour (described in the "Just browsing" section), I visited sites by clicking hypertext links, which is the typical way to browse a Web page. Sometimes, however, you want to go directly to a Web page whose URL you know. Suppose that you want to visit the White House home page at the URL:

```
http://www.whitehouse.gov/
```

Tip   To go to this page, select Open Location from Netscape Navigator's File menu.
Netscape Navigator, in turn, displays the Open Location dialog box. Enter the URL for
the White House home page in the text field of the dialog box, as shown in Figure 4-16.

Figure 4-16: You can open a Web page directly by specifying its URL.

Then click the Open button in the Open Location dialog box. Netscape Navigator
immediately downloads and opens the White House home page, as shown in
Figure 4-17.

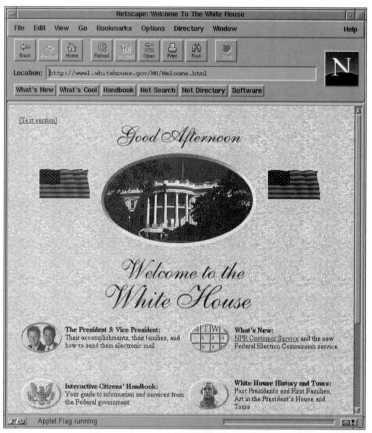

Figure 4-17: Netscape Navigator, showing the White House home page.

From the White House home page, you can visit the President's and the Vice President's offices. You can even sign an electronic guest book with your message.

 Tip You can also enter a URL directly in the text field where Netscape Navigator displays the location of a document. All you have to do is click on the text field and begin typing the new URL. When you finish, press Enter; Netscape Navigator jumps to that URL.

Summary

As a Webmaster, your focus is primarily on the Web server that provides documents and other information to the end-user. However, you also need to learn about the client side of the Web — the Web browsers — because the end-user accesses the information from that end. This chapter presents the Web from the user's perspective. The next chapter summarizes the roles that a Webmaster is expected to fulfill.

Where to go next . . .

✦ To learn about the roles of the Webmaster, go to Chapter 5.

✦ If you are not familiar with the Internet and the information services it supports, refer to Chapters 1 and 2.

✦ For information on choosing a Web server, read Chapter 6.

✦　　✦　　✦

The Role of the Webmaster

Chapters 1 through 4 summarize the Internet information services that Webmasters typically install and maintain. The Web server features prominently among these services. However, being a Webmaster involves more than setting up a Web server and writing HTML documents.

If you are a practicing Webmaster, you know from your experience that a Webmaster has many different roles. At times you are a software developer, downloading software from the Net or writing your own Perl scripts and C programs for specific tasks. When setting up your Web site's Internet connection and Web server, you are a system administrator with intimate knowledge of the operating system (in this case, UNIX), TCP/IP, and the Web server software. You're a graphics designer and HTML expert when laying out the images and text for a Web page. Finally, when you have a Web site up and running, you have to be a salesperson to sell your site to the world. After all, what good is a Web site if users don't visit it often enough? Anyway, you get the point — a Webmaster wears many different hats.

This chapter gives you a broad view of the Webmaster's roles. You learn what users expect from a Webmaster in each role and how this book can help you prepare for these roles.

Webmaster — A Master of Many Trades

You have probably heard the expression "jack of all trades, master of none." The Webmaster, it seems, must be the master of many trades, if not all. As the person responsible for providing information to users on the Internet, a Webmaster's job spans several different areas. At a minimum, a Webmaster alternates between the following roles:

✦ **System administrator:** You need system administrator skills to set up and maintain the Web server and other Internet services such as FTP and Gopher.

✦ **Software developer:** As a Webmaster, you have to modify and compile code and build tools for the Web site. You may also write Perl and Java programs to implement interactive Web pages. For these tasks, you have to be a software developer.

✦ **Graphics designer:** You wear the hat of a graphics designer when you create the Web pages — the content of your Web site. Even if your organization has other staff members responsible for designing the content of the Web site, they'll look to you for help with HTML.

✦ **Salesperson:** A Web site is successful only if users visit the site. You have to be a salesperson to promote your site and make sure potential users know about the site.

The following sections briefly describe each of these roles.

System administrator

To set up a Web site, you must connect your UNIX system to the Internet (typically through an Internet Service Provider) and install the Web server on that system. You also have to configure many Internet services such as anonymous FTP (which allows anyone on the Net access to a selected set of your system files). To perform these tasks, you'll be modifying various configuration files under UNIX. You must have an understanding of UNIX to correctly make changes to system files. Essentially, you have to be a system administrator to ensure smooth operation of your Web site.

Cross Ref Typically, your first assignment as a Webmaster may be to decide how to host your Web site. For example, you may decide to rent disk space from an Internet Service Provider (ISP) and put your Web pages on that system. Another choice may be to locate a complete UNIX system at an ISP's facility (so that you can connect the system to the Internet with a high-bandwidth network connection) and run a Web server on that system. A third option may be to connect your UNIX system (or your organization's local network) to the Internet. Chapter 6 presents these options with the pros and cons of each option so you can decide which one best meets your need.

Cross Ref If you decide to connect your network (or, at a minimum, your UNIX system) to the Internet, you will have to set up TCP/IP networking on your system. Chapter 1 summarizes TCP/IP networking on UNIX systems.

Cross Ref If you connect your network to the Internet, you should be concerned about security — the threat of someone accessing systems on your internal network. You can make your system more secure by taking some precautions when you install various Internet services. If you have enough resources, you may opt for an Internet firewall — a complete system that isolates your internal network from the Internet while still allowing a controlled flow of network traffic to and from the internal network. For more information on security, see Chapter 9.

Cross
Ref

After you connect your system to the Internet (or, if you use the Web on an internal network), you must select a Web server and install it on your system. You can choose from several Web servers for UNIX systems. Several popular Web servers (such as the NCSA and CERN Web servers) are freely available. A few other Web servers (such as the Netscape Commerce Server) are commercial products. Chapters 7 and 8 guide you through the process of selecting and setting up a Web server. These are the tasks where you need your system administrator skills the most.

Software developer

Many of the tools you use as a Webmaster typically come in the form of freely available source code. Usually, you'll download the source code from the Net. Then, you may have to compile the source code to build an executable program for your system before you can install and use the software. For example, the popular NCSA and Apache Web servers are available in source form. Although precompiled versions of these Web servers are available for most UNIX systems, you must compile the server again after you apply patches to fix bugs.

To run the Web site, you'll need many more utility programs besides the Web server. For example, you'll need software to manipulate images and track how many users are accessing your Web site. Often you'll find this type of software in source code form. To build the executable programs, you have to use software development tools such as make. You'll wear your software developer hat when performing these tasks.

Cross
Ref

Building the Web server or utility programs are only the first steps in setting up a Web site. When you have your Web server up and running, you'll want to use features of the Web that require additional computer programs. For example, if you implement interactive Web pages where the user may enter data on a form, you'll have to write a Perl script or a C program to handle the input sent by the user. This is what's known as the *Common Gateway Interface (CGI)*. Chapters 19 through 22 cover the software development tasks you have to perform to support CGI and other ways of providing customized data to the user.

Cross
Ref

The recently released Java programming language offers yet another way you can provide information to the user. With Java, you can send an application to the Web browser where the application runs on the user's computer. For example, you may provide some data along with a Java application that allows the user to view and manipulate the data. Here I don't go into the details of Java programming except to say that you'll need software developer skills to build Java applications (commonly called *applets*). You'll learn more about Java in Chapter 23.

Graphics designer

The Web server and all the supporting tools are useless without the Web pages — the content that your Web site offers to the users. This content must be interesting enough to attract and hold the user's interest. Creating the Web pages requires a knowledge of page layout, graphics design, and writing skills.

If your Web site is a one-person show, you may have to be the graphics designer who prepares the Web pages. In a larger organization, the Web page design may be handled by a professional graphics designer or artist. However, as a Webmaster, you'll still be the expert who helps implement the Web page using HTML.

Cross Ref Chapters 10 through 17 focus on the subject of designing and preparing Web pages. Although writing HTML code may seem mechanical, you do need some graphics design skills to layout a page using HTML. Chapter 15 presents some guidelines for designing Web pages.

Salesperson

No matter what a Web site offers, all sites have the same goal — to attract users to the site and, after they visit once, keep them coming back often. As a Webmaster, you are responsible for this task of marketing your Web site. After all, a Web site has to be promoted on the Net and who better to do the marketing than you — the person who knows the Net most. At least, that's how the logic goes.

Cross Ref Even if you are not that much of a salesperson, you can follow a few simple steps to ensure that your Web site gets the initial exposure. Chapter 18 presents some tips and tricks on promoting your Web site.

After the initial visit by a user, the Web site's content is the key to capturing the user's attention. You'll get repeat visits from only those users who find your site's content useful. The key to a successful Web site, therefore, is still the information you provide through the Web pages.

Webmaster Job Description

Webmaster is a new kind of position that has emerged as the Web gains popularity. Broadly speaking, everyone assumes that the Webmaster takes care of a Web site. However, the Webmaster job description is not as well understood as that of a UNIX system administrator.

Note This section provides a job description for the Webmaster — you can use this job description as a starting point if you plan to hire a Webmaster (for example, although you may be a Webmaster, you may need to hire one or more assistant Webmasters).

The previous sections presented the Webmaster role in terms of several other well-known roles. You can construct a Webmaster job description based on those roles. A good way to prepare the Webmaster job description is to break it down into several sections:

✦ **Job overview:** Includes a statement that captures the essence of the Webmaster job. The overview may include background information about the organization, as well as how the organization expects the Webmaster to serve its mission.

✦ **Responsibilities:** Lists the major duties of the Webmaster. The list is not exhaustive.

✦ **Knowledge and skills:** Lists the minimum education and work experience needed for the job.

✦ **Salary and benefits:** Provides a salary range and briefly mentions the benefits (such as insurance and retirement).

✦ **How to apply:** Includes information on how to apply for the Webmaster position.

Job overview

The overview section of the job description should provide the "mission statement" of the Webmaster — it's a high-level description of what the Webmaster is expected to do for the organization.

For example, a generic job overview may include:

> The Webmaster will be responsible for the implementation, operation, and support of XYZ Corporation's World Wide Web site. The selected individual must proactively develop and maintain the site's information content so that the Web site serves as a strategic business tool for XYZ Corporation.

 Tip You may want to augment this overview with a brief statement of XYZ Corporation's mission. The additional information will help the prospective applicant understand the strategic needs of the corporation. For example, the strategic need of an educational institute (such as a university) is different from that of a computer company.

Responsibilities

The job description should clearly indicate the major responsibilities of the Webmaster. Although you don't want a laundry list of tasks listed as responsibilities, it is easier to derive the broad areas of responsibility from a list of specific tasks the Webmaster performs. For example, here are some specific tasks that a Webmaster may perform:

✦ Design the layout of individual Web pages with image maps (users can click on such images to jump to a new URL) and links.

✦ Use HTML to implement the Web pages.

✦ Use graphics software (possibly on PC or Macintosh) to create images in GIF or JPEG formats.

✦ Manipulate images with various tools; in particular, create transparent GIF images (these images appear to float on a Web page — more on this in Chapter 11).

✦ View Web pages with different Web browsers to make sure the pages are useable (in particular, make sure that pages present the information even on a text-based Web browser such as Lynx).

✦ Diagnose problems with Web pages (such as nonfunctioning image maps and errors in HTML tags) and fix them.

✦ Periodically test all hypertext links and make sure they are current.

✦ Promote the Web site by submitting links to various Web indexes.

✦ Use freeware tools or develop scripts to generate reports of Web site statistics such as the number of times a page is accessed, the top users of the site, and so on.

✦ Write Common Gateway Interface (CGI) scripts (in Perl, C, or C++) to let a user provide information through interactive forms, as well as return information requested by the user.

✦ Set up and maintain anonymous FTP server with files that users can download.

✦ Connect a Web server to a corporate database (typically in a commercial RDBMS — relational database management system — such as Oracle, Informix, or Sybase).

✦ Search the Web to locate specific information.

✦ Help others in the organization develop Web pages consistent with the overall style and layout of the Web site.

✦ Download freeware or shareware from the Internet and use the software at the Web site.

✦ Browse selected Web sites, Internet newsgroups (such as `comp.infosystems. www.*`), and computer journals to keep up with the latest developments in Web technology (HTML and HTTP standards, new ways of connecting to a corporate database, use of Intranets, and so on).

✦ Experiment with new Web technology (such as Java, JavaScript, and VRML).

✦ Use TELNET and FTP to communicate with a remote Web server (this may be necessary when the Web server is hosted at an Internet Service Provider's site).

✦ Respond to e-mail from customers on the Web.

This list is not exhaustive. In particular, I did not include many system and network administration tasks that Webmasters often have to perform. This list should, however, give you an idea of the kinds of tasks a Webmaster may be asked to perform. From this list, you can aggregate some items and arrive at some high-level bullets that you could use in the Responsibilities section of the Webmaster job description:

✦ Develop and maintain Web site's content (including interactive interfaces, consistent with the organization's business mission).

✦ Manage the quality of the Web site's content (including evaluation of the links and the usability of the site).

✦ Ensure delivery of information to the end-users through various Internet information services (such as FTP, Gopher, and the Web CGI).

✦ Maintain cross-platform and cross-browser compatibility of the Web pages so that the Web site is accessible from a wide variety of systems.

✦ Manage Web site security.

✦ Routinely generate report on Web site usage statistics.

✦ Provide training and technical support to Web content-development team in areas of HTML authoring and use of tools to create content.

✦ Keep abreast of technological advances in Web-site deployment and Web programming and integrate these technologies into the Web site.

✦ Develop software for Web servers, CGI, and database access.

✦ Respond to e-mail from customers on the Web.

You can pick all or a few of these as the responsibilities of the Webmaster position.

Knowledge and skills

This section of the job description summarizes the kind of person you want as the Webmaster. You may list both technical (such as experience in C or C++) as well as personal skills (such as good oral and written communication skills).

Here is a list of experience and skills that can serve as the starting point for what you may list in the Webmaster job description:

✦ Bachelor's degree in Computer Science, Engineering, or equivalent.

✦ Minimum two or three years of related work experience (such as a UNIX system administrator or Webmaster).

✦ Hands-on experience with the installation and configuration of NCSA and CERN Web servers.

✦ Knowledge of HTML, including familiarity with CGI programming.

✦ Familiarity with Netscape Navigator and other Web browsers running on a variety of systems (Windows 95, Windows NT, and Macintosh).

✦ Excellent working knowledge of UNIX, TCP/IP networking, and Internet services (such as FTP and Gopher).

✦ Experience in Perl, C, and C++ programming.

✦ Experience in designing graphical user interfaces.

✦ Knowledge of Internet firewalls.

✦ Good understanding of relational databases and SQL.

✦ Skills in graphics design and experience with PC- or Macintosh-based graphics software.

✦ Excellent written and oral communication skills.

✦ Good organizational skills.

Tip   You may want to make the list of required skills more specific to your organization by indicating the exact version of UNIX your site uses (for example, Solaris or HP-UX) and the type of database you have (Oracle, Informix, Sybase, or none at all).

Salary and benefits

You should provide an indication of the salary and benefits that your organization is willing to offer. The statement could be something generic such as the following:

> This is a full-time permanent position with excellent medical and retirement benefits. Salary commensurate with experience.

Although a generic statement may be sufficient for medical and retirement benefits, it's best to include a salary range, especially if you are trying to attract talented people with a somewhat higher salary.

Tip   If your organization offers other unique benefits (such as stock options), be sure to mention these benefits in the job description.

Currently, Webmaster salaries range from $30,000 to $60,000 (U.S.) plus typical medical and retirement benefits. The demand for Webmasters is increasing steadily, however, and the salaries are expected to rise with the demand.

Tip   You can get a good idea about Webmaster salaries from the Web itself. For example, a recent search on AltaVista (http://www.altavista.digital.com/) with the keywords webmaster salary, yielded a Web site (http://techknowledge.com) that lists a Webmaster opening with an annual salary of $50,000 to $65,000 (U.S.).

The Internet newsgroup misc.jobs.offered lists many Webmaster openings — you may find salaries listed in some of these announcements. I have seen Webmaster job openings with annual salaries up to $75,000 (U.S.). Most Webmaster positions, however, are advertised for salaries in the $40,000 to $50,000 (U.S.) range.

How to apply

Last, but not the least, you should include information on how to apply for the position. You may want to include a mail address, as well as voice and FAX phone numbers.

Because Webmaster is an Internet position, you may want to accept applications by e-mail or even through your Web page (if you have one up already). In fact, you could post the job announcement itself on the Internet — a good place is the Internet newsgroup `misc.jobs.offered`.

Summary

The Webmaster is a new breed of Information System professional that has emerged because of the Web's popularity as the information delivery system of choice. The exact description of a Webmaster is still evolving, but the consensus is that Webmasters wear quite a few hats at the job. This chapter describes the multiple roles of the Webmaster. In the next part of the book, you learn how to get your Web site up and running.

Where to go next . . .

✦ If you are starting a new Web site, Chapters 6 through 9 show you how to set up, configure, and secure a Web server.

✦ If you already have a Web server set up and you want to start with Web page design, go to Chapter 10.

✦   ✦   ✦

Getting Your Web Site Up and Running

✦ ✦ ✦ ✦

✦ ✦ ✦ ✦

Your Options for a Web Site

The first part of this book summarizes the Internet including several prominent Internet information services such as FTP, Gopher, and the Web. Because this book focuses on the Web, Chapters 3 and 4 summarize the Web from both the server and the client side. From this chapter on, the book focuses on helping you fulfill your Webmaster duties.

Unless you are joining as a Webmaster at an established Web site, one of your first duties is to set up the Web site. More specifically, you need to set up the basic infrastructure for your Web site: physical access to the Internet, Web server software, and an initial set of Web pages.

If you are lucky, your organization has an Internet connection and all you have to do is install a Web server. Typically, only universities, major government agencies, and large corporations have existing physical connection to the Internet. For most small businesses and individuals, arranging an Internet connection is the first (and most important) step in setting up a Web site.

When you have Internet access, Web server setup is relatively simple. Several times, I have set up an NCSA HTTP server (one of the most common Web servers) in less than an hour. Of course, in all cases, the UNIX system already had full Internet access. All I had to do was download the Web server from an Internet site, prepare its configuration file, and run the server.

You learn the details of setting up common UNIX Web servers in Chapters 7 and 8, but first you need to consider all the options you have for setting up a Web site. After analyzing the options, you may decide that you don't need direct Internet access. You may find it adequate to put your Web pages on an off-site Web server maintained by an Internet Service Provider (ISP). This chapter presents your options for the Web site to help you select an approach that best suits your needs.

Overall Options for a Web Site

When you plan a Web site, your first reaction may be to begin making a list of what you need to run the Web site. For example, you may think of the Web server software, a UNIX workstation (or PC running Linux or BSDI) on which to run the Web server, and a high-speed Internet connection — that is, high-capacity, or, more accurately, high-bandwidth connection.

If you have already started shopping around for Internet access, you may have found the Internet connection to be rather expensive. Internet connection can be expensive because you need a full-time connection for a Web site (after all, anyone from around the globe may access the Web site at any hour of the day).

Before you connect your own UNIX system to the Internet, you need to consider your overall options for a Web site. At the least, you need to consider the following options (listed roughly in the order of increasing cost):

✦ **Option 1: Setting up a personal page at an ISP's Web server.** Many ISPs allow you to put up a Web page when you sign up for Internet access. For modest needs, this option may be sufficient.

✦ **Option 2: Using a Web site maintained by the ISP.** In this option, the ISP maintains the Web server on an ISP-owned system, but gives you a fully qualified domain name, FQDN, (such as www.your-company.com) for your Web page.

✦ **Option 3: Collocating your system at the ISP site.** You can arrange to place your own computer at the ISP's site. In doing so, you get the benefit of the ISP's high-speed connection to the Internet.

✦ **Option 4: Arranging a dedicated Internet connection for your system.** In this case, you connect your computer system to the Internet through a high-speed Internet connection such as a 56 Kbps or T1 leased line (T1 has a capacity of 1.544 Mbps). Of course, if your organization already has a high-speed Internet connection, you don't have to agonize with these options; you can choose Option 4 by default.

✦ **Option 5: Setting yourself up as an ISP.** With this option, you set yourself up as an ISP with several high-bandwidth connections to the Internet. You can put up your own Web site plus offer Options 1 and 2 to other customers.

Many small businesses should be able to manage a successful Web presence with Option 2 — putting up your Web pages on a Web server maintained by an ISP. For organizations with the resources, Option 4 — getting a dedicated Internet connection — makes sense. The following sections further explain these options so that you can make up your own mind about the option that best suits your need.

Option 1: Personal page at an ISP's Web server

If you have recently signed up for an Internet account with an ISP, you may already have everything you need to put up your home page. Today, most ISPs offer a personal Web page automatically when you sign up with the ISP. Follow these steps for using the personal Web-page feature offered by the ISP:

1. You sign up with an ISP for dial-up PPP access. The ISP gives you a phone number and other information you need to set up your system for the PPP connection. The ISP also gives you a shell account (which assumes that the ISP runs UNIX — the case for most ISPs) with a username and password.

2. You set up your system (Windows 95 PC or a UNIX workstation) to dial out and make a PPP connection with the ISP's system (follow the ISP's instructions).

3. After establishing a PPP connection to the ISP, run TELNET and log into the ISP's system (using the user name and password that were assigned to you).

4. At the UNIX shell prompt, type `ls` to look at the directory listing. You should see a directory named `public_html` (if you don't, ask your ISP where you can place your HTML files). Go to the `public_html` directory and create the file named `index.html`. This `index.html` file is your home page.

5. Run a Web browser and try out your personal home page. If your ISP's Web site's URL is `http://www.my-isp.net/` and your user name is `xyz-corp`, then your personal page is `http://www.my-isp.net/~xyz-corp/`.

The personal home page is obviously adequate for an individual, but you can also use the personal page for a home business or even a small business. You can use a text editor (such as `vi`) to edit the Web pages. To use these features, you need a working knowledge of HTML, which this book provides in Chapters 10 through 17.

The personal page option can be a cost effective way to get a Web presence on the Net. ISPs typically charge anywhere from $15 (U.S.) to $30 (U.S.) per month for dial-up PPP access to the Internet. For that price, you automatically get the personal page option and the ability to provide information on the Web. Another benefit to using the personal Web page is that it resides on the ISP's system, which has much higher speed connection to the Internet than you can afford (at least, as an individual).

The main drawback of the personal page is the restriction that ISPs place on that page. You typically have a limited amount of disk space (5MB to 10MB) and you have a limit on the volume of data transfer from your Web page (for example, 200MB per month). Also, you cannot have any interactive Web pages with forms because ISPs generally do not allow personal pages access to the Common Gateway Interface (CGI) — you can only offer static information through the personal pages.

In spite of the limitations, the personal page is a perfect place to try out HTML authoring and learn some of the skills you need as a Webmaster. Consider setting up a personal page just for the educational experience.

Option 2: Web site maintained by ISP

Most ISPs offer this option , which allows you to place your Web pages in a directory on the ISP's system. Best of all, for an extra fee, the ISP provides an FQDN for your Web pages. In other words, instead of using `http://www.my-isp.net/~xyz-corp/` as your Web site's URL, users can refer to your site with a more intuitive URL such as `http://www.xyz-corp.com/`. This unique name leads the outside world to believe that your Web pages are located at your company's Web site.

Cross Ref The ability to refer to a site with several different names is implemented through the Web server's ability to support virtual hosts. Chapter 8, "Installing Other Web Servers," explains how the Apache Web server supports virtual hosts.

In this option, you store the documents the same way you would store the documents in Option 1. The ISP provides a directory in which you can place the HTML files. Typically, however, you get more storage space (for example, 25MB instead of 5MB) and a higher limit on data volume (for example 1GB per month instead of 200MB).

You also can use CGI scripts — you can have interactive Web pages where you may solicit input from the user. Many ISPs reserve the right to inspect your CGI scripts to ensure that you do not inadvertently undermine the site's security.

Because the Web pages are located on the ISP's system, your Web site also benefits from the ISP's high-speed connection to the Net. For many businesses, this option is very attractive. However, it does cost somewhat more than Option 1. Most ISPs charge anywhere from $80 (U.S.) to $120 (U.S.) per month for Option 2.

The only significant drawback of Option 2 is lack of control. You cannot select the Web server software and you cannot set up the site exactly as you want. Also, if your site becomes successful, the volume of traffic (the amount of Web pages and images transferred during a month) may be too much for the ISP to handle.

Despite the lack of control, Option 2 is ideal for small to medium businesses that cannot justify the cost of getting a high-speed Internet connection. This option can be a convenient way to get started with your Web site. You can focus on the content and leave the Web site management chores to the ISP.

Option 3: Collocated system at the ISP site

Even if you plan to set up a Web site on your own hardware, you may be stumped by the cost of getting a dedicated Internet connection (of adequate bandwidth). As you research more into the basic necessities of a Web site, you will realize that the toughest part of setting up a Web site is getting a high-speed connection to the Net. The cost of a 1.544 Mbps T1 connection can be around $18,000 (U.S.) a year.

One way out of this quandary is to place your system on the ISP's Local Area Network (LAN) so that your system can benefit from the ISP's high-speed Internet access (typically 1.544 Mbps T1 or even 45 Mbps T3 connection).

Not all ISPs offer this option, but if you ask, you can get a price quotation. This option's cost should be lower than getting your own high-speed Internet connection, but higher than Options 1 or 2. Typically, an ISP charges $800 (U.S.) to set up the system (this does not include the cost of the computer) and anywhere from $350 (U.S.) to $500 (U.S.) per month to maintain the system at the ISP's site.

With this option, you'll provide a computer that your ISP places in their offices and connects to their network, which, in turn, is connected to the Internet. You may want to opt for a Pentium PC running a UNIX operating system such as Linux. When the computer is located at the ISP's facilities, you can get a dial-up shell or PPP account from the same ISP so that you can log into your system and control it from a remote location (such as your home or office). You must be quite knowledgeable about UNIX and you have to manage the Web server yourself.

The biggest benefit of this option is high-speed Internet access and complete control over what Web server to run and how your Web site is organized.

A drawback of this option is that your computer is at the mercy of the ISP. If the ISP were to go out of business, you may have trouble reclaiming your computer.

Not many ISPs offer the option of collocating your system on their premises. A more common offering is a dedicated ISP-owned computer that you get to use exclusively for your Web site. Typically, the ISP sets up and manages the Web server on this dedicated system and you provide the content (the HTML documents and any files that users can download). If you are the Webmaster for an established business with a healthy budget allocated for Web presence, you may seriously consider leasing such a full-service Web server from an ISP.

Option 4: System with dedicated Internet connection

If you want full control of your Web site, the best approach is to connect your system to the Internet. This is easiest if your site already has an Internet connection; otherwise, you have to spend a lot to get a decent Internet connection.

To set up a Web site that's useful to your customers, you must have the site up and running day and night. You should not turn off the Web site just because it's nighttime where you live; after all, it's always working hours somewhere in the world. The implication is that you need a dedicated Internet connection to your Web server.

ISPs sell dedicated connections of various capacities starting with full-time PPP connection through 28.8 Kbps modems. In this case, the ISP provides a dedicated phone number for your use — you need a dedicated phone line as well. Your computer establishes a dial-up PPP connection with the ISP's system and maintains the connection 24-hours a day. For this, ISPs charge around $100 (U.S.) to $150 (U.S.) per month. Of course, you have to also pay a monthly fee for the second phone line.

From the cost perspective, you may find it reasonable to have a permanent 28.8 Kbps connection. However, a 28.8 Kbps data transfer rate is not enough for a Web site; this bandwidth cannot sustain multiple simultaneous connections with an acceptable response time. Even when a single Web browser accesses a site through a 28.8 Kbps connection, it takes around 10 seconds to load a Web page with 30K of data (images contribute to the hefty size of most Web pages). Clearly, when you have only a 28.8 Kbps connection, it's best to keep your Web pages as small as possible. You also have to contend with the issue of multiple users attempting to access your site at the same time. Although the Web server will accept and attempt to serve all the users, each user will see a very slow response from your server.

If your budget can only handle a full-time 28.8 Kbps connection, you would be better off with Option 2 — putting your Web pages on the ISP's Web site, but under your company's name (such as www.my-business.com).

If you want a dedicated Internet connection for your Web site, at the very least you need a 56 Kbps Frame Relay or 64 Kbps ISDN (you can get up to 128 Kbps with ISDN) connection to your ISP. These connections cost several hundred dollars a month, but such costs may be justified if your business benefits from having a Web site. (You learn more about ISDN in the "ISDN" section later in this chapter.)

If you can afford it, you may want a T1 line between your system and the ISP. A T1 line has a data transfer rate of 1.544 Mbps — that's 1,544,000 bits per second or roughly 193,000 bytes per second compared to 7,000 bytes per second for a 56 Kbps line. With a T1 link, your Web site should appear very responsive to users.

The biggest drawback of a T1 connection is its cost, which is around $1,200 (U.S.) per month (the cost depends on the distance between your site and the ISP's offices). The exact location of your site also affects the cost. If your computer is in an office building that already has T1 access, it may cost less to arrange a T1 line for your site.

When you opt for a high-speed Internet connection such as 56 Kbps Frame Relay or T1, you also need extra networking equipment such as a router and devices known as CSU (Channel Service Unit) and DSU (Data Service Unit) to complete the installation. You have to spend several thousand dollars up front for this networking equipment.

Option 5: You as the ISP

In this option, you decide to go all the way and set yourself up as an Internet Service Provider, or, more appropriately, as a Web Presence Provider (who provides room for Web pages and even builds the Web pages for customers). You could offer customers a number of options for Web pages (much like Options 1 and 2). If you can attract enough customers, you could finance your own Web site with customer fees.

This option, however, is easier said than done. First, you have to invest in several powerful computers running UNIX. You can use a Pentium PC with enough memory (32MB) and a large disk (32GB) running Linux or some other UNIX clone. Next, you have to get a high-speed Internet access from a Network Service Provider (NSP) — NSPs sell high-speed connections to the Internet backbone (you learn more about the Internet's networking architecture in the "Internet Connection Options" section of this chapter). You also need many 28.8 Kbps modems and phone lines for customers to dial into your system and routers and CSU and DSU devices to connect your network to the NSP.

As if the upfront cost of setting up shop as ISP were not enough to put a damper on your plans, competition is intense in the ISP marketplace. Nearly all ISPs offer Web services. To further muddy the waters, many established telecommunications companies are now getting into the ISP business. These large companies have much better networking infrastructure than you may be able to afford and they can direct many resources (money as well as people) at the ISP business. The point is that you should think carefully before going into business as an ISP.

If you already have an established business, you may consider setting up shop as an ISP as a side-business. This is especially true if your current business is in publishing or advertising; these businesses have the people who can design and lay out Web pages (and provide a service to others in need of Web page design).

Internet Connection Options

If you decide to get a dedicated Internet connection for your UNIX system (to run a Web server), you have to select from one of several networking options. These options deal with the physical connection between your system and your ISP's system. To make an informed decision, you need to know a bit about the Internet's network architecture.

The overview of the Internet in Chapter 1 tells you that the Internet is a set of inter-connected networks that spans the globe. However, Chapter 1 does not give you any clue about the Internet's physical connections. The following sections give you an overview of the Internet's current network architecture and connection options.

Recent Internet history

The Internet's current physical networking infrastructure owes its existence to NSFNET, which started as a pioneering effort by a U.S. government agency — the National Science Foundation (NSF) — to promote high-speed networking. The first NSFNET backbone (a backbone is a high-speed physical connection between a number of physical sites) became operational in 1986. The initial backbone connected six sites — five NSF supercomputer centers and the National Center for Atmospheric

Research (NCAR) in Boulder, Colorado. These centers included San Diego Supercomputer Center, National Center for Supercomputing Applications (the famous NCSA that originated Mosaic and the NCSA Web server), Cornell Theory Center, Pittsburgh Supercomputing Center, and the John von Neumann Supercomputer Center (Princeton University).

In 1987, NSF funded a partnership of IBM, MCI, and the state of Michigan to improve the initial backbone; that partnership cost NSF $58 million (U.S.). The following is a list of the partnership's goals:

✦ Expand the number of backbone sites from 6 to 13.

✦ Increase the speed of the backbone from 56 Kbps to 1.544 Mbps (T1) and eventually to 45 Mbps (T3).

✦ Improve the reliability and stability of the network.

URL   From 1987 through early 1995, Merit Network, Inc., a nonprofit organization located in Ann Arbor, Michigan, managed the NSFNET backbone project. You can read the complete report of the NSFNET backbone project (1987 – 1995) by visiting the URL `http://nic.merit.edu/nsfnet/final.report/`.

NSFNET used a three-tiered network architecture as illustrated in Figure 6-1.

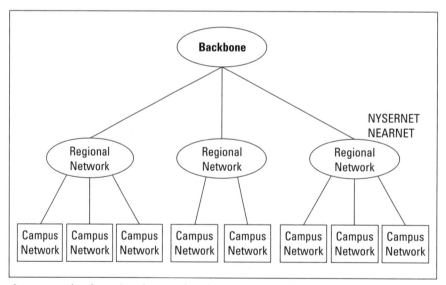

Figure 6-1: The three-tiered network architecture of NSFNET.

The NSFNET backbone constitutes the topmost tier of the architecture. The next tier is comprised of various regional networks such as NYSERNET, NEARNET, and Westnet. The lowest tier includes various campus networks. This basic multi-tiered network architecture is used in today's Internet as well.

During 1987 – 1989, the NSFNET project focused on building the T1 backbone service. The tremendous growth in the use of NSFNET prompted the project's partners to propose an upgrade of the backbone to T3 (45 Mbps) speed. Ultimately, the upgrade from T1 to T3 was completed in 1992, with the number of backbone sites increasing from 13 to 16. This T3 backbone linked over 3500 networks.

The NSFNET project was the catalyst for many important Internet networking technologies. For example, in deploying the T3 backbone, IBM pioneered the development of high-performance T3 routers. Eventually, these routers evolved to the point where they could switch 100,000 IP packets per second. NSFNET also spurred IBM and Cisco Systems to develop the Border Gateway Protocol (BGP), a protocol for routing among networks, now used extensively on the Internet. NSFNET backbone was the first network to use BGP in an operational environment.

NSFNET also originated another important routing concept — Classless Inter-Domain Routing or CIDR — that's used widely in the Internet. Engineers noticed the exponential growth of the routing tables (each entry in the table specifies how to route packets to a specific network) as new IP networks joined NSFNET. One problem was IP address classes (see Chapter 1) where each Class C address is a separate network and requires a unique entry in the routing table. CIDR alleviates the problem by allowing grouping of multiple Class C IP addresses into a single logical network.

By 1994, NSFNET connected 50,766 networks from 93 countries. Of these networks, 28,470 were in the U.S. (remember, this is from 1994; since then, the number of networks has grown tremendously). NSFNET's role in interconnecting the networks of various countries contributed to the global nature of today's Internet.

Current Internet architecture

On April 30, 1995, NSFNET transitioned to a new architecture with a more commercial orientation. The following is a list of the key elements for NSFNET's new architecture:

✦ A high-speed backbone service (vBNS) that links the five NSF supercomputer centers at a minimum operating speed of OC-3 (155 Mbps). The service also provides high-speed data transfer capabilities to scientists and researchers. MCI runs the vBNS.

✦ A number of Network Access Points (NAPs) that serve as interconnection points for commercial network service providers (these organizations sell high-speed network connections to ISPs). Currently, there are four NAP managers: Sprint for a New York NAP, Metropolitan Fiber Systems Datanet (MFS Datanet) for a Washington, D.C. NAP, Ameritech for a Chicago NAP, and Pacific Bell for a California NAP.

✦ Seventeen regional and mid-level networks that connect to the NAPs. The funding for these regional networks will be phased out over four years.

✦ A Routing Arbitrer who manages the routing tables and databases for the network service providers who connect to the NAPs. The current Routing Arbitrer team consists of Merit Network and Information Sciences Institute (ISI) of the University of Southern California.

Today's Internet operates and evolves within this structure. The physical network connections are still organized in tiers. Each tier constitutes one layer of physical connection. Figure 6–2 illustrates the physical network with all the layers of connections. (In Figure 6–2, the thickness of lines denotes the bandwidth — the thicker the line the higher the bandwidth.)

The first layer is the backbone that provides the interconnection between the NAPs. These are high-speed connections ranging in speed from 45 Mbps to 155 Mbps. The backbones use a variety of connections such as T3 (45 Mbps), FDDI (100 Mbps), or OC-3 (155 Mbps).

At the second layer, you find the Network Service Providers (NSPs) that connect to the NAPs. You can think of an NSP as a large-scale ISP — the NSPs offer network access to many ISPs in a region. The NSPs connect to each other and the interconnection of NSPs tie to the backbone at the NAPs. Typically, an NSP connects to the NAP at speeds ranging from T1 (1.544 Mbps) to T3 (45 Mbps).

The third layer is made up of ISPs who typically connect to NSPs only. However, some ISPs also connect to NAPs. Most small businesses and individuals connect to the Internet through ISPs. ISPs offer connections at speeds ranging from 28.8 Kbps dial-up modem to T1 (1.544 Mbps) leased line.

 To learn about the latest Internet network architecture, consult the URL `http://nic.merit.edu/.internet.html`.

Current Network Access Points

Currently, the four NAP managers — Sprint, Ameritech, Pacific Bell, and MFS Datanet — operate the following NAPs across the country:

✦ Sprint NAP in Pennsauken, New Jersey, runs a 100 Mbps Fiber Distributed Data Interface (FDDI) network with a number of routers and an Ethernet bridge. Customers connect through T1 or T3 links, and an Ethernet interface is also available upon request. For more information about the Sprint NAP, visit the URL `http://nic.merit.edu/nsf.architecture/Sprint/`.

✦ Ameritech Advanced Data Service (AADS) NAP in Chicago, Illinois, maintains a 100 Mbps FDDI network with a number of high-speed routers to which customers connect through T3 (45 Mbps) links. For more information on the Chicago NAP, visit the URL `http://www.ameritech.com/products/nap/`.

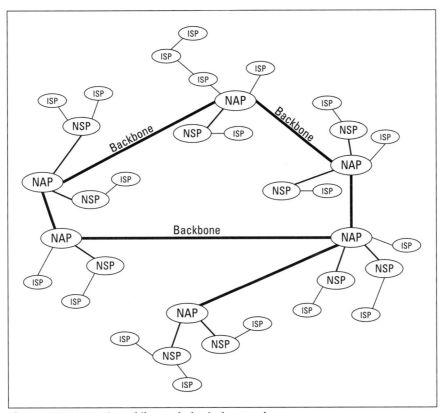

Figure 6-2: Internet's multilayered physical network.

✦ Pacific Bell NAP in San Francisco, California, provides a combination of FDDI and 155 Mbps Asynchronous Transfer Mode (ATM) network with Cisco 7000 routers. Customers can connect at speeds of up to 36.8 Mbps or 139 Mbps (the higher speed is using SONET — Synchronous Optical Network). For more information, visit the URL `http://www.pacbell.com/Products/NAP/`.

✦ MAE East is the Washington, D.C. NAP run by MFS Datanet. MAE East provides FDDI and Ethernet connections. MFS Datanet also runs two more NAPs — MAE West in San Jose, California, and MAE Chicago in Chicago, Illinois. (MAE access points are planned for Houston, Dallas, and Los Angeles.) Visit the URL `http://ext2.mfs-datanet.com/mfs-datanet/internet-services/`.

Each NAP is a local network with a high-speed backbone to other NAPs. The NAPs use Cisco 7010 routers, which seem to be the universal routers of choice on the Internet backbones. Each NAP also has a Route Server maintained by the Routing Arbitrer (RA). The Routing Server exchanges routing information among various ISP's routers.

Webmaster If you examine the path that an IP packet takes between your system and another, you see that the packet goes through one of these NAPs. In most UNIX systems, you can use the `traceroute` command to view the gateways (the routers) through which an IP packet travels on its way to its destination. For example, here is a `traceroute` command that shows the route between Digital Express (`digex.net`) — a Maryland-based ISP — and IDG Books (`idgbooks.com`) in Indianapolis, Indiana:

```
traceroute idgbooks.com
traceroute to idgbooks.com (198.70.168.2), 30 hops max, 40 byte packets
 1  border1-ether3-2.belt.dca.digex.net (205.197.245.1)  2 ms  2 ms  3 ms
 2  core2-fddi-2.belt.dca.digex.net (206.205.242.2)  3 ms  4 ms  4 ms
 3  core1-hssi-1.vienna.dca.digex.net (206.205.247.2)  105 ms  4 ms  4 ms
 4  mae-east.ans.net (192.41.177.140)  5 ms  4 ms  5 ms
 5  t3-3.cnss56.Washington-DC.t3.ans.net (140.222.56.4)  8 ms  6 ms  6 ms
 6  t3-0.cnss32.New-York.t3.ans.net (140.222.32.1)  18 ms  12 ms  11 ms
 7  t3-0.enss218.t3.ans.net (140.222.218.1)  20 ms  18 ms  16 ms
 8  sl-pen-2-F4/0.sprintlink.net (192.157.69.9)  251 ms  41 ms  37 ms
 9  sl-chi-3-H2/0-T3.sprintlink.net (144.228.10.38)  144 ms  211 ms  78 ms
10  sl-chi-5-F0/0.sprintlink.net (144.228.50.5)  72 ms  77 ms  79 ms
11  sl-idgbooks-1-S0-T1.sprintlink.net (144.228.55.34)  84 ms  92 ms  83 ms
12  idgbooks.com (198.70.168.2)  80 ms  79 ms  70 ms
```

URL As this sample output from `traceroute` shows, from the `digex.net` system, the IP packet enters the Internet backbone at the MAE East NAP (as indicated by the gateway named `mae-east.ans.net`). Then the packet travels through various T3 lines from Washington, D.C. to New York and then to Chicago (`sl-chi-5-F0/0.sprintlink.net`). On its last leg to `idgbooks.com`, the packet travels over a T1 link provided by SprintLink (`http://www.sprintlink.net/`) as indicated by the gateway `sl-idgbooks-1-S0-T1.sprintlink.net`. You can learn a lot about the physical network paths of the Internet by trying out the `traceroute` command for various destinations.

If you want to become an ISP, you may get your high-speed Internet connection directly from one of the organizations that run the NAPs. You may also get the connection from an NSP who already has high-speed access to the Internet.

If you do not want to be an ISP, you can get the physical Internet connection from any ISP. If you need high-speed access (T3 or ATM) to the Internet backbone, you can become a customer of one of the NAPs.

URL If you are a new NAP customer, you have to go through many different steps to ensure that packets from your network go out properly, and that packets addressed to your network are delivered correctly. All this is accomplished through what is called *peering agreement* — an agreement with another ISP to carry each other's routes. You should also use the services of the Routing Arbitrer. For more information on the steps to follow, consult the URL `http://www.ra.net/nap_customer/`.

Internet networking organizations

In the early days of NSFNET, the core physical network infrastructure of the Internet was subsidized by the U.S. government. In the new architecture, the Internet backbones and physical networks are gradually migrating to a commercial model where customers pay for access. That fee, in turn, allows telecommunications companies to build the necessary high-speed networks. The commercial Internet providers — the NSPs and ISPs — are the early pioneers in the commercialization of the Internet.

The pioneer NSPs and ISPs needed to ensure that packets originating in one NSP made their way through the routers maintained by other NSPs. Toward this end, in 1992, a group of Internet providers joined to form the Commercial Internet eXchange (CIX) Association, a nonprofit trade association of Public Data Internetwork service providers.

URL CIX maintains a Cisco 7000 router in Santa Clara, California. All CIX members can get IP routing service from the CIX router, thus ensuring interconnection to each other's networks. If you are an ISP, you may want to join the CIX Association so that your network is properly connected to other ISP's networks. For more information about the CIX Association, visit the URL `http://www.cix.org/`. Another helpful organization for NSPs is the North American Network Operators Group (NANOG). Organized in 1994 by Merit Network, Inc., NANOG has these goals:

✦ Hold 3 meetings of NSPs every year.

✦ Provide a forum for technical information exchange.

✦ Hold discussions of network implementation issues that require cooperation and coordination among NSPs.

✦ Promote and coordinate interconnection of networks within North America and to other countries.

URL For detailed information on NANOG, visit the URL `http://nic.merit.edu/ routing.arbiter/NANOG/NANOG.html`. In particular, you'll find the NANOG meeting reports very interesting. For example, the NAPs report the network traffic statistics at the NANOG meetings. These statistics will help you understand the growth rate of the Internet and the volume of traffic carried by the NAPs (NAPs are the entry points into the Internet backbone).

Types of Internet connections

Depending on how you plan to implement your Web site, you have a number of choices for the physical connection to the Internet. These physical connections vary in capacity from the low 28.8 Kbps modem to the 45 Mbps T3 line. To run a Web site on your computer, you need bandwidths between 56 Kbps and 1.544 Mbps (T1 line). Listed here are your physical connection options:

✦ Dial-up modem connections at speeds of up to 28.8 Kbps

✦ 56 Kbps leased line

✦ Integrated Services Digital Network (ISDN) at typical speeds of 128 Kbps

✦ Frame Relay at speeds of up to 1.5444 Mbps

✦ 1.544 Mbps T1

✦ 45 Mbps T3

Dial-up modem connection

Dial-up modems operate at speeds of up to 28.8 Kbps. As an individual, if you have Internet access from home, you probably use a 28.8 Kbps modem for the connection.

By running a protocol such as SLIP or PPP, you can establish a TCP/IP connection through the modem and make your computer a part of the Internet. With such Internet connections, you can run Web browsers to surf the Net through the modem.

Although a 28.8 Kbps modem can provide acceptable performance for browsing Web sites, this bandwidth is not adequate to serve Web pages to others on the Net. By using the dial-up PPP connection for your Web site, you must maintain the connection 24 hours a day, 7 days a week. Maintaining a permanent 28.8 Kbps PPP connection can cost from $100 (U.S.) to $150 (U.S.) a month (plus the phone bill for the phone line). You may be better off leasing space on an ISP's Web server; you can benefit from the ISP's higher-speed (typically 1.544 Mbps) Internet connection.

I cannot think of a good reason to use a 28.8 Kbps modem connection to serve Web pages. If you do, make sure that your ISP provides you with a *static IP address* (a *permanent* IP address), which does not change whenever you disconnect and reconnect.

56 Kbps leased line

You can lease (from your phone company) a permanent physical line connecting your site to the ISP. One of the most common is the one that can carry data at 56 Kbps. Data is transmitted over such a line using a *Digital Signal Level 0 (or DS0)*. Data transmission using DS0 requires a 64 Kbps bandwidth, but 8 Kbps of this bandwidth is used for control information. Thus, 56 Kbps is available for transmitting your data.

When you connect to your ISP with a 56 Kbps leased line, you (and the ISP) must have a device called the *Channel Service Unit/Data Service Unit (CSU/DSU)* for each end of the line. Additionally, you need a router to connect your local Ethernet network to the leased line. Along with the cost of this hardware, you have the initial installation charges and the monthly charge from the phone company for the leased line. Your ISP also charges a monthly fee for accessing the Internet through the 56 Kbps leased line.

Listed here is an itemization of the typical costs of setting up and using a 56 Kbps leased line for Internet access as of the spring of 1996 (shown in U.S. dollars):

Description	One-Time Cost	Monthly Cost
Phone company setup fees	$1,000	–
CSU/DSU for 56 Kbps	$150–$250	–
Router	$1,500–$2,500	–
ISP setup fee	$500–$1,000	–
Phone company monthly charges (may depend on distance)	–	$325
ISP monthly charges	–	$250–$500
Domain name registration fee	–	$50 per year

Many ISPs also charge for the CSU/DSU that they need at their end to connect to your site. In that case, their setup fees may be even higher. An alternative to 56 Kbps leased line is the 56 Kbps (or higher) Frame Relay service that's becoming increasingly popular.

Frame Relay

Unlike the dedicated point-to-point connection offered by leased lines, Frame Relay is based on the switching of variable-length packets over a shared digital network. The key word here is *shared* — all packets travel over the same network, but each packet is switched to its destination.

Frame Relay is appropriate for bursty data transfers with mid- to high-bandwidth (128 Kbps to 1.544 Mbps) needs. Frame Relay forwards packets to their destination without performing any internal error detection or error correction. This approach is in direct contrast to X.25, an older packet switching network, that incurs the overhead of error handling during transmission. Its simple packet-switching approach allows Frame Relay to make efficient use of the available bandwidth. Frame Relay is ideal as a data transport mechanism in layered protocol suites (such as TCP/IP) because a higher level protocol can take care of the error detection and error correction chores.

To use Frame Relay, your site and your ISP's site must be physically connected to a telephone company facility (maybe different facilities). The phone company can establish a permanent virtual circuit (PVC) between your site and your ISP. You get a guaranteed data transfer rate, called *Committed Information Rate (CIR)*, but when extra network capacity is available, data transfer can burst to higher rates. For example, you can buy a Frame Relay circuit with a CIR of 32 Kbps that can burst up to 56 Kbps.

For Frame Relay service, you need a Subscriber Network Access Line (SNAL) from your site to the central office where the Frame Relay switch resides. This access line can be a 56 Kbps line or a 1.544 Mbps T1 line. For example, you may connect with a 56 Kbps access line whereas your ISP may have a T1 access line. Then, several subscribers with 56 Kbps PVCs could come into the ISP's facility on a single T1 line (the single line can handle up to 24 56 Kbps PVCs). When this approach is used, the ISP can handle many Frame Relay customers with a single T1 line and a single CSU/DSU.

With a 56 Kbps access line, you can opt for one of several CIRs (you pay according to the CIR you want); typically customers get 32 Kbps or 56 Kbps CIRs with burst rates to 56 Kbps. A T1 Frame Relay access line provides more options for the CIR. For instance, a typical offering may give you the following options:

✦ 128 Kbps CIR with bursts up to 256 Kbps

✦ 256 Kbps CIR with bursts up to 512 Kbps

✦ 512 Kbps CIR with bursts up to 1.024 Mbps

✦ 768 Kbps CIR with bursts up to 1.544 Mbps

The cost of Frame Relay service depends on the bandwidth of the access line to the Frame Relay switch and the CIR. You need a CSU/DSU and a router for your site. Because Frame Relay is connection-oriented, each end of the connection needs an identifier (much like a telephone number). In Frame Relay terminology, the identifier is called a Data Link Connection Identifier (DLCI). Some Frame Relay providers charge a nominal fee for each DLCI (on a T1 access line, you may have as many as 24 DLCIs, one for each 56 Kbps Frame Relay circuit).

You also must pay a setup fee and a monthly fee to both the Frame Relay service provider (telephone company) and your ISP. Listed here are the typical costs for a 56 Kbps Frame Relay connection as of the spring of 1996 (shown in U.S. dollars):

Description	One-Time Cost	Monthly Cost
Phone company setup fees	$800–$1,000	—
CSU/DSU for 56 Kbps and router	$1,250–$1,500	—
ISP setup fee	$500–$1,000	—
Phone company monthly charges	—	$250–$450
ISP monthly charges	—	$250–$450

Of course, the charges vary from one Frame Relay provider to another. Also, the ISP's charges may differ greatly from one ISP to another. Therefore, you should shop around carefully before selecting a service.

The costs for a T1 Frame Relay are higher because you need a T1 access line between your site and the Frame Relay switch. Typically, the access line costs around $1,000 (U.S.) to setup. The T1 CSU/DSU and router costs roughly $3,000 (U.S.). The ISP charges around $1,000 (U.S.) to set up a T1 connection. The phone company may charge a monthly fee of anywhere from $500 (U.S.) to $750 (U.S.) while the ISP's monthly charges are nearly $1,000 (U.S.). As you can see, it can be quite expensive to have a T1 Frame Relay service.

Typically, the costs of a 56 Kbps Frame Relay should be less than that of a 56 Kbps leased line, but you have to remember that with Frame Relay you are using a shared digital network (as opposed to a dedicated connection with a leased line). When you use a shared digital network at times of heavy traffic, you may not get the full bandwidth of the connection.

URL   Frame Relay service is available from most local telephone companies (the Regional Bell Operating Companies or RBOCs such as Pacific Bell and Bell Atlantic) as well as AT&T, BT North America, MCI, Network Services, US Sprint, and Wiltel. On the Web, you can find more information about Frame Relay service when you visit your local telephone company's Web site (as well as many other ISP sites). Listed here are a few sample sites that include pricing information that you may find helpful:

- ✦ Pacific Bell: `http://www.pacbell.com/Products/FR-RELAY/`

- ✦ Bell Atlantic: `http://www.bell-atl.com/internet/html/access.htm`

- ✦ Direct Network Access (an ISP in the San Francisco Bay Area): `http://www.dnai.com/services/frame.html`

Note   A recent development on the Internet front is the interest among local telephone companies in offering Internet access to individuals and businesses. For example, in the Mid-Atlantic region, Bell Atlantic formed a new business unit, Bell Atlantic Internet Solutions, to provide Internet services to business and residential customers (visit `http://www.bell-atl.com/internet/` for more information). In other words, the telephone companies are becoming the ISPs instead of being the provider of the communication link only. When you get Internet access from the telephone company, you receive a single consolidated bill instead of two bills: one from the communications provider and the other from your ISP.

ISDN

Integrated Services Digital Network (ISDN) has been on the drawing board for quite a while — phone companies have started marketing the service only recently. ISDN can provide T1 speeds (1.544 Mbps) over a T1 line, but the most exciting feature of ISDN is its ability to provide up to 128 Kbps bandwidth over an existing phone line.

Phone companies offer ISDN service in the following two forms:

✦ **Basic Rate Interface (BRI):** Provides two 64 Kbps bearer channels (B channels) that carry your data and a 16 Kbps data channel (D channel) that carries control information. Works over a single twisted-pair connection. The shorthand for BRI ISDN is 2B+D (2 bearer channels and 1 data channel).

✦ **Primary Rate Interface (PRI):** Provides 24 channels, each 64 Kbps in capacity. Requires a specially conditioned T1 line. Of the 24 channels, 23 are used as bearer channels and 1 serves as the data channel that controls the bearer channels. Thus, the PRI service is called 23B+D in telephone jargon.

If you are contemplating a T1 connection for your Web site, you may want to consider the PRI ISDN option, which may be less expensive. PRI ISDN is also more flexible than T1 because you can use the channels for different tasks at different times. You also can use several channels at the same time (using a technique called *bonding*) to provide a higher aggregate bandwidth. You can use bonding with the two B channels of BRI ISDN as well, and get an effective bandwidth of 128 Kbps from BRI ISDN.

To use a BRI ISDN connection for your Web site (which, I assume has a Ethernet LAN), you need a device called the Network Terminator (NT-1) and an ISDN router. However, presently the ISDN routers that are on the market include built-in NT-1. Listed here are two popular ISDN routers with a built-in NT-1:

✦ Livingston's PortMaster ISDN Office Router is available for $1,195 (U.S.). For more information, visit the URL http://www.livingston.com/Marketing/Products/isdnor.html.

✦ Ascend Pipeline 50 ISDN router is available for a street price of $1,695.00 (U.S.) For pricing information and a data sheet, visit the URL http://www.dfw.net/dfwnet/store/hardware/isdn/p50.html.

Today, a typical ISDN router includes the following:

✦ One Ethernet port (15-pin AUI connector and 10BASE-T) to connect to your local Ethernet network

✦ One ISDN BRI port to connect to the ISDN phone line

✦ One 115.2 Kbps serial port (Typically, you connect a terminal or PC to this port to control and set up the ISDN router.)

✦ An integrated NT-1 device (inside the BRI port) that supports two 64 Kbps B channels for data transmission and one 16 Kbps D channel for ISDN signaling

✦ Software necessary to configure and set up the router

Basically, you connect the ISDN BRI line (the phone line that has ISDN) to the router's ISDN port. Then, you connect the router's Ethernet port to your LAN's Ethernet hub. If you have a single computer, you can build an Ethernet network between the router and your computer (you'll need an Ethernet card on the computer).

The ISDN switch needs a unique identification number for each ISDN port to which it sends calls and signals. This ID is called a Service Profile Identifier or SPID. You get a SPID from the phone company when you order ISDN service. You have to enter the SPID into the ISDN router when you set up the router.

The exact pricing structure of ISDN service depends on your local telephone company. Today, most telephone companies aggressively market ISDN. Most phone companies charge a one-time installation fee (as well as a monthly fee) for BRI ISDN service. Additionally, you typically pay a usage fee, charged by the minute (the rate depends on peak hours and off-peak hours, much like long-distance phone calls). Listed here is a typical rate schedule from Bell Atlantic as of the spring of 1996 (for residential ISDN users in Maryland):

Description	Cost
Installation fee	$125-$175
Monthly fee	$35 (approximately)
Usage fee	$0.02 per minute for each B channel during business hours (Monday–Friday, 7:00 a.m.–7:00 p.m.) and $0.01 per minute for each B channel during evenings and weekends

URL For Bell Atlantic's latest pricing information, visit `http://www.bell-atl.com/isdn/consumer/` for residential ISDN and `http://www.bell-atl.com/isdn/sbs/` for small business ISDN.

The lack of a flat usage fee makes it difficult to use ISDN for a Web site. For example, with the sample pricing schedule, the price for a week's usage fee for continuous use is as follows (in U.S. dollars):

Type of Day	Cost
2 weekend days (48 hours at $0.60 per hour)	$28.80
5 weekdays (each day 12 hours at $1.20/hour and 12 hours at $0.60/hour)	$108.00
Total for one week's use of 1 B channel (64 Kbps)	$136.80

You have approximately 4.33 weeks in a month. Therefore, the total phone company charges (in U.S. dollars) for using a single B channel (64 Kbps) is $4.33 \times 136.80 + 35 =$ $628 (approximately). Of course this amount nearly doubles if you use two B channels. I have not even mentioned the charges that your ISP levies on an ISDN connection — those charges are above and beyond what the phone company charges you.

Without a flat usage fee, the ISDN rate structure is not yet conducive to the continuous use of an ISDN line for a Web site. You may be better off arranging a 56 Kbps Frame Relay circuit (which does not require any per-minute usage fee) rather than a single B channel ISDN.

Some telephone companies (such as Pacific Bell) offer what is called *Centrex ISDN* — a service that allows you to use a permanent ISDN connection within a limited area and pay no per-minute usage fee. If you and your ISP are within such an area, you can use this option to get an Internet connection for your Web site. For example, Direct Network Access, Inc., an ISP in the San Francisco Bay Area, provides Centrex ISDN connections with the following rate schedule as of the spring of 1996 (shown in U.S. dollars):

Description	ISDN 1B (64 Kbps)	ISDN 2B (112K/128 Kbps)
ISDN hardware (router)	$2,400	$2,400
Phone company setup fee	$200	$200
Phone company monthly fee	$60	$60
ISP setup fee	$800	$800
ISP monthly fee	$275	$325

Prices may change; you should check `http://www.dnai.com/services/centrex.html` for the latest pricing information.

If you are lucky enough to be near an ISP and a phone company that offers a flat-rate Centrex ISDN service, you may want to opt for the ISDN solution for your Web site because the monthly fees will then be reasonable for the bandwidth you get from ISDN.

For typical ISDN pricing and ordering details, visit one of these Web pages:

✦ Ameritech: `http://www.ameritech.com/products/data/`

✦ Bell Atlantic: `http://www.bell-atl.com/isdn/sbs/`

✦ Pacific Bell: `http://www.pacbell.com/Products/SDS-ISDN/`

✦ NYNEX: `http://www.nynex.com/iibxxpge.html`

✦ US West: `http://www.uswest.com/ISDN.HTM`

✦ BellSouth: `http://www.smlbiz.bellsouth.com/bssbi.html`

✦ GTE: `http://www.gte.com/Cando/Business/Docs/Wired/isdn.html`

✦ Direct Network Access (an ISP in the San Francisco Bay area):
`http://www.dnai.com/services/centrex.html`

Another good source of ISDN information on the Web is Dan Kegel's ISDN page at `http://alumni.caltech.edu/~dank/isdn/`.

T1

Most phone companies (and other data communications companies) offer a type of leased line called a T1 line that can sustain data transfer rates of up to 1.544 Mbps. The data transmission service over T1 lines is called *DS1*.

Many ISPs use a T1 line as their physical connection to the Internet. As a result, the data traffic from all of that ISP's customers travels to the Internet over that single T1 link. The point is that a T1 link is definitely adequate for a Web site. In fact, a T1 link can easily serve as the Internet connection for a small to medium business.

Many larger ISPs offer T1 connection to Internet. In such a scenario, you pay the phone company for the T1 link to the ISP, then you pay monthly charges to both the phone company and the ISP. You also have to buy or lease a CSU/DSU and a router for the Internet connection.

If you get T1 Internet access through an ISP, check and make sure that the ISP has adequate bandwidth to the Internet. For example, some ISPs may have only one T1 line to the Internet, but they may have several customers with T1 service — all sharing the single T1 to the Internet.

For a T1 Internet connection, get the service from your local telephone company or a major long distance carrier; the ISPs (who offer T1 connection) typically buy the connection from the long distance carrier and resell the bandwidth to several customers. (The full T1 bandwidth may not be available to you even if you pay for a T1 connection.) Most local and long-distance carriers offer T1 service. For example, you can get T1 service from Pacific Bell, Bell Atlantic, Ameritech, AT&T, MCI, and Sprint, to name a few. These companies even sell the T1 connectivity as an Internet access (the connection is properly routed through one of the NAPs to the Internet backbone).

The costs for a T1 leased line depend on the distance between the locations that the T1 line connects. A typical T1 Internet connection costs $2,000 (U.S.) to set up, and you pay a monthly fee of $1,500 (U.S.). At this range of prices, packages from carriers such as Sprint and Ameritech include the following:

✦ Rental fee for equipment (CSU/DSU and router with software)

✦ Dedicated access line

✦ Maintenance of router

✦ Access to Internet and IP address registration with NIC

Many large corporations opt for such standard package Internet access at T1 speed.

An alternative to leased line T1 service is Frame Relay T1, which provides a more flexible option than a leased T1 line. See the "Frame Relay" section for a discussion of Frame Relay T1 service.

T3

T3 is a high-end data transmission service that provides almost 30 times the bandwidth of a T1 line. T3 lines carry DS3 format signals at 44.746 Mbps. Most literature rounds off the 44.736 Mbps and lists a T3 line's capacity as 45 Mbps.

T3 lines serve as Internet backbones. Gradually, however, many backbones are moving to ATM — Asynchronous Transfer Mode. ATM is a packet switching technology that transfers fixed-size (53 bytes — 48 bytes of data and 5 bytes of routing information) packets over Synchronous Optical Network (SONET) lines. Currently, ATM works over OC-3 (155.52 Mbps) lines, but ATM can scale up to OC-12 lines that support data transfer rates of 622.08 Mbps.

Of course, a T3 line is more than adequate for a Web site. Many large corporations, government laboratories, and universities have T3 connections to the Internet. Such connections usually go to one of the NAPs. You can get a T3 connection from one of the organizations (such as Sprint, MFS Datanet, Pacific Bell, and Ameritech) that manage NAPs. Some high-end ISPs also sell T3 connections to the Internet.

URL To get T3 service, you typically pay an installation fee of $3,000 (U.S.) to $5,000 (U.S.) and a monthly service charge of $5,000 (U.S.) to $10,000 (U.S.). For a typical pricing information, consult Pacific Bell's URL `http://www.pacbell.com/Products/NAP/nap2-3.html` where you'll find the price schedule for connecting to the Pacific Bell NAP in the San Francisco Bay area.

SMDS: Another choice for high-speed Internet access

Between the 1.544 Mbps T1 and the 45 Mbps T3, you have another choice for high-speed Internet access: the Switched Multimegabit Data Service (SMDS). SMDS is another packet delivery service. Like Frame Relay, SMDS is "distance insensitive," available at a flat monthly rate. While Frame Relay service is limited to T1 speed, SMDS service can go up to 34 Mbps. Typical SMDS speeds start at 56 Kbps (as does Frame Relay) but are available at many more incremental speeds such as 1.17, 4, 10, 16, 25, and 34 Mbps.

You may find SMDS the most flexible and cost-effective solution for high-speed Internet connectivity. For example, Bell Atlantic Internet Solutions offers a 1.17 Mbps SMDS connection at a monthly rate of $800 (U.S.) with a one-time charge of $500 (U.S.). However, you still need to buy or lease the router and CSU/DSU. The connection prices are lower if you sign a 1- or 2-year contract.

ISP choices

Whether you plan to run a Web server on your own computer with direct Internet connection or use the services of an ISP to host the Web server, you must first select an ISP. Until recently, the ISP business used the following model:

✦ The ISP purchased high-speed access to the Internet backbone from one of the major regional Internet providers.

✦ The ISP sold various types of Internet services to customers. These services range anywhere from dial-up PPP accounts to Web hosting services. In particular, the ISP took care of chores such as domain name registration, e-mail setup, and DNS.

The distinction between the network access provider (the people who moved the bits) and the ISP (the people who provided specific Internet service) is getting blurred. Many network access providers (such as major telecommunications companies and local telephone companies) are beginning to offer Internet service also. Because of the new players on the market, the ISP business is currently in a state of flux.

URL When it comes to selecting an ISP, your best source of information is the Web itself. Mecklermedia maintains a comprehensive list of all major ISPs at the following URL:

```
http://thelist.iworld.com/
```

As of April 1996, this list included 1,966 ISPs worldwide and the list continues to grow. From this Web page, you can look for ISPs by country and, for United States and Canada, by area code. The page even has a graphic map for U.S. and Canada from which you can select your region and view a list of ISPs who provide service in your region. Best of all, the list of providers shows the services each ISP offers and includes pricing information. I found this list very helpful in comparing ISPs and narrowing down the search for an ISP.

URL Another place to look for ISPs is Yahoo. Point your Web browser to `http://www.yahoo.com/` and type `Internet Service Provider` as the search text. Yahoo reports back a list of matching descriptive categories of items about ISPs. From this category list, you can click on an appropriate category to browse lists of ISPs. The services range from basic Internet access to full Web presence provider.

URL If you want to go directly to Yahoo's ISP category, try the following URL:

```
http://www.yahoo.com/Business_and_Economy/Companies/Internet_Services/
          Internet_Access_Providers/
```

URL The United States has quite a few national level ISPs. These national ISPs provide a wide variety of Internet connectivity and services to most parts of the country. Table 6-1 lists some of the major national ISPs and their Web addresses.

Table 6-1
Major National Internet Service Providers

Company	URL
ANS CO+RE Systems Inc.	`http://www.ans.net`
AT&T WorldNet	`http://www.att.com/worldnet`
BBN Planet	`http://www.bbn.com`
CERFNET, Inc.	`http://www.cerf.net`
IBM Internet Connection	`http://www.ibm.com/globalnetwork`
MCI Telecommunications, Inc.	`http://www.internetmci.com`
Netcom Online Communications Services, Inc.	`http://www.netcom.com`
PSINet, Inc.	`http://www.psi.net`
Sprint	`http://www.sprintbiz.com`
UUNet Technologies, Inc.	`http://www.uu.net`

Computer System Options

In addition to a physical connection (with adequate bandwidth) to the Net, you'll need a computer system to run the Web server. Try a UNIX system; you can find a plethora of Web-site administration tools for UNIX. (Keep in mind, though, you have many other incentives to choose UNIX, such as availability of many other tools, documentation, and helpful advice from experts who participate in newsgroups on the Net. You still have to decide, though, exactly what type of computer to buy and which version of UNIX to use on that computer. You have the following options for the computer system:

✦ A RISC (Reduced Instruction Set Computer) UNIX workstation such as those from Sun Microsystems, HP, IBM, DEC, and Silicon Graphics.

✦ An Intel Pentium PC running one of the freely available (or nearly free) UNIX clones such as Linux, BSDI, or FreeBSD. You can also choose one of the commercial UNIX (such as SCO UNIX or Sun Solaris x86) for Intel x86 processors.

As you may have already guessed, the total cost of a Pentium PC running freeware UNIX is much less than an equally capable commercial UNIX workstation (a well-equipped Pentium PC costs less than $5,000 whereas a low-end RISC UNIX workstation still costs over $10,000). I recommend that you seriously consider a PC running something like Slackware Linux Version 3.0 as the computer for your Web site.

Make sure that the PC has adequate memory — at least 16MB, preferably 32MB. Also, get as large a disk as you can — you need the room to hold files that you may download from the Net and files that you offer to your users through anonymous FTP or Gopher. Today, you can get a 4GB SCSI hard disk drive for a little over $1,000 (U.S.).

Web Server Options

If you opt to place your Web pages on an ISP's Web site, you do not have to worry about selecting a Web server; the ISP makes that choice for you. However, if you decide to run the Web site on your own computer, you have to choose the Web server software. The next few sections provide an overview of the Web server choices for UNIX systems, together with a discussion of server features that you may consider when making your selection.

Webmaster Note that a Web server is also known as an HTTP server because HTTP is the underlying protocol of the Web. The term HTTPD (pronounced *HTTP-dee*) is also used for a Web server. That name comes from the UNIX practice of calling persistent programs daemons and naming them with a *d* as the suffix. Thus, the FTP server is called `ftpd` and the Gopher server program is called `gopherd`. Similarly, the HTTP server program is named `httpd` (I write it in uppercase — as HTTPD — when referring to the HTTP server in the text).

The following sections refer to several UNIX Web servers by name. Table 3-2 of Chapter 3 lists the commonly available UNIX Web servers. Note, however, that the commercial Web server market is in a state of flux. If you opt for a commercial Web server, you may find more choices than the ones listed in Table 3-2 of Chapter 3. Among the free Web servers, the following two are the most popular:

✦ According to surveys, until April 1996, the NCSA HTTP server was the most popular Web server; it is the easiest free server to install and configure. The NCSA server is reputed to be less demanding of system resources, such as memory and processor time. The NCSA HTTP server is still very popular. If you know how to set up and configure it, you can also easily set up the Apache server, because Apache evolved from NCSA HTTP server.

✦ The Apache HTTP server began life as the NCSA HTTP server with various bug fixes and improvements. Recently, the Apache server has garnered a huge following. As of April 1996, the Apache server has surpassed the NCSA HTTP server in number of installed sites. The Apache server has gained the reputation of being robust and efficient. The ApacheSSL variant of the Apache server supports secure transactions through Secure Socket Layer (SSL).

Another free Web server that's worth mentioning is the CERN server, known as the W3C HTTP server (because the World Wide Web Consortium has taken over the CERN server). The CERN server is the original Web server. The server was developed at CERN, the European laboratory for particle physics, where the concepts of the Web and HTTP were invented. Although the CERN server is complex to set up, it is very flexible. A selling point of the CERN server is its ability to act as an HTTP proxy (systems inside an Internet firewall — an access-controlled gateway — can use a CERN server as an intermediary for access to Web servers anywhere on the Net).

Web server survey

If you want to pick a Web server based on popularity, you can do so based on information widely available on the Web. A number of Web sites conduct surveys to count the numbers of specific Web servers in use. Some of the surveys even provide information on the operating system used by various Web sites. You can browse through these survey results and select a popular server.

URL The majority of Web sites run UNIX, and most sites run one of the freely available UNIX Web servers (NCSA and Apache). To locate the latest Web server surveys, point your Web browser to the following URL at Yahoo:

```
http://www.yahoo.com/Computers_and_Internet/Internet/World_Wide_Web/HTTP/
        Servers/Surveys/
```

In the April 1996 list of Web server surveys, the Netcraft Web Server Survey at `http://www.netcraft.co.uk/Survey/` had the most up-to-date survey results.

Netcraft is an automated Web server survey. All Web servers respond to the HEAD command by returning information about the server's name and version number. Try this out with a TELNET session. For example, listed here is how you can check out the version number of the site `www.lnbsoft.com` (user input is in boldface; comments are in italics):

```
telnet www.lnbsoft.com 80
Trying 206.161.69.39...
Connected to www.lnbsoft.com.
Escape character is '^]'.
HEAD / HTTP/1.0
...(Press Enter again to enter a blank line)
HTTP/1.0 200 OK
Date: Mon, 29 Jul 1996 01:22:43 GMT
Server: Apache/1.0.0
Content-type: text/html
Content-length: 4320
Last-modified: Wed, 24 Jul 1996 02:03:06 GMT

Connection closed by foreign host.
```

As the output shows, the server reports its name and version on the Server line. In this case, the server is Apache Version 1.0.0.

Essentially, an automated Web server survey program sends the HEAD command to as many Web sites as possible and collates the responses as reports that show the relative popularity of various Web servers.

The April 1996 results of the Netcraft survey includes 150,295 Web sites (the March survey showed 135,396 sites — that's an increase of 15,000 sites in a month) and shows the following:

✦ The Apache 1.0 server is the most popular Web server with a 29 percent share of all Web sites. Until April 1996, NCSA HTTPD was more popular than Apache.

✦ NCSA HTTPD is close behind Apache; 26 percent of the sites use the NCSA HTTPD server.

✦ The other free UNIX Web server, CERN (now called W3C HTTPD), is used at 8 percent of the sites.

✦ Taken together, the three Web servers — NCSA HTTPD, Apache, and CERN — are in use at 63 percent of all Web sites.

✦ Among the commercial Web servers, Netscape Commerce Server has an 8 percent share and Netscape Communications Server has a 7 percent market share. Netscape's total market share, then, is 15 percent. Recently, Netscape has announced new servers (FastTrack and SuiteSpot); the April 1996 survey has just started to show some sites that use these new Netscape servers.

The Netcraft Web Server Survey provides reports by different domains (such as .COM and .GOV) as well. In the April 1996 survey, of the 96,735 sites in the .COM domain, 33 percent use Apache, 22 percent use NCSA HTTP, and 5 percent use CERN. A total of about 60 percent of sites use one of these 3 servers. In the .COM domain, Netscape's Communications and Commerce servers together have a respectable 17 percent market share.

Web server features

Along with considering the relative popularity of Web servers, you may also want to know the key features of various servers. That way, you can compare the Web servers based on features. As expected, you can find such a feature's comparison on the Web; visit the following URL for a chart that compares all popular Web servers (including those that run on various types of UNIX, Windows NT, and Macintosh operating systems):

```
http://www.webcompare.com/server-main.html
```

You can read that chart at your leisure; here I provide an overview of the desired features from the perspective of a UNIX Webmaster.

Because HTTP is the protocol used to distribute HTML documents, all Web servers support HTTP, which is why the Web servers are often called HTTP servers. Web server, however, is a better name because typically a Web server does much more than simply respond to HTTP requests. Besides the core HTTP support, listed here are some important Web server features:

✦ **Support many versions of UNIX:** You can use a specific Web server only if it runs on your version of UNIX (such as Linux, BSDI, FreeBSD, SunOS, Solaris, HP-UX, AIX, SCO UNIX, and Digital UNIX). The freeware NCSA HTTPD, Apache, and CERN servers run on nearly all versions of UNIX. The commercial offerings, such as the ones from Netscape Communications Corporation, run on most major versions of UNIX (such as SunOS, Solaris, and HP-UX).

✦ **Write multiple log files:** Log files allow you to monitor how many users are accessing your Web site and the types of document that are most popular with users. Most Web servers (including NCSA HTTPD, Apache, and CERN) can write several types of log files.

✦ **Allow different document directories for different IP addresses:** This feature allows a single Web server to service a number of IP addresses, each with a different domain name. This feature is important if you want to go into business as an ISP. With this feature, you can use a single Web server to set up several virtual Web sites with unique domain names (such as www.abc.com and www.xyz.com). Both the NCSA HTTPD and Apache servers support this feature.

✦ **Select documents based on the Accept header:** The Accept header in the client's request specifies the document types that the client can accept (the client is the Web browser). Both Apache and NCSA HTTPD can select documents based on the Accept header, but the CERN server does not.

✦ **Has built-in capability to handle image maps:** An image map is a single image with several hypertext links, each link associated with a part of the image. Most Web servers (including NCSA HTTPD and Apache) support image maps.

✦ **Act as HTTP proxy:** You need a proxy — an intermediary server — to let users on a protected network access Web sites in outside networks. (A protected network connects to the Internet through a firewall — a controlled access gateway.) The CERN server can act as an HTTP proxy server, and this is one of the selling points of the CERN server.

✦ **Allow server-side includes:** Server-side include refers to the ability of the server to include the contents of a file or a script into the HTML document returned to the client. Usually, a comment in the HTML file specifies the file to include. Server-side includes first appeared in the NCSA HTTPD server; the Apache server also supports this feature.

✦ **Deny access by IP address:** As a security measure, many servers allow you to prohibit specific IP addresses from accessing your Web site. Both NCSA HTTPD and Apache servers can prohibit access based on IP address.

✦ **Deny access by domain name:** Similar to denying access to specific IP addresses, many servers (including NCSA HTTPD and Apache) can deny access to specific domain names. With this feature, you can allow one or more selected domains.

✦ **Support password-based authentication:** Many servers, including NCSA HTTPD and Apache, allow you to enable password-based authentication where a user must enter a user name and a password before the server sends the requested document.

✦ **Control file access on a per directory basis:** This feature implies that the server lets you enforce password-based access for all files in a specific directory (whereas another directory may be accessible by anyone).

✦ **Support Secure Socket Layer (SSL):** If you plan to conduct monetary transactions that require users to provide credit card account numbers, make sure that the credit card information is secure. SSL is one of the protocols for transferring information in a secure manner through encryption. For such encrypted data transfers to work, both the Web server and the Web browser must support the secure protocol. SSL is supported by Netscape, currently the most popular Web browser. That's why SSL support is a good feature. Of the free Web servers, a variant of Apache, called ApacheSSL, supports SSL (for more information, visit the URL `http://apachessl.c2.org/`). ApacheSSL is free for noncommercial use, but you need a digital ID, which is available for a fee from VeriSign, Inc. (details at URL `http://www.verisign.com/apachessl-us/`).

✦ **Provide full source code:** You don't really need source code to use a Web server, but when you rely on a freeware Web server, it is nice to know that you have all the source code (in case you need to rebuild the server). You can get the full source code for NCSA HTTPD, Apache, and CERN servers. As expected, commercial Web servers do not include the source code. The commercial servers, however, come with technical support from the vendor.

Summary

Unless you join as a Webmaster at an established Web site, one of your first tasks is deciding how to set up the Web site. You have a wide array of options, ranging from renting space on an ISP's system to setting up the Web site on your own computer with a dedicated connection to the Internet. This chapter explores options for aspects of the Web site, from the physical Internet connection to the Web server software. The next chapter takes you through the steps of installing a Web server.

Where to go next . . .

✦ If you decide to install the NCSA Web server, go to Chapter 7.

✦ To learn how to install the Apache or CERN Web servers, go to Chapter 8.

✦ If you are joining as a Webmaster at an existing site and you want to get into authoring HTML documents, proceed to Chapter 10.

✦   ✦   ✦

Setting Up the NCSA HTTP Server

Chapter 6 presents you with many options for a Web site. Depending on the option you choose, you may or may not have to set up a Web server. For example, if you decide to place your Web pages on an ISP-maintained Web server, you can ignore the Web server setup chores and start preparing the Web pages. In that case, you do not need to read Chapters 7–9.

If you want to set up a Web site on your computer, you must install and configure the Web server. This chapter shows you how to download and install the popular NCSA HTTP server. I start with the NCSA server because it's a popular Web server. Also, the most popular Web server, Apache, is derived from the NCSA HTTPD and, therefore, has similar configuration steps.

The next chapter shows you how to set up the other popular UNIX Web servers: Apache and CERN (now called W3C HTTPD). Although the CERN server is not widely used, it can act as an HTTP proxy that acts as an intermediary between Web clients inside a protected network and Web servers outside the network. (Such protected networks access the outside world through a gateway called a firewall; Chapter 9 describes firewalls.)

Installing the NCSA HTTP Server

You already know how it feels to use the Web. Now you can learn to set up a Web server so that you, too, can provide information to the world through Web pages. To become an information provider on the Web, you have to run a Web server on your UNIX system (and that system must have a physical network connection to the Internet). You also have to prepare the Web pages — a task that may turn out to be more demanding than the server setup, as you'll see in Chapters 10–17. The first step, however, is to install the Web server.

Note Web servers provide information by using HTTP, which is why they are also called HTTP daemons — continuously running server processes are called *daemons* in UNIX (or HTTPD, for short). The Web server program is usually named `httpd` and pronounced *HTTP-dee*.

URL NCSA HTTPD happens to be one of the popular freely available Web servers for UNIX systems. You can download NCSA HTTPD using anonymous FTP from `ftp.ncsa.uiuc.edu`. If you have a Web browser running, you can download the software directly from NCSA's Web page at `http://hoohoo.ncsa.uiuc.edu/`. Incidentally, you can also read the latest NCSA HTTPD documentation at `http://hoohoo.ncsa.uiuc.edu/`.

The following section describes how to download and set up the NCSA HTTPD software for a Linux system. The same steps apply to any other UNIX system.

Download the NCSA HTTPD software

Webmaster The NCSA HTTPD software is available from the FTP site `ftp.ncsa.uiuc.edu`. To download NCSA HTTPD, follow these steps:

1. Make sure that your Linux system is connected to the Internet.

2. Type the following commands, shown in boldface (my comments are in italics):

```
ftp ftp.ncsa.uiuc.edu
Connected to ftp.ncsa.uiuc.edu.
220 larry FTP server (Version wu-2.4(25) Thu Aug 25 13:14:21 CDT 1994) ready.
Name (ftp.ncsa.uiuc.edu:naba): anonymous
331 Guest login ok, send your complete e-mail address as password.
Password:   (Type your e-mail address and then press Enter)

...(Lines deleted)
```

3. At the `ftp>` prompt, type the following command, shown in boldface:

```
ftp> cd Web/httpd/Unix/ncsa_httpd
250-This directory contains NCSA's public domain HTTP server. The current
250-release is 1.5.  Comments to httpd@ncsa.uiuc.edu.
250-
250-All documentation is online in the World Wide Web under URL
250-http://hoohoo.ncsa.uiuc.edu/
250-
250-
250 CWD command successful.
```

4. Type the ls command to view the contents of this directory, as follows:

```
ftp> ls
200 PORT command successful.
150 Opening ASCII mode data connection for /bin/ls.
total 42
drwxr-xr-x   8 12873     wheel        2048 Nov 10 12:48 .
drwxr-xr-x   4 12873     wheel        2048 May 29  1995 ..
-rw-r--r--   1 12873     wheel          66 Jul  7  1994 .accountrc
-rw-r--r--   1 12873     other         344 Aug 22  1994 .index
-rw-r--r--   1 12873     wheel         212 Nov 10 18:46 .message
drwxr-xr-x   3 12873     wheel        2048 Jul  6  1995 cgi
drwxr-xr-x   2 12873     wheel        2048 May  2  1995 contrib
lrwxr-xr-x   1 19056     wheel           9 Nov 10 12:48 current -> httpd_1.5
drwxr-xr-x   3 19019     202         2048 Dec 22 01:46 documents
-rw-r--r--   1 12873     wheel          61 Jul  7  1994 gsql.note
drwxr-xr-x   2 19056     wsstaff     2048 Jun 22  1995 httpd_1.4
drwxr-xr-x   2 19056     wsstaff     2048 Mar 21 13:34 httpd_1.5
drwxr-x---  10 12873     wheel        2048 May  3  1995 old
226 Transfer complete.
```

5. Change the directory to the current version, as follows:

```
ftp> cd current
250-Please read the file README
250-  it was last modified on Thu Mar 21 13:36:45 1996 - 10 days ago
250 CWD command successful.
```

6. Get a listing of that directory with the ls command, as follows:

```
ftp> ls
200 PORT command successful.
150 Opening ASCII mode data connection for /bin/ls.
total 18282
drwxr-xr-x   2 19056     wsstaff     2048 Mar 21 13:34 .
drwxr-xr-x   8 12873     wheel        2048 Nov 10 12:48 ..
-rw-rw-r--   1 19056     wsstaff     3342 Mar 21 13:36 README
-rwxr-xr-x   1 19056     wsstaff   167941 Mar 21 13:32 httpd_1.5c-
    export_aix3.2.5.Z
-rw-r--r--   1 19056     wsstaff   610389 Mar 21 13:32 httpd_1.5c-
    export_aix3.2.5.tar.Z
-rwxr-xr-x   1 19056     wsstaff   138099 Mar 21 13:32 httpd_1.5c-
    export_hpux9.0.5.Z
-rw-r--r--   1 19056     wsstaff   541007 Mar 21 13:33 httpd_1.5c-
    export_hpux9.0.5.tar.Z
-rwxr-xr-x   1 19056     wsstaff   263747 Mar 21 13:33 httpd_1.5c-
    export_irix4.0.5.Z
-rw-r--r--   1 19056     wsstaff   975225 Mar 21 13:33 httpd_1.5c-
    export_irix4.0.5.tar.Z
-rwxr-xr-x   1 19056     wsstaff   172823 Mar 21 13:33 httpd_1.5c-
    export_irix5.3.Z
```

(continued)

```
-rw-r--r--   1 19056    wsstaff    583067 Mar 21 13:33 httpd_1.5c-
      export_irix5.3.tar.Z
-rwxr-xr-x   1 19056    wsstaff    107591 Mar 21 13:33 httpd_1.5c-
      export_linux1.2.13_ELF.Z
-rw-r--r--   1 19056    wsstaff    487185 Mar 21 13:33 httpd_1.5c-
      export_linux1.2.13_ELF.tar.Z
-rwxr-xr-x   1 19056    wsstaff    192437 Mar 21 13:33 httpd_1.5c-export_osf3.0.Z
-rw-r--r--   1 19056    wsstaff    641999 Mar 21 13:33 httpd_1.5c-
      export_osf3.0.tar.Z
-rwxr-xr-x   1 19056    wsstaff    117343 Mar 21 13:33 httpd_1.5c-
      export_solaris2.3_sparc.Z
-rw-r--r--   1 19056    wsstaff    517684 Mar 21 13:33 httpd_1.5c-
      export_solaris2.3_sparc.tar.Z
-rwxr-xr-x   1 19056    wsstaff    115851 Mar 21 13:33 httpd_1.5c-
      export_solaris2.4_sparc.Z
-rw-r--r--   1 19056    wsstaff    499363 Mar 21 13:33 httpd_1.5c-
      export_solaris2.4_sparc.tar.Z
-rwxr-xr-x   1 19056    wsstaff    113733 Mar 21 13:34 httpd_1.5c-
      export_solaris2.4_x86.Z
-rw-r--r--   1 19056    wsstaff    501153 Mar 21 13:34 httpd_1.5c-
      export_solaris2.4_x86.tar.Z
-rw-r--r--   1 19056    wsstaff    285386 Mar 21 13:34 httpd_1.5c-
      export_source.tar.Z
-rwxr-xr-x   1 19056    wsstaff    251609 Mar 21 13:34 httpd_1.5c-
      export_sunos4.1.3.Z
-rw-r--r--   1 19056    wsstaff    669272 Mar 21 13:34 httpd_1.5c-
      export_sunos4.1.3.tar.Z
-rwxr-xr-x   1 19056    wsstaff    250755 Mar 21 13:34 httpd_1.5c-
      export_ultrix4.3.Z
-rw-r--r--   1 19056    wsstaff   1018327 Mar 21 13:34 httpd_1.5c-
      export_ultrix4.3.tar.Z
-rw-r--r--   1 19056    wsstaff      1285 Nov 14 11:42 patch-1.5a
-rw-r--r--   1 19056    wsstaff    116035 Mar 21 13:34 patch-1.5c
226 Transfer complete.
```

This listing tells you the UNIX variants for which NCSA HTTPD is available. As this list shows, NCSA HTTPD Version 1.5c is available (in precompiled binary plus source form) for the following UNIX versions:

- HP-UX 9.0.5

- SGI IRIX Versions 4.0.5 and 5.3

- Linux 1.2.13 (binaries are in ELF — Executable Linking Format, but you can recompile to create binaries in the older a.out format)

- DEC OSF 3.0

- Sun Solaris Versions 2.3 and 2.4 for both SPARC and x86

- SunOS 4.1.3

- DEC Ultrix 4.3

7. Notice that two files have `linux` in their names. The smaller file is the NCSA HTTP server binary; the `httpd_1.5c-export_linux1.2.13_ELF.tar.Z` file is larger because it contains the source code and other support files. You should download the `.tar.Z` file so that you can recompile the program (if you are not yet using the ELF version of Linux). Set the file type to binary and download the Linux version of the NCSA HTTPD with the following commands:

```
ftp> binary
200 Type set to I.
ftp> mget *linux*.tar.Z
mget httpd_1.5c-export_linux1.2.13_ELF.tar.Z? y
```

8. After the file transfer is complete (which could take a few minutes over a dial-up SLIP or PPP connection), type **bye** to quit the `ftp` program.

After completing these steps, you have downloaded Version 1.5 of NCSA HTTPD.

Unpack the NCSA HTTPD software

Webmaster The `httpd_1.5c-export_linux1.2.13_ELF.tar.Z` file that you downloaded from NCSA's FTP server has to be uncompressed and unpacked before you can use the HTTPD software. Move this file to a directory where you plan to install the HTTPD software. The default installation directory is `/usr/local/etc/httpd`. Follow these steps to unpack the HTTPD software in its proper directory:

1. If you use the default installation directory for the HTTPD software, copy the downloaded file to the `/usr/local/etc` directory, as follows:

```
mv httpd_1.5c-export_linux1.2.13_ELF.tar.Z /usr/local/etc
```

2. Change the directory to `/usr/local/etc` and uncompress the file, as follows:

```
cd /usr/local/etc
uncompress httpd_1.5c-export_linux1.2.13_ELF.tar.Z
```

3. Use the `tar` command to extract the files from the archive:

```
tar xvf httpd_1.5c-export_linux1.2.13_ELF.tar.Z
httpd_1.5c-export/
httpd_1.5c-export/BUGS
httpd_1.5c-export/CHANGES

...(Lines deleted)

httpd_1.5c-export/support/dbmgroup
httpd_1.5c-export/support/dbmpasswd
httpd_1.5c-export/httpd
```

The output of the `tar` command shows the files that constitute the NCSA HTTPD software distribution. In particular, the COPYRIGHT file tells you the terms under which you can use the NCSA HTTPD software. The COPYRIGHT file specifically states that a commercial organization does not have to pay any license fee to use NCSA HTTPD as the World Wide Web server as long as it does not redistribute NCSA HTTPD.

4. When `tar` unpacks the archive, it creates the `httpd_1.5c-export` (a name that reflects the version of HTTPD) subdirectory in the `/usr/local/etc` directory. Rename that directory `httpd` with the `mv` command, as follows:

```
mv httpd_1.5c-export httpd
```

Now you have the necessary files for NCSA HTTPD in the `/usr/local/etc/httpd` directory. This directory contains the following items:

```
total 198
-rw-r--r--   1 root     root          145 Mar 21 13:35 BUGS
-rw-r--r--   1 root     root        10062 Mar 21 13:35 CHANGES
-rw-r--r--   1 root     root         3251 Mar 21 13:35 COPYRIGHT
-rw-r--r--   1 root     root         4880 Mar 21 13:35 CREDITS
-rw-r--r--   1 root     root         1838 Mar 21 13:35 Makefile
-rw-r--r--   1 root     root         3340 Mar 21 13:35 README
drwxr-xr-x   2 root     root         1024 Mar 21 13:44 cgi-bin/
drwxr-xr-x   2 root     root         1024 Mar 21 13:44 cgi-src/
drwxr-xr-x   2 root     root         1024 Mar 21 13:35 conf/
-rwxr-xr-x   1 root     root       168084 Mar 31 21:18 httpd*
drwxr-xr-x   2 root     root         1024 Mar 21 13:35 icons/
drwxr-xr-x   2 root     root         2048 Mar 31 21:18 src/
drwxr-xr-x   3 root     root         1024 Mar 21 13:45 support/
```

The following is a list of what these files and directories contain:

✦ `BUGS` is a list of known bugs.

✦ `CHANGES` contains a list of changes made in each version of the software.

✦ `COPYRIGHT` contains the copyright notice that applies to NCSA HTTPD 1.5.

✦ `CREDITS` is a list of all the people who have contributed to the development of NCSA HTTPD.

✦ `Makefile` is for use by the `make` utility when you want to rebuild the NCSA HTTPD binaries.

✦ `README` is a summary description of the software distribution.

✦ `cgi-bin` is a directory that contains sample scripts and binaries for Common Gateway Interface (CGI) — the mechanism by which NCSA HTTP server can execute other programs.

✦ `cgi-src` is a directory that contains the source code for the binaries in `cgi-bin`.

✦ `conf` is a directory with sample configuration files. You can copy these samples and edit them to create the required configuration files for NCSA HTTPD.

✦ `httpd` is the NCSA HTTPD binary — the executable program.

✦ icons is a directory that contains some sample icons and images.

✦ src is the directory with the complete source code for NCSA HTTP server.

✦ support is a directory with the source code for many support programs (such as the htpasswd program that can create password files used by NCSA HTTPD).

Compile the NCSA HTTPD software

After you install the NCSA HTTPD files in the /usr/local/etc/httpd directory, you should have everything you need to run the Web server. If, however, your system is not one of the select few for which NCSA provides pre-compiled binaries, you may have to compile the software and create new binaries.

Sometimes you may have to create a new binary even if NCSA includes the binaries for your version of UNIX. For example, recently Linux began supporting the Executable and Linking Format (ELF) — a standard format for binary files used in UNIX System V Release 4. The latest NCSA HTTPD for Linux comes with ELF binaries. However, I have an older Linux 1.2.13 system that does not have the ELF support. On that system, I had to rebuild the NCSA HTTPD binaries in the older a.out format (in Linux the default name of a binary file created by a compiler is a.out).

Compiling and building the NCSA HTTPD binaries is easy when you use the make command. The make utility works when you read and interpret a *makefile* — a text file that has a specified syntax. The makefile (usually named Makefile) describes which files constitute a program and how to compile and link the files. Whenever you change one or more files, make determines which files should be recompiled and issues the appropriate commands to compile those files and rebuild the program.

What is make?

When an application is made up of more than a few source files, compiling and linking the files by manually typing the compiler command (such as cc for the C compiler) is no longer convenient. Besides, you do not want to compile every file whenever you change something in a single source file. This situation requires the help of the make utility.

The make utility works by reading and interpreting a *makefile* — a text file with a specified syntax. The makefile describes which files constitute a program; it also explains how to compile and link the files to build the program. Whenever you change one or more files, make determines which files should be recompiled;

then it issues the appropriate commands for compiling those files and rebuilding the program.

In UNIX systems, it is customary to use Makefile as the name of the makefile because it appears near the beginning of the directory listing where the uppercase names appear before the lowercase ones.

When you download software from the Internet, you will usually find a Makefile with the source files. To build the software, type make at the shell prompt; make takes care of all the steps necessary to build the software.

The NCSA HTTPD software comes with a Makefile that can build the NCSA HTTPD binaries for many UNIX systems. Just type the following command:

```
make type
```

where *type* is a word that identifies your UNIX system. Table 7-1 lists the type words and associated UNIX systems that the Makefile supports.

Table 7-1
UNIX System Types Identified in Makefile for NCSA HTTPD 1.5

Type	UNIX Version
aix3	IBM AIX 3.2.x
aix4	IBM AIX 4.1.x
aux	Apple Unix A/UX
bsdi	BSDI BSD/OS 2.x systems
hp-cc	HP-UX 9.x machines using HP C compiler (cc)
hp-gcc	HP-UX 9.x machines using GNU C compiler (gcc)
linux	Linux systems
netbsd	NetBSD systems
next	NeXTStep 3.x systems
osf1	DEC Alpha-based systems running OSF/1 operating system
sgi4	Silicon Graphics IRIX 4.x
sgi5	Silicon Graphics IRIX 5.x
solaris	Sun Solaris 2.x
sunos	Sun SunOS 4.1.x (also called Solaris 1.x)
svr4	UNIX System V Release 4 systems
ultrix	DEC Mips-based systems (Ultrix)

Thus, to build the NCSA HTTPD binaries for Linux, type the following command from the /usr/local/etc/httpd directory:

```
make linux
```

This command causes make to build the programs in the src, cgi-src, and support subdirectories. The end result of the command is a file named httpd — the NCSA HTTPD binary — in the /usr/local/etc/httpd directory.

If you are unsure about your UNIX system's version, use the uname command with -a option. For example, listed here is the result of that command on a Sun SPARC system:

```
uname -a
SunOS lnbsun 4.1.3_U1 2 sun4c
```

In this case, the operating system is SunOS 4.1.3, the system's name is lnbsun, and the system's hardware is sun4c (which means SPARCstation).

On the other hand, on a Linux 1.2.13 system, the uname command displays the following output:

```
uname -a
Linux lnbp75 1.2.13 #2 Fri Oct 13 23:04:49 EDT 1995 i586
```

In this case, uname displays the Linux Version (1.2.13), as well as the date, when the system was built (Fri Oct 13 23:04:49 EDT 1995).

On a BSDI system, the uname command even shows the name of the user who compiled the operating system. For example, listed here is the output of uname on a BSDI system:

```
uname -a
BSD/OS hq.vni.net 2.0.1 BSDI BSD/OS 2.0.1 Kernel #0: Tue Aug 1 09:29:38 MDT 1995
polk@demiurge.BSDI.COM:/home/polk/sys_2.0.1/sys.src/compile/GENERIC  i386
```

The point is that the output of the uname command varies from one system to another, but in all cases you should be able to tell the name of the operating system and the version number. In the example uname output, you can see that the BSDI system runs BSD/OS 2.0.1.

Getting NCSA HTTPD Up and Running

To fully configure the NCSA HTTPD software takes time. If you simply want to get the Web server up and running (to see that it works), you can do so easily *provided* you install NCSA HTTPD in the /usr/local/etc/httpd directory. If you do, follow these steps to get the NCSA HTTP server up and running:

1. Create three configuration files (httpd.conf, srm.conf, and access.conf) by copying sample files that come with the NCSA HTTPD software.

2. Edit a few key items in the httpd.conf file.

3. Create a directory for the HTML documents to be served by the Web server.

4. Create a directory for various log files.

5. Log in as root and run the httpd program.

The following sections guide you through these steps.

Create initial configuration files

To run NCSA HTTPD, you need three configuration files. These configuration files should be in the `/usr/local/etc/httpd/conf` directory. After you install NCSA HTTPD, you'll find the following files (with the string `conf` in their names) in the `/usr/local/etc/httpd/conf` directory:

```
access.conf-dist
httpd.conf-dist
localhost_srm.conf-dist
srm.conf-dist
```

These files are meant to be sample configuration files. Make copies of the following files to use as the actual configuration files:

```
cp access.conf-dist access.conf
cp httpd.conf-dist httpd.conf
cp srm.conf-dist srm.conf
```

The `localhost_srm.conf-dist` file is meant as a sample for `localhost_srm.conf`, a file that configures the server resources (such as the directory where the HTML documents are located) when NCSA HTTPD is set up to serve Web pages for the local host.

You learn more about these configuration files in the "Configuring NCSA HTTPD" section later in this chapter. For now, just locate the `ServerName` line in the `httpd.conf` file and set it to the name of your Web site. Listed here is an example:

```
ServerName www.lnbsun.com
```

Of course, the name you use must be a name recognized by the domain name server. This name is the name by which Web browsers refer to the server.

Create document and log directories

By default, all Web documents must be in the directory specified by the `DocumentRoot` directive in the resource configuration file (`srm.conf`). The default directory is `/usr/local/etc/httpd/htdocs`.

Webmaster That directory does not exist, so you must create the directory; otherwise, `httpd` won't run. To create the directory, log in as `root` and type the following commands:

```
cd /usr/local/etc/httpd
mkdir htdocs
```

Webmaster When `httpd` encounters errors, it logs them in a file specified by the `ErrorLog` directive in the `httpd.conf` file. The default directory for the error log file is the `logs` subdirectory of the `ServerRootDirectory` — the directory where you installed the NCSA HTTPD software. For the default installation directory (`/usr/local/etc/httpd`), use the following commands to create the error-logs directory:

```
cd /usr/local/etc/httpd
mkdir logs
```

Check out the Web server version

After you prepare the configuration files, but before you start `httpd` — the NCSA HTTPD program — as a daemon, you can run it with the `-v` option and see information about the program's version.

The following listing shows what NCSA HTTPD 1.5 displays when you run it with the `-v` option:

```
httpd -v
NCSA HTTPd NCSA/1.5.0c
Documentation online at http://hoohoo.ncsa.uiuc.edu/

Compiled in Options:
        DBM_SUPPORT
        DIGEST_AUTH
        HTTPD_ROOT = /usr/local/etc/httpd
        DOCUMENT_ROOT = /usr/local/etc/httpd/htdoc

Usage: httpd [-d directory] [-f file] [-v]
-d directory    : specify an alternate initial ServerRoot
-f file         : specify an alternate ServerConfigFile
-v              : version information (this screen)
```

Webmaster You do not have to be `root` to run `httpd` with the `-v` option. Anyone (with access to the system) can run NCSA HTTPD with the `-v` option.

Start the Web server

Webmaster After completing these setup steps, you are ready to run `httpd` — the NCSA Web server program. You can run `httpd` two ways:

✦ *From* `inetd`. In this case, you must specify the `httpd` program in the `/etc/inetd.conf` file. Whenever a client attempts to connect to the HTTP port (80), the `inetd` daemon launches the `httpd` program.

✦ *Stand-alone*. In this case, you run the `httpd` program at system startup; it runs all the time as a daemon.

Webmaster For best performance, run httpd in stand-alone mode; the server is always ready to respond to client requests. When you run NCSA HTTPD 1.5 as a stand-alone program, it creates many child processes that are ready to service HTTP requests from multiple clients. This pre-launching of child processes further improves performance by avoiding the delay associated with creating a new process to handle a new connection from a Web client.

Webmaster To ensure that httpd runs whenever your system reboots, add a few lines to one of the scripts that the init process executes at startup. On a Linux system, the /etc/rc.d/rc.local script is a good place to add these lines because that's where you should place any local initializations. Log in as root, and use your favorite text editor to add the following lines to the /etc/rc.d/rc.local file:

```
# Start the httpd
if [ -x /usr/local/etc/httpd/httpd ]; then
  echo -n " httpd"
  /usr/local/etc/httpd/httpd
else
  echo "No httpd found!"
fi
```

These lines check for the existence of the Web server (httpd); they also start the server — that is, if it exists. Although you added these lines to the script, the script won't run until the system reboots. For now, log in as root and start httpd by hand with the following command:

```
/usr/local/etc/httpd/httpd
```

If you don't see any error messages, the Web server should be running successfully. You can also type the following command to verify that the server has started:

```
ps -aux | grep httpd
```

You should see six httpd processes because NCSA HTTPD starts five child processes by default (you see the five child httpd processes plus the parent httpd process).

Tip If you install NCSA Web server in a directory other than the default (/usr/local/etc/httpd), you must start the server with the -d command-line option that allows you to specify the installation directory. For example, if you install the software in /usr/local/web/httpd, start the httpd program with the following command:

```
/usr/local/web/httpd/httpd -d /usr/local/web/httpd
```

Try the Web server

You need Web pages to use the Web server. After all, the Web server's job is to "serve" Web pages to its clients: the Web browsers. Even though you may not have a Web page yet, you can manually test the server. Follow these steps:

Webmaster

Webmaster

1. From a system on the Internet (or your local network), type `telnet your.system.domain 80`, where *your.system.domain* is your system's fully-qualified domain name. (If you want to test the server without connecting to the Internet, use `localhost` as the system name.)

2. When you see the `Connected ...` message from `telnet`, type the following:

   ```
   HEAD / HTTP/1.0
   ```

   After typing this line, press Enter twice.

These steps should generate a response from the Web server on your system. The following is what I got when I tried this procedure to test a Web server on one of my systems:

```
telnet www.lnbsun.com 80
Trying 206.197.168.2...
Connected to lnbsun.
Escape character is '^]'.
HEAD / HTTP/1.0

HTTP/1.0 200 Document follows
Date: Tue, 02 Apr 1996 02:51:24 GMT
Server: NCSA/1.5
Content-type: text/html
Last-modified: Mon, 01 Apr 1996 02:31:09 GMT
Content-length: 910

Connection closed by foreign host.
```

As the listing shows, the server replies with information about the requested document and closes the connection after sending the reply.

Configuring NCSA HTTPD

The NCSA HTTPD uses the following configuration files with the `.conf` extension:

✦ `httpd.conf` is the basic HTTPD configuration file that controls how the HTTP daemon runs, where its files are, and what TCP/IP port the daemon uses.

✦ `srm.conf` is the server resource map file that tells the Web server (the HTTP daemon) how to serve the Web pages.

✦ `access.conf` is the server access configuration file that controls who can access the Web server.

As the "Getting NCSA HTTPD Up and Running" section (in this chapter) explains, you can get an initial version of the configuration files by renaming sample files that come with the NCSA HTTPD software distribution.

Each of these initial configuration files already contains most of the configuration items set up properly. You only need to fill in information that is specific to your system, such as the Web site's name, to run the Web server. Each configuration file, however, has many more directives and you should know about them.

General configuration through `httpd.conf`

When initially starting the server, you only set the `ServerName` directive. You also need to specify the e-mail address of the Webmaster. You can edit the `httpd.conf` file with your favorite text editor and specify the Webmaster's e-mail address:

1. Find the line `ServerAdmin you@your.address`

2. Change `you@your.address` to the e-mail address of the Webmaster.

Many more directives in the `httpd.conf` file control the way that the Web server works. The following list summarizes the directives that you can use in the `httpd.conf` file. You can leave most of these directives in their default settings, but you need to know about these directives because, as a Webmaster, you are maintaining the Web server.

`ServerType` *type* — Specifies how the HTTP server is executed by Linux. The *type* can be `inetd` (to run the server through the `inetd` daemon) or `standalone` (to run the server as a stand-alone process). Run the server as a stand-alone process for better performance.

`Port` *num* — Specifies that the HTTP daemon should listen to port *num* (a number between 0 and 65,535) for requests from clients. The default port for HTTPD is 80. You should leave the port number at its default value, because clients assume the HHTP port to be 80. If your server does not use port 80, the URL for your server must specify the port number.

`User` *name* [*#id*] — Specifies the user name (or ID) used by the HTTP daemon when running in stand-alone mode. You can leave this directive at the default setting (`nobody`). If you specify a user ID, use a pound-sign (#) prefix for the numeric ID.

Group `name [ #id]` — Specifies the group name (or ID) of the HTTP daemon when running in stand-alone mode.

ServerAdmin `webmaster@company.com` — Provides the server the e-mail address of the person who maintains the Web server. In case of errors, the server provides this address so that users can report errors.

ServerRoot `pathname` — Specifies the directory where you installed `httpd` (the directory where the `httpd` program resides). The default ServerRoot is `/usr/local/etc/httpd`, but you can install HTTPD anywhere you want; just set ServerRoot to that directory. Most other files, including the Web pages, are expected to be in directories relative to the ServerRoot.

ServerName `www.company.com` — Sets the server's host name to `www.company.com` instead of its real host name. You cannot simply invent a name; the name must be a valid name from the Domain Name System (DNS) for your system.

StartServers `num` — Sets the number of child processes that start when NCSA HTTPD runs. (The Linux version of NCSA HTTPD does not support this directive.)

MaxServers `num` — Sets the maximum number of children that `httpd` will launch to handle increased loads. (The Linux version of NCSA HTTPD does not support this directive.)

TimeOut `numsec` — Sets the number of seconds that the server waits for a client to send a query after the client establishes connection. The default TimeOut is 1,200 seconds (20 minutes).

ErrorLog `filename` — Sets the file where `httpd` logs the errors that it encounters. The filename is taken to be relative to ServerRoot. The default ErrorLog is `logs/error_log`. For a ServerRoot of `/usr/local/etc/httpd`, the absolute location of the error log is `/usr/local/etc/httpd/logs/error_log`. Typical ErrorLog entries include events such as server restarts and any warning messages, such as the following:

```
[Sat Apr 13 09:18:28 1996] HTTPd: caught SIGHUP, restarting
[Sat Apr 13 09:18:28 1996] HTTPd: successful restart
```

TransferLog `filename` — Sets the file where `httpd` records all client accesses (including failed accesses). The default TransferLog is `logs/access_log`. The following example shows the log entries when a Web browser accesses a single Web page:

```
lnbsun - - [13/Apr/1996:09:47:41 -0400] "GET / HTTP/1.0" 200 910
lnbsun - - [13/Apr/1996:09:47:41 -0400] "GET /image/lnbimage.gif HTTP/1.0" 200
    3575
lnbsun - - [13/Apr/1996:09:47:42 -0400] "GET /image/constT.gif HTTP/1.0" 200 403
```

The first entry is for the text of the file; the next two entries are for two embedded images. The last two items on each line show the status code returned by the server, followed by the number of bytes sent by the server. Note that a single Web page can create quite a few entries in the `TransferLog` — one for each embedded image. Keep this in mind when you use these logs to determine the number of people who have accessed your Web site.

`AgentLog` *filename* — Sets the file where `httpd` records the name of the client software. The default `AgentLog` file is `logs/agent_log`. Following are some typical entries in the `AgentLog` file, showing records of accesses from Lynx and various versions of Netscape Navigator (which reports its name as Mozilla) and NCSA Mosaic:

```
Lynx/2-4-2  libwww/2.14
Mozilla/2.0 (Win95; I)
Mozilla/2.0 (Macintosh; I; 68K)
Mozilla/2.01 (X11; I; SunOS 4.1.3_U1 sun4c)
Mozilla/2.0 (X11; I; Linux 1.2.13 i586)
Mozilla/3.0b2 (X11; I; HP-UX A.09.01 9000/750)
Mozilla/2.0 (X11; I; HP-UX A.09.05 9000/755)
Mozilla/2.01 (X11; I; SunOS 4.1.3_U1 sun4c)  via proxy gateway  CERN-
        HTTPD/3.0 libwww/2.17
NCSA Mosaic/3.0.0 A2 (Macintosh)
NCSA_Mosaic/2.6 (X11;AIX 2 000019623500)  libwww/2.12 modified
NCSA_Mosaic/2.6 (X11;SunOS 4.1.3_U1 sun4c)  libwww/2.12 modified
NCSA_Mosaic/2.6 (X11;Linux 1.2.13 i586) libwww/2.12 modified
```

One of the Mozilla entries shows how the entry appears when a Web browser accesses your site through a proxy server. The entry shows the Web browser's name as well as the name of the proxy gateway (in this case, the CERN HTTP running in proxy mode — see Chapter 8 for information on how to install and run the CERN HTTP proxy).

`RefererIgnore` *string* — Instructs `httpd` to ignore any `Referer` (the server that had a link to your page) whose `Referer` header contains the specified string. Specify your own host name as the string, so that references between pages within the site are not recorded.

`PidFile` *filename* — Sets the file where `httpd` stores its process ID. The default `PidFile` is `logs/httpd.pid`. You can use this information to kill or restart the HTTP daemon. The following example shows how to restart `httpd`:

```
kill -HUP 'cat /usr/local/etc/httpd/logs/httpd.pid'
```

This example assumes the default settings for `ServerRoot` and `PidFile`.

`AccessConfig` *filename* — Specifies the file that controls access to the server. The default `AccessConfig` file is `conf/access.conf`.

ResourceConfig *filename* — Specifies the resource configuration file that indicates the location of Web pages and the supported formats. The default ResourceConfig file is conf/srm.conf.

TypesConfig *filename* — Specifies the file that contains the mapping of file extensions to MIME data types. (MIME stands for *Multipurpose Internet Mail Extensions*, which defines a way to package attachments in a single message file.) The server reports these MIME types to clients. If you do not specify a TypesConfig directive, httpd assumes that the TypesConfig file is conf/mime.types. Listed here are a few lines from the default mime.types file:

```
...(Many lines deleted)
audio/basic        au snd
audio/x-wav        wav
image/gif          gif
image/ief          ief
image/jpeg         jpeg jpg jpe
text/html          html htm
text/plain         txt
video/mpeg         mpeg mpg mpe
```

Each line shows the MIME type (such as text/html), followed by the file extensions for that type (html and htm).

IdentityCheck off [on] — Turns on or off the logging of the remote user name. By default, IdentityCheck is off.

<VirtualHost *hostname*> *directives* </VirtualHost> — A new feature, introduced in NCSA HTTPD 1.5, that allows you to define a multihomed Web server — a server that can serve documents from different directories based on domain names. The "Supporting virtual hosts" section in Chapter 8 describes how to set up a virtual host. To use this feature, your version of UNIX must support multiple IP addresses on a single network interface.

Server resource configuration through srm.conf

The resource configuration file, srm.conf (the default filename), specifies the location of the Web pages, as well as how to specify the data types of various files. To begin, leave the directives at their default settings. These are the resource configuration directives for NCSA HTTPD Version 1.5:

DocumentRoot *pathname* — Specifies the directory where the HTTP server finds the Web pages. The default DocumentRoot is /usr/local/etc/httpd/htdocs. If you place your HTML documents in another directory, set DocumentRoot to that directory.

`UserDir` *dirname* — Specifies the directory below a user's home directory where the HTTP server looks for the Web pages when a user name appears in the URL (in a URL such as `http://www.lnbsoft.com/~naba/`, for example, which includes a user name with a tilde prefix). The default `UserDir` is `public_html`, which means that a user's Web pages will be in the `public_html` subdirectory of that user's home directory. If you do not want to allow users to have any Web pages, specify `DISABLED` as the directory name in the `UserDir` directive.

`DirectoryIndex` *filename* — Indicates the default file to be returned by the server when the client does not specify any document. The default `DirectoryIndex` is `index.html`. If `httpd` does not find this file, it returns an index (basically, a nice-looking listing of the files) of that directory.

`AccessFileName` *filename* — Specifies the name of the file that may appear in each directory that contains documents and that indicates who has permission to access the contents of that directory. The default `AccessFileName` is `.htaccess`. The syntax of this file is the same as that of the `access.conf` file, discussed in the following section.

`AddType` *type/subtype extension* — Associates a file extension with a MIME data type (of the form `type/subtype`, such as `text/plain` or `image/gif`). Thus, if you want to the server to treat files with the `.asc` extension as plain-text files, you would specify the following:

```
AddType text/plain asc
```

The default MIME types and extensions are listed in the `conf/mime.types` file.

`AddEncoding` *type extension* — Associates an encoding type with a file extension. If you want the server to mark files ending with `.gz` as encoded with the `x-gzip` encoding method (the standard name for the GZIP encoding), you would specify the following:

```
AddEncoding x-gzip gz
```

`DefaultType` *type/subtype* — Specifies the MIME type that the server should use if it cannot determine the type from the file extension. If you do not specify `DefaultType`, `httpd` assumes the MIME type to be `text/html`. In the default `srm.conf` file that you get with the NCSA HTTPD software, `DefaultType` is specified as `text/plain`.

`Redirect` *requested-file actual-URL* — Specifies that any requests for the `requested-file` be redirected to the `actual-URL`.

`Alias` *requested-dir actual-dir* — Specifies that the server use `actual-dir` to locate files in the `requested-dir` directory (in other words, `requested-dir` is an alias for `actual-dir`). If you want requests for `/images` directory to go to `/ftp/pub/images`, you would specify the following:

```
Alias /images /ftp/pub/images
```

Cross Ref

`ScriptAlias` *`requested-dir actual-dir`* — Specifies the real name of the directory where scripts for the Common Gateway Interface (CGI) are located. (You learn about CGI in Chapter 19.) The default `srm.conf` file contains the following directive:

```
ScriptAlias /cgi-bin/ /usr/local/etc/httpd/cgi-bin/
```

This directive means that when a Web browser requests a script such as `/cgi/bin/test-cgi`, the HTTP server runs the script `/usr/local/etc/httpd/cgi-bin/test-cgi`.

`FancyIndexing on [off]` — Enables or disables the display of fancy directory listings, with icons and file sizes.

`DefaultIcon` *`iconfile`* — Specifies the location of the default icon that the server should use for files that have no icon information. By default, `DefaultIcon` is `/icons/unknown.xbm`.

`ReadmeName` *`filename`* — Specifies the name of a README file whose contents are added to the end of an automatically generated directory listing. The default `ReadmeName` is README.

`HeaderName` *`filename`* — Specifies the name a header file whose contents are prepended to an automatically generated directory listing. The default `HeaderName` is HEADER.

`AddDescription` *`"file description" filename`* — Specifies that the `file description` string be displayed next to the specified `filename` in the directory listing. You can use a wildcard, such as `*.html`, as the `filename`.

`AddIcon` *`iconfile extension1 extension2 ...`* — Associates an icon with one or more file extensions. The following directive associates the icon file `/icons/movie.xbm` with the file extensions `.mpeg` and `.qt`:

```
AddIcon /icons/movie.xbm .mpeg .qt
```

`AddIconByType` *`iconfile MIME-types`* — Associates an icon with a group of file types specified as a wildcard form of MIME types (such as `text/*` or `image/*`). To associate an icon file of `/icons/text.xbm` with all `text` types, specify the following:

```
AddIconByType (TXT,/icons/text.xbm) text/*
```

This directive also tells the server to use TXT in place of the icon for clients that cannot accept images. (Browsers tell the server what types of data they can accept.)

`AddIconByEncoding` *`iconfile encoding1 encoding2 ...`* — Specifies an icon to be displayed for one or more encoding types (such as `x-compress` or `x-tar`).

`IndexIgnore` *filename1 filename2* ... — Instructs the server to ignore the specified filenames (they typically have wildcards) when preparing a directory listing. To leave out README, HEADER, and all files with a leading period (.), specify the following:

```
IndexIgnore */.??* */HEADER* */README*
```

`IndexOptions` *option1 option2* ... — Indicates the options that you want in the directory listing prepared by the server. Options can include one or more of the following:

✦ `FancyIndexing` turns on the fancy directory listing.

✦ `IconsAreLinks` makes the icons act like links.

✦ `ScanHTMLTitles` shows a description of HTML files.

✦ `SuppressLastModified` stops display of the last date of modification.

✦ `SuppressSize` stops display of the file size.

✦ `SuppressDescription` stops display of any file description.

`ErrorDocument` *errortype filename* — Specifies a file that the server should send when an error of a specific type occurs. If you do not have this directive, the server sends a built-in error message. Some of the common `errortype` are as follows:

✦ 302–URL redirected to another document

✦ 304–Document had not changed since last access

✦ 400–Bad request

✦ 401–Authorization required

✦ 403–Access is forbidden

✦ 404–URL Not Found

✦ 500–Server error

✦ 501–Method (either GET or POST) not implemented

✦ 503–Service not available (server is out of resources)

Access control through `access.conf`

The `access.conf` file allows you to control who can access different directories in your Web site. This file is the global access configuration file. In each directory, you can have another access configuration file with the name specified by the `AccessFileName` directive in the `srm.conf` file. (That per-directory access configuration file is named `.htaccess` by default.)

NCSA HTTPD's sample `access.conf` file contains the following:

```
# access.conf: Global access configuration
# Online docs at http://hoohoo.ncsa.uiuc.edu/
# I suggest you consult them; this is important and confusing stuff.

# /usr/local/etc/httpd/ should be changed to whatever you set ServerRoot to.
<Directory /usr/local/etc/httpd/cgi-bin>
Options Indexes FollowSymLinks
</Directory>

# This should be changed to whatever you set DocumentRoot to.

<Directory /usr/local/etc/httpd/htdocs>

# This may also be "None", "All", or any combination of "Indexes",
# "Includes", or "FollowSymLinks"

Options Indexes FollowSymLinks

# This controls which options the .htaccess files in directories can
# override. Can also be "None", or any combination of "Options", "FileInfo",
# "AuthConfig", and "Limit"

AllowOverride All

# Controls who can get stuff from this server.

<Limit GET>
order allow,deny
allow from all
</Limit>

</Directory>

# You may place any other directories you wish to have access
# information for after this one.
```

As you may have noticed from the listing, the access configuration file has a different syntax than the server and resource configuration files. The layout and syntax of the access configuration file are similar to those of an HTML file. The file is organized in sections, with each section enclosed by opening and closing directives. There are two directives to define sections:

✦ `Directory` is used to group all the access control directives for a specified directory. A `Directory` section has the following format:

```
<Directory directory-name>
Other Directives
</Directory>
```

✦ `Limit` is used to specify which clients can access the contents of a directory. As the sample `access.conf` file shows, one or more `Limit` sections appear inside a `Directory` section. A `Limit` section has the following format:

```
<Limit GET>
Other Directives (order, deny, allow, require)
</Limit>
```

The following example shows what the access control options for the `cgi-bin` directory look like:

```
<Directory /usr/local/etc/httpd/cgi-bin>
Options Indexes FollowSymLinks
</Directory>
```

The first line is the opening directive; the last line is the closing directive. In between, a single line lists the access control options that apply to the `cgi-bin` directory. In this case, there are two options:

✦ `Indexes` allows clients to request indexes (directory listings) for this directory (to turn this feature off, just remove the word `Indexes` from the `Options` line).

✦ `FollowSymLinks` enables the server to follow symbolic links.

The following list describes some of the other access control directives . In particular, notice the `AuthUserFile` directive, which allows you to implement password-based access control for specific directories.

`Options opt1 opt2 ...` — Specifies the access control options for the directory section in which this directive appears. The options can be one or more of the following:

✦ `None` disables all access control features.

✦ `All` turns on all features for the directory.

✦ `FollowSymLinks` enables the server to follow symbolic links.

✦ `SymLinksIfOwnerMatch` follows symbolic links only if the linked directory is owned by the same user as this directory.

✦ `ExecCGI` allows execution of CGI scripts in the directory.

✦ `Includes` allows server-side include files in this directory.

✦ `Indexes` allows clients to request indexes (directory listings) for this directory.

✦ `IncludesNoExec` disables the Exec feature.

AllowOverride *directive1 directive2* ... — Specifies which access control directives can be overridden on a per-directory basis by placing a file named .htaccess in a directory for which you want to override access control. The directive list can have one or more of the following:

✦ None stops any directive from being overridden.

✦ All allows overriding of any directive on a per-directory basis.

✦ Options allows the use of the Options directive in the directory-level file.

✦ FileInfo allows the use of AddType and AddEncoding directives.

✦ AuthConfig allows the use of the AuthName, AuthType, AuthUserFile, and AuthGroupFile directives.

✦ Limit allows the use of Limit directives in a directory's access configuration file.

AuthName *name* — Specifies the authorization name for a directory.

AuthType *type* — Specifies the type of authorization to be used. The only supported authorization type is Basic.

AuthUserFile *filename* — Specifies the file where user names and passwords are stored for authorization. The following directive sets the authorization file to /usr/local/etc/httpd/conf/.htpasswd:

```
AuthUserFile /usr/local/etc/httpd/conf/.htpasswd
```

Tip

You have to create the authorization file with the htpasswd support program, located in the /usr/local/etc/httpd/support directory. To create the authorization file and add the password for a user named jdoe, specify the following:

```
/usr/local/etc/httpd/support/htpasswd -c /usr/local/etc/httpd/conf/
        .htpasswd jdoe
Adding password for jdoe.
New password: (Type the password)
Re-type new password: (Type the same password again)
```

AuthGroupFile *filename* — Specifies the file to consult for a list of user groups for authentication.

order *ord* — This directive appears only in a Limit section. The order ord directive specifies the order in which two other directives — allow and deny — are evaluated. The order can be one of the following:

✦ deny,allow evaluates the deny directive before allow.

✦ allow,deny evaluates the allow directive before deny.

✦ `mutual-failure` allows only those hosts that are in the `allow` list.

`deny from host1 host2...` — This directive, which appears only in a `Limit` section, specifies the hosts that are denied access.

`allow from host1 host2...` — This directive, which appears only in a `Limit` section, specifies the hosts that are allowed access. If you want all hosts in a specific domain to access the Web documents in a directory, specify the following:

```
<Limit GET>
order deny,allow
allow from .nws.noaa.gov
</Limit>
```

`require entity en1 en2...` — This directive, which appears only in a `Limit` section, specifies which users can access a directory. The `entity` can be one of the following:

✦ `user` allows only a list of named users.

✦ `group` allows only a list of named groups.

✦ `valid-user` allows all users listed in the `AuthUserFile` access to the directory (provided that they enter the correct password).

Password-protect a directory

Suppose that you want to provide some information to a specific group of users through your Web site, but you do not want the whole world to access the information. In this case, you can use a password-protected directory.

With NCSA HTTPD 1.5 software, you can create a password-protected directory by following these steps:

1. Assume that you are preparing the password-protected Web pages in the `public_html` subdirectory of your home directory. Create a password file with the following commands:

```
/usr/local/etc/httpd/support/htpasswd -c .htpasswd username
Adding password for username.
New password: (Type the password; it does not echo)
Re-type new password: (Type the password again; it does not echo)
```

Provide a `username` — the name that a user has to use to access the Web pages in this directory. You can add more user names with the same command; just leave out the `-c` option, which creates the password file. Note that there is no relationship between the system-level password file (`/etc/passwd`) and the password file generated by the `htpasswd` utility program.

2. Use a text editor to prepare the `.htaccess` file in the `public_html` directory, and add the following lines to that file:

```
AuthName GroupName
AuthType Basic
AuthUserFile yourhomedir/public_html/.htpasswd
AuthGroupFile /dev/null

<Limit GET>
require valid-user
</Limit>
```

Provide a *GroupName* to identify this group of users, and fill in your home directory to fully specify the password file's location.

After you complete these two steps, only users who have passwords in the specified password file (.htpasswd) will be able to access the Web pages in this directory. When a user attempts to access the contents of this directory, the Web browser prompts the user for a user ID and a password, as shown in Figure 7-1.

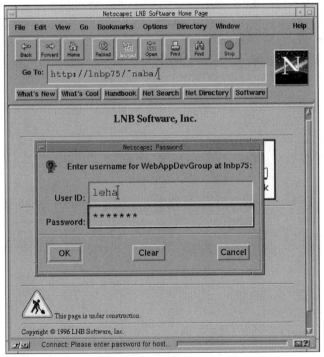

Figure 7-1: When a user tries to access a password-protected Web page, the browser prompts for the user ID and password.

The WebAppDevGroup part of the dialog-box title comes from the group name that I specified in my .htaccess file.

Summary

To set up a Web site on your Internet-connected computer, you need a Web server — the software that runs on your computer and serves the Web pages to users. The NCSA Web server is a good choice for a Web site. This chapter guides you through the process of downloading, compiling, and installing the NCSA Web server. The next chapter shows you how to install the Apache and CERN Web servers.

Where to go next . . .

✦ If you want to install the Apache HTTP server rather than the NCSA Web server, go to Chapter 8.

✦ To learn how to install the CERN Web server, go to Chapter 8.

✦ If you have finished installing the NCSA Web server and want to begin preparing the HTML documents, proceed to Chapter 10.

✦　　✦　　✦

Installing Other Web Servers

Chapter 7 describes how to install and configure the NCSA HTTP server. This chapter describes two more Web servers.

The first one is Apache, which started out as an improved version of the NCSA HTTP server, but soon grew into a separate development effort. Like NCSA HTTPD, the Apache server is developed and maintained by a team of collaborators. Apache is freely available over the Internet.

The second server is the CERN HTTP server — the original Web server developed at CERN, the European laboratory for particle physics, where the concepts of the Web, HTTP, and HTML were invented. Today, the CERN server is called W3C HTTPD — the new name reflects the change of ownership — the World Wide Web Consortium (W3C) now owns the CERN server. The main attraction of the CERN server is that it can serve as an HTTP proxy server — an intermediary that provides access to other HTTP servers. This feature makes the CERN server useful as the Web gateway for systems on protected corporate networks that must access the Internet through a firewall.

Note Although the CERN server is officially referred to as W3C HTTPD, I continue to call it the CERN server because that's how Webmasters still call this venerable Web server.

This chapter shows you how to download, install, and configure the Apache and CERN servers. You learn about the proxy capability of the CERN server. The examples are from a Linux system, but most of the information applies to any UNIX system.

Why is it called "Apache"?

According to the information about the Apache HTTP server project on `http://www.apache.org/info.html`, the Apache group was formed in March 1995 by a number of people who provided patch files that had been written to fix bugs in NCSA HTTPD 1.3. The result after applying the patches to NCSA HTTPD was what they called *A PATCHy* server; that's how the name Apache began. Nearly a year later, Apache Version 1.0 is in widespread use, having surpassed NCSA HTTPD in popularity (as reported by the Netcraft Web Server Survey at `http://www.netcraft.co.uk/Survey/`).

Apache HTTP Server

Because it originated as a bug-fixed version of NCSA HTTPD 1.3, the Apache server is a plug-in replacement for NCSA HTTPD 1.3 and even NCSA HTTPD 1.4. Even as NCSA HTTPD and Apache evolve on separate paths, the configuration files and directory organizations of the two servers — Apache and NCSA HTTPD — remain similar. If you know how to set up NCSA HTTPD, you can easily transfer that knowledge to the Apache server. If the Apache server is your first Web server, carefully read the next few sections; they show you how to download, build, and setup the Apache server.

Before you download and install the Apache HTTP server, here are the general steps that you have to follow to get the Apache HTTP server running on your system:

1. Download the Apache HTTP software distribution from `http://www.apache.org/`. For certain systems, you may be able to download precompiled binaries that are ready-to-run.

2. Unpack the downloaded archive. This step involves using `compress` (or `gzip`) and `tar`.

3. If you download the source-only distribution, you have to compile and build the binaries. The steps involve editing a `Configuration` file, running a `Configure` script, and running the `make` utility. This step generates the server binary, which is called `httpd` (the name is the same for NCSA HTTPD and CERN servers as well).

4. Edit the configuration files: `httpd.conf`, `srm.conf`, and `access.conf`. You can get the initial versions from samples that come with the software distribution.

5. Start the Apache HTTP server by running the `httpd` program with appropriate options. You have to log in as `root` to do this (previous steps may also require you to be `root` because you'll be placing files in directories that may not be accessible to you as an ordinary user).

After you get the server running, you may have to tweak the configuration files (and even the operating system) to improve performance and make the server secure.

Downloading the Apache HTTP server

The latest version (1.1.1 as of this writing) of the Apache HTTP server is available from the Apache Group's Web site at `http://www.apache.org/`. What you find on this page is a number of links organized by country. Click on an appropriate link to download the server.

As is customary for software distributed on the Internet, the Apache HTTP server's directories and files are packaged as a compressed tar archive. The Apache Group distributes the server software using the following two forms of compression:

✦ *UNIX* `compress`: The filename has a `.tar.Z` extension and you have to use the `uncompress` command to get back the tar file.

✦ *GNU* `gzip`: The filename ends with a `.tar.gz` and you have to use the `gunzip` command to uncompress the file.

The `gzip`-ed version is smaller than the file generated by UNIX `compress`. Although the UNIX `compress/uncompress` utilities are available on all versions of UNIX, you may have to download and install GNU `gzip` yourself; many UNIX systems do not come with `gzip` (Linux includes nearly all GNU tools including `gzip`).

The filename for the `gzip`-ed version of Apache HTTP server 1.1.1 is `apache_1.1.1.tar.gz`. This file weighs 282K whereas the `apache_1.1.1.tar.Z` file (created with `compress`) is a much heftier 456K.

URL From your Web browser, click on one of the filenames (`apache_1.1.1.tar.Z` or `apache_1.1.1.tar.gz`) from the URL `http://www.apache.org/dist/` and save the downloaded file in a directory of your choice. For example, I save the files in the `/usr/local/src` directory on my Linux system.

What's GNU and how do I get it?

GNU, which stands for *GNU Is Not UNIX*, is a project of the Free Software Foundation in Cambridge, Massachusetts, which aims to develop a free version of UNIX. The GNU project has generated many high-quality programming tools, ranging from the `emacs` editor to the famous GNU C and C++ compilers (`gcc` and `g++`) that run on virtually any computer system. All GNU software and derivative work are covered by the GNU General Public License (GPL), which allows the author to copyright the software but gives everyone legal permission to copy, distribute, and modify the software. Note that any modifications are also covered by GPL and you must distribute the source if you distribute binaries.

To download GNU `gzip` as well as any other GNU software for free from the Internet, use your Web browser to visit the URL `ftp://prep.ai.mit.edu/pub/gnu/`. If you want to use anonymous FTP, connect to `prep.ai.mit.edu` and look in the `/pub/gnu` directory.

Unpacking the compressed archive

After downloading the Apache server software, you have to uncompress and unpack the archive. If you downloaded the apache_1.1.1.tar.Z file, use the following command to unpack the distribution (I assume the downloaded file is in the /usr/local/src directory of your UNIX system):

```
cd /usr/local/src
zcat apache_1.1.1.tar.Z | tar xvf -
```

This example uses the zcat command together with tar to uncompress and extract the files from the tar archive.

If you downloaded the apache_1.1.1.tar.gz file, you must first run gunzip and then use the tar command. On Linux, you can perform these steps with the z option of the tar command as follows:

```
tar zxvf apache_1.1.1.tar.gz
```

The z option tells tar to expect a gzip-ed file.

After you unpack the software distribution, tar creates a subdirectory named apache_1.1.1 with all the files for the Apache HTTP server.

Tip   Because it's cumbersome to type a long directory name such as apache_1.1.1, I always set up a symbolic link with a more generic shorter name. For example, you may set up a symbolic link apache that points to the apache_1.1.1 directory with the following command:

```
ln -s apache_1.1.1 apache
```

After you set up this symbolic link, you can change to the Apache directory with the command:

```
cd apache
```

In the apache directory, you'll find the following files and subdirectories (the slash at the end of a name indicates a directory):

Name	Description
CHANGES	Text file with a summary of the new features of this release.
LICENSE	Text file with the copyright notice from Apache Group detailing the terms of distribution and use of the Apache server.
README	Text file with a brief description of the Apache HTTP server and where to go for more information (http://www.apache.org).

Name	Description
cgi-bin/	Directory with sample scripts and binaries for Common Gateway Interface (CGI). You'd put your own CGI scripts in this directory.
conf/	Directory with sample configuration files. You can rename the sample files and edit them to suit your needs. The configuration files control the operation of the Apache HTTP server.
icons/	Directory with icons used when the Web server displays the contents of a directory that does not contain a default index document (such as index.html).
logs/	Directory in which Web server access logs and error logs are kept.
src/	Directory with all the source files for the Apache HTTP server.
support/	Directory with support tools such as the programs used to control who can access the documents in specific directories.

If you download a binary distribution (see next section), you'll also find a ready-to-run binary version of the Apache HTTP server (the program's name is httpd — the same as in NCSA HTTP server).

Downloading Apache HTTP server binaries

If you are in a hurry and you don't want to build the Apache HTTP server from scratch, you can download a read-to-run binary version. If you are not in a hurry, however, you may want to try building the Apache HTTP server from scratch; the process is not that difficult.

URL

Binaries of the Apache HTTP server are available from http://www.apache.org/dist/binaries/ for the following versions of UNIX:

Directory Name	UNIX Version
aux_3.1	Apple A/UX 3.1
bsdi_1.1	BSDI BSD/OS 1.1
bsdi_2.0	BSDI BSD/OS 2.0
freebsd_2.1	FreeBSD 2.1
hpux_9.07	HP-UX 9.07
linux	Linux (ELF binaries; Slackware Linux 3.0 supports ELF)
netbsd_1.1	NetBSD 1.1

(continued)

Directory Name	UNIX Version
irix_5.3	SGI IRIX 5.3
solaris_2.4	Solaris 2.4
sunos_4.1.3	SunOS 4.1.3
unixware_1.1.2	Unixware 1.1.2

To download the files for a specific version of UNIX, click on the directory name. When the new directory listing appears, select the file to download. The steps for unpacking the file are the same as those for the source version of Apache HTTP server (see the "Unpacking the compressed archive" section in this chapter).

Tip After you unpack a binary distribution, you should find the server binary, httpd, in the src subdirectory of the directory in which you install the software.

Compiling the Apache HTTP server

Although it began life as a bug-fixed version of the NCSA HTTPD server, the Apache HTTP server source code has been rearranged to make the server more modular. As explained in the Apache Group's README file (in the src directory), the server has been organized as a core and many optional modules. Each module has a standard interface to the server core. The design is such that (if you are a programmer) you can easily add a new module or replace an existing module with one that provides customized functionality.

URL For examples of Apache HTTP server modules, visit the URL http://www.apache.org/dist/contrib/modules/.

To incorporate modules into the Apache HTTP server, you have to generate a short C source file called modules.c that lists the modules to be included in the server binary you are going to build. You have to edit a file named Configuration and then run a script named Configure. This step generates a new modules.c file as well as a new Makefile file that you must use to compile the program (do not use the modules.c and Makefile that come with the distribution; they may not be exactly what you need).

To build the Apache HTTP server on a Linux system, make the following changes to the Configuration file in the src subdirectory (use your favorite text editor):

1. Comment out the options for all non-Linux operating systems. (To comment a line, place a pound sign character, #, at the beginning of the line.)

2. Uncomment the compiler option for Linux so that the enabled option is as follows (if this is already uncommented, leave it as is):

```
For Linux -m486 ONLY IF YOU HAVE 486 BINARY SUPPORT IN KERNEL
AUX_CFLAGS= -DLINUX -m486
```

3. Near the end of the Configuration file you'll see a list of modules. If you had a new module, you have to list it in this section. Also, you can uncomment one or more modules following the instructions in the file. By default, the following list of modules is used to build the Apache HTTP server:

```
# Basic modules (i.e., generally useful stuff that works everyplace):

Module mime_module          mod_mime.o
Module access_module        mod_access.o
Module auth_module          mod_auth.o
Module negotiation_module   mod_negotiation.o
Module includes_module      mod_include.o
Module dir_module           mod_dir.o
Module cgi_module           mod_cgi.o
Module userdir_module       mod_userdir.o
Module alias_module         mod_alias.o
Module env_module           mod_env.o
Module common_log_module    mod_log_common.o
Module asis_module          mod_asis.o
Module imap_module          mod_imap.o
Module action_module        mod_actions.o
```

After editing the Configuration file, type the following command to complete the configuration step:

```
Configure
Using 'Configuration' as config file
```

This command runs the Configure script, which consults the Configuration file and generates a new Makefile file and a source file named modules.c. The modules.c file is essentially a list of modules to be included in the Apache server.

If you want, you can create a configuration file with a name other than Configuration and maintain another configuration of the Apache HTTP server. Suppose you have an alternate configuration file named config.new. Then, you can create a Makefile and modules.c file for the new configuration with the command:

```
Configure -file config.new
Using alternate config file config.new
```

After you run the Configure script, type the following command to build the Apache HTTP server program:

```
make
```

After make finishes, you'll find the server binary httpd in the src directory. The next step is to edit the server configuration files.

Configuring the Apache HTTP server

Like the NCSA HTTPD, the Apache server's operation is controlled by three configuration files located in the `conf` subdirectory. The configuration files control how the server runs, what documents it serves, and who can access these documents.

The three configuration files are:

Filename	Purpose
httpd.conf	Configuration file for the Apache server. The file specifies general attributes of the server (such as port number and directory in which the server's directories are located).
srm.conf	Configuration file for the server resources — the documents and other information that the Web server provides to the users. For example, the srm.conf file specifies where the documents are located. (Note that srm stands for *server resource map*.)
access.conf	Configuration file that controls access to the Web server. You can control access to the entire Web server as well as to specific directories.

The next few sections show you the minimal amount of configuration file editing that you must do to get the Apache HTTP server up and running.

Cross Ref

Copy the sample configuration files

The Apache software distribution comes with three sample configuration files. If you install the server software in the `/usr/local/src/apache` directory, you'll find the following files in the `/usr/local/src/apache/conf` directory:

```
access.conf-dist
httpd.conf-dist
srm.conf-dist
```

These files are meant to be sample configuration files. To use these files as the actual configuration files, make copies of them as follows:

```
cp access.conf-dist access.conf
cp httpd.conf-dist httpd.conf
cp srm.conf-dist srm.conf
```

There is another file named `mime.types` that associates file extensions with a MIME (Multipurpose Internet Mail Extensions) data type. For example, the following line in `mime.types` associates the `.html` extension with the `text/html` MIME type:

```
text/html               html
```

Tip   You don't need to modify the `mime.types` file unless you want to associate a new file extension with a MIME type. For now, you can safely ignore the `mime.types` file.

Edit the configuration files

As you edit the configuration files, keep the following syntax rules in mind:

✦ All comment lines begin with a #.

✦ Each line can have only one directive.

✦ Extra spaces and blank lines are ignored.

✦ All entries except pathnames and URLs are case-insensitive.

Next, I'll show you the minimal amount of editing that you have to do to get the server up and running.

Basic `httpd.conf` configuration

The `httpd.conf` file controls how the Apache HTTP server runs. For example, in the `httpd.conf` file you specify the port number the server uses, the name of the Web site, and the e-mail address of the Webmaster.

To run the Apache HTTP server as a stand-alone daemon, you need to edit certain items (listed here) in the `httpd.conf` file:

✦ If your system does not have a user named `nobody` (it should be in the `/etc/passwd` file), change the `User` and `Group` directives to an appropriate user name and group ID. The default values of `User` and `Group` are as follows:

```
User nobody
Group #-1
```

The `Group` directive says that the group ID is –1 — the syntax for specifying numerical values (with a # prefix).

✦ Change `ServerAdmin` to be your e-mail address (for example, `webmaster@your.domain`). Make sure you define the `webmaster` alias in the `sendmail` aliases file (`/usr/lib/aliases` or `/etc/aliases`).

✦ Change `ServerRoot` to the absolute pathname of the directory in which you plan to install the Apache HTTP server program and in which the configuration files and logs are located. The default is `/usr/local/etc/httpd`.

✦ Set `ServerName` to the hostname of your Web site (of the form `www.your.domain`). The name should be a registered domain name that others can locate through their name server. Listed here is an example:

```
ServerName  www.lnbsoft.com
```

Basic `srm.conf` configuration

The `srm.conf` file controls the location and type of the documents that the Apache HTTP server provides to clients (Web browsers). For example, the `srm.conf` file specifies where the HTML documents are located. To quickly bring up the Apache server, you must specify the following items in the `srm.conf` file:

✦ Change `DocumentRoot` to the directory in which you plan to keep the documents that your Web site offers to the users. The default location is `/usr/local/etc/httpd/htdocs`.

✦ If you do not want users to serve Web pages from their home directories, set the `UserDir` directive to `DISABLED` as follows:

```
UserDir DISABLED
```

The default setting of `UserDir` is `public_html`, which means when a request of the form `http://www.your.domain/~user` comes in, the Web server looks for documents in the `~user/public_html` directory (that's the `public_html` directory in the user's home directory).

Basic `access.conf` configuration

The `access.conf` file controls what types of access Web browsers (the HTTP clients) have to documents on your server. There are global access control directives that apply to all documents as well as access control directives that apply to specific directories.

Stripped of most of the comment lines, the initial `srm.conf` file has the following default content:

```
# The directory name should match the location of the cgi-bin directory
<Directory /usr/local/etc/httpd/cgi-bin>
    Options Indexes FollowSymLinks
</Directory>
# The following directory name should match DocumentRoot in srm.conf
<Directory /usr/local/etc/httpd/htdocs>
    Options Indexes FollowSymLinks
    AllowOverride All
    <Limit GET>
        order allow,deny
        allow from all
    </Limit>
</Directory>
```

Note that the `access.conf` file uses a different syntax than the `httpd.conf` and `srm.conf` files. If you know HTML, you can see that the syntax is similar to that of HTML. Various access control directives are enclosed within pairs of tags such as `<Directory>` ... `</Directory>` and `<Limit>` ... `</Limit>`.

The default `access.conf` file has minimal access control, a situation you want to remedy before you fully deploy your Web site. For now, you may need to make the following changes:

✦ Change the directory name in the first `<Directory>` directive if your `cgi-bin` directory is in a different location than `/usr/local/etc/httpd/cgi-bin`.

✦ If you do not want users to look at the content of the `cgi-bin` directory, remove the `Indexes` option from the `Options` directive.

✦ Change the directory name in the second `<Directory>` directive to the directory in which the Apache HTTP server binary is installed.

✦ The `AllowOverride All` line in the second `<Directory>` directive means that local directory-level access control (you learn about access control in the "Password-protect a directory" section in Chapter 7) can override any global constraints. To ensure that global access control cannot be overridden, change this directive to:

```
AllowOverride None
```

Installing the Apache HTTP server

After you edit the configuration files to reflect the directory in which you have installed the server and the directory in which the documents are located, you have to make sure that the server is indeed in the specified directory and all necessary subdirectories exist.

If you decide to leave the default choices for the `ServerRoot` directive, the Apache HTTP server binary, `httpd`, should be in the `/usr/local/etc/httpd` directory. If you unpacked the Apache server's files in `/usr/local/src/apache` directory, here are the commands to use to install everything in the proper place:

```
cd /usr/local/src/apache
mkdir /usr/local/etc/httpd
cp -r httpd conf logs icons cgi-bin /usr/local/etc/httpd
```

You also need to create the directory specified in the `DocumentRoot` directive. If you left it at the default setting of `/usr/local/etc/httpd/htdocs`, you have to create that directory as well:

```
mkdir /usr/local/etc/httpd/htdocs
```

Starting the Apache HTTP server

After you install the Apache HTTP server binary (`httpd`) in the appropriate directory (the default is `/usr/local/etc/httpd`) and create the necessary subdirectories, you are ready to start the server.

If you left the `ServerRoot` at its default setting of `/usr/local/etc/httpd`, you can start the server with the command:

```
/usr/local/etc/httpd/httpd
```

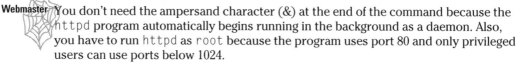 You don't need the ampersand character (&) at the end of the command because the `httpd` program automatically begins running in the background as a daemon. Also, you have to run `httpd` as `root` because the program uses port 80 and only privileged users can use ports below 1024.

If you changed `ServerRoot` to a directory other than `/usr/local/etc/httpd`, you have to start the server with the `-d` command-line option. For example, if your `ServerRoot` is `/usr/local/etc/apache`, then you'd start the Apache HTTP server with the following command:

```
/usr/local/etc/apache/httpd -d /usr/local/etc/apache
```

Instead of specifying the `ServerRoot` directory on the command line, you can also indicate the full pathname of the `httpd.conf` file (which can specify the `ServerRoot`). Suppose you left the Apache HTTP binary (`httpd`) in the `/usr/local/src/apache/src` directory and the configuration file is in `/usr/local/src/apache/conf/httpd.conf`. You can start the server with the following command:

```
/usr/local/src/apache/src/httpd -f /usr/local/src/apache/conf/httpd.conf
```

You can verify that the server has started by typing the following command:

```
ps -ax | grep httpd
```

With the default configuration of the server, you should see a total of six `httpd` processes: one parent process and five child processes ready to handle requests from Web browsers.

Testing the Apache HTTP server

You can test the Web server even before you have the documents ready in the `DocumentRoot` directory. From one of the systems on your network TELNET to port 80 of the host that's running the Apache HTTP server. After a connection is established, send the HTTP command like a Web browser. One good way is to send `HEAD /  HTTP/1.0` command. Note that the Web server responds only after receiving a blank

line, so press Enter twice after typing the HEAD / HTTP/1.0 command. Listed here
is a sample session when I tried the test on my network (lnbp75 is the host that runs
the Apache Web server):

```
lnbsun% telnet lnbp75 80
Trying 206.197.168.200 ...
Connected to lnbp75.
Escape character is '^]'.
HEAD / HTTP/1.0

HTTP/1.0 200 OK

Date: Mon, 29 Jul 1996 03:05:54 GMT
Server: Apache/1.1.1
Content-type: text/html
Content-length: 1046
Last-modified: Sun, 07 Jul 1996 20:21:43 GMT

Connection closed by foreign host.
lnbsun%
```

As the listing shows, the response to the HEAD command includes the name and
version of the Web server (Apache/1.1.1). This information tells you if your Web
server is up and running.

For a more exciting test, place an index.html file in the directory specified in the
DocumentRoot directive and try to access the server from a Web browser.

Supporting virtual hosts with Apache HTTP server

Until Version 1.5 of NCSA HTTPD, one of the features that distinguished the Apache
server from NCSA HTTPD was Apache's ability to handle virtual Web servers. This
enables a single server to respond to many different IP addresses and serve Web
pages from different directories depending on the IP address. As a result, you can set
up a single Web server to respond to both www.big.org and www.tiny.com and
serve a unique home page for each hostname. A server with this capability is vari-
ously known as *multi-homed Web server*, *virtual host support*, and *virtual Web server*.

As you may guess, virtual host capability is used by ISPs who offer virtual Web sites to
your customers. You need the following to support virtual hosts:

✦ The Web server must be able to respond to multiple IP addresses (each with a
   unique domain name) and must allow you to specify document directories, log
   files, and other configuration items for each IP address.

✦ The UNIX system must be able to associate multiple IP addresses with a single
   physical network interface.

✦ Each domain name associated with the IP address must be a unique registered
   domain name with proper DNS entries.

Many UNIX systems allow you to associate multiple IP addresses with a single physical interface. In UNIX, the `ifconfig` command binds an IP address to a physical network interface. In some versions of UNIX, the `ifconfig` command takes an `alias` option that associates multiple IP addresses with the same physical interface.

URL For the latest step-by-step instructions on how to set up Linux to support multiple IP addresses at a single interface, consult the following URL:

```
http://www.qosina.com/apache/
```

This URL also includes information on how to configure DNS and `sendmail` to support the multiple hostnames on a single host.

Virtual host options

URL As explained in the document at URL `http://www.apache.org/docs/ virtual-host.html`, the Apache HTTP server can respond to different hostnames with different home pages. You have two options to support virtual hosts:

✦ Run multiple copies of the `httpd` program, one for each IP address. In this case, you create a separate copy of the `httpd.conf` configuration file for each host and use the `BindAddress` directive to make the server respond to a specific IP address.

✦ Run a single copy of the `httpd` program with a single `httpd.conf` file. In the configuration file, set `BindAddress` to * (so that the server responds to any IP address) and use the `VirtualHost` directive to configure the server for each virtual host.

Run multiple HTTP daemons only if your system does not expect heavy traffic; the system may not be able to respond well because of the overhead associated with running multiple daemons. However, you may need multiple HTTP daemons if each virtual host has a unique configuration need for the following directives:

✦ `ServerType` (specifies whether the server runs standalone or through `inetd`)

✦ `UserId` and `GroupId` (the user and group ID for the HTTP daemon)

✦ `ServerRoot` (the root directory of the server)

✦ `TypesConfig` (the MIME type configuration file)

For a site with heavy traffic, you should configure the Web server so that a single HTTP daemon can server multiple virtual hosts. Of course, this implies that you have only one configuration file. In that configuration file, use the `VirtualHost` directive to configure each virtual host.

Note Today, most ISPs use the `VirtualHost` capability of Apache HTTP server to provide virtual Web sites to their customers. They charge around $1,000 (U.S.) per year for a virtual site where you get your own domain name, but share the server and the actual host with many other customers.

VirtualHost directive

The syntax of the VirtualHost directive is as follows:

```
<VirtualHost hostaddr>
    ... directives that apply to this host
    ...
</VirtualHost>
```

With this syntax, you use `<VirtualHost>` and `</VirtualHost>` to enclose a group of directives that will apply only to the particular virtual host identified by hostaddr parameter. The hostaddr can be an IP address or the FQDN of the virtual host.

You can only place certain directives within the `<VirtualHost>` block. At a minimum, Webmasters include the following directives in the `<VirtualHost>` block:

✦ DocumentRoot specifies where this virtual host's documents reside.

✦ Servername identifies the server to the outside world.

✦ ServerAdmin is the e-mail address of this virtual host's Webmaster.

✦ ErrorLog specifies the file in which errors related to this virtual host are to be logged.

✦ TransferLog specifies the file in which accesses to this virtual host are logged.

Along with these common directives, you may also include any of the following directives in the `<VirtualHost>` block:

✦ AccessConfig (the configuration file for access to this virtual host)

✦ AccessFileName (the file that controls access to specific directories of this virtual host)

✦ AgentLog (the file in which the Web server records the names of browsers used to access this virtual host's documents)

✦ DefaultType (the default MIME type of documents with unknown filename extensions)

✦ `<Directory> ... </Directory>` (the access control directives for a specific directory on this virtual host)

✦ ErrorDocument (the file to return when specific errors occur)

✦ Options (the command that specifies access control options for files in a specific directory)

✦ ResourceConfig (the configuration file for this virtual host's resources — the documents managed by this virtual host)

✦ ScriptAlias (the directory in which this virtual host's CGI programs are located)

When the server receives a request for a document in a particular virtual host's `DocumentRoot` directory, it uses the configuration parameters within that server's `<VirtualHost>` block to handle that request.

Listed here is a typical example of a `<VirtualHost>` directive that sets up the virtual host `www.lnbsoft.com`:

```
<VirtualHost www.lnbsoft.com>
    DocumentRoot    /usr/home/naba/httpd/htdocs
    ServerName    www.lnbsoft.com
    ServerAdmin    webmaster@lnbsoft.com
    ScriptAlias    /cgi-bin/    /usr/home/naba/httpd/cgi-bin/
    ErrorLog    /usr/home/naba/httpd/logs/error_log
    TransferLog    /usr/home/naba/httpd/logs/access_log
</VirtualHost>
```

CERN HTTP Server

URL The CERN HTTP server is the original Web server, having been developed at CERN (European Particle Physics Laboratory, Geneva, Switzerland), the birthplace of the World Wide Web. Today, the World Wide Web Consortium (W3C) has taken over the role of developing common standards for the evolution of the World Wide Web. You can learn more about the W3C by visiting their home page at the URL `http://www.w3.org/pub/WWW/`.

Along with the responsibility for the Web standards, the World Wide Web Consortium has also taken over all CERN-developed software, including the CERN HTTP server. Officially, the CERN server is now called W3C `httpd`. However, I'll continue to use the name CERN HTTP server (or, simply, the CERN server) because that's how most people still refer to this Web server.

As with NCSA HTTPD and the Apache server, you must follow these general steps to install and use the CERN HTTP server:

1. Download the CERN HTTP server for free from the W3C Web site (`http://www.w3.org/pub/WWW/Daemon/`). You can get binary versions for many popular UNIX systems. Otherwise, you have to download the source code and build the server. After downloading, unpack the files.

2. If you downloaded the source files, you have to compile and build the server binary. If you already have the binary, you can skip this step.

3. Install the server binary in appropriate directories and edit the configuration files.

4. Start the server and test to make sure it's working.

The following sections guide you through the installation process on a Linux system.

Downloading the CERN HTTP server

The best way to download the CERN HTTP server is to use a Web browser and open the URL `http://www.w3.org/pub/WWW/Daemon/`. On that Web page, you find links that point to information about the CERN (W3C) Web server. One of the links lists the systems on which the CERN server runs and the systems for which binaries are available. As you learn by browsing through the information, the CERN server is available for the following versions of UNIX:

UNIX Version	Binary Available
Apple A/UX 3.1	NO
BSDI BSD/386	NO
DEC OSF/1 3.0	YES (see notes in the URL `http://www.w3.org/pub/WWW/Library/User/Platform/OSF.html`)
DEC Ultrix 4.3	YES
FreeBSD	NO
HP-UX 9.0	YES (see notes in the URL `http://www.w3.org/pub/WWW/Library/User/Platform/HP.html`)
IBM AIX 3.2	YES
Linux 1.2.10	YES (a.out format)
NetBSD	NO
SCO UNIX 3.0/3.2	YES (read the notes from SCO in the URL `http://www.w3.org/pub/WWW/Library/User/Platform/SCO.html`)
SGI IRIX 5.2	YES
Solaris 2.3 SPARC	YES (see notes in the URL `http://www.w3.org/pub/WWW/Library/User/Platform/Solaris.html`)
Solaris 2.4 x86	YES (see notes in the URL `http://www.w3.org/pub/WWW/Library/User/Platform/sun_x86_5.4.html`)
SunOS 4.1.3	YES (see notes in the URL `http://www.w3.org/pub/WWW/Library/User/Platform/SunOS.html`)

For all the UNIX versions for which precompiled binaries are available, you can download the files by clicking on a link that appears on the Web page at `http://www.w3.org/pub/WWW/Daemon/`. That link takes you to the URL `ftp://ftp.w3.org/pub/httpd/` where you'll find the following binary distributions for UNIX systems:

Filename	*Size*	*Description*
`httpd_2.16beta_bin.sgi_405.gz`	197K	GNU Zip Compressed Data
`httpd_3.0_bin.dec_osf1.tar.Z`	545K	Compressed Data
`httpd_3.0_bin.hp_ux9.tar.Z`	648K	Compressed Data
`httpd_3.0_bin.linux_aout.tar.gz`	204K	GNU Zip Compressed Data
`httpd_3.0_bin.rs_aix32.tar.Z`	1031K	Compressed Data
`httpd_3.0_bin.sgi_51.tar.Z`	362K	Compressed Data
`httpd_3.0_bin.sun4_41+lresolv.tar.Z`	651K	Compressed Data
`httpd_3.0_bin.sun4_41+wais+lresolv.tar.Z`	846K	Compressed Data
`httpd_3.0_bin.sun4_41+wais.tar.Z`	834K	Compressed Data
`httpd_3.0_bin.sun4_41.tar.Z`	744K	Compressed Data
`httpd_3.0_bin.sun4_53+wais.tar.Z`	918K	Compressed Data
`httpd_3.0_bin.sun4_53.tar.Z`	838K	Compressed Data
`httpd_3.0_bin.sun4_54_x86.tar.Z`	1419K	Compressed Data

To download the binary distribution, click on the selected filename in the Web browser window.

The source files are available in two formats (also in `ftp://ftp.w3.org/pub/httpd/`) with the following filenames:

`httpd_3.0_src.tar.Z`	317K	Compressed Data
`httpd_3.0_src.tar.gz`	195K	GNU Zip Compressed

If you download the source distribution, you must also get Version 2.17 of the W3C Reference Library (also known as `libwww`) in order to build the CERN HTTP server. This library is available at the URL `ftp://ftp.w3.org/pub/libwww/` under the following filename:

`libwww_2.17_src.tar.Z`	583K	Compressed Data

Because I plan to install the CERN HTTP server on a Linux system, I downloaded the binary distribution file `httpd_3.0_bin.linux_aout.tar.gz`.

Webmaster Unlike Netscape HTTPD and the Apache Web server, the binary distribution of CERN HTTP server does not come with the support directories and files (for example, the configuration files). So, when you download the binary, you should also download the file `server_root.tar.Z` from `ftp://ftp.w3.org/pub/httpd/` (the same place where you find the binaries). The `server_root.tar.Z` file gives you the directory structure you need to set up the binary server.

Unpacking the CERN HTTP files

After downloading the binary distribution and the `server_root.tar.Z` file, follow these steps to unpack and place the CERN HTTP files in their appropriate places:

1. Copy the `server_root.tar.Z` file to `/usr/local/etc` with the following command:

   ```
   mv server_root.tar.Z /usr/local/etc
   ```

2. Unpack the `server_root.tar.Z` archive with the following command:

   ```
   zcat server_root.tar.Z | tar xvf -
   ```

   This command creates a `/usr/local/etc/server_root` directory and places a number of files in subdirectories.

3. Copy the server binary, `httpd_3.0_bin.linux_aout.tar.gz` to the `/usr/local/etc/server_root/bin` directory as follows:

   ```
   mv httpd_3.0_bin.linux_aout.tar.gz /usr/local/etc/server_root/bin
   ```

4. Unpack the `httpd_3.0_bin.linux_aout.tar.gz` file with the following commands:

   ```
   cd /usr/local/etc/server_root/bin
   tar zxvf httpd_3.0_bin.linux_aout.tar.gz
   ```

   These commands extract the binary files in the `/usr/local/etc/server_root/bin` directory.

5. Move the `htimage` program to the `server_root/cgi-bin` directory; the `htimage` program is used to handle clicks on images. Use the following command:

   ```
   mv htimage ../cgi-bin
   ```

Taking inventory of the CERN HTTP files

After completing the preceding steps, you'll find the following files and directories in the `/usr/local/etc/server_root` directory of your Linux system:

```
lnbp75:/usr/local/etc/server_root$ ls -l
-rw-r--r--  1 12516    69          2883 May  4  1994 README
-rw-r--r--  1 12516    69          2830 Apr  4  1994 README~
drwxr-xr-x  2 root     root        1024 Apr 11 00:26 bin
drwxr-sr-x  2 12516    69          1024 Apr 11 00:26 cgi-bin
drwxr-sr-x  2 12516    69          1024 May  2  1994 config
drwxr-sr-x  2 12516    69          1024 May  3  1994 icons
```

These files and directories serve the following purposes:

✦ README is a May 3, 1993, statement from CERN releasing the CERN W3 software into public domain. README also lists the contents of the distribution (although the URLs listed in this file are now outdated).

✦ bin is a directory with the CERN HTTP server binary (httpd) and several utility programs (cgiparse, cgiutils, and htadm).

✦ cgi-bin is a directory that contains the htimage program used to handle clicks on images (the cgi-bin directory holds any binaries for Common Gateway Interface — CGI).

✦ config is a directory with sample configuration files for the CERN HTTP server.

✦ icons is a directory that contains some icons to be used for directory listings and FTP listings.

Tip   You need a directory to keep logs and another directory for the HTML documents that the CERN HTTP server provides to Web browsers. Create subdirectories named logs and htdocs in the /usr/local/etc/server_root directory for these files:

```
cd /usr/local/etc/server_root
mkdir logs
mkdir htdocs
```

Tip   If you are using a UNIX system other than Linux, you can still repeat the same steps to install the CERN server binaries except that you have to download a different binary distribution. If you cannot find binaries for your system, you have to download the source code and build the binaries.

Configuring the CERN HTTP server

If you unpack the CERN HTTP server software according to the instructions in the "Unpacking the CERN HTTP files" section, the sample server configuration files will be placed in the /usr/local/etc/server_root/config directory.

The sample configuration files in the /usr/local/etc/server_root/config directory include the following:

Filename	Purpose
all.conf	Lists all the configuration directives understood by CERN httpd; it is *not* a real configuration file
caching.conf	Configuration file when CERN httpd is running as a proxy HTTP server or with caching
httpd.conf	Configuration file when CERN httpd is running as a normal HTTP server
prot.conf	Configuration file when CERN httpd is running as a normal HTTP server with access control
proxy.conf	Configuration file when CERN httpd is running as a proxy HTTP server without caching

As you can see, each configuration file controls the operation of the CERN HTTP server in a specific operational mode. To start the server in a specific mode, you must run the httpd program and specify the appropriate configuration file as a command-line option. For example, to start the CERN HTTP server in a normal mode of operation using the httpd.conf configuration file, log in as root and type the following commands (of course, you should do this only *after* you edit the configuration file):

```
cd /usr/local/etc/server_root
bin/httpd -r config/httpd.conf
```

Webmaster If you start the CERN httpd program without any options, it looks for the default configuration file /etc/httpd.conf. Unless you place the httpd.conf file in the /etc directory, you must start the server by specifying a configuration file through the -r option.

Cross Ref The CERN HTTP server accepts many configuration directives. Because you can run the CERN HTTP server several ways, I cover some interesting cases separately in the following sections.

Running CERN HTTP server in normal mode

The easiest way to get the CERN server up and running is in the normal (unprotected) mode. To run as a normal HTTP server, you should first edit the httpd.conf configuration file (in /usr/local/etc/server_root/config directory), as follows:

✦ Set ServerRoot to the directory where the httpd program is installed. If you follow this book's example, you have to define ServerRoot as follows:

```
ServerRoot    /usr/local/etc/server_root
```

✦ Define AccessLog and ErrorLog as follows:

```
AccessLog       /usr/local/etc/server_root/logs/httpd-log
ErrorLog        /usr/local/etc/server_root/logs/httpd-errors
```

✦ Change Exec to the cgi-bin directory in the ServerRoot directory, as follows:

```
Exec    /cgi-bin/*       /usr/local/etc/server_root/cgi-bin/*
```

✦ Change the Pass directive to the name of the directory in which the HTML documents are located. For example, if you place the HTML documents in /usr/local/etc/server_root/htdocs, you should define Pass to:

```
Pass    /*       /usr/local/etc/server_root/htdocs/*
```

Now you can put your home page — the index.html file — and other HTML files in the /usr/local/etc/server_root/htdocs directory and start the CERN HTTP server.

To begin serving documents, start the CERN HTTP server with the following command:

```
cd /usr/local/etc/server_root
bin/httpd -r config/httpd.conf
```

To see if the CERN HTTP server is working, use TELNET to connect to the server host at port 80 and send the string HEAD / HTTP/1.0. Then press Enter twice. The following listing shows the response from the CERN HTTP server (the server host is lnbp75 and the connection is made from the host named lnbsun):

```
lnbsun% telnet lnbp75 80
Trying 206.197.168.200 ...
Connected to lnbp75.
Escape character is '^]'.
HEAD / HTTP/1.0
...(Press Enter again)...
HTTP/1.0 200 Document follows
MIME-Version: 1.0
Server: CERN/3.0
Date: Thursday, 11-Apr-96 23:05:32 GMT
Content-Type: text/html
Content-Length: 910
Last-Modified: Thursday, 11-Apr-96 23:01:54 GMT

Connection closed by foreign host.
lnbsun%
```

As the server's response to the HEAD command shows, the server name and version appears as CERN/3.0, which means the host is running the CERN HTTP server, Version 3.0.

CERN HTTP server command-line options

The CERN httpd program accepts the following command-line options:

Command-Line Options	Meaning
-r configfile	Use specified configuration file (default is /etc/httpd.conf).
-p port	Listen to specified port.
-l logfile	Log the requests in specified logfile.
-restart	Restart an already running httpd process. (You must also provide the configuration file with the -r option.)
-gc_only	Perform garbage collection (clean up old cache files) only and exit (applies to servers running in proxy mode).
-v	Run in verbose mode (display debugging messages).
-vv	Run in very verbose mode (display even more debugging messages).
-version	Display the version number of httpd and libwww (the common WWW library).
-dy	Enable directory browsing (can also be set with the DirAccess configuration directive). This command-line option is the default.
-dn	Disable directory browsing
-ds	Allow browsing only those directories listed in a file named .www_browsable.
-dt	If a browsable directory contains a README file, display the contents of that file at the top of the directory listing (can also be set with the DirReadme configuration directive).This command-line option also is the default.
-db	Same as -dt, but the README file's content appears after the directory listing.
-dr	Disable the README file display.

Running CERN HTTP server as a caching proxy server

One common use of the CERN HTTP server is to use it as a proxy HTTP server through which systems inside a firewall can access other Web sites on the Internet. (For more information on firewalls, see Chapter 9.) To get the most benefits, you should run the CERN server as a caching proxy server. Read further to see how it works.

As a proxy server, the CERN HTTP server runs on the firewall system that isolates an internal network from the wide-open Internet. When a Web browser running on an internal host wants to access a Web site on the Internet, it first connects to the CERN HTTP server at a specified port (port 8080 is typically used for a proxy HTTP server — that means the CERN server listens for connections on port 8080) and sends the request. The CERN server, in turn, connects the actual Web site, downloads the Web documents, and forwards them to the Web browser running on the internal host.

The term *caching proxy server* simply means that when the CERN HTTP server downloads a document from a specific URL, it caches the document by storing it temporarily on disk. If another client requests the same URL, the CERN HTTP server can serve that document from the cache instead of having to download the document again from the original Web site.

Figure 8-1 illustrates the concept of a caching proxy server.

As Figure 8-1 illustrates, the CERN HTTP server runs (with the `caching.conf` configuration file) on the firewall host F. When internal Client A requests a document from O through the CERN server, the server fetches the document, returns it to A, and caches it locally. When internal Client B also requests the same document from O, the CERN server serves that document from its cache thus avoiding a second trip to host O.

To set up the CERN HTTP server as a caching proxy server, edit the `caching.conf` configuration file (in the `/usr/local/etc/server_root/config` directory):

✦ Set `ServerRoot` to the directory in which the `httpd` program is installed. If you follow this book's example, you must define `ServerRoot` as follows:

```
ServerRoot     /usr/local/etc/server_root
```

✦ Define `AccessLog` and `ErrorLog` as follows:

```
AccessLog      /usr/local/etc/server_root/logs/proxy-log
ErrorLog       /usr/local/etc/server_root/logs/proxy-errors
```

✦ Change `CacheRoot` to the directory in which you want the CERN HTTP server to store the cached documents. For example, you can define `CacheRoot` as follows:

```
CacheRoot      /usr/local/etc/server_root
```

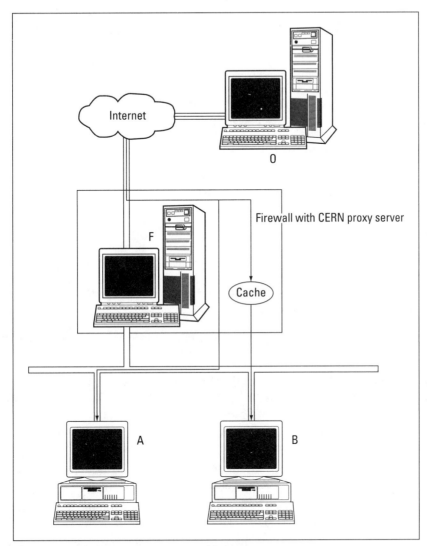

Figure 8-1: CERN HTTP server as a caching proxy server.

If you want to allow a specific set of hosts (such as those on your internal network) access to the CERN proxy server, you can specify the restrictions through the Protection directive in the caching.conf file. For example, listed here is how I ensure that only the 206.197.168 network and the noaa.gov domain can access the proxy server:

```
Protection LNB-ProxyProt {
    ServerId    lnbproxy1
    Mask        @(206.197.168.*, *.noaa.gov)
}
Protect  *  LNB-ProxyProt
```

The string `LNB-ProxyProt` identifies this protection block. `ServerId` is just an identifier sent to the client; it does not have anything to do with your Web site's name. The `Mask` directive indicates groups of IP addresses or domain names that are allowed access to the proxy server. If you do not want to restrict access to the proxy server, leave these lines untouched (by default, they are commented out).

Another important directive in the `caching.conf` file is `CacheSize`, which specifies the size of the cache in megabytes of disk space. The default setting for `CacheSize` is 5MB, but if you plan to use CERN HTTP server as a caching proxy server, consider increasing `CacheSize` to 50MB (or even 100MB).

To start the CERN HTTP server as a caching proxy server, log in as `root` and start the `httpd` program with the following commands:

```
cd /usr/local/etc/server_root
bin/httpd -r config/caching.conf
```

You can test the proxy server by running a proxy-capable Web browser (such as Netscape Navigator 2.0 or later) on one of the systems on your network (a system that does not have a direct Internet connection and has to go through the CERN proxy server to access outside Web sites).

You have to first configure Netscape Navigator to use the CERN HTTP proxy server by performing the following steps:

1. Select Network Preferences from the Option menu in Netscape Navigator. Netscape Navigator displays the Preferences dialog box. (Click on the Proxies tab to make sure that the Proxies page is visible.)

2. Click on the Manual Proxy Configuration radio button in the Preferences dialog box. That radio button appears selected after you click on it.

3. Click on the View button next to the Manual Proxy Configuration radio button. The Manual Proxy Configuration dialog box appears.

4. In the HTTP Proxy text field of the Manual Proxy Configuration dialog box, enter the IP address (or the FQDN) of the host that runs the CERN HTTP proxy server.

5. In the Port field, type 8080. (By default, the CERN HTTP proxy server listens for connections on this port.)

6. Close the dialog boxes by clicking on the OK buttons.

Now you should be able to access any Web site from that internal host using Netscape Navigator. I tested this configuration successfully with Netscape Navigator running on a Windows 95 PC as well as on a Sun workstation. Each system successfully accessed the Web through a CERN HTTP proxy server running on a Linux host (that has a direct Internet connection and that serves as the firewall).

Configuring access control in CERN HTTP server

The CERN HTTP server supports many configuration directives that let you control who has access to which documents (or directories) in your Web site. To implement access control, follow these steps:

- ✦ Define groups of users so that you can grant access to directories by group name.

- ✦ Create a password file to which the server can consult to authenticate a user.

- ✦ Use server directives to protect (or control access to) specific directories.

Creating a group file

You define groups so that you can give access to directories by group. To define groups, you have to prepare a text file that lists groups of users and gives each group a name. The following example shows the typical contents of a group file:

```
all_internal_users: @206.197.168.*
webprog: naba, leha
trusted: naba@140.90.*.*
```

The first line defines the group `all_internal_users` to be any user from the 206.197.168 Class C network. The `webprog` group refers to just two users with user IDs `naba` and `leha`. The trusted group consists of the user named `naba` on any system in the 140.90 Class B network.

You can store the group file wherever you want. However, you may want to keep them in the same directory where the server configuration files are kept (`/usr/local/etc/server_root/config` in this book's example for CERN HTTP server).

Creating a password file

If you want to grant per-user access to some files, you can create a password file and store passwords for users. Use the `htadm` utility program (in the `/usr/local/etc/server_root/bin` directory) to create and maintain the password file. For example, to create an empty password file, use the following command:

```
cd /usr/local/etc/server_root/bin
htadm -create /usr/local/etc/server_root/config/htpasswd
```

To add a user, type the following command:

```
htadm -adduser /usr/local/etc/server_root/config/htpasswd
WWW: Username: naba
Password:    (Type the password and press Enter)
Verify:      (Retype the same password)
WWW: Real name: Naba Barkakati
```

As the listing shows, the `htadm` program prompts you for the username and password. Use the `htadm -deluser` command to remove a user and type `htadm -passwd` to change a user's password.

Protecting a directory

When you control access to a directory, you want to allow a specific group of users access to it, but prohibit everyone else from accessing it. In CERN HTTP, you must use two specific directives in the configuration file to protect a directory:

✦ Embed the `Protection` directive in the configuration file to define a specific protection scheme, and give that scheme a name. A protection scheme specifies the exact details of access control (such as the group file, the password file, and the names of users or groups).

✦ Use the `Protect` directive to apply a specific protection scheme to control access to a specific directory.

The CERN HTTP software distribution comes with the `prot.conf` configuration file (in the `config` subdirectory) that shows sample use of the `Protection` and `Protect` directives. You may understand it better if I explain these directives with an example.

On a Web site, I store the documents in the `/usr/local/etc/server_root/htdocs` directory. That means in the CERN server's configuration file, I define the `Pass` directive as follows:

```
Pass    /*      /usr/local/etc/server_root/htdocs/*
```

I also have two subdirectories of information that I want to provide to a select group of users:

✦ `/usr/local/etc/server_root/htdocs/webprog` has HTML documents with information about Web programming. I want the users in the `webprog` group to access this directory.

✦ `/usr/local/etc/server_root/htdocs/lnbnews` has information of interest to all users on the internal network. Therefore, I want anyone on the internal network (206.197.168) to access this directory.

Webmaster Note that the Web browser refers to these two directories as `/webprog/` and `/lnbnews/`. However, on my Web host, the actual directory names have the `/usr/local/etc/server_root/htdocs` prefix (because the root directory of documents is `/usr/local/etc/server_root/htdocs`)

To implement this protection scheme, I first create the group file and password as illustrated in the last two sections. Then, I edit the `prot.conf` configuration file (in `/usr/local/etc/server_root/config` directory), as follows:

✦ Define `ServerRoot` as follows:

```
ServerRoot    /usr/local/etc/server_root
```

✦ Define AccessLog and ErrorLog as follows:

```
AccessLog        /usr/local/etc/server_root/logs/httpd-log
ErrorLog         /usr/local/etc/server_root/logs/httpd-errors
```

✦ Change Exec to the cgi-bin directory in the ServerRoot directory, as follows:

```
Exec    /cgi-bin/*        /usr/local/etc/server_root/cgi-bin/*
```

✦ Change the Pass directive to the name of the directory in which the HTML documents are located. For example, if you place the HTML documents in /usr/local/etc/server_root/htdocs, you should define Pass to:

```
Pass    /*        /usr/local/etc/server_root/htdocs/*
```

✦ Define the PROT-SETUP-USERS protection scheme as follows:

```
#
#        Protection setup by usernames; specify groups in the group
#        file [if you need groups]; create and maintain password file
#        with the htadm program
#
Protection PROT-SETUP-USERS {
        UserId           nobody
        GroupId          nogroup
        ServerId         LNB-Intranet
        AuthType         Basic
        PasswdFile       /usr/local/etc/server_root/config/htpasswd
        GroupFile        /usr/local/etc/server_root/config/htgroup
        GET-Mask         webprog
}
```

The GET-Mask option indicates the group that has permission to run the GET command (which the Web browser uses to retrieve a document from the Web server).

✦ Define the PROT-SETUP-HOSTS protection scheme as follows:

```
#
#        Protection setup by hosts; you can use both domain name
#        templates and IP number templates
#
Protection PROT-SETUP-HOSTS {
        UserId           nobody
        GroupId          nogroup
        ServerId         LNB-Intranet
        AuthType         Basic
        PasswdFile       /usr/local/etc/server_root/config/htpasswd
        GroupFile        /usr/local/etc/server_root/config/htgroup
        GET-Mask         @(206.197.168.*)
}
```

In this scheme, the `GET-Mask` option indicates that all users of a specific IP address range can have GET permission.

✦ Apply the `PROT-SETUP-USERS` protection to the `/webprog/` directory as follows:

```
Protect /webprog/*        PROT-SETUP-USERS
```

✦ Apply the `PROT-SETUP-HOSTS` protection to the `/lnbnews/` directory as follows:

```
Protect /lnbnews/*        PROT-SETUP-HOSTS
```

That's it! Now, only users from the IP addresses 206.197.168 network should be able to access the `/lnbnews/` URL, whereas only the `webprog` group (as defined in the group file `/usr/local/etc/server_root/config/htgroup`) can access the `/webprog/` URL.

When a user from a host with an IP address outside 206.197.168.* tries to access the `/lnbnews/` URL, the CERN HTTP server displays an error message, as shown in Figure 8-2.

On the other hand, access to the `/webprog/` directory is restricted by user (that means only specific users can access the directory). When a user tries to access the `/webprog/` URL, the CERN HTTP server prompts the user for a username and password, as shown in Figure 8-3.

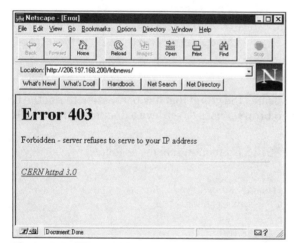

Figure 8-2: CERN HTTP server returns an error message when a user attempts access from an unauthorized IP address.

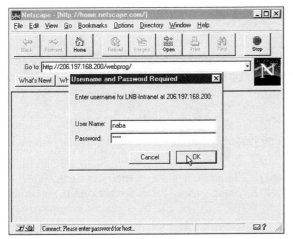

Figure 8-3: CERN HTTP server prompt for a username and password before providing access to a directory that is restricted by user.

After the user enters a username and password in the dialog box (see Figure 8-3) and clicks on the OK button, the CERN server consults the password file to authenticate the user. If the username and password match an entry in the password file (and the username is in the group that has access to the /webprog/ URL), then the CERN server gives access to that URL.

Using Access Control List

After you protect a directory with a `Protect` directive, you can further tighten access through an access control list. For example, in the previous section's example, the /lnbnews/ URL is open to all users in the 206.197.168 network. Suppose I want to allow only a handful of users access to that URL. I can do so by placing a text file named .www_acl in the /usr/local/etc/server_root/htdocs/lnbnews directory (the directory that corresponds to the /lnbnews/ URL) and putting access control information in that file.

For example, if I only wanted the users naba and leha to access the HTML documents in the /lnbnews/ URL, I could do so with the following line in the .www_acl file:

```
*.html : GET : naba, leha
```

This line says that all files with the names that match the pattern *.html can be accessed (which is what GET does) by the users naba and leha only.

Webmaster If you inadvertently place a .www_acl file in a directory that does not have a `Protect` directive in the configuration file, the CERN HTTP server will return an error message when any user attempts to access that directory.

Server Maintenance Tasks

No matter which Web server you use — NCSA, Apache, or CERN — you must perform some routine maintenance tasks as a Webmaster. Most of these maintenance tasks have to do with the log files that the Web server generates. Listed here are typical Web-server maintenance tasks:

✦ Manage the log files so they don't grow in size and fill up the disk.

✦ Analyze the log files to generate various statistics to help you understand how the Web site is being used.

✦ If users report performance problems (or you find problems during your own tests), adjust some of the system parameters to optimize the server's performance.

Manage log files

Both NCSA HTTPD and Apache servers share the same original design and generate log files with similar formats. By default, these Web servers generate three log files (usually located in the `/usr/local/etc/httpd/logs` directory):

✦ `access_log` is a record of all accesses to the server. This file contains a one-line entry for each access to the server.

✦ `agent_log` contains the names of clients (Web browsers) that have accessed the server. This file contains a one-line entry that contains the name of the Web browser each time the browser accesses the server.

✦ `error_log` is a log of error messages that includes any failed accesses due to authorization failure (when a user attempts to access a protected directory, but fails to provide a valid username and password), server restarts, and other program errors.

✦ `referer_log` is a log of the URLs that refers to Web pages on your server.

The basic maintenance task is to ensure that these log files do not grow too much in size. Of the four log files, `access_log` is the biggest because it records each access to the server. The `agent_log` and `referer_log` files are about the same size and usually half the size of the `access_log` file. The `error_log` file should not be too large because it only records problems. If the `error_log` file is growing in size, that may indicate some fundamental problem such as errors in access control (for example, someone trying to override the global access control directives).

One strategy for reducing the storage requirements of log files is to eliminate some of the files. For example, if you don't care to know what Web browser your users use, you can safely eliminate the `agent_log` file (just comment out the `AgentLog` directive in the configuration file and restart the server with the `kill -HUP` command). Similarly, if you do not need to know how the users reach your site, you do not need the `referer_log` file.

Note The two log files that are essential are the `access_log` and `error_log` files. The `access_log` file tells you who is visiting your site and how often; the `error_log` file is essential in determining whether your Web server is working properly.

Webmaster The `access_log` file typically grows by 1MB for each 10,000 requests. You need to periodically replace the `access_log` and `error_log` files; they can get too big and they may be full of information you don't need.

Webmaster The proper way to remove a log file is to use the mv command to rename the current log file and then restart the server. The following commands illustrate how to replace the current log file:

```
cd /usr/local/etc/httpd/logs
mv access_log access_log.old; kill -HUP 'cat httpd.pid'
```

You can save the old log file for a while and eventually archive it to a tape or delete it. (Note that the `httpd.pid` file in the logs directory contains the process ID of the NCSA, Apache, or CERN Web server.) Many Webmasters use this method of moving the log file and restarting the server to replace (and backup) their log files on a nightly basis.

Analyze log files

You need to analyze the contents of the log files to make sure the Web server is up and running and to extract information that can help you understand how users are using the information you provide through your Web site.

Each log file helps you with some aspect of your Webmaster job. Consider, for example, the `referer_log` file that tells you which Web site sent a user to your site. By studying this file, you can tell who may have put links to your site or how the users are finding out about your site. Suppose a user accesses a URL at your site after performing a search at Alta Vista. Then, the entry in the `referer_log` file may look like this:

```
http://www.altavista.digital.com/cgi-bin/query?pg=q&what=web&fmt=.&q=
      %22client+server%22 -> /addl/swsarch.html
```

Everything to the left of `->` is the query to Alta Vista (this query searches for the words `client` and `server`) that resulted in the reference to the URL `/addl/swsarch.html`.

The most interesting log is the access log file. All Web servers write a one-line entry in this log file each time someone attempts to access the Web server. You can specify the access log file's name with the `TransferLog` directive in the `httpd.conf` file. By default, the Web server's access log file is named `access_log` and it's in the `logs` subdirectory of your server's root directory (the default root directory is `/usr/local/etc/httpd`).

When a Web browser connects to your Web server, the server writes an entry that has the following format:

```
dcc05211.slip.digex.net - - [13/Apr/1996:09:47:41 -0400] "GET /image/
        lnbimage.gif HTTP/1.0" 200 3575
```

The meaning of various fields of this line are as follows:

`dcc05211.slip.digex.net`
The FQDN of the host that makes the request. The Web server determines the name by reverse lookup of the IP address to hostname (usually Domain Name Service — DNS — is used to look up the IP address corresponding to a hostname). If the reverse name lookup does not succeed, this field contains the IP address.

`- -`

These two dashes represent two fields that should contain two usernames. The first dash should be a username as determined by the Web server using the RFC 931 authentication server protocol. Unfortunately, most systems do not support this protocol, so the first field is usually empty. The second dash should be the authorized username used to access the file. You'll see a name here for URLs that are in a directory with access control.

`[13/Apr/1996:09:47:41 -0400]`
This is the date and time of the access request. The date is April 13, 1996, and the local time is 9:47:41 (time is reported using a 24-hour clock). The `-0400` is the offset of the local time from GMT (it says the local time is obtained by subtracting four hours from GMT). Because this system is on the East Coast of the United States and daylight saving time is in effect, the local time is four hours ahead of GMT.

`"GET /image/lnbimage.gif HTTP/1.0"`
This is the HTTP request sent by the Web browser to the Web server. In this case, the first word is GET to indicate that this is a request to get a document from the server. The second field of the request is the URL of the document. The third and final field of the request indicates the protocol being used for the request. In this case, the client is using Version 1.0 of HTTP.

`200`
This is the Web server's response code sent to the Web browser. Response code 200 means everything is OK. Other common response codes include the following:

- 302–URL redirected to another document

- 304–Document unchanged since last access (used for caching)

- 400–Bad request received

- 401–Authorization required for this URL

- 403–Access to document forbidden

- 404–Document not found

- 500–Server error

- 501–Application method (GET or POST) not implemented

- 503–Server is out of resources

```
3575
```
This shows the number of bytes transferred to the client.

This log file is the one you need to analyze so you can determine how your Web site is being used. In particular, what you want to know is how many people are visiting your Web site and which documents are they accessing the most.

Webmaster You may think that the most obvious way to count the number of visitors to your site is by the number of lines in the access log (for example, by using the wc command in UNIX). Unfortunately, that type of count will grossly exaggerate the actual number of visitors to your site. Each time someone accesses one of your site's Web pages, the log shows an entry for the initial document as well as a separate entry for each image in that document. Thus, if a page has five images, the access log shows six entries when a single user accesses that page.

You need a more careful analysis of the log file to determine how many unique users may have visited your site. Because the popular Web servers (Apache and NCSA HTTPD) use a standard format and filename for the access log, many developers have written programs that can analyze the log file and generate various reports.

For a complete list of Web-server log analysis tools, visit the following URL at YAHOO!:

```
http://www.yahoo.com/Computers_and_Internet/Internet/World_Wide_Web/HTTP/
        Servers/Log_Analysis_Tools/
```

At this URL, you'll find over two dozen links, each pointing to a log analysis tool. The following is a list of some of the more popular Web server log analysis tools:

✦ analog, written by Stephen Turner of the University of Cambridge Statistical Laboratory, is a C program that can analyze NCSA format log files and generate reports as an HTML document that you can view in any Web browser. The analog program is fast compared to other log analysis tools. To learn more about analog, visit the URL http://www.statslab.cam.ac.uk/~sret1/analog/.

✦ getstats, written by Kevin Hughes of Enterprise Information Technology, is a C program that analyzes Web server logs and generates server statistics (it's shown in YAHOO! as EIT's Getstats). For more information about getstats, visit the URL http://www.eit.com/software/getstats/. From this Web page, you can read the license agreement and download the program.

✦ wusage, developed by Thomas Boutell, is a C program that analyzes server access logs and generates GIF images showing graphs of server statistics. You can download an evaluation copy of wusage from the URL http://www.boutell.com/wusage/.

✦ wwwstat, developed by Roy Fielding of the University of California, Irvine, is a Perl program that can analyze NCSA HTTPD compatible log files (that means wwwstat can handle Apache server logs also). To learn more about wwwstat and to download the software, visit the URL http://www.ics.uci.edu/WebSoft/wwwstat/. Qiegang Long at the University of Massachusetts, Amherst, has developed a companion program called gwstat that takes the output from wwwstat and generates a set of GIF images with graphs that show server traffic by hour, day, week, or client's domain. To learn more about gwstat, visit the URL http://dis.cs.umass.edu/stats/gwstat.html.

Most of these log analysis tools generate similar statistics, so you can use any one you choose. I used the analog program because it is very fast. For example, analog processed a log with 2,700 entries (totaling 235K in size) and generated an HTML report in a second.

To download and install analog on your system, follow these steps (the examples are based on installation on a Linux system):

1. Get the 71K analog.1.2.6.tar.gz file from one of the following sites (choose the site nearest to you):

Location	URL
Austria	http://gd.tuwien.ac.at/infosys/logeval/analog/
Germany	ftp://mabuse.phil.uni-passau.de/pub/mirrors/analog/index.html
Russia	http://www.gamesdomain.ru/analog/
Sweden	http://ftp.sunet.se/pub/www/utilities/analog/
UK	http://www.statslab.cam.ac.uk/~sret1/analog/ http://www.gamesdomain.co.uk/analog/
USA	http://www.gamesdomain.com/analog/

If you want to get the analog program by anonymous FTP, you can download it from ftp.statslab.cam.ac.uk/pub/users/sret1/analog/.

2. Move the analog.1.2.6.tar.gz file to a directory in which you keep such utility programs (I keep them in /usr/local/src), and then use gunzip followed by tar to extract the files. Listed here are the commands I use on a Linux system:

```
mv analog.1.2.6.tar.gz /usr/local/src
cd /usr/local/src
gunzip analog.1.2.6.tar.gz
tar xvf analog.1.2.6.tar
```

These commands create a subdirectory named `analog` in `/usr/local/src;` in that subdirectory the commands place the source files for the `analog` tool.

3. Create the directory `/usr/local/etc/httpd/analog` and copy the `domains.tab` file to that directory, as follows:

```
mkdir /usr/local/etc/httpd/analog
cp domains.tab /usr/local/etc/httpd/analog
```

4. Edit the header file `analhead.h` and check the definition of the macros DOMAINSFILE and LOGFILE, which specify the location of the `domians.tab` file and the access log file. You should also change the definitions of HOSTNAME and HOSTURL to match your Web server's hostname and URL.

5. Build the program with the following command:

```
make
gcc           -02        -c alias.c
gcc           -02        -c analog.c
gcc           -02        -c formgen.c
gcc           -02        -c hash.c
gcc           -02        -c init.c
gcc           -02        -c output.c
gcc           -02        -c sscanf.c
gcc           -02        -c utilities.c
gcc           -02        alias.o analog.o formgen.o hash.o init.o
          output.o sscanf.o utilities.o -o analog
```

As long as your system has the GNU C compiler (GCC), `make` should succeed. If you do not have GCC, you must edit the `Makefile` and provide appropriate compiler options.

When you finish building `analog`, type `analog` to run it. By default, it sends its output to `stdout` (the display screen). To save the report in a file, redirect the output to the file, as follows:

```
analog > lnbstat_13Apr96.html
```

Then, you can view the report with a Web browser on any system.

Summary

Until April 1996, the NCSA Web server was the most popular Web server on the Internet (as reported by The Netcraft Web Server Survey, `http://www.netcraft. co.uk/Survey/`). However, since April 1996, the Apache HTTP server has overtaken the NCSA Web server when it comes to installed base. Additionally, the original Web server from CERN continues to enjoy a small but devoted installed base. This chapter shows you how to download and install the Apache and CERN HTTP servers. The next chapter focuses on an important aspect of setting up a Web site — how to maintain a presence on the Internet without jeopardizing the security of your organization's internal network.

Where to go next . . .

✦ To learn how to keep your internal network secure while you set up shop on the Internet, read Chapter 9.

✦ If you want to move on to HTML authoring, read Chapter 10.

✦ To learn more about specific HTML features, read one of Chapters 11 through 17.

✦   ✦   ✦

Securing Your Web Site

Chapters 7 and 8 show you how to install and configure a Web server on your system. After you install and test the Web server, you may think you are ready to move on to preparing your site's content. However, before you proceed to prepare HTML documents, you should pay attention to one more crucial detail — security.

By its very nature, an Internet connection makes your system accessible to any other system on the Internet. The Internet connects a large number of networks across the globe. In fact, the client/server architecture of Internet information services (such as FTP and HTTP) relies on the wide-open network access that the Internet provides. Unfortunately, the easy accessibility to Internet services running on your system also means that anyone on the Net can easily access your system.

As a Webmaster who provides information to others, you certainly want everyone to access your system's Internet services (such as FTP and Web servers). However, these servers often have vulnerabilities that unscrupulous users can exploit and cause harm to your system. You need to know about the potential security problems of the Internet services and the precautions you can take to minimize the risk of someone exploiting the weaknesses of the FTP or Web server.

You may also want to protect your company's internal network from outsiders even though your goal is to provide information to the outside world through a Web server. You can protect your internal network by setting up an Internet firewall — a controlled access point to the internal network — and place the Web server on a host outside the firewall.

This chapter provides the information you need to secure Internet services running on your Web server. You also learn about setting up an Internet firewall and running a Web server on the firewall where users cannot break through and access your company's internal network.

Internet Security Issues

The issue of security comes up when you connect your organization's internal network to the Internet. This happens to be true even if you connect a single computer to the Internet. However, the security concerns are more acute when an entire internal network is potentially opened up to the world (because you connect that network to the Internet). If your organization's network is not already connected to the Internet, it will become connected if you decide to set up a Web server on one of the systems and make the Web server accessible to anyone on the Internet.

If you are an experienced Webmaster, you already know that when you seek management approval for a Web presence on the Internet, it's not the cost that worries the corporate management; their main concern is security. To get your management's backing for the Web site, lay out a plan to keep the corporate network secure.

You may think that a way to avoid jeopardizing the internal network is to connect only the Web server host to the Internet, as shown in Figure 9-1. This simplistic approach of total separation between the internal network and your Web server is not a wise approach. The decision to separate is like deciding not to drive because you may have an accident. Besides, not having a network connection between your Web server and your internal network has the following drawbacks:

✦ You cannot use network file transfers (such as FTP) to copy documents and data from your internal network to the Web server.

✦ Users on the internal network cannot access the corporate Web server.

✦ Users on the internal network do not have access to any Web servers on the Internet. Such a restriction makes a valuable resource — the Web — inaccessible to the users in your organization.

A practical solution to this problem is to set up an Internet firewall and then put the Web server on a highly-secured host outside the firewall. You'll find more information about firewalls in the next section "Internet Firewalls."

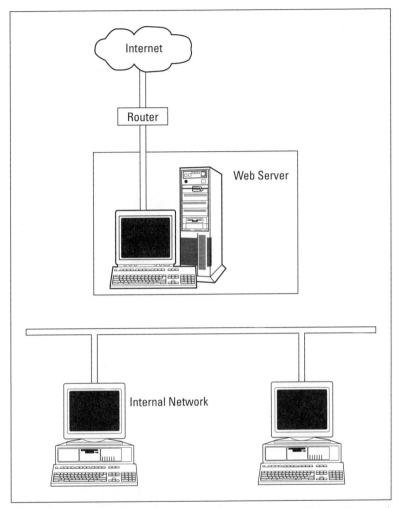

Figure 9-1: Total separation between Web server host and internal network protects the internal network.

With a firewall in place, the strategy is to run the Internet information services (such as FTP server and Web server) on a system that's outside the firewall. This system serves as your Internet host and is accessible to anyone on the Internet. This means that anyone can exploit existing security vulnerabilities in the Internet information services that you run on your Internet host. You need to learn about these vulnerabilities and take the necessary precautions to plug any security holes. The "Web Server Security" section includes information on securing the HTTP server.

Firewall terminology

Computer magazines and experts on Internet firewall technology use a number of terms with unique meanings. You need to know these terms to understand discussions about firewalls (and to effectively communicate with the firewall vendors).

Term	Meaning
Application gateway	A proxy service that acts as a gateway for application-level protocols such as FTP, Gopher, and HTTP.
Bastion host	A highly secured computer that serves as an organization's main point of presence on the Internet. A bastion host typically resides on the perimeter network, but a dual-homed host is also a bastion host.
DMZ	Another name for the perimeter network. (DMZ stands for *De-Militarized Zone* — the buffer zone separating North and South Korea.)
Dual-homed host	A computer with two network interfaces (think of each network as a home).
Firewall	A controlled access gateway between an organization's internal network and the Internet.
Host	A computer on any network (called a host because it offers many services).
Packet	A collection of bytes that serve as a basic unit of communication on a network. On TCP/IP networks, the packet may be referred to as an IP packet or a TCP/IP packet.
Packet filtering	Selective blocking of packets based on the type of packet (as specified by the source and destination IP address or port).
Perimeter network	A network between the Internet and the protected internal network. The bastion host resides on the perimeter network.
Proxy server	A server on the bastion host that lets internal clients access external servers (and let external clients access servers inside the protected network). Various Internet services (such as FTP, HTTP, and Gopher) have proxy servers.
Screening router	An Internet router that filters packets.

Internet Firewalls

An Internet firewall is an intermediary between your internal network and the Internet. The firewall controls access to and from the protected internal network.

If you connect an internal network directly to the Internet, make sure that every system on the internal network is properly secured — this can be nearly impossible to do because it takes only one careless user to make the entire internal network vulnerable. With a firewall, you have a single point of connection to the Internet and you can spend all of your efforts to make that firewall system a daunting barrier to external users.

The firewall's job is to keep outside users out but let internal users access selected information services on the Internet. To be useful, a firewall should have the following general characteristics:

✦ Must control the flow of packets between the Internet and the internal network.

✦ Must not provide dynamic routing because dynamic routing tables are subject to *route spoofing* — use of fake routes by intruders. Instead, the firewall should use static routing tables (set up by the `route` command on UNIX systems).

✦ Must not allow any external user log in as `root`. That way, even if the firewall system is compromised, the intruder may not be able to become `root` from a remote login.

✦ Must be kept in a physically secure location.

✦ Must distinguish between packets that come from the Internet or from the internal protected network. This feature allows the firewall to reject packets that come from the Internet but which have an IP address of a trusted system on the internal network (an attack where packets use fake IP addresses is called *IP spoofing*).

✦ Should act as the SMTP mail gateway for the internal network. The `sendmail` software should be set up so that all outgoing appears to come from the firewall system.

✦ Should not have any user accounts. However, the firewall system may need to have a few user accounts for those internal users who need access to external systems and external users who need access to the internal network.

✦ Should keep a log of all system activities such as successful and unsuccessful login attempt.

✦ Should provide Domain Name Service to the outside world for any host names that should be known to the outside world.

✦ Should provide good performance so that it does not hinder the internal users access to specific Internet services (such as World Wide Web and FTP).

A firewall can take many different forms. Listed here are three common forms:

✦ *Screening router with packet filtering*: This simple form of security uses a router capable of filtering (blocking) packets based on IP addresses. Such routers are called *screening routers*.

✦ *Dual-homed host with proxy services*: A host with two network interfaces — one on the Internet and the other on the internal network — that runs proxy services that act as gateways for services such as FTP and HTTP.

✦ *Perimeter network with bastion host*: This firewall configuration includes a perimeter network between the Internet and the protected internal network. A well-secured bastion host resides on the perimeter network and provides various services.

 Tip In a large organization, you may need to isolate smaller internal networks from the corporate network using internal firewalls. You can set up internal firewalls the same way you set up Internet firewalls.

Screening router with packet filtering

If you were to directly connect your organization's internal network to the Internet, you would have to use a router to ensure proper exchange of packets between the internal network and Internet. Most routers include a facility to block packets based on the source or destination IP address (as well as port number) of a packet. The router's packet filtering capability can serve as a simple firewall. Figure 9-2 illustrates the basic concept of packet filtering.

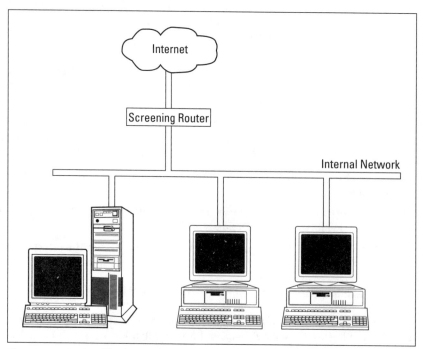

Figure 9-2: Packet filtering with a screening router provides a simple firewall.

Many router vendors (such as Cisco, 3Com, Digital, and Wellfleet) offer routers that can be programmed to perform packet filtering. The exact details of filtering depend on the router vendor, but the filtering is based on rules that refer to the basic attributes of an Internet packet as listed here:

✦ Source IP address

✦ Destination IP address

✦ Protocol (TCP, UDP, or ICMP)

✦ Source port number (if protocol is TCP or UDP)

✦ Destination port number (if protocol is TCP or UDP)

✦ ICMP message type

The router also knows the physical interface on which the packet arrived and the interface on which the packet will go out (if it is not blocked by the filtering rules).

Most packet filters operate in the following sequence:

1. You define the rules for allowing or blocking specific types of packets based on IP addresses and port numbers. These packet filtering rules are stored in the router.

2. For each packet that arrives, the screening router examines the packet's header for the information (such as IP addresses and port numbers) needed to apply the filtering rules.

3. The screening router applies the rules in the order in which they were stored.

4. If a rule allows the packet to be forwarded, the router sends the packet to its destination.

5. If a rule blocks the packet, the router drops the packet — that is, it stops processing the packet.

6. If none of the rules apply, the packet is blocked.

The last rule epitomizes the security philosophy that says "deny unless expressly permitted."

Although packet filtering with a screening router is better than having no security, packet filtering suffers from the following drawbacks:

✦ It is easy to inadvertently introduce errors in the filtering rules.

✦ Packets are filtered by their IP addresses, which represent specific hosts. Essentially, packet filtering either blocks or routes all packets from a specific host. Anyone who breaks into a trusted host can immediately gain access to the protected network.

✦ Because packet filtering is based on IP addresses, it can be defeated by a technique called *IP spoofing* — a process in which packets are sent with the IP address of a trusted host (by simply appropriating the IP address of a trusted host and setting up an appropriate route).

✦ Packet filtering is susceptible to routing attack programs that can create a bogus route that allows an intruder to receive all packets meant for a protected internal network.

✦ Screening routers that implement packet filtering do not keep logs of activities. This absence makes it hard to determine if anyone is attempting to break into the protected network. As you will see in the next section, a dual-homed host can provide logging.

✦ A screening router does not hide the host names and IP addresses of the internal network. Outsiders can access and use this information to mount attacks against the protected network.

A more sophisticated approach than using a screening router is to use an application gateway that controls network traffic based on specific applications instead of on a per packet basis. You can implement an application gateway with a dual-homed host or a bastion host.

Dual-homed host

A dual-homed host is a system with two network interfaces — one interface is connected to the Internet and the other is on an internal network that needs to be protected. The term *dual-homed* refers to the fact that the host "lives" in two networks (homes). Sometimes a dual-homed host is also called a *multihomed host*.

In fact, if the operating system supports *IP routing* — the ability to forward network packets from one interface to another — the dual-homed host can serve as a router. However, you must turn off the IP forwarding feature to use the dual-homed host as a firewall system. Many UNIX variants support the IP forwarding feature. If you plan to use a dual-homed host as the firewall, you have to reconfigure the operating system to disable IP forwarding.

With IP forwarding turned off, systems on both networks — the internal network as well as the Internet — can reach the dual-homed host, but no one from the Internet can access the internal network (nor can anyone from the internal network access the Internet). In this configuration, the dual-homed host completely isolates the two networks. Figure 9-3 illustrates the basic architecture of a dual-homed host.

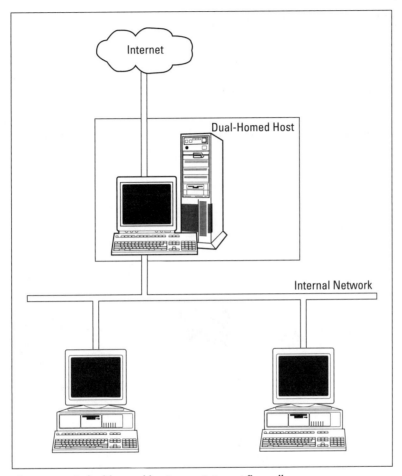

Figure 9-3: A dual-homed host as an Internet firewall.

The firewall function of the dual-homed host is implemented by running application gateways — proxy services — on the dual-homed host. These proxy services allow specific applications (such as FTP and HTTP) to work across the dual-homed host. This means that the firewall can be configured such that internal clients (on the internal network) can access Web servers on the Internet.

Caution This also means that your public Web site can run on the dual-homed host and be accessible to everyone on the Internet. Note that you should not allow user logins on the dual-homed host. Anyone logged into the host can get access to both the internal network as well as the Internet. Because the dual-homed host is your only barrier between the Internet and the internal network, it's best not to increase the chances of break-in by allowing users to log into the firewall system. If you have user accounts, you increase the chances of an intruder gaining access to the firewall by cracking one of the users' passwords.

Perimeter network with bastion host

Often an Internet firewall is more complicated than a single dual-homed host that connects to both the Internet and the protected internal network. In particular, if you provide a number of Internet services, you may need more than one system to host the services. For example, you may have two systems: one to run the Web and FTP servers and the other to provide mail (SMTP) and domain name service (DNS). In this case, you would place these two systems on a network that sits between the Internet and the internal network. Figure 9-4 illustrates this concept of an Internet firewall.

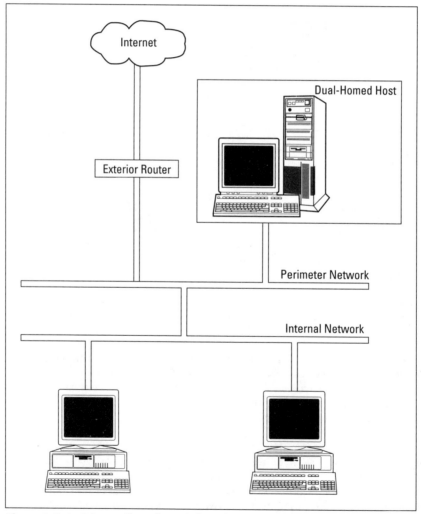

Figure 9-4: An Internet firewall consisting of a perimeter network and bastion hosts.

As Figure 9-4 illustrates, the firewall consists of a perimeter network that connects to the Internet through an exterior router. The perimeter network, in turn, connects to the internal network through an interior router. The perimeter network has one or more hosts that run Internet services including proxy services that allow internal hosts access to Web servers on the Internet.

Note The term *bastion host* is used to describe any system on the perimeter network because such a system is on the Internet and must be protected. The dual-homed host is also a bastion host because the dual-homed host is also accessible from the Internet and must be protected.

Note In the firewall configuration of Figure 9-4, the perimeter network is called a *DMZ (De-Militarized Zone)* network because that network acts as a buffer between the Internet and the internal network (just as the real-life DMZ sits between North and South Korea).

Typically, you would combine packet filtering with a bastion host. The external router is typically provided by your Internet Service Provider. You do not have much control over that router's configuration. Because you provide the internal router, you can choose a screening router and employ some packet filtering rules on the router. For example, you would typically employ the following packet filtering rules:

✦ From the internal network, allow only packets addressed to the bastion host.

✦ From the DMZ, allow only packets originating from the bastion host.

✦ Block all other packets.

These rules ensure that the internal network communicates with the bastion host (or hosts, if you have more than one bastion host) only. Like the dual-homed host, the bastion host also runs an application gateway that provides proxy services for various Internet services such as TELNET, FTP, SMTP, and HTTP.

Application gateway

The bastion host or the dual-homed host is the system that acts as the intermediary between the Internet and the protected internal network. As such, that system serves as the internal network's gateway to the Internet. To fulfill the gateway role, the system runs software to forward and filter TCP/IP connections for various services such as TELNET, FTP, and HTTP. The software for forwarding and filtering TCP/IP connections for specific applications is known as proxy services. Figure 9-5 illustrates a proxy server's role in a firewall.

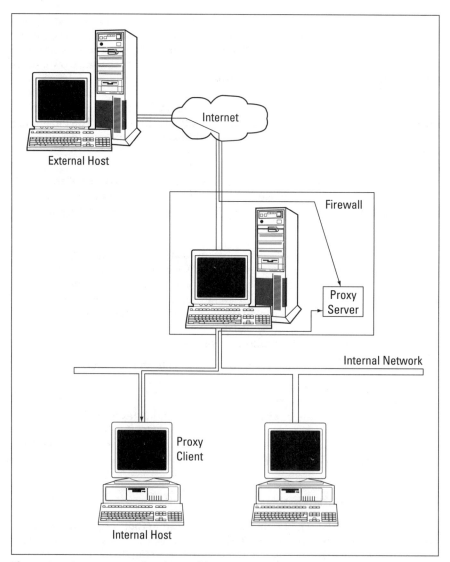

Figure 9-5: A proxy server lets internal hosts access Internet servers.

As Figure 9-5 shows, a proxy server accepts a connection for a specific protocol (such as FTP) and forwards the request to another server. In other words, the proxy server acts as a proxy for an actual server. Because it acts as a gateway for a specific application (such as TELNET or FTP), a proxy server is also known as an *application gateway*.

Unlike a screening router that blocks packets only by their information in the packet header (such as source and destination IP addresses), a proxy server actually uses the packet's data to decide what to do. For example, a proxy server does not blindly forward packets to an Internet services. The proxy server can enforce a site's security policy and disallow certain operations, depending on the specific application. For example, an FTP proxy server can stop users (from internal networks) from using the FTP `put` command to send files out to the Internet.

The typical steps involved in accessing an Internet service through a proxy server can be a bit more involved than directly accessing that service. For example, a user on the internal network can establish a TELNET session with an Internet host by following these steps:

1. The user establishes a TELNET session with the *firewall host* — the system that runs the TELNET proxy. To do this, the user enters a username and password so that the firewall host can verify that the user has permission to connect to the Internet.

2. The user enters a command (that the TELNET proxy accepts) to connect to the Internet host. The TELNET proxy, in turn, establishes a TELNET connection between itself and the Internet host.

3. The TELNET proxy on the firewall begins passing packets back and forth between the Internet host and the user's system. The TELNET proxy passes packets until the user ends the TELNET session with the Internet host.

Besides acting as a gateway, the TELNET proxy also logs the user's session with the Internet host. The logging is part of an application gateway's security feature because the log file keeps track of all firewall accesses (as well as attempted accesses that may fail because of a wrong username or password).

Although the TELNET session involves two steps — first establishing a TELNET session with the firewall host and then connecting to the Internet host — the process of accessing services through a proxy need not be too cumbersome. The exact steps of accessing services through a firewall depend on the proxy software and the client program used to access a service. With the right client program, proxies can be transparent to the user. For example, the Netscape Navigator Web browser makes it easy to access a Web site through an HTTP proxy. Just indicate, through a menu choice, the HTTP proxy you want to use.

Firewall software

You need some sort of proxy or application gateway software to make the firewall work. (I prefer to use the generic term *firewall software* to refer to the proxy software.) The primary purpose of the proxy software is to allow internal users to access servers on the Internet.

Listed here are the most popular firewall software packages (all freely available on the Internet):

✦ *CERN HTTP server.* This Web server supports a proxy mode in which it can handle requests for documents made by Web browsers on the internal network. Chapter 8 describes how to set up and use the CERN HTTP server in proxy mode.

✦ *SOCKS:* This is a general-purpose proxy system that relays TCP data streams from a client (inside the firewall) to the Internet and back. To use the SOCKS proxy, users need versions of the client programs (TELNET, Web browser) linked with the SOCKS library.

✦ *TIS Firewall Toolkit (FWTK):* This freeware software package from Trusted Information Systems (TIS) includes several proxy servers. With TIS FWTK proxies, users can use unmodified versions of client programs to access Internet services, but the access becomes a two-step process — users must first log into the firewall before they can connect to the Internet service.

The "Firewall Installation Example" section describes how to set up a dual-homed host with a SOCKS proxy as well as the TIS Firewall Toolkit.

SOCKS

SOCKS is a freely available software package (originally developed by David and Michelle Koblas and currently maintained by Ying-Da Lee) that acts as a generic proxy for Internet services such as HTTP, FTP, and TELNET. At this writing, SOCKS Version 4 (SOCKS4) is the most commonly used version of SOCKS. However, SOCKS Version 5 (SOCKS5) is in beta testing and should become prevalent soon.

SOCKS5 improves upon SOCKS4 in the following ways:

✦ SOCKS4 can act as proxy for TCP connections only, but SOCKS5 can provide proxy service for UDP as well. Utilities such as `ping` and `traceroute` use UDP (connectionless protocol) whereas services such as FTP, TELNET, and HTTP use TCP (connection-oriented protocol).

✦ SOCKS5 includes username/password authentication.

✦ SOCKS5 clients can use a SOCKS5 server to perform DNS name lookups whereas SOCKS4 clients must be able to resolve any hostname (convert a hostname to an IP address) on its own.

URL   Because of its popularity, SOCKS has become the de facto standard proxy software for Internet firewalls. An Internet Draft has been written, proposing SOCKS5 as an Internet standard for proxy services. You can find the latest drafts at the URL `http://www.socks.nec.com/draft/`. For a host of other information that supplements this section's brief description of SOCKS, visit the URL `http://www.socks.nec.com/`.

What does SOCKS stand for?

According to the SOCKS Frequently Asked Questions (FAQ), the name SOCKS came from parts of the word **sock**ets. That name was used during the software's development and the name stuck.

If you want to read the SOCKS FAQ, you can find the latest FAQ files at `http://www.socks.nec.com/ftp/`.

SOCKS5 supports what is known as authenticated traversal of multiple firewalls (or Authenticated Firewall Traversal or AFT). This is just a fancy way of saying that you can connect several SOCKS5 servers in sequence and still maintain the firewall security. By hooking up the SOCKS5 proxy servers, you can build a virtual private network that connects two or more geographically separate networks (see Figure 9-6).

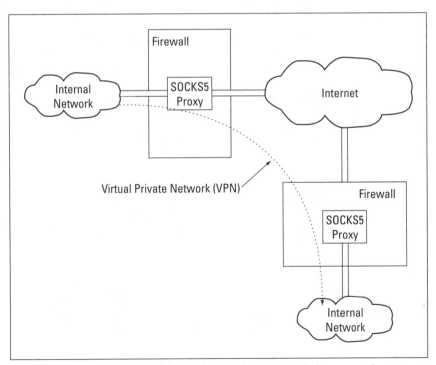

Figure 9-6: Using SOCKS5 to build a virtual private network that spans the Internet.

URL The SOCKS4 software package (as well as the Beta version of SOCKS5) is available from `http://www.socks.nec.com/ftp/socks4/socks.cstc.4.2.tar.gz`. Use your Web browser to visit the URL `http://www.socks.nec.com/socks4.html`. The relative Web page has the links to download the SOCKS4 software package. If you prefer to download the code through anonymous FTP, connect to `ftp.nec.com` and look for the files in `/pub/security/socks.cstc` directory.

The SOCKS4 software can work on a wide variety of UNIX systems including SunOS 4.1.3, Solaris 2.3 and 2.4, HP-UX 9.0.5, AIX, IRIX, Linux, SCO Open Desktop, DEC OSF/1, Ultrix 4.3, and FreeBSD.

The SOCKS4 software has the following components:

✦ *SOCKS Server*. The generic SOCKS proxy server. Clients use the SOCKS client library to communicate with the SOCKS server, which, in turn, provides access to the Internet services such as TELNET, FTP, and HTTP.

✦ *SOCKS Client Library*. A nearly compatible replacement for standard Berkeley socket functions such as `bind`, `connect`, `accept`, and `listen`.

✦ *SOCKS-ified Clients*: Standard clients such as TELNET and FTP that have been linked with the SOCKS library. The *SOCKS-ified* adjective is used to refer to client programs that have been linked with the SOCKS client library.

Because SOCKS provides a single generic proxy server, the basic arrangement of a SOCKS firewall is as shown in Figure 9-7. As Figure 9-7 illustrates, all clients know the protocol for communicating with the SOCKS server and the SOCKS server can handle connections to many Internet services including TELNET, FTP, and HTTP.

SOCKS allows users on the protected network transparent access to servers on the Internet, provided the user runs a SOCKS-ified client. (You can use the SOCKS server's configuration file to control the hosts that can access the Internet.) To SOCKS-ify a client, the client program needs to be compiled and linked with the SOCKS library. This process replaces the standard Berkeley sockets calls with SOCKS version calls. (Chapter 1 describes the Berkeley sockets.)

Of course, a client program can be recompiled only if you have the source code for the client program. Because SOCKS is popular, many vendors already include SOCKS support in their clients. For example, the Netscape Navigator 2.0 Web browser includes support for SOCKS — you just have to specify the SOCKS server in Navigator's Network options. The "Firewall Installation Examples" section shows how to set up a SOCKS server on a Linux system.

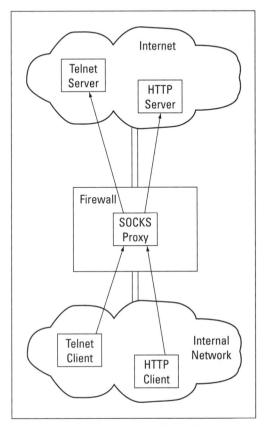

Figure 9-7: In a SOCKS firewall, all clients go through the same proxy server.

TIS Firewall Toolkit

The TIS Firewall Toolkit from Trusted Information Systems includes a number of proxy servers that work with the standard client programs. While SOCKS provides a single proxy that works for all TCP connections, TIS Firewall Toolkit provides individual proxy servers for each service such as FTP, HTTP, TELNET, and Gopher. For example, `tn-gw` is the TELNET proxy and `http-gw` is the HTTP and Gopher proxy. Figure 9-8 shows the architecture of the TIS Firewall Toolkit proxy servers. As Figure 9-8 shows, each client works through a specific proxy server dedicated to handle that client's protocol.

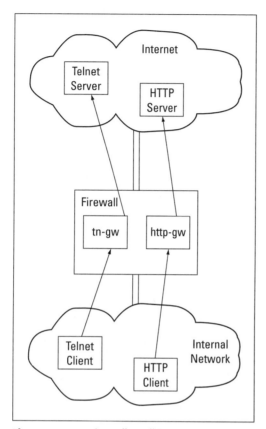

Figure 9-8: TIS Firewall Toolkit provides proxy servers for each client.

TIS Firewall Toolkit allows the use of standard (unmodified) client applications to access Internet services. However, users must first access the proxy server and then initiate connection to the server on the Internet. For example, when a user on the internal network wants to use TELNET to connect to an external host, the user has to go through the following two-step process:

1. The user runs TELNET and connects to the bastion host where the TELNET proxy (tn-gw) runs. The tn-gw proxy asks for username and password and authenticates the user.

2. The user types the connect remotehost (where remotehost is the external host's name) command at the proxy prompt (tn-gw>). The TELNET proxy establishes the connection between the user's system and the external host.

The user follows similar steps to use the FTP proxy (ftp-gw).

Cross Ref You learn how to install TIS Firewall Toolkit in the "Firewall Installation Examples" section.

More on Internet security and firewalls

This chapter gives you an overview of Internet firewalls and shows you how to set up the TIS Firewall Toolkit on a Linux system. This one chapter cannot list all the information that you need to know about firewalls and Internet security. Because of the Internet's popularity, you can find quite a few resources about Internet security and firewalls, ranging from books to FTP sites. The following is a short list of Internet firewall resources:

✦ **Books:** You can choose from several popular books on Internet security and firewalls. One of the most definitive guides on this subject is the recent book by D. Brent Chapman and Elizabeth Zwicky. This book includes detailed information about firewall design and implementation, including a lengthy chapter on how to configure various Internet services. The book by K. Siyan and C. Hare covers the basics of firewalls; it also provides a list of commercial firewall vendors.

[1] D. Brent Chapman and Elizabeth D. Zwicky, *Building Internet Firewalls*, O'Reilly & Associates, Inc., 1995.

[2] K. Siyan and C. Hare, *Internet Firewalls and Network Security*, New Riders Publishing, 1995.

✦ **Internet Resources:** A number of Web and FTP sites contain information about Internet security in general and firewalls in particular. The following list uses the Uniform Resource Locator (URL) syntax. You can use a Web browser (such as Netscape, Mosaic, or Lynx) and enter the URL as shown. The browser then displays appropriate information about the contents of the site. In particular, to keep up with the latest security problems, visit the CERT home page (`http://www.cert.org/`) and read the CERT summaries posted periodically at CERT's FTP site. (CERT once stood for Computer Emergency Response Team, but today it is simply CERT — a service mark of Carnegie Mellon University.)

```
ftp://ftp.greatcircle.com/
       pub/firewalls/FAQ
http://www.netcraft.co.uk/
       security/http/
http://www.netcraft.co.uk/
       security/diary.html
http://www.cert.org/
ftp://info.cert.org/pub/
       cert_summaries/
```

Firewall Installation Examples

Now that you have an overview of Internet firewalls, you are ready for some concrete examples of firewalls. An ideal host for a firewall is a dual-homed host — a UNIX system with one network connection to the Internet and another to your organization's internal network. A cost effective choice is a Pentium PC running Linux.

For the examples in the following sections, I use the following system configuration:

✦ A 75MHz Pentium PC with 16MB of RAM and two 500MB hard disk drives.

✦ Linux 1.2.13 operating system. (Linux is a UNIX clone for 386, 486, and Pentium PCs.)

✦ A 3Com 3C509 Ethernet card that connects the PC to the internal Ethernet network.

✦ A PPP connection to an Internet Service Provider through a 28.8 Kbps modem.

The other systems on my internal Ethernet network include several PCs running Windows 95, a Sun workstation, and a Macintosh. In setting up the Linux system as a firewall, my goal is to allow users on the internal systems to run Web browsers and TELNET and access any host on the Internet.

Linux is freely available from the Internet, or you can buy a book with Linux on a CD-ROM. (For example, this book's companion CD-ROM includes Slackware Linux. If you need detailed instructions on installing Linux, consider my recent book, *Linux SECRETS*, published by IDG Books, which includes the latest Slackware Linux distribution on a CD-ROM and comes with detailed installation instructions.)

Tip When you use Linux as the operating system for a dual-homed firewall host, you must configure Linux to turn off the *IP Forwarding/Gatewaying* and turn on *IP Firewalling*. This step requires that you recompile Linux so that Linux does not automatically forward IP packets from one network interface to another (use the firewall software to control what IP packets pass between the two network interfaces). To complete a firewall setup, you must secure the firewall host by removing all unneeded Internet services and making sure that it runs only proxy services.

After you secure the firewall host, you need to install the firewall software. You should first make sure that both network interfaces on your Linux system work. Establish a PPP connection to your ISP and make sure that you can access other Internet hosts (try the command `ping home.netscape.com`). Also make sure that all systems on the internal network can access the Linux system and vice versa.

For firewall software, you have two good choices:

✦ *SOCKS4*: SOCKS Version 4 provides a universal proxy server that can serve as a gateway for the Web. In particular, Netscape Navigator can use the SOCKS proxy server.

✦ *TIS Firewall Toolkit*: Trusted Information Systems Firewall Toolkit provides proxy servers for specific services such as TELNET and FTP. TIS Firewall Toolkit is a good choice to provide internal users TELNET and FTP access to the Internet.

Securing the firewall host

After you configure Linux appropriately (by turning off IP Forwarding and enabling IP Firewall), secure the dual-homed host by turning off the unneeded Internet services. Then disable the following two types of services:

✦ Services are started by `inetd`. These services are listed in the `/etc/inetd.conf` file.

✦ Stand-alone daemons (servers) that are started from the startup shell scripts. In Linux, these scripts are located in the `/etc/rc.d` directory.

To turn off services in the `/etc/inetd.conf` file, put a comment character (#) in front of a service to be turned off. For example, listed here is how you comment out the TELNET service:

```
#telnet  stream  tcp  nowait  root  /usr/sbin/tcpd  /usr/sbin/in.telnetd
```

From the `/etc/inetd.conf` file, remove the following services (that is, as many as are present in your system's `inetd.conf` file):

✦ `bootp` is used to boot diskless workstations; firewall systems do not need to support this service.

✦ `finger` provides information about users; you can safely disable it.

✦ `ftp` allows you to provide FTP service through a proxy such as TIS Firewall Toolkit.

✦ `login` is a remote login service; use TIS Firewall Toolkit to provide this service.

✦ `netstat` provides information about network connections; it is not needed on a firewall.

✦ `nntp` is the news transfer protocol; it is not needed on a firewall.

✦ `ntalk` allows users to send lines of text to one another across the network; it is not needed on a firewall.

✦ `pop3` is a mail delivery protocol; you should run a properly configured sendmail program.

✦ `shell` is a remote shell service; you don't need to offer this in a firewall.

✦ `smtp` is a mail transfer protocol; you can run `sendmail` with proper security precautions.

✦ `systat` provides status information about the system; it should be turned off on a firewall.

✦ `talk` is the same as `ntalk`.

✦ telnet allows you to provide TELNET service through a proxy such as TIS Firewall Toolkit.

✦ tftp is used by diskless workstations and X terminals to download a boot program; it not needed on a firewall.

✦ uucp is a UNIX file copying protocol; it is not needed on a firewall.

After you install firewall software (such as TIS Firewall Toolkit), add the proxy services to the /etc/inetd.conf file.

Of the daemons started by the Linux startup scripts in /etc/rc.d directory, pay close attention to the ones listed in the file rc.inet2. Because the rc.inet2 file is a shell script, you can avoid starting a daemon by putting a comment character (#) on the lines that start the daemon. For example, the following shows you how to turn off the Sun RPC (Remote Procedure Call) services including NFS — Network File System:

```
# Constants.
NET="/usr/sbin"

...(Lines deleted)

# # Start the various SUN RPC servers.
# if [ -f ${NET}/rpc.portmap ]; then
#   # Start the NFS server daemons.
#   if [ -f ${NET}/rpc.mountd ]; then
#     echo -n " mountd"
#     ${NET}/rpc.mountd
#   fi
#   if [ -f ${NET}/rpc.nfsd ]; then
#     echo -n " nfsd"
#     ${NET}/rpc.nfsd
#   fi
```

Comment out the startup commands for the following servers from the rc scripts:

✦ routed

✦ rpc.mountd

✦ rpc.nfsd

✦ rpc.portmap

✦ rwhod

If you are running a Web server on the firewall system, retain the httpd startup that may be in one of these startup scripts. After you install a proxy server (such as SOCKS4), you may want to start sockd (the name of the SOCKS4 proxy server) from a startup script.

After cleaning up the /etc/inetd.conf file and the startup scripts in /etc/rc.d directory, reboot the system. Then use the command ps -aux and carefully examine the list of processes for any other servers that you should turn off.

Tip To check if any Sun RPC services are still running, type the following command (shown with the command's typical output on a Linux system):

```
/usr/sbin/rpcinfo -p
   program vers proto   port
   100000    2   tcp    111  portmapper
   100000    2   udp    111  portmapper
   100005    1   udp    653  mountd
   100005    1   tcp    655  mountd
   100003    2   udp   2049  nfs
   100003    2   tcp   2049  nfs
```

After rebooting, if you see a report such as this, you have not successfully turned off all RPC services. After you turn off all unnecessary services, install the firewall software, which includes proxy servers for some necessary services. The proxy servers allow users on the internal network access to Internet services.

Using SOCKS4

To install the SOCKS4 on the Linux system, you must first download the software. You can download the software using anonymous FTP from ftp.nec.com located in the /pub/security/socks.cstc/socks4 directory.

Download and Unpack SOCKS4

To download and unpack SOCKS4 follow these steps:

1. Download the SOCKS4 software using the following sample session as a guideline (user input appears in boldface; my comments are in italics):

```
ftp ftp.nec.com
Connected to handel.inoc.dl.nec.com.
220 handel FTP server (Version wu-2.4(3) Sun Mar 26 02:15:39 CST
     1995) ready.
Name (ftp.nec.com:naba): anonymous
331 Guest login ok, send your complete e-mail address as password.
Password: (Type your e-mail address and press Enter)
230-Welcome to the anonymous FTP database on ftp.nec.com.
230-Local time is Mon Apr  8 19:48:56 1996.
230-
230-The Socks5, SOCKS.CSTC, and SocksCap collections have
```

(continued)

```
230-moved to the /pub/socks directory.
230-
230-Drivers, updates, and technical support for NEC PC and
230-PC peripheral products can be found at:
230-    Ftp: ftp.nectech.com
230-    CompuServe: GO NECTECH
230-    BBS: 508-635-4706
230-    -->     Email: tech-support@nectech.com <-
230-Please direct questions and comments concerning PC
230-peripherals and drivers to that email address.
230-
230-==========================================================
230-ftp@ftp.nec.com
230-
230-Please read the file README
230-  it was last modified on Wed Mar  6 08:25:14 1996 - 33 days ago
230 Guest login ok, access restrictions apply.
Remote system type is UNIX.
Using binary mode to transfer files.
ftp> cd /pub/security/socks.cstc/socks4
250-This directory contains SOCKS version 4 servers.
250-
250 CWD command successful.
ftp> ls
200 PORT command successful.
150 Opening ASCII mode data connection for /bin/ls.
total 1113
-r--r--r--  1 root     0              49 Mar 20 14:08 .message
-r--r--r--  1 root     0            8230 Feb 24  1995 CHANGES.4.2
-r--r--r--  1 root     0            1670 Aug 20  1995 CHANGES.4.2.1
-r--r--r--  1 root     0            1359 Apr  3 17:41 FILES
drwxr-xr-x  2 root     0             512 Apr  3 17:35 PC_Socks_Pack
-r--r--r--  1 root     0           12071 Feb 24  1995 README.4.2
drwxr-xr-x  2 root     0             512 Apr  3 17:35 client
-r--r--r--  1 root     0          278805 Sep  6  1995
        export.socks.cstc.4.2.2.tar.gz
-r--r--r--  1 root     0          242783 Feb 24  1995
        export.socks.cstc.4.2.tar.gz
drwxr-xr-x  2 root     0            1024 Apr  3 17:48 old
-r--r--r--  1 root     0          249342 Aug 28  1995
        socks.cstc.4.2.2.tar.gz
```

```
-r--r--r--  1 root      0          30991 Aug 20  1995
        socks.cstc.4.2.p1
-r--r--r--  1 root      0           4162 Aug 28  1995
        socks.cstc.4.2.p2
-r--r--r--  1 root      0         250908 Feb 24  1995
        socks.cstc.4.2.tar.gz
226 Transfer complete.
ftp> get socks.cstc.4.2.2.tar.gz
200 PORT command successful.
150 Opening BINARY mode data connection for socks.cstc.4.2.2.tar.gz
        (249342 bytes).
226 Transfer complete.
249342 bytes received in 124 seconds (2 Kbytes/sec)
ftp> bye
 221 Goodbye.
```

After completing this step, you would have downloaded a compressed tar file (you can tell the file type from the .tar.gz extension).

2. Copy the compressed tar file to an appropriate directory such as /usr/local/src using the following command:

```
cp socks.cstc.4.2.2.tar.gz /usr/local/src
```

3. Uncompress and extract the files. On Linux, you can use the following tar command to perform both steps (uncompress and unpack) at once:

```
tar zxvf socks.cstc.4.2.2.tar.gz
```

This command creates a directory named socks.cstc.4.2.2 and places the SOCKS4 source files in that directory.

4. Set up a symbolic link to the socks.cstc.4.2.2 directory so that you can refer to this directory as socks by using the following command:

```
ln -s  socks.cstc.4.2.2 socks
```

Build the SOCKS4 proxy server

After you download and unpack the SOCKS4 software, you need to compile and link the SOCKS4 server. Read the README.4.2 file in the /usr/local/src/socks directory (if that's where you placed the SOCKS4 source code) for some guidance on how to build the SOCKS4 server.

To compile and link the server on Linux, you must first edit the Makefile file in the /usr/local/src/socks directory. (Note that the subdirectories also contain Makefile files.) Make the following changes to the Makefile file:

1. Locate the PWD variable and define it to be the directory in which you installed the SOCKS4 software. If you installed the software in /usr/local/src/socks directory, define PWD as follows:

   ```
   PWD=/usr/local/src/socks
   ```

2. Comment out the current operating system specific options. The Makefile comes with the IRIX 5 options enabled. Place a pound sign (#) in front of the lines you want to comment out.

3. To build the SOCKS4 programs under Linux, uncomment the lines that come after the following line:

   ```
   # LINUX should use
   ```

   However, leave the following commented line as is:

   ```
   #NEED_STRUCT_LINGER = -DNEED_STRUCT_LINGER
   ```

   because this line refers to a specific data structure that you do not need.

   Also, ignore the comments about the older versions of Linux; those comments do not apply to Linux 1.2.13 (the latest stable version of Linux).

4. If you want to install the server binaries anywhere other than /usr/etc, edit the SERVER_BIN_DIR variable. For example, to install the SOCKS4 server program in the /usr/local/etc directory, define SERVER_BIN_DIR as follows:

   ```
   SERVER_BIN_DIR = /usr/local/etc
   ```

Next you must edit the file socks.h in the /usr/local/src/socks/include directory (the include subdirectory of the directory in which you installed SOCKS4). Make the following changes to the socks.h file:

1. Set the macro SOCKS_DEFAULT_SERVER to the name of the host that runs the SOCKS proxy server. For example, I define SOCKS_DEFAULT_SERVER as the name of a local host as follows:

   ```
   #define SOCKS_DEFAULT_SERVER     "lnbsun"
   ```

2. Define the SOCKS_DEFAULT_NS macro as the IP address of your name server. For example, to set the default name server as 164.109.1.3, I write the following:

   ```
   #define SOCKS_DEFAULT_NS     "164.109.1.3"
   ```

3. Define the ORIG_FINGER macro as follows:

   ```
   #define ORIG_FINGER     "/usr/bin/finger.orig"
   ```

4. Because the Linux system is a dual-homed host, you have to define the macro MULTIHOMED_SERVER. Locate the line that defines the macro MULTIHOMED_SERVER and uncomment the line (remove the enclosing /* and */) so that it reads as follows:

```
#define MULTIHOMED_SERVER
```

5. By default the SOCKS server runs through inetd. For better performance, however, you can run the SOCKS server standalone. (For this choice, you pay the penalty in the memory and processing time devoted to the server at all times, even when the server is not in use.) To run the SOCKS server standalone, uncomment the following line:

```
#define NOT_THROUGH_INETD
```

After you finish editing the socks.h file, rename the finger program with the following commands (you have to log in as root):

```
cd /usr/bin
mv finger finger.orig
```

You must also make the following changes to the source code to compile the SOCKS4 code under Linux:

1. Edit the shell_cmd.c file in /usr/local/src/socks/lib directory. Comment the line that includes the <arpa/inet.h> header file and include a new header file as follows:

```
/* #include <arpa/inet.h> */
#include "/usr/src/linux/include/linux/inet.h"
```

2. Edit the sockd.c file in /usr/local/src/socks/sockd directory. Comment the line that includes the <arpa/inet.h> header file and include the following new header files as follows:

```
/* #include <arpa/inet.h> */
#include "/usr/src/linux/include/linux/inet.h"
#include "/usr/src/linux/include/linux/stat.h"
```

To make the SOCKS4 proxy server and the SOCKS4 library, type the following commands:

```
cd /usr/local/src/socks
make server
```

You'll see a number of informational messages as well as warning messages. You can safely ignore the warnings.

Install SOCKS4 proxy server

After you build the SOCKS4 server, you have to install it. To complete this step, log in as `root` and type the following commands:

```
cd /usr/local/src/socks
make install.server
```

This command copies the server program (called `sockd` and pronounced *sock-dee*) to its installation directory and installs the online documentation for SOCKS4.

Configure the SOCKS4 server

After installing the `sockd` program and its online documentation, read about the SOCKS4 server configuration file with the following command:

```
man sockd.conf
```

The online documentation tells you how to allow specific internal hosts access to the Internet through the SOCKS4 server. Before you can start the SOCKS4 server, you need two configuration files:

✦ `/etc/sockd.conf` is the SOCKS4 server configuration file that specifies which hosts can use the services of the server.

✦ `/etc/sockd.route` specifies how the SOCKS4 server should route packets on a dual-homed host.

For the `/etc/sockd.conf` file, copy the sample configuration file `sockd.conf.sample` to the `/etc/sockd.conf` as follows:

```
cd /usr/local/src/sockd
cp sockd.conf.sample /etc/sockd.conf
```

In the sample `sockd.conf` file, the first few lines are as follows:

```
# replace 'client_IP' below with an actual IP address before trying it
permit        client_IP 255.255.255.255
deny          0.0.0.0 0.0.0.0 :  (...Long shell command deleted)
```

To try out the SOCKS4 proxy server, replace the word `client_IP` with the IP address of a host on your internal network. For example, to provide access to the hosts 206.197.168.2 and 206.197.168.100 from my internal network, I put the following lines in `/etc/sockd.conf`:

```
permit        206.197.168.2      255.255.255.255
permit        206.197.168.100    255.255.255.255
```

Each of these lines permit a specific host to access the services of the SOCKS4 proxy server. The `deny` line at the end of the file (see earlier listing of `sockd.conf` file) ensures that access is denied to all other hosts.

The `/etc/sockd.route` file can be simple. To set up this file, you need the IP address for your Internet gateway (for a PPP link, this is the IP addresses of the remote end of the link). For example, if your Internet gateway address is 206.197.168.1, then the `/etc/sockd.route` file contains the following line:

```
206.197.168.1        0.0.0.0        0.0.0.0
```

This line tells the SOCKS4 proxy server to route all packets to the IP address 206.197.168.1. For detailed syntax of the `sockd.route` file, type the following command:

```
man sockd.route
```

Start SOCKS4 proxy server

To start the SOCKS4 proxy server, log in as `root` and type:

```
/usr/local/etc/sockd
```

This command assumes that you installed the server binary (named `sockd`) in the `/usr/local/etc` directory.

Test SOCKS4 proxy server

To test the SOCKS4 proxy server in action, run Netscape Navigator on one of your internal hosts whose IP address appears on a `permit` line in the `/etc/sockd.conf` file. (On my network, I ran Netscape Navigator 2.0 on a Windows 95 system.) Follow these steps to configure Netscape Navigator to use the proxy server:

1. Select Network Preferences from the Options menu. Netscape Navigator will then display the Preferences dialog box.

2. Click on the Proxy tab and then click on the Manual Proxy Configuration radio button. The Preferences dialog box now appears as shown in Figure 9-9.

3. Click on the View button next to the Manual Proxy Configuration radio button. Netscape Navigator displays a Manual Proxy Configuration dialog box, as shown in Figure 9-10.

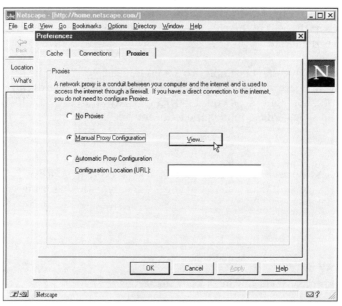

Figure 9-9: Netscape Navigator's Preferences dialog box lets you configure proxy services.

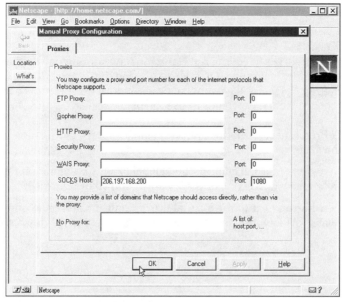

Figure 9-10: Specify the SOCKS proxy server in Netscape Navigator's Manual Proxy Configuration dialog box.

4. In the SOCKS Host text field type the IP address of the firewall host that runs the SOCKS4 proxy server. In the Port field, type 1080; it is the standard port that SOCKS clients and servers use to communicate with each other.

5. Click on the OK button to close the Manual Proxy Configuration dialog box. Then click on the OK button again in the Preferences dialog box.

URL After configuring Netscape to use the SOCKS proxy server, you can try accessing a Web site on the Internet. First try a URL with an explicit IP address. For example, try the following URL to reach the SOCKS Web page:

```
http://143.101.182.11/
```

In a more readable form that URL appears as follows:

```
http://www.socks.nec.com/
```

Webmaster Unfortunately, if you refer to a host by name instead of an IP address, the test is likely to fail unless you have a *DNS server* (also known as a *name server*) running on the internal network. If you do not have a DNS server running on the internal network, you cannot refer to hosts by name. To solve this problem, run a minimal DNS server on the Linux firewall system.

Run a minimal DNS server on the firewall

The internal hosts can use SOCKS-compliant client applications (such as Netscape Navigator) to access Internet hosts through the SOCKS4 server running on the Linux system. However, the internal hosts cannot resolve Internet host names unless they can access a DNS server that translates IP addresses to host names.

A solution to this problem is to provide a minimal DNS server on the Linux firewall host. The goal is to allow internal hosts to resolve names of outside hosts. By a minimal DNS server I mean the following implementation:

✦ Connect the Linux host to an ISP so that it has access to the ISP's name server.

✦ Set up a name server on the Linux host and use the forwarding feature (explained later in this section) to send any name server requests to the ISP's name server.

The name server program is known as named (pronounced *name-dee*); you have to configure it through the /etc/named.boot file. Because it is a text file, you can use any text editor to modify the file.

The named server has a forwarding feature that resolves name server queries (requests for IP address corresponding to a host name such as lnbsoft.com) by forwarding each query to another name server and then relaying the results back to the original requester. The idea is to use your ISP's name server to perform the actual DNS lookup; your Linux host's DNS server simply acts as an intermediary for the internal clients that require DNS service.

The DNS server (with forwarding) provides a name server proxy for clients on the internal network. When a client needs to look up a name, it sends the request to the firewall host (the client system should be configured to use the firewall system as the name server). The DNS server on the firewall forwards that request to another DNS server on the Internet (this should be the ISP's name server), gets a response back, and returns that response to the client on the internal network. This process allows the clients (such as Netscape Navigator) on the internal network to use well-known Internet host names in URLs.

Your ISP should provide you with the IP addresses of one or more name servers. To configure the `named` server as a forwarding DNS server, add a `forwarders` line with the IP addresses of your ISP's name servers. Listed here is a sample `/etc/named.boot` file that shows the syntax of the `forwarders` line:

```
;     File: /etc/named.boot
;     Boot file for name server (named)
;
forwarders 205.197.245.224 164.109.1.3 164.109.10.23 192.33.4.10
slave
```

This example shows four name servers on the `forwarders` line. Typically, you have at least two name servers — one primary and one backup — on the `forwarders` line. All name server queries will be forwarded to these name servers in the order shown. When you configure `named` on your system, use the name server addresses that your ISP provides.

As you may have guessed by looking at the sample, in the `named.boot` file, comment lines begin with a semicolon (`;`). The `slave` line specifies that the name server should be configured to use the forwarding feature only.

After you log in as `root` and prepare the `/etc/named.boot` file with the appropriate forwarders line, start the `named` server with the following command:

```
/usr/sbin/named
```

Now, clients on your internal network can refer to Internet hosts by name.

Webmaster Make sure that the internal systems are configured to use the firewall host as the DNS server. For example, on a Windows 95 system, you must specify the DNS server (through the TCP/IP Properties dialog box) that you can access through the Network icon in the Control Panel.

Tip To test the DNS server on the firewall, run Netscape Navigator on an internal system, configure it to use the SOCKS4 proxy server on the firewall, and access an Internet Web site (for example, `http://www.socks.nec.com/`).

Using TIS Firewall Toolkit

The Trusted Information Systems Firewall Toolkit (TIS FWTK) provides many separate proxy servers for services such as TELNET, rlogin, FTP, and HTTP. You can edit the /etc/inetd.conf file and replace the existing servers for these services with the proxy versions that come with TIS FWTK.

TIS Firewall Toolkit Version 1.3 includes the following proxy servers:

Proxy Server	Description
ftp-gw	FTP proxy server
http-gw	HTTP and Gopher proxy servers
plug-gw	Generic socket-to-socket proxy server
rlogin-gw	Proxy for rlogin (remote login)
tn-gw	TELNET proxy server
x-gw	Proxy for the X Window System server

The proxy servers are named with a -gw suffix to indicate that these are application gateways for specific applications such as TELNET and FTP.

To use the TIS Firewall Toolkit, you must first download the source code and build the program. To ensure controlled access, you must also edit the /usr/local/etc/netperm-table file that controls the TIS Firewall Toolkit proxy servers.

Download and unpack TIS Firewall Toolkit

The TIS Firewall Toolkit software is available through anonymous FTP from ftp.tis.com. As is customary with free software distributions on the Internet, TIS Firewall Toolkit is distributed as a compressed tar archive (the file name has a .tar.Z extension). To download and unpack TIS Firewall Toolkit, follow these steps:

1. Download TIS Firewall Toolkit from the host ftp.tis.com. Use the following listing of a sample anonymous FTP session as a guideline to complete this step (user input appears in boldface; my comments are in italics):

   ```
   ftp ftp.tis.com
   Connected to neptune.tis.com.
   220 neptune FTP server (Version 5.60mjr) ready.
   Name (ftp.tis.com:naba): anonymous
   331 Guest login ok, send ident as password.
   Password: (Type your e-mail address and press Enter)
   ```

(continued)

```
230 Guest login ok, access restrictions apply.
Remote system type is UNIX.
Using binary mode to transfer files.
ftp> cd /pub/firewalls/toolkit
250 CWD command successful.
ftp> ls
200 PORT command successful.
150 Opening ASCII mode data connection for /bin/ls.
total 3600
-rw-r--r--    1 rick      staff        9078 Nov  4  1994 CHANGES
-rw-r--r--    1 rick      staff         549 Nov  4  1994 CHECKSUMS
-rw-r--r--    1 rick      staff        1465 Nov  4  1994 DISCLAIMER
-rw-r--r--    1 rick      staff        4632 Feb 12 11:26 LICENSE
-rw-r--r--    1 rick      staff        1366 Nov  4  1994 README
drwxr-xr-x    2 rick      staff         512 Nov  4  1994 US-only
drwxr-xr-x    2 rick      staff         512 Dec 30  1994 contrib
drwxr-xr-x    2 120       daemon       1024 Apr  1 03:15 fwall-users-
        archive
-rw-r--r--    1 rick      staff      452499 Mar 31 23:26 fwtk-
        2.0alpha.tar.Z
-rw-r--r--    1 rick      staff      418175 Nov  4  1994 fwtk-doc-
        only.tar.Z
-rw-r--r--    2 rick      staff      444950 Feb 12 13:58 fwtk-
        v1.3.tar.Z
-rw-r--r--    2 rick      staff      444950 Feb 12 13:58 fwtk.tar.Z
drwxr-xr-x    2 rick      staff         512 Nov  4  1994 old-versions
drwxr-xr-x    2 rick      staff         512 Mar 17  1995 patches
226 Transfer complete.
ftp> get fwtk.tar.Z
200 PORT command successful.
150 Opening BINARY mode data connection for fwtk.tar.Z (444950
        bytes).
226 Transfer complete.
444950 bytes received in 225 secs (1.9 Kbytes/sec)
ftp> bye
221 Goodbye.
```

After completing this step, you would have downloaded TIS Firewall Toolkit.

2. Copy the `fwtk.tar.Z` file to the directory in which you want to unpack and build the software. Use the `/usr/local/src` directory as follows:

```
cp fwtk.tar.Z /usr/local/src
```

3. Uncompress the file with the following command:

```
uncompress fwtk.tar.Z
```

This command creates the `fwtk.tar` file — a `tar` archive.

4. Extract the TIS Firewall Toolkit source files with the following command:

```
tar xvf fwtk.tar.Z
```

This command creates a directory named `fwtk` and places all the source files in various subdirectories under the `fwtk` directory.

Build and install the Firewall Toolkit proxy servers

After unpacking the software, you have to edit a file named `Makefile.config` in the `/usr/local/src/fwtk` directory, build the various proxy servers, and install them in appropriate directories.

Edit the `Makefile.config` file using a text editor and make the following changes:

✦ Comment out the definition of `AUXLIB` by placing a pound-sign (#) character at the beginning of the line because Linux does not use this library. The commented line is as follows:

```
#AUXLIB= -lresolv
```

✦ Define `FWTKSRCDIR` as the directory in which you installed the TIS Firewall Toolkit source code. If you install everything in `/usr/local/src/fwtk`, you have to define `FWTKSRCDIR` as follows:

```
FWTKSRCDIR=/usr/local/src/fwtk
```

✦ Define DBMLIB as the link option that links with the `dbm` library. In Linux, define DBMLIB as follows:

```
DBMLIB= -ldbm
```

To build the TIS Firewall Toolkit libraries and proxy servers, type the following command at the top-level directory (`/usr/local/src/fwtk`):

```
make
```

As the libraries and proxy servers are compiled and linked, you'll see a number of warning messages, which you can safely ignore.

The `make` command builds all Firewall Toolkit libraries and proxy servers except for the X Server proxy, `x-gw`, which does not fully build due to some errors. I did not attempt to build `x-gw` because you don't have to run X across the firewall.

After successfully building the Firewall Toolkit servers, log in as `root` and type the following command (from the `/usr/local/src/fwtk` directory) to install the programs:

```
make install
```

By default, the Firewall Toolkit programs are installed in the `/usr/local/etc` directory.

Configuring TIS Firewall Toolkit

The `/usr/local/etc/netperm-table` file serves as the common configuration file for all proxy servers and tools of the TIS Firewall Toolkit. After you install the Firewall Toolkit programs, you'll find a sample configuration file `/usr/local/etc/netperm-table`.

The comments in the `netperm-table` file provide hints on how to specify permissions for various services. A comment at the beginning of the file says the following:

```
#
# Sample netperm configuration table
#
# To get a good sample working netperm-table, just globally
# substitute YOURNET for your network address (e.g.; 666.777.888)
#
```

As this comment suggests, you can get a working configuration file by replacing the string YOURNET with the network address of your internal network. For example, my internal network has a Class C IP address (206.197.168), which means I should replace all occurrences of YOURNET with 206.197.168.

The `netperm-table` file has access rules for each proxy service. For example, listed here is a rule that allows all hosts on my network access to the TELNET proxy (`tn-gw`) on the Linux firewall host:

```
tn-gw:        timeout 3600
tn-gw:        permit-hosts 206.197.168.* -passok -xok
```

To make the TELNET gateway active, you have to next edit the `/etc/inted.conf` file. Comment out the current line that begins with `telnet` and, in its place, put in a new line that launches the TELNET gateway (`tn-gw`), as shown here:

```
#telnet stream  tcp  nowait  root  /usr/sbin/tcpd  /usr/sbin/in.telnetd
telnet  stream  tcp  nowait  root  /usr/local/etc/tn-gw tn-gw
```

You can have much more elaborate setups in which users must pass through username and password authentication before they can access the TELNET gateway.

However, this simple configuration is sufficient to allow users from trusted internal networks access to the hosts on the Internet.

After making changes to the `/etc/inetd.conf` file, you have to make `inetd` read the configuration file again. On a Linux system, use the following command to find the process ID of `inetd`:

```
ps -aux | grep inetd
```

From the output, note the process ID (a number) of `inetd`. If the process ID is 1234, type the following command to cause `inetd` to restart (and thereby read the contents of `/etc/inetd.conf` again):

```
kill -HUP 1234
```

Testing the TELNET proxy

To test the TELNET proxy, try the following steps to log into an Internet host:

1. Run telnet and connect it to the firewall host. The TELNET gateway should start and display its prompt (`tn-gw>`).

2. Type `c hostname` to log into the specified Internet host. The TELNET gateway should establish connection to the Internet host and open up a network connection between your system and the host.

The following listing shows a sample TELNET session through the TIS Firewall Toolkit's `tn-gw` proxy (the host inside the firewall is `lnbsun` and the firewall is `lnbp75`):

```
lnbsun% telnet lnbp75
Trying 206.197.168.200 ...
Connected to lnbp75.
Escape character is '^]'.
lnbp75 telnet proxy (Version V1.3) ready:
tn-gw-> c access.digex.net
Trying 205.197.245.196 port 23...

Express Access(tm) Online Communications Service
A service of Digital Express Group, Inc.

Login as "new" (no password) if you don't have an account (8-N-1)
Can't log in? Call 301-847-5050/410-898-5050 for assistance.


SunOS UNIX 4.1 (access1) (ttyp1)

login:
```

Web Server Security

The proxy servers provide Internet access to users on the internal network. However, you typically run a few Internet servers (such as HTTPD and anonymous FTP) directly on the firewall host because you are offering these services to others on the Internet. For these services, you must take precautions to close all known security holes.

When discussing Web server setup, Chapters 7 and 8 also present the basic access control mechanisms of each Web server. For example, the `access.conf` file controls how the Web server protects directories and how the server executes external programs (often as Perl scripts) through a mechanism called *Common Gateway Interface (CGI)*.

Most of the Web server's known vulnerabilities appear when the Web server allows the user to send commands that cause execution of a script (or a computer program) on the host that runs the Web server. The two common problem areas are the following:

✦ Server-side includes

✦ CGI scripts

URL For the latest developments in Web server security, consult the following URL at NCSA:

```
http://hoohoo.ncsa.uiuc.edu/security/
```

URL One of the links on this Web page is "The World Wide Web Security FAQ" (FAQ stands for Frequently Asked Questions). You may want to go straight to that FAQ at the following URL:

```
http://www-genome.wi.mit.edu/WWW/faqs/www-security-faq.html
```

Webmaster As you set up your Web server, download this FAQ and read it. One of the first links on the HTML version of the FAQ provides the URL
```
http://www.genome.wi.mit.edu/WWW/faqs/www-security-faq.tar.gz,
```
which you can use to download the entire FAQ.

The following sections briefly discuss security risks. For the latest information on securing your Web server, consult "The World Wide Web Security FAQ."

Server-side includes

Server-side include refers to a feature of the Web server that can include a file or the value of an environment variable into an HTML document. The feature is like the include files in many programming languages such as C and C++. Just as a pre-processor processes the include files in a programming language, the Web browser processes the server-side includes before returning the document to the Web browser.

Server-side include provides a convenient way to include date, file size, and any file into an HTML document. For example, you can show the size of a graphics file by placing the following directive in the text:

```
File size = <!-#fsize file="nbphoto.gif"->
```

The Web server replaces everything to the right of the equal sign with the size of the file `nbphoto.gif`. This section discusses the security problems of server-side includes.

From the standpoint of security, one problem of server-side includes is the ability to execute a command on the server. For example, the following line of HTML includes the contents of the `/etc/passwd` file in the document returned to the browser:

```
<!-#exec cmd="/bin/cat /etc/passwd"->
```

If you want to retain some of the benefits of server-side includes but minimize the security risks, turn off the `#exec` keyword with the following directive on an Options line in `access.conf`:

```
Options IncludesNoExec
```

CGI scripts

The Web server's CGI feature lets you write interactive forms-based Web pages. Such Web pages can accept input from a user and run external programs (typically scripts written in the Perl programming language) to handle the user's request. You need to run CGI scripts to provide useful services such as database queries or a running count of the number of visitors to your Web page.

Unfortunately, the convenience of CGI comes with some risks. Remember the following potential problems with CGI scripts:

- ✦ A user can trick the CGI scripts or other CGI programs into doing something harmful.
- ✦ A user can modify one of the CGI scripts or upload a new script and have your Web server execute the new script.

With a badly written CGI script, a malicious user can execute a harmful command (such as `rm -rf /` to delete all files) by simply providing the shell command as part of input that a Web page requests. To contain the problem, restrict the directories from which the server can execute CGI scripts. For NCSA HTTPD and Apache servers, the `ScriptAlias` directive in the `srm.conf` configuration file specifies the directory in which CGI scripts reside.

By limiting CGI scripts to special directories, you can control what goes into those directories. You must still check the CGI scripts for any potential vulnerabilities. One of the most common problems is the use of the `system()` and `exec()` function calls to execute any arbitrary command received from the user.

Many Web sites enforce a policy whereby each CGI script is tested for potential security holes before the script is placed in an executable directory.

Summary

With all the publicity surrounding various break-ins on the Internet, you must convince your organization's management that you have arranged to protect the organization's internal network from any break-ins. You can meet the security needs of your organization by setting up a firewall between the internal network and the Internet and placing the Web site outside the firewall. This chapter explains the basics of Internet firewalls and shows you how to build a firewall. In the next part of the book, you learn how to publish HTML documents on the Web.

Where to go next . . .

✦ If you are relatively new to HTML authoring, start with the basics in Chapter 10.

✦ To learn more about specific HTML features, read one of Chapters 11 through 17.

✦ If you already know about creating Web pages with HTML, read Chapters 19 and 20 to learn about CGI programming.

✦ For information on Java programming, go to Chapter 23.

✦   ✦   ✦

Publishing on the Web

P A R T

III

✦ ✦ ✦ ✦

In This Part

Chapter 10
Getting Started
with HTML

Chapter 11
Formatting
Documents in HTML

Chapter 12
Adding Images,
Sound, and
Animation

Chapter 13
Adding Image Maps

Chapter 14
Using HTML
Extensions

Chapter 15
Designing Web
Pages

Chapter 16
Converting Existing
Documents to
HTML

Chapter 17
Using Web
Authoring Tools

Chapter 18
Promoting Your
Web Site

✦ ✦ ✦ ✦

Getting Started with HTML

As a Webmaster, your primary responsibility is to publish information on the Web. Before you can focus on the information content, you have to set up a Web site. Chapters 6 through 9 guide you through various options for setting up a Web site. By now, you should have your Web site physically up and running, so you can turn your attention to the information content for your Web site.

In the next nine chapters, you learn about publishing on the Web. Hypertext Markup Language (HTML) features prominently in these chapters because HTML is the accepted language of the Web.

Note HTML includes a relatively simple set of keywords and tags that you embed in a text document to indicate how that document should be formatted. The Web browser interprets the HTML tags and displays the formatted document. This chapter introduces the major features of HTML by taking you through the process of preparing a typical Web page. (I use the terms *HTML document* and *Web page* to refer to files formatted in HTML.)

Cross Ref Following the overview of HTML in this chapter, Chapters 11 through 14 focus on specific details of Web page preparation, from adding images and animation to exploiting Netscape and Microsoft's HTML extensions. Chapter 15 provides guidelines for designing Web pages. Chapters 16 and 17 cover some of the tools that can help you prepare documents in HTML format. Chapter 18 wraps up this part of the book with information on how to promote your Web site after you finish preparing the site's content.

Learning HTML

Now that you have the Web server up and running, you can turn to the business of preparing the Web pages. For that, you have to learn HTML. Although the name Hypertext Markup Language sounds like a programming language, HTML is really much simpler than a programming language. As its name suggests, HTML is a *markup* language, which means that you embed special *tags* — formatting commands — in the text to describe how the text should be *rendered* (that is, displayed or printed).

Markup languages

The idea of markup languages has been around for a while. Before the days of graphical interfaces, typesetting with the computer meant preparing a text file with embedded typesetting commands and then processing that marked-up text file with a computer program that generated commands for the output device: a printer or some other typesetter.

For example, in the late '70s and early '80s, I prepared all my correspondence and reports on a DEC VAX/VMS system, using a program named RUNOFF. That program formatted output for a line printer or a daisy-wheel printer. The VAX/VMS RUNOFF program accepted embedded commands like these:

```
.page size 58,80
.spacing 2
.no autojustify
```

As you might guess, the first command sets the number of lines per page and the number of characters on each line. The second command generates double-spaced output. The last command turns off justification. Essentially, I would pepper a text file with these commands, run it through RUNOFF, and send RUNOFF's output to the line printer. The resulting output looked as good as a typewritten document, which was good enough for most work in those days.

UNIX came with a more advanced typesetting program called troff (which stands for *typesetting runoff*) that could send output to a special device called a typesetter. A typesetter could produce much better output than a line printer. troff allows you to choose different fonts and to print text in bold and italic. To handle output on simpler printers, UNIX also included nroff (which stands for *nontypesetting runoff*) to process troff files and generate output, ignore fancy output commands, and generate output on a line printer.

Although markup languages were originally used to generate printed output, they have also been used to format output on your computer's monitor. For example, on UNIX systems, the troff markup language is used to prepare the man pages that provide online help to users. Man pages are the files that contain the information users can view by typing the command `man progname`. This command shows online help information on `progname`. The subject of a man page can be anything from an overview of a software package to the programming information for a specific C function such as `fopen` (for example, try `man fopen` on your UNIX system).

Markup languages such as `troff` are device-specific because the markup commands specify exact fonts to be used for specific parts of the document. A more general approach is to specify the layout of a document and leave the final processing to the software that renders the document. That's where the concept of generalized markup languages comes in.

Note   In a generalized markup language, you specify *what* you want to display not *how* you want to display it. For example, instead of saying you want some text typeset in italics, you'd say that you want the text emphasized with tags such as: `<em>this text is emphasized</em>`. In this case, the software that renders the document displays the text within the `<em>`...`</em>` tags emphasized in some way (typically by using italics).

There is, in fact, a Standard Generalized Markup Language (SGML) that standardizes the concept of a generalized markup language by defining parts of the document and the way tags are used to define a document's layout. SGML was standardized by the International Standards Organization (ISO) in 1986 (ISO standard 8879).

An SGML document can have up to three parts, as follows:

✦ A declaration section with global elements such as the character set used in the document

✦ A document type definition (DTD) that defines the structure of the document, including the tags that the document uses

✦ An instance of the structured document with embedded tags

HTML is an SGML-derived language with a set of tags that include support for hypertext links (also known as *hyperlinks*). To be precise, HTML is an SGML DTD that Web browsers understand. You don't really need to know much about an SGML DTD to use HTML.

HTML by example

Tip   The best way to learn HTML is to prepare a simple HTML document and view it in a Web browser. (As you know, you can have the viewer on a different computer on the network.) Then keep adding new HTML elements to that document and see the effect in the rendered version in a Web browser's window.

This chapter introduces you to HTML by taking you through the process of creating a sample Web page. The sample page includes nearly all the features you might use in your Web pages, from clickable images to interactive forms. However, this chapter does not describe all the HTML features in detail. You learn the details in later chapters of this book.

Tip As you begin learning HTML, you should also look at sample HTML documents with good layout. With a Web browser such as Netscape Navigator, select Document Source from the View menu to view the HTML source of the document that the browser is currently displaying. Whenever you see a particularly interesting Web page, you can view the HTML source to learn how specific visual effects are accomplished.

Creating a Web Page

Webmaster Typically, when a client (a Web browser) connects to your Web server, it requests a default page with a URL, such as http://yoursys.com/. The server looks for an HTML document named index.html in the /usr/local/etc/httpd/htdocs directory, which is the default directory for the Web pages.

Because you need the index.html file anyway, I'll introduce HTML by creating an index.html file and improving it through iterations. In the process, you'll see most of the important HTML features. To begin, I log in as root and create the index.html file in the /usr/local/etc/httpd/htdocs directory, with the following lines of text:

```
<html>

<head>
<TITLE>
LNB Software Home Page
</TITLE>
</head>

<body>

<center>
<h1>
LNB Software, Inc.
</h1>
</center>

<hr>

This page is under construction.
```

```
<hr>

Copyright &copy; 1996 LNB Software, Inc.
<address>
webmaster@lnbsoft.com
</address>

</body>

</html>
```

When you prepare the file you should, of course, use your company name and address.

After preparing the bare-bones HTML file, I view it in a Web browser. A good way is to run the Web browser while you edit the Web page. That way, you can save the HTML document periodically and load it in the Web browser to see the result.

Tip   When you want to view a Web page that you prepared recently, chances are that there is no hypertext link that allows you to jump to your newly minted page. To view the new page, use the Web browser's `Open File` menu option, and select the HTML file from the file browser.

I used Netscape Navigator to view the bare-bones Web page. Figure 10-1 shows how the page looks.

At this point, you should correlate the displayed Web page with the HTML document so that you can see the effect of each HTML tag. In particular, notice the following things:

✦ HTML tags are not case sensitive. Thus, you can type `<title>` or `<TITLE>`; both mean the same.

✦ The `<html>` ... `</html>` tag pair simply indicates that the document is an HTML document; these tags do not have any visual effect.

✦ The `<head>` ... `</head>` tags enclose the header information. In this case, the header defines the title of the page. That title appears in the title bar of the Netscape Navigator window.

✦ The `<body>` ... `</body>` tag pair encloses the entire HTML document.

Webmaster   ✦ The body of the Web page shows the text `LNB Software, Inc.` in header level 1 (`<h1>` ... `</h1>`) and centered (`<center>` ... `</center>`). The `<center>` tag is an HTML extension supported by both Netscape Navigator and Microsoft Internet Explorer. However, HTML version 3.2 includes `<center>` as a standard tag.

✦ The `<hr>` tag causes the browser to display a horizontal rule.

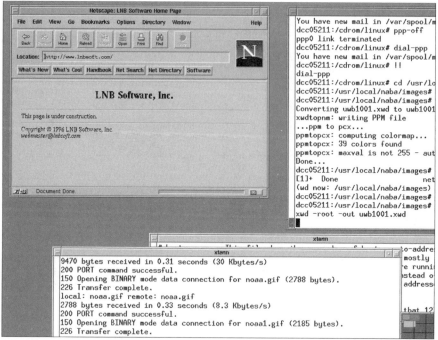

Figure 10-1: The bare-bones Web page.

✦ The HTML keyword `&copy;` displays a copyright symbol (actually an HTML extension added by Netscape Communications Corporation).

✦ The `<address>` ... `</address>` tags display the enclosed text as an address (in italics).

Tip The next few sections illustrate several HTML tags and give you an idea of how HTML documents are organized. The best way to learn HTML is to start with a working page and gradually add new tags. As you add a new feature, you should immediately view the results with a Web browser. That way, you can better understand how a specific HTML tag works.

Hypertext links

The simple Web page (refer to Figure 10-1) is boring, because it does not have much content and, more important, does not exploit any hypertext links. At a minimum, I should make the e-mail address a link so that a user can send mail by clicking the address. To do so, I enclose the address at the end of the document inside an anchor (or link), as follows:

```
<a href="mailto:webmaster@lnbsoft.com">
<address>
webmaster@lnbsoft.com
</address>
</a>
```

I show the new lines added to the HTML file in boldface. The first line illustrates the syntax of a link. In this case, the link associates with a URL that designates a mail address; you can use the same syntax to add a link to another Web page. When I view the Web page after making this change, the address appears as a link (typically shown as blue underlined text by Netscape Navigator).

Webmaster If you were already viewing the Web page that you just finished editing, you have to click Netscape's Reload button to force the Web browser to get the page from the server again. Otherwise, the browser simply displays the image of the page from its cache, in which case you won't see the effect of the latest editing.

Note All the lines between the start tag `<a href="mailto:webmaster@lnbsoft.com">` and the end tag `</a>` is called the anchor (or `<a>`) *element*. The keyword `href` that appears in the start tag of the anchor element is called an attribute. Thus, you'll see sentences such as "the HREF tag in the anchor element specifies a URL."

Note that some elements such as `<hr>` and `<img>` (see the "Embedded images" section) do not have an end tag. The entire element is a single tag.

Web page hierarchy and links

If you have a great deal of information for users, you want to organize the information in a logical manner. Just as you organize your files in directories and subdirectories, you can use hypertext links to organize Web pages in a hierarchy. In your main Web page, you can provide a few links to major categories of information and services. Following is a hypothetical list of categories for a software company:

✦ *What's New:* provides links to descriptions of new products and services offered by your company; should be updated often.

✦ *Company Overview:* describes what the company does and provides links to pages that describe specific parts of the company.

✦ *Web Programming Services:* provides a description of one of your company's specialties. Include links so that visitors can contact you to discuss your company's services further.

✦ *Software Store:* lists the products that you sell and provides any input forms that are necessary to allow the visitor to purchase products. As an incentive, you might allow visitors to download trial copies of the products.

✦ *Search:* brings up a form that takes a keyword and returns a page with links to all the pages that contain the keyword.

✦ *Feedback:* displays a form in which visitors can enter comments.

On your main Web page — the home page — you would show these categories as links to individual pages. Each page provides the information for that category. At the end of each page, you should include a link that returns the user to the home page. You end up with a Web-page hierarchy such as the one shown in Figure 10-2.

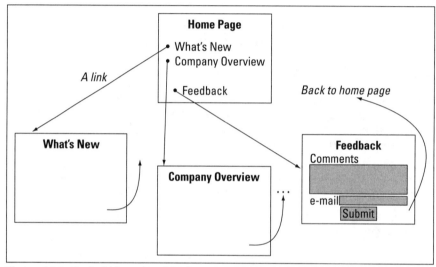

Figure 10-2: Typical hierarchy of Web pages.

On the sample Web page, here's how I add the six links:

```
<ul>
<li> <a href="http://www.lnbsoft.com/new.html"> What's new</a>
</ul>

<ul>
<li> <a href="oview.html"> Company Overview</a>
<li> <a href="webprog.html"> Web Programming Services</a>
<li> <a href="store.html"> Software Store</a>
<li> <a href="search.html"> Search</a>
<li> <a href="feedback.html"> Feedback</a>
</ul>
```

I use two unordered lists (`<ul>` ... `</ul>`) to format the items. The first list has the What's New link; I place this link in a separate list so that it stands out from the other items.

The rest of the links are in another unordered list. Each item starts with ⟨li⟩, and each link is defined using the ⟨a href=URL⟩ ... ⟨/a⟩ syntax.

After I add the new items, the Web page appears as shown in Figure 10-3.

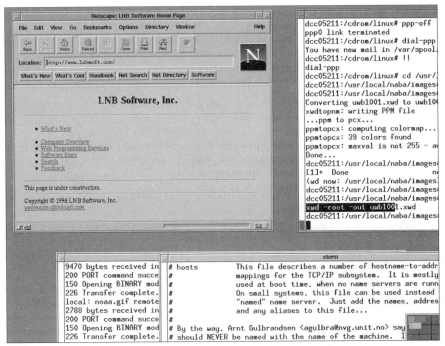

Figure 10-3: The Web page, with links to major categories of information.

Note that, in this sample Web page, I show the links using two forms of URL:

✦ *Absolute URL*: In this case the URL starts with http:// and includes the full hostname and pathname of the HTML document. The following link uses an absolute URL:

```
<a href="http://www.lnbsoft.com/new.html"> What's new</a>
```

With an absolute URL, the Web browser knows precisely which machine to contact (www.lnbsun.com) to download the Web page (new.html in the root directory).

✦ *Relative URL*: In this case, the URL only shows a pathname. The following link is an example of a relative URL:

```
<a href="search.html"> Search</a>
```

With a relative URL, the Web browser has to use information from the current document's URL to fully resolve the link. For example, if the current document's absolute URL is `http://www.lnbsoft.com/index.html`, then the browser strips off the filename (`index.html`) and appends the relative URL to the rest. Thus, the relative URL `search.html` yields the absolute URL `http://www.lnbsoft.com/search.html`. On the other hand, if the relative URL were `links/search2.html`, the absolute URL would be `http://www.lnbsoft.com/links/search2.html`.

Note There is no difference in performance between the two URL styles (absolute or relative). However, if you use relative URLs you can easily move the entire HTML document hierarchy to a new root directory (or a different machine) without having to edit all the URLs because the relative URLs do not explicitly refer to a machine name or an absolute pathname.

Getting back to the sample Web page, note that each of the URLs for the newly added links refers to a different HTML document. I'll have to prepare each of these to complete the suite of Web pages. I won't show you the complete set; instead, I'll focus on adding some new features.

Embedded images

Adding an image to an HTML document is easy. First, you need the image, preferably in a GIF (Graphics Interchange Format) file. Then you add the file with the `<img ...>` tag. Suppose you want to add to the page an "Under Construction" sign like those signs you see at the roadside. Follow these steps to add the image:

1. Get an image in GIF format. If you have a clip-art collection, use a paint or draw program to save the image as a GIF file.

2. Use the following commands to create an image directory in the HTML document directory:

   ```
   cd /usr/local/etc/httpd/htdocs
   mkdir image
   ```

   That way you can put all your images in one place.

3. Copy the new GIF file to the image directory.

Webmaster

4. Add the `<image ...>` directive to insert the image. If the image file's name is `const.gif`, the directive appears as follows:

   ```
   <img alt="Under Construction" align=bottom src="image/const.gif">
   ```

This directive says that the server should return Under Construction if the browser does not support images, that the text and the image should be aligned along the bottom edge, and that the image file is image/const.gif.

Figure 10-4 shows the appearance of the sample Web page after I added an image with the <img ...> tag.

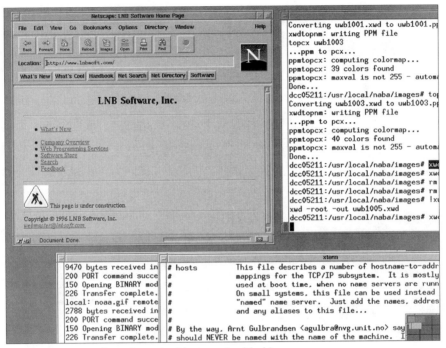

Figure 10-4: Sample Web page with an embedded image.

Cross Ref Figure 10-4 illustrates a common problem of embedded images: When the image's background does not match the window background, the embedded image does not look nice. You can fix this problem by using one of the freely available tools that allow you to create transparent GIFs (that means one of the colors in the GIF file is designated as the transparent color — Web browsers replace this color with the window's background color). Chapter 11 describes how to download and use one such tool known as giftool. You'll also find giftool on this book's companion CD-ROM.

Suppose you use giftool to create a transparent GIF version of the construction sign. To use the new transparent GIF in the sample Web page, edit the reference to const.gif and replace it with constT.gif, so that the <img> directive reads as follows:

```
<img alt="Under Construction" align=bottom src="image/constT.gif">
```

Figure 10-5 shows the new appearance of the Web page with the embedded image. The image now blends in nicely with the background.

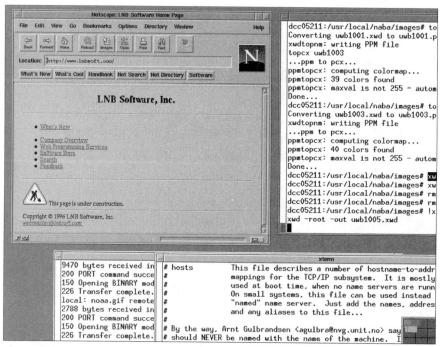

Figure 10-5: Sample Web page after embedded image is converted to transparent GIF.

Image maps

If you have used the World Wide Web, you probably have seen *image maps* — images that take you to different Web pages, depending on where you click. Typically, an image map is used on a Web page as a pictorial menu. Rather than displaying the major categories of information in a bulleted list, as in Figure 10-5, you may want to display an image map.

The best way to learn about an image map is to create one. To add an image map to the Web page shown in Figure 10-5, follow these steps:

1. Create a rectangular image, with icons and text representing the categories in your Web page. For the Web page in Figure 10-5, a suitable image might be the one shown in Figure 10-6.

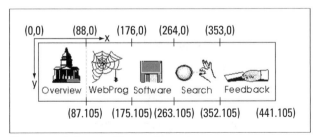

Figure 10-6: A typical image for an image map.

Tip

You can create images such as the one shown in Figure 10-6 by cutting and pasting pieces of clip art and adding annotations in a drawing program, such as CorelDraw. In particular, use a drawing program that identifies the cursor position in pixels, so that you can easily determine the corner points of rectangles (that you need to complete the next step).

2. Identify the rectangles for each category. Each rectangle is identified by the coordinates of the upper left and lower right corner points (when the rect keyword, described in step 3 is used). Figure 10-6 illustrates the coordinate system and shows the corner points for the five rectangles in that image. Look carefully at the leftmost rectangle; then you'll understand how the coordinates are specified.

3. Create a *map file* that associates each rectangle with a link. This file is called a map file because it maps parts of the image to a Web page. A map file is a text file, so you can use any text editor to prepare it. For the image shown in Figure 10-6, I created the map file /usr/local/etc/httpd/lnbimage.map, which contains the following lines:

```
default http://www.lnbsoft.com/

rect http://www.lnbsoft.com/oview.html       0,0   87,105
rect http://www.lnbsoft.com/webprog.html     88,0  175,105
rect http://www.lnbsoft.com/store.html       176,0 263,105
rect http://www.lnbsoft.com/search.html      264,0 352,105
rect http://www.lnbsoft.com/feedback.html    353,0 441,105
```

Each line that starts with a rect associates a URL with a rectangle. Compare the rectangle coordinates with those shown in Figure 10-6, and you'll get the picture. The default line specifies the Web page that the server should display if the user clicks outside the defined rectangles.

4. Use a text editor to edit the file `/usr/local/etc/httpd/conf/`
`imagemap.conf`, and add a line that associates a name for the image map with
the full pathname of the map file. In my case, I added the following line:

```
lnbimage : /usr/local/etc/httpd/htdocs/lnbimage.map
```

This line says that I refer to the map as `lnbimage` and that the actual map file
is `/usr/local/etc/httpd/htdocs/lnbimage.map`. As you will see next,
the map name is used in the HTML file when you are defining the link for the
image map.

5. Embed the image in the HTML file and specify a link, using the following syntax:

```
<a href="/cgi-bin/imagemap/mapname">
<img alt="*" src="imagefile" ismap>
</a>
```

As you might guess, you have to provide the name of the map entry in the
`imagemap.conf` file and the pathname of the image file relative to the HTML
document directory. In my case, the image file is `lnbimage.gif` and the map
name is `lnbimage`, so I added the following lines to my HTML file
(`index.html`):

```
<hr>
<center>
<a href="/cgi-bin/imagemap/lnbimage">
<img alt="imagemap" src="image/lnbimage.gif" ismap>
</a>
</center>
<hr>
```

I also added a horizontal rule and centered the image map by embedding it
within the `<center>` ... `</center>` tags.

6. Load the modified Web page in a Web browser, and give it a try.

Figure 10-7 shows how my sample Web page looks with the newly added image map.

**Cross
Ref**   Chapter 12 provides further details on how to add and use image maps in your Web
pages. Chapter 14 describes another type of image map, known as a *client-side image
map*, which is supported by Netscape Navigator and Microsoft Internet Explorer and
which was recently incorporated into HTML 3.2.

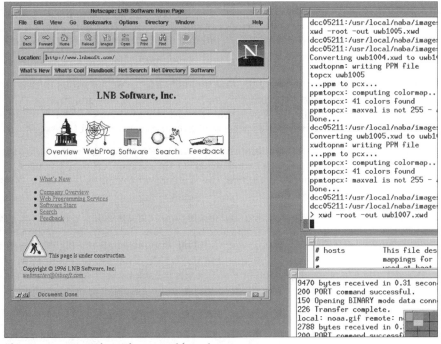

Figure 10-7: Sample Web page with an image map.

Interactive Web pages (HTML forms)

So far the sample Web pages have been one-sided Web pages wherein the user requests a page (through the browser), and the Web server returns the requested page. You have not seen any example of sending data back to the Web server. Interactive Web pages are very useful, because the user can send a query to the server and the server can return information that depends on what the user has sent. For example, the user might enter a keyword in a form and then submit the form; the Web server, in return, sends back a new Web page that contains a list of documents that contain the keyword entered by the user. This capability allows you to deploy the World Wide Web as an information system in a company, because users can query the corporate database through a Web browser and also submit information that the Web server can store in the database.

Cross Ref In the next few sections, I'll show you the basic steps of creating interactive Web pages through a simple example. You'll find detailed information about creating interactive Web pages in Chapters 19 and 20.

CGI scripts

Common Gateway Interface (CGI) scripts provide the means to create interactive Web pages. Using CGI scripts, the Web server interacts with the user in a three-step process:

✦ The server displays a Web page that includes a form with various user-input items (such as a text field and checkboxes), including a Submit button. The form has an attribute, called `action`, that is a URL; that URL specifies the name of an executable program or script in a special directory on the Web server.

✦ When the user clicks the Submit button, the browser activates the URL associated with the form and passes to the server the data entered by the user. Because the URL specifies a script, the Web server executes the script, passing to it the user-entered data.

✦ The script, which can be a Perl or Tcl script, or even a C or C++ program (that has been compiled into an executable), processes the user-entered data and displays any results by generating an HTML document on the fly. (Generating an HTML document on the fly means that the HTML document does not already exist; the script creates each line and sends it back by writing to the standard output.)

Note On Netscape and Apache Web servers, CGI scripts reside in the `cgi-bin` subdirectory of the server's root directory (`/usr/local/etc/httpd`, by default). Thus, the scripts also are referred to as `cgi-bin` scripts.

User input through a form

Use the `<form>` ... `</form>` tags to provide the user interface through which the user sends data back to a designated Web server. In the sample Web page described in earlier sections, one of the links is for user feedback — an example of requesting user input.

Suppose that you want to provide a multiple-line text entry area where the user can enter comments in free-form text. Then, you might prompt specifically for an e-mail address. A button labeled Submit allows the user to send the completed form to the server. Another button, marked Reset, causes the form to revert to its initial state. For this form, the sample HTML page looks like this:

```
<html>

<head>
<TITLE>
LNB Software: Feedback
</TITLE>
</head>
<body>
```

```
<center>
<h2>
Feedback
</h2>
</center>

<hr>
<form method="post" action="/cgi-bin/test-post">

<h3>
Comments:
<br>
<textarea name="feedback" rows="10" cols="40">

</textarea>
<br>

E-mail address:
<br>
<input type="text" name="e-mail" size=40 maxlength=60>
<br>

<input type=submit> <input type=reset>
</h3>
</form>

<hr>

Copyright &copy; 1996 LNB Software, Inc.
<a href="mailto:webmaster@lnbsoft.com">
<address>
webmaster@lnbsoft.com
</address>
</a>
<p>

<h2>
Back to
<a href="http://www.lnbsoft.com/">Home Page</a>

</body>
</html>
```

The form part of the listing appears in boldface. Figure 10-8 shows the appearance of the form in Netscape.

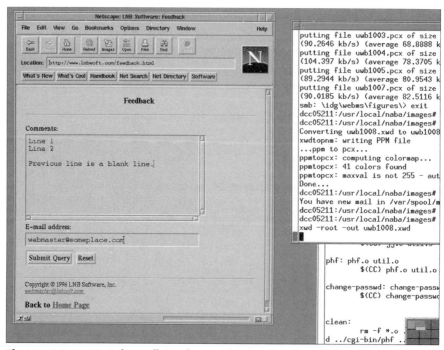

Figure 10-8: An HTML form allows the user to send input to a Web server.

All the user has to do is click in a text entry area and type. After typing the input, the user clicks the Submit button to send the input to the server specified in the `action` attribute of the form.

User-input transmission

The attributes of the `<form ...>` tag control how and where the Web browser delivers the user's input. Notice that the `<form ...>` tag has the following attributes:

✦ `method` specifies the manner in which the user input is sent to the Web server. There are two methods: `GET` and `POST`.

✦ `action` specifies the CGI script to be executed when the form is submitted to the server.

Webmaster The `GET` method sends data to the server by appending all the form parameters to the URL. The server then separates the user input from the URL and passes it to the script through the `QUERY_STRING` environment variable. It's fine for limited amounts of user input, but for a large amount of text input, the `GET` method may not work (because there may be limits on how many characters an environment variable can hold).

Webmaster The POST method is designed to send data from the client to the server. In this method, the browser sends each field of the form encoded in the following way:

✦ Spaces are sent as plus signs.

✦ Special characters (including carriage returns, line feeds, and exclamation points) are sent as hexadecimal values representing the ASCII code, with a percent-sign (%) prefix. Thus, a carriage return appears as %0D, and a line feed is sent as %0A.

✦ Successive fields of the form are separated by ampersands (&).

Webmaster For any significant amount of user input, you should use the POST method.

CGI processing

The CGI script or program at the server receives the POST data through its standard input. If the CGI program has to return anything to the browser (to acknowledge an input, for example, or to return the result of a database query), the CGI program simply writes an HTML document on the standard output. A simple example will make this clear.

For the fields of the sample form shown in Figure 10-8, the CGI script receives the following array of characters through the standard input (which comes as a single line, even though it appears broken up here):

```
feedback=Line+1%0D%0ALine+2%0D%0A%0D%0APrevious+line+is+a+blank+line.&e-
        mail=webmaster@someplace.com
```

The values of the fields reflect the text entered in Figure 10-8.

A simple CGI program in C

As you might guess, the job of the CGI program is to parse this line and take any necessary action. Following is a simple C program that I used to capture the input lines in a log file and basically echo the lines back to the browser in an HTML document:

```
/*-------------------------------*/
/* File: test-post.c
 *
 * 1. Build test-post program with the following command:
 *    gcc test-post.c -o test-post
 * 2. Put executable (test-post) in cgi-bin directory.
 * 3. Create a "feedback.log" file in htdocs directory
 *    and make sure that file has read-write permission
 *    for the world.
 */
```

(continued)

```
#include <stdio.h>
#include <stdlib.h>

char *line;
char fname[] = "/usr/local/etc/httpd/htdocs/feedback.log";

main(int argc, char *argv[])
{
  int cl;
  FILE *of;

  printf("Content-type: text/html\n\n");

  printf("<H1>You submitted</H1>\n");
  printf("<pre>\n");
  cl = atoi(getenv("CONTENT_LENGTH"));
  line = calloc(cl+1, sizeof(char));
  printf("%d bytes\n", cl);

/* Read the entire user input from stdin */
  gets(line);
  printf("%s\n", line);

/* Save raw user input in a file */
  of = fopen(fname, "a");
  if(!of) printf("Error opening: %s\n", fname);
  else printf("Saving in: %s\n", fname);
  fprintf(of, "\n-------------------\n");
  fprintf(of, "%s", line);
  fclose(of);

/* Provide a link to return to Home Page */
  printf("<h1>\nReturn to <a href=\"http://www.lnbsoft.com/\">\
Home Page</a>\n</h1>");

}
```

You should follow the instructions at the beginning of this file to compile and create the test-post CGI program and place it in the cgi-bin directory. When I use this CGI program as the action for the form shown in Figure 10-8, the resulting response is as shown in Figure 10-9.

Obviously, the feedback shown in Figure 10-9 is not what you'd want to provide your users, but this example illustrates how you can process users' input with a CGI program.

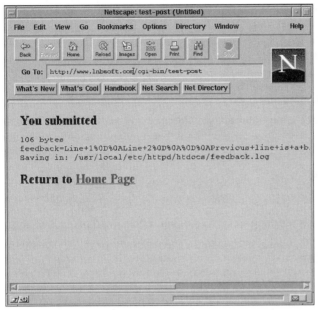

Figure 10-9: Result of submitting a form to a CGI program.

Environment variables in CGI programs

In the sample C program, you may have noticed the call to the `getenv` function to read the value of the `CONTENT_LENGTH` environment variable. That variable happens to hold the number of bytes that the client has sent through the POST method. In addition to `CONTENT_LENGTH`, the Web server uses a host of environment variables to pass information to the CGI program.

Webmaster If you are going to write any meaningful CGI programs, you have to use these environment variables. Following is a list of the most important environment variables:

✦ `AUTH_TYPE` is the authentication (if any) used by the server.

✦ `CONTENT_LENGTH` is the number of bytes being sent by the client.

✦ `CONTENT_TYPE` is the type of data being sent by a `POST` or `PUT` method.

✦ `GATEWAY_INTERFACE` is the version number of the CGI specification that this server follows. A typical example is `CGI/1.1`.

✦ `HTTP_ACCESS` is a list of the MIME data types that the client can accept (for example, `image/gif`, `image/jpeg`).

✦ `HTTP_REFERER` is the URL from which the current request came.

✦ HTTP_USER_AGENT is the name and version number of the Web browser that sent the request. Mozilla/2.01 (X11; I; SunOS 4.1.3_U1 sun4c) is a typical Web browser name.

✦ PATH_INFO is any path information provided by the client.

✦ PATH_TRANSLATED is the translated version of PATH_INFO to account for any virtual-to-physical mapping.

✦ QUERY_STRING is anything that follows the question mark (?) in the URL. (This is how the GET method sends data to the server.)

✦ REMOTE_ADDR is the IP address of the client system.

✦ REMOTE_HOST is the host name of the client that made the request.

✦ REMOTE_IDENT is the remote user name retrieved from the server.

✦ REMOTE_USER is the user name (applies only for password-protected access).

✦ REQUEST_METHOD is the method used for the request. For HTTP, the methods are GET, POST, and HEAD.

✦ SCRIPT_NAME is the name of the script that is being executed.

✦ SERVER_NAME is the host name or IP address of the server system.

✦ SERVER_PORT is the port number (such as 80) at which the request was received.

✦ SERVER_PROTOCOL is the protocol and version. For HTTP, the SERVER_PROTOCOL might be HTTP/1.0.

✦ SERVER_SOFTWARE is the name and version of the Web server software. For NCSA 1.5 HTTPD, SERVER_SOFTWARE is set to NCSA/1.5.

Getting an Overview of HTML Tags

The previous sections illustrate several HTML tags and give you an idea of how to use HTML to build Web pages. One of the best ways to learn HTML is to start with a working page and gradually add new elements. As you add a new feature, you should immediately view the results with a Web browser. That way, you can better understand how a specific HTML tag works.

Cross Ref The latest HTML standard is 2.0. Although there was a draft HTML 3.0 standard, it did not materialize because no one could agree on the details. Instead, popular Web browsers (such as Netscape Navigator and Microsoft Internet Explorer) began to incorporate extensions to HTML. Some of these extensions are described in Chapter 14. In May 1996, the World Wide Web Consortium released the specification for HTML 3.2, which incorporates many of the HTML extensions supported by Netscape Navigator and Microsoft Internet Explorer.

Table 10-1 summarizes the standard HTML tags (as of version 3.2) by category. Appendix C includes detailed reference pages on these tags as well as various Netscape Navigator and Microsoft Internet Explorer extensions.

Table 10-1 HTML 3.2 Tags by Category	
Category	**Tags**
Comments	`<!- comment->`
Overall structure	`<html> <head> <body> <title> <link> <base> <isindex> <meta> <nextid>`
Header levels	`<h1> <h2> <h3> <h3> <h4> <h5> <h6>`
Hyperlinks (anchors)	`<a>`
Images and rules	`<img> <hr>`
Applet	`<applet> <param>`
Client-side image map	`<map> <area>`
Content flow	`  <p> <pre> <blockquote> <div>`
Physical styles	`<b> <big> <font> <i> <small> <strike> <sub> <sup> <tt> <u>`
Logical styles	`<address> <cite> <code> <dfn> <em> <kbd> <samp> <strong> <var>`
Lists	`<ul> <ol> <li> <dir> <menu> <dl> <dt> <dd>`
Forms	`<form> <input> <select> <option> <textarea>`
Tables	`<table> <tr> <th> <td> <caption>`
Reserved for future use	`<script> <style>`

Summary

After you set up a Web server on a UNIX system with an appropriate Internet connection, you have to turn your attention to creating the site's content — the information that users access at your site. Much of the Web site's content is in the form of HTML documents and, as a Webmaster, you must have a good grasp of HTML. This chapter introduces HTML through a sample Web page (that includes nearly all major HTML features). The next chapter provides further details on basic document formatting in HTML.

Where to go next . . .

✦ If you have not yet decided how to set up your Web site, consult Chapter 6 for a discussion of various options for setting up a Web site.

✦ To learn more about formatting a document in HTML, proceed to Chapter 11.

✦ To work with images in HTML documents, see Chapters 12 and 13.

✦ To learn more about additional HTML features supported by specific Web browsers such as Netscape Navigator and Microsoft Internet Explorer, go to Chapter 14.

✦ For guidelines on designing Web pages, see Chapter 15.

✦ If you need to convert existing documents into HTML, consult Chapter 16.

✦ In Chapter 17 you'll find information about HTML authoring tools.

✦ If you already know about creating Web pages with HTML, you may want to proceed to Chapters 19 and 20 to learn about CGI programming.

✦ For information on Java programming go to Chapter 23.

✦   ✦   ✦

Formatting Documents in HTML

Chapter 10 shows you a nearly complete Web page and, in the process of creating that Web page, illustrates the use of many important HTML elements. This chapter presents the bulk of HTML elements in greater detail.

This chapter uses many short examples to illustrate the effect of each HTML element — you'll see the HTML source as well as a screen shot of how a typical browser renders that HTML.

Cross Ref This chapter's focus is on the document formatting aspect of HTML. Chapter 12 provides information on adding images and other multimedia data such as sound and video. Chapter 13 explains image maps — the use of an image as a launching point for different Web pages.

Cross Ref Discussions in this chapter focus on the standard features of HTML (corresponding to HTML 2.0). Some of the well-known Netscape Navigator and Microsoft Internet Explorer extensions to HTML are described in Chapter 14. Recently, the World Wide Web Consortium released the specification for HTML 3.2, which incorporates many of these extensions and makes them standard. Chapter 14 identifies the Netscape Navigator and Microsoft Internet Explorer extensions that are now part of HTML 3.2. Also, the use of forms in interactive Web pages is covered in Chapter 19.

HTML Document Structure

A bare-bones HTML document has the following form:

```
<html>
<head>
<title>My company's home page</title>
</head>

<body>

<h3>Your Home Page</h3>

This is where the document's body appears.
<!- This is a comment line ->

<address>Your Name and Address</address>

</body>
</html>
```

On a Web browser such as Netscape Navigator, this HTML document appears as shown in Figure 11-1.

Your Home Page

This is where the document's body appears.
Your Name and Address

Figure 11-1: Rendered version of a bare-bones HTML document.

As you can see, only part of the HTML source file appears in the browser's window. All the tags, enclosed between a pair of less than (<) and greater than (>) signs, are stripped off — the tags convey formatting information to the browser.

Note All the HTML tags shown in the bare-bones sample document have a start and an end tag. For example, the entire document is enclosed by the tags <html> and </html>. Here <html> is the start tag and </html> is the end tag. The end tag looks like the start tag except for an extra slash (/) at the beginning of the end tag name.

HTML comments

HTML comments begin with <!- and end with ->. The Web browser ignores every-thing between the <!- and -> marks. You can have single- as well as multiline comments:

```
<!- A single line comment ->
<!- This comment spans
  two lines. ->
```

You do need to pay attention to the following specific details:

✦ There must be a space after the initial <!− mark.

✦ There must be a space before the final −> mark.

Webmaster Some Web servers take advantage of the HTML comments — they interpret the comments as special instructions for the Web server. This is the case with server-side includes where the Web server preprocesses the HTML file, interprets specially formatted comment lines, and alters the HTML document prior to sending the document to the Web browser.

HTML document major structures

Everything between the <html> and </html> tags is the <html> *element*, which defines the overall document structure. If you examine the bare-bones document carefully, you'll see that there are two major structures in the HTML document:

✦ The "head" contains information about the document such as its title (in a <title> element). The Web browser does not display the document's head (although the browser displays the document's title in its window's title bar).

✦ The body contains the document's content including all the text, any images, and hyperlinks. You spend most of your time preparing the document's body because that's where the content goes. The Web browser displays the content in its window.

HTML tags and elements

The term tag refers to a single HTML keyword enclosed between a less-than (<) and a greater-than (>) sign. Thus, <h3> and </h3> are HTML tags. The <h3> tag starts header level 3 and the </h3> tag ends that header level.

The term *HTML element* refers to everything between a start tag and an end tag, including both the start tag and the end tag. Thus the following line shows an <h3> element:

```
<h3>The entire line is an
   element.</h3>
```

Document head

An HTML document's head is where you place information about the document. The head is enclosed within the `<head>` and `</head>` tags. You can have one of the following tags in the document head (they can occur in any order you want):

✦ `<base>` is used to specify the base URL of the document.

✦ `<isindex>` is used to implement a simple interactive query.

✦ `<link>` is used to establish a relationship between this HTML document and another document.

✦ `<meta>` is used to provide extra information about the document that the browser might be able to use.

✦ `<nextid>` is used by HTML editors to store the next identifier to be used as the name of a hyperlink in the document.

✦ `<title>` is used to indicate the document's title and should be present in each HTML document.

The `<title>` element should appear in the document's head. The rest of these elements are optional. Nevertheless, I provide a brief discussion of some of these elements so you know what purpose they serve.

Document title

You specify the document's title through the `<title>` element. Web browsers typically display the document title in the window's titlebar. Suppose you use the following `<title>` element:

```
<title>My company's home page</title>
```

When a user views this Web page in Netscape Navigator on Windows 95, the window title appears as shown in Figure 11-2.

Figure 11-2: Document title in Netscape Navigator.

On the other hand, Microsoft Internet Explorer shows the document title in the window's title as shown in Figure 11-3.

Figure 11-3: Document title in Microsoft Internet Explorer.

Webmaster The automatic Web indexing tools also use the information in the document's `<title>` element when indexing the document's content.

Note If you do not include a `<title>` element in an HTML document, the Web browser displays the document's URL in the browser window's titlebar.

Other header elements

Besides the `<title>` element, the other header elements do not have any visible effects, but they can provide useful information to the browser.

You can use the `<base>` element to specify a base URL for the document. The `<base>` element takes an `href` attribute where you specify the base URL.

You might use the `<base>` element to ensure that all relative URLs in the document refer to the proper document. For example, suppose you use the following `<base>` element:

```
<head>
<base href="http://www.lnbsoft.com/">
</head>
```

This tells the browser that all relative URLs in the document should be treated as being relative to the root directory on the `www.lnbsoft.com` system.

The `<link>` element is a strange one. It looks like the `<a>` tag and has the same attributes (see the "Hyperlinks Revisited" section). You can use the <link> element to indicate the relationship of the current document to another document or URL.

The `<meta>` and `<nextid>` elements are typically used by HTML editors. HTML editors (that let you create and edit HTML documents) use the `<nextid>` element to store the next identifier to be used as the name of a link. (Read the "Hyperlinks Revisited" section for more on link names.)

Webmaster You can use the `<meta>` element to provide more information about the HTML document — information that goes beyond the header that the Web server sends. Typically, HTML editors embed information using `<meta>` elements. You can have more than one `<meta>` element in the header. For example, here is a document header generated by Netscape Navigator Gold, which allows you to create and edit HTML documents:

```
<head>
    <title>Yet Another Home Page</title>
    <meta name="Author" content="Naba Barkakati">
    <meta name="GENERATOR" content="Mozilla/2.01Gold (Win32)">
    <meta name="Classification" content="boring">
    <meta name="Description" content="Sample created using Netscape Navigator
    Gold.">
    <meta name="KeyWords" content="HTML, sample, home page">
</head>
```

As this example shows, the HTML editor uses `<meta>` elements to insert lots of information about the document in the document's head. Each `<meta>` element has two attributes:

✦ `name` defines the name of any new information about the document (such as `Author`, `KeyWords`, and so on).

✦ `content` specifies the value of that piece of information (such as the name of the author or a comma-separated list of attributes about the document).

Cross Ref In the sample document head, some of the `<meta>` elements such as `GENERATOR` can be filled in by the HTML editor (because this attribute is simply the name of the tool that generated the document). For other `<meta>` elements, you must provide the information as you create the document. In Netscape Navigator Gold, you can specify information about the document by selecting the Document option from the Properties menu. (Chapter 17 further discusses Web authoring tools.)

Cross Ref In addition to the name and content attributes, the `<meta>` element also accepts the `http-equiv` attribute that allows you to request that the Web server add a specific name/value pair to the header that the server returns to the Web browser. (Chapter 12 describes the header that the server sends to the Web browser.) For example, if you were to specify the following `<meta>` element in the HTML document:

```
<meta http-equiv="Expires" content=" Fri, 16 Aug 1996 21:35:40 GMT">
```

the Web server may include the following field in the header sent to the Web browser:

```
Expires: Fri, 16 Aug 1996 21:35:40 GMT
```

Webmaster Note, however, that Web servers are not required to consult a document's `<head>` element for the header fields being returned to the browser. In fact, the popular NCSA and Apache Web servers ignore the document's `<head>` element when responding to an HTTP request from a Web browser.

Document body

You put the text and images that constitute the content of the Web page in the document's body. The document's body is enclosed in a `<body>` element that starts with a `<body>` tag and ends with the `</body>` tag. The body contains the document's text and images. The following list summarizes the standard HTML elements commonly used in a document's body:

✦ **Headings:** `<h1>` `<h2>` `<h3>` `<h4>` `<h5>` `<h6>`

✦ **Paragraphs and line breaks:** `<p>` `<br>`

✦ **Preformatted text:** `<pre>`

- ✦ **Listings:** `<listing>` `<xmp>`
- ✦ **Address:** `<address>`
- ✦ **Quoted text:** `<blockquote>`
- ✦ **Lists:** `<ul>` `<li>` `<ol>` `<dir>` `<menu>` `<dl>` `<dt>` `<dd>`
- ✦ **Logical styles:** `<cite>` `<code>` `<em>` `<kbd>` `<samp>` `<strong>` `<var>`
- ✦ **Physical styles:** `<b>` `<i>` `<strike>` `<tt>`
- ✦ **Horizontal rule:** `<hr>`
- ✦ **Hyperlink anchors:** `<a>`
- ✦ **Images:** `<img>`
- ✦ **Interactive forms:** `<form>` `<input>` `<select>` `<option>` `<textarea>`

Webmaster The `<listing>` and `<xmp>` elements are both meant to display a block of text without any formatting. Although these elements are supported for historical reasons, you should use the `<pre>` element instead. Like `<listing>` and `<xmp>`, `<pre>` is also for displaying text without any formatting. However, unlike `<listing>` and `<xmp>`, you can embed some HTML tags (such as a hyperlink anchor) in a `<pre>` element (see the "Preformatted text" section).

Cross Ref Chapters 12 and 13 describe how to include images in your HTML documents. Chapter 14 presents the extensions to these HTML elements as well as some new HTML elements supported by specific Web browsers such as Netscape Navigator and Microsoft Internet Explorer (of course, many of these extensions are now part of the HTML 3.2 specification). Chapter 19 covers the creation and use of interactive forms. The next few sections go into the details of text layout.

Text Layout in HTML

You could simply enclose all of your document's text inside the `<body>` element. If you do this, you'll quickly notice that the Web browser ignores all extra lines and turns all of your text into a single paragraph. Thus, at a minimum, you need to know the HTML elements to specify paragraph breaks.

As soon as you have a number of paragraphs, you may also want to organize them under headings. Within the paragraph, you may want to emphasize the text to draw the user's attention to the text. You may need to display embedded computer listings in a different way (typically with a fixed-pitch typeface) so that the listing is readable. You also need ways to display lists of items. HTML includes a number of elements to handle these text formatting and layout chores.

Paragraphs and line breaks

The simplest organization of text is to break it into paragraphs. In a typical word processor, you indicate the end of a paragraph by pressing Enter on the keyboard. However, the Web browser ignores blank lines and extra spaces. In HTML, you have to indicate the *start* of a paragraph with the <p> tag. You are also supposed to mark the end of the paragraph with the </p> tag.

Tip   In practice, you can omit the </p> tag because the start of a new paragraph automatically ends the previous paragraph. Also, you do not have to indicate the start of the first paragraph in the document. The following document body shows a typical use of the <p> tag:

```
<body>
The first paragraph does not need an explicit paragraph
tag because the browser starts with a new paragraph.

Extra lines are ignored, so this is also part of the
first paragraph.

The layout of the paragraph (the location of the line
breaks, for instance) depends on the size of the
browser's window.

<p>
This is the beginning of the second paragraph.
You don't really need
to use any "end-of-paragraph" tag because the start of a
new paragraph means the end of the previous one.

<p>
And this is the last paragraph.

</body>
```

Figure 11-4 shows how the Netscape Navigator renders this paragraph.

The exact locations of line breaks depend on the size of the browser window. If you resize the browser window of Figure 11-4, the paragraph rendering looks different.

If you need to break lines at a specific point, you can do so by inserting a <br> tag. The <br> tag stops the browser from automatically filling the lines and wrapping the paragraphs at the edges of the browser window. There is no end tag for <br>.

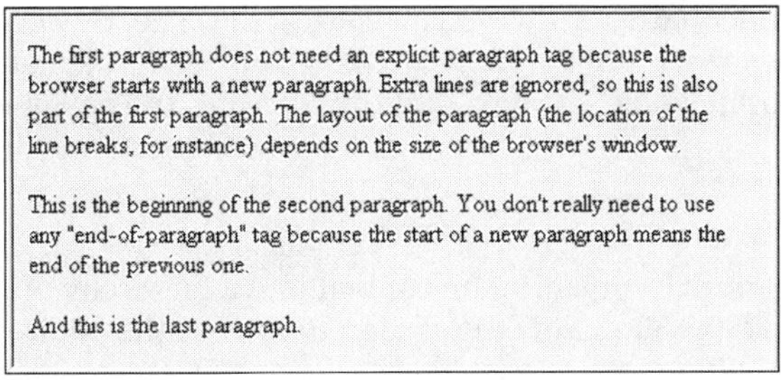

The first paragraph does not need an explicit paragraph tag because the browser starts with a new paragraph. Extra lines are ignored, so this is also part of the first paragraph. The layout of the paragraph (the location of the line breaks, for instance) depends on the size of the browser's window.

This is the beginning of the second paragraph. You don't really need to use any "end-of-paragraph" tag because the start of a new paragraph means the end of the previous one.

And this is the last paragraph.

Figure 11-4: Paragraph rendering in a Web browser.

Tip You may need explicit line breaks when formatting addresses or poems. For example, the following HTML document shows the formatting for a poem where each line ends with a `<br>` tag:

```
<body>
<h3>Reading</h3>
<p>
by Ivy Barkakati
<p>

Reading<br>
A never-ending process<br>
Can be done anywhere, anytime<br>
Traveling to new worlds<br>
Musty, old pages, yellowed with age<br>
Absorbing information like a sponge soaking up water<br>
Spine-tingling suspense<br>
Creating vivid visions in my mind<br>
Meeting new friends and making new enemies<br>
"To be or not to be, that is the question!"<br>

</body>
```

Figure 11-5 shows how the Netscape Navigator renders this paragraph.

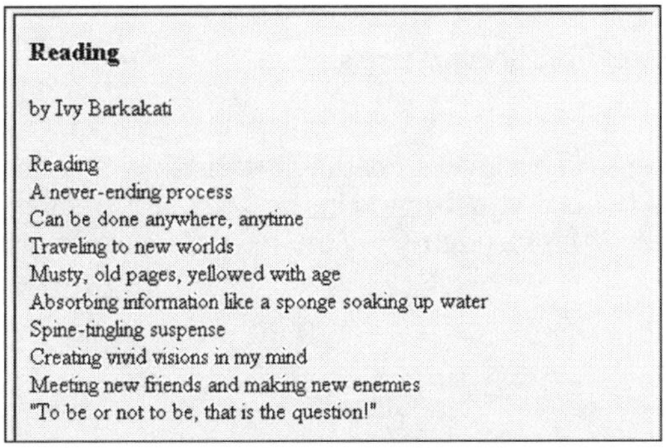

Reading

by Ivy Barkakati

Reading
A never-ending process
Can be done anywhere, anytime
Traveling to new worlds
Musty, old pages, yellowed with age
Absorbing information like a sponge soaking up water
Spine-tingling suspense
Creating vivid visions in my mind
Meeting new friends and making new enemies
"To be or not to be, that is the question!"

Figure 11-5: A poem formatted with explicit line breaks (`<br>`).

Notice that when the browser encounters a `<br>` tag, it starts a new line. However, with a paragraph tag (`<p>`), the browser inserts some extra space before the new paragraph. The `<h3>` tag starts a heading; the next section describes the headings.

Headings

Books such as this one use headings to organize the content into a hierarchy of chapters and sections. The headings allow you, the reader, to browse the book's content more easily than if everything were presented as a large collection of paragraphs. Headings serve the same purpose in HTML documents; they break down the document into smaller chunks that are easy to understand.

Just as word processors provide a number of heading levels, HTML provides six heading elements that begin with the following tags:

```
<h1> <h2> <h3> <h4> <h5> <h6>
```

Each heading tag has a corresponding end tag with the usual format:

```
</h1> </h2> </h3> </h4> </h5> </h6>
```

Thus, all text between `<h1>` and `</h1>` are displayed as a level 1 heading. As you might guess, the browser displays the level 1 heading using large characters. The character sizes grow progressively smaller as you go from a level 1 heading to a level 6 heading, as illustrated by the rendering of the headings shown in Figure 11-6.

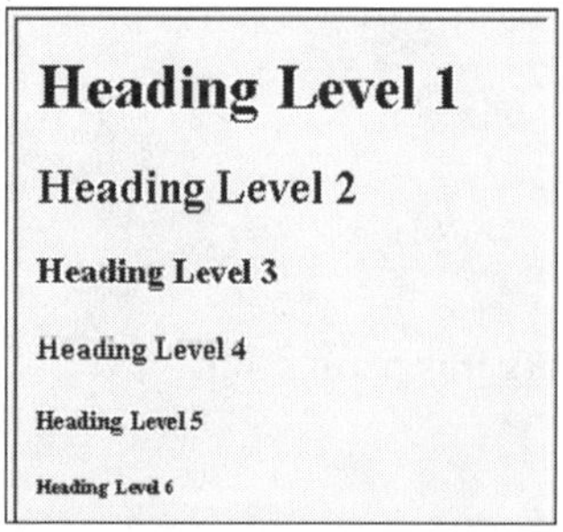

Heading Level 1

Heading Level 2

Heading Level 3

Heading Level 4

Heading Level 5

Heading Level 6

Figure 11-6: Typical rendering of the six HTML heading levels.

By convention, most HTML documents use a level 1 heading for the document's title (typically, you use the same title as the one you provide in the `<title>` element in the document's head). The headings `<h2>` through `<h6>` are used for section and subsection headings.

> **Tip**
> If you feel that the level 1 heading is too large, set the title in an ⟨h2⟩ element and use ⟨h3⟩ for the major sections of the document.

Preformatted text

Sometimes you want to display a block of text without any formatting. For example, you may want to embed the source code of a computer program on your Web page. In that case, you can simply add a ⟨pre⟩ tag, insert the source code, and mark the end with a ⟨/pre⟩ tag. The Web browser treats all text in the ⟨pre⟩ element as preformatted and displays the text as is, without any additional formatting.

You can embed the following HTML tags in a ⟨pre⟩ element:

✦ Hyperlink anchors (⟨a⟩)

✦ Logical and physical text styles

✦ Inline images (⟨img⟩)

✦ Horizontal rules (⟨hr⟩)

> **Webmaster**
> Because you can embed HTML tags in a ⟨pre⟩ element, you cannot have less-than (⟨), greater-than (⟩), and ampersand (&) characters in the preformatted text. Use the following equivalents for any literal less-than (⟨), greater-than (⟩), and ampersand (&) characters in the preformatted text:

✦ Replace ⟨ with the string < (you need everything up to and including the semicolon)

✦ Replace ⟩ with >

✦ Replace & with &

The following example shows how to format a typical C program in an HTML document and add a hyperlink anchor for printf, one of the standard C library functions:

```
<body>

Here is a sample program:

<pre>
#include &lt;stdio.h&gt;

void main(void)
{
    <a href="printf.html">printf</a>("Hello, World!\n");
}
</pre>

</body>
```

Figure 11-7 shows how Netscape Navigator renders the text inside the ⟨pre⟩ element. A typical Web browser uses a monospace font to display text in a ⟨pre⟩ element. Notice how the printf function name is displayed as a hyperlink anchor.

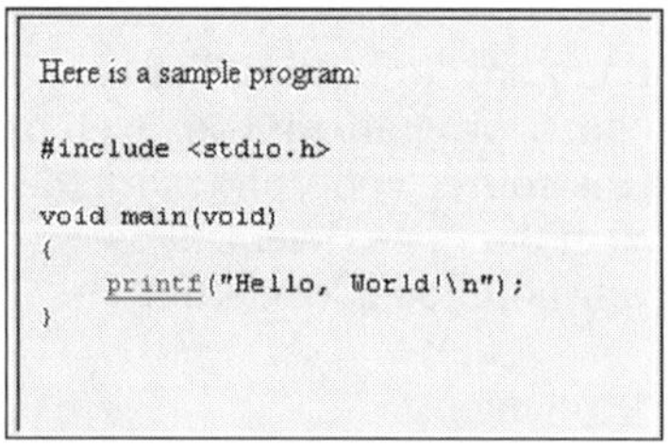

```
Here is a sample program:

#include <stdio.h>

void main(void)
{
    printf("Hello, World!\n");
}
```

Figure 11-7: Typical rendering of text inside a ⟨pre⟩ element.

Address format

An HTML document typically includes the name and address of the person who maintains the document. HTML includes a special ⟨address⟩ element for formatting the address information. Here is a typical example of an ⟨address⟩ element:

```
<address>
  Webmaster<br>
  LNB Software, Inc.<br>
</address>
```

The browser treats the text between the ⟨address⟩ and ⟨/address⟩ tags as an address and formats it in a distinctive manner.

Note In the ⟨address⟩ element, you can use other HTML tags. In particular, it is customary to include a link to the Webmaster's e-mail address so that the user can send mail to the Webmaster by clicking on the link. The following example shows how to add such a link:

```
<address>
  <a href="mailto:webmaster@lnbsoft.com">
  Webmaster</a><br>
  LNB Software, Inc.<br>
</address>
```

Figure 11-8 shows how a typical Web browser displays this HTML source (usually a browser displays the address in italics).

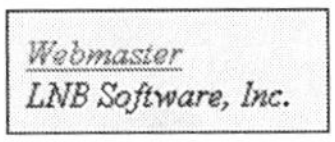

Webmaster
LNB Software, Inc.

Figure 11-8: A Web browser displays an ⟨address⟩ element.

Quoted text

When a report or a book uses a block of text from another source, the convention is to show the quoted text with indented left and right margins. HTML includes the ⟨blockquote⟩ element for this purpose. The Web browser treats the text between the ⟨blockquote⟩ and ⟨/blockquote⟩ tags as a chunk of quoted text and displays that text with indented left and right margins. The following example uses the ⟨blockquote⟩ element to set off a block of text from the rest of the text:

```
<p>
The County law concerning security deposits stipulates that:

<blockquote>
  If any portion of the security deposit is withheld,
  the landlord must send the tenant a written list of damages or
  reasons why any amount is being withheld along with actual costs,
  within 30 days after the lease is terminated.  This list must be
  sent by first class mail to the tenant's last known address.
  Failure to comply with this requirement shall cause the
  forfeiture of the landlord's right to withhold any part of the
  security deposit for damages.
</blockquote>

  Keep this law in mind when you terminate a lease.  If the
  landlord does not provide a damage list within 30 days, send a
 ~letter to the landlord quoting this law and ask for a refund of
  the security deposit.
```

Figure 11-9 shows how Netscape Navigator renders this HTML source. Notice how the Web browser displays the ⟨blockquote⟩ text with extra left and right indentations.

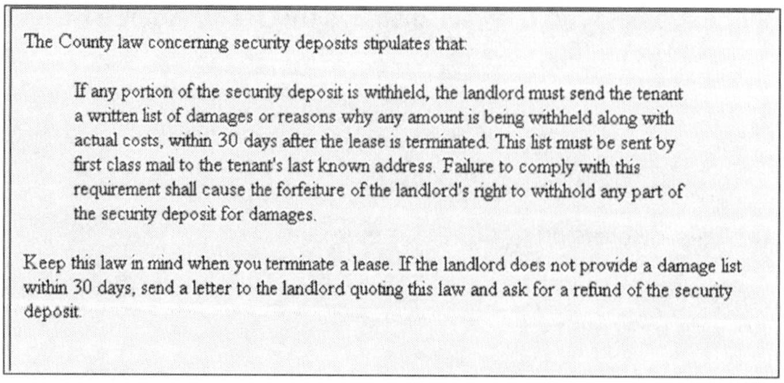

The County law concerning security deposits stipulates that:

> If any portion of the security deposit is withheld, the landlord must send the tenant a written list of damages or reasons why any amount is being withheld along with actual costs, within 30 days after the lease is terminated. This list must be sent by first class mail to the tenant's last known address. Failure to comply with this requirement shall cause the forfeiture of the landlord's right to withhold any part of the security deposit for damages.

Keep this law in mind when you terminate a lease. If the landlord does not provide a damage list within 30 days, send a letter to the landlord quoting this law and ask for a refund of the security deposit.

Figure 11-9: Rendering of a `<blockquote>` element by Netscape Navigator.

Logical styles

In addition to specifying the layout of text blocks, you may also set parts of a sentence apart. For example, you may want to emphasize a word in a sentence or cite the name of a book. HTML provides a set of formatting elements that let you indicate the text style logically. That means instead of saying "display this text in italic," you say "this text should be emphasized" and leave the actual formatting to the browser.

Note   Logical styles are in keeping with the basic philosophy of HTML — you describe your document's content, but not how the document is formatted. In other words, you say "here's the document body," "this text is a citation," "this part needs strong emphasis," and so on. However, as you will see in the next section, HTML does include a few physical formatting tags that let you set text in boldface or italic.

HTML 2.0 provided the following logical style elements:

✦ `<cite>` for citations such as a book or magazine title

✦ `<code>` for computer source code

✦ `<em>` to indicate emphasis

✦ `<kbd>` to show text typed on a keyboard

✦ `<samp>` for a sequence of literal characters

✦ `<strong>` to indicate strong emphasis

✦ `<var>` to show user-supplied variable names

Each style element applies to the text between the start tag and a corresponding end tag. For example, the text between `<cite>` and `</cite>` is treated as a citation and formatted in an appropriate style (typically in italics).

Here are a few sentences that use the logical style tags:

```
<body>

Here is a <cite>citation</cite> embedded in the text.<br>
Here is <code>some code</code> in the text.<br>
You can <em>emphasize</em> text.<br>
Here is how to show <kbd>keyboard</kbd> text.<br>
A <samp>few</samp> literal characters.   <br>
If necessary, use <strong>strong emphasis</strong> in your text.<br>
Here is a variable <var>name</var> embedded in text.<br>

</body>
```

Figure 11-10 shows how Netscape Navigator renders this HTML source text.

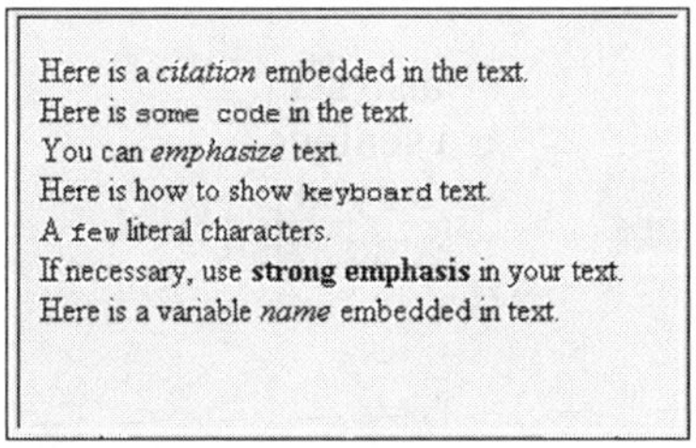

Figure 11-10: Typical rendering of various logical HTML styles.

As Figure 11-10 shows, a Web browser renders several logical styles using a single physical style. For example, the browser displays <cite>, <em>, and <var> elements in italic. The <strong> element appears in boldface. The rest of the styles — <code>, <kbd>, and <samp> — are shown in a monospace font (usually Courier).

Although some of these logical styles appear the same in the browser, there may be future browser enhancements that present the logical styles in a different manner. For example, the <cite> style is used to set apart a book or magazine citation. If you follow the convention that all of your HTML documents use <cite> for citations, you could easily search the documents and locate all citations.

Tip Use these HTML elements sparingly. Use emphasis (<em>) only when appropriate — for example, when you first use a new term or the name of a file or device. Because <strong> appears in boldface, use <strong> even more sparingly than <em>.

Physical styles

Although HTML encourages you to use logical styles to format text, HTML does provide a few physical styles. As the name implies, a physical style specifies exactly how you want the text to appear. For example, with a physical style you can say "this text should appear in italics."

HTML 2.0 provided four physical styles:

✦ `<b>` to display text in boldface

✦ `<i>` to show text in italics

✦ `<strike>` to display text in strikethrough (where a line is drawn through the characters)

✦ `<tt>` for teletype or monospace font

The `<strike>` tag was not really a part of HTML 2.0 standard, but HTML 3.2 includes that style and many browsers support the `<strike>` tag.

Although you can probably guess how these styles look, the following HTML source shows a few sentences that demonstrate the physical style tags:

```
This is <b>boldface< b>. Here is <i>italic</i> and
<strike>strikethrough</strike>. This is <tt>teletype</tt> style.
```

Figure 11-11 shows how these physical styles look in a Web browser.

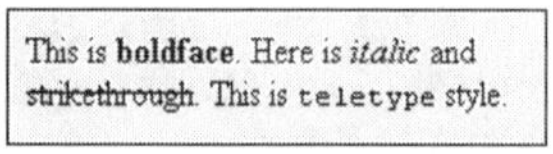

This is **boldface**. Here is *italic* and
~~strikethrough~~. This is `teletype` style.

Figure 11-11: An example of physical HTML styles.

Most popular Web browsers render the physical styles as shown in Figure 11-11. However, if a browser cannot display text in a specific physical style, the browser is free to substitute one style for another. For example, if boldface font is not available, a browser might display the `<b>` style in reverse video or as underlined text.

Tip You should use logical style tags where possible, resorting to the physical styles only when you cannot think of any appropriate logical style. In other words, if you want to emphasize some text, use the `<em>` tag instead of the `<i>` tag. On the other hand, if you have to show some text in strikethrough, you have no choice but to use the `<strike>` tag.

Inserting special characters

Three characters — the less-than sign (<), the greater-than sign (>), and the ampersand (&) — have special meaning in HTML. The less-than and greater-than signs are used in tags and the ampersand is used to insert special characters (which include the less-than, greater-than, and ampersand) into HTML documents.

Webmaster To insert a special character in an HTML document, you have to enclose a representation of the character between an ampersand and a semicolon. For example, to insert a less-than sign, you have to write < in place of the less-than sign. Here, lt is a standard name for the less-than character in the ISO Latin-1 character set (this is a standard character set with 256 characters that most browsers support).

There are two representations of characters:

   ✦ A symbolic name such as lt for less-than and amp for ampersand.

   ✦ A number sign (#) followed by the numeric value of character in the ISO Latin-1 character set. For example, #62 is the greater-than sign (>) and #34 is the double quotation mark (").

Cross Ref Appendix D shows the names as well as the numerical value of the ISO Latin-1 character set.

Tip You can use the numeric value to insert any special character in an HTML document. For example, type &#169 to insert a copyright symbol (©):

```
<p>Copyright &#169 1996 Naba Barkakati
```

The Web browser displays this line as shown in Figure 11-12.

```
Copyright © 1996 Naba Barkakati
```

Figure 11-12: Using special characters such as the copyright symbol in HTML documents.

Lists

Lists help you present information in an organized manner. Throughout this book, you have seen examples of lists. Typically, a bulleted list is used to show a number of related items whose order does not matter. This book uses numbered lists to show sequences of steps where the order *does* matter.

HTML supports five types of lists:

✦ *Unordered lists* are enclosed in ⟨ul⟩ and ⟨/ul⟩ tags, and are good for displaying lists of hyperlinks and displaying short, unordered blocks of text.

✦ *Ordered lists* are enclosed in ⟨ol⟩ and ⟨/ol⟩ tags. These lists are used to show sequences of instructions, tables of contents, or lists of items where the item number is needed to refer to each item.

✦ *Directory lists*, enclosed in ⟨dir⟩ and ⟨/dir⟩ tags, are like unordered lists, but are meant for displaying lists of filenames (directory listings).

✦ *Menu lists*, enclosed in ⟨menu⟩ and ⟨/menu⟩ tags, are used to display a list of choices to the user. Typically, each list entry is a link to other documents.

✦ *Definition lists*, enclosed in ⟨dl⟩ and ⟨/dl⟩ tags, are useful for displaying glossaries and any lists of name-value pairs (essentially, a term and its definition).

Inside each of these lists, you have to use a specific tag to indicate the list items. The ⟨ul⟩, ⟨ol⟩, ⟨dir⟩, and ⟨menu⟩ lists, use the ⟨li⟩ tag to specify each list item (there is no end tag for ⟨li⟩). The ⟨dl⟩ lists use the ⟨dt⟩ and ⟨dd⟩ tags to define terms that appear in the list.

Unordered lists

An unordered list is essentially a laundry list of items that do not have any specific order. Most of us have many examples of unordered lists in our daily lives: shopping lists, lists of ingredients in recipes, and lists of things to do. Books, such as this one, use unordered lists to present information in a visually appealing manner. For example, in the "Lists" section, I use a bulleted list rather than describing the different types of lists in a long and confusing sentence.

Tip   In an HTML document, you can also use unordered lists to organize information. One common use of unordered lists is to present a list of links to the user:

```
<ul>
<li> <a href="oview.html"> Company Overview</a>
<li> <a href="webprog.html"> Web Programming Services</a>
<li> <a href="store.html"> Software Store</a>
<li> <a href="search.html"> Search</a>
<li> <a href="feedback.html"> Feedback</a>
</ul>
```

You must enclose the list inside the ⟨ul⟩ and ⟨/ul⟩ tags and start each list item with a ⟨li⟩ tag. In this case, the text in each item happens to be a link to another HTML document.

A typical browser renders such a list as a bulleted list with a round bullet symbol, as shown in Figure 11-13.

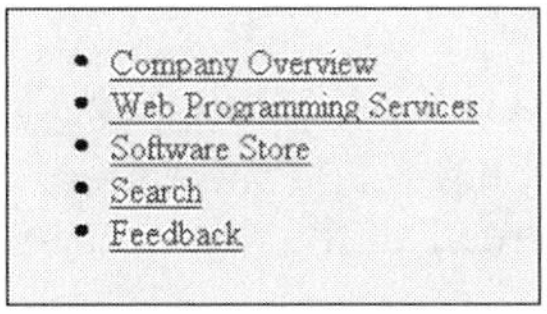

- Company Overview
- Web Programming Services
- Software Store
- Search
- Feedback

Figure 11-13: An unordered list where each item is a link to another document.

Browsers are free to use any type of bullet symbol for the unordered list. Most browsers use a round or a square bullet symbol. The text-only Lynx browser uses an asterisk to mark the start of each list item.

Note that you can *nest* lists — that is, place one list inside another. If you have a nested list, the browser displays the inner list with extra indentation on the left-hand side.

Ordered lists

Ordered lists are useful to show a sequence of steps. For example, this book uses ordered lists to provide step-by-step instructions for a specific task. Typically, the items in an ordered list are numbered so that you can tell the order of the items.

The syntax of an ordered list is similar to that of an unordered list except that you must enclose the ordered list in `<ol>` and `</ol>` tags. Here is a typical ordered list:

```
<ol>
<li> Enter your total income on line 1.
<li> Enter your total deductions on line 2.
<li> Subtract line 2 from line 1. If zero or less, enter -0-
<li> Enter amount of tax from Tax Table.
</ol>
```

Figure 11-14 shows how Netscape Navigator renders this ordered list. The list elements are numbered sequentially, starting at 1.

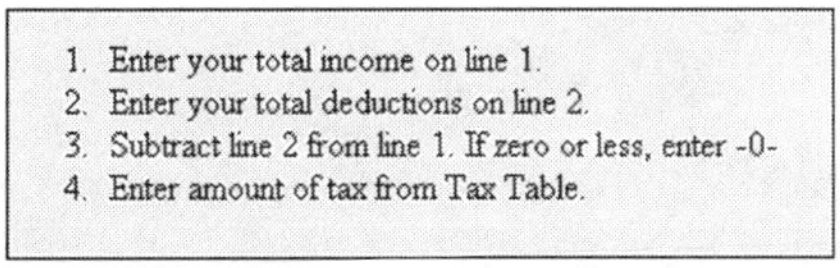

1. Enter your total income on line 1.
2. Enter your total deductions on line 2.
3. Subtract line 2 from line 1. If zero or less, enter -0-
4. Enter amount of tax from Tax Table.

Figure 11-14: An ordered list as rendered by Netscape Navigator.

Directory lists

Directory lists are essentially unordered lists, meant to display a list of filenames. The entire directory list is enclosed in ⟨dir⟩ and ⟨/dir⟩ tags. Like unordered lists, you have to use the ⟨li⟩ tag to specify the items in a directory list.

Directory lists are supposed to contain short items, typically up to 20 characters each. A browser may arrange the directory listing in multiple columns. Because most browsers format a ⟨dir⟩ list the same way as an unordered list, the ⟨dir⟩ list is not commonly used.

Menu lists

Menu lists are yet another form of unordered lists. A menu list can have only one item per line — that means a menu list is more compact than an unordered list that can have somewhat longer items.

You have to enclose a menu list inside the ⟨menu⟩ and ⟨/menu⟩ tags. As in an unordered list, the list items are marked by the ⟨li⟩ tag. When displayed by a Web browser, a menu list looks the same as an unordered list.

Definition lists

Definition lists are a unique type of list that you can use to provide definitions of items. An example of a definition list is a book's glossary that provides definitions of key words. Each definition list entry has a pair of items:

✦ The term being defined

✦ The text that constitutes the term's definition

Typically, the term is shown on a new line starting at the left margin of the page. The term's definition appears slightly indented to the right. If the definition extends to multiple lines, all of these lines appear in an indented paragraph.

You have to enclose the definition list inside the ⟨dl⟩ and ⟨/dl⟩ tags. Each entry in the list requires two items: the term and its definition. HTML provides two separate tags to enter these items:

✦ The ⟨dt⟩ tag to start the term

✦ A ⟨dd⟩ to begin the term's definition

Note that there are no end tags for ⟨dt⟩ and ⟨dd⟩.

Here is an example of a typical glossary formatted as a definition list:

```
<dl>

<dt> abstract class
<dd> A class that cannot have any instance. Usually
defined to specify the behavior of classes that will
be derived from it.

<dt> base class
<dd> In C++, a class from which other classes are
derived. The derived classes inherit from the base class.

</dl>
```

Figure 11-15 shows how a Web browser renders this definition list.

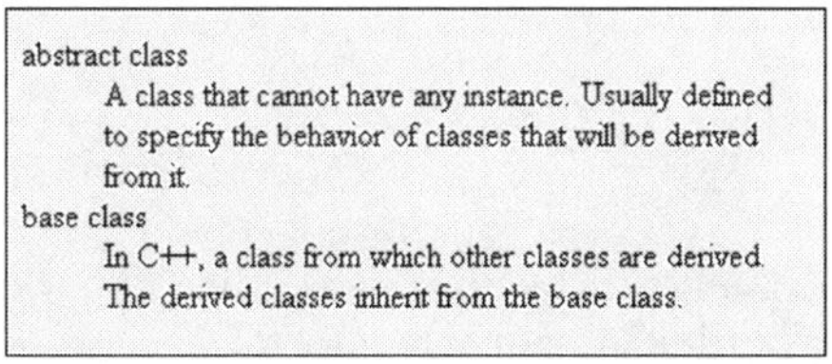

abstract class
    A class that cannot have any instance. Usually defined
    to specify the behavior of classes that will be derived
    from it.
base class
    In C++, a class from which other classes are derived.
    The derived classes inherit from the base class.

Figure 11-15: A definition list lets you define terms.

Horizontal rules

The horizontal rule is not specifically for text layout, but it serves as a separator between various parts of your Web page. You use the ⟨hr⟩ tag to insert a horizontal rule in your HTML document. There is no corresponding end tag for ⟨hr⟩.

For example, here is a typical HTML document showing how to use horizontal rules:

```
<html>
<title>The Water Lily</title>
<body>
<img src="wlily.gif">
<hr>
Welcome to the Water Lily!
<p> Our grand opening celebration is this weekend.
Please come and visit us then,
<hr>
<address> Webmaster, The Water Lily </address>
</body>
</html>
```

Figure 11-16 shows how Netscape Navigator renders this HTML document. Two horizontal rules separate the document into the header (with the image), the body, and the footer.

Figure 11-16: A typical HTML document that uses horizontal rules as separators.

Hyperlinks Revisited

One of the important aspects of HTML documents is the ability to embed hyperlinks. You have to use the `<a>` tag to embed a hyperlink in your document:

```
While in Maui, we took the 30 mile long, winding road to
<a href="hana.html">Hana</a>, one of the most special places in Hawaii.
```

A typical Web browser renders this sentence as shown in Figure 11-17.

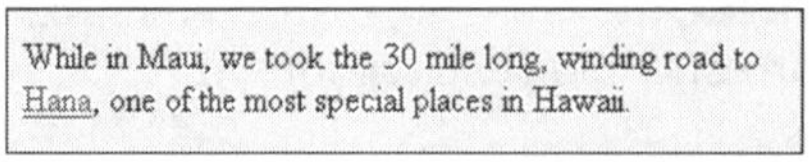

While in Maui, we took the 30 mile long, winding road to
Hana, one of the most special places in Hawaii.

Figure 11-17: An embedded hyperlink in an HTML document.

The browser displays the hyperlink in a distinctive format. When the user places the mouse cursor over the hyperlink, the cursor shape changes. If the user clicks the word *Hana*, the browser loads the HTML document `hana.html` from the server that provided the page shown in Figure 11-17. Presumably, the `hana.html` document contains further information about Hana, Maui.

Note The document containing a hyperlink is referred to as the *source* document. The URL in an anchor (`<a>`) tag is known as the *target* document (target of the hyperlink).

In its simplest form, a hyperlink anchor is enclosed in the tags `<a>` and `</a>`. At a minimum, you need to provide the `href` attribute, which is set to the name of the HTML document to be activated by this hyperlink.

However, the `<a>` element accepts several attributes besides `href`:

✦ `href` specifies the displayed document's URL when the user clicks this link.

✦ `method` tells the Web browser to specially process the document specified by the `href` attribute (most browsers do not use the `method` attribute).

✦ `name` associates a name with a specific location in the document (once defined, you can use the name as the target of a hyperlink).

✦ `rel` specifies the relationship between the source document and link target (if the target document comes after the source, you'd write `rel=next`).

✦ `rev` indicates the reverse relationship — the relationship between the target document (that appears in the link's URL) and this document. For example, if this document precedes the target document, you'd write `rev=prev`.

✦ `title` provides a title for the target document to which you are linking.

✦ `urn` defines a more general Universal Resource Name (URN) for the target document. A URN is supposed to be a location-independent form of the currently well-known URL. However, the URN specification is not yet ready, so this attribute is essentially a placeholder for the future.

Note Of these attributes, `href` and `name` are most commonly used. The `rel` and `rev` attributes provide a good way to document the sequence in which documents are linked, but most Web browsers ignore the `rel` and `rev` attributes.

Making the links

The mechanics of specifying a hyperlink with the `href` attribute of the anchor element (`<a>`) is fairly simple. The basic syntax is

```
<a href="URL">link text</a>
```

where URL specifies the target document that the browser displays when the user clicks this link. The text between the `<a>` and `</a>` tags serves as the link where the user clicks. You can also embed an image that serves as the link.

To set up the hyperlink, you need to know how to specify various URLs. You are already familiar with the `http` URL that establishes a link to another HTML document. For example, here are some typical `http` URLs:

```
http://www.idgbooks.com/
http://www.idgbooks.com/info.html
http://www.sun.com/sunsoft/Developer-products/java/literature/idc.html
```

The first URL refers to the top-level home page on the `www.idgbooks.com` server. The second references the HTML document `info.html` stored in this server's root directory. The third URL refers to the Web document `idc.html` in the `sunsoft/Developer-products/java/literature` directory on the server `www.sun.com`.

You can have URLs for many different types of Internet services:

✦ ftp (File Transfer Protocol) URL to initiate a file transfer.

✦ news URL to access a newsgroup from a USENET news server.

✦ mailto URL to send mail to a specified e-mail address.

✦ gopher URL to access a Gopher server.

✦ telnet URL to initiate a TELNET session

The ftp URL

URL Use the ftp URL to set up a hyperlink that allows the user to download a file from a FTP server. The syntax of the ftp URL is

```
ftp://user:password@server:port/path;type=code
```

where the various parts of the URL mean the following:

✦ user:password specifies the username and password to be used when accessing the FTP server (if you do not specify these fields, anonymous is used as the username). Never put the username and password in an HTML document, because anyone may be able to access your system using that information.

✦ server is the name of the FTP server (for example, ftp.ncsa.uiuc.edu).

✦ port specifies the port to be used (if you omit the port, the default port of 21 is used). Nearly all FTP servers use the default port.

✦ path is the full pathname of the file to be downloaded.

✦ type=code is an optional field that specifies how the file should be downloaded (if you omit this, the file is downloaded as a binary file). The code can be a to indicate ASCII and i to indicate binary.

The typical URL to access a file through anonymous FTP is simple (see Chapter 2 for a description of anonymous FTP). For example, the HTML source includes a link with an ftp URL that allows the user to access NCSA's anonymous FTP server:

```
NCSA HTTPD remains a popular Web server for UNIX systems. You may
<a href="ftp://ftp.ncsa.uiuc.edu/Web/httpd/Unix/ncsa_httpd/current/">
download</a> a copy for evaluation.
```

Figure 11-18 shows how Netscape Navigator renders that HTML source.

NCSA HTTPD remains a popular Web server for UNIX
systems. You may download a copy for evaluation.

Figure 11-18: A hyperlink with an ftp URL in an HTML document.

As Figure 11-18 shows, the word `download` serves as the hyperlink. When the user clicks this word, Netscape Navigator establishes an anonymous FTP session with the FTP server `ftp.ncsa.uiuc.edu` and displays the contents of the `Web/httpd/Unix/ncsa_httpd/current` directory on that server, as shown in Figure 11-19.

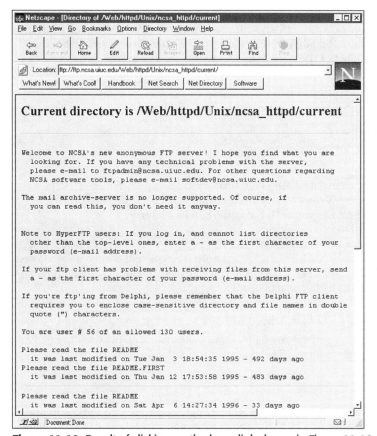

Figure 11-19: Result of clicking on the hyperlink shown in Figure 11-18.

Scroll down in the Netscape Navigator window (Figure 11-19) to see a list of files that can be downloaded (this directory contains the latest NCSA Web server). Clicking a file causes Netscape Navigator to download it via anonymous FTP.

The `news` URL

You can use a `news` URL to let the user access a USENET newsgroup or a specific article in a newsgroup. The basic format of the `news` URL is

```
news:newsgroup
```

where `newsgroup` is the name of a newsgroup in the standard format (for example, `comp.os.linux.announce` or `comp.infosystems.www.announce`). Here is an example of how you might use a `news` URL in a hyperlink:

```
Visit the <a href="news:comp.infosystems.www.authoring.html">
comp.infosystems.www.authoring.html</a> newsgroup for discussions on
writing HTML documents for the Web.
```

Figure 11-20 shows how this HTML source appears on a Web page. In this example, when the user clicks the newsgroup's name, the Web browser contacts a news server and gets the contents of the specified newsgroup.

Visit the comp.infosystems.www.authoring.html newsgroup for discussions on writing HTML documents for the Web.

Figure 11-20: A hyperlink with a `news` URL.

Webmaster If you want to try a `news` URL, the Web browser must support access to a news server, and you must set the Web server to contact this news server (your Internet service provider should provide you with the name of a news server).

Netscape Navigator does support access to a news server. If you click the link (shown in Figure 11-20), Navigator brings up a separate window that displays the contents of the `comp.infosystems.www.authoring.html` newsgroup. You can then click a specific article from the list of articles displayed.

The `mailto` URL

The `mailto` URL lets you specify a link that causes the Web browser to send an e-mail message to a specific address. The syntax of this URL is

```
mailto:address
```

where `address` is the e-mail address where mail should be sent. A typical use of the `mailto` URL is to provide a link that sends an e-mail to the Webmaster of a site:

```
<address>
  <a href="mailto:webmaster@someplace.com">Webmaster</a>
</address>
```

Clicking the link (`Webmaster`) sends mail to `webmaster@someplace.com`.

Webmaster Like the `news` URL, the `mailto` URL works only if the user has configured the browser with the name of a mail server.

The gopher **URL**

Just as the ftp URL is for connecting to an FTP server, the gopher URL is for connecting to a Gopher server. The general syntax of a gopher URL is

```
gopher://server:port/type/selector
```

where server is the fully qualified domain name of a Gopher server, port is the port number of the Gopher service, type is the type of Gopher resource, and selector is the path of a Gopher resource on the Gopher server (see Chapter 2).

If you omit the port number, the default Gopher port of 70 is used. You can also safely omit the type and selector. When you omit these, the Gopher server returns the top-level index of its directory. Here is a typical use of a gopher URL:

```
One of the original Gopher servers is the one in
<a href="gopher://gopher.tc.umn.edu">University of Minnesota</a>.
```

If the user clicks this link, the Web browser should connect to the Gopher server at the host gopher.tc.umn.edu and display the top-level directory of that server.

The telnet **URL**

Suppose you allow users to log into your system as a guest and try out some software. You can actually embed a hyperlink on your Web page that lets users click the link and begin a TELNET session. The syntax of such a telnet URL is

```
telnet://user:password@server:port/
```

where user and password are the username and password used to log in, server is the name of the host, and port is the port number. If you skip the port number, the default TELNET port of 23 is used. If you do not provide a username and password, the TELNET software may prompt for this information.

This telnet URL allows a user to log into a system by clicking a hyperlink:

```
If you want to try out our new software,
<a href="telnet://guest:bemyguest@someplace.com/">login</a> now.
```

For this to work, the Web browser needs a helper application that can establish a TELNET session. On UNIX systems, the browser can use the standard telnet command. TELNET is also available on Windows 95 and Windows NT.

Naming links

The name attribute of the anchor element allows you to assign a name to a specific chunk of text within a document. Then, you can set up a hyperlink so that the browser loads the HTML document and positions it at the named anchor point.

Tip   Suppose you have a rather long HTML document named design.html and one of the sections is titled Display Subsystem. You could define that section header as a named anchor point as follows:

```
<h3><a name="display">Display Subsystem</a></h3>
```

Then, you could provide hyperlinks to jump directly to the display subsystem's description. Here is an example of a realistic use of a named anchor point:

```
The <a href="design.html#display">display subsystem</a> supports plug-ins.
```

When the user clicks this link, the Web browser displays the design.html document, positioning it so that the named anchor is visible in the window.

Summary

When you prepare a Web site's content, much of the work is in formatting text documents. To do this well, you need to know the basic text formatting elements in HTML. This chapter shows the overall structure of an HTML document and how to use various text formatting elements to prepare Web pages. The next chapter explores multimedia data (images, sound, and video clips) in HTML documents.

Where to go next . . .

✦ If you want to spruce up your Web page with images, see Chapters 12 and 13.

✦ To use HTML extensions provided by Netscape Navigator and Microsoft Internet Explorer, go to Chapter 14. (Chapter 14 also indicates which HTML extensions are now part of the HTML 3.2 specification.)

✦ For information on designing Web pages, see Chapter 15.

✦ To learn about HTML authoring tools, proceed to Chapter 17.

✦ Proceed to Chapters 19 and 20 to learn how to create interactive HTML forms.

Adding Images, Sound, and Animation

O ne of the reasons for the Web's popularity is that the Web makes it fun to use information. Users can see text with interspersed images. A click on a link lets the user hear a recorded sound. Another link might bring up an MPEG (Motion Pictures Experts Group) video. Users find the Web fun because of its multimedia integration of images, sound, and video.

Inclusion of images, sound, and video (for that matter, any other type of data) in a Web page is as simple as using the <img> tag or adding an HTML link with the name of the multimedia file. Typically, a Web browser has the built-in capability to display a number of image formats. However, for some other types of multimedia files (such as sound files and MPEG video), the Web browser needs helper applications to handle the multimedia data.

This chapter gives you detailed information on various multimedia file formats and how to use multimedia — images, sound, and video — in your Web pages.

Multimedia File Formats on the Web

When you include any type of multimedia — images, sound, or animation — in a Web page, you do so by specifying the multimedia filename in a URL. Each type of multimedia data can be stored in a file in a number of different formats. For example, images can be stored in GIF (Graphics Interchange Format) or JPEG (Joint Photographic Experts Group) formats. Sound files can be in Windows WAV format or the Sun mu-law (also called au) format. Video clips may be stored in AVI (Audio Video Interleaved) or MPEG formats.

The next few sections discuss various multimedia file formats used on the Web and how you can use multimedia files in your Web pages.

How a Web browser handles multimedia files

The way a Web browser handles a multimedia file is not any different from the way it handles a plain text or HTML document. Just as an HTML document is identified by a URL that includes a filename, a multimedia file is also identified by a URL with a filename. Typically, what differs is the file extension — HTML files have `.html` or `.htm` as extensions, whereas an image might have a `.gif` or `.jpg` extension. As you might guess, the `.gif` extension refers to a GIF image and `.jpg` is a JPEG image.

 The Web server uses the file extension and tells the Web browser the type of data the browser has to process. The basic sequence of steps is:

1. The Web browser sends a `GET` command to the Web server with the filename being requested.

2. The Web server checks the file extension and determines the type of data.

3. The Web server sends a header to the browser informing the data type being sent.

4. The Web server sends the contents of the file.

5. The Web browser processes the data based on the data type (as indicated by the header that precedes the data). For some multimedia data (such as GIF and JPEG images), the browser simply displays the image. For others, the browser may prompt the user for information on how to process the downloaded data.

To understand the header better, you need to see how the Web server sends requested information to the Web browser.

Web server and Web browser interaction

When it needs a file from the server, the Web browser sends a `GET` command. For example, to download a GIF file, the browser might send the following command:

```
GET /image/const.gif HTTP/1.0
```

Immediately after this line, the browser sends a blank line to indicate the end of the command. Here is how a typical Web server responds to this `GET` command:

```
HTTP/1.0 200 OK
Date: Thu, 25 Apr 1996 23:21:47 GMT
Server: Apache/1.0.3
Content-type: image/gif
Content-length: 395
Last-modified: Tue, 14 Nov 1995 04:41:15 GMT

(data from the /image/const.gif file follows)
```

All the lines preceding the actual file contents constitute the header. A blank line separates the header from the file contents. Notice that the header includes information such as the date, the name of the Web server, and the date the file was last modified. All the header information appears in the following format:

```
name: value
```

which specifies a value for a field identified by name. For example, the size of the file in bytes is specified by the `Content-length` field.

Webmaster The header's `Content-type` field indicates the type of the data that the Web server sends to the Web browser. Specifically, the content type is expressed in terms of a type and a subtype. For example, if the `Content-type` field is `image/gif`, then the type is `image` and the subtype is `gif`. The `Content-type` field is crucial for the browser because that field tells the browser what to do with the data that follows from the Web server.

MIME types

Note The `Content-type` field specifies the MIME type of the data that the Web server sends to the Web browser. MIME stands for *Multipurpose Internet Mail Extensions*, an Internet standard for attaching any type of data to a mail message. (MIME is specified in RFC 1521.)

Webmaster Originally, MIME was developed so that the data contained in mail messages and attachments could be identified properly. Because any file can be an attachment to a mail message, MIME defines types for all kinds of data, from text and images to applications.

The Web server associates one or more file extensions with a MIME type. If you use the NCSA or Apache Web server, a file named `mime.types` associates a MIME type to one or more file extensions. For example, here are some excerpts from the `mime.types` file:

```
audio/basic              au snd
audio/x-aiff             aif aiff aifc
audio/x-wav              wav
image/gif                gif
image/jpeg               jpeg jpg jpe
image/tiff               tiff tif
text/html                html htm
text/plain               txt
video/mpeg               mpeg mpg mpe
video/quicktime          qt mov
video/x-msvideo          avi
```

On each line, you see a MIME type followed by one or more file extensions for that MIME type (the file extensions appear without the leading period). Notice that the text/html MIME type uses the file extensions html and htm, which the MIME type of HTML documents. Table 12-1 lists the common MIME data types found on the Web.

Table 12-1
Multimedia Data Formats on the Web

MIME Type	File Extensions	Description
Text types		
text/html	html htm	HTML documents (plain text file with embedded HTML tags).
text/x-sgml	sgml sgm	Text file with SGML tags.
text/plain	txt	Plain text file.
text/tab-separated-values	tsv	Text file with tab-separated fields (used to store spreadsheet data).
Image types		
image/gif	gif	Compressed image file stored in CompuServe's Graphics Interchange Format (GIF). Widely used on the Web for icons and line drawings.
image/jpeg	jpeg jpg jpe	JPEG image file. Popular format for storing photographic images.
image/tiff	tiff tif	Tagged Image File Format (TIFF).
image/x-portable-bitmap	pbm	Portable bitmap format file. A portable format for monochrome images.
image/x-portable-pixmap	ppm	Portable pixmap format file. A portable format for color images.
image/x-xbitmap	xbm	X Window System bitmap file for monochrome images.
image/x-xpixmap	xpm	X Window System pixmap file used to store color images.

MIME Type	File Extensions	Description
`image/x-xwindowdump`	xwd	X Window System screen dump format.
Sound types		
`audio/basic`	au snd	An audio format created by sampling the audio signal at 8KHz (that means sampling 8,000 times per second). Also known as mu-law format. Popular sound file format on Sun and other UNIX workstations.
`audio/x-aiff`	aif aiff aifc	Audio Interchange File Format (AIFF) file. Commonly used on Macintoshes.
`audio/x-wav`	wav	Waveform files used to store digitized sound. Most popular sound format on Microsoft Windows systems.
Animation types		
`video/mpeg`	mpeg mpg mpe	Full-motion video with sound stored using the MPEG format.
`video/quicktime`	qt mov	Quicktime movie. Commonly used on Macintosh.
`video/x-msvideo`	avi	Audio-video interleaved (AVI) file format used to store full-motion video with sound. Popular video format on Microsoft Windows systems.
Other types		
`application/pdf`	pdf	Adobe's Portable Document Format (PDF) for storing formatted documents that can be viewed with Adobe Acrobat software.
`application/postscript`	ai eps ps	PostScript files including Encapsulated PostScript (EPS) and Adobe Illustrator (AI) files that contain ready-to-print formatted documents.
`application/rtf`	rtf	Rich Text Format (RTF) file with formatted document.

(continued)

Table 12-1 *(continued)*

MIME Type	File Extensions	Description
application/x-mif	mif	FrameMaker document (FrameMaker is a high-end page layout software available on a variety of operating systems, including UNIX).
application/x-netcdf	nc cdf	NetCDF files (a popular storage format for scientific data).
application/x-tcl	tcl	Tool Command Language (Tcl) script (a text file that has to be interpreted by the Tcl interpreter).
application/zip	zip	Compressed file in ZIP format.
application/x-tar	tar	A UNIX tar file that has to be unpacked with the tar command.

Webmaster Notice that some of the MIME subtypes in Table 12-1 start with x- (the subtype follows the slash). The x- prefix means that the MIME type is not recognized as an official type by the Internet Assigned Numbers Authority (IANA).

Helper applications for Web browsers

Table 12-1 lists a large number of MIME types, but the Web browser can handle only a handful of formats. For example, Netscape Navigator can handle the following MIME types without any external program:

```
image/x-xbitmap
image/gif
image/jpeg
text/html
text/plain
```

Basically, that says Netscape Navigator can handle plain text and HTML files plus the popular GIF and JPEG image files. The X Bitmap file format is not that popular, but Netscape Navigator supports that format as well.

For a few other MIME types, Netscape Navigator requires a helper application. Essentially, the user can configure a Web browser to launch a application to handle a specific MIME type. For example, the Windows 95 version of Netscape Navigator comes with a helper application named NAPLAYER that handles a number of sound formats such as au, snd, and aiff. Also, on Windows 95 or Windows NT, Netscape Navigator can display AVI video clips by running the Windows MPLAYER (multimedia player) program. The user can configure the Windows 95 Netscape Navigator to launch other helper applications through the Helpers tab in the Preferences dialog box (select General Preferences from the Options menu).

Webmaster On UNIX systems, a user has to specify the helper applications through the .mailcap file in the home directory. For example, to launch the xanim program when the Web browser downloads a QuickTime movie, the .mailcap file should have the following line:

```
video/quicktime;        xanim %s
```

Tip The bottom line is that even though you can include any MIME type in your Web pages, most Web browsers are equipped to handle a handful of prominent file types such as HTML, plain text, GIF and JPEG. Therefore, it's best if you stick to these MIME types in your Web pages.

Popular image file formats

The trouble with images is that they can be quite large. For example, each *pixel* (a *picture element* or dot) of a 256-color image requires a single byte of storage space. Therefore, a 300 pixel by 200 pixel (300x200) image requires 60,000 bytes of storage. For a 24-bit image that uses 8 bits of storage for each of the primary color components (red, green, and blue), the storage triples; a 24-bit 300x200 image requires 180,000 bytes of storage.

Note To minimize the storage requirements (and consequently the time needed to download an image from the Web server to the browser), images are generally stored in compressed form. Two of the popular image file formats are GIF and JPEG.

Most popular Web browsers such as Netscape Navigator, Mosaic, and Microsoft Internet Explorer can display GIF and JPEG images, so these two file formats are safe bets for any images you use in your Web pages. Although you don't need to know the exact details of image file formats, a general understanding can help you use the appropriate formats in a Web page.

JPEG

The JPEG (pronounced "jay-peg") format is a lossy compression algorithm that can handle 24-bit color images. *Lossy compression* means that you cannot get back some of the details in the original image from the JPEG version of that image. In other words, you lose information when you compress an image using JPEG. However, the loss of details is not a problem for photographic images, especially when you can achieve very good compression ratios with the JPEG algorithm.

Unlike GIF, which is only a widely accepted standard, JPEG is a fully defined International standard (ISO 10918-1) for image compression.

Webmaster JPEG compresses images by breaking the image into 8x8 blocks of pixels and performing a mathematical operation known as Discrete Cosine Transform (DCT) on each 8x8 block. DCT breaks down the 8x8 subimage into spatial frequencies that essentially identify small-scale and large-scale features of the image. Then, the small-scale, fine-grained details are discarded (this is why JPEG is *lossy* — it throws away information). The remaining DCT output is first encoded using a Run-Length Encoding (RLE) technique that replaces a sequence of similar values with a count followed by a single value. The run-length encoded DCT output is then further compressed with a variable-length code known as Huffman code.

Webmaster The amount of lossiness of a JPEG image can be controlled by the software that applies the JPEG compression to an image. Typically, JPEG compression software lets you set the image quality of the JPEG image. There is no standard scale of quality settings. However, most JPEG software uses a 0 to 100 scale, with 100 referring to the highest quality. Most JPEG images use a quality setting in the range of 75 to 95.

Webmaster The JPEG standard specifies a compression algorithm, but JPEG does not specify any file format. Of course, people needed some sort of file format to store and exchange JPEG images. A popular JPEG file format is JFIF (JPEG File Interchange Format), which was coordinated by C-Cube Microsystems, Inc. JFIF is a simple file format that uses a simple header followed by the JPEG-compressed image. Currently, JFIF has emerged as the accepted standard for exchanging JPEG images on the Internet.

URL For more information on JPEG, you should consult the JPEG Frequently Asked Questions (FAQ) at the URL `http://www.cis.ohio-state.edu/hypertext/faq/usenet/jpeg-faq/top.html`.

GIF

GIF (pronounced "jif") was developed by CompuServe for compact storage of images with up to 256 colors. GIF files store images using the LZW (named after the scheme's authors, Lempel-Ziv and Welsh) compression scheme. Unlike JPEG, GIF is a *lossless compression scheme*; that means you can reverse the compression process and get back the original data. Also, unlike JPEG, GIF specifies a file format as well as the compression scheme used to compress the image.

Webmaster A GIF file is organized into blocks, and there may be more than one graphic image in a file. A GIF file has the following overall structure:

✦ The file starts with a six-byte header with the text `GIF87a` or `GIF89a`. The header indicates the version of GIF reader required to decode the contents of the file. A GIF89a-capable reader can also handle GIF87a files.

✦ Next comes the Logical Screen Descriptor that provides information about the screen area where the GIF image is to be displayed. The Logical Screen Descriptor includes information such as the width and height, the background color, and some flags. If the most significant bit of the flags field is set, the GIF file includes a color table. This color table is called the Global Color Table because it applies to all images contained in the GIF file.

✦ The Global Color Table follows the Logical Screen Descriptor. The Global Color Table is an array of red-green-blue (RGB) color levels.

✦ The rest of the file contains a series of blocks. The first byte of each block identifies the type of the block. One of the most important blocks is the Image Descriptor block that starts with a comma (,) and contains information about the image about to follow. Specifically, information in the Image Descriptor block specifies the position of the image in the logical screen, the width and height of the image, and some flags. As with the Logical Screen Descriptor, a 1 in the most significant bit of the flags in the Image Descriptor block indicates that another color table, known as the local color table, follows this block.

✦ If there is a local color table, it appears next in the GIF file. A single byte follows the local color table. The value in this byte indicates the number of bits needed to represent an actual pixel value of the image. For example, this byte is 8 for a 256-color image because 8 bits can express any value between 0 and 255. This byte determines the initial code size used by the LZW compression algorithm.

✦ Next comes the image data in a sequence of blocks with, at most, 255 bytes in each block. These values are stored in a compressed format encoded using the LZW algorithm with variable-length codes.

✦ If the GIF file contains multiple images, the sequence of image descriptor and image data blocks is repeated.

✦ A trailer block containing a single semicolon (;) marks the end of the GIF data stream in the file.

Both GIF87a and GIF89a have similar file layouts, but GIF89a adds the following new features to the GIF87a format:

Cross Ref

✦ Application Extension blocks that contain information for use by specific programs (typically, only the program that defines these Application Extension blocks can understand them). For example, Netscape Navigator 2.0 interprets an Application Extension block in a GIF89a file to set some parameters that Navigator uses to animate multiple images in a GIF89a file. Chapter 14 describes the Netscape Application Extension block.

✦ Graphics Control blocks that specify whether the image has a transparent pixel (all transparent pixels are displayed using the background color of the Web browser's window), whether a time delay (specified in hundredths of a second) should be used before displaying the image that follows, and what should be done after displaying the image. A Graphics Control block affects the image immediately following the block, so it always precedes the Image Descriptor block.

✦ Plain Text blocks that contain lines of text. Many GIF display programs do not support the plain text blocks.

The Graphics Control blocks provide two important features: the ability to designate one of the pixels as transparent and animation of multiple images contained in a single GIF89a file.

Cross Ref

The "Creating transparent GIFs" section describes how to use a shareware tool to designate a color as transparent. GIF89a animation is explained in the "Creating GIF89a animation loops" section of this chapter.

GIF or JPEG?

You don't have to exclusively use a single image format in your Web pages. Each image file format has its place. The general guidelines for choosing between GIF and JPEG formats are as follows:

✦ The GIF format is good for line art and images that have large areas of solid colors. For such images, GIF provides very good compression and also preserves the accuracy of the image. That means you should use GIF for graphs and line-art icons with solid colors.

✦ The JPEG format is best for photographic images (remember the *P* in JPEG stands for *Photographic*). Because JPEG is a lossy compression, you should not use JPEG for line drawings where the loss of information is easily noticeable.

The trouble with GIF

In December 1994 CompuServe (the creator of GIF) announced that the LZW compression algorithm (which is used in GIF) infringes on a patent held by Unisys. CompuServe now pays a royalty for using LZW compression in GIF. Unisys expects developers of commercial, for-profit software to secure a license from Unisys and pay royalties for the use of GIF. (Unisys requires such licensing for all GIF-based software marketed beginning in 1995.)

URL

You can read about CompuServe's 1994 announcement at the URL `http://www.lpf.org/Patents/Gif/origCompuServe.html` and read a clarification from Unisys on use of GIF at the URL `http://www.lpf.org/Patents/Gif/unisys.html`.

Note

Basically, Unisys requires a royalty for any commercial software that supports GIF. Non-commercial and non-profit GIF-based applications do not require any licensing. This includes any GIF-based freeware offerings on the Internet. Unisys also indicates that no license is necessary for use of GIF images on Web pages.

This sudden development — the need to pay royalty for use of GIF in commercial software — has spurred the development of an alternate graphics algorithm called Portable Network Graphics or PNG (pronounced "ping").

PNG

In March 1995, a group of graphics developers developed a free standard for *lossless image compression* using algorithms that do not have the legal problems associated with GIF. PNG addresses some of the weaknesses of GIF and is specifically designed for those developers who need to display images over the network.

Note PNG will support multiple compression schemes. However, the only currently defined compression method is an algorithm derived from the LZ77 algorithm. The compression algorithm has been used in GNU ZIP (GZIP), PKZIP, and other programs. Portable C implementation of the compression/decompression code is freely available.

Webmaster PNG retains many of the features of GIF including support for palette-based 256-color images, interlaced images (that appear to fade in when displayed), and transparent pixels. Additionally, PNG improves upon GIF by adding the following new features:

✦ Supports true color images with up to 48 bits per pixel and grayscale images with up to 16 bits per pixel

✦ Allows a transparency mask through an alpha channel (that means each pixel can have an associated transparency level)

✦ Supports gamma correction (gamma correction compresses or expands the dark or light shades in an image)

✦ Detects file corruption

Unlike GIF, however, PNG does not support the storage of multiple images in a single file.

URL You can read about PNG at the URL `http://www.group42.com/png.htm`. Through the links on this Web page, you can download the latest PNG specification as well as an application programming interface (API), a compression library, and a set of test images. The URL `http://quest.jpl.nasa.gov/PNG/` is another good location to check for information on PNG.

Note Because PNG is relatively new, many Web browsers still do not support the PNG format. In particular, the most popular Web browser, Netscape Navigator, does not yet have built-in support for PNG format images.

Digitized sound files

Most Windows and Macintosh Web browsers can play sound files, but many users on UNIX systems do not have the necessary hardware. Additionally, sound files can be rather large. For these reasons, you should use sound files sparingly.

Note Sound files contain digitized sound generated by converting the *analog* (continuously varying) sound waves into 8-bit or 16-bit numbers, sampling the wave at rates from 8 to 44KHz (8,000 to 44,000 times a second). Higher sampling rates and higher numbers of bits (16-bit) provide better quality, but you need more disk space to store high-quality sound.

For example, a 30-second sound digitized at 8KHz and stored with 8 bits per sample requires 30 x 8,000 = 240,000 bytes of storage. Increasing the sampling rate to 22Khz and using 16 bits per sample increases the sound file size to 1,320,000 bytes! If you want CD-quality audio, the sampling rate goes up to 44KHz and samples are stored as 16-bit values.

Webmaster On the Web, the following sound file formats are popular:

✦ **Mu-law** sound files are standard on Sun and NeXT workstations. The file extension is `.au` and the MIME type is `audio/basic`. Mu-law files store sound waves digitized at 8KHz and stored using 8 bits of data per sample. The sound quality of mu-law sound files is similar to that of standard telephone receivers. On UNIX systems with sound capability, you can play a mu-law sound file with the following command:

```
cat soundfile.au > /dev/audio
```

where `soundfile.au` is the name of the mu-law sound file.

URL If you want to try out some mu-law sound files, visit the URL `http://sunsite.unc.edu/pub/multimedia/sun-sounds/`. This site has hundreds of sample sound files.

✦ **AIFF** (Audio Interchange File Format) was originally developed by Apple for use on the Macintosh. AIFF is also popular on Silicon Graphics (SGI) workstations. AIFF typically uses 22.3KHz sampling at 8 bits per sample, which is the default sampling rate for sound on Apple Macintosh systems.

URL ✦ **WAV** (file extension `.wav` and MIME type `audio/x-wav`) is the Microsoft Windows standard for digitized sound. Typically, WAV files are supported only by Web browsers on Microsoft Windows systems. The sampling rate for WAV files can vary anywhere from 8 to 44KHz with sample sizes from 8 to 16 bits. You can find a large collection of WAV files at the URL `http://sunsite.unc.edu/pub/multimedia/pc-sounds/`.

If you provide sound files at your Web site, you may want to use the mu-law format, which is more readily supported on a variety of systems including UNIX, Windows 95, and Windows NT.

Video clips

If you think images and sound files can be large, wait till you see the size of video clips. Even with compression, a 10-second movie can take 1.4MB of storage. That's quite a lot of data to download for 10 seconds worth of motion picture.

Users need the following to enjoy video clips:

✦ High-speed Internet access to download the video clip in a reasonable amount of time

✦ Hardware with enough processing power to decompress and play the video clip at a fast enough display rate (otherwise, the user does not see the video effect)

✦ Software to decompress and display the video frames

Tip   Just because many users do not have a high-speed Internet connection or fast hardware does not mean that you should not provide video clips at your Web site. You just need to keep in mind that many users cannot readily access and view the video clips.

If you plan to provide video clips at your Web site, use one of these file formats:

✦ **MPEG** (Motion Photographers Experts Group) is a standard for compressing and decompressing a video in real-time. MPEG allows for the inclusion of digitized sound with the movie. MPEG compression is quite complex; each frame of video is compressed based on how that frame changes with respect to neighboring frames. MPEG viewer software is available on most UNIX systems.

✦ **QuickTime** was originally developed by Apple for the Macintosh, but the format has become more popular since Apple has released QuickTime video player for Microsoft Windows. On UNIX systems, the `xanim` program can play QuickTime videos.

✦ **AVI** (also known as *Video for Windows*) is Microsoft's proprietary format for storing video clips with the image frames and the sampled sound that accompany the images. The AVI format is most popular among Windows users, which certainly is a large percentage of users on the Web.

Multimedia Files in Web Pages

In a Web page, you can add images, sound, and other multimedia files in one of the following ways:

✦ As a hyperlink that the user must click to download

✦ As an inline image that the Web browser automatically downloads and displays at the same time it downloads the current Web page

Tip Typically, you use inline images to display images that are integral parts of your Web page. This includes company logos or mastheads on the Web page, small icons that spruce up the page, and image maps — clickable images — on the Web page.

Tip The hyperlink format is common for large images (so that the user gets to decide whether to download the image) and other multimedia files such as sound and video clips.

Adding multimedia hyperlinks

In the sample Web page of Chapter 10, you saw how a hyperlink is embedded in an HTML document. The general syntax of a hyperlink is

```
This is a <A HREF="URL">link</A>.
```

The word `link` acts as a hyperlink and, when the user clicks this hyperlink, the Web browser accesses the specified URL. That URL could be the name of another Web page or the name of a multimedia file such as an image file or a sound file.

One way to embed multimedia files in a Web page is to add hyperlinks with the name of the multimedia file as the URL. When the user clicks the link, the Web browser sends an HTTP request to the Web server. The Web server responds with a header that includes the MIME type of the file followed by the raw data in the file. The MIME type tells the Web browser what to do with the downloaded file.

External images through hyperlinks

For images, use a hyperlink when you want the image to open as a separate document after the user explicitly activates the link. Typically, this is the way you should offer large images. It's even better if you include the image's size as well as a smaller inline version of the image so that the user has enough information to decide whether to download the image or not.

For example, here's how NASA's Jet Propulsion Laboratory makes interesting images of the Galileo space probe's journey to Jupiter available to the public (see the URL `http://www.jpl.nasa.gov/archive/gll.html`). The image index is a unnumbered list with links to GIF files that contain the actual images. Parts of the HTML source of the image index page follow:

```
<pre>
<ul>
<li><A HREF=http://www.jpl.nasa.gov/files/images/browse/
       galprobe.gif>galprobe.gif</A>   139K
Artist's conception of probe entry.   P-31528Ac
<li><A HREF=http://www.jpl.nasa.gov/files/images/browse/
       gllant.gif>gllant.gif</A>      231K
Work on ground to diagnose stuck antenna
```

Figure 12-1 shows how these links appear to the user.

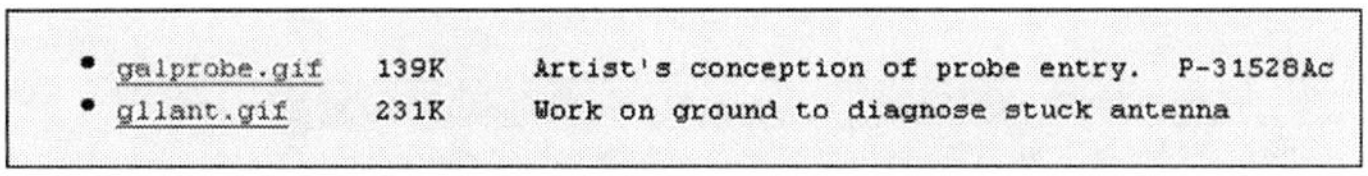

```
  •  galprobe.gif    139K     Artist's conception of probe entry.  P-31528Ac
  •  gllant.gif      231K     Work on ground to diagnose stuck antenna
```

Figure 12-1: Image hyperlinks with size indications.

The user can see a description of the image as well as its size before deciding whether to download the image for viewing.

It's even better when the user can see a small version of the image as well as the size before clicking the link. Figure 12-2 shows a Web page from NASA (the U.S. Space Agency) that shows a thumbnail image along with the size of the full-size image (120K).

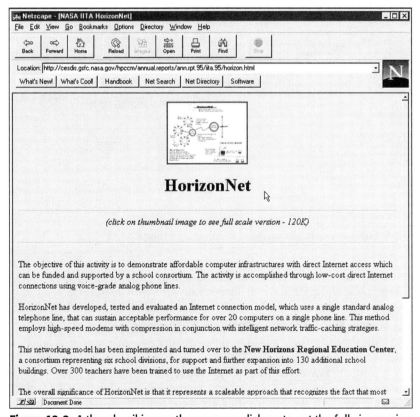

Figure 12-2: A thumbnail image the user can click on to get the full-size version.

Figure 12-3 shows the full-size image that the Web browser displays when the user clicks on the thumbnail version shown in Figure 12-2.

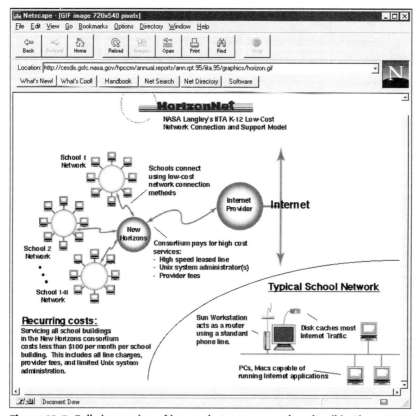

Figure 12-3: Full-size version of image that appears as thumbnail in Figure 12-2.

I show both the thumbnail and the full-size images (in Figures 12-2 and 12-3) so that you can see how a typical thumbnail image compares with its full-size version.

External sound and animation through hyperlinks

While you can provide images as either inline images or hyperlinks, you *must* use hyperlinks to provide sound files and video clips on your Web pages. (In fact, you can make any type of file available through hyperlinks.)

Tip   As with large image files, you should indicate the size of the sound or video file on the hyperlink text so that the user can make an informed decision whether to download the file. Figure 12-4 shows a video offering from the National Weather Service that follows this practice and shows thumbnail images together with links that indicate the size of the videos.

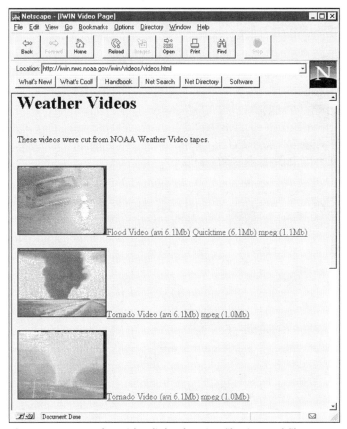

Figure 12-4: Weather video links showing file size and file type.

As you can see, the videos are available in multiple formats and the links indicate the size for each. The following HTML listing shows the links for the first video (starting with the horizontal rule):

```
<HR>
<A HREF="http://iwin.nws.noaa.gov/iwin/videos/chn001tv.avi"> <IMG
    SRC="ch1tv.gif">Flood Video (avi 6.1Mb)</A>
<A HREF="http://iwin.nws.noaa.gov/iwin/videos/chn001tv.mov">Quicktime
    (6.1Mb)</A>
<A HREF="http://iwin.nws.noaa.gov/iwin/videos/chn001tv.mpg">mpeg
    (1.1Mb)</A>
<BR><BR>
```

You can offer sound files through hyperlinks in the same way. As with videos, it's good practice to use an icon to indicate that a sound file follows and provide an indication of the file's size and format on the link. Figure 12-5 shows a Web page where NASA provides audio from the launch of the XTE satellite.

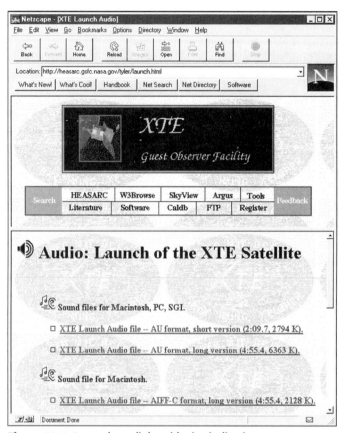

Figure 12-5: Image hyperlinks with size indications.

As Figure 12-5 shows, each audio link shows an icon (to indicate it's audio) as well as the file type and size. The HTML source for the audio links of Figure 12-5 (beginning with the horizontal rule) is shown here:

```
<hr>
<ul>
<img src="/Images/heasarc/icons/sound03.gif">
Sound files for Macintosh, PC, SGI.
<p>
<ul>
<li><a href="http://legacy.gsfc.nasa.gov/tyler/launch.au">XTE Launch
        Audio file — AU format, short version (2:09.7, 2794 K).</a>
<p>
<li><a href="http://legacy.gsfc.nasa.gov/tyler/launch2.au">XTE Launch
        Audio file — AU format, long version (4:55.4, 6363 K).</a>
<p>
</ul>
```

```
<img src="/Images/heasarc/icons/sound03.gif">
Sound file for Macintosh.
<p>
<ul>
<li><a href="http://legacy.gsfc.nasa.gov/tyler/launch.aifc">XTE Launch
        Audio file — AIFC format, long version (4:55.4, 2128 K).</a>
<p>
</ul>
```

Including inline images in a Web page

To include an inline image in a Web page, use the `<img>` element of HTML. For example, suppose you have a small image that you want to use as a masthead on your Web page (a *masthead* is usually a rectangular image that's wide, but not too tall). If the image is stored in the file named `banner.gif` in your Web server's document directory, the following `<img>` element inserts that image in a Web page:

```
<img src="banner.gif">
```

The `src` attribute tells the Web browser to request the image named `banner.gif` and render the image when the Web server sends back the image data.

If the image were stored in the `image` subdirectory of the Web server's document directory, then the `<img>` element would be

```
<img src="/image/banner.gif">
```

You can also include an image from a specific Web site on your Web page. For example, to include the GIF image from the file `/samples/image/banner.gif` from the Web server `www.othersite.com`, use the following `<img>` element:

```
<img src="http://www.othersite.com/samples/image/banner.gif">
```

Image alignment

In addition to the `src` attribute, an `<img>` element can also have an `align` attribute that instructs the Web browser how to align the image with nearby text. For example, to align the bottom of the adjoining text with the middle of the image, use the following `<img>` element:

```
<img align=Middle SRC="/image/banner.gif">
```

`Align=Top` aligns the top of the image with the top of the tallest item on that line (including other images on the line). `Align=Bottom` is the default setting that aligns the bottom of the text with the bottom of the image. Figure 12-6 illustrates the results of the three types of alignment.

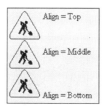

Figure 12-6: Result of different `align` attribute settings.

These alignments are useful only for simple captions. With these alignments you cannot embed an image in the Web page's text and have the text flow around the image.

Cross Ref Netscape has added a number of additional attributes to the `<img>` element including a number of other `align` attributes. Chapter 14 describes some of the Netscape extensions to the `<img>` element.

Providing alternate text for text-only Web browsers

As you add inline images to your Web page, remember that most Web browsers let users turn off inline images. That means there is no guarantee that the images are visible at all times. Therefore, you should not make your Web page totally dependent on the inline images. Additionally, some browsers (such as Lynx) may not support any images at all. For such text-only browsers, you should provide a text label with the `alt` attribute in an `<img>` element.

The purpose of the `alt` attribute is to provide some text that text-only browsers can display in lieu of the image. For example, when you add an inline image with a mast-head showing your company name, you might specify an `alt` attribute as follows:

```
<img alt="LNB Software masthead" SRC="/image/banner.gif">
```

Then, when the user views this Web page using Lynx, the text `LNB Software masthead` appears in place of the image. If you do not provide the `alt` attribute, Lynx users see the text `[INLINE]` or `[IMAGE]` in place of the image.

Tip What text you provide as the `alt` attribute depends on the image. Here are some guidelines for the `alt` attribute:

✦ If the inline image is a simple marker of some sort (for example, a fancy looking bullet in a bulleted list), use `alt="*"`.

✦ If the inline image is a company masthead, use a descriptive title in the `alt` attribute. Here's an example:

```
<img src="banner.gif" alt="LNB Software, Inc.">
```

✦ If the image is an image map (Chapter 12 describes image maps), leave out `alt` atttribute or use `alt="imagemap"`.

✦ If the inline image is purely decorative, use `alt=""` (an empty string). That way, text-only browsers won't see anything in place of the image.

✦ If the inline image is a thumbnail image that allows the user to get some other multimedia file (such as a sound file), use an `alt` attribute with descriptive text to tell the user what that link does. For example, an image that links to a sound file might have the following `<img>` element:

```
<a href="launch.au"><img src="spkr.jpg" alt="[Listen to launch audio]"></A>
```

Using inline images wisely

Tip   Inline images can improve your Web page's appearance, but the vast majority of users do not have high-speed connections to the Internet. At best, most users have only a 28.8Kbps connection, which means a 30K image takes roughly 10 seconds to load. Considering that users may not want to wait more than 10 to 15 seconds for a Web page to load, try to keep the total size of all inline images down to a minimum.

Typically, a Web page might use the following types of images:

✦ A masthead image with the company's name and logo (the masthead may also serve as an image map that lets the user jump to other Web pages)

✦ Several small icons to set apart the major parts of the Web page

✦ One or more horizontal rules as decorative separators (although you could use the <HR> element and forego the inline image version of horizontal rules)

Figure 12-7 shows a Web page layout with a typical set of inline images.

Tip   If you use icons next to hyperlinks, you should make the icons act as links as well. All you have to do is place the `<img>` element inside the anchor element:

```
<a href="music.au"><img src="music.gif" alt="[listen to music]"></a>
```

Unfortunately, when you make an inline image a link, the browser displays the image with a box around the icon. Nevertheless, users typically expect to click an icon and see something happen, especially if the icon is next to another link. Therefore, you should make the icon a link.

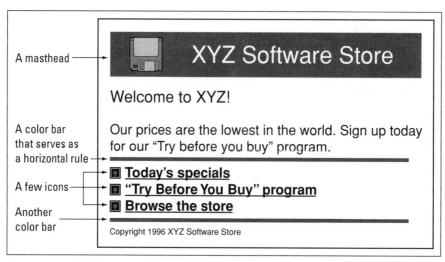

Figure 12-7: A Web page with a typical complement of inline images.

Image File Creation

The preceding sections of this chapter explain various image file formats and how you can include such files in a Web page. The next few sections gives you some guidance on the tools and techniques used to create image files.

Creating images

You need to use a paint or drawing program to create images. The difference between a paint program and a drawing program is that a paint program works directly with a raster image, which the user sees as an array of pixels. Some examples of paint programs include MacPaint on Macintosh, PC Paintbrush or the Windows 95 Paint program on Microsoft Windows systems, and xpaint on the X Window System (which runs on most UNIX systems).

A drawing program, on the other hand, lets you draw graphic objects such as lines, polygons, and text. You can move objects around and resize them. Essentially, the drawing program's objects do not become a raster image until you print them. CorelDraw is an example of a drawing program that runs on Microsoft Windows. Many drawing programs, including CorelDraw, allow you to mix raster images with graphics objects. Additionally, CorelDraw can save an entire drawing as an image in one of several image formats including GIF and JPEG.

Tip You can use both paint and drawing programs to prepare images. The paint programs naturally work with images. Most drawing programs can save the drawings in well-known image formats such as GIF and JPEG.

Converting GIFs to transparent GIFs

Webmaster *Transparent GIF* simply means that one of the colors (*pixel values*) in the GIF file is designated as the transparent color. Web browsers such as Netscape Navigator replace the transparent pixel's color with the window background, thus making the image blend into the background.

Webmaster One of the best freely available tools for creating transparent GIFs is giftool. (You'll also find giftool in the GraphicTools/giftool directory of this book's companion CD-ROM.) To download and prepare giftool on a Linux system, follow these steps:

1. Begin an anonymous FTP session with ftp.homepages.com, as follows:

```
ftp ftp.homepages.com
Connected to point.HomePages.com.
220 point FTP server (Version wu-2.4(26) Mon Nov 7 12:06:06 PST 1994) ready.
Name (ftp.homepages.com:root): anonymous
331 Guest login ok, send your complete e-mail address as password.
Password: (type your e-mail address and press Enter)
230 Guest login ok, access restrictions apply.
Remote system type is UNIX.
Using binary mode to transfer files.
```

2. Change the directory to giftool, and look at the following directory listing:

```
ftp> cd giftool
250 CWD command successful.
ftp> ls
200 PORT command successful.
150 Opening ASCII mode data connection for /bin/ls.
total 1166
drwxr-xr-x  2 4789    1000      512 Jun 19  1995 .
drwxrwxr-x 11 4788    1001      512 May 13 07:01 ..
-rw-rw-r--  1 4789    1001    48836 Jun 19  1995 giftool.alpha-dec-osf2.0.tar.Z
-rw-rw-r--  1 4789    1000   135680 Jun 19  1995 giftool.exe
-rw-r---r-- 1 4789    1000    36101 Jun 19  1995 giftool.hppa1.1-hp-
        hpux9.05.tar.Z
-rw-rw-r--  1 4789    1001    81920 Jun 19  1995 giftool.i86-unknown-linux.tar.Z
-rw-rw-r--  1 4789    1001     3605 Jun 19  1995 giftool.man
-rw-rw-r--  1 4789    1001    66073 Jun 19  1995 giftool.mips-sgi-irix4.0.tar.Z
-rw-rw-r--  1 4789    1001    35409 Jun 19  1995 giftool.mips-sgi-irix5.2.tar.Z
-rw-r--r--  1 4789    1000    44859 Jun 19  1995 giftool.rs6000-ibm-unknown.tar.Z
-rw-rw-r--  1 4789    1001    34226 Jun 19  1995 giftool.sparc-sun-
        solaris2.3.tar.Z
-rw-rw-r--  1 4789    1001    33292 Jun 19  1995 giftool.sparc-sun-sunos4.1.tar.Z
-rw-rw-r--  1 4789    1001    24204 Jun 19  1995 giftool.src.zip
-rw-rw-r--  1 4789    1001    34267 Jun 19  1995 giftool.tar.Z
226 Transfer complete.
```

3. Download the source-code archive `giftool.tar.Z`, and quit `ftp`. (Although there is a binary file for Linux, I could not uncompress the file after downloading, even though the transfer mode was binary. That's why I decided to download the source code.)

```
ftp> get giftool.tar.Z
200 PORT command successful.
150 Opening BINARY mode data connection for giftool.tar.Z (34267 bytes).
226 Transfer complete.
34267 bytes received in 19.1 secs (1.8 Kbytes/sec)
ftp> bye
221 Goodbye.
```

4. Decompress and unpack the archive with the following command sequence:

```
uncompress giftool.tar.Z
tar xvf giftool.tar
README
COPYRIGHT
main.c
readGIF.c
writeGIF.c
gif.h
 Makefile
```

5. Build the `giftool` program with the following command:

```
make CC=gcc
```

That's it! You should have `giftool` ready to run. Use the following command to move the program to a common directory such as `/usr/local/bin`, so that everyone can access it:

```
mv giftool /usr/local/bin
```

If you prefer to download the `giftool` source through your Web browser, use the following URL:

```
http://www.homepages.com/tools/
```

To convert a GIF file to transparent GIF, you have to decide which pixel to designate as the transparent one. You can look at the pixel values in an image with the `-p` option of `giftool`. Here is what `giftool` shows for the `const.gif` image:

```
giftool -p const.gif
GIF Image const.gif (58x52)
Image Colormap
 1:  0  0  0 (0x00 0x00 0x00) black
```

```
 2: 128   0   0 (0x80 0x00 0x00)
 3:   0 128   0 (0x00 0x80 0x00)
 4: 128 128   0 (0x80 0x80 0x00)
 5:   0   0 128 (0x00 0x00 0x80) navy
 6: 128   0 128 (0x80 0x00 0x80)
 7:   0 128 128 (0x00 0x80 0x80)
 8: 128 128 128 (0x80 0x80 0x80)
 9: 192 192 192 (0xc0 0xc0 0xc0) gray
10: 255   0   0 (0xff 0x00 0x00) red
11:   0 255   0 (0x00 0xff 0x00) green
12: 255 255   0 (0xff 0xff 0x00) yellow
13:   0   0 255 (0x00 0x00 0xff) blue
14: 255   0 255 (0xff 0x00 0xff) magenta
15:   0 255 255 (0x00 0xff 0xff) cyan
16: 255 255 255 (0xff 0xff 0xff) white
Image at 0,0 size 58x52
```

Webmaster While viewing the `const.gif` file in a paint program, I noticed that its background is white. The listing from `giftool` indicates that pixel number 16 is white. Therefore, I used the following command to create a transparent GIF:

```
giftool -16 const.gif > constT.gif
```

This command creates the new GIF file `constT.gif`. When I check this file's colors with `giftool`, it reports the following:

```
giftool -p constT.gif
GIF Image constT.gif (58x52)
Image Colormap
 1:   0   0   0 (0x00 0x00 0x00) black

... (Lines deleted)

16: 255 255 255 (0xff 0xff 0xff) white
Image at 0,0 size 58x52
   Transparent pixel = 16
```

Notice that pixel 16 now is reported as the transparent pixel. To use the new transparent GIF in the sample Web page, edit the reference to `const.gif` and replace it with `constT.gif`, so that the `<img>` directive reads as follows:

```
<img alt="Construction sign" align=bottom src="image/constT.gif">
```

Figure 12-8 shows the appearance of the embedded image.

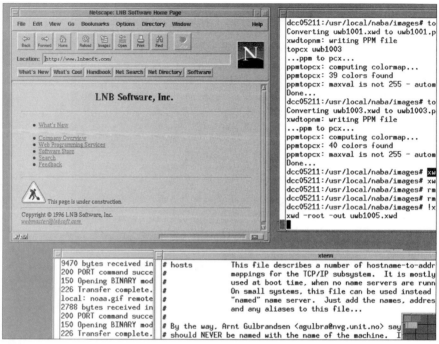

Figure 12-8: The transparent image blends in nicely with the background.

Tip   If you use GIF images in HTML documents, you should use a tool such as `giftool` to make the images transparent.

Creating GIF89a animation loops

An interesting feature of GIF89a is the ability to store multiple images in a single file. Netscape Navigator 2.0 is capable of animating such GIF89a images. With the right tool, creating a GIF89a animation sequence is simple.

URL   A good image manipulation package for UNIX systems is ImageMagick, available from the URL `http://www.wizards.dupont.com/cristy/ImageMagick.html`. Although the software is copyrighted by E. I. du Pont de Nemours and Company, ImageMagick is available for free and can be freely redistributed.

URL   To see some interesting uses of ImageMagick, visit the Imaging Machine Web site at the URL `http://www.vrl.com/Imaging/`. This site lets you submit images for conversion to GIF89a animations, which you can download to your system. In other words, the Imaging Machine site serves as a remote image manipulation facility that you can use if you do not have a system to install and run ImageMagick. You might begin by reading the user's manual at the Imaging Machine site.

URL The ImageMagick software compiles readily on a Linux system. First, you should download the software from the URL `ftp://ftp.wizards.dupont.com/pub/ImageMagick/`. As of this writing, the latest version is ImageMagick 3.7.5. Get the file `ImageMagick-3.7.5.tar.gz`. (Things change fast on the Web, so new versions of software may be available by the time you read this chapter. Please download the latest version of software from the ImageMagick FTP site.) Then, follow these steps to extract and compile the programs on a Linux system:

1. Copy the downloaded file to an appropriate directory. For example, you might place the file in `/usr/local/src` as follows:

   ```
   mv ImageMagick-3.7.5.tar.gz /usr/local/src
   ```

2. Extract the files from the compressed tar file with the following Linux command:

   ```
   tar zxvf ImageMagick-3.7.5.tar.gz
   ```

   This creates a directory named ImageMagick with all ImageMagick files in it.

3. Change directory to ImageMagick and read the `README` file with the following commands:

   ```
   cd ImageMagick
   more README
   ```

4. To compile and build the ImageMagick software, type the following commands:

   ```
   xmkmf
   make Makefiles
   make depend
   make -k
   ```

To learn more about the image processing tools in ImageMagick, all you have to do is use a Web browser such as Netscape Navigator and open the HTML files in the `www` subdirectory of the ImageMagick installation directory. For example, Figure 12-9 shows the ImageMagick `README` file, which is in HTML format.

Like many UNIX software packages, ImageMagick is a set of programs that perform specific image manipulation tasks. The tool that you use to create GIF89a animations is called `convert`. In fact, `convert` is a multipurpose tool that can perform a variety of image operations including conversion from one image format to another.

Cross Ref ImageMagick supports creation of GIF89a animations for use in Netscape Navigator 2.0 (or later versions). These GIF89a files contain a Netscape Application Extension block that tells the browser how many times to loop the image (see Chapter 14 for a description of the Netscape Application Extension in a GIF89a file).

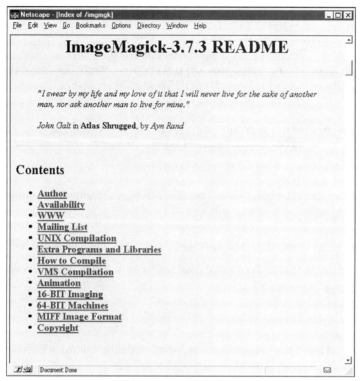

Figure 12-9: ImageMagick README file is in HTML format.

Webmaster

To create a GIF89a animation that can be displayed by Netscape Navigator:

1. Prepare the sequence of GIF images using any drawing or paint software. Name files in a sequence such as frame1.gif, frame2.gif, frame3.gif, and so on. Make sure these images are in the order in which you want to animate them. (I often prepare drawings in CorelDraw and save each frame as a GIF file.)

2. Use the convert program (in the ImageMagick directory) with the -delay and -loop options to create the GIF89a animation. To create the GIF89a animation file anim.gif out of all the frame*.gif files, use this command:

```
convert -delay 25 -loop 10 frame*.gif anim.gif
```

Here the -delay option specifies a delay (between successive frames) in hundredths of a second (thus 25 means 25/100 or 0.25 second delay) and -loop specifies the number of times the animation should loop (although Netscape Navigator 2.0 appears to treat any nonzero count as an infinite loop).

Tip   Use the resulting GIF89a animation file on your Web page just as you would use any other inline image (with the <img> tag). On Netscape Navigator 2.0 or later, the image will be animated; on other browsers, only the first image will be displayed.

Summary

You use images on Web pages to enhance their appearance. When necessary, you can also include other multimedia data such as sound files and video clips in HTML documents. This chapter describes various multimedia file formats and how they can be embedded in HTML documents. The next chapter shows how to create image maps — clickable images that serve as launching points for documents in a Web site.

Where to go next . . .

✦ To read up on the text formatting elements of HTML, see Chapter 11.

✦ To learn how to create image maps, consult Chapter 13.

✦ For information on Netscape Navigator and Microsoft Internet Explorer HTML extensions, go to Chapter 14.

✦ For Web page design guidelines, go to Chapter 15.

✦ To learn about HTML authoring tools, proceed to Chapter 17.

✦ For information on how to create interactive HTML forms, consult Chapters 19 and 20.

✦   ✦   ✦

Adding Image Maps

CHAPTER

13

Most Web pages use images to enhance the information content of the page. Some of the images also act as links — that means when a user clicks the image, the Web browser accesses a new URL that's linked to the image. Another common and innovative use of an image is as a graphical menu system — different parts of the image serve as links to different URLs. Such an image is called an *image map.*

Note An image map is essentially an inline image that, when the user clicks the image, causes the Web browser to send the coordinates of the click to a CGI program on the server. On the server, the CGI program redirects the browser to another document based on the location of the user's mouse click. In this way, the image map implements a graphical menu.

Cross Ref The type of image map described in this chapter is known as a *server-side image map* because the server has to process the mouse clicks on the image. Netscape Navigator and Microsoft Internet Explorer also support a client-side image map where the client handles the mouse clicks on the image map. Chapter 14 describes client-side image maps. You saw an example of an image map in Chapter 10. This chapter further explores image maps in great detail.

Cross Ref This chapter shows you how to implement an image map through the `imagemap` CGI program that accompanies the NCSA and Apache Web servers. Netscape Communications Corporation has introduced an extension to HTML, known as a *client-side image map*, that makes it possible for the Web browser to handle the image map without any CGI scripts on the server. Chapter 14 describes client-side image maps along with many more Netscape Navigator and Microsoft Internet Explorer extensions to HTML.

Image Map Examples

A typical use of image maps is to provide a graphical jumping-off point for the Web site. In this case, a somewhat large image is used as the focal point of the Web page. The image serves as the image map through which users access other Web pages at the site.

URL For example, Figure 13-1 shows a typical image map on the home page of the Climate Prediction Center (`http://nic.fb4.noaa.gov/`), which is part of NOAA — the National Oceanic and Atmospheric Administration (a U.S. Government organization).

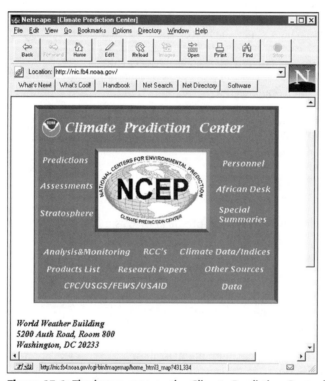

Figure 13-1: The image map on the Climate Prediction Center home page.

In this case, the image map shows a logo of the organization in the center and a number of labels identifying specific topics. If you position the cursor on the image map, the status area at the bottom of the browser's window shows the name of the CGI program (called `imagemap`) and the location of the mouse (the comma-separated numbers following the question mark). If you click the image map, the Web browser invokes the CGI program, passing the location of the mouse click as the input parameter. The CGI program then redirects the browser to the document indicated by the mouse click.

Another common use of an image map is as a button bar. For example, the Climate Prediction Center home page displays an image map button bar that appears at the bottom of the page, as shown in Figure 13-2. The button bar looks like a number of small images laid out in a line. Each image serves as a link to a specific URL.

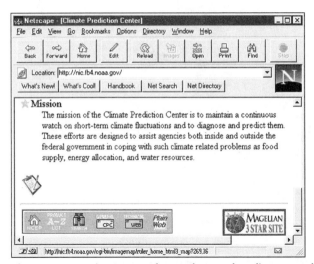

Figure 13-2: An image map button bar on the Climate Prediction Center home page.

URL   Sometimes an image map may combine a button bar with the organization's logo. A good example is the U.S. Air Force home page (`http://www.af.mil/`) shown in Figure 13-3. In this case, the image map includes the row of buttons appearing along the bottom edge as well as the larger image depicting the basic theme of the U.S. Air Force.

URL   Image maps are not only for graphical menus. On the Internet, you can find quite a few Web pages that use image maps in innovative ways. A good example is the Virtual Frog Dissection Kit (`http://george.lbl.gov/ITG.hm.pg.docs/dissect/dissect.html`) that lets you dissect a frog without all the mess. Figure 13-4 shows one of the steps during the frog dissection.

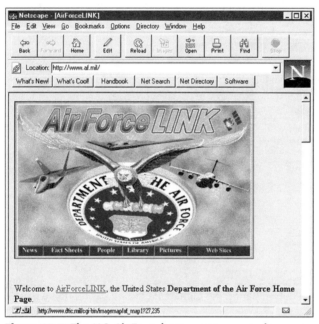

Figure 13-3: The U.S. Air Force home page uses an image map button bar underneath an impressive rendering of the Air Force logo.

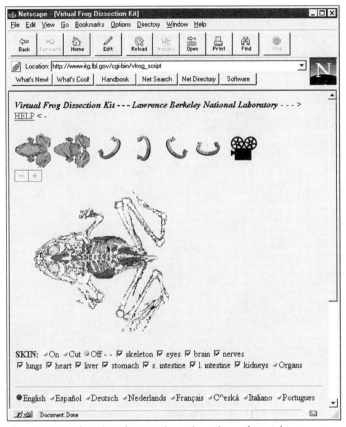

Figure 13-4: The Virtual Frog Dissection Kit on the Web.

Another interesting use of an image map is to display a geographic map and let users click on specific areas to get more information about a specific feature. For example, Figure 13-5 shows an image map that the U.S. National Park Service uses (http://www.nps.gov/wro/nps/cencal.htm) to provide information about national parks in the Central California region.

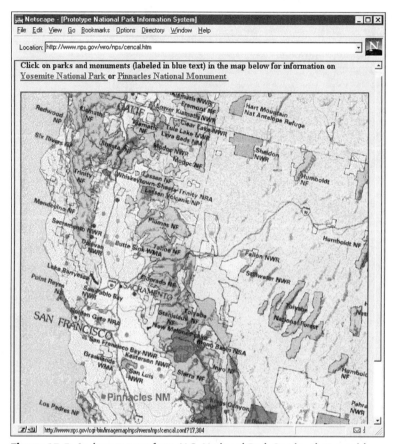

Figure 13-5: An image map from U.S. National Park Service that provides information on parks and monuments in the Central California region.

No matter how the image map is used — whether as a button bar or a large complex image — you have to use the same basic steps to prepare and set up an image map for a Web page.

Image Map Step-by-Step

A well-designed image map can certainly make your Web page appealing to users, but adding image maps is not a simple task. You have to take care of several steps before the image map is ready to use. To create the image map, you need the following items:

✦ An image for the image map. This is the image on which the user can click different parts to activate different hyperlinks.

✦ A way to identify hotspots — areas of the image — in terms of circles, polygons, or rectangles. These are the areas that the `imagemap` CGI program uses to determine which link to activate based on the location of the user's mouse click.

✦ An image map file (or simply, a map file) that associates specific hotspots of the image map with URLs. You could say that this file maps hotspots to hyperlinks.

You also need some tools to prepare these items. At a minimum, you need a paint program to prepare the image and a helper application that lets you identify the areas of the image you want to associate with different hyperlinks.

Preparing the image for the image map

Cross Ref Use a paint or drawing program to prepare the image map. Because image maps are nothing more than images that act as a graphical menu system, use the same program you normally use to prepare all of your images. Some of the common paint programs are mentioned in Chapter 12.

I typically use CorelDraw on Windows 95 to prepare the drawings and save them as GIF images. If you use a Macintosh, you could use a program such as Adobe Photoshop to prepare images.

Tip Although UNIX systems are well suited as Web servers, Macintosh and Microsoft Windows systems have better tools for creating and editing images. Not that you cannot do image editing on UNIX systems, it's just that the necessary image processing software is usually much more expensive than comparable software on Macintosh and Microsoft Windows.

The type of image you choose for an image map depends on how you plan to use the image map. As the "Image Map Examples" section discusses, Web sites use image maps in a variety of ways. Here are a few unique uses of image maps:

A map of the country that users can click to get some information for a specific state (or a region). For example, users may click a state and get the dollar amount of last month's sales for that state.

A plan view of a building where users can click a room to get more information. For example, as the adjoining figure shows, the White House home page (http://www.whitehouse.gov/WH/glimpse/tour/html/index.html) gives users an electronic tour of the White House with such an image map.

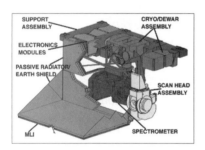

A view of a scientific instrument that lets users click a specific part to get more detailed information about that part. For example, NASA's Jet Propulsion Laboratory provides information about the Atmospheric Infrared Sounder (AIRS) instrument (for NASA's Earth Observing System) on its Web site (http://www-airs.jpl.nasa.gov/test/image.html) using such an image map.

For some of the unique uses, you have no choice but to use a large image. For other routine uses of image maps, follow these guidelines:

✦ Keep the size of the image as small as possible. This is especially true if the image map is the primary way to navigate through your Web site because the user has to wait for the whole image to download before being able to make a selection. Even if you use an image for a unique purpose (such as allowing users to click a geographic map), you should try to reduce the size of the image. Some of the ways to keep down image size are to reduce the physical size of the image and to reduce the number of colors used in the image.

✦ Clearly identify the hotspots on the image so that users can tell where to click to activate a link. You can help the users by putting some type of distinct border around each hotspot and by marking the hotspot with a keyword. You want to make sure that users can tell that they can access other information by clicking the image; otherwise, all of your efforts in preparing the image map will be wasted.

Marking the hotspots

After you prepare an image, you must designate the hotspots on the image. The hotspots are the areas where the user can click to activate specific hyperlinks. The user's mouse clicks on the image map are handled by the `imagemap` CGI program on NCSA and Apache Web servers. The `imagemap` program can handle four types of hotspots:

✦ A rectangle defined by the coordinates of the upper left and lower right corners.

✦ A circle defined by the coordinates of the center point and the radius (in number of pixels).

✦ A polygon defined by the array of vertices.

✦ A point defined by the coordinates of a single point (when the user clicks anywhere, the `imagemap` program activates the URL linked to the point closest to the location of the mouse click).

If you have a simple rectangular image map (such as the one in the sample Web page of Chapter 10), you can designate the hotspots as rectangular areas for which you figure out the coordinates manually. Even for simple images, however, it's tedious to determine the coordinates needed to define the hotspots of the image map. And, even if you were to work out the hotspots by hand, you still have to use a text editor to add the hotspot coordinates to a file that the `imagemap` CGI program uses.

Tip You can combine these two steps — mark the hotspots and generate the map file — with one of several shareware tools available on the Internet. One of the well-known programs is Mapedit, sold as shareware by Boutell.Com, Inc.

URL You can download a 30-day evaluation copy of Mapedit from `http://www.boutell.com/mapedit/`. The software is available in binary form for the following systems:

✦ Microsoft Windows 3.1

✦ Microsoft Windows 95 and Windows NT

✦ Solaris 2.x

✦ SunOS 4.1.x

✦ Linux (`a.out` format binary)

✦ DEC OSF/1 (DEC Alpha)

If your system is not on this list, you can download the UNIX and X11 sources that should compile on any UNIX system. If you plan to use Mapedit, you have to send in a registration fee of $25 (U.S.) to Boutell.Com (detailed registration instructions come with the software).

Mapedit lets you load a GIF or JPEG image into its window and specify the hotspots by drawing rectangles, circles, and polygons on the image. For each hotspot, Mapedit prompts you for the URL of the link associated with that hotspot. Mapedit generates the map file for you. Figure 13-6 shows how Mapedit lets you draw a rectangle and specify a URL that should be accessed when the user clicks that rectangle.

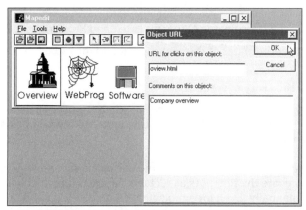

Figure 13-6: Defining the hotspots of an image map with Mapedit.

For each hotspot, you can define a URL as well as a comment. After you define all the hotspots and associate URLs with those hotspots, the end result is a map file. For the rectangular image map in Figure 13-6, the map file is as follows:

```
default http://www.lnbsoft.com/
rect oview.html 3,1 85,103
#Company overview
rect oview.html 49,37 50,38
rect webprog.html 86,0 172,103
rect swstore.html 173,1 250,102
rect search.html 250,1 333,102
rect feedback.html 333,1 433,101
```

Note This listing shows the map file for the `imagemap` CGI program used by the NCSA and Apache Web servers. The Mapedit tool can also generate appropriate map files for the CERN Web server. For example, the CERN format file for the image map of Figure 13-6 is

```
default http://www.lnbsoft.com/
rect (3,1) (85,103) oview.html
rect (49,37) (50,38) oview.html
rect (86,0) (172,103) webprog.html
rect (173,1) (250,102) swstore.html
rect (250,1) (333,102) search.html
rect (333,1) (433,101) feedback.html
```

As you can see, the CERN format is a bit more organized (because of the parentheses around the coordinates of the rectangle's corner points). The CERN server uses a program named htimage to handle the mouse clicks on image maps.

URL If you work on a Macintosh, you can use the Webmap shareware program to draw the hotspots on an image map. Webmap is available from the URL http://www.city.net/cnx/software/webmap.html.

Using the NCSA format map file

Typically, the map files are named with a .map extension. For NCSA format map files meant for use by the imagemap CGI program, you need to add the map file's name to a standard configuration file called imagemap.conf. By default, the NCSA and Apache Web servers expect this configuration file in the conf subdirectory of the directory where the server is installed (typically, /usr/local/etc/httpd).

Tip If the imagemap.conf file does not exist yet, use a text editor to create the file and a line with the name of the newly created map file. Suppose the new map file is named buttonbar.map and that file is located in the /usr/local/etc/httpd/htdocs directory. Then, you might place the following line in imagemap.conf:

```
buttonmap: /usr/local/etc/httpd/htdocs/buttonbar.map
```

This line tells the imagemap CGI program (the imagemap.conf file is interpreted by the imagemap program) that when you use the name buttonmap, you really mean the file /usr/local/etc/httpd/htdocs/buttonbar.map. You use the buttonmap name in the HTML document that uses the image map. If the imagemap.conf file already exists, just add one more line with the name of the new map file.

Writing the HTML to use the image map

The final step in getting the image map working is to use the image map in an HTML document. The basic idea of including the image map is similar to that of adding an inline image. You embed an anchor (<a>) element with the image map as an inline image. The only difference is that you must include the ismap attribute.

Tip For example, if the image file for the image map is buttonbar.gif (stored in the image subdirectory) and you use buttonmap as the name in the imagemap.conf file (see the "Using the NCSA format map file" section), then use the following HTML elements to add the image map to your Web page:

```
<a href="/cgi-bin/imagemap/buttonmap">
    <img alt="[Buttonbar]" src="/image/buttonbar.gif" ismap>
</a>
```

Because of the `ismap` attribute in the `<img>` element, the Web browser sends the x,y coordinates (relative to the upper left corner of the image) of the mouse click to the server. Actually, the browser appends a question mark to the URL specified by the `href` attribute of the anchor element (`<a>`) and then adds the x and y coordinates, separated by a comma. Thus, if the user clicks at the point (100, 50) on the image map identified by the sample HTML elements, the Web browser sends the server the string `/cgi-bin/imagemap/buttonmap?100,50`.

If you use the CERN Web server's `htimage` program to handle clicks on the image map, you should place the full pathname of the map file in the anchor element. In the context of the current example, you have to replace `buttonmap` in the `href` attribute with the full pathname of the CERN-format map file.

Summary

Many Web pages use an image as the launching pad for all other documents on the Web site. The user clicks on a part of the image to access a specific document. Such images are known as *image maps* and they are typically implemented using a built-in facility of the NCSA, Apache, and CERN servers. This chapter shows you samples of image maps and provides step-by-step instructions on creating an image map. The next chapter turns to the coverage of the HTML extensions that have been introduced by Netscape Navigator and Microsoft Internet Explorer.

Where to go next . . .

✦ To learn about the text formatting elements of HTML, see Chapter 11.

✦ For information on HTML extensions supported by Netscape Navigator and Microsoft Internet Explorer, consult Chapter 14.

✦ For Web page design guidelines, go to Chapter 15.

✦ To learn about HTML authoring tools, proceed to Chapter 17.

✦ For information on how to create interactive HTML forms, consult Chapters 19 and 20.

✦ ✦ ✦

Using HTML Extensions

HTML has been instrumental in making the Web possible because HTML provides a common format for exchanging information. However, HTML evolved hastily and it lacks sophisticated formatting commands that give the Web page designer more control over page layout. HTML's philosophy is to specify the logical formatting and leave the physical rendering of the HTML document to the Web browser. The latest formal HTML standard — HTML 2.0 (RFC 1866) — proved too limited for Web site developers. For example, HTML 2.0 does not provide for any way to center text (yes, it's true!) or to format a table.

As the Web grew in popularity, Netscape Communications, the leading provider of Web browsers, took matters into its own hands and added several new tags as well as many new attributes for existing HTML 2.0 tags. The Netscape Navigator Web browser accepted these HTML extensions (also known as the Mozilla extensions because Mozilla is the name of the cartoon dinosaur that appears on Netscape's Web site). Because of Netscape Navigator's popularity, many Web sites started using these extensions. For example, you may have already seen Web pages that use fancy backgrounds, format information in tables, and use frames to display multiple Web pages in the browser's window. These are all HTML extensions pioneered by Netscape.

URL In March 1995, an Internet draft on the HTML 3.0 specification was released (HTML 3.0 would have supported some of the current HTML extensions such as tables and backgrounds). As is the convention of the Internet Engineering Task Force (IETF), Internet drafts are valid for only six months and can be replaced or updated at any time. Essentially, the six-month time limit passed, the HTML 3.0 draft expired, and no standard for HTML 3.0 emerged. However, on May 7, 1996, the World Wide Web

Consortium (W3C) announced HTML 3.2, a new specification for HTML, developed together with vendors such as Netscape Communications Corporation, Microsoft, IBM, Novell, SoftQuad, Spyglass, and Sun Microsystems. To learn more about the status of the HTML standards activities, you should periodically check the W3C Web site (`http://www.w3.org/hypertext/WWW/MarkUp/`).

Tip   Currently, you have to work with HTML 3.2 and the various browser-specific extensions — primarily the Netscape extensions and, to a lesser degree, the Microsoft Internet Explorer extensions. Although you may not want to use any extensions (to ensure that all browsers can view your Web pages), some of them are so handy (for example, tables and frames) that it's difficult to resist using them.

Whether you use extensions or not, you should know what the extensions provide — in case you need a specific feature that only an extension provides. Keep in mind that you can always design a Web page that lets users view a "plain vanilla" Web page if they do not have browsers that support the extensions.

This chapter provides an overview of HTML extensions supported by Netscape Navigator and Microsoft Internet Explorer. Examples and sample screens show you how to use many of these extensions. I focus primarily on the HTML extensions that both Netscape Navigator and Microsoft Internet Explorer support. However, because Netscape Navigator is the most popular Web browser, I also present a few Netscape-only extensions such as frames and GIF89a animations. I also point out which extensions are now part of the recently announced HTML 3.2 specification.

Taking Stock of the HTML Extensions

Because HTML 2.0 is the only adopted standard for HTML (even the recently announced HTML 3.2 is only a specification not a standard), the term "HTML extension" encompasses any element or attribute that is not part of the HTML 2.0 standard. Because the HTML extensions are specific to Web browsers, there are two types:

✦ *Netscape Navigator extensions*: These extensions are supported by Netscape Navigator 1.1 and 2.0 (and later versions). They are also known as Mozilla extensions because Mozilla is the name of the cartoon dinosaur mascot used on Netscape's Web site. The Netscape Navigator extensions include such features as tables, backgrounds, and frames.

✦ *Microsoft Internet Explorer extensions*: The Microsoft Internet Explorer supports many of the HTML extensions pioneered by Netscape. Microsoft also put in a few extensions of its own, including a scrolling text marquee, background sound, and the ability to embed AVI (audio-video interleave) format video clips.

The Netscape extensions came first because Netscape Navigator was available before Microsoft released Internet Explorer. In Internet Explorer, Microsoft implemented many Netscape extensions and introduced a few of its own. In subsequent releases,

Netscape added support for some of the Internet Explorer extensions. In this way, the two Web browsers have been playing a game of catch-up. As a result of supporting each other's extensions, there is a growing common set of HTML extensions.

Cross Ref
The next three sections summarize the various HTML extensions. Later sections describe many useful extensions (such as frames, tables, and client-side image maps) in detail. Most of my focus is on the common extensions — those that both Netscape Navigator and Internet Explorer support. Appendix C includes reference information for all HTML elements, including the extensions summarized in this chapter.

Common HTML extensions

The common set of HTML extensions spans the spectrum from additional attributes in basic HTML tags to new elements such as `<table>`. Table 14-1 summarizes the HTML extensions common to Netscape Navigator and Internet Explorer.

Table 14-1
HTML Extensions Supported by More Than One Web Browser

HTML Element	Description of Extension
`<body>`	Accepts the attributes `background`, `bgcolor`, `link`, `text`, and `vlink` to specify colors of various text and the background of the document.
`<p>`	Accepts the `align` attribute that allows you to align the paragraph.
`<h1>` through `<h6>`	Accepts the `align` attribute that lets you align a heading.
`<basefont>`	Accepts the `size` attribute, which sets the base font size for relative font size changes (with the `<font>` element's `size` attribute).
`<font>`	Lets you set the font color and size. HTML 3.2 includes the `<font>` tag.
` `	Accepts the `clear` attribute that lets you break text flow and resume after an inline image.
`<nobr>`	Does not break text up to the closing `</nobr>` tag.
`<wbr>`	Tells the browser where it may break a line, if necessary.
`<center>`	Centers text enclosed within `<center>` and `</center>`. The `<center>` tag is now part of HTML 3.2.

(continued)

Table 14-1 *(continued)*

HTML Element	Description of Extension
`<hr>`	Accepts the `align`, `noshade`, `size`, and `width` attributes that control the appearance of the horizontal rule.
`<img>`	Accepts the `border`, `height`, `hspace`, `vspace`, `width`, and `usemap` extensions to control placement and appearance of an inline image. The usemap extension defines what is known as a *client-side image map* (see the "Using Client-Side Image Maps" section for more information).
`<map>`	Encloses the image map specification for a client-side image map (see the "Using Client-Side Image Maps" section for more information). HTML 3.2 supports client-side image maps.
`<area>`	Specifies the hotspot area and the associated URL for a client-side image map (see the "Using Client-Side Image Maps" section for more information). HTML 3.2 includes the `<area>` tag.
`<ol>`	Accepts the `start` and `type` attributes that let you set the starting number and the numbering style used to display the items in an ordered list.
`<li>`	Accepts the attributes `type` and `value` that allow you to change the numbering style as well as the item number in an ordered list.
`<textarea>`	Accepts the `wrap` attribute that lets you control how text wraps in a text input area (used in a form). Forms are described in Chapter 19.
`<table>`	Defines a table (see the "Using Tables" section). This tag is now part of HTML 3.2.
`<tr>`	Defines a row in a table (see the "Using Tables" section). This tag is now part of HTML 3.2.
`<th>`	Defines a table header (see the "Using Tables" section). This tag is now part of HTML 3.2.
`<td>`	Defines table data (see the "Using Tables" section). This tag is now part of HTML 3.2.
`<caption>`	Defines a table caption (see the "Using Tables" section). This tag is now part of HTML 3.2.

Netscape Navigator extensions

A number of HTML extensions are specific to Netscape Navigator. This set of extensions includes such popular features as frames that allow you to divide up the browser's window into several subwindows and to display a separate document in each one. Table 14-2 summarizes the HTML extensions supported by Netscape Navigator.

Table 14-2
HTML Extensions Supported by Netscape Navigator

HTML Element	Description of Extension
`<body>`	Supports new attribute `alink` that lets you specify the color of the active link. Also supports `onLoad` and `onUnload` event handler attributes that are used to integrate JavaScript code with HTML (Chapter 24 covers JavaScript).
`<div>`	Marks a new division of the document. Accepts the `align` attribute that specifies the alignment of the text in that division. HTML 3.2 supports the `<div>` tag.
`<big>`	Increases the size of text. This tag is now part of HTML 3.2.
`<blink>`	Blinks text on and off (blinking attracts users' attention but may also annoy them).
`<small>`	Decreases the size of text. This tag is now part of HTML 3.2.
`<sub>`	Displays text as subscript. This tag is now part of HTML 3.2.
`<sup>`	Displays text as superscript. This tag is now part of HTML 3.2.
`<img>`	Accepts the `losrc` attribute through which you can specify a low-resolution image to be downloaded first. (After the entire document has been loaded, Netscape Navigator goes back to the server and downloads the image specified by the `src` attribute.) Also allows a number of new values for the `align` attribute that controls the alignment of an inline image with respect to the remaining text.
`<applet>`	Embeds a Java application in the HTML document. You'll learn more about this HTML extension in Chapter 23. HTML 3.2 supports the `<applet>` tag.
`<a>`	Accepts a `target` attribute that you can use to instruct Netscape Navigator to display the contents of a document in a specific frame (see the "Using Frames in Netscape Navigator" section).
`<isindex>`	Accepts the `prompt` attribute that lets you specify the prompt string displayed by the browser.

(continued)

Table 14-2 *(continued)*	
HTML Element	**Description of Extension**
`<base>`	Accepts the `target` attribute to set the name of a frame where Netscape Navigator displays a redirected link.
`<meta>`	Accepts the `url` attribute that you use with `http-equiv="Refresh"` to specify the name of a document that Netscape Navigator uses to refresh the display at regular intervals.
`<ul>`	Accepts the `type` attribute that lets you specify the bullet symbol (can be one of `disc`, `circle`, or `square`) used for the items in an unordered list.
`<dir>`	Accepts the `type` attribute with which you can change the bullet symbol (can be one of `disc`, `circle`, or `square`) used to display a directory list.
`<menu>`	Accepts the `type` attribute that lets you specify the bullet symbol (can be one of `disc`, `circle`, or `square`) used in front of each menu item.
`<frameset>`	Defines a collection of frames that make up the browser's window (see the "Using Frames in Netscape Navigator" section for details).
`<frame>`	Defines a frame with an associated document (see the "Using Frames in Netscape Navigator" section for details).
`<noframes>`	Provides the content displayed by a browser that cannot display frames (see the "Using Frames in Netscape Navigator" section for details).

Microsoft Internet Explorer extensions

Not to be outdone by Netscape, Microsoft supports many Netscape extensions in Internet Explorer and adds a few Microsoft-specific extensions. For example, Microsoft Internet Explorer supports tags that allow you to add a background sound to a Web page. You can also add AVI video clips to a Web page (AVI is a popular video format used in Microsoft Windows). Table 14-3 lists the Microsoft-specific HTML extensions.

Table 14-3
HTML Extensions Supported by Microsoft Internet Explorer

HTML Element	Description of Extension
`<body>`	New attributes `bgproperties`, `leftmargin`, and `topmargin` to set the text margins and the background properties.
`<dfn>`	A logical style element that sets a definition apart. This tag is now part of HTML 3.2.
`<s>`	A shorthand for `<strike>` element, which displays text with a strikethrough font (a line is drawn through the middle of the text).
`<font>`	Accepts the `face` attribute that lets you set the font face (for example `<font face="Symbol">` displays text in Symbol font).
`<u>`	Underlines text (including spaces and punctuation marks). HTML 3.2 includes the `<u>` tag.
`<img>`	Accepts `controls`, `dynsrc`, `loop`, and `start` attributes to include and let the user play an AVI (audio-video interleave) movie in the Internet Explorer window.
`<bgsound>`	Adds a background sound to the document. Use the `src` attribute to specify the sound file and the `loop` attribute to control how Internet Explorer plays the sound.
`<marquee>`	Adds a scrolling text marquee to the HTML document. You can control the details with the `align`, `behavior`, `bgcolor`, `direction`, `height`, `hspace`, `loop`, `scrollamount`, `scrolldelay`, `vspace`, and `width` attributes.

Using the Extensions to Enhance Your Web Page

Many HTML extensions are meant for enhanced Web page layout and formatting. For example, you may recall from Chapter 11 that HTML 2.0 does not include any formatting element to center text and images. One popular and ubiquitous HTML extension is the `<center>` element that lets you center the content of a Web page. The recently published HTML 3.2 specification includes the `<center>` tag.

Other extensions provide additional attributes for standard HTML tags, which enable you to further control the appearance of text on your Web page. Some of the extensions are new attributes for the `<body>` tag.

Enhancements to `<body>`

In standard HTML, the `<body>` tag does not accept any attributes — it simply serves as the start tag for the document's body. Netscape Navigator and Microsoft Internet Explorer have extended the `<body>` tag with attributes that affect the appearance of the entire Web page. Specifically, the `<body>` tag now accepts the following attributes (notes in parentheses indicate if only a specific Web browser supports the attribute):

✦ `alink` specifies the color of the active link — the link on which the mouse cursor rests (supported by Netscape Navigator only).

✦ `background` specifies a background image for the Web page.

✦ `bgcolor` controls the background color of the Web page.

✦ `bgproperties` lets you stop the background image from scrolling (supported by Internet Explorer only).

✦ `leftmargin` sets the left margin of the Web page (supported by Internet Explorer only).

✦ `link` specifies the color of all links that the user has not yet followed.

✦ `text` specifies the color of text.

✦ `topmargin` sets the top margin for the Web page (supported by Internet Explorer only).

✦ `vlink` specifies the color of all links that the user has already visited.

Background, text, and link colors

In Netscape Navigator or Internet Explorer, you can control the color of various parts of the Web page as follows:

✦ Use the `bgcolor` attribute in the `<body>` tag to set the background to a specific color.

✦ Use the `text` attribute to specify the text color (if you alter the background color, you'll probably have to change the text color as well to ensure the text is still readable).

✦ Use `link`, `vlink`, and `alink` to set the color of hyperlinks.

The basic syntax of color specification is simple:

```
<body attribute=color>
```

Here `attribute` is the name of the attribute such as `bgcolor` or `text` and `color` is the name of a color or the red-green-blue (RGB) components of a color (you'll learn more about RGB color later in this section). For example, to set the background to navy (Navy blue color), you'd write

```
<body bgcolor=navy >
```

If you want the text to appear in white, just add the `text` attribute to the `<body>` tag:

```
<body bgcolor=navy text=white>
```

You can now add color choices for links. You can set one color for all the links that the user has not visited and another for the links that have been visited. Here's a sample HTML document that illustrates a number of color settings in the `<body>` tag:

```
<html>
<head>
<title>Background, text, and link colors</title>
</head>
<body bgcolor=navy text=white link=yellow vlink=lime>

The background color is navy.  Text is white.
<a href="link.html">Unvisited links</a> appear in yellow;
<a href="vlink.html">lime colored links</a> are the ones you have
already visited.

</body>
</html>
```

Figure 14-1 shows how Microsoft Internet Explorer renders this HTML document. If the figure were in color, you'd see white text on a Navy blue background. The unvisited links would be in yellow and the links you have visited would be in lime green.

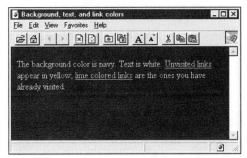

Figure 14-1: An HTML document with a number of color settings as rendered in Microsoft Internet Explorer.

Webmaster In addition to the descriptive name for a color, you can specify it as a hexadecimal number with six hexadecimal digits, which works out to two digits for each of the three components in a color — red (R), green (G), and blue (B). The digits in a 6-digit hexadecimal RGB value of a color are interpreted from left to right, with the most significant pair of digits assumed to be for R, the middle pair for G, and the least significant pair for B. A hash mark (#) precedes the hexadecimal digits to signify that this is a color specification in hexadecimal format. Here are some of the common colors expressed in this format:

black	#000000
red	#ff0000
green	#00ff00
blue	#0000ff
yellow	#ffff00
cyan	#00ffff
magenta	#ff00ff
white	#ffffff

After reviewing how the standard colors are specified, you can start experimenting with new colors you want to see as background or text color of a Web page. For example, you can try out a strange color for the background with the following bgcolor attribute in the <body> tag:

```
<body bgcolor=#cc9090>
```

You can specify text and link colors with this sort of RGB value as well.

Background image

Instead of filling the Web page background with a selected color, you may want to display a pattern. Use the background attribute in the <body> tag to specify a small image that the browser tiles (lays out side by side and in rows to fill the window). Both Netscape Navigator and Internet Explorer support the background attribute.

You must provide the URL of an image file as the value of the background attribute. For example, to use the stone.jpg (that's a JPEG file — one of the image file formats that most Web browsers allow) as the background, write the <body> tag as follows:

```
<body background="stone.jpg">
```

Figure 14-2 shows the appearance of the Netscape Navigator window with this background image.

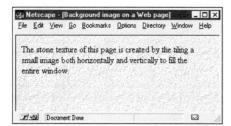

Figure 14-2: An HTML document with a background image.

Tip Although a well-chosen background can greatly enhance a Web page's appearance, you should try to keep the image size as small as possible (around 2KB is a good size). Otherwise, it can take considerably longer to display your Web pages, especially over slower-speed connections. If you can do without an image background, use a solid color instead — flat color backgrounds are faster to display than tiled images.

Tip When picking a background image for your Web page, make sure that the pattern is not too bright and flashy. In particular, you need to make sure that the text is still easily readable. Ideally, you should use a small, light-colored background image to create an unobtrusive background pattern.

Text formatting extensions

Many HTML extensions provide you with more control over the appearance of text. Some of the popular text formatting extensions include the ability to

- ✦ Center text and images with the <center> tag.

- ✦ Justify text with the align attribute (with the values left, right, and center) in HTML elements such as the heading and paragraph (<p>) tags.

- ✦ Control how text breaks occur as well as inhibit text breaks with the <nobr> tag.

- ✦ Blink text.

- ✦ Specify the bullet symbol for unnumbered lists and control the numbering in numbered lists.

- ✦ Control the font size and color so that you can mix and match different font sizes and text colors in a document.

Centering text and images

Centering your document's content with the <center> tag is easy; just enclose the text and images inside a pair of <center> and </center> tags. A browser such as Netscape Navigator or Internet Explorer (that accepts the <center> tag) centers everything between <center> and </center>.

Many Web pages use the <center> tag to center a heading. For example, the following HTML source centers a level 1 heading in the browser's window:

```
<center>
<h1>LNB Software, Inc.</h1>
</center>
```

You can also use another HTML extension to center this heading. That extension involves specifying an align attribute in the <h1> tag, as follows:

```
<h1 align=center>LNB Software, Inc.</h1>
```

This line of HTML source achieves the same result as embedding the level 1 heading inside the `<center>` and `</center>` tags.

Tip Note that on a browser that does not accept the `<center>` tag or the `align=center` attribute your centered text appears as left-justified text. If you are using centering as the only means of emphasizing a line of text, that emphasis may be lost on some browsers. That means you should always use some other form of emphasis (such as formatting the line of text as a heading level) in addition to centering.

Justifying text

In addition to centering text, the `align` attribute also lets you right- or left-justify paragraphs and headings. You can use the `align` attribute with the following tags:

✦ `<p>` for paragraph layouts

✦ `<h1>`, `<h2>`, `<h3>`, `<h4>`, `<h5>`, and `<h6>` for heading levels

You can specify one of three values for the `align` attribute:

✦ `left` to left-justify the text (this is the default)

✦ `center` to center the text in the browser's window

✦ `right` to display the text flush with the right margin of the browser's window

Here is a contrived example showing the use of the `align` attribute in the heading and paragraph tags:

```
<html>
<head>
<title>Text Justification</title>
</head>

<body>

<h1 align=right>Right-aligned heading</h1>
<p align=right>
This paragraph is right-aligned. I am filling it in with some
text so that we have several lines in the browser's window.
That way you get to see the effect of right aligning a paragraph.
<h2 align=center>Centered heading</h2>
<p align=center>
This is a centered paragraph. The browser first formats the paragraph
as if it were left aligned. Then it centers each line.

<h3 align=left> Left-justified heading</h3>
<p align=left>
This is a left-justified paragraph. Left-justified paragraphs are
the default. That means this should be the way most paragraphs
appear in your Web browser.

</body>
</html>
```

Figure 14-3 shows how this HTML source is rendered in Netscape Navigator.

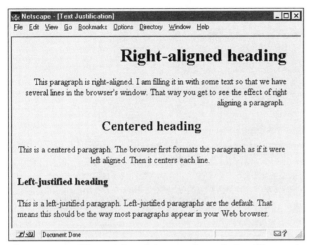

Figure 14-3: Effect of the align attribute in heading and paragraph tags.

Tip For most HTML documents the default setting of left alignment should suffice. However, for some types of text, such as poems and lyrics, you may need the right and center justification options.

Controlling text breaks

In standard HTML, the <br> tag lets you insert a text break anywhere in a line of text. An extension to the <br> tag is a clear attribute that lets you control how the text flows when you have an inline image embedded in a paragraph. Here is a fragment of HTML source that illustrates the use of the clear attribute in a <br> tag:

```
<img src="constT.gif" align=left> An inline image of
of a construction sign. All this text wraps around the image and
continues on the next line.
<p>
<img src="constT.gif" align=left> An inline image of
of a construction sign.<br clear=left>
Because of a <code>&lt;br clear=left&gt;</code> this text
appears directly beneath the image.
```

Both <img> tags use the align=left attribute to align the image along the left edge of the paragraph and have the text wrap along the right edge of the image. For the second image, the <br clear=left> tag forces the browser to break the text flow and start the next line below the image. Figure 14-4 shows the rendering of this example.

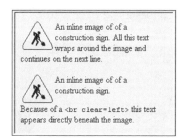

Figure 14-4: Effect of the `clear=left` attribute in a `<br>` tag.

The `<nobr>` tag is an extension that lets you inhibit text breaks and force the browser to display a long line of text as is (without any text wrap). Because `<nobr>` can cause the browser to display very long lines of text, you may want to use the `<wbr>` extension to provide hints where the browser should break lines. The following HTML source and the sample rendering in Figure 14-5 illustrate the effect of `<nobr>` and `<wbr>`:

```
<html>
<head><title>Example of &lt;wbr&gt;</title></head>
<body>
<nobr>
This is a really long line of text that the browser displays
on a single line. If you do not want the line to get too long
<wbr>
add a <code>&lt;wbr&gt;</code> tag to suggest a location
where the browser may break the line. Without these suggested
<wbr>
breaks, the user has to scroll horizontally (a lot) to see the
entire line.
</nobr>
</body>
</html>
```

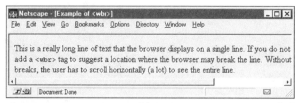

Figure 14-5: Use `<wbr>` with `<nobr>` to suggest good places to break a line.

Note   Note that the `<wbr>` tag affects the line break only if the text between `<nobr>` and `</nobr>` does not fit in the browser window. If a long line fits within the browser window, the browser simply ignores the `<wbr>` tag.

Blinking text

Blinking text can be annoying and only Netscape Navigator supports this feature. However, some Web pages do use this feature to attract the user's attention. The basic syntax is illustrated by the following example (the word `now!` blinks on and off):

```
Send your order <blink>now!</blink>
```

Formatting list items

Standard HTML provides several ways to create lists with the `<ul>`, `<ol>`, `<dir>`, and `<menu>` tags. By default, the browser decides how to render each type of list. For example, each item in an unordered list typically has a solid circle as a bullet.

One of the HTML extensions allows you to specify a bullet character for unordered lists. You use the `type` attribute in the `<ul>` tag to specify the bullet character:

✦ `type=disc` (for a solid circle bullet — the default)

✦ `type=circle` (for a hollow circle)

✦ `type=square` (for a hollow square)

You can also change the numbering format of ordered lists. To change the numbering scheme, use the type attribute with the `<ol>` tag. The allowed values are

✦ `type=1` (for the standard 1,2,3,... numbering — the default)

✦ `type=A` (for A,B,C,... numbering)

✦ `type=a` (for a,b,c,... numbering)

✦ `type=I` (for uppercase Roman numerals: I, II, III, ...)

✦ `type=i` (for lowercase Roman numerals: i, ii, iii, ...)

Additionally, you can use the `start` attribute with the `<ol>` tag to specify a starting number in an ordered list. The following `<ol>` tag begins the list at number 5:

```
<ol start=5>
```

Specifying font size and color

When you use a word processor, you choose the font type and size for various parts of a document. Standard HTML lacks this font control because HTML specifies the content and not the exact physical formatting. One HTML extension supported by both Netscape Navigator and Internet Explorer is control over font size and color (Internet Explorer even allows you to specify the typeface, such as Symbol or Courier).

Webmaster The font size extensions do not let you specify absolute sizes for the font. Instead, you can control the relative size of fonts. The relative size is expressed as an integer, ranging in value from 1 to 7. The base font size is 3. Font sizes 1 and 2 are smaller than the default size and font sizes 4 through 7 are successively larger than the default size.

There are two extended tags for font control:

✦ `<basefont>` lets you specify the initial font size relative to which subsequent size increase and decrease occurs (default base font size is 3).

✦ `<font>` lets you specify font size with the `size` attribute ands lets you specify the font color with the `color` attribute.

Tip   Typically, the `<font>` tag is used with the `size` attribute to increment or decrement the font size for small portions of text. For example, you might want to emphasize the first letter of a sentence with the `<font>` tag as follows:

```
<font size=+1>N</font>ews of the day
```

In this example, the letter N, inside the `<font>` tag, will be a size larger than the base font size. Figure 14-6 shows how Netscape Navigator renders this HTML source.

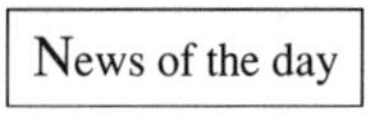

News of the day

Figure 14-6: The `<font>` tag lets you control the font size.

In this case, Netscape Navigator displays the letter N in font size 4 whereas the rest of the letters are in font size 3. You could alter the base font with the `<basefont>` tag. For example, to change the base font size to 4, you'd write the following:

```
<basefont size=4>
```

You can also use the `<font>` tag to specify the absolute font size for text. The following HTML example and Figure 14-7 show the seven available font sizes:

```
<font size=7>Font size 7</font>   <br>
<font size=6>Font size 6</font>   <br>
<font size=5>Font size 5</font>   <br>
<font size=4>Font size 4</font>   <br>
<font size=3>Font size 3</font>   <br>
<font size=2>Font size 2</font>   <br>
<font size=1>Font size 1</font>   <br>
```

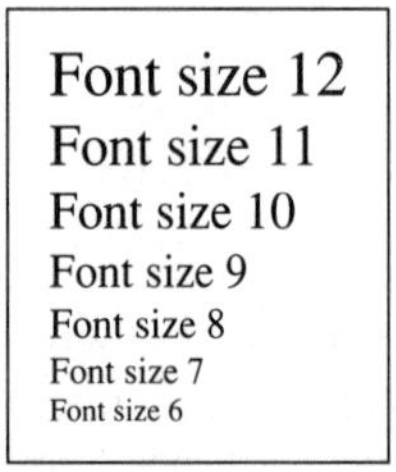

Font size 12
Font size 11
Font size 10
Font size 9
Font size 8
Font size 7
Font size 6

Figure 14-7: The seven font sizes in Netscape Navigator and Internet Explorer.

Internet Explorer supports an additional attribute for the `<font>` tag: You can use the `face` attribute to specify the actual font typeface. For example, you can display a Greek character in Symbol font as follows:

```
I need the value of <font face=symbol>p</font> to 15 decimal places.
```

Figure 14-8 shows how Internet Explorer renders this sentence.

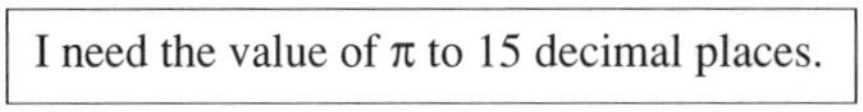

I need the value of π to 15 decimal places.

Figure 14-8: Internet Explorer lets you specify a font face.

On a browser such as Netscape Navigator that does not understand the `face` attribute, the user will see a letter p instead of the Greek letter π.

Horizontal rule extensions

In standard HTML, the horizontal rule (`<hr>`) is a simple element that inserts a separator in your HTML document. The browser typically renders the separator as a 3-D shaded horizontal rule. Netscape Navigator and Internet Explorer give you many more options to customize the horizontal rule. These browsers support the following additional attributes for the `<hr>` tag:

✦ `align` to specify the position of a rule that's shorter than the current text

✦ `noshade` to turn off the 3-D shading on a rule

✦ `size` to specify the thickness (in pixels) of a rule

✦ `width` to specify the absolute width (pixels) or relative width (as a percentage of the text width) of the rule

The following HTML source shows some examples of these additional `<hr>` attributes:

```
<html>
<head><title>Horizontal rule extensions</title></head>

<body>
The following line is the standard horizontal rule:
<hr>
Three 50% rules aligned left, center, and right:
<hr width="50%" align=left>
<hr width="50%" align=center>
<hr width="50%" align=right>
<p>
The next three rules are 6, 12, and 18 pixels in size:
<hr size=6>
<hr size=12>
<hr size=18>
```

(continued)

```
<p>
The next two rules use the <code>noshade</code> attribute:
<hr noshade>
<hr size=6 noshade>
</body>
</html>
```

Figure 14-9 shows how Netscape Navigator renders this HTML source.

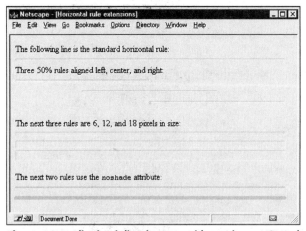

Figure 14-9: Aligning inline images with text in an HTML document.

Inline image extensions

As Chapter 12 shows, the standard HTML `<img>` tag that lets you insert an inline image into a Web page provides minimal control over how the image is positioned with respect to nearby text. Essentially, the standard alignment attribute values of `top`, `center`, and `middle` allow the image to appear on a single line of text. However, print magazines allow the adjoining text to flow around the image.

Netscape Navigator and Microsoft Internet Explorer support additional values for the `<img>` tag's `align` attribute that allow text to flow around an image. The following HTML source demonstrates the use of the `align=left` and `align=right` attributes to place inline images in text:

```
<html>
<head><title>Example of image placement</title></head>
<body>
<img src="constT.gif" align=left> This inline image of
of a construction sign is widely used on Web pages to
indicate that the site is under construction. Because a
```

```
Web site is typically always undergoing renovation,
the construction sign is a constant fixture on many
Web pages. [This is an example of an inline image with
the <code>align=left</code> attribute.]

<p>
<img src="constT.gif" align=right> The <code>align=right</code>
attribute places the image on the right margin of a paragraph
and causes the text to flow around the left side of the image
(as this example illustrates). Notice how the text flows around
the image and continues on to the line following the image.

</body>
</html>
```

Figure 14-10 demonstrates how Netscape Navigator renders this HTML source.

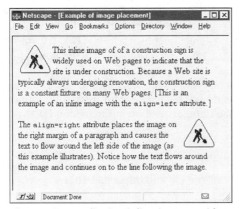

Figure 14-10: Aligning inline images with text in an HTML document.

By default, the browser does not leave much space between the image and the adjoining text. If you want to keep some extra space around the image, you can do so with the hspace and vspace attributes. For example, the following HTML source adds 10 pixels of space around an inline image:

```
<img src=constT.gif align=left hspace=10 vspace=10>
```

Tip   If you know the width and height of the inline image, you can include these dimensions in the <img> tag with the width and height attributes, as follows:

```
<img src="constT.gif" width=58 height=52>
```

This allows the browser to set aside space (on the browser window) for the image even before it actually downloads the image from the server.

The browser automatically displays a border around inline images that are also hyperlinks. By default, the border is 2 pixels wide. If you want to display a different size border around the inline image (displayed only when it's a link), you can do so with the border attribute. The border attribute takes an integer value that specifies the thickness of the border in pixels. For example, to draw a 4-pixel border around an inline image, you'd write the following HTML source:

```
<img src="constT.gif" border=4>
```

If this <img> tag is inside an anchor tag (<a>), the browser displays a 4-pixel border around the image. You can also set the border to zero and turn off the border.

Using Tables

Tables are a logical style of text layout that HTML should support. Unfortunately, HTML 2.0 has no provision for formatting tables. Browsers such as Netscape Navigator, Mosaic, and Internet Explorer have stepped in to correct this deficiency and added extensions that support table layout. The short-lived draft HTML 3.0 standard also included the table element, and any future HTML standard will include support for tables.

Unlike many of the HTML extensions that do not necessarily improve a Web page's content, tables really do help you organize data. The following extended HTML elements are meant for displaying tables:

✦ <caption> to specify a table caption

✦ <table> to enclose a table definition (the closing tag is </table>)

✦ <td> to define a cell that represents the table's data

✦ <th> to define a cell that constitutes part of the table header

✦ <tr> to define a row in a table

HTML table model

The basic HTML table model encloses a table definition inside <table> and </table> tags. The table is made up of rows; you define each row using the <tr> and </tr> pair. Each row consists of a number of cells. There are two types of cells:

✦ A *table header cell* (enclosed in a pair of <th> and </th> tags) is a part of the table's header. Table headers can span entire rows or go down a column.

✦ A *table data cell* (enclosed in a pair of <td> and </td> tags) is part of the table's data.

The total number of cells in the row's definition is the number of columns in the table. Header and data cells can span multiple columns. If a cell spans more than one column, use the colspan attribute to specify the number of columns over which that cell extends. (You'll understand these better when you see an example in the "A sample table" section.) You can optionally provide a caption for the table by enclosing the caption string in `<caption>` and `</caption>` tags.

Here is the skeleton of a simple table with three columns (the number of columns is determined by the cells in each row):

```
<table border>
<caption>Table's caption</caption>
<tr>
    <th>Col 1 Header</th>
    <th>Col 2 Header</th>
    <th>Col 3 Header</th>
</tr>

<tr>
    <td>Row 1, Col 1</td>
    <td>Row 1, Col 2</td>
    <td>Row 1, Col 3</td>
</tr>

<tr>
    <td>Row 2, Col 1</td>
    <td>Row 2, Col 2</td>
    <td>Row 2, Col 3</td>
</tr>

<tr>
    <td colspan=3 align=center>This spans 3 columns.</td>
</tr>

<! - ... more rows... - >
</table>
```

You should be able to discern the pattern of tags that constitute the full table. The `<table>` tag includes the border attribute — this causes Netscape Navigator to display borders around the cells. The last row shows a data cell that spans all three columns (the colspan=3 attribute specifies this) and the contents of that cell are centered (that's indicated by the align=center attribute). In fact, this is a valid table definition that Netscape Navigator renders as shown in Figure 14-11.

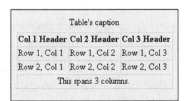

Figure 14-11: A skeletal table rendered by Netscape Navigator.

By comparing the HTML source with the rendered form of the table, you should be able to see how the table layout tags (`<table>`, `<tr>`, `<th>`, and `<td>`) work.

A sample table

For a more realistic table, consider a tax table that shows the amount you owe based on your income range and filing status (whether you are single, married, and so on). Figure 14-12 shows a partial tax table as it appears in Netscape Navigator. 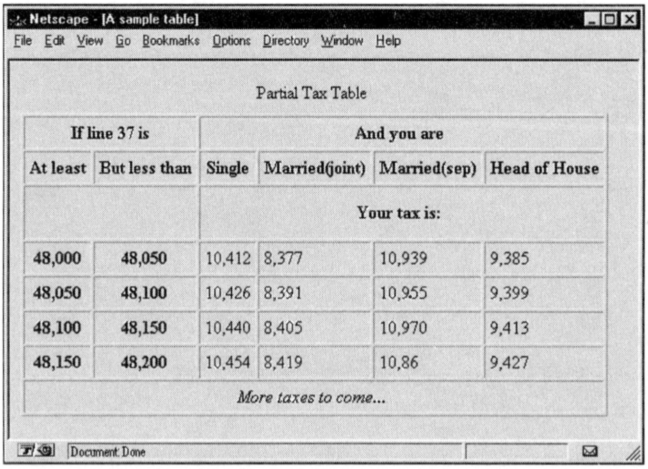

Figure 14-12: A relatively complicated sample table viewed in Netscape Navigator.

To format this table, first you have to realize that there are six columns (even though some of the headers span multiple columns). Next, you have to go down the table row-by-row and specify each row. For example, the first row has only two header cells: the first one spans the first two columns and the next one spans the other four columns. You have to use the `colspan` attribute to specify this. Also, to center the text in the cell, use the `align=center` attribute.

Netscape Navigator accepts the `cellpadding` attribute whose value sets the spacing between the edge of a cell and its contents. If you do not specify the `cellpadding`, the browser leaves a one-pixel border between a cell's edge and its contents.

Another useful attribute is `cellspacing` — this attribute controls the amount of space between adjacent cells in a table. The value of `cellspacing` is also used as the space between the table border and the cells that lie along the edges of the table.

If you go through the table row by row, here is the HTML source you'll end up creating (Figure 14-12 corresponds to this HTML source):

```
<html>
<head><title>A sample table</title></head>
<body>

<table border cellpadding=4>
<caption>Partial Tax Table</caption>

<tr>
    <th colspan=2 align=center>If line 37 is</th>
    <th colspan=4 align=center>And you are</th>
</tr>

<tr>
    <th>At least</th>
    <th>But less than</th>
    <th>Single</th>
    <th>Married(joint)</th>
    <th>Married(sep)</th>
    <th>Head of House</th>
</tr>

<tr>
    <th colspan=2><br></th>
    <th colspan=4 align=center>Your tax is:</th>
</tr>

<tr>
    <th>48,000</th>
    <th>48,050</th>
    <td>10,412</td>
    <td>8,377</td>
    <td>10,939</td>
    <td>9,385</td>
</tr>

<tr>
    <th>48,050</th>
    <th>48,100</th>
    <td>10,426</td>
    <td>8,391</td>
    <td>10,955</td>
    <td>9,399</td>
</tr>

<tr>
    <th>48,100</th>
    <th>48,150</th>
    <td>10,440</td>
    <td>8,405</td>
    <td>10,970</td>
    <td>9,413</td>
</tr>
```

(continued)

```
<tr>
    <th>48,150</th>
    <th>48,200</th>
    <td>10,454</td>
    <td>8,419</td>
    <td>10,86</td>
    <td>9,427</td>
</tr>

<tr>
    <td colspan=6 align=center><em>More taxes to come...</em></td>
</tr>

</table>

</body>
</html>
```

Using Frames in Netscape Navigator

Frames are a recent innovation that first appeared in Netscape Navigator 2.0 (Netscape's home page is one of the places where you can see an example of frames). They allow you to divide up the browser window into two or more regions and display a separate document in each region. Each region of the window is called a *frame*. Each frame essentially acts as an independent Web browser.

A new `target` attribute for the anchor tag (`<a>`) allows you to specify the frame where a selected document appears. When the user clicks a link in one frame, the document appears in a different frame. This is useful in creating a frame-based Web page layout where one side of the window serves as a table of contents for your site and another, larger frame displays the selected document.

A typical use of frames

One of the common use of frames is to implement a table of contents for a Web site. The idea is to divide the Netscape Navigator window into two parts, one smaller than the other, as shown in Figure 14-13.

You can divide the window in two ways:

✦ *Divide the columns*: This divides the window into two side-by-side frames. Usually, the frame on the left-hand side is tall and thin and contains the links that constitute the table of contents. Clicking any of these links brings up the new document in the larger window on the right-hand side.

✦ *Divide the rows*: This creates two frames, one on top of the other. The short and wide frame at the bottom displays the table of contents. Clicking any link in this frame brings up the referenced document in the frame on the top.

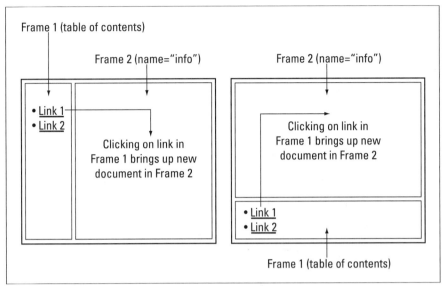

Figure 14-13: Typical use of frames to implement a table of contents for a site.

Typically, you would specify the dimension of the frame as a percentage of the entire browser window.

Frame definition

Netscape provides three new HTML elements to define frames:

✦ ⟨frameset⟩ defines the set of frames that make up the browser's window (the ⟨frameset⟩ element replaces the ⟨body⟩ element of an ordinary HTML document).

✦ ⟨frame⟩ specifies which document the frame initially displays (you may also assign a name to the frame).

✦ ⟨noframes⟩ lets you provide the content that will be displayed by any browser that cannot display frames.

A frame document looks just like a normal HTML document except that the ⟨body⟩ element is replaced by the ⟨frameset⟩ element. Inside the ⟨frameset⟩ element, you place the frame definitions (using ⟨frame⟩ elements) and a ⟨noframes⟩ element that provides the content that non-frame-capable browsers display:

```
<html>

<head>
</head>
```

(continued)

```
<frameset cols="20%,*">

<frame src="doc1.html">
<frame src="doc2.html">

<noframes>
</noframes>

</frameset>

</html>
```

In this HTML source, the `cols="20%,*"` attribute in the `<frameset>` tag tells Netscape Navigator to divide the window into two parts along the columns (or the width). The first frame gets 20 percent of the columns, the other frame gets the rest (that's what the asterisk indicates).

A frame example

Suppose you want to divide the window into two side-by-side frames and use the left side as a table of contents (essentially a list of links). Here is an HTML document that sets up the frames:

```
<html>
<head>
<title>A typical frame-based document</title>
</head>

<frameset cols="20%,*">
<frame src="contents.html">
<frame src="top.html" name="info">

<noframes>
This document uses frames (supported by Netscape Navigator 2.0).
A <a href="contents.html">non-frames version</a> is available
for your convenience.
</noframes>

</frameset>
</html>
```

When Netscape Navigator renders this document, the window is divided into two frames, the left one occupying 20 percent of the window width and the right one taking up the remainder of the window (the order is determined by the order of `<frame>` tags). The right frame is assigned the name `info`.

Initially, the left frame displays the `contents.html` document; the right frame displays the `top.html` document. The `contents.html` document is defined as follows:

```
<ul>
<li> <a href="top.html" target="info">Top</a>
</ul>
```

```
<ul>
<li> <a href="new.html" target="info"> What's New</a>
</ul>
<ul>
<li> <a href="oview.html" target="info"> Overview</a>
<li> <a href="webprog.html" target="info"> WebProg</a>
<li> <a href="store.html" target="info"> Software</a>
<li> <a href="search.html" target="info"> Search</a>
<li> <a href="feedback.html" target="info"> Feedback</a>
</ul>

<p>
<ul>
<li> <a href="http://www.yahoo.com/" target="info">Yahoo</a>
<li> <a href="http://iwin.nws.noaa.gov/iwin/iwdspg1.html"
     target="info">Weather</a>
</ul>
```

As the listing shows, `contents.html` includes a set of links that use the target attribute to display the selected document in the right-hand frame. For example, when the user clicks the `Weather link`, the `http://iwin.nws.noaa.gov/iwin/iwdspg1.html` URL appears in the right-hand frame, as shown in Figure 14-14.

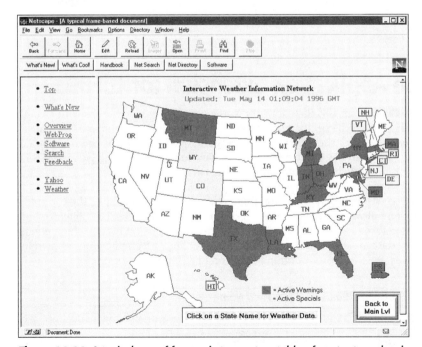

Figure 14-14: A typical use of frames is to create a table of contents and a view area.

As this figure shows, the left-hand frame still shows the list of links, whereas the right-hand frame now displays a different document.

Caution You should get permission from a site's owner before displaying that site's page in a frame of your Web page, making it appear as if the other site is somehow part of your Web site. Of course, you can always organize your own Web site using frames so one shows a table of contents and another (larger) frame shows the currently selected link.

You can safely use frames as long as you provide some content in the `<noframes>` element for browsers that do not support frames. This section's sample frame document provides a `<noframes>` section with a link that lets the user access the top-level links on your Web site. Figure 14-15 shows how Microsoft Internet Explorer renders the sample frame document.

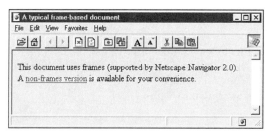

Figure 14-15: The `<noframes>` tag provides for browsers that cannot display frames.

Netscape Application Extension for GIF89a

The latest GIF format, GIF89a, supports Application Extension blocks with data that only makes sense to a specific application. For example, the Netscape Navigator browser can interpret the information in a Netscape Application Extension in a GIF89a image file. The contents of the Netscape Application Extension tell Netscape Navigator how to loop multiple images contained in the GIF89a file.

The Netscape Application Extension must appear immediately after the Global Color Table, which follows the Logical Screen Descriptor. Only Netscape Navigator 2.0 (or later versions) recognize the Netscape Application Extension block, which consists of 19 bytes of data arranged in the following manner (hexadecimal values shown in parentheses use the C programming notation of a `0x` prefix):

Byte	Value	Field Name
1	33 (0x21)	Extension introducer (identifies the block as an extension).
2	255 (0xff)	Extension label.
3	11 (0x0b)	Block size (up to but not including the beginning of the application data).

Byte	Value	Field Name
4 to 11	"NETSCAPE"	Application identifier (8 bytes).
12 to 14	"2.0"	Application authentication code.
15	3 (0x03)	Application data sub-block (this byte is the length of the block).
16	1 (0x01)	First byte of application data.
17 to 18	0 to 65535	A 2-byte unsigned integer (low-order byte followed by high-order byte) that indicates the number of times Netscape Navigator should loop through the images.
19	0 (0x00)	Sub-block terminator.

The value contained in bytes 17 and 18 controls how many times Netscape Navigator loops through the images in a single GIF89a file. If this loop count is nonzero, Netscape Navigator appears to ignore the count and loops the images endlessly.

Cross Ref Chapter 12 summarizes the GIF89a format and describes how to create GIF89a animations with a tool such as ImageMagick. Any image manipulation software capable of creating GIF89a animation can also add the Netscape Application Extension block to the GIF89a image file.

Using Client-Side Image Maps

As Chapter 13 explains, you have to follow quite a few steps to support image maps on your Web pages. You need an image, a file that maps parts of the image to specific URLs, and a reference to the `imagemap` CGI program on the Web server. Chapter 13's image map approach depends on the type of Web server your site uses because clicks on the image map are processed by the Web server.

Netscape Navigator and Microsoft Internet Explorer provide a way to allow the client (the Web browser) to process the image map. Unlike the server-side image map, the client-side image map does not have to be embedded in an `<a>` tag. Instead, you use the `usemap` attribute in the `<img>` tag. The `usemap` attribute specifies the name of a `<map>` tag — another new HTML element that associates areas of the image with specific document names. The `<map>` tag is also part of the HTML 3.2 specification.

Inside the `<map>` element, you define specific areas of the image with a number of `<area>` tags; each `<area>` tag associates the area with a URL. Here is an example of how you might define a client-side image map:

```
<img src="lnbimage.gif" usemap="#lnbmap">

<map name="lnbmap">
    <area coords="0,0,87,105"    href="oview.html">
```

(continued)

```
        <area coords="88,0,175,105"  href="webprog.html">
        <area coords="176,0,263,105" href="store.html">
        <area coords="264,0,352,105" href="search.html">
        <area coords="353,0,441,105" href="feedback.html">
    </map>
```

The first line inserts an inline image and uses the usemap attribute to indicate that this is a client-side image map. The value of the usemap attribute, #lnbmap, specifies that the browser should look in the same document for a <map> element with the name lnbmap. The # character preceding the map's name in the usemap attribute tells the browser to look for a <map> element in the current document. You can specify a URL as the value of the usemap attribute.

The <map> element takes the name attribute through which you specify the map's name. Inside the <map> element, place the <area> elements that define the hotspots on the image. Each <area> element takes two attributes:

> ✦ coords is a string of x,y coordinates enclosing the area (the x-coordinates go from left to right and the y-coordinates go from top to bottom).

> ✦ href is the URL of the document that should be activated when the user clicks this area of the image.

As with server-side image maps, you still have to figure out the coordinates of each hotspot on the image. You can do this inside a paint program. Another way is to use a tool such as Mapedit (described in Chapter 13) to generate the map file for a server-side image map and then use those coordinates in the client-side image map. Figure 14-16 shows a client-side image map that serves as the example in this section.

Webmaster To the user, the client-side image map appears the same as a server-side image map with one key difference. When the user moves the mouse to a specific area of the client-side image map, Netscape Navigator displays the URL associated with that area. In a server-side image map, the associated URL is the same for the entire image (because the mouse click is processed on the server and not by the client).

Note The advantage of client-side image maps is that you can use them in a non-networked environment such as disk- or CD-ROM-based HTML documents because client-side image maps do not require access to a Web server.

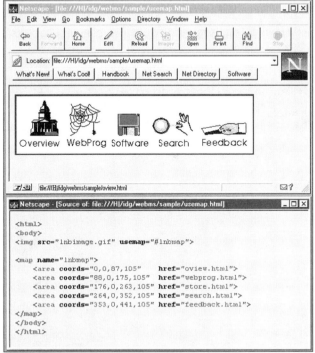

Figure 14-16: A typical client-side image map.

Summary

Standard HTML has only a limited set of formatting tags for page layout — for example, it does not include the ability to center text on a page. Popular Web browsers such as Netscape Navigator and Microsoft Internet Explorer have introduced extensions to HTML to allow more control over some aspects of Web page layout, such as tables and background colors. Some of these HTML extensions are widely used at various Web sites and you may want to know about them so that you can make an informed decision if you need to use them also. This chapter lists all the known HTML extensions and shows you how to use a number of popular ones. The next chapter provides guidelines on how to design effective Web pages.

Where to go next . . .

✦ For information on standard HTML formatting elements, consult Chapters 11 through 13.

✦ To learn about Web page design guidelines, go to Chapter 15.

✦ For information on HTML authoring tools, proceed to Chapter 17.

✦ If you want to create interactive HTML forms, you'll find the relevant information in Chapters 19 and 20.

✦   ✦   ✦

Designing Web Pages

CHAPTER

15

Chapters 10 through 14 show you how to use HTML — the language used for Web page layout. A Web page is more than text and images laid out with HTML tags, however. Because the Web page is a visual medium, you also need to make the page eye-catching and distinct. That means you need graphic design and layout skills, just as print magazines require the skills of art directors and layout editors.

In addition to the graphic design skills, you also need an understanding of the Web's unique organizational features, such as hyperlinked pages, in order to make your Web site easy for your readers to understand and navigate. Before developing the organizational framework for your Web site and designing Web pages, however, you must resolve several design issues. This chapter expolores Web site design and addresses the three steps in the Web site design process shown in Figure 15-1.

Cross Ref Before you start the Web site design, become familiar with the Web and browse existing Web sites. This not only helps you understand the Web as a communication medium, but also gives you a feel for what design best suits your organization's needs. By now, you have probably browsed various Web sites and noticed those that have a look and feel that you want to use. If you have not started using the Web, you should do so or look over the user's view of the Web presented in Chapter 4.

Figure 15-1: Steps in Web site design.

Addressing Overall Design Issues

After you set up the Web server and learn how to write HTML documents, you should address overall Web site design issues before designing your site's organizational framework. Here are some of the important overall Web site design issues:

✦ **Reasons for the Web site:** You need to know what you are planning to accomplish with the Web site. What kind of "image" you are trying to project? Is it serious and all business? Is it light-hearted, playful, and creative?

✦ **Primary audience:** You have to know about the prospective users' behavior before you settle on the form and content of the Web pages at your site. Are the users going to buy products online? Are they going to download technical information about products? What's special about your site that will make users come back repeatedly?

✦ **Technical constraints:** You have to know the limitations of the Web to make the best use of this new medium. What type of network connections do you expect most of your users to have? Does your target audience use 28.8 Kbps modem connections or 1.544 Mbps T1 links? What type of Internet connection speed do *you* have? Do you know what size images you can use in your Web pages without making the pages appear sluggish? Are your images designed for typical 640x480 resolution computer monitors?

Although many sites tend to grow out of a few Web pages, any serious site needs a bit of planning and design to be effective.

Reasons for the Web site

Before you write any HTML, you have to understand why your organization is setting up the Web site. The reason should be more substantive than "Because everyone else has a Web site." Even if your organization decides to establish a Web presence because its competitors are on the Web, what purpose is the new Web site going to serve? This, of course, depends on the type of your organization and what the organization wants to accomplish through the Web site.

You may decide what your Web site should provide if you see some of the Web site categories and what they offer. Here are some general categories of Web sites:

✦ **Online library catalogs:** This category includes sites that provide access to library catalogs. University libraries have typically been the first to offer online library catalogs that users can search to find books and publications.

✦ **Research and educational institutions:** This category includes schools and universities. The main purpose of such sites is to provide information to students. The information contained there can be diverse, containing anything from student and faculty directories to online applications for admission.

✦ **Entertainment:** This includes sports, movies, music, and social activities. Typical offerings include the latest sports scores and sound files with sample recordings.

✦ **Information services:** This category includes newspapers, magazines, and other information providers. Many of these sites enable you to perform searches on the news database to quickly locate all current information about a particular topic. Information providers such as Dow Jones and Standard & Poor offer financial information.

✦ **Corporate sites:** These sites focus on advertising the products and services of a corporation. Some corporate sites offer product literature and online service and support for products. This category includes the majority of commercial sites because all businesses — large and small — fit this category.

✦ **Professional organizations:** This category includes all types of professional organizations, from engineering and scientific societies to membership institutions such as the Commercial Internet Exchange (CIX) — an organization of Internet Service Providers. Professional organizations typically offer services such as member directories, membership renewals, and lists of publications.

✦ **Retail sales:** These sites offer online shopping. Users can browse catalogs, make selections, and pay for products (usually with credit cards). Nowadays online stores sell a variety of products from flowers to computers.

✦ **Intranets:** This category refers to all types of Web sites that run on an organization's internal networks. (Typically, these networks are not connected to the global Internet.) The basic content of an intranet depends on the business, but some common uses seem to be to distribute policy and procedures to employees, provide online employee directories, announce job openings, and even list cafeteria menus (for larger businesses).

In addition to deciding what you want to offer through your Web site, you also have to decide on the type of impression you want to make on the users. This decision determines whether your Web pages have a staid, businesslike appearance or outrageous background colors and multicolor fonts. Your business type dictates your site's online image to some extent, but there is always room for some levity.

Primary audience

Whether you publish a print magazine or software, you have to know your user to build a useful product. A Web site is no different from other products in this respect. You have to decide what type of user you are trying to reach through your Web site. That decision, in turn, leads to other choices such as the information content and presentation. A computer software company's Web site, for example, will probably be of most interest to current and prospective customers of that company's products. Based on this knowledge, the software company's Web site administrator might provide product specifications and new product announcements as well as technical support and a Web-based bulletin board.

After you identify your primary audience, you should determine the characteristics of a typical member of that audience. This will, in turn, enable you to more easily select other details of the Web site's design and content. Here are some characteristics of the audience that may influence your site's overall design:

✦ **Demographics:** The age, educational level, and so on of your target audience will influence your Web site design. Cartoon-like graphics in your Web pages may appeal more to a younger audience than to an older, highly educated audience.

✦ **Knowledge:** You'll need to consider the knowledge level of visitors to your Web site. For example, if you're catering to technical experts, it's okay to use technical jargon in your Web pages. However, if you expect your site to be visited by a lay audience, you should explain technical terminology or avoid its use.

✦ **Nationality:** Because the Web is worldwide, it's possible (if not likely) that people of many nationalities will visit your Web site. If a large portion of your Web site audience is French Canadian, for example, you may want to offer a version of your Web site in French.

 Tip Try not to make the site's content too broad. If you try to do too much, users will end up being confused. Your goal is to decide on the target audience and present information that's useful to that audience.

Technical constraints

To design an effective Web site (one that your target audience can use as designed), you need to be acutely aware of the various technical limitations of the Web. As a Webmaster, you already know a lot about the internal details of how the Web works — how a Web browser downloads HTML documents from a Web server — to understand its limitations. Some of the prominent technical constraints include the following:

✦ **Network speed:** Different users have different network connections with different speeds. The Web site design has to reflect the typical network speeds of the users. For example, a site visited primarily by users with slower connections must have fewer graphics and other large files.

✦ **Users' computer systems:** Different users have different computer systems with different processing capabilities. The processing speed of the user's system partly determines how quickly your Web pages appear on his or her screen.

✦ **Display resolution and colors:** Users have varying display capabilities, depending on the monitors and graphics cards on their computer systems. The colors and details of your Web pages appear differently on different systems.

✦ **Browser types:** Some readers use Netscape Navigator, some use NCSA Mosaic, and others use a text-only browser. Different browsers render your Web page differently — drastically different in the case of a text-only browser.

Network speed

Each time a Web browser displays a document, the entire document with its embedded images must be downloaded over the network. That means the network speed plays a crucial role in how the user perceives your Web site. A slow connection (for example, 28.8 Kbps or slower) can ruin the effect of a fancy graphics-laden Web page. On the other hand, a business user with 1.544 Mbps T1 connection will barely notice the loading time for such a Web page.

Tip

Typical home users have a 28.8 Kbps (or slower) modem connection to the Net. If the home user is your site's primary audience, you should avoid large image files. As a rule of thumb, a 28.8 Kpbs modem can transfer roughly 3K of data each second. To download an HTML document with inline images, the Web browser has to establish a connection to the server for the entire document as well as a separate connection for each image. As you might guess, it takes some time to set up each connection and to download the image from the server. For the sake of home users, you may want to limit the total size of images to 15K per page. Assuming about 3K of text on the Web page, a typical 28.8 Kbps user will be able to download the entire document in under 10 seconds, which should be tolerable.

If your clientele consists mostly of business users, you can use larger images without making the pages slow to load in their browsers. Typical business users have 1.544 Mbps T1 (or better) links to the Internet. At T1 speed, you can transfer up to 193K per second. (In reality the number is lower because of the overhead associated with the TCP/IP and HTTP protocols.) Thus, a page with a 100K image is fine if your primary audience is business users with T1 or better connections to the Net.

For a site on an intranet, you typically have a 10 Mbps or better network connection to all users on a high-capacity internal LAN. That means the pages on your intranet site can use images freely.

In all of this discussion, I have been assuming that your Web site has a T1 or better network connection to the Internet. If you have a slower connection (such as 56 Kbps Frame Relay), then that becomes the bottleneck in the transfers because many of your users' data receiving capabilities will outstrip your site's ability to send data.

Tip   Because a vast majority of users access the Web through relatively low-speed modem connections, you should test your Web pages over a typical modem connection to ensure that your Web pages will be accessible by most users. Of course, an added benefit is that a Web page that loads reasonably fast over a modem connection is bound to appear snappy to those users who have Frame Relay or T1 connections.

Users' computer systems

Users' computers can also be a factor in how they perceive your Web pages because the Web browser has to download the HTML documents, interpret the HTML tags, and render the document. Additionally, for inline images, the browser has to decode the downloaded image (typically in GIF or JPEG format) and then display the image. All this takes processing power. A complex Web page appears lively to users with powerful UNIX workstations but may not be as attractive to users with Intel 486 PCs.

If you develop and test your Web pages on a high-end UNIX workstation, you should also try out the Web pages for performance on less powerful PCs. Better yet, you might want to do all the development and testing on a run-of-the-mill PC (which currently means a 486 or Pentium PC with Windows 95).

Display resolution and colors

A big difference between print media and the Web is that you have to work with much lower resolution (in terms of dots per inch or dpi) and lesser numbers of colors. Most display monitors support one of the following resolutions:

✦ 72 dpi on Macintoshes

✦ 96 dpi on PCs running Windows 95 or Windows NT

✦ 100 dpi (or more) on high-end UNIX workstations such as those from Sun and HP

Although typical monitors are capable of displaying 24-bit color (which allows for about 16 million colors) with the right type of graphics card, many users are limited to 8-bit (256-color) displays because they use their displays in the default 256-color configuration. Another common reason for the 256-color limit is the lack of enough video memory to display 24-bit color at high resolutions (for example, it requires 2,359,296 bytes of video memory to display 24-bit color at a 1024x768 resolution).

Tip   When creating artwork for Web pages, keep screen resolution and color limitations in mind. If you save drawings from software such as CorelDRAW!, specify a resolution of 75dpi (or a value between 75 and 100 dpi) and limit colors to as few as possible. Limiting the number of colors keeps the size of the image file small.

The best way to check the resolution and color limitations is to test your Web pages on a few representative systems (such as a PC, a Macintosh, and a high-end UNIX workstation such as Sun or HP).

Browser types

The differences in browser types — the fact that your users may use many different types of browsers — is a major constraint on designing effective Web pages. In fact, even the same browser, such as Netscape Navigator, may render a document slightly differently on different systems. The differences often stem from display differences such as screen resolution and number of available colors.

If you design your HTML documents and test them using a specific browser on a specific system, you may be surprised by the way the document appears on another browser. Try to make your documents as standard as possible. Use only those HTML tags that are supported by all browsers. Additionally, you should provide enough textual information for inline images (through the `alt` attribute of `<img>` tags) so that users with text-only browsers such as Lynx can also use your Web site.

Tip   If you design your Web pages for a specific browser (such as Netscape Navigator), indicate this on the home page so that prospective users know what to expect. With a little work, you can provide alternatives (such as text-only versions) for those who cannot view your Web pages with the browser you recommend.

Designing an Organizational Framework

After you address the overall Web site design issues, you need to create an organizational framework within which all of your HTML documents reside. The framework specifies the interrelationship of the documents and provides an obvious structure for the Web site's information content. The basic idea is to make it easy for the users to navigate the site. You also must organize HTML files into a directory structure. The following steps can help you arrive at a framework for your Web site:

1. Categorize the site's content and activities into logical groups.

2. Organize the groups into hierarchies of Web pages.

3. Establish navigational links among the groups.

Tip   For a smaller Web site, your initial guess at the organization of the Web pages might be good enough to proceed to implementation. However, for a more complex site, you may also decide to perform a task analysis step to determine how a user performs specific tasks at your site. Task analysis can help you refine the Web page order and relationships, and it involves nothing more than studying the sequence of steps that a user has to take to perform a task. The goal of task analysis is to rearrange the content of the Web pages to let users accomplish certain tasks as efficiently as possible. If you are setting up a Web site that serves as an online shop, make sure that the user can select products and make purchases with a minimal number of steps.

Categories of information

The first design step is to identify the site's content and categorize the information into logical groups. The idea is to group together bits of information that can reside together on a single Web page. You might identify several kinds of information, and plan to create a single Web page for each kind. In later steps, you'll tie these Web pages together with hyperlinks into a cohesive Web site. Suppose you are setting up a Web site that provides some Web programming tools. For this site, a typical grouping of information might be as follows:

Category	Subcategories
Overview	✦ Description of company ✦ Map showing where the offices are located ✦ Job openings (if any)
Software	✦ Free software to download ✦ Product list to browse and select from ✦ Selected products to buy
Web programming	✦ List of Web programming resources ✦ Technical notes about programming ✦ Programming Tip of the Week
Search information	✦ Information to search by keyword ✦ Technical notes to browse
Feedback	✦ Form to submit comments and suggestions

Although the information may differ on another Web site, the basic idea should apply equally well to any Web site design. You begin by selecting the content based on your user base and then group the content into related categories. As you identify major categories of information, you should also settle on one or more subcategories.

You can perform this step using the outline feature of a word processor or other application. I often use Microsoft PowerPoint's Outline mode to organize the categories and subcategories, as shown by the example in Figure 15-2.

Cross Ref An added benefit of organizing the content using PowerPoint is that the individual slides can even serve as the starting point for the Web pages. In fact, you can use the Internet Assistant for PowerPoint to convert the PowerPoint files directly into HTML documents (Chapter 16 describes Internet Assistant for PowerPoint).

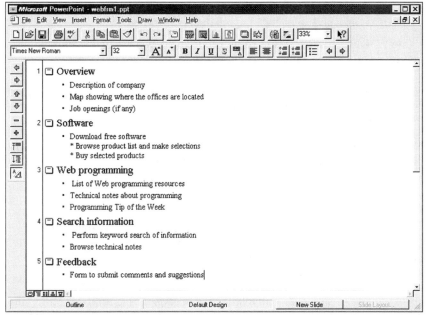

Figure 15-2: You can organize a Web site's content using the Outline mode of software such as Microsoft PowerPoint.

Interrelationship of documents

After you categorize the content, you can transfer the categories into Web pages. Often you can make each major category an individual Web page and link all top-level categories into a home page, the main Web page for your site. Here are some of the points to keep in mind when defining the interrelationship of the documents:

✦ Provide a well-defined entry point to the Web site. This entry point is usually the home page of the Web site.

✦ Make sure the organization of the documents is easy for the users to understand.

✦ Provide navigational links (such as links to previous and next pages) on each Web page.

In HTML documents, you define the relationships by providing hyperlinks that let the users jump from one document to another. You can view the organizational framework of your Web site with a diagram that represents each document with a rectangle and uses lines to show the major hyperlinks. Based on the linkage between the documents, the organization of a Web site can be characterized as follows:

✦ **Hierarchical:** The pages are organized in a well-defined hierarchy that parallels the categories and subcategories of content you have identified.

✦ **Sequential:** Each page is linked to the previous and next pages only. Thus, users progress through the pages in a well-defined sequence.

✦ **Combined hierarchical and sequential:** The pages are in a hierarchy but a subset of the pages may be arranged sequentially where appropriate.

Although you can, in theory, add hyperlinks to any document you want (including links to documents residing on other Web servers), it's important to keep the links organized by following one of these forms of organization.

Tip   I show a few organizational structures in this chapter, but these are by no means the only ways to organize the Web pages at a site. Use whatever suits your needs, as long as it is easy for the users to navigate.

Hierarchical organization

The hierarchical organization meshes well with the way you organize the site's content into categories and subcategories because the Web pages can essentially parallel the organization of categories. Figure 15-3 illustrates the hierarchical organization of Web pages at a site.

This organization is typical of many Web sites because it's simple and straightforward. You can organize the categories and subcategories according to importance and the anticipated frequency of access. Users start at the home page, which serves as an index to the site, enabling them to branch off to various categories of information. From any Web page in the hierarchy, users can always go back to the home page — that means each Web page has a "Back to Home Page" link at a well-defined location on the page.

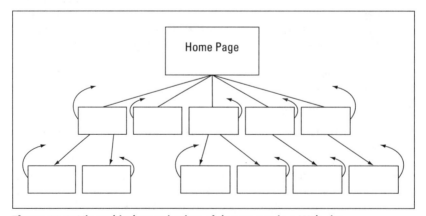

Figure 15-3: Hierarchical organization of documents in a Web site.

When you use a hierarchical organization, you should watch out for hierarchies that are too deep. If you use too many levels, users have to do extra work (clicking on lots of links) and wade through too many pages to reach useful information (because the pages at the lowest levels of the hierarchy tend to have the useful information). It's best to limit the hierarchy to three levels, as shown in Figure 15-3.

Sequential organization

As the name implies, the sequential organization lays out the Web pages one after another in a sequence and lets the user move from a page to the previous or next page only. Figure 15-4 illustrates a sequential layout of Web pages.

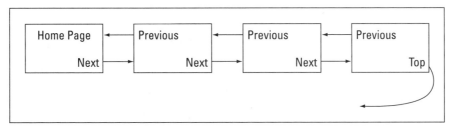

Figure 15-4: Web pages organized sequentially.

The sequential arrangement is appropriate for lengthy documents that you may have broken down into separate Web pages because there is a natural previous and next relationship among the pages.

Tip   Sequential organization of Web pages is also good for any type of information that needs to be presented in a specific sequence. Some examples are step-by-step installation instructions and computer-based training.

Combined hierarchical and sequential organization

It's unlikely that you'll use hierarchical or sequential organization alone. Most of the time, you need to combine the two organizations. Figure 15-5 illustrates a typical combined hierarchical and sequential organization of Web pages.

A good idea is to start with a hierarchical structure with a home page and then use sequential layouts where appropriate.

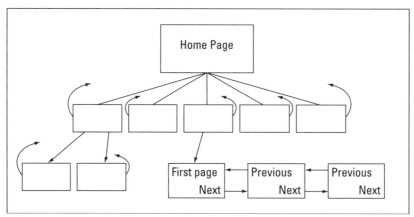

Figure 15-5: Combined hierarchical and sequential organization of Web pages.

Directory structure for the documents

In addition to the organizational framework for the Web pages, you should also lay out how you plan to store the documents in specific directories on the server. Web servers on UNIX systems serve documents from a directory known as the *document root* directory. For example, the NCSA and Apache Web servers use the directory `/usr/local/etc/httpd/htdocs` as the default document root directory. That means when a browser requests the document `/index.html`, the Web server actually sends back the file `/usr/local/etc/httpd/htdocs/index.html` from the system where the server is running.

Within the document root directory, you can organize the HTML files any way you want. Apply some foresight and organize the documents and images into a hierarchy of subdirectories for easier management. When organizing the documents into subdirectories, you should try to make it easy to

✦ Move a subset of documents to another Web site.

✦ Add a whole new set of documents to your Web site (for example, when a new department in your organization wants to add documents to your server).

✦ Move directories and documents to a different system.

Directory layout

If you have several major groups in your company sharing a single Web server, you'll want to provide each group with its own subdirectory under the Web server's document root directory.

Cross Ref
Within each group's directory, documents should use a relative URL (see Chapter 10 for a discussion of relative and absolute URLs), which means the document name does not begin with a slash (/). By using relative URLs, you ensure that the entire subset of documents can be easily moved to another directory or a different Web site.

Each group also can have its own subdirectory to store image files used in the HTML documents. Within a group's subdirectory, there can be other subdirectories depending on how that group organizes its Web pages. Figure 15-6 illustrates a typical directory layout scheme.

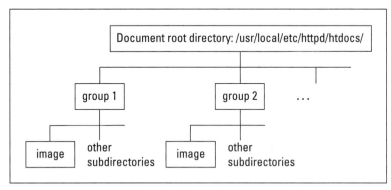

Figure 15-6: Typical directory layout at a large Web site.

If your organization is not large enough to have multiple departments, you can place the home page (the `index.html` file) in the document root directory and create other subdirectories for various top-level categories. You'll still want an image subdirectory in which to place all the images you use in your Web pages.

File and directory names

Tip Although you are implementing your Web server on a UNIX system, you should adhere to a file naming scheme that enables you to easily move the document to a different operating system — Microsoft Windows or Macintosh. To ensure portability among UNIX, Macintosh, and Windows, adhere to the least common denominator of the file naming conventions in these operating systems:

✦ **File name length:** By now most operating systems allow long file names, but Windows 3.1 and MS-DOS still have the 8.3 restriction. That means that their file names can have at most eight characters with a three character extension (such as OVERVIEW.HTM). If you think your files may have to be used on Windows 3.1, you should restrict yourself to the 8.3 file names.

✦ **File extensions:** Web servers rely on the file's extension (such as `.htm`, `.html`, and `.gif`) to determine the file's content type. Although the Macintosh operating system can determine a file's type from information stored inside a file, you should consistently use an extension for all file names.

✦ **Case sensitivity:** It's best if you stick to all lowercase file and directory names so that there is no confusion when you move the files to a system (such as Windows 3.1 and Windows 95) where file names are not case-sensitive.

Specifying the Design

For a smaller Web site, a diagram of the Web site's organization (such as the ones in Figures 15-3 through 15-5) might suffice as a specification of the design. For a more comprehensive Web site, you may need to specify the design with further details so that a larger development team can easily collaborate to create the site's content.

Specification items

You can specify the design through sketches and notes. Here are some of the items you need to document when designing a larger Web site:

✦ **Web site organization:** This can be a simple diagram, as in Figures 15-3 through 15-5, or even a prototype on a corkboard with index cards representing Web pages and strings representing links.

✦ **Web page types:** After you make a list of all the Web pages, classify them into categories such as pages that must display dynamic information (pages that have to be generated on the fly because the information is not known before-hand), interactive forms-based pages, error message pages, a user registration page (for an online shopping service, for instance), and the home page.

✦ **List of hyperlinks:** For each Web page, you should specify all the hyperlinks to other Web pages.

✦ **Web page specification:** For each Web page, you should specify the purpose and any special requirements.

Need for design specification

For many organizations, the site design specification is a must because many stake-holders (people with interest in the Web site) may be involved in approving the Web site. By providing a concrete specification, you enable

✦ System administrators to work on the directory layout and any special network or processing requirements (for example, the need to write scripts and pro-grams to use a corporate database)

✦ Graphics designers to create the graphics elements and design the look-and-feel of typical Web page types

✦ Approving organizations to review the overall design specification and sign off on the implementation of the Web site

Tip   To convey the concept of the Web site fully, you may decide to augment the sketches and diagrams with some limited prototypes that use actual HTML documents and show these on a typical Web browser. These prototypes are most helpful in getting approval from the stakeholders because prototypes speak louder than words.

As a designer of the site, you may appreciate more of an "index card and string" model of the Web site. To do this, write the specification of each Web page on an index card. Arrange the cards on a corkboard and use strings to indicate hyperlinks.

Designing Individual Web Pages

After you have defined an organizational framework for your Web site and, if necessary, specified the design, you can begin designing the individual Web pages. From your overall Web site design, you should have a list of the types of Web pages you need to create. Your goal is to apply a consistent design approach. Some of the typical Web page types are as follows:

✦ **Home page:** Page where users typically enter your site (although a user may save another page as bookmark and go directly to the bookmarked page).

✦ **Login page:** Page where user logs into your site (assuming your site provides access only to members).

✦ **Registration page:** Page where a new user signs up as a member.

✦ **Search page:** Page through which the user can search your site using keywords.

✦ **Feedback page:** Page through which the users can submit comments.

✦ **Error page:** Page that displays an error message in case something goes wrong (such as some requested data not being available).

✦ **Copyright page:** Page with your company's standard copyright message.

✦ **Hierarchical content page:** Page that has links to the home page and that you can use for any type of content in a hierarchical organization (see Figure 15-3).

✦ **Sequential content page:** Page with links to previous and next pages that can be used to display content in a sequential organization (see Figure 15-4).

Regardless of the page type, you can apply some common design themes to each page's design.

Simplicity, order, and consistency

Make your Web pages simple and to the point. The visual elements on the page must have a sense of order to them and all the pages should be consistent. These are common-sense guidelines that you should follow with some discipline.

Keep your Web pages simple

Users are inundated with information on the Web. No one has the time to sift through a lengthy discourse to extract useful information. You need to keep each page clear, concise, and focused on a specific task. Avoid lengthy paragraphs. If you bury important information in a paragraph, users are likely to miss the information. Instead, use headings and lists to make the information easy to scan. In addition, even though "a picture is worth a thousand words," putting large pictures is not the answer for users who have typical 28.8 Kbps modem connections to the Net. Keep graphics small.

Use an orderly page layout

Tip

Just as a newspaper or magazine page uses a well-defined layout (using columns), your Web pages should have an orderly layout. Using an orderly layout does not mean that you cannot be creative about the Web pages. You can still have a variety of page layouts. An orderly layout simply means that you arrange all the elements of the page (such as blocks of text, images, and headings) in a clear, logical manner.

You don't have to duplicate a newspaper's columnar layout in your Web page (although many Web pages do use a tabular layout). You simply need to arrange the visual elements to highlight the central information or activity of the page.

Cross Ref

A good layout is especially important for forms that prompt the user for input. (Forms are described in Chapter 19.) On a form, you should group the text entry fields in a logical manner.

Provide a consistent appearance

For a Web site, a consistent look and feel is like the brand name for a product. Just as brand-name recognition helps businesses sell products, a consistency in Web page appearance helps users recognize your Web site.

A consistent appearance does not mean that all pages are identical. Different types of Web pages can have different layouts, but some key features should be consistent. You can achieve a consistent appearance with a few simple steps:

✦ Place all navigation controls (the links to go back to the home page or go back and forth between related pages) at the same location on each page. On pages that have several screenfuls of content, it is helpful for the users if you place navigation controls both at the top and the bottom of the page.

✦ Use small but distinctive images for the navigation controls.

✦ Use a small identifying image or logo on each Web page. This does not have to be a large image. It can even be just a thick horizontal rule (with distinctive colors or an image of your choice).

HTML style

Although you can design a Web site without paying attention to HTML, it's unwise to do so because ultimately the Web pages have to be implemented using HTML. Therefore, pay attention to HTML capabilities as you design the Web site. After you complete the design, you should establish and follow an HTML style guide for all your documents. This is similar to the situation in programming projects where style guides are used to ensure a consistent coding style among all the programmers.

URL You can find quite a few Web pages on the Net that discuss this very topic — designing good Web pages with HTML. If you want to browse these online resources, the following Web page at NCSA includes a collection of links to documents that discuss HTML writing style:

```
http://union.ncsa.uiuc.edu/HyperNews/get/www/html/guides.html
```

Your goal in creating an HTML style guide is to make the site easy for the user to read and navigate. The following sections highlight some useful HTML styles.

Use short titles

Web page titles appear in the title bar of a browser's window and in bookmarks — the list of saved links. A short title makes the bookmark menu more readable.

The title text is also used by many automatic Web indexing programs to index your Web page. Therefore, your title should include keywords relevant to your site.

Avoid meaningless link text

New Web authors often suffer from the "click here" syndrome; they make the mistake of marking all links with the phrase "click here." Some pages refer to an author home page with a link, for example, as shown in Figure 15-7. This link is supposed to tell the reader how to find out more about the author. A better approach is to make the author's name a link (to the author's home page), as shown in Figure 15-8.

| To learn more about me, click here. |

Figure 15-7: An example of the "click here" syndrome.

| Author: John Doe |

Figure 15-8: A more descriptive link.

Even when a link does not blatantly urge the user to "click here," the link text may still not convey much meaning to the user. A meaningful link should tell the user something about the document at the other end of the hyperlink. In other words, instead of showing the URL as the link text, put a descriptive word or two about that URL and make those descriptive words the link text.

Tip If you use images as links, always use the `alt` attribute to provide some text for each image. Otherwise, your Web page cannot be effectively used by users with text-only browsers or by users who have turned off the display of graphics in their browsers.

Provide a complete copy of multi-page documents

Breaking up a large document into several hyperlinked pages helps readers browse it more easily, but if they want to print the entire document, they must print each Web page individually. This can be time-consuming and annoying to your readers.

Tip If you provide a hypertext version of a long document (with a sequential organization as illustrated in Figure 15-4) on your Web page, you should also include a link to allow the user to download the complete document. This is helpful when the user wants to print the document (especially, if the document happens to be a user guide or installation guide). If you neglect to provide the complete document, the user will be forced to view the pages sequentially and print the pages, one at a time.

Include contact information

Tip At the end of each Web page, you should include some contact information. For a large Web site, this may be a link to the company's Customer Service department. Otherwise, you can provide a link to the author's home page. You should also place a brief copyright notice on the page.

If the information on the page is time-sensitive, include the date when the information was last updated. However, if the page content does not change with time, there is no need to include a date stamp. In fact, it may be a bad idea to add a date stamp to an infrequently revised page because then your site's users will think you are falling behind in your Webmaster duties.

Summary

For a Web site to be useful to its audience, it needs a cohesive overall design. The design should include an organizational framework for the documents, the hyperlinks that tie together the documents, and a consistent layout for all the Web pages. This chapter provides an overview of how to design a complete Web site. The next chapter describes tools that you can use to convert existing documents into HTML format.

Where to go next . . .

✦ For a user's view of the Web, see Chapter 4.

✦ To learn how to convert existing documents into HTML, go to Chapter 16.

✦ For information on HTML authoring tools, proceed to Chapter 17.

✦ If you want to create interactive HTML forms, consult Chapters 19 and 20.

✦   ✦   ✦

Converting Existing Documents to HTML

When you begin preparing the content of a Web site, one of the first tasks is to decide how to make use of any existing material. For example, you may have word processor documents that you want to make available in HTML format. There are a number of tools, commonly referred to as *HTML converters*, that can convert various types of documents to HTML.

Note   Although you are running a Web server on a UNIX system (which is why you are reading this book), many existing documents will be from popular Windows or Macintosh word processors such as Microsoft Word and WordPerfect. This chapter describes some of the tools you can use to convert existing word processor documents into HTML format.

On your UNIX system, you may also have some HTML conversion needs such as the conversion of a man page (the online manual pages that you can view with the man command) to HTML format or the conversion of mail messages to HTML format. This chapter also describes a few such tools.

In most cases, the tools are shareware or freeware programs that you can download from the Internet. Whenever a tool is mentioned, you'll find the URL of the site where you can learn more about the tool and, in most cases, download the software.

HTML Converters

URL HTML converters create HTML documents from various word processor and text files. There are converters that work with specific word processors such as Microsoft Word for Windows and WordPerfect. You can even convert text files (as long as they follow a few specific conventions) into HTML documents. You'll find a comprehensive list of HTML converters at the following Web page in YAHOO!:

```
http://www.yahoo.com/Computers_and_Internet/Internet/World_Wide_Web/
        HTML_Converters/
```

URL Table 16-1 presents a sampling of currently available HTML converters. (The table is by no means exhaustive; it's meant to give you a feel for the kind of conversion tools available on the Internet.)

<table>
<tr><td colspan="2" align="center">Table 16-1
HTML Converters</td></tr>
<tr><td>*Name*</td><td>*URL and Description*</td></tr>
<tr><td>EasyHelp/Web</td><td>`http://www.eon-solutions.com/easyhelp/easyhelp.htm`
A shareware add-on to Microsoft Word for Windows from Eon Solutions Ltd. EasyHelp/Web enables you to create Windows Help files and HTML documents from Word for Windows documents.</td></tr>
<tr><td>HTML Transit</td><td>`http://www.infoaccess.com/products/transit/httoc.htm`
A commercial product from InfoAccess, Inc. that can convert text and tables into HTML. Handles many input formats: ASCII text, Rich Text Format (RTF), Microsoft Word (DOS and Windows versions), WordPerfect (DOS and Windows versions), Lotus AmiPro, FrameMaker MIF files, and Interleaf TPS Files. Accepts graphics in a wide variety of formats: BMP, CDR, CGM, DIB, DRW, DXF, GEM, GIF, HPGL, JPEG, MSP, PCC, PCX, PIC, TIFF, WMF, WPG. You can download a copy of the software (a 3.68MB file) for a 15-day evaluation.</td></tr>
<tr><td>HyperMail</td><td>`http://www.eit.com/software/hypermail/hypermail.html`
A program that converts a file of mail messages in a UNIX mailbox into a set of linked HTML documents. Freely available (for non-commercial purposes) from Enterprise Integration Technologies (EIT).</td></tr>
</table>

Name	URL and Description
Internet Assistant for Microsoft Access for Windows 95	`http://www.microsoft.com/msaccess/ internet/ia/default.htm` A free Microsoft Access add-on from Microsoft that converts database objects (Tables, Queries, Forms, or Reports) into HTML documents.
Internet Assistant for Microsoft Excel	`http://www.microsoft.com/msexcel/ Internet/IA/default.htm` A free Excel add-on from Microsoft to convert Excel spreadsheets into HTML document. The selected spreadsheet cells appear as a table in the HTML document.
Internet Assistant for Microsoft PowerPoint 95	`http://www.microsoft.com/msoffice/ mspowerpoint/internet/ia/` A free PowerPoint add-on from Microsoft to convert PowerPoint presentations into a set of linked HTML documents. It generates both a text and a graphical (GIF or JPEG) version of the presentation.
Internet Assistant for Microsoft Word	`http://www.microsoft.com/msword/ Internet/IA/` A free add-on for Microsoft Word (from Microsoft) that enables you to use Microsoft Word to create new HTML documents as well as convert existing documents into HTML. Available for all versions of Word, including Word for Macintosh.
man2html	`http://www.oac.uci.edu/indiv/ehood/ man2html.doc.html` A Perl program (by Earl Hood) that translates UNIX man pages (the online help that you read using the man command) to HTML.
RTFtoHTML	`http://www.sunpack.com/RTF/ rtftohtml_overview.html` A shareware program (written by Chris Hector) that converts Rich Text Format (RTF) files to HTML.
txt2html	`http://www.cs.wustl.edu/~seth/txt2html/` A Perl script by Seth Golub that converts plain text files into HTML.

(continued)

Table 16-1 *(continued)*	
Name	*URL and Description*
WebMaker	http://www.harlequin.com/webmaker/ A program that converts FrameMaker documents into HTML format. WebMaker was a free software package developed at CERN (the European Laboratory for Particle Physics where the Web began), but now it's marketed as a commercial product by The Harlequin Group Limited.
WordPerfect Internet Publisher 6.1	http://www.novell.com/corp/freesoft/wpip/ A free add-on for WordPerfect 6.1 for Windows (still available from Novell's Web site even though WordPerfect has been purchased by Corel) to create HTML documents in WordPerfect 6.1.

Note As this table indicates, you can find HTML conversion software for most popular word processing programs. Microsoft provides free HTML conversion programs (called Internet Assistants) for all products in the Microsoft Office suite: Word for Windows, Excel, PowerPoint, and Access.

Text to HTML Conversion with `txt2html`

If you are converting existing documents into HTML for distribution over the Internet, your source documents may be in many different formats, including plain text. Although you could convert a plain text file by adding a few HTML tags in a text editor, there are some tools available to help you automatically convert text files to HTML documents.

One of the well-known text-to-HTML conversion tools is `txt2html` by Seth Golub. `txt2html` is a Perl script that converts plain text files into HTML. It does a bit more than simply wrap the text file's contents inside a `<body>` element and intersperse it with paragraph breaks (`<p>`). The `txt2html` Perl script also tries to interpret various nuances of the lines of text and create a surprisingly useful HTML document.

 Tip To use `txt2html`, you must have Perl installed on your system. Perl is available for most common operating systems. You can download Perl from one of the sites in the Comprehensive Perl Archive Network (CPAN). To locate the nearest CPAN site, search for the keyword CPAN in YAHOO! (`http://www.yahoo.com/`).

Downloading and unpacking `txt2html`

 URL To try out `txt2html`, download the software in the form of a 14K Gzip-compressed `tar` file from the following URL:

```
http://www.cs.wustl.edu/~seth/txt2html/txt2html.tar.gz
```

Unpack the file with the following commands:

```
gunzip txt2html.tar.gz
tar xvf txt2html.tar
```

This step creates a directory named txt2html and places the following files in that directory:

File Name	Size (Bytes)	Description
changes.html	5908	History of changes to the software
txt2html.dict	3830	File that specifies patterns for URLs (that way the converter can create a hyperlink when converting the text file)
txt2html.pl	34,301	Perl program that converts text to HTML

Tip The txt2html.pl file is the actual Perl program. Because Perl is an interpreted language, you do not have to compile anything. Provided you have Perl installed on your system, you can begin using the Perl script by typing txt2html.pl.

However, you should edit the first part of the file a bit and save it under the name txt2html so that you can run the script by typing txt2html. If you look at the first few lines of txt2html.pl, you'll find the following:

```
: # Use perl
    eval 'exec perl -S $0 "$@"'
    if 0;

# It's faster to use something like #!/usr/bin/perl but you have to
# know where perl is on your system.  I didn't want to have to tell
# people how to do this, so I don't distribute it that way.  You
# really ought to change it though.  On my machine, it saves about a
# half a second.
```

Use a text editor to comment the first three lines of txt2html.pl and add an extra line at the beginning:

```
#!/usr/local/bin/perl
#: # Use perl
#     eval 'exec perl -S $0 "$@"'
#     if 0;
```

This assumes that Perl is installed in the /usr/local/bin directory of your UNIX system. If not, include the full pathname to Perl on your system.

After making the change, save the txt2html.pl file as txt2html. Make sure its executable attribute is set; use the command chmod +x txt2html to make the file executable. Then you can type txt2html to run the converter.

Webmaster One nice feature of txt2html is that it can identify specific patterns as URLs and add hy-perlinks when converting your text file. If you want to use this feature, you should copy the txt2html.dict file to your home directory under a specific name:

```
cp txt2html.dict  ~/.txt2html-linkdict
```

Using txt2html

Like many UNIX tools, txt2html takes a number of command-line options. To see a list of these options, type the following line shown in boldface:

```
txt2html —help

Usage: txt2html [options]

where options are:
        [-v          ] | [—version                   ]
        [-h          ] | [—help                      ]
        [-t <title> ] | [—title <title>             ]
        [-l <file>  ] | [—link <dictfile>           ]
        [+l          ] | [—nolink                    ]
        [-H <regexp>] | [—heading <regexp>          ]
        [-a <file>  ] | [—append <file>             ]
        [+a          ] | [—noappend                  ]
        [-e/+e       ] | [—extract / —noextract      ]
        [-c <n>      ] | [—caps <n>                  ]
        [-ct <tag>  ] | [—capstag <tag>             ]
        [-m/+m       ] | [—mail     / —nomail        ]
        [-u/+u       ] | [—unhyphen / —nounhyphen    ]
        [-tw <n>     ] | [—tabwidth <n>              ]
        [-iw <n>     ] | [—indent <n>                ]
        [-ul <n>     ] | [—ulength <n>               ]
        [-uo <n>     ] | [—uoffset <n>               ]
        [-s <n>      ] | [—shortline <n>             ]
        [-p <n>      ] | [—prewhite <n>              ]
        [-pb <n>     ] | [—prebegin <n>              ]
        [-pe <n>     ] | [—preend <n>                ]
        [-r <n>      ] | [—hrule <n>                 ]
        [-db <n>     ] | [—debug <n>                 ]

        More complete explanations of these options can be found in
        comments near the beginning of the script.
```

The best way to learn about txt2html is to use it on a number of text files. After a while, you'll get the hang of how txt2html interprets various parts of a text file. Here are a few general guidelines on how you can specify various HTML elements:

HTML Element	What You Use in Text File
<strong>	A LINE IN ALL UPPERCASE

HTML Element	What You Use in Text File
`<p>`	An extra blank line like this: This becomes a new paragraph.
`<h1>`	`ALL UPPERCASE LINE WITH UNDERLINE` `=================================`
`<h2>`	`A line of text in mixed case` `============================`
`<ul>`	`* Bulleted Item 1` `* Bulleted Item 2`
`<ol>`	`1. Numbered Item 1` `2. Numbered Item 2`
`<pre>`	`        Lines with white space in the` `beginning.`

`<a>`	`A URL such as: http://www.altavista.`
	`digital.com/ becomes a hyperlink in`
	`the HTML document.`

Figure 16-1 shows a sample text file and the resulting HTML document generated by `txt2html`. As this example shows, with a little care, you can generate reasonably formatted HTML documents from a plain text file.

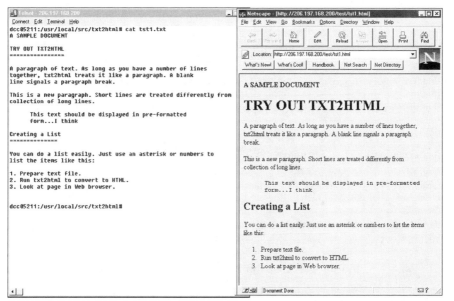

Figure 16-1: The Netscape Navigator window (on right) displays the HTML document created by `txt2html` from the text file that appears on the left.

URL At the `txt2html` home page (`http://www.cs.wustl.edu/~seth/txt2html/`), you'll find links to another sample text page and the HTML document generated by `txt2html`.

From Man Pages to HTML with `man2html`

The term *man page* refers to online help available on UNIX systems through the `man` command. Typically, man pages are formatted using a markup language known as `troff` and viewed with the `man` command. If you set up a Web site to offer support for software tools, you might want to provide Web users access to man pages. To do this, you need to convert man pages to HTML format.

Cross Ref The `man2html` Perl script, by Earl Hood, can take the output of the man command and turn it into HTML. You can use `man2html` as a Common Gateway Interface (CGI) script to serve man pages on the Web. Chapter 19 describes CGI scripts.

Tip To run `man2html`, you must have Perl installed on your system. (See the "Text to HTML Conversion with `txt2html`" section of this chapter for information on how to obtain Perl for your system.)

Downloading and installing `man2html`

URL To download `man2html`, you should use a Web browser to browse through the online documentation at the following URL:

```
http://www.oac.uci.edu/indiv/ehood/man2html.html
```

In that document, you'll find a link to download `man2html`. Or, you can proceed directly to download the file `man2html2.1.0.tar.gz` (50K) from the following URL:

```
ftp://ftp.uci.edu/pub/dtd2html/man2html2.1.0.tar.gz
```

That file corresponds to the version 2.1.0 of `man2html`, which is the latest version as of this writing.

After downloading that file to your UNIX system, unpack it with the following commands:

```
gunzip man2html2.1.0.tar.gz
tar xvf man2html2.1.0.tar
```

This creates a subdirectory named `man2html` and places a number of files in that subdirectory.

After unpacking the software distribution, use the following commands to complete the installation:

```
cd man2html
./install.me
```

The last command is a Perl script that copies `man2html` and its documentation to specific directories.

Using `man2html`

You can generate an HTML file for any man page by redirecting the output of the `man` command into the `man2html` script. The script is designed to send the resulting HTML document to standard output (`stdout`). To save the HTML output, you have to redirect the script's output to a file, using the `man2html` script with the following command:

```
man satview | man2html > satview.html
```

That command generates an HTML file named `satview.html` — a formatted representation of the manual page for a program named `satview` (presumably for viewing satellite images).

Figure 16-2 shows, side by side, a sample man page displayed by the `man` command and the resulting HTML document generated by `man2html`.

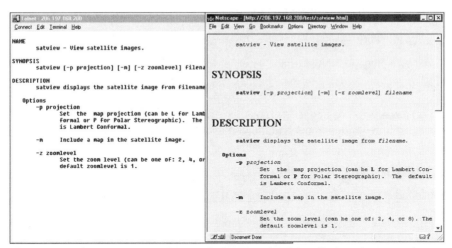

Figure 16-2: The Netscape Navigator window (on the right) displays the HTML document created by `man2html` from the man page that appears on the left.

Rich Text Format to HTML with RTFtoHTML

Rich Text Format, or RTF, was designed by Microsoft as a format for exchanging documents between Microsoft Word and other word processors such as WordPerfect, FrameMaker, and Interleaf. RTF stores formatted text and graphics in a portable text file that uses control words to indicate formatting information. The RTF control words are analogous to the HTML tags — you can say that RTF is a markup language like HTML.

Webmaster If you want to learn more about RTF, the complete format specification is available in the form of a 192K self-extracting executable (for DOS and Windows PCs) from the following URL at Microsoft:

```
http://www.microsoft.com/KB/SoftLib/MSLFiles/Gc0165.EXE
```

After downloading this file, you have to run `Gc0165.EXE` to extract the RTF specification — it appears in the Microsoft Word file `GC0165.DOC`. You can also read the specification as an HTML document at the following URL:

```
http://www.sunpack.com/RTF/Webdocs/RTF-Spec/RTF1-4.htm
```

Webmaster The latest RTF specification is version 1.4. Version 1.4 of the RTF Specification contains all RTF features introduced by Microsoft Word for Windows 95, Version 7.0.

The `www.sunpack.com` site (where you can find information about RTF 1.4) is also the site where Chris Hector makes available RTFtoHTML — a program that converts RTF files into HTML. As of version 3.0 (the latest version as of this writing), RTFtoHTML is being released as a shareware. If you find it useful, you should pay the modest shareware fee (less than US$30) to Chris Hector. RTFtoHTML version 3.0 includes several new features including the capabilities to

✦ Write HTML tables

✦ Use Netscape Navigator and Internet Explorer extensions to HTML

✦ Split large documents into several smaller files

As you'll see in the "Using RTFtoHTML" section earlier in this chapter, you use command-line options to control the converter's behavior.

Downloading RTFtoHTML

URL Download RTFtoHTML from the links on the Web page at the following URL:

```
http://www.sunpack.com/RTF/rtftohtml_overview.html
```

Versions are available for UNIX, Macintosh, and MS-DOS. (You can run the program in a DOS window under Windows 95 or Windows NT.) Because RTF files are mostly created in Microsoft Windows, in this chapter we'll look at the Windows version of RTFtoHTML.

URL The DOS and Windows version of the software is available in the form of a ZIP file that you have to unpack using the PKUNZIP utility program. You can also unpack that file using WinZip, which you can download from the links on the following page:

```
http://www.ncinter.net/~ianh/winzip.html
```

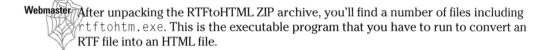

Webmaster After unpacking the RTFtoHTML ZIP archive, you'll find a number of files including `rtftohtm.exe`. This is the executable program that you have to run to convert an RTF file into an HTML file.

Using RTFtoHTML

The syntax for the command to run RTFtoHTML is as follows:

```
rtftohtml [options] file
```

where *file* is the RTF file to convert and *options* denotes one or more command-line options for RTFtoHTML. The RTF file usually has an `.rtf` extension. By default, `rtftohtml` writes the HTML output to a file with the same name, but with the `.rtf` replaced with `.htm`.

An example

Suppose you have the `sample1.doc` document that you have prepared using Microsoft Word for Windows 95. Suppose that file has an embedded bitmap image. You want to convert the file into HTML format.

First, you should save the document in the RTF format. To do this, select Save As from the File menu and then select Rich Text Format from the `Save as type` drop-down list (that's a text entry field with an arrow button to the right; when you click on the arrow button a list appears; you can select items from that list).

After you save the document as an RTF file named `sample1.rtf`, you can convert it to an HTML document by running RTFtoHTML with the following command in an MS-DOS window:

```
rtftohtm -i sample1.rtf
```

Because the RTF document includes one image, RTFtoHTML creates two files:

✦ `sample1.htm` is the HTML document.

✦ `sample1.wmf` is the bitmap image in Windows Metafile format (WMF).

The HTML document references the inline image with the file name `sample1.gif`, but the image itself is saved as a WMF file. Before you can view the document together with the inline image, you have to convert the WMF file into GIF format.

Tip You can use one of several shareware or commercial products to convert the WMF file into a GIF file. One of the well-known shareware image tools is Graphics Workshop. You can download a copy from the following URL:

```
http://www.mindworkshop.com/alchemy/gww.html
```

If you decide to use Graphics Workshop, you should pay the shareware fee of $40.

After you convert the `sample1.wmf` file to `sample1.gif` (GIF format), you can view the converted HTML document in a Web browser. Figure 16-3 shows the original Microsoft Word file next to the HTML document as it appears in Netscape Navigator.

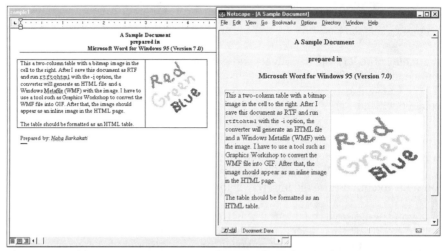

Figure 16-3: The Netscape Navigator window (on the right) displays the HTML document created by `rtftohtm` from the Microsoft Word document that appears on the left.

As Figure 16-3 shows, RTFtoHTML can generate a reasonably close facsimile of the original Microsoft Word document. If you have tables in your Word document, RTFtoHTML uses HTML tables to capture the tabular format. RTFtoHTML can also generate an HTML document with frames — one frame displays a table of contents and the other frame displays parts of the document. You have to use specific RTFtoHTML command-line options to control some aspects of HTML conversion.

Command-line options

RTFtoHTML accepts a number of command-line options. If you run the `rtftohtm` program without a file name, it displays a brief message with the command-line options, as follows:

```
rtftohtm
No input file given.
Usage: rtftohtml [options] file
(Info: This is rtftohtml 3.0c )

Options may be:
  -c        generate a Table of Contents page (req. -h)
  -F        use frames (req. -c and Netscape 2.0 or compatible)
```

```
-G         write no graphics files
-h[n]      split output at headings (at the n'th level)
-i         imbed graphics
-N file    read navigation panel from "file" (req. -h)
-o file    write output to "file"
-P ext     use "ext" as extension for external graphic files
-s         use short filenames when splitting
-t         list external references on top of page (req. -h)
-T title   use "title" as the document title (req. -h)
-V         print version nuber of rtftohtml (only)
-x         create an Index (if there are index entries) (req. -h)
-X text    use "text" as the text for index anchors (e.g. &#183;)
```

Note the F option for generating an HTML document with frames. (See Chapter 14 for a discussion of frames, a Netscape extension to HTML.) When you use frames, you also need to use the -h option to break the document into multiple HTML files and the -c option to generate a table of contents page.

URL

To see an example of a frame-based document generated by RTFtoHTML, take a look at the RTF 1.4 specification page at the following URL:

```
http://www.sunpack.com/RTF/Webdocs/RTF-Spec/RTF1-4.htm
```

You'll find a detailed user's guide to RTFtoHTML at `http://www.sunpack.com/RTF/guide.htm`.

Internet Assistant for Microsoft Word for Windows

Microsoft Word for Windows is a popular word processor and a part of the Microsoft Office suite of applications. Because of its popularity, many organizations have existing documents in Microsoft Word for Windows format. As a Webmaster, you may have the need to convert Microsoft Word files to HTML format. You might also want to use Microsoft Word to prepare a new HTML document. You can accomplish both of these tasks with Internet Assistant for Microsoft Word, a free product from Microsoft.

As of this writing, the latest version of Internet Assistant for Microsoft Word is 2.0z. This version improves upon version 1.0 with the following significant new features:

✦ It saves embedded graphics in separate GIF files and adds <img> tags that reference the GIF files.

✦ It supports HTML extensions such as centering, background color, background image, text color, and hyperlink color.

✦ It converts Word tables into HTML tables.

✦ It installs with minimal user intervention.

Downloading and installing Internet Assistant for Microsoft Word for Windows 95

URL Microsoft freely distributes Internet Assistant for Word. All you have to do is download it from Microsoft's server on the Internet. Just download the file `wrdia20z.exe` (1.2MB) by clicking on a link on the Web page at

`http://www.microsoft.com/msword/Internet/IA/`

and following the instructions on the subsequent Web pages.

After downloading, you should run the `wrdia20z.exe` file. That program automatically extracts the necessary files, runs a setup program, and installs itself as an add-on to Microsoft Word for Windows 95.

Tip Internet Assistant for Word installs its files in the `\Program Files\Internet Assistant` directory. You should use Microsoft Word to open and read the README. DOC file, which contains some useful information about Internet Assistant for Word.

Note Internet Assistant for Microsoft Word adds three basic capabilities to Microsoft Word:

✦ The ability to browse the Web using Word as a browser

✦ The ability to edit an HTML document in Word

✦ The ability to store a Word document as an HTML file

You can access the Web browsing and HTML editing capability through a new Browse Web menu item on the File menu, as shown in Figure 16-4.

Figure 16-4: Internet Assistant for Microsoft Word adds a Browse Web command to Word's File menu.

You can also activate the Web browser and HTML editor mode by clicking on a new button that appears on Word's toolbar, as shown in Figure 16-5.

Figure 16-5: Internet Assistant for Microsoft Word adds a Switch to Web Browse View button on Word's toolbar.

To use the other functionality — the ability to save a document in HTML format — you have to select Save As from the File menu. This opens the Save As dialog box, where you specify the file name and file type. When you open the Save as type drop-down list you'll see that HTML is now an available file type, as shown in Figure 16-6.

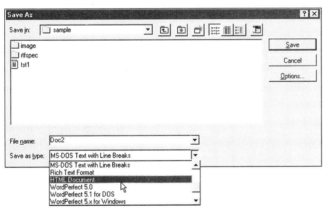

Figure 16-6: After installing Internet Assistant for Microsoft Word, you can save a file as an HTML document.

Using Internet Assistant for Microsoft Word for Windows 95

After you install Internet Assistant, you can easily convert any Microsoft Word document into HTML format. Here are the basic steps:

1. Load the Word document into Microsoft Word.

2. Select Save As from the File menu. Microsoft Word displays the Save As dialog box, as shown in Figure 16-6.

3. Select HTML Document from the Save as type drop-down list and click on the Save button. Word saves the document as an HTML file with a .HTM extension.

4. If there are any embedded graphics, Word displays a dialog box, as shown in Figure 16-7, asking if you want to save the graphics as separate GIF files. If you want to do so, click on the Save Pictures button and Word creates a separate GIF file for each embedded graphic.

Figure 16-7: Internet Assistant for Microsoft Word displays a dialog box that lets you save embedded images as separate files.

After you save the file as an HTML document, Microsoft Word displays the HTML document in a window and you can even edit the HTML source. Figure 16-8 shows an original Microsoft Word file next to the converted HTML document as it appears in Netscape Navigator.

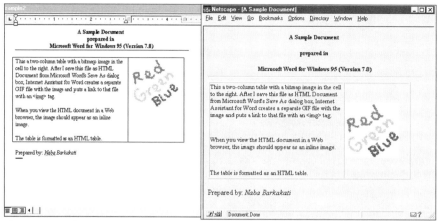

Figure 16-8: The Netscape Navigator window (on right) displays the HTML document saved from the Microsoft Word document that appears on the left.

As Figure 16-8 shows, Internet Assistant for Word creates a useful HTML version of the Word document. Internet Assistant for Word is the tool to use if you have lots of Microsoft Word files and you want to provide them on the Web.

Internet Assistant for Microsoft PowerPoint for Windows

Microsoft PowerPoint for Windows is a presentation program that lets you prepare sets of slides. These collections of slides can be ideal material for the Web, provided you can convert them into HTML documents. You can perform this conversion with Microsoft's Internet Assistant for Microsoft PowerPoint. (The Internet Assistant works only with the Windows 95 version of PowerPoint.)

Downloading and installing Internet Assistant for PowerPoint

URL

Download the file `pptia.exe` (253K) by clicking on a link on the Web page at the following URL:

    http://www.microsoft.com/mspowerpoint/Internet/ia/default.htm

After downloading, run the `pptia.exe` file — it's a self-extracting archive, so when you run it, it generates a number of other files:

Name	Size (Bytes)	Description
IA4PPT95.EXE	281,088	Program for the Internet Assistant for PowerPoint.
IA4PPT95.HTM	19,986	HTML file with installation and user guide for the software.
README.TXT	269	Summary description of the other files.
IA4PPT95.DOC	32,256	Same as IA4PPT95.HTM, but in Word for Windows 95 format.

Open the `ia4ppt95.htm` file in a Web browser (or open `ia4ppt95.doc` in Word for Windows 95). This file tells you how to install and use the Internet Assistant for PowerPoint 95.

To install, first exit PowerPoint if it's running. Then run the `ia4ppt95.exe` program. You can run it by typing `ia4ppt95` in the DOS window within Windows 95 or by double-clicking the file name in My Computer or Windows Explorer. That program automatically performs the installation and informs you that the installation is successful.

Using Internet Assistant for PowerPoint

To use the Internet Assistant for PowerPoint, start PowerPoint and open the presentation that you want to convert to HTML format. Suppose you want to convert a PowerPoint file named `sample1.ppt`. Begin by opening the file in PowerPoint. Then select Export as HTML from the File menu, as shown in Figure 16-9. (Export as HTML appears because you have installed Internet Assistant for PowerPoint.)

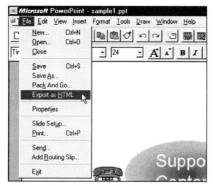

Figure 16-9: Internet Assistant for PowerPoint adds an Export as HTML item in the File menu.

After you select Export as HTML from the File menu, PowerPoint displays the HTML Export Options dialog box, as shown in Figure 16-10. In this dialog box, you specify the directory where all the HTML and graphic files will be stored. You can also select the image file format — the choices are GIF and JPEG.

Figure 16-10: The HTML Export Options dialog appears when you export a presentation as an HTML document.

Webmaster Once you select the HTML Export Options, PowerPoint takes over the conversion process. During the conversion process you should leave the system alone. In particular, do not try to work in another window while the HTML conversion is progressing.

At one stage of the conversion, PowerPoint displays the slides again in a smaller window. Shortly after that, PowerPoint completes the HTML conversion. You can then try out the new HTML documents in a Web browser. As an example, consider the `sample1.ppt`, which is a PowerPoint file with two slides. Figure 16-11 shows how it appears in PowerPoint.

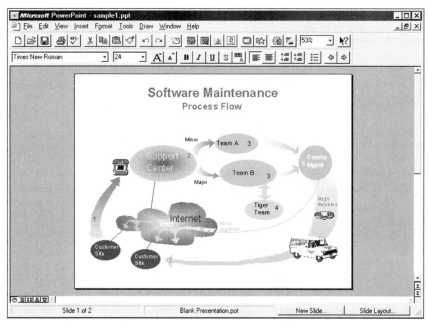

Figure 16-11: A sample presentation as it appears in PowerPoint for Windows 95.

When I export this presentation as HTML, PowerPoint creates a number of files in the `sample1` subdirectory. Here are some of the relevant files:

Name	Description
`index.htm`	Index of the slides
`tsld001.htm`	Text version of slide 1
`sld001.htm`	Graphics version of slide 1
`tsld002.htm`	Text version of slide 2
`sld002.htm`	Graphics version of slide 2
`p2hnext.gif`	Image for the Next button (right arrow)
`p2hprev.gif`	Image for the Previous button (left arrow)

(continued)

Name	Description
p2hup.gif	Image for the Go to Beginning button (two left arrows)
p2htext.gif	Image for button that takes user to text version
sld001.gif	Image for the graphics version of slide 1 (used in sld001.htm)
sld002.gif	Image for the graphics version of slide 2 (used in sld002.htm)

To provide the slides on the Web, all you need to do is create a subdirectory in your Web server's document root directory and place all of these files in that subdirectory. The index.htm file serves as the index file for that directory.

Tip

If your Web server considers index.html (with .html extension instead of .htm extension) to be the default index file, then rename index.htm to index.html.

Webmaster

Make sure that your Web server treats documents with .htm extension as text/html MIME type. (See Chapter 12 for more information on MIME types.) If you run an NCSA or Apache Web server, you may need to add the htm extension next to html in the mime.types file in the /usr/local/etc/httpd/conf directory of your system. Figure 16-12 shows how one of the slides in sample1.ppt appears in Netscape Navigator.

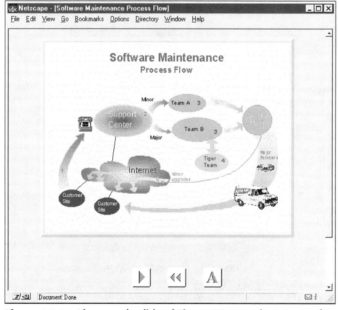

Figure 16-12: The sample slide of Figure 16-11 as it appears after conversion to an HTML format by Internet Assistant for PowerPoint for Windows 95.

Internet Assistant for PowerPoint adds all those navigation buttons underneath the slide. You can use them to go back and forth between the slides. All in all, the resulting HTML document is very impressive. Internet Assistant for PowerPoint can be a very useful tool if you have PowerPoint presentations that you need to serve on the Web.

Summary

When you run a Web site, you invariably must provide some existing documents to the users. Typically, these existing documents come from word processor packages such as Microsoft Word or WordPerfect. Some may even be text files or man pages on UNIX systems. This chapter describes a number of tools that you can use to convert documents from various formats to HTML. The next chapter presents some Web authoring tools (that are primarily for creating new Web pages).

Where to go next . . .

✦ For Web site design guidelines, read Chapter 15.

✦ To learn about tools to create new HTML documents, go to Chapter 17.

✦ If you want to create interactive HTML forms, consult Chapters 19 and 20.

✦ For information on promoting your Web site, proceed to Chapter 18.

✦   ✦   ✦

Using Web Authoring Tools

◆ ◆ ◆ ◆

In This Chapter

Learning about HTML authoring tools

Using X Windows-based UNIX tools

Installing and using popular Windows authoring tools

Finding HTML authoring tools on the Internet

Using Macintosh-based HTML authoring tools

◆ ◆ ◆ ◆

Although HTML is relatively simple, and you can (and should) learn the basic tags with a bit of practice, it's still rather tedious to type all the HTML tags required to lay out a Web page. Additionally, you need good imagination to figure out how the layout is going as you type the HTML elements in a text editor. What you need is an authoring tool — a tool that lets you easily insert HTML tags, add text and images, and view the page layout.

As the Web has grown in popularity, many software vendors have stepped in with Web authoring tools (also known as HTML authoring tools) of varying capabilities. Some are as simple as editor macros that enable you to enter the HTML tags without having to type much. Others are fully graphical tools that let you create a Web page by pointing and clicking at a palette of tools. You can find Web authoring tools for most popular operating systems, including Windows 95, Macintosh, and various flavors of UNIX.

This chapter presents a number of HTML authoring tools, focusing primarily on the shareware and freeware tools that you can download from the Internet. Often, the vendors provide a less capable version of a Web authoring program for free download. After trying out the less capable version, you can get the fully functional version for a price. Prices range from $50–500 (U.S.), with most tools priced at around $100 (U.S.).

Other tools that also help in Web authoring are image manipulation tools and HTML syntax checkers (programs that verify that you are using HTML correctly). A few of these tools are also mentioned in this chapter.

HTML Authoring Tools

You can easily prepare HTML documents with any text editor because HTML documents are all plain text. You can also learn the HTML tags quite easily and, as a Webmaster, you should definitely learn HTML.

However, that does not mean you have to always write all of your HTML documents with a plain text editor. There are a number of tools that can help you prepare HTML documents. Collectively, these tools are called *Web authoring tools* or *HTML editors*. Some of the tools are essentially extensions to text editors so that you can easily enter HTML tags. A number of HTML authoring tools actually let you see what the HTML document may look like in a Web browser (remember that an HTML document may look different in different browsers). However, nearly all HTML authoring tools show you the HTML tags even when they display a tentative rendering of the document. A new trend is to combine the HTML editor with a browser, so you can edit the document and view it as well. Netscape Navigator Gold is one such combined editor-browser.

Tip   The Web authoring tools are available on a wide variety of systems, including UNIX, Microsoft Windows 3.1, Windows 95, and Apple Macintosh. Although you probably run a Web server on a UNIX system, you do not have to prepare all of your Web documents on UNIX. You may want to use a Macintosh or a Microsoft Windows 95 system to prepare the documents because it's easier to prepare the graphics in a Macintosh or Windows system.

URL   Because of the Web's popularity, there is considerable demand for HTML authoring tools. Software developers have sensed the demand for such tools, and there are many Web authoring tools on the market today. Many more authoring tools are available as shareware or freeware on the Internet. You can find a complete list of Web authoring tools at the following URL in YAHOO!:

```
http://www.yahoo.com/Computers_and_Internet/Internet/World_Wide_Web/
        Authoring/
```

URL   Another good starting point for HTML editors is the following URL at NCSA:

```
http://union.ncsa.uiuc.edu/HyperNews/get/www/html/editors.html
```

On this Web page, you'll find a list of HTML editors organized by platform — Macintosh, Windows, UNIX, OS/2, and NeXTstep. You can view the list for a platform and click on a link to read more about a specific tool. For shareware and freeware, you'll also find instructions on how to download the software.

I personally had not used any HTML authoring tools until I began writing this book. I did use HTML converters (see Chapter 16 for a sampling of converters) to convert existing documents to HTML, but for new HTML documents, I simply relied on a text editor. I used graphics programs on Windows or Macintosh to create the graphics, but that was the extent of tools I used. Now that I have seen some of these HTML authoring tools, I have to admit that some of the tools are quite useful.

UNIX Tools

As a Webmaster who runs a Web server on a UNIX system, you probably created your initial HTML documents with a UNIX text editor such as `vi` or Emacs. Plain text editors are fine for a few Web pages, but you need more tools to create and manage all the documents in a large Web site. For starters, you'll probably prefer to prepare the documents in a graphical editor that lets you see the results as you type the HTML tags.

There are quite a few UNIX Web authoring tools available on the Internet. In this chapter I'll introduce you to two popular tools:

✦ ASHE (A Simple HTML Editor) — An X Windows-based HTML editor

✦ tkHTML — A Tcl/Tk program for HTML editing

URL

For a list of latest UNIX tools for HTML authoring, consult the following URLs:

```
http://www.yahoo.com/Computers_and_Internet/Internet/World_Wide_Web/
        HTML_Editors/X_Windows/
http://sdg.ncsa.uiuc.edu/~mag/work/HTMLEditors/unixlist.html
```

ASHE

ASHE stands for A Simple HTML Editor. It's an X Windows-based HTML editor, developed by John Punin of the Department of Computer Science at the Rensselaer Polytechnic Institute. ASHE uses a split-window view to simultaneously show the raw HTML code as well as the formatted output.

ASHE is written in the C programming language and uses Motif for the graphical interface. To display the formatted view of the document, ASHE uses an HTML widget from the NCSA HTML Widget Library.

Downloading and installing ASHE

URL

ASHE is available via anonymous FTP from a server at Rensselaer Polytechnic Institute. You should start with the following URL:

```
ftp://ftp.cs.rpi.edu/pub/puninj/ASHE/README.html
```

This is the ASHE README file with information about the latest release of the software (version 1.3 as of this writing). As you'll learn, the ASHE program itself goes by the name `xhtml`.

URL

You have three options to download the software:

✦ If you have a Sun workstation running SunOS 4.1.3, you can download the following ready-to-run binary file:

```
ftp://ftp.cs.rpi.edu/pub/puninj/ASHE/ASHE-1.3/bin/xhtml-1.3-SunOs-
        static-all-libraries.Z
```

This is a 2MB compressed version of a SunOS 4.1.3 binary that has been statically linked with Motif and X11 libraries. (That means the file contains everything you need to run ASHE.)

✦ Look in the following URL for binaries for a number of UNIX platforms:

```
ftp://ftp.cs.rpi.edu/pub/puninj/ASHE/contrib/bin/
```

These binaries are contributed by various users of ASHE. You'll find binaries for Linux, AIX, HP-UX, SCO UNIX, and SGI IRIX.

✦ For any other UNIX system, you must download the source code as well as some support libraries and then build the executable yourself. If you need the source files, use anonymous FTP to connect to `ftp.cs.rpi.edu` and get the following files (file sizes shown in parentheses):

```
/pub/puninj/ASHE/ASHE-1.3/src/xhtml-1.3.tar.Z (137K)
/pub/puninj/ASHE/ASHE-1.3/libcci/cci.tar.Z (22K)
/pub/puninj/ASHE/ASHE-1.3/libhtmlw-2.7/libhtmlw.tar.Z (246K)
```

The first file is the ASHE source archive in compressed format. The `cci.tar.Z` file is needed so that ASHE can control NCSA Mosaic using the Common Client Interface (CCI) protocol. The `libhtmlw.tar.Z` file is the NCSA HTML widget library — ASHE uses this library to display the formatted HTML document.

Tip If you download the SunOS 4.1.3 binary, copy the file to an appropriate directory and uncompress it with the following command:

```
uncompress xhtml-1.3-SunOs-static-all-libraries.Z
```

This creates the ASHE program file with the name `xhtml-1.3-SunOs-static-all-libraries`. That `static-all-libraries` at the end of the name indicates that this program includes all of the libraries you need to run the program.

If you download the source files and libraries (so that you can build the executable yourself), you can unpack each file in two steps, as follows:

```
uncompress xhtml-1.3.tar.Z
tar xvf xhtml-1.3.tar
```

Using ASHE

Using ASHE is fairly straightforward, especially if you are running on a Sun workstation. Download the binary file (`xhtml-1.3-SunOs-static-all-libraries.Z`), uncompress it, and you are almost ready to run ASHE.

Tip Because the file name is rather long, you should set up a symbolic link as follows:

```
ln -s xhtml-1.3-SunOs-static-all-libraries xhtml
```

With such a symbolic link, you can now refer to the program with the shorter `xhtml` name.

Webmaster For proper operation, ASHE needs to find the file /usr/lib/X11/XKeysymDB to bind keys to specific editing operations (such as deleting a character when you press Backspace). On the Sun workstation, before you run ASHE, you must set the XKEYSYMDB environment variable with the following command:

```
setenv XKEYSYMDB /usr/lib/X11/XKeysymDB
```

Now you can start ASHE with the following command:

```
xhtml &
```

ASHE runs and displays the initial window, as shown in Figure 17-1.

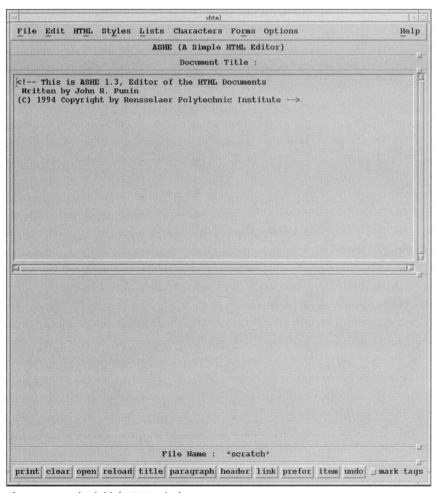

Figure 17-1: The initial ASHE window.

As Figure 17-1 shows, ASHE divides its main window into two major parts. The top part is for viewing and editing raw HTML, and the bottom part is where the formatted document appears.

Viewing an existing HTML document in ASHE

If you want to view and edit an existing HTML document, select Open from the File menu and select the HTML file from the resulting dialog box. Figure 17-2 shows the result of loading a typical HTML document into ASHE.

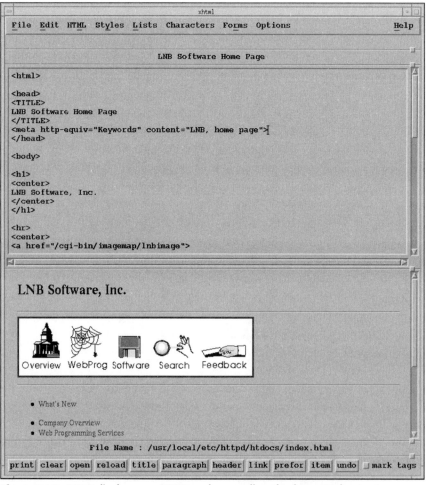

Figure 17-2: ASHE displays raw HTML code as well as the formatted output.

As Figure 17-2 illustrates, ASHE displays the raw HTML file in the upper window and the formatted output in the lower window. As you can see, the formatted output shows the document as it would appear in a typical Web browser. Because ASHE uses NCSA's HTML widget library, the formatted output looks similar to the way the HTML file would have appeared in NCSA Mosaic.

Creating a new HTML document in ASHE

To create a new HTML document in ASHE, start by selecting New from the File menu. ASHE prompts you for the document's title. For example, you could enter the title "A sample page." ASHE then adds the following text to the upper window:

```
<HTML>
<HEAD>
<TITLE>A sample page</TITLE>
</HEAD>
<BODY>

</BODY>
</HTML>
```

Then ASHE positions the text cursor between the `<BODY>` and `</BODY>` tags, which is where the body of the HTML document goes. Even if you know this sequence of tags, ASHE clearly saves you a lot of keystrokes by entering these tags automatically.

ASHE provides menu selections that let you insert other HTML elements such as headers, paragraphs, lists, and forms in a page. In all cases, when you add a tag from the menu, ASHE displays a dialog box to prompt for any attributes, inserts the tags (both the start and end tags), and then positions the text cursor between the two tags.

You can also insert an image by selecting Image from the HTML menu. ASHE displays a dialog box that prompts for an image file name. You can also use a checkbox to make that image an image map. (This simply adds an `ismap` attribute to the `<img>` tag.)

To add a hyperlink, select Hyperlink from the HTML menu. ASHE displays a dialog box that prompts you for the URL. After that, ASHE adds the anchor element and positions the cursor where the link text goes.

As you prepare the HTML document, click the `reload` button at the bottom of ASHE's main window. ASHE then updates the display of the formatted output that appears in the lower window.

tkHTML

tkHTML, developed by Liem Bahneman, is an HTML editor that uses the well-known Tcl/Tk (pronounced "tickle/tee kay") scripting language for graphical applications. In addition to the basic Tcl/Tk tools, tkHTML also uses the Tix widgets that extend Tcl/Tk capabilities. (See the "What are Tcl/Tk and Tix?" sidebar.)

What are Tcl/Tk and Tix?

Tcl stands for Tool Command Language and is pronounced "tickle." The creator of Tcl, John Ousterhout, intended Tcl to be a simple scripting language whose interpreter could be linked with any C program so that the C program could use Tcl scripts. The term *embeddable* refers to this property of Tcl: the capability of any C program to use the Tcl interpreter and run Tcl scripts.

Tk (pronounced "tee-kay") is an extension of Tcl. Tk provides an X Windows-based toolkit that you can use in Tcl scripts to build graphical user interfaces. Tk uses the X Window System for its graphic components, which are known as *widgets*. (A widget represents a user-interface component, such as a button, scrollbar, menu, list, or even an entire text window.) Tk widgets provide a Motif-like three-dimensional appearance. However, you do not need Motif to use Tk.

John Ousterhout created Tcl and Tk when he was at the University of California at Berkeley. (Currently he continues to develop Tcl/Tk at Sun Microsystems.) Tcl first appeared in 1989; Tk followed in 1991. Tcl/Tk are freely available for unrestricted use, including commercial use. At this writing, the Tcl version is 7.5; the Tk version is 4.1. To learn more about Tcl/Tk development and to download the latest version, visit the URL `http://www.sunlabs.com/research/tcl/`. (Tcl/Tk is now available for Windows 95, Windows NT, and Macintosh.)

Tix is a set of widgets that you can use in Tk programs to create more complex graphical interfaces than those possible with Tk alone. Tix was developed by Ioi Lam and is available from `ftp://ftp.xpi.com/pub/`. The latest stable version of Tix is 4.0.5 and the beta version is 4.1.

Up until version 2.0, tkHTML was a set of Tcl/Tk scripts. However, tkHTML 3.11 (the latest version at this writing) is now a single binary program. This simplifies the task of downloading, installing, and running tkHTML 3.11 because all you have to do is unpack a single binary file.

tkHTML 3.11 provides a preview capability by controlling a copy of Netscape Navigator or Mosaic. Earlier versions of tkHTML included a limited built-in preview capability. The new approach to previewing (by feeding the HTML document to an actual browser) lets you see a more complete rendering of the document.

Downloading and installing tkHTML

URL
To download the latest version of tkHTML, you should begin at the tkHTML home page at the following URL:

```
http://www.ssc.com/~roland/tkHTML/
```

URL
I find a brief description of the latest version of tkHTML and a link to download the software. That link for downloading tkHTML takes you to the following URL:

```
ftp://ftp.ssc.com/pub/ssc/roland/tkHTML/binaries/
```

At this anonymous FTP location, you will find the binary distribution of tkHTML 3.11 for a number of UNIX variants. The following list shows the important files in this FTP directory:

File Name	Size	Description
COPYING	1K	Text file with the tkHTML license terms. (Essentially you can download, use, and distribute tkHTML freely for any non-commercial purposes provided you retain the copyright notice.)
config.tcl	1K	Configuration file that you should download and place in the /usr/local/lib/tkHTML directory.
tkHTML-3.11-Irix-5.3-r3000.gz	522K	GNU Zip file with binary for Silicon Graphics workstations (based on MIPS R3000 processor) running the Irix 5.3 operating system.
tkHTML-3.11-Irix-5.3-r4000.gz	522K	GNU Zip file with binary for Silicon Graphics workstations (based on MIPS R4000 processor) running the Irix 5.3 operating system.
tkHTML-3.11-Linux-a.out.gz	380K	GNU Zip file with binary for Linux. (This is an a.out format binary. a.out is an older format for executable files in Linux.)
tkHTML-3.11-Linux-ELF.gz	387K	GNU Zip file with binary for Linux (This is an ELF binary. ELF is Executable and Linking Format, a new standard for Linux binaries.)
tkHTML-3.11-Linux-ELF.gz	358K	GNU Zip file with ELF binary for the m68k-Motorola 68000 version of Linux. (This version of Linux runs on systems with a number of Motorola 68000-based systems.)
tkHTML-3.11-Solaris-2.4.gz	407K	GNU Zip file with binary for Sun workstations running Solaris 2.4.
tkHTML-3.11-SunOS-4.1.3.gz	480K	GNU Zip file with binary for Sun workstations running SunOS 4.1.3.
tkHTML-3.1-OSF1-3.2.gz	592K	GNU Zip file with binary for DEC OSF 3.2.

As this list shows, tkHTML 3.11 binaries are available for a number of workstations: PCs running Linux, Silicon Graphics, Sun, and DEC. Because tkHTML 3.11 is available in binary format only, you are out of luck if you do not have one of the supported systems.

Suppose you want to download and use tkHTML 3.11 on a Linux system. If you have an older Linux installation (older than Slackware 3.0, if you use the Slackware distribution of Linux), download the `tkHTML-3.11-Linux-a.out.gz` file. For newer Linux distributions, download the `tkHTML-3.11-Linux-ELF.gz` file.

After downloading the file, you have to "unzip" it using the `gunzip` command, as follows:

```
gunzip tkHTML-3.11-Linux-ELF.gz
```

This creates the file `tkHTML-3.11-Linux-ELF.` which is the executable program for tkHTML 3.11.

Webmaster When you download a binary for tkHTML 3.11, you should also download the `config.tcl` file because tkHTML 3.11 needs the configuration file to run. After you download the `config.tcl` file, place it in the `/usr/local/lib/tkHTML` directory. (Create the directory if it does not exist on your system.)

Using tkHTML

To use tkHTML, you have to run its executable file. For example, on a Linux system you have to type `tkHTML-3.11-Linux-ELF` to run the file you have downloaded and uncompressed.

Tip To avoid typing the long file name, you can set up a symbolic link with a shorter name such as tkhtml (that way you can avoid changing to uppercase as well) with the following command:

```
ln -s tkHTML-3.11-Linux-ELF tkhtml
```

After completing this step, you can type `tkhtml` to run tkHTML 3.11.

When it starts, tkHTML 3.11 reads the configuration file `config.tcl`, sets up its window appearance (such as font and background color), and displays the main window, as shown in Figure 17-3.

Creating a new HTML document in tkHTML

The main window initially displays the `<head>` and `<body>` elements of an empty HTML document. tkHTML positions the cursor in the `<title>` element so that you can type in the title of the new document.

You can add new HTML elements by selecting items from the menus. The menus are all tear-off menus; each menu has a dotted line as the first element, as shown in Figure 17-4.

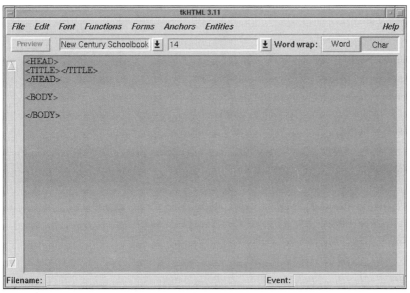

Figure 17-3: The main window of tkHTML 3.11.

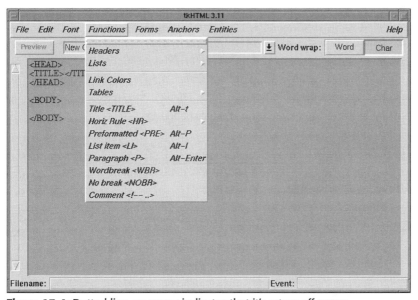

Figure 17-4: Dotted line on menu indicates that it's a tear-off menu.

Figure 17-4 shows the Functions menu. When you click on the dotted line, the menu is detached from the tkHTML window and appears in its own window, as shown in Figure 17-5.

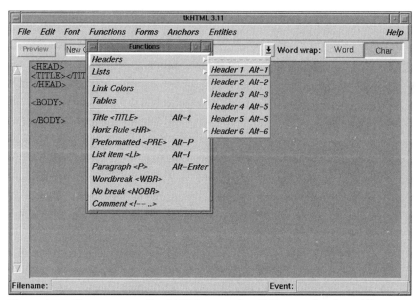

Figure 17-5: You can tear off a tkHTML menu by clicking on the dotted line.

As Figure 17-5 shows, you can then make selections from that menu without having to repeatedly click on the Functions item on the menubar. Figure 17-5 shows a cascading menu that appears when you click on the Headers item in the Functions menu. From this cascading menu, if you select Header 1, tkHTML inserts the following tags

```
<H1></H1>
```

and positions the cursor between the start and end tags.

Note   Because of the tear-off menus, you do not have to always go to the menu bar to activate a menu and then select an HTML element. Instead, you can keep the frequently-used menus open in individual windows (by tearing them off the menu bar) and easily access the menu items.

tkHTML 3.11 provides menu items for most commonly used HTML tags, including some, but not all, of the Netscape Navigator extensions. You'll typically follow these steps to add an HTML element to your document:

1. In the tkHTML main window, click at the location where you want to add the HTML element.

2. Find the menu that lets you insert the HTML element and make the selection (for example, the Anchors menu for inline images).

3. Add additional text required by the HTML element (for example, the image file name in an src attribute of an <img> tag).

When you begin using tkHTML, you have to spend some time becoming familiar with the menus so that you can locate the HTML tags easily. Figure 17-6 shows all the top-level menus in tkHTML 3.11.

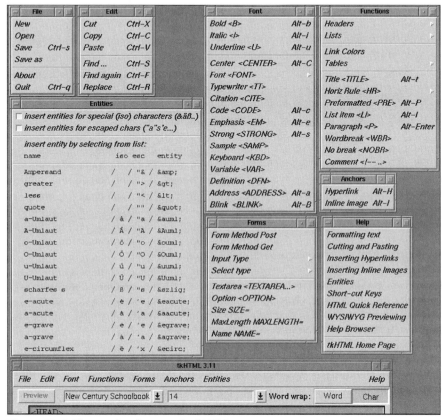

Figure 17-6: The top-level menus in tkHTML 3.11.

As with any software, you can learn to use the menus best by trying them out for awhile. To help you get started, here is a brief summary of each top-level menu in tkHTML 3.11:

✦ **File:** Lets you create a new document, open an existing document, and save the current document. You can also exit tkHTML by selecting Quit from this menu.

✦ **Edit:** Enables you to perform typical text-editing functions such as cut, copy, and paste. You can also search for a string and replace one string with another.

✦ **Font:** Provides a selection of text-formatting tags such as citation (`<cite>`), emphasis (`<em>`), and address (`<address>`). The Netscape `<font>` tag is also on this menu.

✦ **Functions:** Lets you add headers, lists, paragraphs, and horizontal rules. You can also add tables from this menu.

✦ **Forms:** Provides the HTML elements needed to define interactive forms. (See Chapter 19 for more information on how to use forms.)

✦ **Anchors:** Lets you insert hyperlinks (`<a>` tag) and inline images (`<img>` tag).

✦ **Entities:** Enables you to insert special characters such as vowels with accents, umlauts, and circumflexes.

✦ **Help:** Provides online help. You can even connect to the tkHTML home page, provided you have Netscape Navigator up and running.

Previewing an HTML document in tkHTML

As you prepare an HTML document, you may want to see how the document looks when rendered by a Web browser. In versions prior to 3.1, tkHTML included a built-in previewing capability. (Essentially, tkHTML opened a new window and rendered the HTML document in that window.) tkHTML 3.11 does not try to format the HTML document; instead, by default, tkHTML 3.11 relies on Netscape Navigator to display the document. If you want to use Mosaic as the browser, you have to edit the configuration file `config.tcl` (in the `/usr/local/lib/tkHTML` directory) to make Mosaic the default browser (you can locate the appropriate configuration command by opening the `config.tcl` file using a text editor).

To preview the current HTML document, you have to first start the Netscape Navigator browser on your system. Then click on the Preview button in the upper left corner of the tkHTML window. tkHTML then sends the HTML document to Netscape Navigator, which, in turn, displays the document in its window.

You can also load an existing HTML document into tkHTML to edit or preview it. Select Open from the File menu. tkHTML displays the Open File dialog box, shown in Figure 17-7.

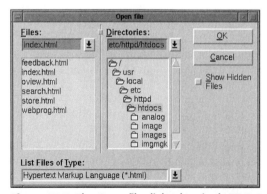

Figure 17-7: The Open file dialog box in tkHTML 3.11.

From the dialog box, you can pick an HTML file to load. Notice the appearance of the Open File dialog box in Figure 17-7. The entire Open File dialog box is an example of a widget provided by the Tix package that tkHTML uses. (See the "What are Tcl/Tk and Tix?" sidebar.)

Windows 95 and Windows NT Tools

URL Window 95 and Windows NT are popular platforms in many corporations and homes. As such, these systems are widely used for many document preparation tasks and HTML is no exception. You can find a long list of Web authoring tools for Windows at YAHOO!:

```
http://www.yahoo.com/Computers_and_Internet/Internet/World_Wide_Web/
        HTML_Editors/MS_Windows/
```

URL Another good list of Windows HTML authoring tools is at the following URL:

```
http://sdg.ncsa.uiuc.edu/~mag/work/HTMLEditors/windowslist.html
```

In the following sections I describe two well-known Web authoring tools for Windows 95:

✦ HotDog 32-bit 1.1

✦ HoTMetaL Free 2.0

HotDog 32-bit

HotDog is a popular shareware HTML editor. It supports Netscape's HTML extensions. The 32-bit version runs under Windows 95.

URL ### Downloading and installing HotDog
Download HotDog 32-bit version from the links on the Web page at the following URL:

```
http://www.sausage.com/hotdog32.htm
```

Specifically, you have to download the following files for HotDog 32-bit:

✦ A 1.9MB support file (`ftp://ftp.sausage.com/pub/hd32supp.exe`)

✦ A 2.8MB installation file (`ftp://ftp.sausage.com/pub/hd32inst.exe`)

To install HotDog, perform the following steps:

1. From an MS-DOS window, type HD32SUPP to install the supporting files. The installation program copies important files to various system directories.

2. From an MS-DOS window, type HD32INST to run the HotDog installation program. A warning dialog box appears with the message that you must run HD32SUPP first. Click on the OK button to dismiss the warning dialog box.

3. A dialog box prompts you for the directory where you want to install HotDog. Select a directory (or accept the default choice) and click on the OK button.

4. A dialog box asks if you want to create backup copies of files replaced during installation. If this is the first time you are installing HotDog, you may answer No. The installation program copies the necessary files to various directories.

5. A dialog box prompts if you want to add a shortcut to the Windows 95 Start menu under the Programs submenu. Click on the Yes button to do this.

6. Read the README.HTM file for more information.

Using HotDog

To run HotDog, click on the Start button, move the mouse pointer to Programs, and select HotDog 32 Bit from the Programs menu. If you have an evaluation copy, HotDog displays an Unregistered Copy dialog box, as shown in Figure 17-8.

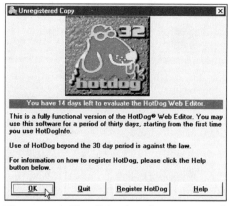

Figure 17-8: The dialog box that appears when you run an unregistered copy of HotDog.

The dialog box tells you how long you can use the software for evaluation purposes.

Tip   To learn how to register the software, click on the Help button. A Help window appears with pricing and ordering information. (You can reach Sausage Software, the developer of HotDog, at the e-mail address sales@sausage.com.au.)

To begin using HotDog, click on the OK button of the Unregistered Copy dialog box. HotDog displays a licensing agreement that you have to accept by clicking the I Agree button. (Of course, you can always quit by clicking the Cancel button.) The license agreement appears only the first time you run HotDog.

Understanding the HotDog tools and menus

After all of these steps, you finally get the initial HotDog windows, as shown in Figure 17-9.

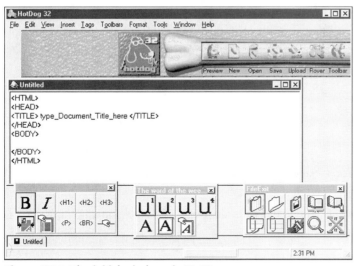

Figure 17-9: The initial windows in HotDog.

HotDog displays a main window where you can work on multiple HTML documents. That window already shows an untitled document with all the tags necessary for a skeletal HTML document. You can change the title and begin typing the body of the document.

In addition to the main window, HotDog also provides the following toolbar windows:

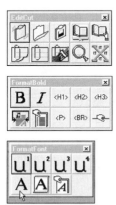

Buttons that act as shortcuts to menu items in the File and Edit menu. (The toolbar's title tells you the function of a button as you position the mouse pointer over that button.)

With this toolbar, you can change text to bold or italics, add headers, center text, add a list, insert a paragraph tag, add a ruler, and add a line break.

You can have up to four user-defined buttons (designated U1 through U4). Right click on any of these buttons to associate a function with the button. (You can right click on any toolbar button to customize the toolbars.) The other buttons on this toolbar let you format font, format document, and insert a text file.

You can move the toolbar windows around. Typically, you'll arrange the main window with the toolbar windows nearby, as shown in Figure 17-10.

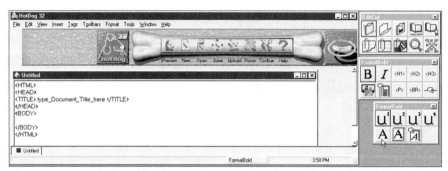

Figure 17-10: Typical working layout of HotDog's main window and toolbar windows.

The main window has a menu bar with ten items. The basic function of these menus are as follows:

Menu		Functions
File	✦	Open a new document, save the current document, and save all documents.
	✦	Preview an HTML document using a Web browser (such as Netscape Navigator).
	✦	Convert a document in preparation for uploading to a Web server. (This option is called "publish a document" in HotDog.)
	✦	Define a project. (A project is a collection of HTML documents.)
Edit	✦	Copy, cut, and paste text. Find and replace text.
	✦	Create new tags or edit current tags. (You can change the syntax of a tag if necessary.)
	✦	Convert URLs from absolute to relative and vice versa.
	✦	Color the tags so they stand out. (I found this option handy.)
View	✦	View the HTML tags.
	✦	Open the HotDog File Manager, which you use to designate the target of a hypertext link.
	✦	Toggle the "Toolbone." (The Toolbone is the bone-shaped toolbar underneath the menu — see Figure 17-10.)
Insert	✦	Insert an image, hyperlink, form, list, horizontal rule, or table.
	✦	Insert the contents of a text file into the document.
	✦	Add a URL. (A dialog box prompts you for further information.)

Menu		Functions
Tags	✦	Insert various types of HTML tags organized by categories: Document, Body, Content, Headings, Attributes, Graphics, Font, Lists, Forms, Tables, Miscellaneous, and Custom. (After you choose category, a dialog box lets you choose the exact tag from a list of tags.)
Toolbars	✦	Turn the toolbar windows on or off.
Format	✦	Format the document (set its title, base URL, colors, links, and `<meta>` tags).
	✦	Select a font size, style, and color.
	✦	Turn on (or off) bold, italic, underline, and blink attributes.
	✦	Center text.
	✦	Make the first letter of the current word larger than the rest.
Tools	✦	Change various HotDog options.
	✦	Customize the toolbars.
	✦	Create a template out of current document.
	✦	Find duplicate links.
	✦	Check HTML syntax. (It reports any syntax errors and also identifies any browser-specific tags.)
	✦	Convert text files into HTML using some simple rules.
	✦	Upload files to a Web server using FTP. (You have to provide a user name, password, and other details through another dialog box.)
	✦	Run the spell checker.
	✦	Find and replace in multiple files.
	✦	Change the sounds that HotDog makes for various HotDog events.
Window	✦	Make one of the currently open document windows active.
	✦	Perform other Windows 95 window management tasks, such as cascading or tiling windows.
Help	✦	Get online help.
	✦	Read the online HTML reference.
	✦	Register HotDog. (You have to insert the content of an e-mail message that you receive from Sausage Software in a dialog box.)
	✦	View the HotDog version number and copyright information.

As a shortcut to some of the menu items, HotDog also provides a Toolbone — a bone-shaped toolbar that appears underneath the menu bar, as shown in Figure 17-11.

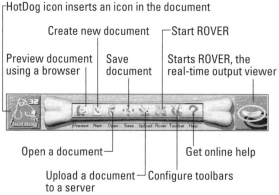

Figure 17-11: The tools in HotDog's Toolbone.

Note HotDog even includes its own Web browser named ROVER (for Real-time Output Viewer). If you click on the sausage on the right edge of the Toolbone, HotDog activates ROVER and connects to the HotDog home page at `http://www.sausage.com/`, as shown in Figure 17-12.

Figure 17-12: HotDog starts ROVER and connects to its home page when you click on the sausage icon on the Toolbone.

Creating an HTML document in HotDog

At startup, HotDog displays an empty HTML document with the `<head>` and `<body>` elements. To create an HTML document, you can begin to flesh out the empty document. You can work in HotDog's document window the same way you work in a typical Windows word processor. Click where you want to enter text and type the text. The only difference is that when you want to add an HTML element, you can go to the menu bar and select an element from the appropriate menu bar.

The first step is to edit the `<title>` element and enter a title for your document. Then you can move the cursor to the `<body>` element and begin work on the document's body. You may want to begin with a level 1 heading that shows your document's title. You can add the heading in one of two ways:

✦ Click on the button labeled `<H1>` on one of the toolbars. This adds the start and end tags for a level 1 heading and places the cursor between the two tags.

✦ Select Headings from the Tags menu. A dialog box appears with all levels of heading. Double-click on the item labeled Heading 1 to add the level 1 heading.

For some HTML elements, you may not have the choice of inserting the tags from a toolbar. For these elements you have to use the menus. For example, to insert a hyperlink to a document on another system, you have to select Jump to a Document on Another System from the Insert menu. This brings up the Build External Hypertext Link dialog box, as shown in Figure 17-13.

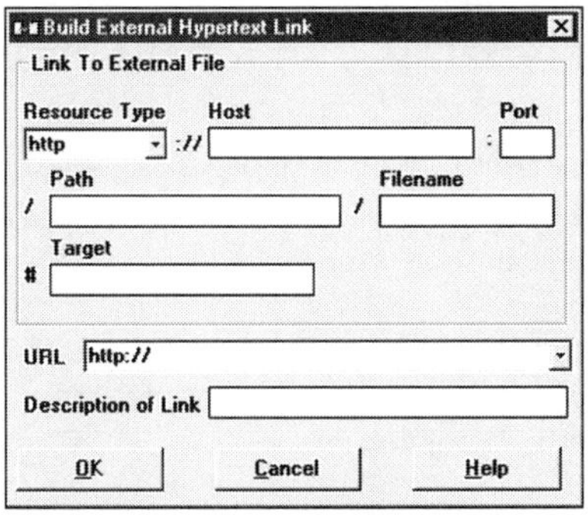

Figure 17-13: HotDog displays a dialog box requesting information needed to insert an external hyperlink.

In the Build External Hypertext Link dialog box of Figure 17-13, you have to fill in the URL of the document to which this hyperlink refers. In the text field labeled Description of Link, type the link text for this hyperlink.

The steps for inserting other HTML elements are similar to the steps for inserting a hyperlink. For simpler HTML tags, the steps are often not as detailed.

After you prepare the document, you will want to preview it. One approach is to save the document in a file and then view that file in a Web browser such as Netscape Navigator. Another approach is to keep Netscape Navigator running and then select Preview Document from the File menu (or click on the Preview button on the Toolbone). HotDog prompts you with the names of the browsers it has found on your system. You can select a browser to use as the previewer; HotDog then transfers the document to the browser and you can view the formatted output.

HoTMetaL Free 2.0

SoftQuad's HoTMetaL Free Version 2.0 is the non-commercial evaluation version of SoftQuad's commercial Web publishing tool HoTMetaL PRO (which is in version 3.0 as of this writing). HoTMetaL is an HTML editor that shows the formatted output as well as the raw HTML tags. You can add HTML elements by selecting them from the editor's toolbar. HoTMetaL also checks for the correct use of HTML tags and lets you insert tags only where they are allowed.

URL

Downloading and installing HoTMetaL Free 2.0

You can download HoTMetaL Free 2.0 from the following URL:

```
http://www.sq.com/products/hotmetal/hm-ftp.htm
```

To download the Windows version, select Windows from the left side of the Web page. A new page (`http://www.sq.com/products/hotmetal/install.htm`) appears with step-by-step instructions for downloading HoTMetaL Free 2.0. The procedure involves clicking on a link to download the file `hmfree2.exe` (1.6MB) from an anonymous FTP server.

The `hmfree.exe` file is a self-extracting archive; that means that when you run it, the program extracts a number of files. You should copy `hmfree.exe` into a temporary directory and then run it by typing `hmfree` in an MS-DOS window.

After you run `hmfree`, a number of files appear in that directory. One of the files is `setup.exe` — the installation program for HoTMetaL Free 2.0. To complete the installation of HoTMetaL Free 2.0, perform the following steps:

1. Type `setup` to run the installation program.

2. The setup program prompts for the installation location. Either accept the default directory or specify a new one. The setup program copies files to that directory.

3. The setup program prompts for a program group name. Accept the default and click on the OK button.

4. The setup program asks if you want to view the Readme file. Click on OK to view the file. That file spells out the terms of the license for HoTMetaL 2.0 for Microsoft Windows. You'll also find information on how to contact SoftQuad.

Using HoTMetaL Free 2.0

Select SoftQuad HoTMetaL 2.0 from the Windows 95 Start menu. (Look for SoftQuad HoTMetaL 2.0 under the Programs menu.) A dialog box appears urging you to upgrade to HoTMetaL PRO 2.0, the professional version of this product. Click on the OK button to continue.

HoTMetaL begins with a blank window with a number of toolbars. The buttons come with tool help — that means if you place the mouse pointer on a button, a small window pops up displaying a short help message that tells you what the button does. Figure 17-14 shows the initial HoTMetaL window with tool help shown for one of the buttons.

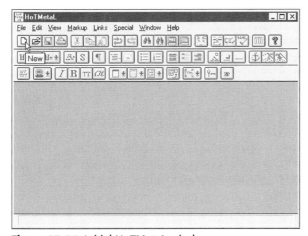

Figure 17-14: Initial HoTMetaL window.

To begin preparing a document, select New from the File menu (or click on the New icon on the first toolbar). HoTMetaL shows a new document with an initial set of HTML elements. The blinking text entry cursor appears in the `<body>` element, as shown in Figure 17-15.

From this point on, you can add text and HTML elements into the document's body. To enter any HTML element (such as a header, image, or hyperlink), you have to click on a toolbar button.

For plain text, simply type as you would in a word processor. That means you should not press Enter unless you want a paragraph break. You'll notice that HoTMetaL automatically inserts paragraph tags when you press Enter.

Tip   If you cannot easily tell which toolbar button is associated with a specific HTML element, simply move the mouse pointer on to a button and pause for a moment. A small window pops up with a brief help message about the button. This feature helps you learn the toolbar buttons. After awhile, you'll begin to remember which button to press to insert a specific HTML tag.

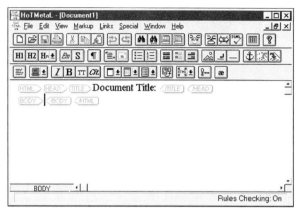

Figure 17-15: Starting a new HTML document in HoTMetaL.

As you click on buttons and add HTML tags, HoTMetaL displays the formatted output as well as the tags. The tags appear dim, and the formatted text is darker. If you add inline images, HoTMetaL displays these in the formatted output as well. Thus, you get a mixture of tags plus formatted output in the HoTMetaL window, as shown by the sample in Figure 17-16.

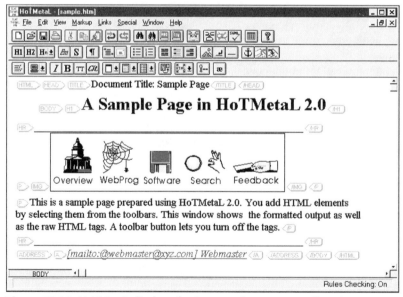

Figure 17-16: HoTMetaL displays the formatted output as well as the tags as you type the HTML document.

Macintosh Tools

Web page design involves graphic design, and the Macintosh is popular among Web designers. As with Windows 95 and Windows NT, there are a number of shareware as well as commercial HTML editors for the Macintosh.

Some well-known HTML editors for Macintosh

URL

Your best bet to find the latest list of available authoring tools is to try a Web index such as YAHOO!. You'll find quite a few HTML editors listed at the following YAHOO! URL:

```
http://www.yahoo.com/Computers_and_Internet/Internet/World_Wide_Web/
        HTML_Editors/Macintosh/
```

Here are some of the well-known HTML editors for Macintosh and the URLs where you can get more information or download the software:

Name	URL and Description
Alpha	`http://www.cs.umd.edu/~keleher/alpha.html` Alpha is a shareware text editor by Pete Keleher. Alpha supports many different editing modes, including HTML. It uses Tcl (Tool Command Language by John Ousterhout) as the scripting language, making it easy to add extensions.
BBEdit	`http://www.barebones.com/bbedit.html` BBEdit is a shareware text editor (from BareBones Software, Inc.) with some features tuned for ease of editing HTML documents. BBEdit includes an HTML-aware spell-checker.
GNNpress	`http://www.tools.gnn.com/press/index.html` GNNpress is a freeware Web browser with HTML editing capabilities. Provided by GNN, a part of America Online, Inc.
HoTMetaL	`http://www.sq.com/products/hotmetal/hm-ftp.htm` HoTMetaL Free Version 2.0 is a freeware HTML editor from SoftQuad. UNIX and Windows 95 versions are also available. SoftQuad sells a commercial product named HoTMetaL Pro with more capabilities.

HTML Web Weaver	`http://webster.northnet.org/Web.Weaver/`
	`        HTMLWW.html`
	HTML Web Weaver is a shareware HTML editor by Miracle Software, Inc. A commercial version is available under the name World Wide Web Weaver.

(continued)

Name	URL and Description
HTML.edit	`http://www.stonehand.com/murray/htmledit.html` HTML.edit is a freeware HTML editor by Murray Altheim. HTML.edit is a HyperCard-based application, but it does not require HyperCard to run.
PageMill	`http://www.adobe.com/prodindex/pagemill/` `main.html` PageMill is a commercial HTML authoring tool from Adobe Systems Inc.

HTML Web Weaver

URL

HTML Web Weaver, written by Robert C. Best III, is a typical shareware HTML editor for the Macintosh. You can download it from one of the following URLs:

```
http://www.sau.edu/CWIS/ComputingServices/HTMLWebWeaver2.5.1.sea.hqx
http://webster.northnet.org/Web.Weaver/HTMLWW.html
```

As with several other shareware products, an enhanced version of HTML Web Weaver is now being marketed as a commercial product by Miracle Software, Inc.

The file you download has the `.sea.hqx` extension; it's a self-extracting archive in BinHex format. (BinHex is a Macintosh utility that converts binary files into text files that can be easily transmitted through e-mail.) You'll have to first use BinHex 4.0 to convert the file into binary format. Then double-click the icon of the resulting binary file to extract everything. Figure 17-17 shows files in the HTML Web Weaver folder.

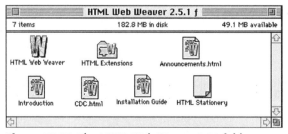

Figure 17-17: The HTML Web Weaver 2.51 folder.

To run HTML Web Weaver, double-click on the HTML Web Weaver icon. If your copy is not yet registered, HTML Web Weaver displays a "nag screen" — a notice — telling you about registration, as shown in Figure 17-18.

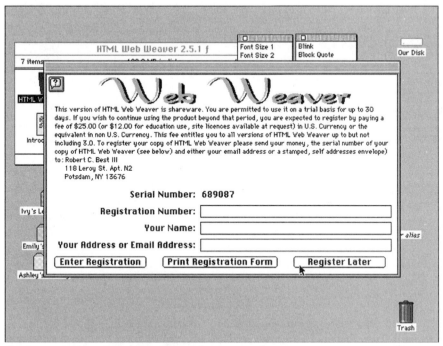

Figure 17-18: The HTML Web Weaver "nag screen."

The nag screen also lets you enter registration information (which you can enter after you send in a shareware fee and receive your registration number). You can also print a registration form from this screen. If you are simply evaluating HTML Web Weaver, click on the Register Later button to begin using the software.

HTML Web Weaver starts up with an untitled HTML document in a window. It also displays three floating toolbar windows:

✦ A toolbar for selecting header levels.

✦ A toolbar for changing various text attributes.

✦ A toolbar for HTML elements such as `<html>`, `<body>`, and `<title>`.

Unlike some other HTML editors, HTML Web Weaver version 2.5.1 does not provide an initial document with some of the HTML elements already inserted in the document; you have to add the tags yourself. When you need a tag as you type the document, you can either get it from the Tags menu or click on that tag on the floating toolbar. Figure 17-19 shows a typical editing session with HTML Web Weaver.

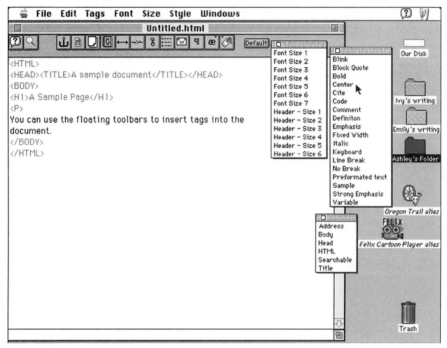

Figure 17-19: Editing an HTML document in HTML Web Weaver.

Summary

You can prepare HTML documents with a text editor and a good knowledge of HTML, but the job can be much easier if you use one of many HTML authoring tools. These tools typically let you add HTML tags with minimal effort and show you how the document will look in a browser. Some tools even check the HTML syntax for correctness. This chapter describes a number of HTML authoring tools for three popular operating systems: Macintosh, Windows 95, and UNIX. The next chapter focuses on the important activity of promoting your Web site.

Where to go next . . .

✦ For Web site design guidelines, read Chapter 15.

✦ For tools that convert existing documents into HTML, see Chapter 16.

✦ If you want to prepare interactive Web pages using Common Gateway Interface (CGI) programs, consult Chapters 19 and 20.

✦   ✦   ✦

Promoting Your Web Site

After you finish preparing the initial set of documents for your Web site, you have to make sure that users can find your site. How you promote your site depends on the type of Web site you maintain. Some sites may require relatively little publicity. For example, if your Web site provides online technical support for a product, it may be enough to list your site's URL in the product's documentation. However, most sites are designed to promote an organization or even sell products online. If you are the Webmaster for one of these sites, you will want to spread the news about your site's existence.

This chapter discusses some of the ways in which you can promote your Web site. Nowadays there are many Web indexing services that let users either browse the content by category or search for a Web site by keyword. This chapter briefly describes how typical Web indexes work and how you might provide information to an index so that anyone on the Net can easily find your site.

Learning How Users Find Information on the Web

To effectively promote your Web site, you need to know how users locate information on the Web. That way, you can make sure that information about your Web site shows up at the places where the user is most likely to search.

Before you decide how to best promote your site, you should try the following:

✦ Browse a Web index and try to locate information similar to what your Web site offers. (Browsing involves starting with a top-level category and going down into subcategories until you find a document that appears relevant.) Note which categories produce the most relevant information, because you'll want to list your sites in the same categories.

✦ Use keywords to locate the same type of information as your own site's offering. Each Web index produces a different result for the same set of keywords. Make notes of which keywords cause the Web index to produce the most relevant documents. You'll want to use these keywords in your documents' titles and content to ensure that your site is indexed properly.

The results of your search can help you decide how to tell the world about your site.

Web search

Nowadays Web indexes are a common way of locating information on the Web. Some of these indexes are maintained by software known as *robots* or *spiders* that automatically access Web sites, download information, and create indexes. A number of these indexes require you to submit information about your Web site.

There are a number of popular Web indexes; some of the well-known ones are the following:

✦ YAHOO! at `http://www.yahoo.com/` is a popular and successful Web directory that organizes information by category (which is ideal for browsing).

✦ AltaVista at `http://www.altavista.digital.com/` is an automatic Web index that has gained a reputation for being comprehensive and extremely fast.

✦ The Net Search page at

```
http://home.netscape.com/home/internet-search.html
```

accessible from the Net Search button on the Netscape Navigator, includes hyperlinks to a number of Web search sites including YAHOO!, AltaVista, Lycos, and Excite.

YAHOO!

YAHOO! is well known as one of the original Web directories that has been commercially successful. When you access the YAHOO! home page (`http://www.yahoo.com/`), you are presented with a simple but versatile search form, as shown in Figure 18-1.

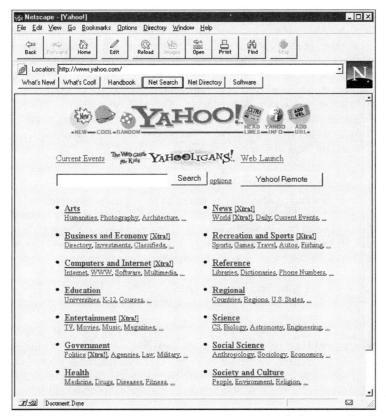

Figure 18-1: The YAHOO! home page presents a simple but versatile search form. (Text and artwork copyright © 1996 by YAHOO!, Inc. All rights reserved. YAHOO! and the YAHOO! logo are trademarks of YAHOO!, Inc.)

You can use the search form in two ways:

✦ Type one or more keywords in the text entry field, and then click on the Search button. (See Figure 18-1.) YAHOO! returns a new page with links to documents or categories that contain all of the keywords.

✦ Click on any of the categories on the home page (which appear as hyperlinks). This brings up another search form with links to subcategories, as well as a text field where you can again type keywords for a new search.

Even though there are other Web indexes with more extensive databases of Web pages, YAHOO! retains a competitive advantage by organizing the information better and by providing more relevant search results.

Note One of YAHOO!'s attractions is that you can browse through the contents by category. YAHOO! organizes the Web sites in a hierarchy of categories and subcategories. You can start with a category of interest and successively proceed to subcategories until you find a relevant Web site. For example, if you click on the Computers and Internet category, a second list appears with subcategories such as Hardware, Software, and Programming Languages. Click on the Programming Languages subcategory and YAHOO! displays a list of programming languages from ABC (yes, there is a BASIC-like programming language called ABC) to the formal specification notation Z (pronounced "Zed"). In fact, I first learned about ABC and Z when I was browsing YAHOO! indexes on Programming Languages.

AltaVista

AltaVista, a search service run by Digital Equipment Corporation, was launched in mid-December, 1995, and it has already become one of the most popular sites on the Web. The reason is that AltaVista literally indexes everything in the Web. The AltaVista database contains 15 billion words indexed from 30 million Web pages around the world. The best part is that you can search this database nearly instantly.

URL Like most Web indexes, the AltaVista home page (`http://www.altavista.digital.com/`) presents a search form, as shown in Figure 18-2.

On this page, you can type one or more keywords and click on the Submit button to initiate a search. Within moments, AltaVista should return with a list of hyperlinks to pages that contain the keywords. The default search type is simple; that means the words you type in the search box are interpreted as keywords or constraints.

Tip To find pages containing all keywords, place a plus sign (+) prefix on each keyword. To exclude pages containing a specific word, specify that word with a negative sign (-) prefix. For example, to locate pages containing the words *HTML, authoring,* and *tools* but not the word *Windows,* you would type the following keywords:

```
+HTML +authoring +tool -Windows
```

Even with simple searches, you can specify constraints such as finding all pages from a specific domain or all Web pages with a specific title. For example, to locate the string "AltaVista" on all Web pages on hosts with the string `digital.com` in the name, you would enter the following:

```
host:digital.com "AltaVista"
```

Tip One of the interesting simple searches is to find out how many pages contain links to your home page. Assuming that your Web site is `www.mysite.com`, the following simple query does the job:

```
+link:http://www.mysite.com -url:http://www.mysite.com
```

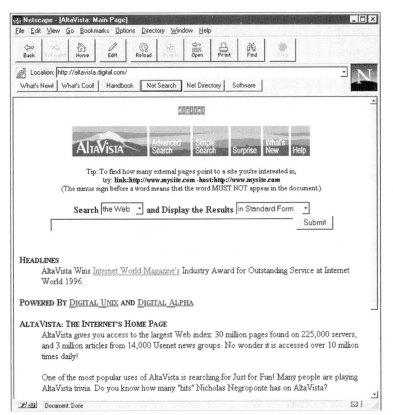

Figure 18-2: You can search AltaVista's extensive database of Web pages from this form at `http://www.altavista.digital.com/`. (Copyright © 1996 by Digital Equipment Corporation.)

This query says find all the pages with links to `http://www.mysite.com`, but exclude the pages with that URL. Just replace `www.mysite.com` with the name of your Web site and you can keep tabs on all sites that have links to your site.

You can also choose to use advanced queries by clicking on the Advanced Search image on the masthead. With advanced queries, you can use operators such as AND, OR, and NOT. You can also use the NEAR keyword to search for two words that must appear within ten words of each other in a document. For example, to locate Web pages that contain any of the strings: "John F. Kennedy" or "Kennedy, John F." or "John Fitzgerald Kennedy", type the following advanced query:

```
John NEAR Kennedy
```

Netscape's Net Search page

If you want to access many of the Web indexes from a single place, you can do so from Netscape's Net Search page. This page is particularly handy if you use the Netscape Navigator Web browser. All it takes is a click on Netscape Navigator's Net Search button to reach Netscape's Net Search page, as shown in Figure 18-3.

URL

As Figure 18-3 shows, you can access many Web search services from Netscape's Net Search page. In addition to YAHOO! and AltaVista, you can also access the following:

✦ Lycos (`http://www.lycos.com/`), a huge Web index that gets its entries by automatically searching the Web

✦ eXcite (`http://www.excite.com/`), a site that supports concept-based search

Figure 18-3: You can access a number of Web indexes from Netscape's Net Search page at `http://home.netscape.com/home/internet-search.html`. (Copyright © 1996 Netscape Communications Corporation. Netscape Communications, the Netscape Communications logo, Netscape, and Netscape Navigator are trademarks of Netscape Communications Corporation.)

✦ Infoseek Guide (`http://guide.infoseek.com/`), a popular search service that lets you search a variety of indexes including the Web, newsgroups, and e-mail addresses

✦ Magellan (`http://www.mckinley.com/`), an Internet guide that lets you search Web sites that have been rated and reviewed

There are many more Web search services listed on Netscape's Net Search page.

Tip If you use Netscape Navigator, you may want to begin your search by clicking on the Net Search button on the Navigator window.

Newsgroup search

The Internet newsgroups provide a bulletin-board system that spans the globe. Web browsers such as Netscape Navigator make it very easy to read various newsgroups and post new items to these newsgroups. Users do need access to a news server to read newsgroups; they get such access from their Internet Service Providers.

Newsgroup hierarchy

Newsgroups are organized into a hierarchy for ease of maintenance and use. A newsgroup's name reflects its position in the hierarchy. A typical newsgroup name is:

```
comp.infosystems.www.announce
```

As you can see, the format of a newsgroup name is a sequence of words separated by periods. These words denote the hierarchy of the newsgroup. This name says that `comp.infosystems.www.announce` is a newsgroup for announcements (`announce`) about the World Wide Web information system (`infosystems.www`) and that these subjects fall under the broad category of computers (`comp`).

Tip Compare the newsgroup name with the path name of a file (such as `/usr/local/etc/httpd/htdocs/index.html`) in UNIX. Just as a file's path name shows the directory hierarchy of the file, the newsgroup name shows the newsgroup hierarchy. In file names, a slash (`/`) separates the names of directories; in a newsgroup's name, a period separates the different levels in the newsgroup hierarchy.

In a newsgroup name, the first word represents the newsgroup category. The `comp.infosystems.www.announce` newsgroup, for example, is in the `comp` category, whereas `alt.books.technical` is in the `alt` category. Table 18-1 lists some of the major newsgroup categories.

Table 18-1
Major Newsgroup Categories

Category	Subject
alt	"Alternative" newsgroups (not subject to any rules), running the gamut from the mundane to the bizarre
bionet	Biology newsgroups
bit	Bitnet newsgroups
biz	Business newsgroups
clari	Clarinet news service (daily news)
comp	Computer hardware and software newsgroups
ieee	Institute of Electrical and Electronics Engineers newsgroups
k12	Newsgroups devoted to elementary and secondary education
misc	Miscellaneous newsgroups
news	Newsgroups about Internet news administration
rec	Recreational and art newsgroups
sci	Science and engineering newsgroups
soc	Newsgroups for discussing social issues and various cultures
talk	Discussions of current issues (such as "talk radio")

This list of categories is deceptive, because it does not tell you about the wide-ranging variety of newsgroups available in each category. Because each newsgroup category contains several levels of subcategories, the overall count of newsgroups runs into several thousands. The comp category alone has more than 500 newsgroups. Typically, you have to narrow your choice of newsgroups according to your interests. If you are interested in topics related to the World Wide Web, for example, you can pick one or more of the following newsgroups:

✦ comp.infosystems.www.advocacy includes postings with comments, arguments, and debates about Web servers, browsers, and other Web software.

✦ comp.infosystems.www.announce contains important announcements about the World Wide Web (including announcements about new Web sites). This newsgroup is *moderated:* When you post an article, that article is automatically mailed to the person running the newsgroup, who will check it for relevancy and post it only if it is of interest to the newsgroup readers.

✦ comp.infosystems.www.authoring.cgi covers discussions on writing Common Gateway Interface (CGI) scripts for the Web.

✦ comp.infosystems.www.authoring.html has articles on various aspects of authoring HTML documents.

✦ `comp.infosystems.www.authoring.images` covers the subject of how to use images and image maps in HTML documents.

✦ `comp.infosystems.www.authoring.misc` covers miscellaneous Web authoring issues that are not covered by the other authoring newsgroups.

✦ `comp.infosystems.www.browsers.mac` is for discussions about Web browsers for Macintosh systems.

✦ `comp.infosystems.www.browsers.misc` covers Web browsers for systems other than Windows, Macintosh, and X Window System. (This newsgroup covers browsers for Amiga, VMS, and UNIX text mode.)

✦ `comp.infosystems.www.browsers.ms-windows` contains articles about Web browsers for Microsoft Windows.

✦ `comp.infosystems.www.browsers.x` covers Web browsers for the X Window System, the graphical windowing system for UNIX workstations.

✦ `comp.infosystems.www.misc` provides a forum for general discussions about the World Wide Web.

✦ `comp.infosystems.www.servers.mac` includes articles about Web servers for the Macintosh platform.

✦ `comp.infosystems.www.servers.misc` covers Web servers for systems other than the Macintosh, Microsoft Windows, and UNIX.

✦ `comp.infosystems.www.servers.ms-windows` is for discussions about Web servers for Microsoft Windows and Windows NT.

✦ `comp.infosystems.www.servers.unix` covers Web servers for UNIX.

Besides the `comp.infosystems.www.*` newsgroups, there are a number of other newsgroups on topics related to the Web, such as Java and Virtual Reality Modeling Language (VRML). Here are a few other Web related newsgroups:

✦ `alt.culture.www`

✦ `alt.hypertext`

✦ `alt.lang.vrml`

✦ `alt.www.hotjava`

✦ `comp.lang.java`

✦ `comp.lang.javascript`

Local newsgroups may also cover the Web.

Newsgroup browsing

As the preceding section shows, there are many newsgroups for each subject area. Typically, a user regularly accesses only a few newsgroups of interest. For the purposes of promoting a Web site, you'll want to target the newsgroups that cover the type of information provided by your Web site. To determine which newsgroups you want, you need to browse the newsgroups for awhile.

Note To browse (or read) newsgroups, you have to use a news reader — a program that lets you access news items from a news server. Some Web browsers, such as Netscape Navigator, include an integrated news reader that enables you to access newsgroups as you visit Web sites.

Most newsgroup hierarchies contain a specific newsgroup for posting announcements (for example, `comp.infosystems.www.announce` or `comp.os.linux.announce`). Look for such a newsgroup (typically with a name ending in `announce`) and read the postings in that newsgroup to learn what sort of postings are appropriate.

Tip In addition to `comp.infosystems.www.announce`, another newsgroup that's worth browsing is `comp.internet.net-happenings`, a moderated newsgroup that includes announcements about new Web sites.

Newsgroup indexes

Many Web indexes that maintain information about Web pages also maintain indexes of the newsgroups (or, more precisely, the articles in each newsgroup). That means you can search these indexes for news items by keyword. Some good newsgroup indexes are

URL

✦ Deja News (`http://www.dejanews.com/forms/dnq.html`) maintains an archive of newsgroup postings that you can search using keywords.

URL

✦ AltaVista (`http://www.altavista.digital.com/`) indexes newsgroup submissions as well as Web sites.

Try searching these indexes with keywords relevant to your Web site to see what type of results users might get.

Tip To search Deja News, start at the URL

```
http://www.dejanews.com/forms/dnq.html
```

which displays a form. Type in keywords for the search. For example, when looking for news about HTML authoring tools for Linux, I type the keywords:

```
Linux HTML Authoring tool
```

Figure 18-4 shows the Deja News search form with the keywords filled in.

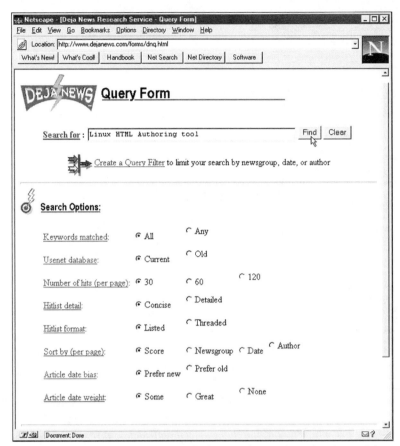

Figure 18-4: Searching news items by keyword on Deja News. (Copyright © 1994-96, Deja News Research Service, Inc.)

To initiate the search, I click on the Find button in the search form. Deja News, in return, presents a new HTML document with links to the news items that contain the keywords, as shown in Figure 18-5.

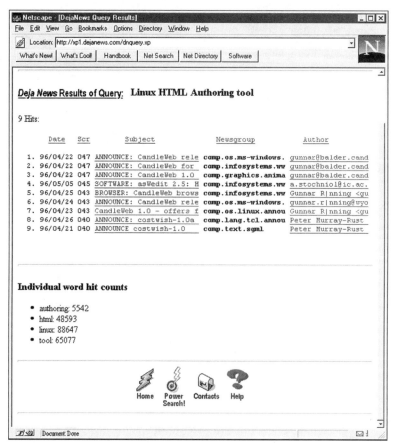

Figure 18-5: Results of a typical keyword search on Deja News. (Copyright © 1994-96, Deja News Research Service, Inc.)

From the document shown in Figure 18-5, I could click on a link in the Subject column and view the full text of that news item. Options available for your search include the ability to limit the search to a selected set of newsgroups. To learn more about the search options, click on the Help link at the bottom of the Deja News search form.

Announcing Your Web Site

Now that you know the ways in which users can search for information on the Web, you can turn to the subject of announcing your new Web site to selected Web index services and newsgroups. The remainder of this chapter tells you how to announce your Web site, but it's up to you to decide where to make the announcement.

Your site's capacity

First, you should consider how much traffic your site can handle. Considering the wide array of search options that users have, your main problem is to decide where, and in which order, to advertise your Web site. You have to be the judge when it comes to deciding what level of attention your site can sustain. Using the information in this chapter, you can easily announce your Web site to a large number of Web indexes and newsgroups. If you provide some unique and useful information, it is likely that a huge number of users will attempt to visit your site. The question you have to answer is: what level of traffic can your Web site sustain?

Note   Your Web site's maximum capacity (measured, for example, by the number of HTTP connections per second) depends a number of factors such as

✦ The bandwidth of the site's connection to the Internet

✦ The average size of the HTML documents at your site

Webmaster   Here is a crude formula to compute the number of HTTP connections per second that your site can sustain. The multiplication by 8 is done to convert bytes to bits.

HTTP transfers/sec = Bandwidth in Kbps / (File size in K x 8)

For example, if the bandwidth of the connection is 56 Kbps and average file size is 10K, then the site can sustain at most 56 / (10 x 8) = 0.7 HTTP transfers per second. This would imply that the site can support up to 0.7 x 3600 x 24 = 60,480 HTTP transfers a day *provided* that the HTTP requests arrive at a uniform rate. In reality, the pattern of HTTP requests during a day has distinct peaks and valleys. The peak rate can be up to five to ten times the average rate for a day. The formula is crude because it ignores the overhead associated with the network protocols such as TCP/IP and HTTP. Table 18-2 shows the number of HTTP transfers per second for a given network bandwidth and an average document size of 10K.

Table 18-2 Maximum HTTP Transfer per Second for a 10K File Size		
Network Connection	*HTTP Transfer/sec*	*Maximum Transfers/day*
14.4 Kbps modem	0.18	15,552
28.8 Kbps modem	0.36	31,104
56 Kbps Frame Relay	0.7	60,480
64 Kbps ISDN (1B channel)	0.8	69,120
128 Kbps ISDN (2B channel)	1.6	138,240

(continued)

Table 18-2 *(continued)*		
Network connection	*HTTP transfer/sec*	*Maximum transfers/day*
1.544 Mpbs T1	19.3	1,667,520
10 M Ethernet	125	10,800,000
45 Mbps T3	562.5	48,600,000
100 Mbps FDDI or Ethernet	1,250	108,000,000
155 Mbps ATM	1,937.5	167,400,000

Webmaster To account for peak arrival rates of HTTP requests, divide the maximum daily HTTP transfers by five to arrive at the total number of requests that your site can sustain in a day. That means with a 56 Kbps link a site can support about 12,000 transfers a day — respectable for a typical site. If the network connection is a 1.544 Mbps T1 link, the site can manage 333,000 transfers daily, which is more than adequate.

The number of maximum HTTP transfer rates do not directly translate to the number of users (because several HTTP transfers are associated with a single user visiting your site). However, they should give you an idea about the kind of traffic your site can sustain. Based on this knowledge, you can decide whether to promote your site aggressively or keep the site relatively obscure.

Note Just to give you some perspective, the AltaVista Web index is reportedly accessed over 10 million times daily. That site, however, has a 135 Mbps connection to the Internet backbone. Most sites have a much smaller network bandwidth and, consequently, can support only modest daily access volumes.

Web site announcement options

As I described in the "Learning How Users Find Information on the Web" section, users typically locate information on the Web by one of the following ways:

✦ Browse Web directories such as YAHOO!.

✦ Search Web indexes such as AltaVista or YAHOO! using keywords.

✦ Read newsgroups in an area of interest and visit sites listed in news items.

✦ Read newsgroups such as `comp.infosystems.www.announce` or `comp.internet.net-happenings` for announcements of new Web sites.

This means that you should announce your Web site in one or more of these places. Typically, the following steps should provide a good coverage:

✦ Add your site to one or more Web indexes.

✦ Announce the site in the newsgroups `comp.infosystems.www.announce` or `comp.internet.net-happenings`. (`comp.infosystems.www.announce` does not allow commercial announcements.)

✦ If you are familiar with a newsgroup that's relevant to the subject of your Web site, you can also announce your Web site in that newsgroup.

Of course, in addition to these announcements on the Internet, you might also consider announcing in the traditional print media through a press release.

"What's New" Web pages

URL Before the proliferation of the Web indexes, the only way to promote a Web site was to list it at one of several "What's New" Web pages — pages that list new Web sites. One of the original "What's New" pages is the NCSA What's New page that you can access from the What's New option in NCSA Mosaic's Help menu. If you want to access this page from another Web browser, use the following URL:

```
http://www.ncsa.uiuc.edu/SDG/Software/Mosaic/Docs/whats-new.html
```

You can add your site to this page by clicking on the Submit an Entry button (actually a small image) on this page or visiting the URL

```
http://www.ncsa.uiuc.edu/SDG/Software/Mosaic/Docs/whats-new-form.html.
```

Netscape Navigator also has a What's New button that displays a listing of new Web sites. However, Netscape picks the sites that appear on the page.

URL Another site announcement page is Open Market's Commercial Sites Index at `http://www.directory.net/`. Click the submit listings link to submit a listing.

Web indexes and directories

Web indexes and directories are essentially listings of Web sites. I am using the term *Web index* to refer to all types of Web site listings that a user can search by keyword. On the other hand, by *Web directory*, I mean a listing that is suitable for browsing. That means a Web directory is organized in a hierarchy of categories.

Note YAHOO! is a Web directory; AltaVista is a Web index. You can browse YAHOO! by category, but you must search the AltaVista index by keywords.

One of the easiest ways to announce your Web site is to add your new Web site to various Web indexes and directories. As the following sections show, there are a number of good Web indexes and directories you can target.

Some Web indexes are automatically created by spiders (see "What are 'spiders'?"). All you have to do to get your Web site listed on these indexes is make sure your site's HTML documents include the appropriate keywords.

What are "spiders"?

Spiders are special network applications that access each Web site and download the Web pages at the site. Also called *Web robots* or *Web crawlers*, these programs are essentially custom Web clients that request documents from a Web server and use the retrieved documents to create a huge index of the Web. The index contains various information about each document (such as its URL, size in bytes, and date of last modification).

Web search services use spiders to gather information about the content of the Web and enable users to search the index by keyword. Some search services also organize the content in categories for ease of browsing.

Digital Equipment Corporation's AltaVista is the ultimate example of using a spider to index the entire Web. AltaVista uses a spider (called Scooter) to gather documents from the Web. Scooter (running on a DEC3000/900 AlphaStation with 1GB RAM and a 48GB disk array) can retrieve over 3 million Web pages a day and send those pages to another workstation (a DEC AlphaServer 4100 with 2 processors and 1GB of memory) for indexing. Users accessing the AltaVista home page (`http://www.altavista.digital.com/`) interact with one of three DEC AlphaServer 8400 5/300 systems, each with 10 processors, 6GB of RAM (yes, six gigabytes of physical memory), and a 210GB hard disk.

The WWW virtual library

The World Wide Web Consortium (W3C) maintains a catalog of all Web sites. For your Web site to appear in the catalog, you must fill out the form at the following URL:

```
http://www.w3.org/hypertext/DataSources/WWW/Geographical_generation/
       new.html
```

URL The Web site listing is maintained by geographic region — in fact, certain countries and regions have their own registration forms. Users can access the listing from the Virtual Tourist Web site at the URL `http://www.vtourist.com/webmap/`.

AltaVista

AltaVista uses a spider to create its index. After you set up the Web site, AltaVista should index your site within a few weeks. To request a visit by AltaVista's spider, click the Add URL link at the bottom of the AltaVista home page (see Figure 18-6).

After you click on the Add URL link, AltaVista displays a form with instructions on how to submit a URL, as shown in Figure 18-7.

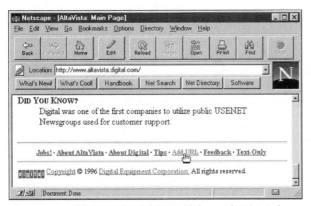

Figure 18-6: Click on the Add URL link on AltaVista's home page to submit a new Web site for indexing. (Copyright © 1996 by Digital Equipment Corporation.)

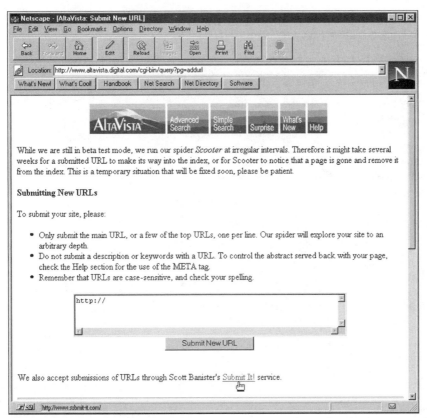

Figure 18-7: This form lets you submit a new URL for indexing by AltaVista. (Copyright © 1996 by Digital Equipment Corporation.)

You need to submit only the URL of your site's main page. The AltaVista spider automatically accesses and indexes all linked Web pages at your site.

Tip AltaVista indexes all the words in your Web pages and uses the first few words of the document as an abstract when it shows that page to the user. You can help AltaVista index your Web page better by providing two `<meta>` tags with the `description` and `keywords` fields. (See Chapter 11 for more information on the `<meta>` tag.) For example, if your Web page is about multimedia software for Windows 95, you might add the following `<meta>` tags in the Web page:

```
<meta name="description" content="We specialize in Windows95 multimedia
     software.">
<meta name="keywords" content="multimedia Windows95 software">
```

AltaVista indexes both the `description` and `keywords` fields and displays the description when serving this page as a search result.

Stopping robots or spiders from indexing parts of your site

What if you don't want any robots or spiders to index the contents of certain Web pages at your site? For example, you may have some transient information (such as the cafeteria menu) that should not be indexed for posterity. There is a way to mark some pages as off-limits to robots. Most well-behaved robots respect a protocol that lets a Webmaster indicate which parts of the Web site should not be accessed and indexed.

All you have to do is create a `robots.txt` file in the root document directory of your Web site. The `robots.txt` file should have the following typical format:

```
User-agent: *
# applies to all robots and
spiders
Disallow: /cgi-bin/sources/
```

```
# no need to index CGI source
code
Disallow: /tmp/
# temporary stuff; don't copy
```

If you want to bar robots from your entire site, simply place the following lines in the `/robots.txt` file:

```
User-agent: *      # that means
all robots and spiders
Disallow: /        # should
avoid this site entirely
```

To learn more about the standards for robot exclusion, consult the Web page at `http://info.webcrawler.com/mak/projects/robots/norobots.html`.

YAHOO!

Unlike AltaVista, YAHOO! does not automatically index all Web sites. YAHOO! instead relies on Webmasters to submit URLs.

Tip   You have to navigate through the hierarchy of categories to the right place before you can submit your site's URL to YAHOO!. If your company specializes in multimedia software, you would go through the following category hierarchy (in the order shown):

```
Business and Economy
Companies
Computers
Software
Multimedia
```

Then click on the Add URL link on the masthead in the YAHOO! home page, as shown in Figure 18-8.

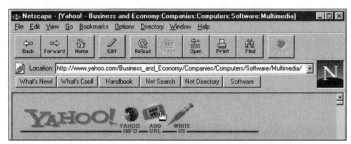

Figure 18-8: Click on the Add URL link on the YAHOO! home page to submit your site to the YAHOO! directory. (Text and artwork copyright © 1996 by YAHOO!, Inc. All rights reserved.)

After you click on the Add URL link, the browser displays a new page, as shown in Figure 18-9.

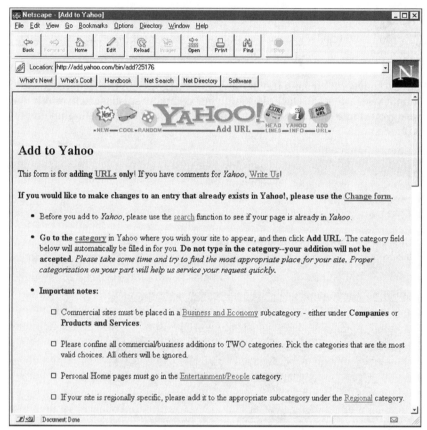

Figure 18-9: You can submit a URL to YAHOO! by filling out the form on this page. (Text and artwork copyright © 1996 by YAHOO!, Inc. All rights reserved.)

This page provides instructions for submitting the URL for inclusion in the YAHOO! directory. After reading the instructions on this page, you should scroll down to view the part of the form where you have to fill in the URL and other requested information. Because you have already gone through the hierarchy of categories, the selected category appears in the Category field of the form. After you have filled in all the requested information, click on the Submit button to send the form to YAHOO!.

Newsgroups

Announcing your Web site in one or more relevant newsgroups is another good way to spread the word about the site. You have to judge which newsgroups are relevant for your Web site based on the focus of your Web site.

Typical newsgroup announcements

URL

To give you a feel for the type of Web site announcements made in various newsgroups, here are some recent examples. (I mention these URLs as examples only; don't take them as endorsements of any kind.)

Newsgroup	Type of Site
`comp.bbs.misc`	Web conferencing software (`http://www.allaire.com/forums/`)
`comp.infosystems`	Collector's network (`http://www.footnet.com/collect`)
`comp.os.ms-windows.programmer`	Visual C++ and Microsoft Foundation Classes (`http://www.webcom.com/sleslie/` `resources.html`)
`misc.invest.stocks`	Standard & Poor's daily stock split report (`http://` `www.stockinfo.standardpoor` `.com/samples/splits.htm`)
`rec.crafts.marketplace`	Art of crochet (`http://www.io.com/` `crochet-guild-of-america/`)
`rec.food.veg.cooking`	Original vegetarian recipes (`http://` `www.wp.com/chflouie/`)
`rec.martial-arts`	Kung Fu martial arts (`http://www.users.fast.net~lilung/`)
`rec.outdoors.fishing.fly`	Delaware River Club fly fishing resort (`http://www.mayfly.com/`)
`rec.sport.baseball`	News about the Boston Red Sox (`http://www.projo.com/horizons/` `offthewall/`)
`rec.sport.baseball.analysis`	Baseball analysis (`http://www.scruznet.com/` `~ewalker/baseball.html`)

As this list indicates, if the focus of a newsgroup matches that of your Web site, you can prepare a brief announcement and post it to the newsgroup.

Newsgroups for announcements

Even if you cannot find a newsgroup that's appropriate for your Web site, you can always post announcements in two newsgroups that are relevant for all Web sites. These are the general-purpose Web announcement newsgroups:

✦ `comp.infosystems.www.announce` for non-commercial Web-related news.

✦ `comp.internet.net-happenings` for new sites, events, publications, and other events on the Internet.

Tip   The `comp.infosystems.www.announce` newsgroup does not allow commercial
announcements. To announce a commercial site, post an article in a relevant
unmoderated newsgroup.

Prepare the announcement

Before you prepare the announcement, read the newsgroup to see how typical
announcements are formatted.

Every week, the `comp.infosystems.www.announce` newsgroup carries an article
about how to announce in that group. Go to the newsgroup (use your favorite news
reader) and look for an article with the following subject line:

```
Subject:  ** How to Announce in comp.infosystems.www.announce **
```

That article tells you exactly how to format your announcement for
`comp.infosystems.www.announce`. Essentially, your announcement should
include a meaningful `Subject:` line and be straightforward without any hype. Try to
include one of the following words (in capital letters) on the `Subject:` line:

ARCHIVE	ENTERTAINMENT	MAGAZINE	SCIENCE
ART	ENNVIRONMENT	MISC	SERVER
BOOK	FAQ	MUSIC	SOFTWARE
BROWSER	GAMES	NEWS	SPORTS
COLLECTION	HEALTH	PERSONAL	TRANSPORTATION
ECONOMY	HUMANITIES	POLITICS	
EDUCATION	INFO	REFERENCE	
EMPLOYMENT	LAW	RELIGION	

If none of these keywords are appropriate, you may skip the word.

The announcement should include the URL in the following format:

```
<URL:protocol://site[:port]/path/to/file/or/directory/>
```

where the items within square brackets (`[...]`) are optional. For example,
`<URL:http://www.altavista.digital.com/>` is a valid URL entry; so is
`<URL:ftp://ds.internic.net/rfc/rfc1738.txt>`.

Post the announcement

Both `comp.infosystems.www.announce` and `comp.internet.net-happenings`
are moderated newsgroups; each has its own way of submitting an article.

Net-Happenings

Tip   To post an announcement to the `comp.internet.net-happenings` newsgroup,
visit the following URL:

```
http://www.mid.net/net/
```

On that Web page, you'll find a link to Net-Happenings Resource Submittal Form (`http://www.mid.net/net/input.html`). Fill out the form and click on the Submit button to send out an announcement that should eventually appear in the `comp.internet.net-happenings` newsgroup.

When filling out the submission form, you must select a category for your announcement to Net-Happenings. Some common keywords and meanings are:

Keyword	Meaning
AD-WWW	Advertisement about the Web
AD-MISC	Other advertisement
BOOK	Books about the Internet.
CONF-NA	Conferences in North America
CONF	Conferences in the rest of the world
CORRECT	Corrections to a previous announcement
EJOUR	Electronic journals (e-journals)
EMAG	Electronic magazines
FAQ	Frequently-Asked Question
FEDGOVT	Federal government
FTP	Anonymous FTP sites
GOPHER	Gopher server
K12	Kindergarten through 12th grade education
LISTS	Mailing lists
MISC	Miscellaneous
NEWSLTR	Newsletters
SEM	Seminars
SOFT	New software
UPDATED	An update of a previous announcement
WRKSHOP	Workshops
WWW	Web servers

Note In addition to the `comp.internet.net-happenings` newsgroup, the Net-Happenings announcement also goes to subscribers of the Net-Happenings mailing list. You can subscribe to the mailing list by sending mail to `listserv@lists.internic.net`. (Just type `subscribe net-happenings` in the message body.) You can also sign up on the Web page at `http://www.mid.net/net/`.

Tip

The `comp.infosystems.www.announce` **newsgroup**
To submit a non-commercial announcement to the
`comp.infosystems.www.announce` newsgroup, you can simply the post the article using a news reader. The article ends up in an e-mail message to the moderator. The moderator makes sure that the article is relevant and posts it to the newsgroup.

You can use any news reader to post a news item to one or more newsgroups. The exact command for posting a news item depends on the news reader. If you read news from a news reader built into a Web browser such as Netscape Navigator, you can post an article by clicking on a button on the news reader. For other news readers, you may have to type a few extra commands.

Summary

After you complete the initial content of your Web site, you have to let the world know about the site. Because most users locate information using Web indexes and newsgroups, you have to promote your Web site using these Internet-based resources. This chapter describes various ways to promote your Web site on the Net. The next chapter turns to the subject of creating interactive Web pages with Common Gateway Interface (CGI) programs.

Where to go next . . .

✦ For Web site design guidelines, read Chapter 15.

✦ For a user's view of the Web, consult Chapter 4.

✦ To learn about Web authoring tools, go to Chapter 17.

✦   ✦   ✦

Developing Web Applications

Programming the Common Gateway Interface (CGI)

The preceding part of this book covered a number of topics about Web publishing, from designing a web site to promoting it on the Web. While those are necessary skills for a Webmaster, an even more important responsibility is providing the computer programming expertise that is needed to support an interactive and dynamic Web page.

Unlike static Web pages that display some preset information, an *interactive* Web page lets the user send information to the Web server and get back a response that differs depending on the input. A Web index such as AltaVista (http://www.altavista.digital.com/) is a good example of an interactive Web page; the user enters one or more keywords and the Web index returns a list of Web pages that contain the search words. The Web page returned by the Web index is also *dynamic* because the content of that page depends on what the user types as search words — it's not a predefined static document.

Another example of an interactive and dynamic Web page might be a form where the user can enter a stock symbol and receive the latest stock quote for that stock. Yet another example might allow the user to subscribe to a magazine or register for a conference. The interaction might be as simple as letting users fill out a feedback form and submit comments that are then recorded in a file at the Web site.

To create an interactive Web page you have to use certain HTML elements (to display the form that solicits user input) and implement special computer programs on the Web server. These computer programs process the user input and return requested information, usually in the form of a dynamic Web page — a page that is constructed on-the-fly by a computer program. These programs are known as gateways because they typically act as a conduit between the Web server and an external source of information such as a database (even if the database may be a collection of UNIX files).

Note The gateway programs exchange information with the Web server using a standard known as *Common Gateway Interface* (*CGI*). That's why the term *CGI programming* is used to describe the task of writing computer programs that handle user requests for information.

As a Webmaster, you have to learn the details of how CGI programs work with the Web server and become an expert on CGI programming. If your Web site uses a database to store information, you may also need to learn how to let users query the database (through forms that you design).

The four chapters in this part of the book cover the subjects of CGI programming and database access. This chapter provides details about CGI — how the Web server provides necessary information to CGI programs and how CGI programs return information to the Web server. You also learn about the HTML tags that you have to use to create forms. The remaining details of CGI programming are relegated to the rest of the chapters in this part of the book. However, you do need to read this chapter to understand the CGI conventions that you must follow when writing a CGI program.

Cross Ref Chapter 20 focuses on CGI programming with Perl, a popular scripting language on UNIX and other systems. Chapter 21 shows how to use programming languages such as C and C++ (as well as scripting languages such as Tcl/Tk) to write CGI programs. Chapter 22 covers a unique aspect of CGI programming — how to access a database from a CGI program and return results of a database query as an HTML document.

HTML Forms

Before I explain the inner workings of CGI, I need to present some information that you need when preparing interactive Web pages — those Web pages that look like data-entry forms where you can type in the requested information and click on a submit button to send the information back to the Web server. CGI specifies how the Web server uses external programs to handle the input you submit through HTML forms. But, as a Webmaster, you also need to know how to create the data entry forms through which you can solicit information from users.

Note There is also a relationship between CGI programs and HTML forms because CGI programs process the data that the user enters in the form. One of the attributes of the form specifies the name of the CGI program that receives the input from the form. Additionally, each element of the form has an identifying name that helps the CGI program separate out the user's input for each form element. You'll learn these details in the next few sections.

A form in action

URL Web indexes use search forms to let the user type the keywords for a search. The well-known AltaVista Web index (`http://www.altavista.digital.com/`), for example, presents a search form where you can type in the keywords and click on a submit button. AltaVista then returns the results of the keyword search as an HTML document. You can learn all about the AltaVista search form from a Web page at AltaVista's Web site, as shown in Figure 19-1.

Figure 19-1: This Web page shows you how to embed AltaVista's search form in your Web page. (Copyright © 1996 by Digital Equipment Corporation.)

The Web page in Figure 19-1 tells you that you can use the following HTML text to display the AltaVista search form (which appears near the bottom of the page in Figure 19-1):

```
<FORM method=GET action="http://altavista.digital.com/cgi-bin/query">
<INPUT TYPE=hidden NAME=pg VALUE=q>
<B>Search <SELECT NAME=what>
<OPTION VALUE=web SELECTED>the Web
<OPTION VALUE=news>Usenet
</SELECT>
and Display the Results <SELECT NAME=fmt>
<OPTION VALUE="" SELECTED>in Standard Form
<OPTION VALUE=c>in Compact Form
<OPTION VALUE=d>in Detailed Form
</SELECT></B><BR>
<INPUT NAME=q size=55 maxlength=200 VALUE="">
<INPUT TYPE=submit VALUE=Submit>
</FORM>
```

This is a good example of the typical HTML elements that you can use for interactive forms. Also, you can see how the `<form>` element associates a CGI program with a form. Here are the key points to note in this HTML sample:

✦ The form begins with a `<form>` tag and ends with a closing `</form>` tag.

✦ The `<input>` tag defines a number of common form elements such as text fields, option menus, and submit buttons.

✦ The `<select>` element defines menus.

✦ The `<option>` tag defines each item within a `<select>` element.

You learn more about these form elements in the next few sections.

The `<form>` element

At the heart of an HTML form is a `<form>` element — the entire form must begin with a `<form>` tag and end with a closing `</form>` tag. The attributes of the starting `<form>` tag specify the CGI program that processes this form's input and how the Web browser sends the user's input to the Web server (which, in turn, forwards this information to the CGI program).

A typical `<form>` element definition has the following structure:

```
<form method="post" action="/cgi-bin/cgi-prog">
...(other form elements appear here)
</form>
```

The action **attribute**

The <form> tag's action attribute specifies a URL for the CGI program that you have designed to handle this form's input. You can use an absolute URL that specifies the full server name as well as the pathname for the CGI program. Often, however, you'd use a relative URL that identifies the directory on your Web server where the CGI programs reside.

In NCSA and Apache Web servers, /cgi-bin is the default directory where the CGI programs reside. That's why you typically see /cgi-bin in the action URL of most forms.

The method **attribute**

The method attribute indicates how the Web browser sends form input back to the server. You can specify one of the following submission methods:

✦ The POST method causes the browser to send the data in a two-step process. First the browser contacts the server specified in the action URL. Then, after a successful connection is established, the browser sends the form's data to the server, which, in turn, sends the data to the CGI program.

✦ The GET method causes the browser to append the form's data to the URL specified in the action attribute and send everything to the Web server in a single step. A question mark (?) separates the data from the URL.

If you don't specify a method, the browser uses the GET method by default.

The enctype **attribute**

The <form> tag accepts a third attribute, enctype, that specifies how the form's data is encoded when it's sent to the server — this is the MIME type of the form's data. Currently, you can use the following encoding types:

✦ application/x-www-form-urlencoded (this the default encoding type)

✦ multipart/form-data

Webmaster The default encoding method — application/x-www-form-urlencoded — is simple:

✦ Send a field's value with a name=value syntax (a field is a distinct element in the form; the name attribute specifies the field's name).

✦ If there is more than one field, separate the fields by ampersands (&).

✦ Convert all spaces into plus signs (+).

✦ Convert any non-alphanumeric character into a percent sign (%) followed by a two-digit hexadecimal number that corresponds to the ASCII code of that character.

✦ Encode line breaks as %0D%0A, which happens to be the ASCII codes of carriage-return followed by line feed.

In the CGI program, you have to use this encoding information to extract the values of various fields in the form. However, typically, you can use an existing function in Perl or C to extract the values.

Webmaster The multipart/form-data encoding allows the user to send back a file to the browser. You can use it only when the form's method attribute is POST. When you specify multipart/form-data encoding, the browser sends each field's content in a separate section just like a mail message with MIME attachments. For example, if a form has two fields, feedback and e-mail-address, a typical submission with the multipart/form-data encoding might be the following:

```
--------------17194870331573
Content-Disposition: form-data; name="feedback"

Very interesting!

--------------17194870331573
Content-Disposition: form-data; name="e-mail-address"

some@someplace.com
--------------17194870331573--
```

Each section of the multipart encoding starts with a *separator line* that has thirty dashes followed by a long random number. The next line contains the MIME header for the data, followed by the data itself. Two extra dashes on a separator line indicates the end of transmission.

Fields in the form

You have to use a handful of other HTML tags to specify the different fields in an HTML form:

✦ The <input> tag specifies a number of different input fields — the type attribute indicates which type of input field you want.

✦ The <textarea> element is for multiline text fields.

✦ The <select> and <option> tags are for creating menus.

Using <input> tags

You can use the <input> tag for several different input fields, from text entry fields to the submit button that actually sends the form's data to the Web server. (For multiline text entry fields, use the <textarea> tag.) The following list summarizes the syntax of the <input> tag in its various forms:

Type of Input	Sample `<input>` Tag
Single-line text	`<input type=text name=fname value="default" size=num>`
Password	`<input type=password name=fname value="default" size=num>`
Hidden field	`<input type=hidden name=fname value="default">`
Checkbox	`<input type=checkbox name=fname value="default">`
Radio button	`<input type=radio name=fname value="default">`
Submit button	`<input type=submit value="button label">`
Reset button	`<input type=reset value="button label">`
Custom button	`<input type=image src="path/to/ image.gif" name=fname>`

The first three `<input>` tags specify text fields; the last five are for buttons. Of these, the Submit and Reset buttons are used on most forms. As you might guess, the Submit button causes the browser to send the form's data to the server. The Reset button changes all fields to their default values (the default value of a field is the value that you assign when you define the field; these values appear when the browser first displays the form).

Text and password fields

The single-line text and password `<input>` tags allow the user to enter text; when you use the password type, the browser does not echo the user's input (the browser displays asterisks instead of the password characters — just what you expect to see in a password field). For example, Figure 19-2 shows a form where the user has to sign in by entering a name and a password.

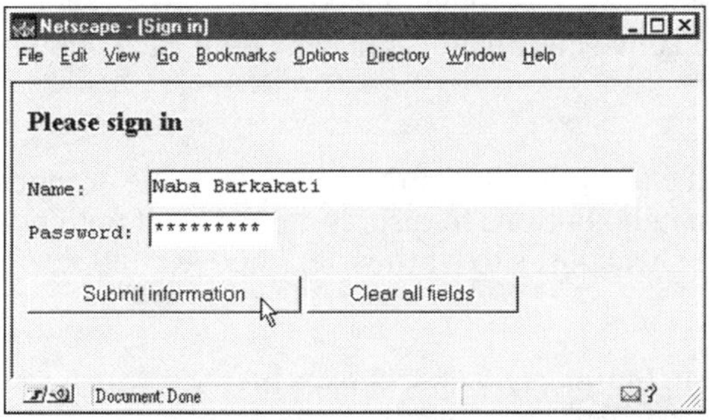

Figure 19-2: Form with text and password fields.

Here's the HTML source that creates the form shown in Figure 19-2:

```
<head>
<title>Sign in</title>
</head>
<body>
<form action="/cgi-bin/login.pl" method=post>
<h3> Please sign in

<pre>
Name:     <input type=text size=40 name=username>
Password: <input type=password size=10 name=passwd>
</pre>

<input type=submit value="Submit information">
<input type=reset value="Clear all fields">

</form>
</body>
```

As this example shows, you can use plain text as well as <input> tags inside the <form> element. You have to use normal HTML formatting tags (such as <pre> and <br>) to provide line breaks and align various fields.

The size attribute specifies the maximum number of characters that the user can enter in that text field. The Web browser uses the field name when sending the form's data to the Web server.

Webmaster The hidden field <input> tag (specified by type=hidden) is useful for storing information on the form. When the user clicks on the Submit button of a form, the browser sends the content of any hidden fields (along with the other fields) to the server. As the name implies, the Web browser does not display the contents of any hidden <input> tags on the HTML form.

Caution Although the password text (type=password) does not appear on the form (as the user types the text), the Web browser does not use any encryption when sending that text to the server. The upshot is that password text is not really protected as it's sent over the network. Therefore, you should not assume that you can use password text to securely accept and transmit sensitive information such as credit card numbers.

Radio buttons and checkboxes

Forms also need radio buttons and checkboxes to let the user select one or more items from a group of choices. Use radio buttons to display a number of options from which the user can select one; use checkboxes to let the user choose multiple options from a set.

You can understand the use of radio buttons and checkboxes better through a simple example. Suppose you want to display an HTML form that lets the user order a serving of ice cream. Figure 19-3 shows the appearance of the form after the user has selected some items.

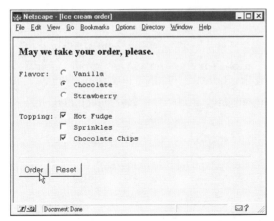

Figure 19-3: An ice cream order form with radio buttons and checkboxes.

This form shows the ice cream flavors as a collection of radio buttons—that means the user can select only one flavor. On the other hand, the user may choose more than one topping, so the toppings are listed in a group of checkboxes.

Here is the HTML source that generates the form of Figure 19-3:

```
<head>
<title>Ice cream order</title>
</head>
<body>
<form action="/cgi-bin/icecream.pl" method=post>
<h3> May we take your order, please.

<pre>
Flavor:  <input type=radio checked name=flavor value="Vanilla"> Vanilla
         <input type=radio name=flavor value="Chocolate"> Chocolate
         <input type=radio name=flavor value="Strawberry"> Strawberry

Topping: <input type=checkbox checked name=topping value="Hot Fudge"> Hot Fudge
         <input type=checkbox name=topping value="Sprinkles"> Sprinkles
         <input type=checkbox name=topping value="Chocolate Chips"> Chocolate
    Chips
</pre>
<hr>
<input type=submit value="Order">
<input type=reset>

</form>
</body>
```

Here are the key points to note when you use radio buttons and checkboxes in a form:

✦ Use `type=radio` for radio buttons and `type=checkbox` for checkboxes.

✦ Present a collection of radio buttons (or checkboxes) as a group. Indicate a group by using the same `name` attribute for all items in a group.

✦ Add a `checked` attribute (without any value) to indicate which items are selected by default.

✦ Provide text next to each `<input>` tag to label the radio buttons and checkboxes.

✦ Use HTML formatting tags such as `<pre>` or `<br>` to break lines and arrange the items on the form.

As long as you give the same name to all radio buttons (or checkboxes) in a group, the Web browser treats the group as a collection. For a group of radio buttons, the browser sends the user's selection in a `name=value` format. For checkboxes, multiple selections are sent as a comma-separated list in the `name=value1,value2,...` format.

For the ice cream flavor and topping selections shown in Figure 19-3, the browser sends `flavor=Chocolate` and `topping=Hot Fudge,Chocolate Chips` to the server. The CGI program at the server has to parse these strings and recognize the user's selections (and send back the right serving of ice cream).

Creating menus with `<select>` and `<option>`

You can create option menus and scrolled lists by placing a number of `<option>` tags inside a `<select>` element. For example, suppose you need a book order form that lets the user select one or more books, select the payment option, fill out the credit card information, and submit the order. Figure 19-4 shows a simple book order.

In this example, the list of books and the payment options use the `<select>` and `<option>` tags. As the highlighted entries in Figure 19-4 show, users can select multiple items from the scrolled list. You get the multiple selection behavior by using the `multiple` attribute in the `<select>` tag.

The following listing shows the HTML source that implements the book order form of Figure 19-4:

```
<head>
<title>Book Order</title>
</head>
<body>
<form action="/cgi-bin/bkorder.pl" method=post>
<h3> Book Order Form
<hr>
<pre>
```

```
Titles to purchase:
                <select name=books size=4 multiple>
                  <option>Linux Secrets
                  <option>UNIX Webmaster Bible
                  <option>Success with Windows 95
                  <option>X Window System Programming
                  <option>Object-oriented programming in C++
                  <option>Visual C++ Developer's Guide
                  <option>Borland C++ Developer's Guide
                  <option>Turbo C++ Bible
                  <option>Microsoft Macro Assembler Bible
                </select>

Method of payment:<select name=card size=1>
                  <option>Visa
                  <option>MasterCard
                  <option>American Express
                </select>
                </select>

Account Number:  <input type=text name=acct size=16>
Expiration Date: <input type=text name=expire size=5>
<hr>
                <input type=submit value="Order">  <input type=reset>
</pre>
</form>
</body>
```

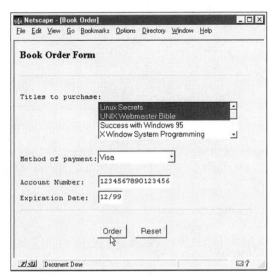

Figure 19-4: A book order form that uses an option menu and a scrolled list.

You should note the following as you compare the HTML listing with the form in Figure 19-4:

✦ The entire list or menu appears between the `<select>` and `</select>` tags.

✦ The `<option>` tag defines items in the list.

✦ The appearance of the `<select>` element depends on the value of the `size` attribute.

✦ If you specify `size=1`, the browser displays the `<select>` element as an option menu (the list of items appears in a drop-down list box when you click on the arrow next to a single visible item).

✦ If the value of `size` is more than one, the browser displays the `<select>` element as a scrolled list. The browser makes the list box large enough to display the number of items you specify in the `size` attribute. Thus, `size=4` means the list box should make 4 items visible.

✦ If you want the user to select more than one item from the list, include the `multiple` attribute in the `<select>` tag (the `multiple` attribute does not need any value).

Using the `<textarea>` element

You must have seen many feedback forms that let you type your comments in a large text entry area. Unlike the one-line text fields that let you type your name or password, the comment fields accept multiple lines of text. The `<textarea>` element lets you provide such multiline text entry fields.

The following example illustrates the syntax of the `<textarea>` element:

```
<textarea name="feedback" rows="10" cols="40">
This is the default text.  This is what
the user sees when the browser
initially displays the form.
</textarea>
```

The element begins with a `<textarea>` tag and ends with a `</textarea>` tag. You may provide some text between the `<textarea>` and `</textarea>` tags—the browser uses this text when initially displaying the text area. If you do not provide any text, the text entry field comes up empty.

The `<textarea>` tag accepts the following attributes:

✦ `name` identifies this text entry field. The browser uses the name when it sends the content of this field to the server.

✦ `rows` specifies the height of the text entry area (these are the visible rows of text; the user can enter more lines of text than that specified by the value of the `rows` attribute).

✦ cols specifies the width of the text-entry area (these is the visible number of characters per line; the user can enter longer lines than that specified by the value of the cols attribute).

Netscape Navigator supports a fourth attribute—wrap—that automatically wraps the text as the user types in the text entry field.

Typically, you'll use <textarea> elements when soliciting comments through a text entry area. For example, Figure 19-5 shows a feedback form that uses a <textarea> element.

Figure 19-5: The <textarea> element is useful for soliciting user feedback.

The following HTML text creates the form shown in Figure 19-5:

```
<head>
<title>Feedback</title>
</head>

<body>
<h2>Your feedback is welcome.</h2>
<hr>

<form method="post" action="/cgi-bin/test-post">
<h3>
Comments:<br>
```

(continued)

```
<textarea name="feedback" rows="10" cols="40">
</textarea><br>

E-mail address:<br>
<input type="text" name="e-mail" size=40 maxlength=60><br><br>
<input type=submit>  <input type=reset>
</h3>
</form>
</body>
```

The Common Gateway Interface (CGI)

If you have set up a Web server, you know how the Web server serves documents from a specific directory. The Web server can provide a variety of documents, but a key characteristic of these documents is that their content is static — the document does not change unless you, as the Webmaster, explicitly edit the it.

On the other hand, sometimes a document's content may not be known in advance. For example, if a Web site provides a search capability, the result of a search depends on which keywords the user enters in the search form. To handle these needs, the Web server relies on external programs called *gateways*.

A gateway program accepts the user input and responds with the requested data formatted as an HTML document. Often, the gateway program acts as a bridge between the Web server and some other repository of information such as a database.

Gateway programs have to interact with the Web server. To allow anyone to write a gateway program, the method of interaction between the Web server and the gateway program had to be specified completely. This is where *Common Gateway Interface (CGI)* comes in. CGI defines how the Web server and external gateway programs communicate. Figure 19-6 shows the interrelationship of the Web browser, Web server, and CGI programs.

As Figure 19-6 shows, the Web browser running on the user's system exchanges information with a Web server using the *Hypertext Transfer Protocol (HTTP)*. The Web server and the CGI programs typically run on the same system where the Web server resides. Depending on the type of request from the browser, the Web server either serves a document from its own document directory or executes a CGI program.

CGI in action

When the user retrieves a dynamic HTML document through CGI, the basic sequence of events is

1. The user clicks on some link that causes the Web browser to request an HTML document that contains a form.

2. The Web server sends the HTML document with the form, which the browser displays.

3. The user fills in the fields of the form and clicks on the submit button. The browser, in turn, sends the form's data using the GET or POST methods (as specified by the <form> tag in the HTML form). In either method, the browser sends the URL specified in the <form> tag's action attribute.

4. From the URL the Web server determines that it should activate the gateway program listed in the URL and send the information to that program. (The "How a Web browser sends form data to the Web server" section in this chapter explains how the Web server sends the form's information to the gateway program.)

5. The gateway program processes the information and returns HTML text to the Web server (which reads the output of the gateway program). The server, in turn, adds a MIME header and returns the HTML text to the Web browser.

6. The Web browser displays the document received from the Web browser. That document contains information that depends on what the user entered in the HTML form (often the information may be nothing more than a confirmation from the server that the user's input has been received).

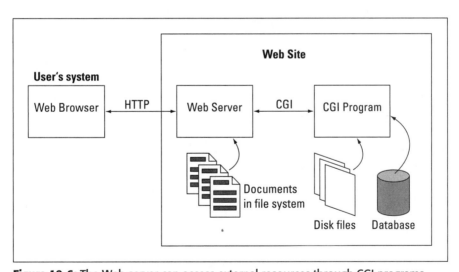

Figure 19-6: The Web server can access external resources through CGI programs.

After reading this sequence of events, you probably have the following questions:

✦ How does the Web browser send data using the GET and POST methods?

✦ How does the Web server determine that a URL specifies a gateway program and not a normal document?

✦ How does the Web server send information to the gateway program and receive information back from the program?

✦ How does the gateway program process the information sent by the Web server?

✦ How does the gateway program return information back to the server?

You'll find answers to these questions and more in the followings sections.

How a Web browser sends form data to the Web server

The Web browser uses the `method` attribute of the `<form>` tag to determine how to send the form's data to the Web server. There are two submission methods:

✦ *GET:* The Web browser submits the form's data as a part of the URL.

✦ *POST:* The Web browser sends the form's data separately from the URL; the server then sends the data to the gateway program's standard input.

Because you design the form as well as the CGI program that processes the form's data, you can select the method that best suits your needs. The "GET vs. POST" section provides some guidelines to help you choose the appropriate data submission method for your forms.

Note If you do not specify a method attribute in the `<form>` tag, the browser uses the GET method by default.

The GET method of data submission

The GET method is so called because the browser uses the HTTP GET command to submit the data. The GET command sends a URL to the Web server. That means, to send a form's contents to the server using the GET method, the browser must include all data in the URL.

This is what is known as the `application/x-www-form-urlencoded` encoding of data (see the "The `enctype` attribute" section for a discussion of this encoding method). The key features are

✦ The values of all the fields are concatenated to the URL specified in the `action` attribute of the `<form>` tag. Each field's value appears in the `name=value` format (you specify each field's name with the `name` attribute of various elements such as `<input>`, `<select>`, and `<textarea>`, that constitute an HTML form).

✦ To ensure that the Web server is not confused by special characters that may appear in the form's data, any character with special meaning is encoded using the `application/x-www-form-urlencoded` encoding.

For example, the AltaVista Web index (`http://www.altavista.digital.com/`) uses a form with the `GET` method of data submission. When you submit a query with the following search keywords:

```
"fairy tale" +frog -dragon
```

the Web browser sends the following URL back to the AltaVista server:

```
http://www.altavista.digital.com/cgi-bin/
        query?pg=q&what=web&fmt=.&q=%22fairy+tale%22+%2Bfrog+-dragon
```

In this URL, everything following the question mark (?) constitutes form data. Each field is separated by an ampersand (&). Each blank space is converted to a plus sign (+); an actual plus sign becomes %2B (that means ASCII code 2B in hexadecimal); and each double quotation mark is changed to %22.

The `POST` method of data submission

In the `POST` method of data submission, the Web browser sends the `POST` command (another HTTP command) to the server and includes the form's data in the body of that command.

Note The Web browser encodes the form's data identically whether you use the `GET` method or the `POST` method of data submission. However, as you will see in the " How the Web server sends data to the CGI program" section, the CGI program receives the information in a different manner when you specify the `POST` method.

GET **vs.** POST

When you design an HTML form, you have the option of specifying either `GET` or `POST` as the data submission method. In the early days of the Web, the `GET` method was the only way a browser could send form data to the server. The server, in turn, passes the data to the CGI program in an environment variable. Both the URL and environment variables have upper limits on the length — that means the `GET` method could not be used to transfer large amounts of form data from the browser to the server. (The upper limit on the length of environment variables depends on your system — some systems allow as little as 1K of data in an environment variable.)

The `POST` method was defined as a new way to transfer data without the limitations of `GET`. `POST` can handle any amount of data because the browser sends the data as a separate stream (which the Web server then sends to the standard input of the CGI program).

`GET` and `POST` are both useful ways of sending data from the browser to the server.

The basic guidelines for choosing a data submission method are

✦ Use GET to transfer a small amount of data and POST to send potentially large amounts of data. For example, GET is appropriate for a search form that solicits a few keywords from the user. On the other hand, you'd want to use POST for a feedback form with a free-form text entry area because the user might enter a large amount of text.

✦ Use the GET method if you want to access the CGI program without using a form. For example, if you want to access a CGI program at the URL http://www.someplace.com/cgi-bin/dbquery with a field named keyword as input, you could invoke the CGI program with a URL such as the following:

    http://www.someplace.com/cgi-bin/dbquery?keyword=Linux

If a CGI program is designed to receive data with the POST method, you cannot activate that program with a URL like this.

When you define a form in an HTML document, use these guidelines to decide whether to use the GET or the POST method of data submission.

How the Web server interprets a CGI URL

The URL specifying a CGI program looks like any other URL, but the Web server can examine the directory name and determine whether the URL is a normal document or a CGI program.

Webmaster Both NCSA and Apache Web servers accept the ScriptAlias directive in the srm.conf configuration file, which is in the /usr/local/etc/httpd/conf directory by default. Through a ScriptAlias directive you specify the directory where the CGI programs are located. You can use multiple ScriptAlias directives to specify multiple directories for CGI programs. Here's a typical ScriptAlias directive:

    ScriptAlias/cgi-bin//usr/local/etc/httpd/cgi-bin/

This tells the Web server that CGI URLs use the /cgi-bin/ directory name. The ScriptAlias directive also specifies that the Web server should substitute the full pathname /usr/local/etc/httpd/cgi-bin/ for /cgi-bin/.

For example, if a URL specifies http://www.someplace.com/cgi-bin/dbquery, then the Web server at www.someplace.com recognizes this as a CGI URL and invokes the dbquery program. The ScriptAlias directive in that Web server's srm.conf configuration file indicates which directory on the server's system contains the CGI programs. In other words for the example ScriptAlias directive, the Web server translates the CGI program name /cgi-bin/dbquery to the full pathname /usr/local/httpd/cgi-bin/dbquery.

For the CERN HTTD server, you have to use the `Exec` directive to specify the directory that contains the CGI programs. The syntax is similar to the `ScriptAlias` directive of NCSA and Apache Web servers. Here is a typical `Exec` directive for the CERN Web server:

```
Exec    /cgi-bin/*        /usr/local/etc/httpd/cgi-bin/*
```

Thus, the alias for the CGI program directory tells the Web server that a URL refers to a CGI program and not to a plain HTML file.

Webmaster The Web server expects the CGI program's name to appear immediately following the CGI directory alias (such as `/cgi-bin/`). If the URL includes other path information following the program name, the Web server passes that information to the CGI program in an environment variable named `PATH_INFO`. For example, if you were to invoke the `/cgi-bin/dbquery` program with the following URL:

```
http://www.someplace.com/cgi-bin/dbquery/misc/items
```

the Web server places the string `/misc/items` in the `PATH_INFO` environment variable before running the `/cgi-bin/dbquery` program. This example illustrates another way to pass extra information to a CGI program.

How the Web server sends data to the CGI program

Some details of how the Web server sends data to the CGI program depend on whether the `GET` or `POST` method is used by the browser to submit a form's data. The browser selects the method from the `method` attribute of the `<form>` tag which you wrote in the first place. That means you are in charge of deciding how you want your CGI program to accept input—through the `GET` or the `POST` method.

Information through environment variables

Whether you use the `GET` method or the `POST` method, the Web server uses a number of environment variables (see sidebar) to transfer helpful information to the CGI program. If you are running an NCSA or Apache Web server, you can see these environment variables using a sample CGI program (called `/cgi-bin/test-cgi`) that comes with the NCSA Web server. The `/cgi-bin/test-cgi` program echoes back the relevant environment variables in an HTML document.

You can also see the effect of various query strings on the environment variables through the examples at the following URL:

```
http://hoohoo.ncsa.uiuc.edu/cgi/examples.html
```

Figure 19-7 shows the result I get by invoking the `/cgi-bin/test-cgi` program on one of my systems running an Apache Web server.

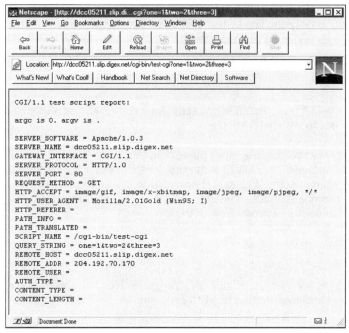

Figure 19-7: The /cgi-bin/test-cgi program displays the environment variables through which the Web server sends information to a CGI program.

As Figure 19-7 shows, the server defines 20 or so environment variables with a variety of information for the CGI program.

The very fact that I am running the `test-cgi` program through a URL implies that the `GET` method is used to send any data to the server. You can see that the `REQUEST_METHOD` environment variable is indeed set to `GET`.

Webmaster Note that everything in the URL after the question mark (?) appears as the value of the environment variable `QUERY_STRING`. This is how the Web server sends a form's contents to the CGI program when the `GET` method is used.

You'll find it instructive to look at the `test-cgi` program — that program happens to be a simple shell script. For a default installation of the NCSA Web server, you can view the file with the following command:

```
cat /usr/local/etc/httpd/cgi-bin/test-cgi
#!/bin/sh

echo Content-type: text/plain
echo

echo CGI/1.1 test script report:
echo
```

```
echo argc is $#. argv is "$*".
echo

echo SERVER_SOFTWARE = $SERVER_SOFTWARE
echo SERVER_NAME = $SERVER_NAME
echo GATEWAY_INTERFACE = $GATEWAY_INTERFACE
echo SERVER_PROTOCOL = $SERVER_PROTOCOL
echo SERVER_PORT = $SERVER_PORT
echo REQUEST_METHOD = $REQUEST_METHOD
echo HTTP_ACCEPT = "$HTTP_ACCEPT"
echo HTTP_USER_AGENT = "$HTTP_USER_AGENT"
echo HTTP_REFERER = "$HTTP_REFERER"
echo PATH_INFO = "$PATH_INFO"
echo PATH_TRANSLATED = "$PATH_TRANSLATED"
echo SCRIPT_NAME = "$SCRIPT_NAME"
echo QUERY_STRING = "$QUERY_STRING"
echo REMOTE_HOST = $REMOTE_HOST
echo REMOTE_ADDR = $REMOTE_ADDR
echo REMOTE_USER = $REMOTE_USER
echo AUTH_TYPE = $AUTH_TYPE
echo CONTENT_TYPE = $CONTENT_TYPE
echo CONTENT_LENGTH = $CONTENT_LENGTH
```

Environment variables

An environment variable is nothing more than a name associated with a string. On a UNIX system, for example, the environment variable named PATH might be defined as follows:

```
PATH=/usr/local/bin:/bin:/usr/
    bin:/usr/X11/bin:.
```

The string to the right of the equal sign is the value of the PATH environment variable. The meaning of an environment variable depends on the program that uses the environment variable. By convention, the PATH environment variable is a sequence of directory names, each name separated from the preceding one by a colon (:). The period at the end of the list of directories also denotes a directory; it represents the current directory.

To see the value of an environment variable in a UNIX shell (the command interpreter for UNIX), use the echo command followed by the environment variable's name with a dollar sign prefix ($). Thus, to see the value of PATH, type the following command:

```
echo $PATH
```

Programs written in C, C++, Perl, or Tcl can query the values of environment variables. Therefore, the environment variables provide a convenient mechanism to transfer information from one program to another. The Web server uses environment variables to send information to a CGI program.

This shell script uses the echo command to display the values of the environment variables.

It happens to be a complete CGI program, and as such demonstrates the basic format of a CGI program's output. Notice the first two `echo` commands:

```
echo Content-type: text/plain
echo
```

These lines send a header that tells the Web server that the CGI program is returning a text document. After that, the script basically prints out the value of each environment variable on a separate line.

You can guess the meaning of some of the environment variables shown in Figure 19-7. Consult Table 19-1 for a description of environment variables commonly used in CGI.

<table>
<tr><td colspan="2">Table 19-1
Useful CGI Environment Variables</td></tr>
<tr><td>*Environment Variable*</td><td>*Description*</td></tr>
<tr><td>SERVER_SOFTWARE</td><td>Name and version of Web server software (such as NCSA/1.5.1 or Apache/1.0.3)</td></tr>
<tr><td>SERVER_NAME</td><td>Hostname or IP address of system where Web server is running</td></tr>
<tr><td>GATEWAY_INTERFACE</td><td>Name and version number of gateway interface (currently CGI/1.1)</td></tr>
<tr><td>SERVER_PROTOCOL</td><td>Name and version number of protocol used for this request (for example, HTTP/1.0)</td></tr>
<tr><td>SERVER_PORT</td><td>Port number where request was received (for example, 80 for HTTP requests)</td></tr>
<tr><td>REQUEST_METHOD</td><td>Data submission method used (for example, GET or POST)</td></tr>
<tr><td>HTTP_ACCEPT</td><td>MIME types that the Web browser accepts (such as image/gif, image/x-xbitmap, image/jpeg. */*)</td></tr>
<tr><td>HTTP_USER_AGENT</td><td>Name and version of Web browser making the request</td></tr>
<tr><td>HTTP_REFERER</td><td>URL of the document from where this request originated</td></tr>
<tr><td>PATH_INFO</td><td>Any extra pathnames following the CGI program's name in the URL</td></tr>
<tr><td>PATH_TRANSLATED</td><td>PATH_INFO appended to the server's document root directory</td></tr>
</table>

Environment Variable	*Description*
SCRIPT_NAME	Name of the CGI program (for example, /cgi-bin/test-cgi)
QUERY_STRING	Everything following the question mark (?) in the URL (this is how a CGI program receives the data from an HTML form that uses the GET method)
REMOTE_HOST	Hostname of the system from where this request was made (this is the system where the user is running the Web browser)
REMOTE_ADDR	IP address of the system from where this request originated
REMOTE_USER	Name of authenticated user (if the CGI program is password-protected, this is the username under which the program is being accessed)
AUTH_TYPE	Name of authentication method used to validate the user
CONTENT_TYPE	MIME type of data being sent to the CGI program (used with the POST method)
CONTENT_LENGTH	Number of bytes of data being sent (used with the POST method)

Note Note that when you specify the GET method, the Web server places all required data in the QUERY_STRING environment variable.

Information through command-line arguments

In UNIX, you run most programs with a command that has the following general format:

```
progname option1 option2 ... optionN
```

where progname is the name of the program's executable file. A single line of command commonly is referred to as a *command line*. On a command line, you enter the name of a computer program followed by one or more arguments (or *options*) known as *command-line arguments* (or *command-line options*). You pass information to the program through its command-line arguments. Of course, the program must be designed to accept and deal with the command-line arguments.

When the Web server runs a CGI program, the server can use command-line arguments to pass information to the program. Indeed, the CGI specification calls for the Web server to send simple queries to a CGI program through command-line arguments (a query is everything following the question mark in a CGI URL). For example, consider the following CGI URL:

```
http://www.someplace.com/cgi-bin/test-cgi?one+two+three
```

In this case, the Web server starts the `/cgi-bin/test-cgi` program with the following command line:

```
/cgi-bin/test-cgi one two three
```

That means `/cgi-bin/test-cgi` receives three command-line arguments. By convention, the Web server replaces any plus signs in the query with spaces and that's how `one+two+three` becomes a sequence of three arguments: `one two three`.

Webmaster If the query contains an equal sign (=), then the Web server does not provide anything in the command-line arguments. In any case, the entire query is always provided in the `QUERY_STRING` environment variable.

Note Note that only the `GET` method uses command-line arguments to pass information to a CGI program. Even then, the technique is used when the query is simple. Because the query is always available in the `QUERY_STRING` environment variable, you are better off using that environment variable to access the query.

Information through standard input

When you use the `POST` method in an HTML form, the Web server sends the form's data to the standard input of the CGI program. In other words, a CGI program must read the standard input in order to accept data sent using the `POST` method.

The `CONTENT_LENGTH` environment variable indicates the total number of bytes to be read. The MIME type of the input data is specified in the `CONTENT_TYPE` environment variable.

Unless you specify a different encoding through the `enctype` attribute of the `<form>` tag, the CGI program receives the form's data in the `application/x-www-form-urlencoded` MIME type and the `CONTENT_TYPE` environment variable is set to `application/x-www-form-urlencoded`. That means the information is URL-encoded: A space is replaced with a plus sign (+), fields are separated by an ampersand (&), and any non-alphanumeric character is replaced with a `%xx` code (where `xx` is the character's ASCII code in hexadecimal format).

How a CGI program processes a form's data

Depending on the data submission method — `GET` or `POST` — a CGI program receives information through the `QUERY_STRING` environment variable or through the standard input. Typically, you associate a CGI program with a form through the `<form>` tag's `action` attribute and, at the same time, specify whether the `GET` method or the `POST` method is to be used to send the form's data. Thus, you could design a CGI program to handle either `GET` or `POST` input.

Note One school of thought is that you should design your CGI program to handle both `GET` and `POST` methods of input. You can do so because you can determine the input method at run-time by checking the value of the `REQUEST_METHOD` environment variable. The reason for handling both GET and POST requests is that you can then use that CGI program in two ways:

✦ To handle input from a form using the POST method

✦ To support predefined requests as part of a URL and that were submitted using the GET method

Here are the basic steps for a CGI program designed to handle URL-encoded data sent through both GET and POST methods:

1. Check the REQUEST_METHOD environment variable to determine whether the request is a GET or a POST.

2. If the method is GET, use the value of the QUERY_STRING environment variable as the input. Also check for any extra path information in the PATH_INFO environment variable. Then go to step 4.

3. If the method is POST, get the length of the input (in number of bytes) from the CONTENT_LENGTH environment variable. Then, read that many bytes from the standard input.

4. Extract the name=value pairs for various fields by splitting the input data at the ampersand character (&), which separates the values of fields.

5. In each name=value pair, convert all %xx sequences into ASCII characters.

6. In each name=value pair, convert all plus signs (+) to spaces.

7. Save the name=value pairs denoting values of specific fields for later use.

After you decode the input and find the values of all the fields, you know what to do with the fields because you designed the form in the first place. For example, if it's a registration form that solicits the user's name and e-mail address, you may simply store the decoded information in a database and return an acknowledgment in the form of an HTML document.

How a CGI program returns information to the server

Regardless of how the Web server passes information to the CGI program, the CGI program always returns information to the server by writing to the standard output. In other words, if the CGI program wants to return an HTML document (typically constructed on the fly), the program must write that document to the standard output. The Web server then processes that output and sends the data back to the Web browser that had originally submitted the request.

The CGI program cannot simply begin sending an HTML document back to the server; the program also must send some header information. The amount of header information depends on whether the CGI program is a *parsed header* or a *non-parsed header* CGI program.

Webmaster The Web server treats the output of parsed header and non-parsed header CGI programs differently:

✦ *Parsed header CGI programs* send a minimal header before sending the actual document. The Web server processes the header before sending the data to the Web browser. Most CGI programs fall in this category.

✦ *Non-parsed header CGI programs* must send a complete MIME header before sending the actual data. For these programs, the Web server simply passes through the CGI program's output to the Web browser.

Parsed header CGI program

By default, most CGI programs fall in the parsed header category. The term *parsed header* is used because the Web server parses the header generated by the CGI program before sending the document to the Web browser. Essentially, the Web server accepts the CGI program's output, adds some HTTP codes and a MIME header, and then sends everything to the Web browser.

A parsed header CGI program must write at least a minimal MIME header before writing the data to standard output. A minimal header includes the MIME type of the data with a line such as the following:

```
Content-type: text/html
```

The MIME type can be anything consistent with the data the CGI program is returning to the Web server. For example, for a plain text file, the MIME header should be

```
Content-type: text/plain
```

From a CGI program, you can also send back an image. For a GIF image, you'd use the following MIME header:

```
Content-type: image/gif
```

 Tip If you return binary data (such as a GIF image) from a CGI program, you must include the `Content-length` header with the size of the data. For example, if you return a GIF image with 10,940 bytes of data, you need the following header line:

```
Content-length: 10940
```

You may also include other header lines. Here is a list of typical header lines:

Header	Description
Content-type	MIME type of data being sent to the Web server
Content-length	Number of bytes being sent (you must provide this for binary data)
Expires	Date and time when document is no longer valid (for example, `Expires: Friday, 31-Dec-99 05:15:10 GMT`)

Header	Description
Location	New URL that the server should send back to the Web browser (you cannot use the Location header with other headers)
Pragma	Cache control (for example, you can turn browser-side caching off with Pragma: no-cache)
Status	Status code such as Status: 200 OK (you cannot use the Status header with other headers)

Tip The only key point you must remember is that the last line of a MIME header block must end with a blank line. After the blank line marking the end of the header, you can begin the CGI program's output, which is usually an HTML document.

Non-parsed header CGI program

Non-parsed header CGI programs are useful when you want to write a CGI program that directly communicates with the Web browser. You might use such a program to

✦ Provide a faster response by bypassing the server

✦ Implement what is known as *server push animation* where you write a CGI program that sends multiple frames of animation directly to the Web browser (using a Content-type: multipart/x-mixed-replace MIME header)

 Webmaster The name of a non-parsed header CGI program must start with the nph- prefix. NCSA, Apache, and CERN Web servers looks for the nph- prefix to determine if a CGI program's output should be sent directly to the Web browser (without any processing by the server).

A non-parsed header program must include some HTTP header information and additional MIME headers because the output goes directly to the Web browser and the browser expects a reply in HTTP format.

From a non-parsed header CGI program, you should send back the following information before sending the data:

✦ An HTTP status line such as the following:

```
HTTP/1.0 200 OK
```

✦ A header line with the name and version of the server software (from the SERVER_SOFTWARE environment variable) in the following format:

```
Server: Apache/1.0.3
```

✦ MIME header with MIME type data, as follows:

```
Content-type: text/html
```

✦ Other MIME headers as needed (for example, Content-length for binary data)

✦ An extra blank line to mark the end of the header information

Summary

The most useful Web sites are the ones that provide customized information. That means instead of static Web pages with predetermined content, users get dynamic Web pages created on-the-fly based on user input. Such dynamic Web pages rely on *Common Gateway Interface (CGI)* programs. This chapter describes how CGI programs work and how you can create HTML forms that invoke CGI programs on the Web server. The next chapter goes into CGI programming in Perl — a popular language for this kind of programming.

Where to go next . . .

✦ For information on CGI programming in Perl, read Chapter 20.

✦ If you want to write CGI programs in C, C++, or Tcl, turn to Chapter 21.

✦ To learn how to access databases from a CGI program, consult Chapter 22.

✦   ✦   ✦

Writing CGI Programs in Perl

Although you can write a CGI program in any language, Perl has become synonymous with CGI programming. Perl is a freely available, popular scripting language with text processing features that make it an excellent tool for writing CGI programs (which involve parsing URLs and preparing HTML text that is sent back to the user).

This chapter introduces you to CGI programming with Perl. The chapter starts with an introduction to Perl programming, followed by examples of typical CGI programs in Perl. You'll need Perl installed on your system to begin developing CGI programs in Perl.

Cross Ref In Chapter 21, I cover CGI programming in C, C++, and Tcl/Tk.

Learning Perl Programming

Officially, *Perl* stands for *Practical Extraction Report Language*. Perl was created by Larry Wall to extract information from text files and then use that information to prepare reports. Programs written in Perl, the language, are interpreted and executed by perl, the program. The version of Linux on this book's companion CD-ROM comes with Perl.

Perl is available on a wide variety of computer systems because Perl can be distributed freely. Also, Perl was popular among many users and system administrators as a scripting language even before the Web became popular. When the need for CGI programs arose, Perl became the natural choice for those already familiar with the language. By now, Perl has become the accepted tool for creating CGI programs (even though you can write CGI programs in any programming language, from C and C++ to Tcl).

As you might know, the term *script* is just a synonym for *program*. Unlike programs written in programming languages such as C and C++, Perl programs do not have to be compiled; the `perl` program simply interprets and executes the Perl programs. The term *script* often is used for such interpreted programs written in a shell's programming language or in Perl. (Strictly speaking, `perl` does not just interpret a Perl program; it converts the Perl program to an intermediate form before executing the program.)

Note If you are familiar with shell programming or the C programming language, you can pick up Perl very quickly. If you have never programmed, becoming proficient in Perl may take a while. I encourage you to start with a small subset of Perl's features and ignore anything that you do not understand. Then you can slowly add Perl features to your repertoire as time goes by.

Do I have Perl?

Before you proceed with the Perl tutorial, check to see whether you have `perl` installed on your system. Type the following command:

```
which perl
```

The `which` command tells you whether it finds a specified program in the directories listed in the `PATH` environment variable. If `perl` is installed, you should see something like the following output:

```
/usr/local/bin/perl
```

If the `which` command complains that no such program exists in the current `PATH`, that message does not necessarily mean that you do not have `perl` installed; it simply means that `perl` is not in any of directories listed in your `PATH` environment variable. Typically, the `perl` program is installed in the `/usr/bin` or `/usr/local/bin` directory. Check to ensure that `/usr/bin` and `/usr/local/bin` are in `PATH`; either type `echo $PATH` or look at the message displayed by the `which` command (that message includes the directories in `PATH`). If `/usr/bin` and `/usr/local/bin` are not in `PATH`, use the following command to redefine `PATH` (this command will work in Bourne and Korn shells):

```
PATH="$PATH:/usr/bin:/usr/local/bin"; export PATH
```

If you have `perl` installed on your system, type the following command to see its version number:

```
perl -v
```

Following is typical output from that command (on a Linux system):

```
This is perl, version 4.0 for Linux {36LA}-ljl-

$RCSfile: perl.c,v $$Revision: 4.0.1.8 $$Date: 1993/02/05 19:39:30 $
Patch level: 36

Copyright (c) 1989, 1990, 1991, Larry Wall

Perl may be copied only under the terms of either the Artistic License or the
GNU General Public License, which may be found in the Perl 4.0 source kit.
```

This output tells you that you have Perl version 4.0, patch level 36, and that Larry Wall, the originator of Perl, holds the copyright. Perl is freely distributed under the GNU General Public License, however.

URL The companion CD-ROM has version 5.003 of Perl. You can get the latest version of Perl via anonymous FTP (use the `ftp` program, and provide `anonymous` as the username) from one of the following sites on the Internet:

```
ftp.uu.net                      137.39.1.2
ftp.netlabs.com                 192.94.48.152
coombs.anu.edu.au               150.203.76.2 (Australia)
archive.cis.ohio-state.edu      128.146.8.52
jpl-devvax.jpl.nasa.gov         128.149.1.143
prep.ai.mit.edu                 18.71.0.38
ftp.cs.ruu.nl                   131.211.80.17  (Europe)
```

Note The Perl examples in this chapter will work with Perl version 4. However, many new Perl libraries require Perl version 5.

Your first Perl script

Perl has many features of C, and, as you may be aware, most books on C start with an example program that displays `Hello, World!` on your terminal. Because Perl is an interpreted language, you can accomplish this task directly from the command line. If you enter:

```
perl -e 'print "Hello, World!\n";'
```

the system responds:

```
Hello, World!
```

This command uses the `-e` option of `perl` to pass the Perl program as a command-line argument to the Perl interpreter. In this case, the following line constitutes the Perl program:

```
print "Hello, World!\n";
```

To convert this line to a script that can be executed directly, all you have to do is place the line in a file and start the file with a directive to run `perl` (as you do in the shell scripts, in which you place a line such as `#!/bin/sh` to run the Bourne shell to process the script).

To try a Perl script, follow these steps:

1. Use a text editor, such as `vi` or `emacs`, to save the following lines in the file named `hello`:

   ```
   #!/usr/local/bin/perl
   # This is a comment.
   print "Hello, World!\n";
   ```

2. Make the `hello` file executable by using the following command:

   ```
   chmod +x hello
   ```

3. Run the Perl script by typing the following at the shell prompt:

   ```
   hello
   Hello, World!
   ```

That's it! You have just written and run your first Perl script.

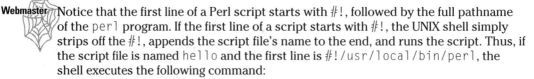

Notice that the first line of a Perl script starts with `#!`, followed by the full pathname of the `perl` program. If the first line of a script starts with `#!`, the UNIX shell simply strips off the `#!`, appends the script file's name to the end, and runs the script. Thus, if the script file is named `hello` and the first line is `#!/usr/local/bin/perl`, the shell executes the following command:

```
/usr/local/bin/perl hello
```

Perl overview

Perl, like most programming languages, has the following features:

✦ *Variables* to store different types of data. You can think of each variable as being a placeholder for data — kind of like a mailbox, with a name and room to store data. The content of the variable is its value.

✦ *Expressions* that combine variables by using *operators*. An expression might add several variables; another might extract a part of a string.

More on Perl

This chapter devotes a few sections to giving you an overview of Perl and showing you a few simple examples. However, this discussion does not teach everything about Perl. If you want to use Perl as a tool, consult one of the following books:

> Larry Wall and Randal L. Schwartz, *Programming Perl* (O'Reilly & Associates, 1991)

> Randal L. Schwartz, *Learning Perl* (O'Reilly & Associates, 1993)

Ellie Quigley, *PERL by Example* (Prentice Hall, 1995)

The book by Perl originator Larry Wall and Randal Schwartz is the authoritative guide to Perl (although it may not be the best resource for learning Perl). The later book by Randal Schwartz focuses more on teaching Perl programming. Ellie Quigley's recent book teaches Perl with short but complete example programs.

✦ *Statements* that perform some action, such as assigning a value to a variable or printing a string.

✦ *Flow-control statements* that allow statements to be executed in various orders, depending on the value of some expression. Typically, flow-control statements include for, do-while, while, and if-then-else statements.

✦ *Functions* (also called *subroutines* or *routines*) that allow you to group several statements and give them a name. This feature allows you to execute the same set of statements by invoking the function that represents those statements. Typically, a programming language provides some predefined functions.

The next few sections provide an overview of these major features of Perl and illustrate the features through some simple examples.

Basic Perl syntax

Perl is free-form; no constraints exist on exact placement of any keyword. Perl programs often are stored in files with names that end in `.pl`, but there is no restriction on the file names that you can use.

Each Perl statement ends with a semicolon (;). A pound sign (#) marks the start of a comment; the `perl` program disregards the rest of the line beginning with the pound sign. Groups of Perl statements are enclosed in braces ({...}), similar to C.

Variables

You don't have to declare Perl variables before using them, as you do in C. You can easily recognize a variable in a Perl script, because variable names begin with special characters: an at symbol (@), a dollar sign ($), or a percent sign (%). These special characters denote the variable's type. The three types are

✦ *Scalar variables*, which represent the basic data types: integer, floating-point number, and string. A dollar sign ($) precedes a scalar variable. Following are some examples:

```
$maxlines = 256;
$title = "UNIX Webmaster Bible";
```

✦ *Array variables*, which are collections of scalar variables. An array variable has an at symbol (@) as a prefix. Thus, the following are arrays:

```
@pages = (62, 26, 22, 24);
@commands = ("start", "stop", "draw", "exit");
```

✦ *Associative arrays*, which are collections of key-value pairs in which each key is a string and the value is any scalar variable. A percent-sign (%) prefix indicates an associative array. You can use associative arrays to associate a name with a value. You might store the amount of disk space used by each user in an associative array such as the following:

```
%disk_usage = ("root", 147178, "naba", 28547, "emily", 55, "ivy", 60,
    "ashley", 45);
```

Because each variable type has its own special character prefix, you can use the same name for different variable types. Thus, %disk_usage, @disk_usage, and $disk_usage can appear within the same Perl program.

Scalars

Scalar variables are the basic data type in Perl. Each scalar's name starts with a dollar sign ($). Typically, you start using a scalar with an assignment statement that initializes it. You can even use a variable without initializing it; the default value for numbers is zero, and the default value of a string is an empty string. If you want to see whether a scalar is defined, use the defined function as follows:

```
print "Name undefined!\n" if !(defined $name);
```

The expression (defined $name) is 1 if $name is defined. You can actually "undefine" a variable by using the undef function. You can undefine $name, for example, as follows:

```
undef $name;
```

Variables are evaluated according to context. Following is a script that initializes and prints a few variables:

```
#!/usr/local/bin/perl
$title = "UNIX Webmaster Bible";
$count1 = 450;
$count2 = 350;

$total = $count1 + $count2;

print "Title: $title — $total pages\n";
```

When you run this Perl program, it produces the following output:

```
Title: UNIX Webmaster Bible — 800 pages
```

As the Perl statements show, when the two numeric variables are added, their numeric values are used, but when the $total variable is printed, its string representation is displayed.

Another interesting aspect of Perl is the fact that it evaluates all variables in a string within double quotation marks ("..."). On the other hand, if you write a string inside single quotation marks ('...'), Perl leaves that string untouched. If you were to write

```
print 'Title: $title — $total pages\n';
```

with single quotes instead of double quotes, Perl would display

```
Title: $title — $total pages\n
```

and not even generate a new line.

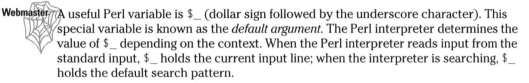

Webmaster A useful Perl variable is $_ (dollar sign followed by the underscore character). This special variable is known as the *default argument*. The Perl interpreter determines the value of $_ depending on the context. When the Perl interpreter reads input from the standard input, $_ holds the current input line; when the interpreter is searching, $_ holds the default search pattern.

Arrays

An *array* is a collection of scalars. The array name starts with an at symbol (@). As in C, array subscripts start at zero. You can access the elements of an array with an index. Perl allocates space for arrays dynamically.

Consider the following simple script:

```
#!/usr/local/bin/perl
@commands = ("start", "stop", "draw" , "exit");

$numcmd = @commands;
print "There are $numcmd commands. The first command is: $commands[0]\n";
```

When you run the script, it produces the following output:

```
There are 4 commands. The first command is: start
```

As you can see, equating a scalar to the array sets the scalar to the number of elements in the array. The first element of the @commands array is referenced as $commands[0] because the index starts at zero. Thus, the fourth element in commands is $commands[3].

Two special scalars are related to an array. The $[variable is the current base index, which is zero by default. The scalar $#arrayname (in which arrayname is the name of an array variable) has the last array index as the value. Thus, for the @commands array, $#commands is 3.

You can print an entire array with a simple print statement like this:

```
print "@commands\n";
```

When Perl executes this statement, it displays the following output:

```
start stop draw exit
```

Associative arrays

Associative array variables, which are declared with a percent sign (%) prefix, are unique features of Perl. Using associative arrays, you can index an array with a string such as a name. A good example of an associative array is the %ENV array that Perl automatically defines for you. In Perl, %ENV is the array of environment variables that you can access by using the environment variable name as an index. The following Perl statement prints the value of the QUERY_STRING environment variable:

```
print " QUERY_STRING = $ENV{QUERY_STRING}\n";
```

When Perl executes this statement, it prints the current setting of QUERY_STRING. In contrast to regular arrays, you have to use braces to index into an associative array. To retrieve the value of QUERY_STRING into a variable, you'd write the following:

```
$query_string = $ENV{QUERY_STRING};
```

Tip When processing the information from an HTML form, you can use an associative array to store the name-value pairs for each field.

Perl has many built-in functions — such as delete, each, keys, and values — that enable you to access and manipulate associative arrays.

Operators and expressions

Operators are used to combine and compare Perl variables. Typical mathematical operators are addition (+), subtraction (-), multiplication (*), and division (/). Perl provides nearly the same set of operators that C has. When you use operators to combine variables, you end up with *expressions*. Each expression has a value.

Following are some typical Perl expressions:

```
error < 0
$count == 10
$count + $i
$users[$i]
```

Predefined variables in Perl

Perl has several predefined variables that contain useful information that you may need in a Perl script. Following are a few important predefined variables:

@ARGV is an array of strings that contains the command-line options to the script. The first option is $ARGV[0], the second one is $ARGV[1], and so on.

%ENV is an associative array that contains the environment variables. You can access this array by using the environment-variable name as a key. Thus, $ENV{HOME} is the home

directory, and $ENV{PATH} is the current search path that the shell uses to locate commands.

$$ is the script's process ID.

$< is the user ID of the user who is running the script.

$? is the status returned by the last system call.

$_ is the default argument for many functions.

$0 is the name of the script.

These expressions are examples of the *comparison operator* (the first two lines), the *arithmetic operator*, and the *array-index operator*.

Caution In Perl, don't use the == operator to find out whether two strings match; the == operator works only with numbers. To test the equality of strings, Perl includes the FORTRAN-style eq operator. Use eq to see whether two strings are identical, as follows:

```
if ($input eq "stop") { exit; }
```

Other FORTRAN-style string comparison operators include ne (inequality), lt (less than), gt (greater than), le (less than or equal), and ge (greater than or equal). You also can use the cmp operator to compare two strings. The return value is -1, 0, or 1, depending on whether the first string is less than, equal to, or greater than the second one.

Perl also provides the following operators that are unique to itself. C lacks an exponentiation operator, which FORTRAN includes; Perl uses ** as the exponentiation operator. Thus, you can enter the following:

```
$x = 2;
$y = 3;
$z = $x**$y;  # z should be 8 (2 raised to the power 3)
$y **= 2;  # y is now 9 (3 raised to the power 2)
```

You can initialize an array to null by using ( ) — the *null-list operator* — as follows:

```
@commands = ();
```

The dot operator (.) allows you to concatenate two strings, as follows:

```
$part1 = "Hello, ";
$part2 = "World!";
$message = $part1.$part2;  # Now $message = "Hello, World!"
```

A curious but useful operator is the *repetition operator*, denoted by x=. You can use the x= operator to repeat a string a specified number of times. Suppose that you want to initialize a string to 65 asterisks (*). The following example shows how you can initialize the string with the x= operator:

```
$marker = "*";
$marker x= 65;  # Now $marker is a string of 65 asterisks
```

Another powerful operator in Perl is the *range ope*rator, which is represented by two periods (..). You can initialize an array easily by using the range operator. Following are some examples:

```
@numerals = (0..9); # @numerals is the list 0, 1, 2, 3, 4, 5, 6, 7, 8 , 9
@alphabet = ('A'..'Z'); # @alphabet is the list of capital letters A
        through Z
```

Regular expressions

If you have used UNIX for a while, you probably know about the grep command, which allows you to search files for a pattern of strings. Following is a typical use of grep to locate all files that have any occurrences of the string make or Make on any line of all files with names that end in .c:

```
cd /usr/local/src/perl5.001m
grep "[Mm]ake" *.c
```

This grep command finds all occurrences of make and Make in the files whose names end in .c.

The grep command's "[Mm]ake" argument is known as a *regular expression*, which is a pattern that matches a set of strings. You construct a regular expression with a small set of operators and rules that are similar to the ones for writing arithmetic expressions. A list of characters inside brackets ([...]), for example, matches any single character in the list. Thus, the regular expression "[Mm]ake" is a set of two strings, as follows:

```
make    Make
```

Perl supports regular expressions just as the grep command does. Many other UNIX programs, such as the vi editor and sed (stream editor), also support regular expressions. The purpose of a regular expression is to search for a pattern of strings in a file.

Perl lets you construct complex regular expressions. The rules, however, are fairly simple. Essentially, the regular expression is a sequence of characters in which some characters have special meaning. Table 20-1 lists the basic rules for interpreting the characters.

Table 20-1
Rules for Interpreting Regular Expression Characters

Expression	Meaning
.	Matches any single character except new line
x*	Matches zero or more occurrences of the character x
x+	Matches one or more occurrences of the character x
x?	Matches zero or one occurrence of the character x
[...]	Matches any of the characters inside the brackets
x{n}	Matches exactly n occurrences of the character x
x{n,}	Matches n or more occurrences of the character x
x{,m}	Matches zero or, at most, m occurrences of the character x
x{n,m}	Matches at least n occurrences, but no more than m occurrences of the character x
$	Matches the end of a line
\0	Matches a null character
\b	Matches a backspace
\B	Matches any character that's not at the beginning or the end of a word
\b	Matches the beginning or end of a word —(when not inside brackets)
\cX	Matches Ctrl-*X*
\d	Matches a single digit
\D	Matches a nondigit character
\f	Matches a form feed
\n	Matches a new-line (line-feed) character
\ooo	Matches the octal value specified by the digits ooo (where each o is a digit between 0 and 7)
\r	Matches a carriage return
\S	Matches a non-white-space character
\s	Matches a white-space character (space, tab, or new line)
\t	Matches a tab
\W	Matches a nonalphanumeric character
\w	Matches an alphanumeric character
\xhh	Matches the hexadecimal value specified by the digits hh (where each h is a digit between 0 and f)
^	Matches the beginning of a line

If you want to match one of the characters $, |, *, ^, [,], \, and /, you have to place a backslash before them. Thus, you would type these characters as \$, \|, *, \^, \[, \], \\, and \/. Regular expressions often look confusing because of the preponderance of strange character sequences and the generous sprinkling of backslashes. As with anything else, however, you can start slow and use only a few of the features in the beginning.

So far, this section has summarized the syntax of regular expressions, but you have not yet seen how to use regular expressions in Perl. Typically, you place a regular expression within a pair of slashes and use the match (=~) or not-match (!~) operators to test a string. You can write a Perl script that performs the same search as the one done with grep earlier in this section. Follow these steps to complete this exercise:

1. Use an editor to type and save the following script in a file named lookup:

```
#!/usr/local/bin/perl

while (<STDIN>)
{
    if ( $_ =~ /[Mm]ake/ ) { print $_; }
}
```

2. Make the lookup file executable by using the following command:

```
chmod +x lookup
```

3. Try the script, using the following command:

```
cat filename | lookup
```

   where filename refers to the file whose content you want to search.

   The cat command feeds the contents of a specific file (which, as you know from the grep example, contains some lines with the regular expression) to the lookup script. The script simply applies Perl's regular expression-match operator (=~) and prints any matching line.

The $_ variable in the script needs some explanation. The <STDIN> expression gets a line from the standard input and, by default, stores that line in the $_ variable. Inside the while loop, the regular expression is matched against the $_ string. All the lookup script's work is done with this single Perl statement:

```
if ( $_ =~ /[Mm]ake/ ) { print $_; }
```

This example illustrates how you might use a regular expression to search for occurrences of strings in a CGI query.

After you use regular expressions for a while, you will better appreciate their power. The trick is to figure out exactly which regular expression performs the task that you have in mind. Following is a search that looks for all lines that begin with exactly seven spaces and end with a right parenthesis:

```
while (<STDIN>)
{
    if ( $_ =~ /\)\n/ && $_ =~ /^ {7}\S/ )  { print $_; }
}
```

Flow-control statements

So far, you have seen Perl statements that are meant to execute in a serial fashion, one after another. Perl also includes statements that let you control the flow of execution of the statements. You have already seen the if statement and a while loop. Perl includes a complete set of flow-control statements just like those in C, but with a few extra features.

Tip

In Perl, all conditional statements take the following form:

```
conditional-statement
{ Perl code to execute if conditional is true }
```

Notice that you *must* enclose within braces ({...}) the code that follows the conditional statement. The conditional statement checks the value of an expression to determine whether to execute the code within the braces. In Perl, as in C, any nonzero value is considered to be true, whereas a zero value means false.

The if and unless statements

The Perl if statement is similar to the C if statement. For example, an if statement might check a count to see whether the count exceeds a threshold:

```
if ( $count > 25 ) { print "Too many errors!\n"; }
```

You can add an else clause to the if statement, as follows:

```
if ($user eq "root")
{
    print "Starting simulation...\n";
}
else
{
    print "Sorry $user, you must be \"root\" to run this program.\n";
    exit;
}
```

If you know C, you can see that Perl's syntax looks quite a bit like C. Conditionals with the if statement can have zero or more elsif clauses to account for more alternatives, such as the following:

```
print "Enter version number:";    # prompt user for version number
$os_version = <STDIN>;            # read from standard input
chop $os_version;                 # get rid of newline at end of line
# Check version number
```

(continued)

```
if ($os_version >= 10 ) { print "No upgrade necessary\n";}
elsif ($os_version >= 6 && $os_version < 9) { print "Standard upgrade\n";}
elsif ($os_version > 3 && $os_version < 6) { print "Reinstall\n";}
else { print "Sorry, cannot upgrade\n";}
```

Note   The unless statement is unique to Perl. This statement has the same form as if, including the use of elsif and else clauses. The difference is that unless executes its statement block only if the condition is *false*. You could, for example, use the following:

```
unless ($user eq "root")
{
    print "You must be \"root\" to run this program.\n";
    exit;
}
```

In this case, unless the string user is "root", the script exits.

The while **statement**

Use Perl's while statement for *looping* — repeating some processing until a condition becomes false. To read one line at a time from standard input and to process that line, you might use the following:

```
while ($in = <STDIN>)
{
# Code to process the line
    print $in;
}
```

Webmaster   If you read from the standard input without any argument, Perl assigns the current line of standard input to the $_ variable. Thus, you can write the preceding while loop as follows:

```
while (<STDIN>)
{
# Code to process the line
    print $_;
}
```

Perl's while statements are more versatile than those in C, because you can use almost anything as the condition to be tested. If you use an array as the condition, for example, the while loop executes until the array has no elements left, as in the following example:

```
# Assume @cmdarg has the current set of command arguments
while (@cmdarg)
{
    $arg = shift @cmdarg;          # extract one argument
# Code to process the current argument
    print $arg;
}
```

The `shift` function removes the first element of an array and returns that element.

You can skip to the end of a loop with the `next` keyword; the `last` keyword exits the loop. The following `while` loop adds the numbers from 1 to 10, skipping 5:

```
while (1)
{
    $i++;
    if($i == 5) { next;}   # Jump to the next iteration if $i is 5
    if($i > 10) { last;}   # When $i exceeds 10, end the loop
    $sum += $i;            # Add the numbers
}
# At this point $sum should be 50
```

The `for` and `foreach` statements

Perl's `for` statement has a similar syntax to C's `for` statement. Use the `for` statement to execute a statement any number of times, based on the value of an expression. The syntax is

```
for (expr_1; expr_2; expr_3) { statement block }
```

`expr_1` is evaluated one time, at the beginning of the loop, and the statement block is executed until expression `expr_2` evaluates to zero. The third expression, `expr_3`, is evaluated after each execution of the statement block. You can omit any of the expressions, but you must include the semicolons. Also, the braces around the statement block are required. The following example uses a `for` loop to add the numbers from 1 to 10:

```
for($i=0, $sum=0; $i <= 10; $sum += $i, $i++) {}
```

In this example, the actual work of adding the numbers is done in the third expression, and the statement controlled by the `for` loop is an empty block (`{}`).

The `foreach` statement is most appropriate for arrays. Following is the syntax:

```
foreach Variable (Array) { statement block }
```

The `foreach` statement assigns to `Variable` an element from the `Array` and executes the statement block. The `foreach` statement repeats this procedure until no array elements are left. The following `foreach` statement adds the numbers from 1 to 10:

```
foreach $i (1..10) { $sum += $i;}
```

Notice that I declare the array with the range operator (..). You also can use a list of comma-separated items as the array.

Webmaster If you omit the `Variable` in a `foreach` statement, Perl implicitly uses the `$_` variable to hold the current array element. Thus, you could use the following:

```
foreach (1..10) { $sum += $_; }
```

The `goto` statement

The `goto` statement transfers control to a statement label. Following is an example that prompts the user for a value and repeats the request if the value is not acceptable:

```
ReEnter:
print "Enter offset: ";
$offset = <STDIN>;
chop $offset;
unless ($offset > 0 && $offset < 512)
{
    print "Bad offset: $offset\n";
    goto ReEnter;
}
```

Access to UNIX commands

You can execute any UNIX command from Perl in several ways:

✦ Call the `system` function with a string that contains the UNIX command that you want to execute.

✦ Enclose a UNIX command within *backquotes* (`'`), which also are known as *grave accents*. You can run a UNIX command this way and capture its output.

✦ Call the `fork` function to copy the current script and process new commands in the child process (if a process starts another process then the new process is known as a *child process*).

✦ Call the `exec` function to overlay the current script with a new script or UNIX command.

✦ Use `fork` and `exec` to provide shell-like behavior (monitor user input and process each user-entered command through a child process). This section presents a simple example of how to accomplish this task.

The simplest way to execute a UNIX command in your script is to use the `system` function with the command in a string. After the `system` function returns, the exit code from the command is in the `$?` variable. You can easily write a simple Perl script that reads a string from the standard input and processes that string with the `system` function. Follow these steps:

1. Use a text editor to enter and save the following script in a file named rcmd.pl:

```
#!/usr/local/bin/perl
# Read user input and process command

$prompt = "Command (or \"exit\"): ";
print $prompt;

while (<STDIN>)
{
    chop;
    if ($_ eq "exit") { exit 0;}

# Execute command by calling system
    system $_;
    unless ($? == 0) {print "Error executing: $_\n";}
    print $prompt;
}
```

2. Make the rcmd.pl file executable, using the following command:

```
chmod +x rcmd.pl
```

3. Run the script by typing rcmd.pl at the shell prompt. Following is some sample output from the rcmd.pl script (the output depends on what commands you enter):

```
Command ("exit" to quit): ps
PID TTY STAT  TIME COMMAND
  112 pp1 S     0:00 -bash
  195 pp1 S     0:00 perl ./rcmd.pl
  196 pp1 R     0:00 ps
Command ("exit" to quit): exit
```

Another way to run UNIX commands is to use fork and exec in your Perl script. Following is an example script — psh.pl — that uses fork and exec to execute commands entered by the user:

```
#!/usr/local/bin/perl

# This is a simple script that uses "fork" and "exec" to
# run a command entered by the user

$prompt = "Command (\"exit\" to quit): ";
print $prompt;

while (<STDIN>)
{
```

(continued)

```
        chop;    # remove trailing newline
        if($_ eq "exit") { exit 0;}
        $status = fork;
        if($status)
        {
# In parent... wait for child process to finish...
            wait;
            print $prompt;
            next;
        }
        else
        {
            exec $_;
        }
    }
```

The following example shows how the `psh.pl` script executes the `ps` command:

```
Command ("exit" to quit): ps
  PID TTY STAT   TIME COMMAND
  508 pp1 S      0:00 -bash
  527 pp2 S      0:02 -bash
 1514 pp2 S      0:00 perl ./psh.pl
 1515 pp2 R      0:00 ps
Command ("exit" to quit): exit
```

UNIX shells use the `fork` and `exec` combination to run commands.

File access

You may have noticed the `<STDIN>` expression in various examples in this chapter. That's Perl's way of reading from a file. In Perl, a file is identified by a *file handle*, which is just another name for an identifier. Usually, file handles are in uppercase characters. `STDIN` happens to be a predefined file handle that denotes the standard input—by default, the keyboard. `STDOUT` and `STDERR` are the other two predefined file handles. `STDOUT` is used for printing to the terminal, and `STDERR` is used for printing error messages.

To read from a file, you write the file handle inside angle brackets (`<>`). Thus, `<STDIN>` reads a line from the standard input.

You can open other files by using the `open` function. The following example shows you how to open the `/etc/passwd` file for reading and for displaying the lines in that file:

```
open (PWDFILE, "/etc/passwd");     # PWDFILE is the file handle
while (<PWDFILE>) { print $_;}     # By default, input line is in $_
close PWDFILE;                     # Close the file
```

By default, the open function opens a file for reading. You can add special characters at the beginning of the file name to indicate other types of access. A > prefix opens the file for writing, whereas a >> prefix opens a file for appending. The following short script reads the /etc/passwd file and creates a new file, named output, with a list of all users without any shell (the password entries for these users end with a : at the end of the line):

```perl
#!/usr/local/bin/perl
# Read /etc/passwd and create list of users without any shell

open (PWDFILE, "/etc/passwd");
open (RESULT, ">output");                    # open file for writing

while (<PWDFILE>)
{
    if ($_ =~ /:\n/) {print RESULT $_;}
}

close PWDFILE;
close RESULT;
```

After you execute this script, you should find a file named output in the current directory. Following is what the output file contains when this script is run on a Linux system:

```
bin:*:1:1:bin:/bin:
daemon:*:2:2:daemon:/sbin:
adm:*:3:4:adm:/var/adm:
lp:*:4:7:lp:/var/spool/lpd:
mail:*:8:12:mail:/var/spool/mail:
news:*:9:13:news:/usr/lib/news:
uucp:*:10:14:uucp:/var/spool/uucppublic:
games:*:12:100:games:/usr/games:
man:*:13:15:man:/usr/man:
nobody:*:-1:100:nobody:/dev/null:
```

Note One interesting file name prefix is the pipe character—the vertical bar (|). If you call open with a file name that begins with |, the rest of the file name is treated as a command. The Perl interpreter executes the command, and you can use print calls to send input to this command. The following Perl script sends a mail message to a list of users:

```perl
#!/usr/local/bin/perl
# Send mail to a list of users

foreach ("root", "naba")
{
    open (MAILPIPE, "| mail -s Greetings $_");
    print MAILPIPE "Remember to send in your weekly report today!\n";
    close MAILPIPE;
}
```

If a file name ends with a pipe character (|), that file name is executed as a command, and you can read that command's output with the angle brackets, as shown in the following example:

```
open (PSPIPE, "ps -ax |");
while (<PSPIPE>)
{
# Process output of ps command — this example simply echoes each line
    print $_;
}
```

Subroutines

Although Perl includes a large assortment of built-in functions, you can add your own code modules in the form of subroutines. In fact, the Perl distribution comes with a large set of subroutines. Here is a simple script that illustrates the syntax of subroutines in Perl:

```
#!/usr/local/bin/perl
sub hello
{
# Make local copies of the arguments from the @_ array
    local ($first,$last) = @_;

    print "Hello, $first $last\n";
}

$a = Jane;
$b = Doe;

&hello($a, $b);      # Call the subroutine
```

When you run this script, it displays the following output:

```
Hello, Jane Doe
```

Here are some points to note about subroutines:

✦ The subroutine receives its arguments in the array @_ (the at symbol, followed by an underscore character).

✦ Variables used in subroutines are global by default. Use the local function to create a local set of variables.

✦ Call a subroutine by placing an ampersand (&) before its name. Thus, subroutine hello is called by &hello.

If you want, you can put a subroutine in its own file. The hello subroutine, for example, can be in a file named hello.pl. When you place a subroutine in a file, remember to add a return value at the end of the file; just type 1; at the end to return 1. Thus, the hello.pl file would be

```
sub hello
{
# Make local copies of the arguments from the @_ array
    local ($first,$last) = @_;

    print "Hello, $first $last\n";
}
1;      # return value
```

Then you have to write the script that uses the `hello` subroutine:

```
#!/usr/local/bin/perl
require 'hello.pl';   # include the file with the subroutine definition

$a = Jane;
$b = Doe;

&hello($a, $b);     # Call the subroutine
```

This script uses the `require` function to include the `hello.pl` file that actually contains the definition of the `hello` subroutine.

Built-in functions in Perl

Perl has more than 160 built-in functions, including ones that are similar to those in the C run-time library as well as functions that access the operating system. You really need to go through the list of functions to see the breadth of capabilities available in Perl. The following list shows a number of Perl functions that you'll find useful for CGI programming:

Function	Meaning
chdir(EXPR)	Change directory to directory specified by EXPR
chop(VARIABLE)	Chop off last character (useful for removing the trailing newline character in a string)
chroot(FILENAME)	Change root directory to specified FILENAME
close(FILEHANDLE)	Close specified file
delete $ASSOC{KEY}	Delete a value from an associative array
die(LIST)	Exit Perl program
do SUBROUTINE (LIST)	Call subroutine
each(ASSOC_ARRAY)	Return next key-value pair of associative array
eof(FILEHANDLE)	Return true if end-of-file is reached

(continued)

Function	Meaning
exec(LIST)	Execute system command
exit(EXPR)	Exit Perl program
fileno(FILEHANDLE)	Return file descriptor for a file handle
flock(FILEHANDLE,OPERATION)	Lock a file so other processes cannot change it (useful when multiple processes need to access a single file)
getc(FILEHANDLE)	Read next character from file
gmtime(EXPR)	Convert time to Greenwich Mean Time (GMT)
grep(EXPR,LIST)	Search LIST for occurrences of expression
hex(EXPR)	Return decimal value of hexadecimal EXPR
index(STR,SUBSTR)	Return position of first occurrence of a string
join(EXPR,LIST)	Return single string by joining list elements
keys(ASSOC_ARRAY)	Return array of keys for an associative array
length(EXPR)	Return length in number of characters
local(LIST)	Make a local list of variables (used in subroutines)
localtime(EXPR)	Convert binary time to local time
open(FILEHANDLE,EXPR)	Open a file
pipe(READHANDLE,WRITEHANDLE)	Open a pipe for reading and writing
pop(ARRAY)	Remove and return last element of an array
print(FILEHANDLE LIST)	Print a string to a file
printf(FILEHANDLE LIST)	Print formatted string like C's printf
push(ARRAY,LIST)	Append values in LIST to end of ARRAY
rand(EXPR)	Return random value between 0 and EXPR
read(FILEHANDLE,SCALAR,LENGTH)	Read specified number of bytes from file
require(FNAME)	Include the file specified by FNAME
reverse(LIST)	Reverse order of elements in LIST
rindex(STR,SUBSTR)	Return last position of substring in string

Function	Meaning
seek(FILEHANDLE,POSITION,WHENCE)	Move to new location in file
shift(ARRAY)	Remove first value off the array and return it
sleep(EXPR)	Sleep for EXPR seconds
sort(LIST)	Sort list and return sorted list in an array
splice(ARRAY,OFFSET,LENGTH,LIST)	Replace some ARRAY elements with LIST
split(/PATTERN/,EXPR,LIMIT)	Split EXPR into array of strings
sprintf(FORMAT,LIST)	Format a string just like sprintf in C run-time library
srand(EXPR)	Set seed for random number generation
stat(FNAME)	Return file statistics for file named FNAME
system(LIST)	Execute the shell command in LIST
tell(FILEHANDLE)	Return current file position in bytes from beginning of file
time	Return number of seconds since 00:00:00 GMT 1/1/1970
times	Return time in seconds for this process
tr/SEARCHLIST/REPLACE_LIST/cds	Translate search list into replacement list
truncate(FILEHANDLE,LENGTH)	Truncate the file FILEHANDLE to a specified LENGTH
unpack(TEMPLATE,EXPR)	Unpack a string into an array and return the array
unshift(ARRAY,LIST)	Prepend LIST to beginning of ARRAY
values(ASSOC_ARRAY)	Return array containing all values from associative array
wait	Wait for the child process to terminate
write(FILEHANDLE)	Write a formatted record to the file

CGI Programming in Perl

Now that you know what Perl offers as a high-level programming language, this section turns to the topic of how to write CGI programs in Perl. As explained in Chapter 19, the basic steps for a CGI program are

1. Read the CGI query into a string. Depending on the method of data submission (GET or POST), the input is either in the QUERY_STRING environment variable or read from standard input (STDIN in Perl).

2. Separate out the fields and their values from the query. In Perl, you can use the split function to separate the fields.

3. Decode the URL-encoded input values.

4. Store the fields in associative arrays.

5. Process the fields as appropriate.

Of these steps, only the last step is specific to a form. The other steps are performed for all types of form data. That means it's best to implement the first four steps using a library of Perl subroutines. In fact, as you'll learn in the "The cgi-lib.pl library for parsing CGI queries" section, you can perform these steps using Steven Brenner's cgi-lib.pl Perl library.

A simple CGI program in Perl

You can easily write a CGI program that displays a welcome message in an HTML page. Because it's simple to get various environment variables from Perl, you can even customize the hello message with the name of the user's system as well as provide a link back to your site's home page.

To implement this simple CGI program, all you need to do is create a Perl script that prints a MIME header followed by the message. Use a text editor to type the following text and save it as the hello.pl file:

```perl
#!/usr/local/bin/perl

# A simple Perl script that displays
# "Hello!" in an HTML page

# First, send the MIME header. Remember to
# end header with an extra newline

print "Content-type: text/html\n\n";

# Next, send the HTML document with
# appropriate tags

print "<html>\n";
print "<head>";
print "<title>Hello from ", $ENV{SERVER_NAME}, "</title>\n";
print "</head>\n";
print "<body>\n";
print "<h3>Hello from ", $ENV{SERVER_NAME}, "</h3>\n";

# Send some interesting information from
# the environment variables that the Web
# server sets up before running this
# script

print "<pre>\n";
print "You're visiting from: ", $ENV{REMOTE_HOST}, "\n";
```

```
print "Your browser is:       ", $ENV{HTTP_USER_AGENT}, "\n";
print "</pre>\n";

print "<hr>\n";

print "Return to: <a href=\"http://", $ENV{SERVER_NAME}, "/\">\n";
print $ENV{SERVER_NAME}, "</a>\n";

print "</body>\n";
print "</html>\n";
```

As the listing shows, this Perl script first prints a MIME header to indicate the document type. The script writes an extra newline (\n) character to mark the end of the header. Then, the script prints lines of an HTML document. The script uses several environment variables (accessed through the $ENV{...} syntax) to prepare a dynamic HTML document whose content changes depending on who accesses the script.

You can best understand the script's output when you see it in action. To test the hello.pl script:

1. Make sure your system has Perl installed and the perl program is in the /usr/local/bin directory. If not, edit the first line of hello.pl to reflect the name of the directory where perl resides.

2. Place the script in a directory where your Web server expects CGI programs. For example, my Internet Service Provider (ISP) has set up the Web server to recognize scripts in the /exec-bin/ directory, so I place the script in that directory.

3. Use a Web browser (you can run the browser on any system on the Net) to access the script with an appropriate URL. For my Web server, the URL is http://www.lnbsoft.com/exec-bin/hello.pl (go ahead and try this; it should work).

Figure 20-1 shows the HTML document generated by the hello.pl script for a typical access.

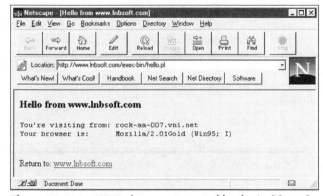

Figure 20-1: An HTML document created by the hello.pl script.

If you access `http://www.lnbsoft.com/exec-bin/hello.pl` from a different system, the script will display the name of your system instead of what Figure 20-1 shows. Also, if you were to copy the script and run it on your Web server, the script would generate an HTML document with a hello message from your server instead of `www.lnbsoft.com`, as shown in Figure 20-1.

This simple script gives you an idea of how to write CGI programs in Perl. However, the `hello.pl` script does not show how to process a query from the user. As you'll see in the next section, the best way to process a query is to use a well-known Perl library named `cgi-lib.pl`.

The `cgi-lib.pl` library for parsing CGI queries

Each CGI program is designed to handle a specific query submitted by the user by filling in a form. However, all form data require similar processing to extract the fields and their values. For this, you could use a common set of subroutines. As you might expect for a popular tool like Perl, there is already such a Perl library and that common library happens to be `cgi-lib.pl` by Steven Brenner.

Just as Perl is the accepted programming language for CGI programs, `cgi-lib.pl` is the accepted library for parsing the CGI query string that the Web server sends to the CGI program. By using the `cgi-lib.pl` library, you can quickly create Perl programs to handle form input.

Obtaining `cgi-lib.pl`

You can download the latest version of `cgi-lib.pl` from the official `cgi-lib.pl` home page at the URL:

```
http://www.bio.cam.ac.uk/cgi-lib/
```

As of this writing, version 2.12 is the latest released version of `cgi-lib.pl`. However, it's easier to understand an earlier version (1.14), which is what I describe in this chapter. This book's companion CD-ROM includes both version 1.14 and version 2.12 of `cgi-lib.pl`.

Because `cgi-lib.pl` is a library of Perl subroutines in a text file, there is nothing much to install. All you need to do is download the latest version of the file and place it in the `/cgi-bin/` directory of your server (for NCSA and Apache Web servers, the default pathname of the CGI binary directory is `/usr/local/etc/httpd/cgi-bin`). If your server is set up to load CGI programs from a different directory, place the `cgi-lib.pl` file in that directory.

Understanding `cgi-lib.pl`

The `cgi-lib.pl` library is popular because it's simple to understand and use. Although version 2.12 is somewhat more complex, you can understand the basic functionality by studying version 1.14.

The `cgi-lib.pl` library includes the following Perl subroutines:

Name	Description
ReadParse	Reads and parses the CGI query for both GET and PUT methods. Places parsed result in associative array that you provide as an argument. Returns TRUE is there is a query; otherwise, returns FALSE.
PrintHeader	Prints the MIME header (Content-type: text/html) with an extra blank line indicating end-of-header.
HtmlTop	Prints the top of the HTML document, including a title that you provide as argument.
HtmlBot	Prints the bottom of the HTML document with the ending </body> and </html> tags.
MethGet	Returns TRUE if the CGI query came as a GET request.
MethPost	Returns TRUE if the CGI query came as a POST request.
MyURL	Returns a complete HTTP URL for your script (such as http://www.someplace.com:8000/cgi-bin/dbquery.pl).
CgiError	Prints an HTML document with an error message. If you provide an array of strings as an argument, the first string is used as a title and the rest are displayed in the body of the HTML document. If you do not provide any arguments, a generic error message is used as the body of the HTML document.
CgiDie	Calls CgiError and then the script quits with a call to the die function.
PrintVariables	Prints the variables in the associative array that you pass as an argument (use this subroutine to print the fields and their values).

Using `cgi-lib.pl`

It's straightforward to use the subroutines from the `cgi-lib.pl` library. The general sequence of subroutine calls are

1. Call the ReadParse subroutine to process the CGI query.

2. If ReadParse returns TRUE, process the query (which is now available in an associative array). Output the desired HTML document by calling PrintHeader, HtmlTop, and HtmlBot.

3. Call CgiDie or CgiError to report any error conditions through an HTML page.

You can understand this sequence best by studying a skeleton script such as the one shown below:

```
#!/usr/local/bin/perl

# Include the cgi-lib.pl library with a require function
require "cgi-lib.pl";

# Read and parse input (in this case result is in the associative array
# named input

if(&ReadParse(*input))
{

# Successfully read and parsed the query string.
# Access specific fields from the input array. For example,
# if you have a field named keyword, access that field's value with
# the construct $input{'keyword'}

# Output HTML using the PrintHeader and HtmlTop subroutines
    print &PrintHeader;
    print &HtmlTop("Title of page");

# Print any other text you want

# End with the string returned by HtmlBot
    print &HtmlBot;
}
else
{
# You might want to generate an error message if ReadParse fails
# Call CgiDieor CgiError to do this
    &CgiDie("Error reading form input",
                    "A descriptive error message.");
}
```

In the next section, you'll see a more complete example of a Perl CGI script that uses the `cgi-lib.pl` library.

A feedback form

One of the common uses of CGI programming is to solicit and accept feedback from users. The next few sections present a simple CGI program to handle the input from a feedback form. The sample Perl program illustrates the use of `cgi-lib.pl` library and also shows how to send mail from a CGI program.

Designing the feedback form

URL The first step is to create an HTML form through which the user can submit comments. Figure 20-2 shows a typical feedback form (at the URL `http://www.lnbsoft.com/feedback.html`) with the fields filled in:

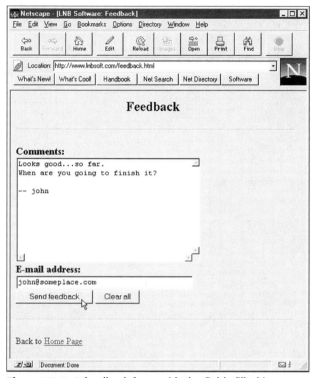

Figure 20-2: A feedback form with the fields filled in.

I use this form at the site `www.lnbsoft.com` to accept user feedback and mail those comments to me (the Webmaster). The HTML source for the form of Figure 20-2 looks like this:

```
<html>

<head>
<TITLE>
LNB Software: Feedback
</TITLE>
</head>

<body>

<h2>
<center>
Feedback
</center>
</h2>
```

(continued)

```
<hr>
<form method="post" action="http://www.lnbsoft.com/exec-bin/feedback.pl">

<h3>
Comments:
<br>

<textarea name="comment" rows="10" cols="40">
</textarea>
<br>

E-mail address:
<br>
<input type="text" name="e-mail" size=40 maxlength=60>
<br>

<input value="Send feedback" type=submit>  <input value="Clear all" type=reset>
</h3>
</form>

<hr>
<p>
Back to
<a href="http://www.lnbsoft.com/">Home Page</a>

</body>

</html>
```

As indicated by the `action` attribute of the `<form>` tag, this form's input is handled by a script named `feedback.pl` at my site. My ISP specifies `/exec-bin/` as the script directory, that's why the script's URL is `http://www.lnbsoft.com/exec-bin/feedback.pl`. On most sites with NCSA and Apache Web servers, the scripts reside in the `/cgi-bin/` directory (of course, the `/cgi-bin/` directory name is an alias for another real directory on the system, usually `/usr/local/etc/httpd/cgi-bin/`).

Note that the feedback form (shown in Figure 20-2) has two fields:

✦ The `comment` field is where the user enters comments.

✦ The `e-mail` field allows the user to enter an e-mail address.

The `method` attribute of the `<form>` tag specifies that the Web browser should send the form's data through a `POST` request.

Processing user feedback

The `feedback.pl` CGI program that processes the feedback form has to perform the following tasks:

✦ If the method is not POST, report an error and exit.

✦ Read and parse the form's data.

✦ Save the comment and e-mail fields in a log file with a date and time stamp and any other relevant information (such as the site from where the user sent the feedback).

✦ Send an e-mail message to the Webmaster with the comment and e-mail fields so that the Webmaster can respond back with a reply (provided the user enters an e-mail address in the e-mail field).

✦ Return a "thank you" note to the user in the form of an HTML document.

Here are some points to help you design the CGI program in Perl:

✦ Include the cgi-lib.pl library to parse the CGI input and the ctime.pl library to get the current date and time.

✦ Use the MethPost subroutine from cgi-lib.pl to check if the method is POST.

✦ Call ReadParse to parse the input. Then, open the log file and append the fields in that file. To add a time stamp, get the date and time by calling the ctime subroutine from the ctime.pl library.

✦ To send e-mail, run the sendmail program with a -t option and send a mail header with the addressee, subject, and body of the message to sendmail (see the send_mail subroutine in the following listing).

The following listing shows the complete feedback.pl program that handles input from the form shown in Figure 20-2:

```
#!/usr/local/bin/perl

# File: feedback.pl
# A simple Perl script to save user comments in a log file.
# Expects a POST request. Mails comment to Webmaster.

# Author: Naba Barkakati

require "cgi-lib.pl";
require "ctime.pl";

# A subroutine to send mail message to the Webmaster
#
# Usage: $to   = "Webmaster@site.com";
#        $sub  = "Feedback from web site";
#        $body = "Body of mail message";
#        &send_mail($to, $sub, $body);
```

(continued)

```perl
sub send_mail
{
    local($addressee, $subject, $message) = @_;
    local($sendmail) = "/usr/lib/sendmail";

    open(SENDMAIL, "| $sendmail -t");

    print SENDMAIL "To: ", $addressee, "\n";
    print SENDMAIL "Subject: ", $subject, "\n\n",
    print SENDMAIL $message;

    close(SENDMAIL);
}

$my_home_page =
  "<a href=\"http://$ENV{SERVER_NAME}/\">$ENV{SERVER_NAME}</a>.";


# If the method is not POST, display error message and quit.

if(!&MethPost)
{
&send_mail("naba", "mtest", "Mail test from $ENV{SERVER_NAME}");
    &CgiDie("Form input only",
            "You need to submit data from a form to use this script.",
            "<hr>",
    "Return to <a href=\"http://$ENV{SERVER_NAME}/\">$ENV{SERVER_NAME}</a>.");
}

# If method is POST, process the input

$logfilename = "feedback.log";

$remote_host = $ENV{"REMOTE_HOST"};
$remote_addr = $ENV{"REMOTE_ADDR"};
$date = &ctime(time);
$separator = "-";
$separator x= 65;   # Separator is a line with 65 dashes
$separator .= "\n";

if(&ReadParse(*input))
{
# open the log file
    open(LOGFILE,">>$logfilename");

# Lock the file to guard against another process updating the
# file as this script uses it
    $lock_exclusive = 2;
    $unclock = 8;
    flock(LOGFILE, $lock_exclusive);
```

```
# Append the comments to the log file
    print LOGFILE $date;
    print LOGFILE "From: $remote_host ($remote_addr)\n\n";
    print LOGFILE "E-mail address: ", $input{'e-mail'}, "\n\n";
    print LOGFILE "Comment: ", $input{'comment'}, "\n";
    print LOGFILE $separator;

# Close the log file
    close(LOGFILE);

# Remember to unlock the file
    flock(LOGFILE, $unlock);

# Send mail message to Webmaster at this host (assumes that server
# name is www.<mailhost> — you may want to change the following)
    $host = substr($ENV{SERVER_NAME}, 4);
    $to = "webmaster\@$host";
    $when = substr($date, 0, 10);
    $sub = "Feedback from: $remote_host on $when";
    $body = "$date\nFrom:$remote_host ($remote_addr)\nE-mail:\
            $input{'e-mail'}\n\nComment: $input{'comment'}\n";

    &send_mail($to, $sub, $body);

# Send back a response
    print &PrintHeader;
    print &HtmlTop("Thank you for the feedback");
    print "Thank you for the feedback. Your input will be forwarded \n",
          "to the Webmaster ($to). You should receive a response soon.\n";
}
else
{
    print &PrintHeader;
    print &HtmlTop("Empty form");
    print "You did not fill out anything!\n";
}

# Output a link to return to home page of this site
    print "<hr>\n";
    print "Return to ", $my_home_page;

    print &HtmlBot;
```

When the user submits the comments from the form shown in Figure 20-2, the feedback.pl program appends the comments to the file feedback.log and also mails the comments to the Webmaster. Finally, the feedback.pl program sends a thank-you message to the user, as shown in Figure 20-3.

Figure 20-3: "Thank you" message returned by the `feedback.pl` CGI program.

Summary

Although you can write CGI programs in any programming language, Perl has become the language of choice. Perl's text processing capabilities make it ideal for CGI programming where you need to parse and extract information from a query. This chapter provides a tutorial-style introduction to Perl and shows how to write CGI programs in Perl. The next chapter turns to CGI programming in other popular languages: C, C++, and Tcl.

Where to go next . . .

✦ For a general introduction to CGI programming, read Chapter 19.

✦ If you want to write CGI programs in C, C++, or Tcl, turn to Chapter 21.

✦ If you need to access databases from a CGI program, consult Chapter 22.

✦   ✦   ✦

CGI Programming in Other Languages

Although Perl is the language of choice for CGI programming, you can write CGI programs in any programming language. As long as a programming language allows you to access the environment variables and read the standard input, you can use it to create a program to process CGI queries. Many programming languages such as C, C++, and Tcl (Tool Command Language) have these basic capabilities and can be used to write CGI programs.

This chapter shows how to accomplish basic CGI programming tasks in C, C++, and Tcl. When it comes to CGI programming, these three languages happen to be popular alternatives to Perl.

This chapter assumes that you are already familiar with C and C++.

CGI Programming in C and C++

If you are proficient in C or C++, you can go ahead and use either of these languages to write CGI programs. As you probably know, you can use C syntax (most of it anyway) and call C run-time routines in a C++ program. So, you may not decide to do anything different in a C++ program. However, if you know object-oriented programming, you may decide to create a C++ class that handles CGI queries. The following sections shows you how to handle the common CGI processing chores in C and C++.

Implementing a CGI processing library in C

As you learned in Chapter 20, Perl CGI programmers can use the well-known `cgi-lib.pl` library to handle common chores such as reading and parsing the CGI query. You can use a similar strategy in your C and C++ programs — create a library of C routines that help you with the CGI programming chores.

Cross Ref One good way to create the library of routines is to borrow from the popular `cgi-lib.pl` library that Perl programmers use to parse CGI queries (see Chapter 20 for more information on the `cgi-lib.pl` library). However, C does not have string-handling functions that are as convenient as those in Perl. Therefore, you have to write extra code to parse the query string and manage the storage space needed to store the query string and the fields. In this section, I present the design and implementation of `cgi-lib.c` — a CGI processing library that I implemented in C.

I decided to use the following strategy for the `cgi-lib.c` library of routines (you'll find the listings later in this section):

✦ Read the query string into a character array and parse the fields in place by using the `strtok` function that extracts tokens from a string.

✦ Create a data structure named `Field` that has two pointers: one points to the field's name and the other points to the field's value. For each field, there is a `Field` structure and that structure's name and value pointers point to the appropriate locations in the query string.

✦ Use a `FieldArray` structure to hold the query string, the total number of fields and the array of `Field` structures. The caller is expected to create a `FieldArray` structure and pass that structure's address as an argument to the `ReadParse` function, which parses the query string. Because the parsing process allocates some memory (specifically the array of `Field` structures), the caller must call a `Cleanup` function to release the memory when the field values are no longer needed.

✦ The parsing process first counts the number of ampersands (&) in the query string to determine the total number of fields. Then, I allocate an array of `Field` structures, call `strtok` to separate the fields at the ampersand, and call `strtok` again to separate each field into name and value pairs (by using the equal sign as a separator). After that, both name and value strings are processed to convert plus (+) signs to spaces and all `%xx` string fragments into single characters.

With this basic strategy in mind, I create the following header file, `cgi-lib.h`, that defines the necessary data structures and the function prototypes (a function's prototype specifies how the function is called and what the function returns — the prototype looks like a function declaration without the body):

```
/*----------------------------------------------------------*/
/* File: cgi-lib.h
 *
 * Header file for CGI query processing routines.
 *
 * Author: Naba Barkakati
 */

#ifndef __CGI_LIB_H
#define __CGI_LIB_H

typedef struct Field
{
    char *name;   /* Pointer to the name */
    char *value;  /* Pointer to value    */
}Field;

typedef struct FieldArray
{
    int   count;    /* Number of fields in query */
    Field *fields;  /* Array of Field structures */
    char  *query;   /* The query string          */
} FieldArray;

/* Function prototypes */

int ReadParse(FieldArray *fa);
int ParseQuery(FieldArray *fa);
int MethGet(void);
int MethPost(void);
const char *GetValue(const FieldArray *fa, const char *name);
void PrintVariables(const FieldArray *fa);
void PrintHeader(void);
void HtmlTop(const char *title);
void HtmlBot(void);
void Cleanup(FieldArray *fa);

#endif
```

Then I implemented these functions in a file named cgi-lib.c, as follows:

```
/*----------------------------------------------------------*/
/* File: cgi-lib.c
 *
 * CGI query processing routines in C (patterned after the
 * cgi-lib.pl Perl routines).
 *
 * Author: Naba Barkakati
 */
```

(continued)

```
#include <stdio.h>
#include <stdlib.h>
#include <string.h>
#include <ctype.h>
#include "cgi-lib.h"

static char *FieldSep = "&";
static char *ValueSep = "=";
/*-------------------------------------------------------------*/
/* R e a d P a r s e
 *
 * Read and parse the query string. This is the heart of this
 * library of routines. Define a FieldArray structure and pass
 * a pointer to that structure as the first argument. For example,
 *    FieldArray fa;
 *    ReadParse(&fa);
 * On return, the fa->count is the number of fields in the query and
 * fa->fields[] is the array of fields.
 *
 * Returns nonzero if everything goes well; zero in case of error.
 */

int ReadParse(FieldArray *fa)
{
    if(fa == NULL) return 0;

/* Initialize the FieldArray structure */
    fa->count = 0;
    fa->fields = NULL;
    fa->query = NULL;

    if(MethGet())
    {
/* Method is GET; retrieve query from QUERY_STRING environment
 * variable
 */
        char *p_env = getenv("QUERY_STRING");
        if(p_env == NULL) return 0;

/* Copy the environ variable's value into another string */
        if((fa->query = strdup(p_env)) != NULL)
            return ParseQuery(fa);
        else
        {
            Cleanup(fa);
            return 0;
        }
    }

    if(MethPost())
    {
```

```
/* Method is POST; read query from stdin; read number of bytes
 * specified in CONTENT_LENGTH environment variable.
 */
        char *p_env = getenv("CONTENT_LENGTH");
        int numbytes;
        if(p_env == NULL) return 0;
        numbytes = atoi(p_env);

/* Allocate memory to hold the query */
        fa->query = malloc(numbytes + 1);
        if(fa->query != NULL)
        {
            int n = fread(fa->query, sizeof(char), numbytes, stdin);
            fa->query[n] = '\0';
            return ParseQuery(fa);
        }
        else
        {
            Cleanup(fa);
            return 0;
        }
    }
/* Unknown method */
    return 0;
}
/*----------------------------------------------------------------*/
/* P a r s e Q u e r y
 *
 * Parses a query string "in-place" using strtok and returns
 * results in an FieldArray structure (through an array of
 * pointers). Returns non-zero if all goes well.
 */

int ParseQuery(FieldArray *fa)
{
    int i, nf = 1;
    if(fa->query == NULL) return 0;

/* Count the ampersands in the query to find out number of fields */
    for(i = 0; fa->query[i] != '\0'; i++)
    {
        if(fa->query[i] == '&') nf++;
    }
    fa->count = nf;

/* Allocate that many array of Field structures */
    if((fa->fields = (Field*)calloc(nf, sizeof(Field))) == NULL)
    {
        Cleanup(fa);
        return 0;
    }
```

(continued)

```
/* Split up the fields by looking for the ampersands */
    fa->fields[0].name = strtok(fa->query, FieldSep);

/* Now get the rest of the fields */
    for(i = 1; i < nf; i++)
    {
        fa->fields[i].name = strtok(NULL, FieldSep);
    }

/* Now, split each field into name and value at the = sign */
    for(i = 0; i < nf; i++)
    {
        fa->fields[i].name = strtok(fa->fields[i].name, ValueSep);
        fa->fields[i].value = strtok(NULL, ValueSep);
    }

/* Translate plus signs to spaces and %xx to single characters */
/* First work through the names */
    for(i = 0; i < nf; i++)
    {
        int j;
/* First convert + to space */
        for(j = 0; fa->fields[i].name[j] != '\0'; j++)
        {
            if(fa->fields[i].name[j] == '+')
                fa->fields[i].name[j] = ' ';
        }
/* Next convert each %xx to a single character */
        for(j = 0; fa->fields[i].name[j] != '\0'; j++)
        {
            if(fa->fields[i].name[j] == '%')
            {
                int k;
                fa->fields[i].name[j] =
                    16 * HexNum(fa->fields[i].name[j+1]) +
                        HexNum(fa->fields[i].name[j+2]);
/* Move rest of string two spaces to the left */
                for(k = j+3; fa->fields[i].name[k] != '\0'; k++)
                    fa->fields[i].name[k-2] = fa->fields[i].name[k];
/* Place a null character to mark end of string */
                fa->fields[i].name[k-2] = '\0';
            }
        }
    }

/* Now process the values */
    for(i = 0; i < nf; i++)
    {
        int j;

/* Skip if the field value is NULL */
        if(fa->fields[i].value == NULL) continue;
```

```
/* First convert + to space */
        for(j = 0; fa->fields[i].value[j] != '\0'; j++)
        {
            if(fa->fields[i].value[j] == '+')
                fa->fields[i].value[j] = ' ';
        }
/* Next convert each %xx to a single character */
        for(j = 0; fa->fields[i].value[j] != '\0'; j++)
        {
            if(fa->fields[i].value[j] == '%')
            {
                int k;
                fa->fields[i].value[j] =
                    16 * HexNum(fa->fields[i].value[j+1]) +
                        HexNum(fa->fields[i].value[j+2]);

/* Move rest of string two spaces to the left */
                for(k = j+3; fa->fields[i].value[k] != '\0'; k++)
                    fa->fields[i].value[k-2] = fa->fields[i].value[k];
/* Place a null character to mark end of string */
                fa->fields[i].value[k-2] = '\0';
            }
        }
    }
    return 1;
}
/*------------------------------------------------------------*/
/* C l e a n u p
 * Cleans up all allocated memory in the FieldArray structure fa->
 */

void Cleanup(FieldArray *fa)
{
    if(fa == NULL) return;
    if(fa->query != NULL) free(fa->query);
    if(fa->fields != NULL) free(fa->fields);
}
/*------------------------------------------------------------*/
/* M e t h G e t
 * Returns nonzero if method is GET.
 */

int MethGet(void)
{
    char *p_env = getenv("REQUEST_METHOD");
    if(p_env == NULL) return 0;

    return(strcasecmp(p_env, "get") == 0);
}
/*------------------------------------------------------------*/
```

(continued)

```c
/* M e t h P o s t
 * Returns nonzero if method is POST.
 */

int MethPost(void)
{
    char *p_env = getenv("REQUEST_METHOD");
    if(p_env == NULL) return 0;

    return(strcasecmp(p_env, "post") == 0);
}
/*--------------------------------------------------------------*/
/* G e t V a l u e
 *
 * Return the value of a field (specified by name), if found.
 * Else, return NULL.
 */

const char *GetValue(const FieldArray *fa, const char *name)
{
    int i;
    for(i = 0; i < fa->count; i++)
    {
        if(strcmp(name, fa->fields[i].name) == 0)
            return fa->fields[i].value;
    }
    return NULL;
}
/*--------------------------------------------------------------*/
/* P r i n t V a r i a b l e s
 *
 * Prints the name and value of the fields (like the subroutine
 * with the same name in cgi-lib.pl Perl library).
 */

void PrintVariables(const FieldArray *fa)
{
    int i;
    printf("<dl>\n");
    for(i = 0; i < fa->count; i++)
    {
        printf("<dt>%s</dt>\n", fa->fields[i].name);
        printf("<dd>%s</dd>\n", fa->fields[i].value);
    }
    printf("</dl>\n");
}
/*--------------------------------------------------------------*/
/* P r i n t H e a d e r
 *
 * Print the MIME header
 */
void PrintHeader(void)
{
    printf("Content-type: text/html\n\n");
```

```
}
/*-----------------------------------------------------------*/
/* H t m l T o p
 *
 * Print the top part of the HTML document
 */
void HtmlTop(const char *title)
{
    printf("<html>\n<head>\n<title>%s</title></head>\n", title);
    printf("<body>\n<h1>%s</h1>\n", title);
}
/*-----------------------------------------------------------*/
/* H t m l B o t
 *
 * Print the bottom part of the HTML document
 */
void HtmlBot(void)
{
    printf("</body>\n</html>\n");
}
/*------------------------------------------------------------*/
/* H e x N u m
 *
 * Returns the decimal value corresponding to a hexadecimal
 * digit.
 */

int HexNum(int c)
{
    if(isdigit(c))
    {
        return c - '0';
    }
    else
    {
        int cl = toupper(c);
        return cl - 'A' + 10;
    }
}
```

You can understand the parsing logic by studying the code in this listing. However, you can use the routines even if you do not fully understand how the query string is parsed. The next section shows a sample program that uses the cgi-lib.c library.

Using the C CGI parsing library

A simple C program together with an HTML form can show you how to use the cgi-lib.c routines. The C program will serve as the CGI program that processes the user's input from a form. Here is the listing of the C program, which I call, test-ccgi.c:

```
#include <stdio.h>
#include "cgi-lib.h"

void main(void)
{
    FieldArray fa;

/* Parse the query and display the fields */
    if(ReadParse(&fa))
    {
        int i;
        PrintHeader();
        HtmlTop("Testing C CGI library");
        printf("<h2>%d fields</h2>", fa.count);
        PrintVariables(&fa);
    }

/* Now clean up everything */
    Cleanup(&fa);
}
```

This program parses the CGI query (by calling ReadParse) and then displays the values of all fields in the query. Before exiting, the program calls Cleanup to free any memory allocated during parsing. These are the general steps of any CGI program that uses the cgi-lib.c library.

Note   The test-ccgi.c example program simply prints the values of the fields of a form. However, in a real CGI program, you'll do some more processing with that input (what you do depends on the form). In particular, you'll get the value of specific fields and use them in the CGI program. For example, if the HTML form solicits comments from the user, you may retrieve and store the comments in a log file and return an acknowledgment.

Tip   Use the GetValue function in the cgi-lib.c library to retrieve the value of a field.

To compile and link the test-ccgi program, you can use the following simple Makefile:

```
all: test-ccgi

test-ccgi: test-ccgi.c cgi-lib.c cgi-lib.h
        cc -o test-ccgi test-ccgi.c cgi-lib.c
```

To see the test-ccgi program in action:

1. Build the test-ccgi program using the Makefile shown.

2. Place the program in the /cgi-bin/ directory on your Web server.

3. Create an HTML form and specify `/cgi-bin/test-ccgi` as the `action` attribute in the `<form>` tag.

4. Load the HTML form in a Web browser and submit the form's data.

Figure 21-1 shows a sample HTML form for which I specified `test-ccgi` as the CGI program.

URL

To access and try out this form and browse the source code online, use the following URL:

```
http://www.lnbsoft.com/webprog.html
```

After filling in the form, if you submit the form's data, the `test-ccgi` program should display the values for all the fields in the form. Figure 21-2 shows the output from the `test-ccgi` program after I submitted the data from the form shown in Figure 21-1.

Note that multiple selections are reported as separate instances of a field with the same name. In this example, the two selected books are reported as two instances of the `books` field.

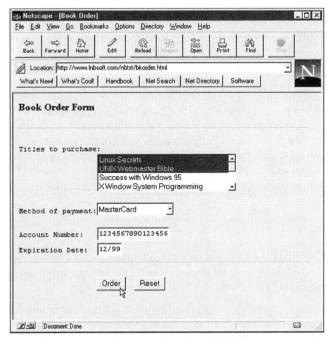

Figure 21-1: A sample HTML form for which the `test-ccgi` program is designated as the action.

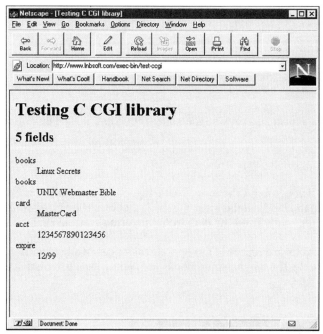

Figure 21-2: Result of submitting the data from the form shown in Figure 21-1.

Implementing a `CgiQuery` **class in C++**

You can certainly use the `cgi-lib.c` library of the preceding section in a C++ program, but it's easier to manage the CGI processing if you make use of object-oriented programming techniques that C++ supports. In particular, you can use C++'s `class` construct to define a `CgiQuery` data type that reads and parses the CGI query string. You can include member functions in the `CgiQuery` class to access the fields of the form. In this section, I show you the design and implementation of the `CgiQuery` class.

My approach to designing the `CgiQuery` class is as follows:

✦ The `CgiQuery` class holds the query string as well as the results of parsing the query: the total count of fields and an array of `Field` structures where each `Field` structure contains pointers to the field's name and value.

✦ The constructor of the `CgiQuery` class gets the query string and parses it. That means you can create an instance of the `CgiQuery` class and immediately begin accessing the fields.

✦ The destructor of the `CgiQuery` class frees all memory allocated during parsing. Because the C++ compiler automatically calls the destructor at an appropriate time, there is no need for an explicit cleanup step (which was necessary in the `cgi-lib.c` library).

✦ Use the code from `cgi-lib.c` library to parse the query string in the `CgiQuery` class.

✦ A status variable in the `CgiQuery` class indicates whether the contents of the class are valid. A nonzero status variable means CGI parsing was successful.

The following listing shows the specification of the `CgiQuery` class:

```
//--------------------------------------------------------------------
// File: cgiquery.h
//
// Defines the CgiQuery class that loads a CGI query string and
// makes it all ready for use by programs.
//
// Author: Naba Barkakati
//--------------------------------------------------------------------

#if !defined(__CGIQUERY_H)
#define __CGIQUERY_H

#include <ctype.h>
#include <iostream.h>

struct Field
{
    char *name;   /* Pointer to the name */
    char *value;  /* Pointer to value    */
    Field() : name(NULL), value(NULL) {}
};

class CgiQuery
{
public:
    CgiQuery();
    ~CgiQuery();

    int MethGet(void);
    int MethPost(void);
    const char *GetValue(const char *name);
    int Status(void) { return status;}
    int Count(void) { return count; }
    void PrintVariables(void);

private:
    char  *query;  /* The query string              */
```

(continued)

```
    int    count;   /* Number of fields in query  */
    Field *fields; /* Array of Field structures  */
    int    status;  /* Non-zero if CgiQuery if OK */

    void ParseQuery(void);
};

inline void PrintHeader(void)
{
    cout << "Content-type: text/html\n\n";
}

inline void HtmlTop(const char *title)
{
    cout << "<html>\n<head>\n<title>"
         << title << "</title></head>\n";
    cout <<"<body>\n<h1>" << title << "</h1>\n";
}

inline void HtmlBot(void)
{
    cout << "</body>\n</html>\n";
}

inline void CgiError(const char *title, const char *body)
{
    PrintHeader();
    HtmlTop(title);
    cout << body << endl;
    HtmlBot();
}

inline int HexNum(int c)
{
    if(isdigit(c))
    {
        return c - '0';
    }
    else
    {
        int cl = toupper(c);
        return cl - 'A' + 10;
    }
}

#endif
```

The cgiquery.h header file also includes a number of inline functions that are useful in CGI programming.

The following listing shows my version of the implementation, which I store in a file named cgiquery.cc:

```
//-------------------------------------------------------------
// File: cgiquery.cc
//
// Implementation of the CgiQuery class
//
// Author: Naba Barkakati
//-------------------------------------------------------------
#include <stdio.h>
#include <stdlib.h>
#include <string.h>
#include "cgiquery.h"

static char *FieldSep = "&";
static char *ValueSep = "=";
//-------------------------------------------------------------
// CgiQuery::  C g i Q u e r y
//
// Constructor for the CgiQuery class (reads and parses the
// query string). Works for both GET and POST queries.

CgiQuery::CgiQuery() : fields(NULL), count(0), query(NULL),
                       status(0)
{
    if(MethGet())
    {
// Method is GET; retrieve query from QUERY_STRING environment
// variable
        char *p_env = getenv("QUERY_STRING");
        if(p_env == NULL) return;

// Copy the environment variable's value into another string
        if((query = strdup(p_env)) != NULL)
            ParseQuery();
    }

    if(MethPost())
    {
/* Method is POST; read query from stdin; read number of bytes
 * specified in CONTENT_LENGTH environment variable.
 */
        char *p_env = getenv("CONTENT_LENGTH");
        if(p_env == NULL) return;
        int numbytes = atoi(p_env);

/* Allocate memory to hold the query */
        query = new char[numbytes + 1];
        if(query != NULL)
        {
```

(continued)

```
                int n = fread(query, sizeof(char), numbytes, stdin);
                query[n] = '\0';
                ParseQuery();
            }
        }
}
//--------------------------------------------------------------_
// CgiQuery:: ~ C g i Q u e r y
//
// Destructor for the CgiQuery class (frees up any memory
// allocated by this class).

CgiQuery::~CgiQuery()
{
    if(fields != NULL) delete fields;
    if(query != NULL) delete query;
}
//--------------------------------------------------------------_
// CgiQuery:: P a r s e Q u e r y
//
// Private member function that actually parses the query string
// and creates the fields array.

void CgiQuery::ParseQuery(void)
{
    int i, nf = 1;
    if(query == NULL) return;

/* Count the ampersands in the query to find out number of fields */
    for(i = 0; query[i] != '\0'; i++)
    {
        if(query[i] == '&') nf++;
    }
    count = nf;

/* Allocate that many array of Field structures */
    if((fields = new Field[nf]) == NULL) return;

/* Split up the fields by looking for the ampersands */
    fields[0].name = strtok(query, FieldSep);

/* Now get the rest of the fields */
    for(i = 1; i < nf; i++)
    {
        fields[i].name = strtok(NULL, FieldSep);
    }

/* Now, split each field into name and value at the = sign */
    for(i = 0; i < nf; i++)
    {
        fields[i].name = strtok(fields[i].name, ValueSep);
        fields[i].value = strtok(NULL, ValueSep);
    }
```

```
/* Translate plus signs to spaces and %xx to single characters */
/* First work through the names */
    for(i = 0; i < nf; i++)
    {
        int j;
/* First convert + to space */
        for(j = 0; fields[i].name[j] != '\0'; j++)
        {
            if(fields[i].name[j] == '+')
                fields[i].name[j] = ' ';
        }
/* Next convert each %xx to a single character */
        for(j = 0; fields[i].name[j] != '\0'; j++)
        {
            if(fields[i].name[j] == '%')
            {
                int k;
                fields[i].name[j] =
                    16 * HexNum(fields[i].name[j+1]) +
                        HexNum(fields[i].name[j+2]);
/* Move rest of string two spaces to the left */
                for(k = j+3; fields[i].name[k] != '\0'; k++)
                    fields[i].name[k-2] = fields[i].name[k];
/* Place a null character to mark end of string */
                fields[i].name[k-2] = '\0';
            }
        }
    }

/* Now process the values */
    for(i = 0; i < nf; i++)
    {
        int j;

/* Skip if the field value is NULL */
        if(fields[i].value == NULL) continue;

/* First convert + to space */
        for(j = 0; fields[i].value[j] != '\0'; j++)
        {
            if(fields[i].value[j] == '+')
                fields[i].value[j] = ' ';
        }
/* Next convert each %xx to a single character */
        for(j = 0; fields[i].value[j] != '\0'; j++)
        {
            if(fields[i].value[j] == '%')
            {
                int k;
                fields[i].value[j] =
                    16 * HexNum(fields[i].value[j+1]) +
                        HexNum(fields[i].value[j+2]);
```

(continued)

```
               /* Move rest of string two spaces to the left */
                          for(k = j+3; fields[i].value[k] != '\0'; k++)
                              fields[i].value[k-2] = fields[i].value[k];
               /* Place a null character to mark end of string */
                          fields[i].value[k-2] = '\0';
                      }
                  }
           }

       status = 1;
   }
   //-------------------------------------------------------------
   // CgiQuery:: G e t V a l u e
   //
   // Returns the value of a field; returns NULL if the field is
   // not found or if there were problems parsing the query

   const char *CgiQuery::GetValue(const char *name)
   {
       if(!status) return NULL;

       int i;
       for(i = 0; count; i++)
       {
           if(strcmp(name, fields[i].name) == 0)
               return fields[i].value;
       }
       return NULL;
   }
   //-------------------------------------------------------------
   // CgiQuery:: M e t h G e t
   // Returns nonzero if method is GET.

   int CgiQuery::MethGet(void)
   {
       char *p_env = getenv("REQUEST_METHOD");
       if(p_env == NULL) return 0;

       return(strcasecmp(p_env, "get") == 0);
   }
   //-------------------------------------------------------------
   // CgiQuery:: M e t h P o s t
   // Returns nonzero if method is POST.

   int CgiQuery::MethPost(void)
   {
       char *p_env = getenv("REQUEST_METHOD");
       if(p_env == NULL) return 0;

       return(strcasecmp(p_env, "post") == 0);
   }
   //-------------------------------------------------------------
```

```
// CgiQuery:: P r i n t V a r i a b l e s
//
// Prints the name and value of the fields (like the subroutine
// with the same name in cgi-lib.pl Perl library).

void CgiQuery::PrintVariables(void)
{
    cout << "<dl>\n";

    int i;
    for(i = 0; i < count; i++)
    {
        cout << "<dt>" << fields[i].name << "</dt>\n";
        cout << "<dd>" << fields[i].value << "</dd>\n";
    }
    cout << "</dl>\n";
}
```

If you know C++, you'll find the implementation of the CgiQuery class straightforward. The CgiQuery constructor reads the query string and parses the string by calling a private member function named ParseQuery. The ParseQuery function borrows heavily from the function with the same name in the C library (cgi-lib.c).

Using the C++ CgiQuery class

To learn how to use the CgiQuery class, you need to go through a simple example. The following test program, named trycppcgi.cc, is designed to be a general-purpose CGI program that simply prints all fields in a query string:

```
//-------------------------------------------------------------
// File: trycppcgi.cc
// Test the C++ CGI class (CgiQuery)

#include "cgiquery.h"

void main(void)
{
    CgiQuery cq;

    if(cq.Status())
    {
        PrintHeader();
        HtmlTop("Testing C++ CGI library");
        cout << "<h2>" << cq.Count() << " Fields</h2>" << endl;
        cq.PrintVariables();
    }
    else
    {
        CgiError("Error in CGI Program",
                 "Could not parse query!");
    }
}
```

As this program shows, to read and parse a CGI query all you need to do is create a `CgiQuery` object. After that, you can begin accessing the fields with the `GetValue` function. For example, if your form has a field named `keyword`, you can get the value of `keyword` with the following code:

```
CgiQuery cq;
if(cq.Status())
{
// Get the value of the "keyword" field
    const char *kw = cq.GetValue("keyword");
//...
}
```

The `trycppcgi.cc` program just prints all fields in the query string. Thus, you can use this program with any HTML form (provided all you want to do is see the fields).

To compile and link the `trycppcgi` program, use the following Makefile:

```
all: trycppcgi

trycppcgi: trycppcgi.cc cgiquery.cc cgiquery.h
        g++ -o trycppcgi trycppcgi.cc cgiquery.cc
```

After you build the program, place it in the directory where your system's CGI programs are located.

To see the `trycppcgi` program in action, specify it in the `action` attribute of the `<form>` attribute. For example, here's a simple ice cream order form:

```
<head>
<title>Ice cream order</title>
</head>
<body>
<form action="/exec-bin/trycppcgi" method=post>
<h3> May we take your order, please.</h3>

<pre>
Flavor:  <input type=radio checked name=flavor value="Vanilla"> Vanilla
         <input type=radio name=flavor value="Chocolate"> Chocolate
         <input type=radio name=flavor value="Strawberry"> Strawberry

Topping: <input type=checkbox checked name=topping value="Hot Fudge"> Hot Fudge
         <input type=checkbox name=topping value="Sprinkles"> Sprinkles
         <input type=checkbox name=topping value="Chocolate Chips"> Chocolate
    Chips
</pre>
<hr>
<input type=submit value="Order">
<input type=reset>

</form>
</body>
```

Figure 21-3 shows this HTML form with some user selections.

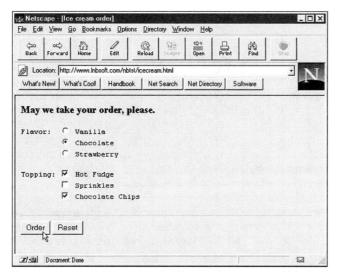

Figure 21-3: An ice cream order form to be processed by the C++ `CgiQuery` class.

After the form's data is submitted to the server, the `trycppcgi` program processes the query and displays the values of all fields, as shown in Figure 21-4.

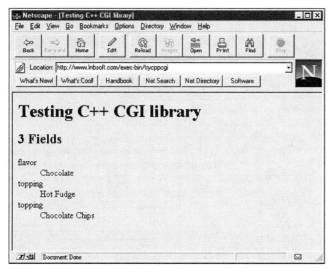

Figure 21-4: The output from the `trycppcgi` program after processing the data from the form shown in Figure 21-3.

Tip   You can view the source code for the `CgiQuery` class and try out the test program at the following URL:

```
http://www.lnbsoft.com/webprog.html
```

Writing CGI Programs in Tcl

Although Perl is very popular as a scripting language (especially for CGI programming), Tcl is another capable scripting language that you can use to write CGI programs. Tcl stands for Tool Command Language and is pronounced "tickle." The creator of Tcl, John Ousterhout, intended Tcl to be a simple scripting language with an interpreter that could be linked with any C program so that the C program could use Tcl scripts. The term *embeddable* refers to this property of Tcl: the capability of any C program to use the Tcl interpreter and run Tcl scripts.

Just like Perl, Tcl includes all the facilities you need to write CGI programs. You can easily access environment variables, read the standard input, manipulate strings, and print to the standard output. As you'll see in the next two sections, Tcl is a capable language for writing CGI programs.

A simple CGI program in Tcl

One of the simple CGI programs is to display the CGI environment variables in an HTML page. (By CGI environment variables, I mean the environment variables that are used by the Web server to communicate with a CGI program.) You can perform this chore easily in Tcl.

More on Tcl

There just is not enough room in this chapter to list all the information that you need to fully exploit the power of Tcl (and its popular companion, X toolkit, called Tk). Because of Tcl/Tk's popularity, you can find quite a few resources about it, ranging from books to FTP sites.

Two prominent books on Tcl and Tk are available. The first book is *Tcl and the Tk Toolkit* (Addison-Wesley, 1994), by John K. Ousterhout, the originator of Tcl and Tk. John's book provides a broad overview of Tcl and Tk, including an explanation of the way that Tcl

command strings are parsed. The other book is *Practical Programming in Tcl and Tk* (Prentice Hall, 1995), by Brent B. Welch. This book provides more Tcl and Tk examples.

Tcl and Tk are freely available for unrestricted use, including commercial use. At this writing, the Tcl version is 7.5; Tk is 4.1. To learn more about Tcl/Tk development and to download the latest versions of the software, visit the URL `http://www.sunlabs.com/research/tcl/`.

Just to make the output interesting, I decided to prepare a Tcl script that presents the environment variables in a tabular format. Here is the Tcl script that does the job:

```
#!/usr/local/bin/tclsh
# File: showenv.tcl
# Print out the environment variables
# Author: Naba Barkakati

# Array of environment variables
set envvars { SERVER_SOFTWARE SERVER_NAME GATEWAY_INTERFACE SERVER_PROTOCOL \
              SERVER_PORT REQUEST_METHOD PATH_INFO PATH_TRANSLATED \
              SCRIPT_NAME QUERY_STRING REMOTE_HOST REMOTE_ADDR REMOTE_USER \
              AUTH_TYPE CONTENT_TYPE CONTENT_LENGTH HTTP_ACCEPT \
              HTTP_USER_AGENT HTTP_REFERER }

# Print a MIME header. Because puts always prints a newline, we need only
# one more newline character (\n) to mark the end of the MIME header
puts "Content-type: text/html\n"

# Print HTML tags
puts "<html>"
puts "<head>"
puts "<title>Environment variables</title>"
puts "</head>"

puts "<body>"
# Display the environment variables as a table

puts "<table border>"
puts "<caption>List of environment variables</caption>"
puts "<tr><th>Variable</th><th>Value</th></tr>"

foreach var $envvars {
    if {[info exists env($var)]} {
        puts "<tr>"
        puts "<td><strong>$var</strong></td>"
        puts "<td>$env($var)</td>"
        puts "</tr>"
    }
}
puts "</table>"
puts "</body>"
puts "</html>"
```

Tip   Remember to edit the first line of the Tcl script to reflect the exact location of the `tclsh` program on your system. On most systems, `tclsh` is in the `/usr/local/bin` directory, but it could be in some other arbitrary location such as `/usr/contrib/bin`.

To test the sample Tcl script, place the script in the location where your server expects CGI programs. Then, use a Web browser to invoke the script by providing its URL. For example, on my server I use the following URL:

```
http://www.lnbsoft.com/exec-bin/showenv.tcl
```

Figure 21-5 shows the result of running the script on my server.

Notice the complete URL shown in the Location line of the Netscape browser in Figure 21-5. As the URL shows, you can submit a query to the script by appending the query to the URL — a question mark separates the URL proper from the query string. That query string is reported as the value of the QUERY_STRING environment variable.

A CGI processing library in Tcl

As Chapter 20 describes, Perl programmers often use the cgi-lib.pl library to read and parse the CGI query sent by the Web server. I could not find a similar CGI processing library in Tcl, so I wrote cgi-lib.tcl — a set of Tcl procedures for CGI programming. As the similarity of the names suggests, I patterned cgi-lib.tcl after the Perl library, cgi-lib.pl. However, I have not tried to reproduce everything that the Perl library offers.

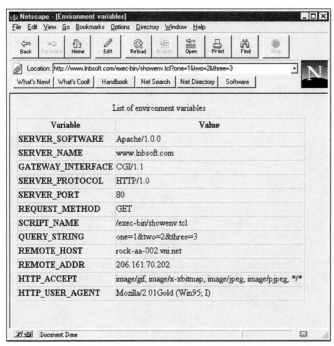

Figure 21-5: The list of environment variables displayed by the showenv.tcl program.

URL

The following listing shows `cgi-lib.tcl` (which is also available on the Net at `http://www.lnbsoft.com/code/tcl/`):

```tcl
###########################################################################
# File: cgi-lib.tcl
#
# Tcl procedures for CGI programming (patterned after the Perl
# cgi-lib.pl subroutines)
#
# Author: Naba Barkakati
###########################################################################

proc ReadParse { input } {
    global env
    upvar $input FIELDS

    set method $env(REQUEST_METHOD)

# Retrieve the query string
    if { [string compare $method "GET"] == 0} {
        set query $env(QUERY_STRING)
    } elseif { [string compare $method "POST"] == 0} {
        set query [read stdin $env(CONTENT_LENGTH)]
    } else {
        CGIError {Unknown Method!} {Method must be GET or POST}
    }

# Split the name and value pairs at the ampersands
    set name_value_pairs [split $query &]

# Split each name-value pair into name and value
    foreach name_value $name_value_pairs {
        set name_and_value [split $name_value =]
        set name [lindex $name_and_value 0]
        set value [lindex $name_and_value 1]

# Replace + signs with space
        regsub -all {\+} $value { } value

# Convert occurrences of %xx into single ASCII characters
        while {[regexp {%[0-9A-Fa-f][0-9A-Fa-f]} $value found]} {
            scan $found "%%%x" decimal
            set ASCIIchar [format "%c" $decimal]
            regsub -all $found $value $ASCIIchar value
        }

# Store the field name and value in the FIELDS array
        if {[info exists FIELDS($name)]} {
            append FIELDS($name) "|" $value
        } else {
```

(continued)

```
            set FIELDS($name) $value
        }
    }
}

proc PrintHeader {} {
    puts "Content-type: text/html\n"
}

proc HtmlTop { title } {
    puts "<html>"
    puts "<head>"
    puts "<title>$title</title>"
    puts "</head>"
    puts "<body>"
    puts "<h1>$title</h1>"
}

proc HtmlBot {} {
    puts "</body>"
    puts "</html>"
}

proc CGIError { title message } {
    PrintHeader $title
    HtmlTop $title
    puts $message
    HtmlBot
}

proc PrintVariables { input } {
    upvar $input FIELDS

# Print all fields
    puts "<dl compact>";
    foreach index [array names FIELDS] {
        puts "<dt><b>$index</b></dt>"
        set value $FIELDS($index)
        puts "<dd>"

# Print the values (multiple values are separated by "|")
        foreach item [split $value "|"] {
            puts "$item<br>"
        }
        puts "</dd>"
    }
    puts "</dl>"
}
```

As you study the listing, you should note the following interesting points about cgi-lib.tcl:

✦ This script does not begin with a line that runs tclsh because you have to use this script in other Tcl scripts with the following command:

```
source "cgi-lib.tcl"
```

✦ The CGI query is parsed by the ReadParse procedure. That procedure uses the split command to separate the name-value pairs that constitute the fields of a form.

✦ The regsub command replaces all plus signs with spaces.

✦ The regexp command is used to find occurrences of %xx strings. The format command converts each %xx string to an ASCII character and another regsub command replaces each %xx string with the equivalent ASCII character.

✦ The parsed field names and values are stored in an array that you provide as an argument to the ReadParse procedure.

To show how to use the cgi-lib.tcl procedures, I'll write another Tcl script that displays all fields in a CGI query. The following listing shows the testcgi.tcl script that performs this task of echoing the field names and values:

```
#!/usr/contrib/bin/tclsh
# File: testcgi.tcl
# A sample CGI program that uses cgi-lib.tcl
#
# (Edit the first line to reflect where tclsh is installed on
# your system)
#############################################################

# Use the cgi-lib.tcl procedures
source "cgi-lib.tcl"

# Read and parse the form data
ReadParse myform

# Print all fields of the form
PrintHeader
HtmlTop "Testing cgi-lib.tcl"
puts "<hr>"
puts "List of fields in the form:"
PrintVariables myform
HtmlBot
```

This script starts with a line that runs the tclsh — the Tcl shell. You may need to edit this line to reflect the location of tclsh on your system (on most systems the full pathname is /usr/local/bin/tclsh).

A source command brings in the `cgi-lib.tcl` procedures. Then, I use the `ReadParse` procedure to read and parse the query and get the results back in an array named `myform`.

To test the `testcgi.tcl` script, create an HTML form and specify `testcgi.tcl` as the `action` attribute of the `<form>` tag. Figure 21-6 shows a filled-in form that's to be processed by `testcgi.tcl`.

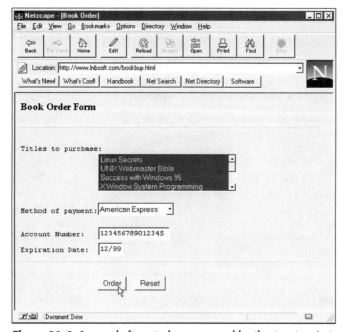

Figure 21-6: A sample form to be processed by the `testcgi.tcl` program.

URL

You can view this form (as well as the Tcl scripts) at the URL `http://www.lnbsoft.com/code/tcl/`.

After I submit the form in Figure 21-6, the `testcgi.tcl` script displays the form's fields in an HTML document, as shown in Figure 21-7.

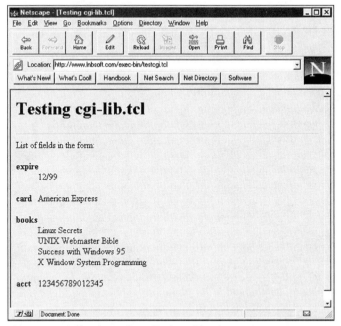

Figure 21-7: The form data displayed by the `testcgi.tcl` program.

Summary

Although Perl is the most popular language for CGI programming, you can write CGI programs equally well in other languages such as C, C++, or Tcl. All of these languages remain popular alternatives to Perl. Therefore, this chapter describes how to write CGI programs in C, C++, and Tcl. Because Tcl may be new to you, this chapter also provides an introduction to Tcl, which is another freely available scripting language. In the next chapter, you'll learn how to access databases from CGI programs.

Where to go next . . .

✦ For a general introduction to CGI programming, read Chapter 19.

✦ To learn about CGI programming in Perl, turn to Chapter 20.

✦ For information on how to access databases from a CGI program, consult Chapter 22.

✦   ✦   ✦

Providing Access to Databases through the Web

I n the previous three chapters, you have seen the details of CGI programming in Perl, Tcl, C, and C++. The examples have been simple CGI programs that save the user's input in a file and return an acknowledgment in an HTML document. This chapter introduces another valuable use of CGI programming — as a gateway to information stored in various corporate databases.

Typically, businesses store information in industry-standard *relational database management systems* (RDBMS). In a client/server architecture, users access the data through client applications that usually run on a PC. Programmers use Structured Query Language (SQL) to retrieve data from the RDBMS. A new trend is to use *middleware* — software that acts as an intermediary between the application program and the RDBMS — to access many different databases in a uniform manner. Microsoft's Open Database Connectivity (ODBC) is an example of such middleware. It is used for database programming on Windows 95 and Windows NT.

Until the Web became popular, database applications tended to be custom designed for a specific platform, even for a specific database. Now that the Web browser is becoming the standard client application for information access, the trend is to use the Web server as the gateway to corporate relational databases. A benefit of this approach is that you no longer need to write custom client applications for database access; instead you write CGI programs that access the RDBMS and return results in an HTML document.

This chapter shows you how to write CGI programs in Perl and C to access relational databases. It also describes mSQL (or MiniSQL) — a low-cost SQL database developed by David Hughes — which you can use as a database for your Web server.

You'll learn how to write C++ CGI programs to access and use an mSQL database, where you might store information such as a product catalog, customer information, or registration information for a conference.

Relational Databases

To develop CGI programs that access relational databases, you need to understand how information is organized in and retrieved from such databases. As you will see in the following sections, relational databases store information in tabular format, and SQL is used as the standard way to access and manipulate the information. A database CGI application may use embedded SQL to access the database, or it may interact with an SQL interpreter by sending SQL commands.

Relational database model

A relational database organizes information into multiple tables. The columns in the table represent attributes or fields (such as name, identification number, and salary in an employee database) that apply to the rows. Each row in the table is a database record (for instance, the record of a specific employee in an employee database). Each record has a fixed set of fields. Figure 22-1 shows how employee information might be organized in a number of tables — note that the employee ID ties the two tables together.

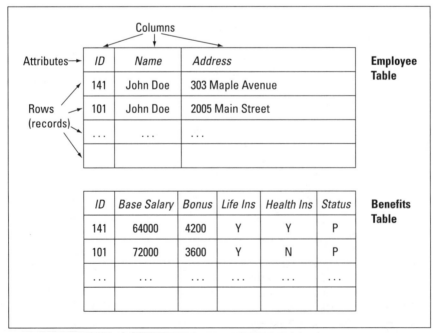

Figure 22-1: Tabular data organization in a relational database.

More on relational databases

To learn more about the relational model and relational databases, consult the following classic references:

✦ E.F. Codd, *The Relational Model for Database Management: Version 2* (Addison-Wesley, 1990).

✦ C.J. Date, *Relational Database Selected Writings* (Addison-Wesley, 1986).

✦ C.J. Date, *An Introduction to Database Systems, Sixth Edition* (Addison-Wesley, 1995).

When you work with a relational database, you work with tables. The database structure — the collection of tables and the fields in each table — is known as the *schema*.

The relational model was developed by E.F. Codd in 1969. Informally, you can think of each relation as a table of values. However, more formally, the relational model lets you view data at several different levels:

✦ *External* level is the user's view of the data.

✦ *Conceptual* level models the data as a collection of entities and relationships between entities (through entity-relationship diagrams).

✦ *Logical* level is the database schema — a collection of relational tables and the attributes of each table.

✦ *Physical* level refers to the actual storage of data (for example, UNIX files, raw disk partitions, or B-trees).

SQL lets you access the data at the *logical* level. Thus, SQL-based applications do not need to be changed when the physical implementation of the database is changed.

Introduction to SQL

SQL originated from the relational data model, which is based on organizing data into tables. SQL is now a widely accepted industry standard for defining, manipulating, and managing tables. Even databases that do not use the relational data model support SQL. SQL was adopted as an industry standard in 1986 and was revised in 1992. Another revision, called SQL3, is now in progress. SQL3 will support objects (a higher level abstraction of data than relational tables).

SQL is not a programming language. It lacks flow control (such as the `if-else` statements in C). Essentially, SQL provides operators for manipulating tables. For example, the SQL `SELECT` statement queries tables with the following general syntax:

```
SELECT attributes
FROM table1, table2, ...
WHERE condition
```

Here `attributes` refers to the columns you want to retrieve from the tables (identified by the names `table1, table2, ...`). The `FROM` clause identifies the tables with the specified columns, and the `WHERE` clause specifies the rows you want to see. The `SELECT` query returns the rows for which the `condition` is true. A typical query from a database (with two tables named `employees` and `benefits`) might be as follows:

```
SELECT employees.name, benefits.base_salary
FROM employees, benefits
WHERE employees.id = benefits.id
and benefits.base_salary > 65000
```

The `SELECT` statement can have many other clauses such as `GROUP BY` and `ORDER BY` clauses.

In addition to `SELECT`, there are many other SQL statements available for a wide variety of database operations, from creating a new table to inserting rows of information into tables. You will see examples of some common SQL statements in the remainder of this chapter.

SQL references

The following standards apply to Structured Query Language (SQL):

✦ *Database Language – SQL with Integrity Enhancement*, American National Standards Institute (ANSI), 1989 ANSI X3.135-1989.

✦ *X/Open and SQL Access Group (SAG) SQL Common Applications Environment (CAE) specification* (1992).

✦ *Database Language – SQL: ANSI X3H2 and ISO/IEC JTC1/SC21/WG3 9075:1992* (SQL-92). This is the latest SQL standard (known as *SQL-92* or *SQL2*).

Work continues on SQL3, but at this writing the SQL3 standard is far from complete. In addition to these standards and the SQL guides that accompany most databases, there are many books that describe SQL, including the following classic reference on SQL:

✦ C.J. Date and Hugh Darwen, *A Guide to The SQL Standard,* Third Edition (Addison-Wesley, 1993).

1989 SQL Standard (SQL1)

SQL was first standardized by the American National Standards Institute (ANSI) in 1986. In the first ANSI standard, SQL was defined as a query language independent of any programming language. In the 1989 revision of the ANSI stadard for SQL, three programming interfaces were defined:

✦ *Module language* allows the definition of procedures in compiled programs (modules). These procedures are then called from programs written in traditional programming languages.

✦ *Embedded SQL* allows SQL statements to be placed directly inside a program written in a standard programming language. The 1989 SQL standard defines embedded statements for COBOL, FORTRAN, Pascal, and PL/1.

✦ *Direct invocation* provides access that is implementation-dependent.

Embedded SQL has been the most popular programming interface for applications that need to access databases with SQL. The 1989 SQL standard supported the embedding of static SQL statements; the 1992 SQL standard allows embedding of dynamic SQL statements. These are briefly described in the following sections.

1992 SQL Standard (SQL2)

The 1992 SQL standard (SQL-92 or SQL2 for short) is the most recent ANSI standard for SQL. SQL2 is now an international standard adopted by the International Organization for Standardization (ISO). SQL2 defines three levels of functionality:

✦ Entry

✦ Intermediate

✦ Full

SQL2 added many new features to the 1989 SQL standard, including the following:

✦ Additional data types such as date and time

✦ The notion of a connection to a database environment to address the needs of client-server architectures

✦ Support for dynamic SQL so that applications can generate and execute SQL statements at run time

✦ Scrollable cursors (that keep track of records) for access to result sets (available only in full level of functionality)

✦ Outer joins that allow you to combine rows from two tables, regardless of whether there is a matching row between the tables (available only in intermediate and full levels of functionality)

Embedded SQL

Databases supporting SQL offer an interactive mode in which the user can use SQL statements to access the data. An SQL interpreter accepts SQL commands and performs the requested tasks.

Applications, however, need another way to send SQL statements to the RDBMS. Embedded SQL allows you to place SQL statements into a program written in a standard programming language such as COBOL, Pascal, or FORTRAN. (You can have embedded SQL statements in C and C++ as well, but these were not part of the SQL standard.) The SQL standard refers to the programming language used to write the application as the *host language*.

The embedded SQL approach is to use specific starting and ending statements of the host language to delimit SQL statements placed in an application's source code. Source files with embedded SQL statements are compiled in a two-step process:

1. A precompiler translates the SQL statements into the equivalent host- language source code.

2. The host-language compiler compiles the resulting source code.

Static SQL

The ANSI 1989 SQL standard allowed the embedding of static SQL statements only. Embedding static SQL statements is done as follows:

✦ Define each SQL statement as well as the number of result columns and their data types within the program source code.

✦ Host variables (fully defined prior to compilation) are accessible to both the host-language code and to SQL statements. However, host variables cannot be used for table names or column names.

✦ For SQL statements that are expected to return more than one row of data, define a cursor that points to one row of result at a time.

✦ Declare standard data-storage areas for status and error information.

Static SQL requires definition of all SQL statements before the application runs. This approach is efficient because all SQL statements can be precompiled prior to execution and run multiple times without recompiling. However, static SQL has the following drawbacks:

✦ Because the table names and column names are fixed, the application becomes bound to a particular RDBMS when it is compiled.

✦ The application cannot create queries on-the-fly and provide the flexibility needed in client-server architecture where there is often a need to connect dynamically to a database.

Dynamic SQL

The most recent ANSI specification, SQL2, includes dynamic SQL, which allows an application to generate and execute SQL statements at run time. SQL2 supports the notion of a database environment that is responsible for handling dynamic SQL statements. When an SQL statement is prepared at run-time, the database environment generates an access plan and a description of the result set. To retain the efficiency advantages of static SQL, a dynamic SQL statement can be executed multiple times with the previously generated access plan, thus minimizing the processing overhead of parsing and generating the access plan.

Dynamic SQL statements can accept arguments. When embedding a dynamic SQL statement, the arguments are in the form of host variables to which you assign values prior to executing the SQL statement. Although dynamic SQL is not as efficient as static SQL, it is very useful because it allows an application to do the following:

✦ Construct SQL statements at run time.

✦ Connect to a database at run time.

Call Level Interface

Although embedded SQL (especially with support for dynamic SQL statements) provides a powerful mechanism for writing database applications, embedded SQL does not provide a standard callable Application Programming Interface (API). The Call Level Interface (CLI) for SQL consists of a library of functions that support execution of dynamic SQL statements.

The industry standards group X/Open and the SQL Access Group (SAG) issued the SQL Common Application Environment (CAE) specification in 1992. This specification defines a CLI for SQL that is straightforward to use because of the function call interface. The function call interface does not require concepts from embedded SQL, such as host variables or a precompiler.

The SQL CLI lets you place an SQL statement in a text buffer and execute that SQL statement by providing the text buffer as an argument in a function call. The CLI function's return values indicate the status of execution of the submitted SQL statement.

Microsoft's ODBC API is a CLI for SQL. That means ODBC provides a set of functions that you can call from a C program to access a database.

mSQL — The MiniSQL Database

You need an SQL database to experiment with CGI programs that access databases using SQL. For this chapter, I selected mSQL — the capable MiniSQL database engine, developed by David Hughes of Bond University, Australia. mSQL is a lightweight database engine that uses a subset of ANSI standard SQL as its query interface.

mSQL is an ideal database for most Web sites. You can download mSQL from the following URL:

```
ftp://bond.edu.au/pub/Minerva/msql/
```

You'll also find an evaluation copy of mSQL on this book's companion CD-ROM.

Note that mSQL is not free — it's distributed as shareware. If you want to use mSQL, you have to register and pay a nominal fee (the cost is much less than what you would pay for a commercial database such as Oracle or Informix).

Downloading and installing mSQL

If you decide to try out mSQL, first visit the MiniSQL home page at the following URL:

```
http://hughes.com.au/product/msql/
```

On this page, you'll find lots of information about mSQL as well as a link to download the latest version of mSQL. When you click on the link to download mSQL, you'll get to an FTP site (`ftp://bond.edu.au/pub/Minerva/msql/`) with a number of files and directories. You can then click on specific files to download them.

Here's a listing of the files I downloaded from this site:

Name	Size	Description
faq.html	165K	Frequently Asked Questions (FAQ) about mSQL (in HTML format)
faq.txt	137K	The mSQL FAQ in plain text format
msql-1.0.14.tar.gz	189K	mSQL distribution in a tar archive, compressed using GNU Zip

At the time of this writing, the latest version of mSQL is 1.0.14. By the time you download mSQL, the version is likely to be different.

After you download the mSQL distribution, follow these steps to build and install the software:

1. Copy the downloaded file to an appropriate directory. On my Linux system, I placed the file in the `/usr/local/src` directory with the following command:

```
mv msql-1.0.14.tar.gz /use/local/src
```

2. Use the `gunzip` command (you'll need GNU Zip installed on your system) to uncompress the file, as follows:

```
gunzip msql-1.0.14.tar.gz
```

This command creates the file `msql-1.0.14.tar`.

3. Unpack the tar archive with the following command:

```
tar xvf msql-1.0.14.tar
```

The unpacking process creates a subdirectory named `msql-1.0.14` and places all files in that subdirectory.

4. In the newly created subdirectory, you'll find a `README` file with installation instructions. You can read this file with the following commands:

```
cd msql-1.0.14
more README
```

5. As the `README` file instructs, type the following command in the top-level directory (this is the directory where you find the `README` file):

```
make targets
```

This step creates a `targets` subdirectory.

6. Type `cd targets` to change to the `targets` subdirectory where you'll find another subdirectory with a name that depends on your operating system. For example, on my Linux system, this subdirectory is named `Linux-1.2.13-i586`.

7. Use the `cd` command to change to the subdirectory corresponding to your operating system and type the `setup` command. Thus, on my Linux system, I type the following commands:

```
cd Linux-1.2.13-i586
setup
```

The `setup` command runs the `autoconf` utility that asks you some questions. For ease, accept the default answers that `autoconf` provides.

8. To build the mSQL programs, type the following command:

```
make all
```

9. To install the mSQL programs in various directories, type the following command:

```
make install
```

By default, the mSQL programs and library files are installed in the `/usr/local/Minerva` directory. The executable programs are placed in the `/usr/local/Minerva/bin` directory.

Creating a sample database

Webmaster After you build and install mSQL, you can create databases and populate the database with tables. First, log in as root and start the database server with the following command:

```
/usr/local/Minerva/bin/msqld &
```

The database server is a daemon (a background process that runs continuously) that accepts database queries from the SQL interpreter (or C and C++ programs that use the msql library).

Tip You should also add the mSQL binary directory to your PATH environment variable. If you installed in the default location, you need to add the /usr/local/Minerva/bin directory to PATH. In Korn shell or Bash, use the following command to modify PATH:

```
PATH=$PATH:/usr/local/Minerva/bin; export PATH
```

In C shell, use the following command to modify the PATH environment variable (when you update the path variable, C shell automatically changes PATH):

```
set path = ( $path /usr/local/Minerva/bin )
```

To illustrate how to create and load a database, I'll set up a simple book-catalog database in the following section. I'll use the same database in CGI programming examples in other sections of the book.

Reviewing the steps to build the database

The basic sequence of steps to build a database are as follows:

1. **Design the database.** In this step you define the tables and attributes that will be used to store the information.

2. **Create an empty database.** Before you can add tables, database systems require you to build an empty database.

3. **Create the tables in the database.** In this step, you define the tables using the CREATE TABLE statement of SQL.

4. **Load the tables with any fixed data.** For example, if you had a table of manufacturer names or publisher names, you'd want to load that table with information that's already known.

5. **Back up the initial database.** This step is necessary to ensure that you can create the database from scratch, if necessary.

6. **Load data into tables.** You may either load data from an earlier dump of the database or interactively through forms.

7. **Use the database.** Make queries, update records, or insert new records using SQL commands.

Designing the database

In my simple example, I won't follow all the steps of database building. For example, the database design step is going to be trivial because my book catalog database will include a single table. The attributes of the table are as follows:

✦ Book's title with up to 50 characters

✦ Name of first author with up to 20 characters

✦ Name of second author (if any) with up to 20 characters

✦ Name of publisher with up to 30 characters

✦ Page count as a number

✦ Year published as a number (such as 1996)

✦ International Standard Book Number (ISBN), as a 10-character text (such as 156884798X)

I store the ISBN without the dashes embedded in a typical book's ISBN. I also use the ISBN as the primary key of the table because ISBN is a world-wide identification system for books. This means that each book entry must have a unique ISBN, which we know to be true for books.

Creating an empty database

To create the empty database in mSQL, I use the `msqladmin` program. For example, to create an empty database named `books`, I type the following command:

```
msqladmin create books
```

It is necessary to log in as `root` to run the `msqladmin` program. As the name suggests, `msqladmin` is the database administration program for mSQL. If I were to type `msqladmin` without an argument, the program would display a help message, as follows:

```
msqladmin


usage : msqladmin [-h host] [-q] <Command>

where command =  drop DatabaseName
                 create DatabaseName
                 shutdown
                 reload
                 version

 -q     Quiet mode.  No verification of commands.
```

In addition to creating a database, I can use `msqladmin` to remove a database, shutdown the database server, and check the mSQL version. For example, to see the version information, I would type the following command:

```
msqladmin version

Version Details :-

        msqladmin version      1.0.14
        mSQL connection        Localhost via UNIX socket
        mSQL server version    1.0.14
        mSQL protocol version  6
        mSQL TCP socket        1112
        mSQL UNIX socket       /dev/msql
        mSQL root user         root
```

The output shows that I am running version 1.0.14 of the mSQL server.

Using `msql` — the SQL interpreter in mSQL

After I create the empty database, all my interactions with the database will be through the `msql` program — the SQL interpreter of mSQL. It is necessary to run `msql` with the name of a database as argument. The `msql` program then prompts for input. Here is an example that shows user input in boldface:

```
msql books

Welcome to the miniSQL monitor.  Type \h for help.


mSQL > \h


MiniSQL Help!

The following commands are available :-

        \q      Quit
        \g      Go (Send query to database)
        \e      Edit (Edit previous query)
        \p      Print (Print the query buffer)

mSQL > \q


Bye!
```

Tip When creating tables or loading data into tables, a typical approach is to place the SQL statements (along with `msql` commands such as `\g`) in a file and then run `msql` with the standard input directed from that file. For example, suppose a file named `sample.msql` contains some SQL commands that you want to try out on a database named `books`. Then you should run `msql` with the following command:

```
msql books < sample.msql
```

I'll use `msql` in this manner to create a database table.

Defining a table

To create a table named `books`, I edited a text file named `makedb.sql` and placed the following line in that file:

```
#
# Table structure for table 'books'
#
CREATE TABLE books (
  isbn CHAR(10) NOT NULL PRIMARY KEY,
  title CHAR(50),
  author1 CHAR(20),
  author2 CHAR(20),
  pubname CHAR(30),
  pubyear INT,
  pagecount INT
) \g
```

`CREATE TABLE books` is an SQL statement to create the table named `books`. The `\g` at the end of the statement is an `msql` command. The attributes of the table appear in the lines enclosed in parentheses.

If a table contains fixed data, you could also include other SQL statements (such as `INSERT INTO`) to load the data into the table right after the table is created.

To execute the SQL statements in the `makedb.sql` file create the `books` table, I run `msql` as follows:

```
msql books < makedb.sql
```

Now the `books` database should have a table named `books`. You can now begin loading data into the table.

Inserting records into a table

One way to load data into the table is to prepare SQL statements in another file and then run `msql` with that file as input. For example, suppose I want to add the following book information into the `books` table:

```
isbn = '156884798X'
title = 'Linux SECRETS'
author1 = 'Naba Barkakati'
author2 = NULL
pubname = 'IDG Books Worldwide'
pubyear = 1996
pagecount = 900
```

The following `msql` statement loads this information into the `books` table:

```
INSERT INTO books VALUES
( '156884798X', 'Linux SECRETS', 'Naba Barkakati', NULL,
'IDG Books Worldwide', 1996, 900) \g
```

On the other hand, suppose you had the various fields available in a different order (than the order in which the table's attributes are defined by the `CREATE TABLE` statement). In that case, you can use a different form of the `INSERT INTO` command to add the row, as shown in the following example:

```
INSERT INTO books (pubyear, author1, author2, title, pagecount, pubname,
       isbn) values
(1996, 'Naba Barkakati', NULL, 'Linux SECRETS', 900, 'IDG Books World-
       wide', '156884798X')\g
```

You have to specify the list of attributes as well as the values, and make sure that the order of the attributes matches that of the values.

A less tedious way to add new entries is through a form. With a CGI gateway, you can make that form an HTML form so that you can enter data from a Web browser. A typical use of this capability is in a conference registration application where users register through the Web and the CGI program stores the information in an SQL database.

CGI Gateway to Relational Database

A CGI-based database-access scenario starts with the Web browser displaying an HTML form in which the user enters items that define the search criteria. For example, in an online book catalog, the form might allow the user to enter the author's name or a subject.

When the user submits the form, the Web server sends the form's data to a CGI program (the `<form>` tag's `action` attribute specifies the name of the CGI program that processes the form's data).

The CGI program processes the form's data, constructs an SQL query, and sends the query to the RDBMS. The results of the query come back to the CGI program. The CGI program then converts the results into an HTML document and sends that document to the Web server. Finally, the Web server returns the HTML-formatted results back to the Web browser.

Figure 22-2 shows the basic concept of how a CGI gateway retrieves and displays information stored in a relational database.

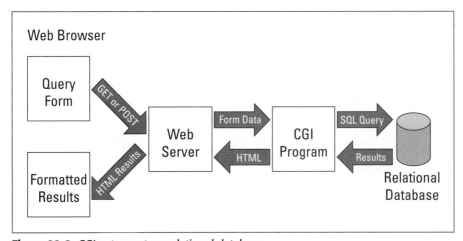

Figure 22-2: CGI gateway to a relational database.

The CGI gateway converts the form's data into an SQL query, accepts the results returned by the RDBMS, and then converts the search results into an HTML document.

You can use one of the following approaches to implement the CGI gateway to a database:

✦ Start an SQL interpreter from the gateway program and send SQL queries to the interpreter.

✦ Use an embedded SQL interface (or call an RDBMS-specific API) in the CGI program to directly access and query the database.

Gateway through an SQL interpreter

Note Most commercial RDBMS (such as Oracle, Informix, Sybase, and IBM DB2) include an SQL interpreter — a computer program that accepts SQL queries and returns results. You can write a short Perl program to open a pipe to the SQL interpreter's standard input and then send the SQL statements to the interpreter. The SQL interpreter then returns results as lines of text, which your Perl script can parse and convert into an HTML document.

In the following sections, I show two examples — a data entry form and a database query form — that use the mSQL interpreter to access an mSQL database. Although I developed these examples for mSQL, you can use them as the basis for interacting with other SQL interpreters such as the Oracle SQL interpreter.

A data entry program

Suppose I want to use a Web browser to add new book information to the books database that I created in mSQL. I can do so with the following steps:

1. Design an HTML form that includes the necessary fields to be filled in.

2. Assign a Perl CGI program to process the data from the form.

3. In that Perl program, parse the CGI query (use the cgi-lib.pl library, as described in Chapter 20). Open a pipe to the SQL interpreter and send a format-ted query string with the INSERT INTO command to add the new book. Return some status information to the user in HTML format.

Creating the data-entry form in HTML

Cross Ref For a simple table, you can design the data-entry form in a straightforward manner. Because my books database has only one table, all I need is a form with a field corresponding to each table attribute. To design the form, I use the HTML <form> and <input> tags that were described in Chapter 19.

Here is the HTML form that I use to enter new book information into the database:

```
<html>
<head>
<title>Add a new book</title>
</head>
<body>
<h3>Enter new book information:</h3>
<form action="/cgi-bin/addbook.pl">
<pre>
Title:   <input type=text name="title" size=50 maxlength=50>
Author:   <input type=text name="author1" size=20 maxlength=20>
        Author2:<input type=text name="author2" size=20 maxlength=20>
Publisher:<input type=text name="pubname" size=30 maxlength=30>
        ISBN:<input type=text name="isbn" size=10 maxlength=10>
```

```
Year:      <input type=text name="pubyear" size=4 maxlength=4>
Page Count:<input type=text name="pagecount" size=5 maxlength=5>
<br><br>

          <input type=submit>  <input type=reset>
</pre>

</form>

</body>
</html>
```

Figure 22-3 shows the form with the necessary information filled in.

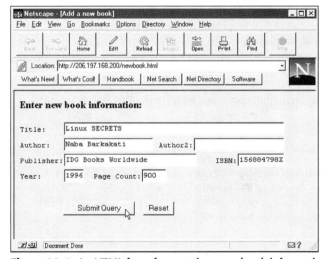

Figure 22-3: An HTML form for entering new book information into a database.

After filling in the form, if I were to click on the submit button, the Web server will run the addbook.pl CGI program to process the form's data. That's the Perl script that handles the database interactions.

Implementing the data entry program in Perl
The basic steps in the CGI gateway program are as follows:

1. Use the cgi-lib.pl subroutines to parse the CGI query that contains the values of various fields.

2. Because we use single quotes to delimit strings in SQL statements, the script converts any single quotes in the field values into \' (a backslash followed by a single quote).

3. Run the SQL interpreter and open a connection to the interpreter.

4. Send an SQL query to the SQL interpreter.

5. Read the results returned by the SQL interpreter and report the results back in an HTML document.

It's simple enough to launch a program in Perl — call the open function as if you are opening a file, but in place of the file name provide the program name with a vertical bar (|) prefix. The open function then opens a pipe to that program.

Caution When you run the SQL interpreter and establish a connection to the interpreter with the open function, you get back a pipe. Through this pipe you can send SQL statements to the SQL interpreter. However, you also want to accept any results sent back by the SQL interpreter. Although you can use the same pipe to send and receive data, doing so may create a deadlock condition. Suppose, for example, that the CGI program sends a command to the SQL interpreter and waits to receive a reply; but the command happens to be incomplete and the SQL interpreter waits for further input. In this case, both the CGI program and the SQL interpreter could be waiting for input indefinitely.

A better approach is to create a child process, which calls the SQL interpreter and sends SQL commands to it. The parent process can then wait and read data from the pipe to the interpreter.

Tip To create a child process, use the open function with a special file name. If you call open with -| (a minus sign followed by a vertical bar) as the file name, Perl creates a child process and returns a process ID. As with the fork function in UNIX, the returned process ID is zero in the child process and non-zero in the parent process. The following code fragment illustrates how to use this facility:

```
    $pid = open(PIPE, "-|");

# Check if it's the child process
    if($pid == 0)
    {
# Place code here for the child process to execute.
# For database interface, run the SQL interpreter and send it the query
# ...
    }

# This part is in the parent process
# Read the results in the parent process
    @result = <PIPE>;
```

The following listing shows the complete addbook.pl script that I used to insert a new record in a database table:

```perl
#!/usr/local/bin/perl

# File: addbook.pl

# A Perl script that adds an entry to a book database
# (This program works with mSQL — the mini-SQL database by
# David Hughes).

# You need to create the books database and a table named
# books.

# Author: Naba Barkakati

    require "cgi-lib.pl";

    $msql = "/usr/local/Minerva/bin/msql";
    $dbname = "books";

# Read and parse the query string
    &ReadParse(*input);

    $title = $input{'title'};
    $author1 = $input{'author1'};
    $author2 = $input{'author2'};
    $pubname = $input{'pubname'};
    $pubyear = $input{'pubyear'};
    $pagecount = $input{'pagecount'};
    $isbn = $input{'isbn'};

# Convert any single quote (') into \'
    $title =~ s/'/\\'/;
    $author1 =~ s/'/\\'/;
    $author2 =~ s/'/\\'/;
    $pubname =~ s/'/\\'/;

# Create a child process to send query to SQL intrepreter
# First unbuffer stdout and flush it
    select((select(STDOUT), $| = 1)[0]);
    print ("");

    $pid = open(PIPE, "-|");
# In child process, pid is zero
    if($pid == 0)
    {
# Run the SQL interpreter and send it the query
        open(MSQL, "| $msql $dbname") ||
                die("Could not start SQL interpreter");
        print MSQL "insert into books\n";
        print MSQL "(title, author1, author2, pubname, pubyear,";
        print MSQL "pagecount, isbn) values\n";
        print MSQL "('$title', '$author1', '$author2', '$pubname',";
```

(continued)

```
        print MSQL "$pubyear, $pagecount, '$isbn')\\g";
        print MSQL ("\\q\n");
        close MSQL;
        exit;
    }

# Process the results in the parent process
    @result = <PIPE>;

# Print the HTML header
    print &PrintHeader;
    print &HtmlTop("Results SQL query");
    print "<pre>\n";

# Print out the query
    print "insert into books\n";
    print "(title, author1, author2, pubname, pubyear,";
    print "pagecount, isbn) values\n";
    print "('$title', '$author1', '$author2', '$pubname',";
    print "$pubyear, $pagecount, '$isbn')\\g";
    print ("\\q\n");

# Ignore some of the lines and display the rest
    for(@result)
    {
        next if /miniSQL/;
        next if /mSQL/;
        next if /Bye\!/;
        print $_;
    }
    print "</pre>\n";
    print "<hr>";
    print "<pre>\n";
    print "<a href=\"/newbook.html\">Add another book</a>
        <a href=\"/bkquery.html\">Look for a book</a>\n";
    print "</pre>\n";
    print &HtmlBot;
```

> **Note**   Before you can use this script, you have to install mSQL and set up a database named
> books; then in that database define a books table with the appropriate attributes (see
> the "Creating a sample database" section earlier in this chapter).

With the HTML form of Figure 22-3 and the addbook.pl script, I can now enter new book information from a Web browser. I bring up the HTML form in the browser, fill in the information, and click on the submit button. The addbook.pl program starts the SQL interpreter and sends it a properly formatted SQL statement to insert the new book information into the database. After completing the database transaction, the addbook.pl script returns an HTML page with status information. Figure 22-4 shows the HTML document returned in response to the form shown in Figure 22-3.

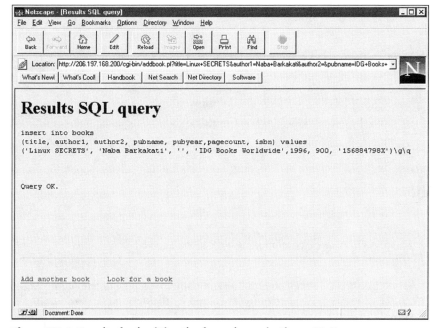

Figure 22-4: Result of submitting the form shown in Figure 22-3.

In this case, I wrote the `addbook.pl` script to return the SQL query and the status reported by the SQL interpreter. I used the SQL statement to confirm that the script sends the correct commands to the SQL interpreter.

A database query program

Another common database interaction is to query the database and find information that meets certain criteria that the user specifies through an HTML form. For the `books` database, one such query is to look for a book by a specific author. The following HTML source implements a simple form to submit a query:

```
<head>
<title>Find book</title>
</head>
<body>
<form action="/cgi-bin/dbquery.pl" method=get>
<h3>Search for books:</h3>
<p>You may enter a partial name.
<p>
Author: <input type=text size=20 name=author>

<input type=submit value="Submit query">
<input type=reset value="Clear">

</form>
</body>
```

Figure 22-5 shows the appearance of the form in Netscape Navigator.

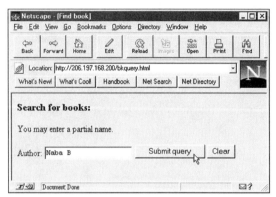

Figure 22-5: An HTML form for submitting a database query.

To look for a book, type either the first or last name (or a part of the name) of the author, and the dbquery.pl script (as specified by the action attribute of the <form> tag) receives the query to process.

Like the addbook.pl script shown in the "Implementing the data entry program in Perl" section, the dbquery.pl script first parses the query string, runs the SQL interpreter, and sends an SQL statement to the SQL interpreter. The following listing shows the dbquery.pl script (which requires the books database and a table named books):

```
#!/usr/local/bin/perl

# File: dbquery.pl

# A simple query interface to a SQL interpreter (this example
# works with mSQL — the mini-SQL database by David Hughes).

# You need to create the books database and a table named
# books.

# Author: Naba Barkakati

    require "cgi-lib.pl";

    $msql = "/usr/local/Minerva/bin/msql";
    $dbname = "books";

# Read and parse the query string
    &ReadParse(*input);
    $author = $input{'author'};
```

```perl
# Replace any single quote (') with \' because the SQL
# intrepreter uses single quotes as string delimiters
    $author =~ s/'/\\'/;

# Create a child process to send query to SQL intrepreter
# First unbuffer stdout and flush it
    select((select(STDOUT), $| = 1)[0]);
    print ("");

    $pid = open(PIPE, "-|");
# In child process, pid is zero
    if($pid == 0)
    {
# Run the SQL interpreter and send it the query
        open(MSQL, "| $msql $dbname") ||
                die("Could not start SQL interpreter");
        print MSQL "select title, pagecount, pubyear, isbn\n";
        print MSQL "from books\n";
        print MSQL "where author1 like '%$author%' OR ";
        print MSQL "author2 like '%$author%'\\g";
        print MSQL ("\\q\n");
        close MSQL;
        exit;
    }

# Process the results in the parent process
    @result = <PIPE>;

# Print the HTML header
    print &PrintHeader;
    print &HtmlTop("Results of query");
    print "<pre>\n";

# Ignore some of the lines and display the rest
    for(@result)
    {
        next if $_ eq "\n";
        next if /miniSQL/;
        next if /mSQL/;
        next if /Query OK\./;
        next if /Bye\!/;
        print $_;
    }
    print "</pre>\n";

    print &HtmlBot;
```

When I submit the query shown in the HTML form of Figure 22-5, the `dbquery.pl` script returns the result in an HTML document, as shown in Figure 22-6.

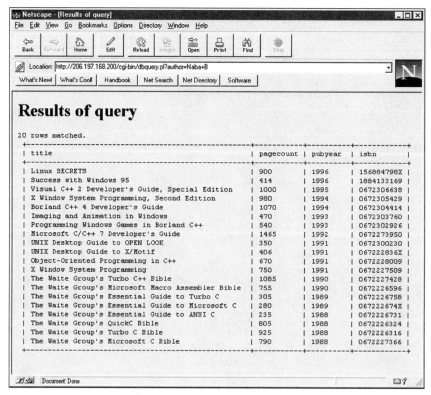

Figure 22-6: Result of submitting the query shown in Figure 22-5.

As Figure 22-6 shows, the dbquery.pl script displays the results exactly as reported by the SQL interpreter. The only formatting is to remove some blank lines and any lines that include the prompt strings of the msql program (this is the SQL interpreter of mSQL). Of course, if you prefer, you can further process the SQL interpreter's output and present the result in a nicer format.

Pros and cons of using an SQL interpreter

The advantage of using an SQL interpreter to access the database is that you don't have to use any special library functions or modify the Perl interpreter to access the database.

However, there is a significant drawback in using the SQL interpreter as an intermediary. For each database query, the CGI gateway must start the SQL interpreter, and the interpreter in turn must set up a connection to the database server. This can be a time-consuming process and may result in poor response times for queries. An alternative approach is to write programs that call special library functions to access the database server directly.

Gateway with an embedded interface to SQL

Instead of using an existing SQL interpreter, you can write a CGI program with an embedded SQL interface that directly accesses the database server. The benefit of this approach is that you don't incur the overhead of starting the SQL interpreter process for each query.

Using an embedded SQL interface in Perl programs

Perl programmers who need to access Oracle or Sybase databases may use the following customized versions of Perl 4.036 interpreter to accomplish the task:

✦ `oraperl` is a Perl extension that provides a number of functions to access and interact with Oracle databases. `oraperl` is available from the following URL:

> `http://sunsite.doc.ic.ac.uk/packages/perl/db/perl4/oraperl/`

✦ `sybperl` is a Perl extension that uses the Sybase DB-Library to provide access to Sybase databases. You can download `sybperl` from the following URL:

> `http://sunsite.doc.ic.ac.uk/packages/perl/db/perl4/sybperl/`

Currently, a common database interface is being developed in Perl 5. This common interface, known as DBI or DBperl, supersedes the custom database interfaces such as `oraperl` and `sybperl`. You can get the latest version of DBI from the following URL:

> `ftp://ftp.demon.co.uk/pub/perl/db/`

Another way to use an embedded SQL interface is to write the CGI program in C or C++ and then use the programming library provided by your database. For example, most databases include Embedded SQL (ESQL), which allows you to embed SQL statements in a C program. The MiniSQL database (mSQL) comes with its own programming library, which is illustrated in the next section.

Using an embedded SQL interface in a C++ program

When you build and install mSQL following the steps outlined in the "Downloading and installing mSQL" section of this chapter, the installation process creates the `libmsql.a` library and places it in the `lib` subdirectory of your mSQL installation directory (which is `/usr/local/Minerva` by default). The `libmsql.a` library contains a number of functions that you can call from a C or C++ program to access and manipulate mSQL databases.

To use the `libmsql.a` library, you have to include the `msql.h` header file in your program. This header file is located in the `/usr/local/Minerva/include` directory.

In this section, I present a C++ program that can query the `books` database and find the books by a particular author. To parse the CGI query, I use the `CgiQuery` C++ class described in Chapter 21.

The basic processing steps in the C++ program (that I call bkquery) are as follows:

1. Parse the CGI query string that contains the form's data. With the CgiQuery class, I implement this step with the following declaration:

   ```
   // Read and parse the CGI query
      CgiQuery cq;
   ```

   The initialization of the CgiQuery class instance reads and parses the CGI query string.

2. Call msqlConnect to establish a connection to the mSQL database server. The msqlConnect function returns an integer identifier that serves as a handle to the database server.

3. Call msqlSelectDB to select a database by name. For this example, the database name is books.

4. Construct an SQL query string and call msqlQuery to send the query to the mSQL database server. The msqlQuery function returns -1 in case of error.

5. If msqlQuery returns without any error, call msqlStoreResult to store the results in an m_result structure from which you can retrieve the rows one by one.

6. Call msqlFetchRow in a loop to get each row and then access each field in the row. See the listing of bkquery.cc for details.

7. When the query results are no longer needed, call msqlFreeResult to free the storage allocated for the rows retrieved from the database.

The following listing shows the bkquery.cc file — the C++ source code for the bkquery program:

```
//-------------------------------------------------------------
// File: bkquery.cc
//
// C++ program that serves as CGI gateway to an mSQL database.
// You must install mSQL and build a books database to use this
// program.
//
// Uses the CgiQuery class to parse the CGI query string.
//
// Author: Naba Barkakati
//-------------------------------------------------------------
#include <strstream.h>
#include "cgiquery.h"
#include <msql.h>

// Name of database and table
char *DBNAME = "books";
```

```
const char *TBNAME = "books";
//-----------------------------------------------------------------
// m a i n
//
// The main function.

int main(void)
{
// Read and parse the CGI query
    CgiQuery cq;

    if(!cq.Status())
    {
        CgiError("Parse Error",
                "Error parsing CGI query");
        exit(1);
    }

// Connect to the MSQL database server
    int db_id = msqlConnect(NULL);

    if(db_id < 0)
    {
        CgiError("Connect Error",
                "Cannot connect to SQL server");
        exit(2);
    }

// Open the database
    if(msqlSelectDB(db_id, DBNAME) < 0)
    {
        CgiError("Database Error",
                "Cannot open database");
        exit(0);
    }

// Construct SQL query
    char query[256];
    ostrstream s_query(query, 256);

    s_query << "SELECT title, pagecount, pubyear, isbn "
            << "from " << TBNAME << " where "
            << "author1 like '%" << cq.GetValue("author")
            << "%' OR author2 like '%" << cq.GetValue("author")
            << "%'" << ends;

// Run the query
    int result = msqlQuery(db_id, query);

    if(result == -1)
```

(continued)

```
        {
            CgiError("SQL Query Error", msqlErrMsg);
            exit(3);
        }


// Get the results of the query */
    m_result *bklist = msqlStoreResult();
    if(bklist == NULL)
    {
        msqlFreeResult(bklist);
        CgiError("Failed to store results",
                "Error allocating storage for results");
        exit(4);
    }

// Format and display search results in an HTML table
    PrintHeader();

    char title[60];
    ostrstream s_title(title, 60);
    s_title << "Books by: " << cq.GetValue("author") << ends;

    HtmlTop(title);
    cout << "Found " << msqlNumRows(bklist) << " books.<p>" << endl;
    cout << "<table border align=center>" << endl;

// Print the table header (only if some rows were found)
    if(msqlNumRows(bklist) > 0)
    {
        cout << "<tr>" << endl;
        cout << "<th>Book title</th>" << endl;
        cout << "<th>Pages</th>" << endl;
        cout << "<th>Year</th>" << endl;
        cout << "<th>ISBN</th>" << endl;
        cout << "</tr>" << endl;
    }
    else
    {
        cout << "<tr><th>No books found!</th></tr>" << endl;
    }
// Now print each row
    m_row row;
    while((row = msqlFetchRow(bklist)) != NULL)
    {
        cout << "<tr>" << endl;
        int i;
        for(i = 0; i < msqlNumFields(bklist); i++)
        {
            cout << "<td>" << row[i]
                << "</td>" << endl;
        }
```

```
        cout << "</tr>" << endl;
    }
    cout << "</table>" << endl;

    HtmlBot();

// Free the storage allocated for the query result
    msqlFreeResult(bklist);

    return 0;
}
```

To build the `bkquery` program and copy the binary to the `/cgi-bin/` directory, I used the following `Makefile` on a Linux system:

```
############################################################
# File: Makefile
#
# Build the bkquery program that acts as a gateway to an
# mSQL database.
#
# Author: Naba Barkakati
############################################################
CGIBINDIR= /usr/local/etc/httpd/cgi-bin
CFLAGS= -I/usr/local/Minerva/include
LIBS=   -L/usr/local/Minerva/lib -lmsql

# Make sure that this directory contains cgiquery.h and cgiquery.o
OBJS= cgiquery.o

all: bkquery

bkquery: bkquery.cc
        g++ -o bkquery $(CFLAGS) bkquery.cc $(OBJS) $(LIBS)
        cp bkquery $(CGIBINDIR)
```

To test the `bkquery` program, copy the program into the `/cgi-bin/` directory on your Web server. The full directory name depends on your Web server; it's usually `/usr/local/etc/httpd/cgi-bin/` for NCSA and Apache Web servers. Then use the HTML form shown in Figure 22-5 as the query form, but edit the HTML source so that `/cgi-bin/bkquery` is specified as the `<form>` tag's `action` attribute. Now you can enter an author's name in the form and click the submit button to see the results.

Figure 22-7 shows a typical tabular output from the `bkquery` program.

Figure 22-7: Tabular output showing the results of a database search performed by the `bkquery` CGI program.

Summary

Most businesses store information in *relational database management systems* (RDBMS) and use specific client applications to let users access the information. Nowadays, however, Web browsers are becoming the universal client applications and there is a need to provide access to databases through the Web. This can be done best by developing CGI programs that act as gateways to RDBMS.

This chapter describes some of the ways in which you can create CGI gateways to databases. In the next chapter, you'll learn about another exciting new subject — Java programming — that also promises to bring new capabilities to the Web.

Where to go next . . .

✦ For a general introduction to CGI programming, read Chapter 19.

✦ To learn about CGI programming in Perl, turn to Chapter 20.

✦ If you want to use C or C++ for CGI programs, consult Chapter 21.

✦ ✦ ✦

Extending Web Applications

Writing Java Applications

In previous chapters you have seen examples of Web pages that are prepared on the server (either as predefined files or prepared dynamically by CGI programs) and sent to the Web browser to display. However, a new programming language called Java introduces the concept of Web pages with *executable content* — small application programs called *applets* that are downloaded and executed on your system where the Web browser resides. To be more precise, these Java programs are transmitted as sequences of bytes that can be executed by a Java Virtual Machine (JVM) embedded in a Web browser. To run Java applets, you need a Java-capable Web browser such as Netscape Navigator, version 2.0 or later, or Microsoft Internet Explorer, version 3.0 or later.

Java applets allow you to provide information in a unique way. You can write an applet that downloads data from your server and plots the data in various ways based on the user's selection. The key is that the Web server sends the applet's code, and the applet then downloads the data once. After that, all data manipulation and displays are handled by the applet running inside your Java-capable Web browser (a *Java-capable* Web browser includes a JVM — Java Virtual Machine — that can run Java code).

Because Java applets run on a user's machine, there is obvious concern over security. For example, users worry that a rogue Java applet might transfer sensitive data from the user's system back to the host (where the Java applet originated) or, worse yet, destroy data stored in the local hard disk. To alleviate such concerns, security has been a built-in feature of the Java programming language. Among many security restrictions imposed on Java applets, a significant one is that applets are not allowed access to the local disk. The Java Virtual Machine uses a byte-code verification process to ensure that a Java applet's code does not violate Java's security restrictions.

This chapter provides an overview of the Java language and shows you a few simple examples. As you might guess, a single chapter cannot do full justice to Java; but this chapter can get you started with Java. With that goal in mind, I focus immediately on the tools you need to create Java applications and show you several examples to illustrate specific Java programming techniques.

Cross Ref You also may have heard of JavaScript, which is a scripting language supported by Netscape Navigator (version 2.0 and later). Although the names are similar, JavaScript is not Java. JavaScript is a scripting language that you place inside `<script>...</script>` tags in an HTML document. Like Java, a JavaScript script also executes entirely within the Web browser. I'll cover JavaScript in Chapter 24.

Getting Ready for Java Programming

As with any programming language, the best way to learn Java is to begin writing some programs. Of course, you need an overview of the language as well, but if you already know C++ and understand the basics of object-oriented programming, you can quickly become proficient in Java.

This section gets you started with the hands-on aspects of Java programming by showing how to download and install the Java Development Kit (JDK) on a Windows 95 system. Even though you are running a Web server on a UNIX system, like the HTML content, you can develop Java applets on a Windows 95 system and then place the applet on the UNIX Web server for distribution on the Web.

Downloading and installing Java Developers Kit (JDK)

URL To develop Java applications, you need the JDK. You can download the latest version (1.0.2 as of this writing) of JDK by following the links at the following Sun Microsystems Web site:

```
http://java.sun.com/products/JDK/CurrentRelease/
```

This book's companion CD-ROM also includes JDK 1.0.2.

Sun Microsystems has released JDK 1.0.2 for the following systems:

✦ Microsoft Windows 95 and Windows NT

✦ Sun SPARC workstations running Solaris 2.3, 2.4, or 2.5

✦ Apple Macintosh System 7.5

To download and install JDK 1.0.2 for Microsoft Windows 95, perform the following steps (the same procedure works under Windows NT as well):

1. Download the file named `JDK-1_0_2-win32-x86.exe` (3,751KB) from the following URL:

   ```
   ftp://ftp.javasoft.com/pub/JDK-1_0_2-win32-x86.exe
   ```

   You can complete this step from your Web browser.

2. Copy the file to the directory where you want to install the JDK. For example, if you want to place the JDK in the `c:\java` directory, copy the `JDK-1_0_2-win32-x86.exe` file to the root directory of the C drive (`c:\`).

3. Execute that file by typing the following line in an MS-DOS window under Windows 95:

   ```
   JDK-1_0_2-win32-x86
   ```

   This program creates a java directory and all the necessary subdirectories with the files that constitute this release of JDK.

4. Set the `CLASSPATH` environment variable to `java\lib\classes.zip` and the `PATH` environment variable to include the `java\bin` directory. For example, if you install the JDK in `c:\java`, add the following lines in your system's `autoexec.bat` file:

   ```
   set PATH=%PATH%;c:\java\bin
   set CLASSPATH=c:\java\lib\classes.zip
   ```

   (On Windows NT, set environment variables through the Control Panel.)

Taking stock of the JDK

The JDK comes with a number of files organized into several directories. The top-level directory contains the following files and subdirectories:

Name	Description
README	Information about the JDK contents.
COPYRIGHT	The copyright and license information for this release of the JDK. Read this file before using the JDK.
index.html	An HTML document with a link to Sun's site, with additional information about the JDK.
src.zip	JDK source code in a ZIP archive. If you want to unzip this archive, make sure that you use an unzip program that can handle long filenames. You don't need the source files to write Java applets.
bin	Directory with the executable programs and Dynamic Link Libraries (DLLs) for Windows (include this directory in the `PATH` environment variable).

(continued)

Name	Description
lib	Java class library in the `classes.zip` file (set the CLASSPATH environment variable to this file).
demo	Directory with many sample Java applets with source code.
include	Header files for the JDK source.

The tools you'll use most are in the `bin` subdirectory. Following are some tools that you'll use when creating Java applications:

Name	Description
appletviewer	Java applet viewer program to load and run Java applets that are designed to be embedded in an HTML document. You can also load applets in a Java-capable browser by embedding the applet in an HTML document using the `<applet>` tag.
java	Java interpreter that runs stand-alone Java programs specified by a class name. It expects to find the class in a file with the same name as the class, but with a `.class` extension. Stand-alone Java applications are Java classes with a `main` method (in Java, functions are called *methods*).
javac	Java compiler that converts Java source code into "byte code" (that's the instruction set of the Java Virtual Machine). The compiler takes source code that is in a `.java` file and generates compiled code in a `.class` file.
javad	Java debugger with a command syntax like that of the UNIX `dbx` or `gdb` debuggers.
javadoc	Java documentation generator that extracts documentation from source files with special comments that begin with `/**` and endwith `*/`.
javah	Java C file generator that generates C .h and .c files for a Java class.
javap	Java class disassembler that takes a class name and prints a human-readable description of the class.

Of these programs, the three that you'll use most are the following:

✦ You'll use `javac` a lot because that's the Java compiler program. The `javac` program converts a Java source file (you'll see some examples in the next section) into a binary file that contains Java byte code — the instruction set of the Java Virtual Machine.

✦ If you write a stand-alone Java application — one that can run without being embedded in a Web browser — you'll use the `java` interpreter to run the application.

✦ If you write Java applets — mini-applications that run inside a Web browser — you'll use the `appletviewer` program to test the applets. You can also test applets using a Java-capable Web browser such as Netscape Navigator (version 2.0 or later).

Writing Your First Java Program

Following the grand old tradition of C programming books, I'll begin by showing you how to display "Hello, World!" from a Java program. However, before I proceed I should point out the difference between two types of Java programs:

✦ **Stand-alone Java application:** This is a Java program that can be executed by a Java interpreter. A Java stand-alone application is just like the stand-alone C or C++ programs that you may know. The application has a `main` method, and the Java interpreter program `java` can run the application. General-purpose Java applications take the form of stand-alone application.

✦ **Java applet:** This is a Java class that can be loaded and executed by the `appletviewer` program or by a Java-capable Web browser. You first have to embed the applet inside an HTML document using the `<applet>` tag and then load that HTML document to activate the applet. As a Webmaster, you'll mostly write Java applets.

Whether you write a stand-alone application or an applet, the basic steps are similar except for the last step when you execute the program. You use the `java` interpreter to run stand-alone programs and `appletviewer` to test applets. These development steps are as follows:

1. Use a text editor to create the Java source file. A Java application is a class (a type of object — a collection of data and methods). The source file's name must be the class name with a `.java` extension.

2. Process the source file with `javac` (the Java compiler) to generate the class file with a `.class` extension.

3. If it's a standalone application, run the class with the `java` interpreter with the following command:

   ```
   java classname
   ```

4. If the program is an applet, create an HTML document and embed the applet using the `<applet>` tag. (See "Using the `<applet>` tag" section for the syntax.) Then load that HTML document using `appletviewer` or a Java-capable Web browser. Loading the document also activates all embedded Java applets.

Writing a stand-alone "Hello, World!" program

The classic C-style "Hello, World!" application is easy to write in Java. That's because many of Java's syntactical details are similar to those of C and C++. The following code implements a simple "Hello, World!" program in Java:

```
public class HelloWorld
{
    public static void main(String[] args)
    {
        System.out.println("Hello, World!");
    }
}
```

This simple Java program illustrates some key features of Java:

✦ Every Java program is a public-class definition.

✦ A stand-alone application contains a `main` method that must be declared
  `public static void`. The interpreter starts execution at the `main` method.

Save this program in a file named `HelloWorld.java`. Then compile it with the
following command:

```
javac HelloWorld.java
```

This step creates a class file named `HelloWorld.class`. To run the application, use
the Java interpreter and specify the class name as a parameter, as follows:

```
java HelloWorld
```

The program prints "Hello, World!" on the Java console. If you run the program from an
MS-DOS window, the output appears in that window.) Figure 23-1 shows the result of
running the stand-alone `HelloWorld.class` in an MS-DOS window under Windows 95.

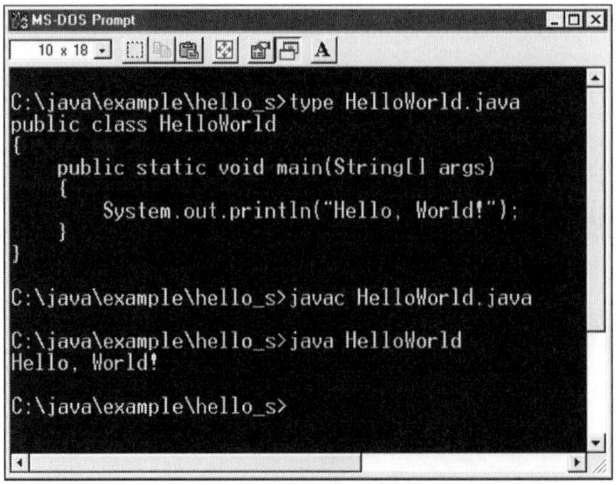

Figure 23-1: Running a stand-alone "Hello, World!" Java application.

Note Although I'll focus mostly on Java applets (because they are used in Web pages), stand-alone Java applications are important in their own right. The stand-alone application model lets you use Java as a general-purpose programming language. In fact, Java is already gaining ground as a more structured version of C++ that's well-suited for developing multi-platform applications (because Java applications can run wherever Java Virtual Machines exist).

Creating a "Hello, World!" applet

The other model of a Java program is an applet that runs inside the `appletviewer` program or a Java-capable Web browser. A Java applet is a class in the Java Abstract Windowing Toolkit (AWT). In an applet, you do not have to provide a `main` method. Instead, you provide a `paint` method where you place code to draw in an area of a window. You can use the applet model to implement a graphical user interface (GUI) and other graphical programs.

For a "Hello, World!" applet, do the following:

✦ Instead of displaying the message in a default font, pick a specific font to display the message.

✦ Use the information about the font sizes to center the message within the area where the applet is required to display its output.

✦ Draw the text in red instead of the default black color.

Here is the Java code that implements the "Hello, World!" applet:

```
//------------------------------
// File: HelloWorld.java
//
// Displays "Hello, World!" in Helvetica font and in red color.
//------------------------------

import java.applet.*;
import java.awt.*;

//------------------------------
// H e l l o W o r l d
//
// Applet class to display "Hello, World!"

public class HelloWorld extends java.applet.Applet
{
    String hellomsg = "Hello, World!";

//------------------------------
// p a i n t
//
// Method that paints the output
```

(continued)

```
    public void paint(java.awt.Graphics gc)
    {
// Draw a rectangle around the applet's bounding box
// so we can see the box
        gc.drawRect(0, 0, size().width-1, size().height-1);

// Create the font to be used for the message
        Font helv = new Font("Helvetica", Font.BOLD, 24);

// Select the font into the Graphics object
        gc.setFont(helv);

// Get the font metrics (details of the font size)
        FontMetrics fm = gc.getFontMetrics();
        int mwidth = fm.stringWidth(hellomsg);
        int ascent = fm.getAscent();
        int descent = fm.getDescent();

// Compute starting (x.y) position to center string
// The size() method returns size of the applet's
// bounding box
        int xstart = size().width/2 - mwidth/2;
        int ystart = size().height/2 + ascent/2 - descent/2;

// Set the color to red
        gc.setColor(Color.red);

// Now draw the string
        gc.drawString(hellomsg, xstart, ystart);
    }
}
```

By browsing through this code, you can learn a lot about graphics output in Java. Here are some key points to note:

✦ The import statement lists external classes that this program uses. The name that follows the import statement can be the name of a class or can be a name with a wildcard (*), which tells the Java compiler to import all the classes in a package. This example uses the Applet class as well as a number of graphics classes that arc in the java.awt package.

✦ The HelloWorld applet is defined as an extension of the Applet class. That's what the statement public class HelloWorld extends java.applet.Applet means.

✦ An applet's paint method contains the code that draws the output. The paint method receives a Graphics object as argument. You have to call methods of the Graphics object to display output.

✦ The `size` method returns the size of the applet's drawing area.

✦ To use a font, you first have to create a `Font` object and then call the `setFont` method of the `Graphics` object.

✦ To draw text in a specific color, invoke the `setColor` method of the `Graphics` object with an appropriate `Color` object as argument.

✦ If you know C++, you'll notice that Java's method invocation is similar to the way you call the member function of a C++ object.

Save the listing in a file named `HelloWorld.java`. Then compile it with the command:

```
javac HelloWorld.java
```

This step creates the applet class `HelloWorld.class`. To test the applet, create an HTML document and embed the applet in it, as shown in the following example:

```
<html>
<head>
<title>Hello, World! from Java</title>
</head>

<body>

<h3>"Hello, World!" from Java</h3>

A Java applet is given an area where it displays
its output. In this example, the applet draws a
border around its assigned area and then displays
the "Hello, World!" message centered in that box.
<br>

<applet code=HelloWorld width=200 height=60>
If you see this message, then you do not have a
Java-capable browser.
</applet>

Here is the applet!
</body>
</html>
```

As this HTML source shows, you have to use the `<applet>` tag to insert an applet in an HTML document.

You can use two tools to test the applet. The first one is `appletviewer`, which comes with JDK. To view the `HelloWorld` applet, you have to run the `appletviewer` program and provide the name of the HTML document that includes the applet. Suppose, for example, that the HTML document is in the file named `hello.html`. Then you'd run `appletviewer` with the following command:

```
appletviewer hello.html
```

Figure 23-2 shows how `appletviewer` displays the applet.

Figure 23-2: Running a stand-alone "Hello, World!" Java application.

Notice that `appletviewer` displays only the applet; the rest of the text in the HTML document is ignored. However, the appearance of the display is quite different in a Java-capable Web browser. Figure 23-3 shows how Netscape Navigator renders the HTML document containing the `HelloWorld` applet.

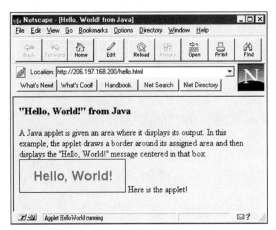

Figure 23-3: Viewing the HTML document with the "Hello, World!" Java applet.

Unlike `appletviewer`, Netscape Navigator displays the entire HTML document, and the Java applet appears embedded in the document like an image. The applet draws inside the rectangle assigned to it through the `width` and `height` attributes of the `<applet>` tag.

Using the `<applet>` tag

You have to use the `<applet>` tag to embed Java applets in an HTML document. Embedding a Java applet is a lot like embedding an image. The applet has a width and a height and it can be placed anywhere within the document. A simple use of the `<applet>` tag is as follows:

```
<applet code=HelloWorld width=200 height=60>
If you see this message, then you do not have a
Java-capable browser.
</applet>
```

The `<applet>` attributes

The complete `<applet>` element starts with an `<applet>` tag and ends with an `</applet>` tag. The beginning `<applet>` tag takes a number of attributes. The following three are always required:

✦ `code` specifies the name of the applet class (without the `.class` extention).

✦ `width` and `height` specify the size of the box (in pixels) assigned to the applet. This is the area where the applet draws its output.

> **Tip**　Java-capable browsers and the `appletviewer` program ignore the text between the `<applet>` and `</applet>` tags. However, Web browsers that do not support the `<applet>` tag simply ignore the tag. This means that, if you place some text between the `<applet>` and `</applet>` tags, that text is displayed only by browsers that do not support Java. This can be a good way to display an informative message to users who access your site with browsers that do not support Java applets.

The `<applet>` tag also accepts the following attributes:

✦ `codebase = URL` specifies the location of the code. If you do not specify this attribute, the HTML document's URL is used to locate the applet's code.

✦ `alt = text` specifies a message that a Java-capable browser can display if the browser is somehow unable to run the Java applet.

✦ `name = instance name` specifies the name of this instance of the applet. This allows you to embed multiple instances of an applet in a single HTML document.

✦ `align = alignment` indicates how the browser aligns the applet's area with text adjoining the applet. This is similar to the `align` attribute of the `<img>` tag.

✦ `vspace = vpad` tells the Web browser how many pixels of padding to apply above and below the applet's rectangle.

✦ `hspace = hpad` tells the Web browser how many pixels of padding to apply to the left and the right of the applet's box.

The `<param>` tag

Between the `<applet>` and `</applet>` tags, you can include one or more `<param>` tags that specify values of parameters that the applet uses. To understand the use of `<param>` tags, consider the `HelloWorld` applet that displays a "Hello, World!" message. Suppose you want a more general-purpose applet (I'll call the new applet `Message`) that displays any selected message in its display area. Instead of including the message text inside the Java class, you want to pass the message as an argument at run-time. In a normal C or C++ program, you might do this through command-line arguments. In a Java applet, you can pass arguments through the `<param>` tag.

Here's how to implement the Message applet in Java:

```
//------------------------------
// File: Message.java
//
// Displays a specified message in Helvetica font and in
// red color. You have to specify the message in a
// <param> tag with name=message.
//------------------------------

import java.applet.*;
import java.awt.*;

//------------------------------
// M e s s a g e
//
// Applet class to display message from <param> tag of <applet>

public class Message extends java.applet.Applet
{
    private Font helv;
    private String message;

    //------------------------------
    // i n i t
    //
    // Initialization method

    public void init()
    {
    // Create the font to be used for the message
        helv = new Font("Helvetica", Font.BOLD, 24);

    // Retrieve the message to be displayed
        message = getParameter("message");
    }
    //------------------------------
    // p a i n t
    //
    // Method that paints the output

    public void paint(java.awt.Graphics gc)
    {
    // Draw a rectangle around the applet's bounding box
    // so we can see the box
        gc.drawRect(0, 0, size().width-1, size().height-1);


    // Select the font into the Graphics object
        gc.setFont(helv);
```

```
    // Get the font metrics (details of the font size)
        FontMetrics fm = gc.getFontMetrics();
        int mwidth = fm.stringWidth(message);
        int ascent = fm.getAscent();
        int descent = fm.getDescent();

    // Compute starting (x.y) position to center string
    // The size() function returns size of the applet's
    // bounding box
        int xstart = size().width/2 - mwidth/2;
        int ystart = size().height/2 + ascent/2 - descent/2;

    // Set the color to red
        gc.setColor(Color.red);

    // Now draw the string
        gc.drawString(message, xstart, ystart);
    }
  }
```

The following code fragment shows how you can extract a parameter named `message` from what you specify in the `<param>` tag:

```
    String message;
// Retrieve the message to be displayed
    message = getParameter("message");
```

After you write the Java applet and compile it into a `Message.class` file, you can embed the `Message` applet in an HTML file and pass it different text messages to display. To specify a message text for the `Message` applet, you have to embed a `<param>` tag in an `<applet>` element (that means between `<applet>` and `</applet>` tags). The general syntax of the `<param>` tag (without the `<applet>` element) is:

```
<param name=parameter-name value=parameter-value>
```

Use the `name` and `value` attributes of the `<param>` tag to specify the name of a parameter and its value. For example, to specify the string "Hello, World!" as the value of the parameter named `message`, you'd write the following:

```
<param name="message" value="Hello, World!">
```

For example, here is a sample HTML file that uses two instances of the `Message` applet, each with a different message text:

```
<html>
<head>
<title>Testing messages</title>
</head>
```

(continued)

```
<body>
Here is one instance of the applet:
<applet code=Message width=200 height=60>
<param name="message" value="First message">
</applet>

<p>You can embed the applet again, with a
different message:
<applet code=Message width=250 height=60>
<param name="message" value="Another message">
</applet>

</body>
</html>
```

Figure 23-4 shows how this HTML document appears in Netscape Navigator. Each instance of the Message applet displays the message that was specified in the <param> tag in the respective <applet> element.

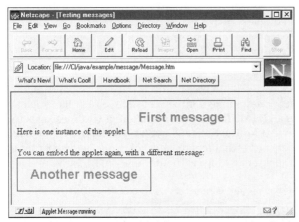

Figure 23-4: Two instances of the Message applet displaying different messages.

Running an applet as a stand-alone application

Suppose you have an applet and you want to run it as a stand-alone application using the Java interpreter (without having to embed the applet in an HTML document). You can accomplish this by extending the applet class and adding a main method. You'll need a window where the applet can display its output. One simple solution is to extend the Frame class and use that frame's window for the applet.

The following listing shows the SayHello class that converts the HelloWorld applet into a stand-alone Java application:

```
//--------------------------------
// File: SayHello.java
//
// A stand-alone version of the HelloWorld applet.

import java.applet.*;
import java.awt.*;

public class SayHello extends HelloWorld
{
    public static void main(String args[])
    {
        Applet applet = new SayHello();
        Frame frame = new HelloFrame("Hello, World!",
                                     applet, 300, 200);
    }
}

class HelloFrame extends Frame
{
    public HelloFrame(String title, Applet applet,
                      int width, int height)
    {
// Create a frame with the title
        super(title);

// Add a menu bar with a File menu and an Exit option
        MenuBar mbar = new MenuBar();
        Menu fmenu = new Menu("File", true);

        mbar.add(fmenu);
        fmenu.add("Exit");
        setMenuBar(mbar);

// Add the applet to this window...centered
        add("Center", applet);
        resize(width, height);
        show();

// Start the applet
        applet.init();
        applet.start();
    }

// Exit when user clicks on the Exit option
    public boolean action(Event evt, Object obj)
    {
```

(continued)

```
        if(evt.target instanceof MenuItem)
        {
            if(obj.equals("Exit"))
                System.exit(0);
        }
        return false;
    }
}
```

This example subclasses the `Frame` class to define the `HelloFrame` class. In the `HelloFrame` constructor, I add a menu bar with a `File` menu and an `Exit` button. Then I add the applet to the frame, resize the window, show the window (make it visible), and start the applet.

Note Note that in the `HelloFrame` constructor, the frame is created by calling the super-class constructor with the `super` keyword. The `super` keyword refers to the super-class — the class from which the current class inherits.

The `action` method is called whenever the user clicks on the frame or the menu bar. The method checks to see if the mouse click is on a menu item; if that menu item's label is Exit, the method calls `System.exit` to quit the program.

To compile the `SayHello.java` file, use the `javac` program, as follows:

```
javac SayHello.java
```

Then run the resulting `SayHello` applet with the Java interpreter program (`java`) with the following command:

```
java SayHello
```

The interpreter creates the frame and loads the applet, and then the applet's output appears in the frame. You can close the program by selecting Exit from the File menu, as shown in Figure 23-5. By converting an applet into a stand-alone program, you can run the applet without having to embed it in an HTML document.

Figure 23-5: A stand-alone version of the HelloWorld applet.

VisitCount — A visit-counter applet

This section turns to a simple but useful Java applet — a visit counter that demonstrates how a Java applet can access a CGI program to perform some useful task. You may have seen visit counters on many Web sites. A visit counter tells you how many visitors have accessed the Web site. A Java applet coupled with a CGI script provides an effectiveway to implement a visit counter. The basic idea is as follows:

✦ Write a CGI program that updates a count stored in a file. When run, the CGI program updates the count and sends back a text document with the current count.

✦ Embed a visit-counter applet in your Web site's home page. Whenever a user accesses the home page, the visit-counter applet is executed. Write the applet so that it, in turn, executes the CGI program that updates the count stored in a file at your Web server. The visit-counter applet can also display the current count.

`count.pl` — Perl script to update visitor count

To illustrate this technique, I'll first write a simple Perl script to increment the count stored in a file. The script `count.pl` performs the following tasks:

✦ Opens a file named `counter` and reads the current count stored in that file.

✦ Increments the count and stores the new count back in the `counter` file.

✦ Prints the count as a single line of text preceded by a `MIME` header.

The following listing shows my implementation of the `count.pl` script:

```perl
#!/usr/local/bin/perl
###############################################################
# Increments a visit count stored in the file named
# "counter" and send the count as a plain text document.
#
# I invoke this script from a Java applet embedded in
# the index.html document of my site. The formatting
# and display of the count is handled by the Java applet.
#
# Author: Naba Barkakati
###############################################################

# Print a minimal MIME header
    print "Content-type: text/plain\n\n";

    $counterfile = "counter";

# Open the counter file and get current count
    open(COUNTER, "$counterfile");
```

(continued)

```
# Lock the file to guard against another process updating the
# file as this script uses it
    $lock_exclusive = 2;
    $unlock = 8;
    flock(COUNTER, $lock_exclusive);

# Read and increment the count
    $line = <COUNTER>;
    close(COUNTER);

    chop($line);
    $count = $line;
    $count++;

# Save the new count in the file
    open(COUNTER, ">$counterfile");
    print COUNTER ("$count\n");
    close(COUNTER);

# Remember to unlock the file
    flock(COUNTER, $unlock);

# Send count to caller
    print "$count\n";
```

To test and use this script, place the `count.pl` file in the `cgi-bin` directory (that's the directory where your Web server looks for CGI programs). Then use a text editor to create a file named `counter` and enter a single line with a zero.

`VisitCount.java` — **Java applet that invokes** `count.pl`

The `VisitCount` Java applet does its job by opening a connection to a URL (by using the URL class in the `java.net` package). The URL specifies the host and the `count.pl` script. The net effect of connecting to the URL is to execute the `count.pl` script that updates the visit count and returns the current count.

After opening the URL, the applet calls the URL's `openStream` method and constructs a `DataInputStream` object to read a line of text from the URL. As you know from the description of the `count.pl` script, this single line should include the current visitor count for the Web site (specified in the URL). The `VisitCount` applet then formats the count and displays it on the Web page where the applet is embedded. The following listing shows the Java source code for the `VisitCount` applet:

```
//--------------------------------
// File: VisitCount.java
//
// Accesses a CGI program to update visit count and display
// the current count.
```

```
//
// Compile with: javac VisitCount.java
//
// Author: Naba Barkakati
//--------------------------------
/**
 * The VisitCount class is a Java applet that accesses a CGI
 * program at the host URL and retrieves the visitor count (the
 * CGI program also updates the count). Then it displays the
 * current count. Use an <applet> tag to embed this applet
 * at the location where you want to display the count.
 *
 * You'll need the count.pl script installed in your cgi-bin
 * directory.
 *
 * @author Naba Barkakati
 * @version 1.00 July 8, 1996
 */
//--------------------------------
import java.awt.*;
import java.applet.*;
import java.net.*;
import java.io.*;
//--------------------------------
// V i s i t C o u n t
//
// Applet class to display visitor count at a site

public class VisitCount extends java.applet.Applet
{
    String visitCount;  // String to store visitor count

//--------------------------------
// i n i t
//
// Class initialization method

    public void init()
    {
        try
        {
// Open the URL that counts visitors to this site
// *** Edit URL before using at your site ***
            URL url = new URL(
                "http://www.lnbsoft.com/exec-bin/count.pl");

// Open a data stream and read a single line
            try
            {
```

(continued)

```
                    DataInputStream in = new
                        DataInputStream(url.openStream());
                    visitCount = in.readLine();
                }
            catch(IOException e) {}
        }
        catch(MalformedURLException e) {}
    }
//---------------------------------
// p a i n t
//
// Method that paints the output

    public void paint(java.awt.Graphics gc)
        {
// Display the visitor count that was read from the URL
// Use whatever font style and color you want
// I used Helvetica for a message and a Courier font
// for the visitor count

        Font helv = new Font("Helvetica", Font.BOLD, 16);
        Font courier = new Font("Courier", Font.BOLD, 24);

        gc.setFont(helv);
        FontMetrics fm = gc.getFontMetrics();
        String message = "Visitor number: ";
        int xstart = 0;
        int ystart = fm.getHeight();
        gc.drawString(message, xstart, ystart);

// Advance horizontally by amount needed to display message
        xstart += fm.stringWidth(message);

// Change font to Courier and display the count
        gc.setFont(courier);
        gc.setColor(Color.red);
        gc.drawString(visitCount, xstart, ystart);
    }
}
```

Tip   I embedded the URL in this Java program, but a better approach would be to specify the URL through a `<param>` tag in the HTML document. In that way you would not have to edit the Java program when you change the URL.

Note   The implementation of the `VisitCount` class also demonstrates the exception-handling mechanism in Java. Any code that might cause an exception — an error condition — is enclosed in a `try` block (enclosed in a pair of curly braces {...}). The exception-handling code follows in one or more `catch` blocks following the `try` block. You also can enclose one `try` block inside another.

To compile the `VisitCount` applet and create the `VisitCount.class` file, use the `javac` program from the JDK as follows:

```
javac VisitCount.java
```

You should place the resulting `VisitCount.class` file in the same directory as the HTML document where you want to embed the applet. Because the `VisitCount` applet functions as a visit counter, you may want to embed the applet in your Web site's home page (usually, the `index.html` file in the Web server's document root directory). In that way, the visit count will be incremented whenever someone accesses your home page.

To see the `VisitCount` applet in action, visit the Web site at the URL `http://www.lnbsoft.com/`. The upper-left corner of the document in Figure 23-6 shows visitor count as displayed by the `VisitCount` applet.

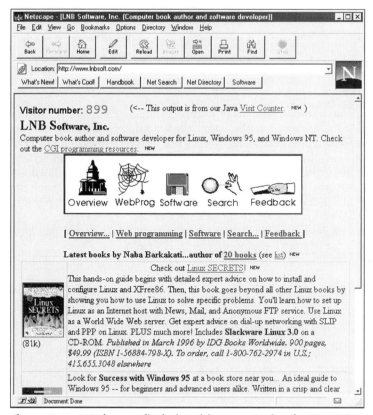

Figure 23-6: A Web page displaying visitor count using the `VisitCount` applet.

By studying the HTML source of the document at `http://www.lnbsoft.com/`, you can see how the `VisitCount` applet is embedded in a Web page. The `<applet>` tag corresponding to the display in Figure 23-6 is as follows:

```
<body>

<applet code=VisitCount width=200 height=26 align=middle>
<strong>You do not have a Java-capable browser. Otherwise,
you would have seen a visit count here :-)</strong>
</applet>

... other parts of the document deleted ...
</body>
```

In this case, the `<applet>` tag is the first item in the document's `<body>` element. You can place the `VisitCount` applet anywhere you want.

Tip   Use the `VisitCount` applet as a model for any Java applet that downloads data from your Web site and displays it in a user-selected format. For example, you could download stock prices for your company and plot the trends with a Java applet.

Learning Java

Now that you have seen some examples of Java programming, you are ready for an overview of Java. In the earlier examples, you have seen that Java can be used to create both stand-alone applications and applets that can be embedded in an HTML document. As you learn the features of Java, you'll notice that Java has everything you need from a general-purpose programming language. Although Java has been associated mostly with the creation of applets to be embedded in Web pages, many people have discovered that Java is also ideal for developing general-purpose applications.

One of the reasons for Java's popularity is its true portability. The compiled Java code runs on any system for which a Java interpreter is available.

Objects in Java

Java is an object-oriented language. This is so much the case that Java does not allow any stand-alone procedures at all; all data and procedures must be inside an object. In fact, the entire Java application is an object as well.

The basic concepts of object-based programming with Java are the same as with other object-oriented programming languages such as Smalltalk or C++:

✦ Data abstraction

✦ Inheritance

✦ Polymorphism

Data abstraction

To understand data abstraction, consider the file input/output (I/O) routines in the C run-time library. These routines allow you to view the file as a stream of bytes and to perform various operations on this stream by calling the file I/O routines. For example, you can call `fopen` to open a file, `fclose` to close it, `fgetc` to read a character from it, and `fputc` to write a character to it. This abstract model of a file is implemented by defining a data type named `FILE` to hold all relevant information about a file. The C constructs `struct` and `typedef` are used to define `FILE`. You will find the definition of `FILE` in the header file `stdio.h`. You can think of this definition of `FILE`, together with the functions that operate on it, as a new data type. like C's `int` or `char`.

To use the `FILE` data type in C, you do not have to know the data structure that defines it. In fact, the underlying data structure of `FILE` can vary from one system to another. Yet, the C file I/O routines work in the same manner on all systems. This is possible because you never access the members of the `FILE` data structure directly. Instead you rely on functions and macros that essentially hide the inner details of `FILE`. This is known as *data hiding*.

Data abstraction is the process of defining a data type, often called an abstract data type (ADT), together with using data hiding. The definition of an ADT involves specifying the internal representation of the ADT's data as well as the functions to be used by others to manipulate the ADT. With data hiding, the internal structure of the ADT can be altered without breaking the programs that call the functions provided for operations on that ADT. Thus, C's FILE data type is an example of an ADT (see Figure 23-7).

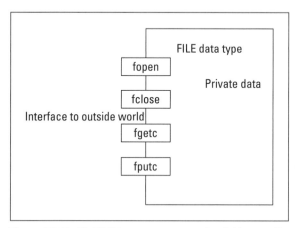

Figure 23-7: C's FILE type as an example of Abstract Data Type (ADT).

In object-oriented languages, you create an *object* from an ADT. An ADT is a collection of variables combined with the procedures necessary to operate on those variables. The variables represent the information contained in the object while the procedures define the operations that can be performed on that object. You can think of the ADT as a template from which specific instances of objects can be created as needed. The term *class* is often used for this template; consequently class is synonymous with an ADT. In fact, Java provides the class keyword precisely for the purpose of defining an ADT. The ADT is a template for objects in the sense that creating an object involves setting aside a block of memory for the variables of that object.

In Java, the procedures that operate on an object are known as *methods*. This term comes from the object-oriented language Smalltalk. Methods define the behavior of an object. Another common element of object-oriented programming that also originated with Smalltalk is the process of sending messages to an object, causing it to perform an operation by invoking one of the methods. In Java, you do this is by calling the appropriate method of the object.

In Java, you use the class keyword to define the blueprint of an object. This means that a class defines the data and methods that constitute a type of object. Then you can create instances of the object by using the new keyword. For example, you might create an instance of a Circle class as follows:

```
Circle c1 = new Circle(100.0, 60.0, 50.0);
```

This example invokes the Circle class constructor that accepts three floating-point numbers as argument (presumably, the coordinates of the center and the radius of the circle). You'll see a complete example of classes in the "Geometric shapes in Java" section, later in this chapter.

Inheritance

Data abstraction does not cover an important characteristic of objects. Real-world objects do not exist in isolation. Each object is related to one or more other objects. In fact, you can often describe a new kind of object by pointing out how the new object's characteristics and behavior differ from that of a class of objects that already exists.

This notion of defining a new object in terms of an old one is an integral part of object-oriented programming. The term *inheritance* is used for this concept because you can think of one class of objects inheriting the data and behavior from another class. Inheritance imposes a hierarchical relationship among classes where a child class inherits from its parent class. In Java terminology, the parent class is known as the *superclass*; the child class is the *subclass*. In a Java program, you use the extends keyword to indicate that one class is a subclass of another.

Note Unlike C++, Java does not support multiple inheritance (multiple inheritance allows a class to inherit from multiple superclasses). Java allows a class to have only one superclass. In Java, all classes inherit from a single root class named Object. (The Smalltalk programming language also provides a class hierarchy of this type.) Here the term *root class* refers to a class that does not have any superclass.

Polymorphism

In a literal sense, *polymorphism* means the quality of having more than one form. In the context of object-oriented programming, polymorphism refers to the fact that a single operation can have different behavior in different objects. In other words, different objects react differently to the same message. For example, consider the operation of addition. For two numbers, addition should generate the sum. In a programming language that supports object-oriented programming, you should be able to express the operation of addition by an operator, for example +. When this is possible, you can use the expression *x+y* to denote the sum of *x* and *y* for many different types of x and y: integers, floating-point numbers, and even strings (for strings the + operation means the concatenation of two strings).

Similarly, suppose a number of geometrical shapes all support a method, draw. Each object reacts to this method by displaying its shape on a display screen. Obviously, the mechanism for displaying the object differs from one shape to another, but all shapes perform this task in response to the same method.

Polymorphism allows you to simplify the syntax of performing the same operation on a collection of objects. For example, by exploiting polymorphism you can compute the area of each geometrical shape in an array of shapes with a simple loop:

```java
// Assume "shapes" is an array of shapes (rectangles, circles,
// etc.) and "computeArea" is a function that computes the
// area of a shape

for(int i=0; i < shapes.length; i++)
{
    double area = shapes[i].computeArea();
    System.out.println("Area = "+area);
}
```

This is possible because each object, regardless of the geometrical shape, supports the computeArea method and computes the area in a way appropriate for that shape.

Geometric shapes in Java

For an illustration of object-oriented programming in Java, consider the following example. Suppose you want to write a computer program that handles geometric shapes such as rectangles and circles. The program should be able to draw any shape and compute its area.

Shape **class**

The first step in implementing the geometric shapes in Java is to define the classes. You can start with an abstract class that defines the behavior of the shape classes by defining the common methods. The following listing shows the abstract Shape class that you should save in the Shapes.java file:

```
//-------------------------------
// File: Shape.java
//
// Abstract class for Shape objects

abstract public class Shape
{
    abstract public void draw();
    abstract public double computeArea();
}
```

As this listing shows, the abstract keyword indicates that a class cannot be instantiated because it does not implement all the methods.

Caution If you know C++, you'll notice some superficial similarities between C++ and Java class definitions. However, the similarities are truly superficial. I suggest you approach Java as a brand-new object-oriented language rather than as a mutation of C++. You can still use your knowledge of C syntax, but when it comes to the object-oriented features of Java, don't try to extrapolate from your knowledge of C++.

Circle **class**

After you define the abstract Shape class, you can create concrete versions of Shape classes such as a Circle and Rectangle. Here is a simple implementation of the Circle class that you can save in a file named Circle.java:

```
//-------------------------------
// File: Circle.java
//
// Circle class

public class Circle extends Shape
{
    double x, y;
    double radius;

    public Circle(double x, double y, double r)
    {
        this.x = x;
        this.y = y;
        this.radius = r;
    }

    public double computeArea()
```

```
    {
        return Math.PI * radius * radius;
    }

    public void draw()
    {
        System.out.println("Circle of radius "+radius+
                           " at ("+x+", "+y+")");
    }
}
```

As this definition of the Circle class shows, the Shape class implements the computeArea and draw methods that were declared as abstracts in the Shape class. The Circle class also defines three double variables — x, y, and radius — that denote the coordinates of the center and the radius of the circle. Such variables are referred to as *instance variables* of the class.

The extends keyword in the Circle class definition indicates that Circle is a subclass of the Shape class. The public qualifier specifies that the Circle class is accessible from other packages (in Java, a *package* is a collection of classes).

Rectangle **class**

In the following example, I define the Rectangle class using the same pattern as was used in defining the Circle class:

```
//--------------------------------
// File: Rectangle.java
//
// Rectangle class

public class Rectangle extends Shape
{
    double x1, y1;
    double x2, y2;

    public Rectangle(double x1, double y1,
                     double x2, double y2)
    {
        this.x1 = x1;
        this.y1 = y1;
        this.x2 = x2;
        this.y2 = y2;
    }

    public double computeArea()
    {
        return Math.abs((x1-x2)*(y1-y2));
    }
```

(continued)

```
        public void draw()
        {
            System.out.println("Rectangle with corners "+
                               "("+x1+", "+y1+") and "+
                               "("+x2+", "+y2+")");
        }
    }
```

Just as the `Circle` class is saved in the `Circle.java` file, the `Rectangle` class can be saved in the `Rectangle.java` file. This is how Sun's JDK expects the class to be defined.

Note   The `computeArea` method of the `Rectangle` class calls the `Math.abs` method to get the absolute value of an argument. Although this looks like the invocation of an object's method, there is no object named `Math`; instead `Math` is the name of a class. The `abs` method is a static method in the `Math` class. You can invoke a static method without having to create an instance of the class.

MakeShape **class — The test program**

Now that I have defined the `Circle` and `Rectangle` classes, it's time to test them with a simple program. In Java, the program itself must be another class; and for a stand-alone Java program, the class must include a `public static void` method called `main` (this is akin to the `main` function in a C program).

The following listing shows the `MakeShape` class (in a file named `MakeShape.java`) that includes a `main` method to test the geometric shapes:

```
//--------------------------------
// File: MakeShape.java
//
// Java application to try out various shapes

public class MakeShape
{
    public static void main(String args[])
    {
        Shape shapes[] = new Shape[2];

        shapes[0] = new Circle(100.0, 100.0, 50.0);
        shapes[1] = new Rectangle(80., 40., 120., 60.);

        System.out.println("\n"+shapes.length+" shapes\n");

        for(int i=0; i < shapes.length; i++)
        {
            double area = shapes[i].computeArea();
            System.out.println("Shape #"+i);
            shapes[i].draw();
```

```
            System.out.println("Area = "+area);
            System.out.println("-----");
        }
    }
}
```

The `main` method creates an array of `Shape` objects and initializes the array with different shapes. Then, the `computeArea` and `draw` methods of each shape are invoked.

Webmaster Note that you use the `new` keyword to create instances of objects in Java. There is no corresponding `delete` or `free` keyword to get rid of objects. Instead, Java supports a technique called *garbage collection* to automatically destroy objects that are no longer needed. Java keeps track of all references to an object and removes the object when there are no more references to it. This means that you do not have to worry about freeing memory in Java. Because memory management is a source of many errors in C and C++ programs, Java's support for garbage collection helps eliminate a major source of potential errors in your applications.

In this example, the `MakeShape` class is the Java application. To compile the program, type the following command:

```
javac MakeShape.java
```

This step takes care of compiling the `MakeShape.java` file and all the related classes (the `Shape.java`, `Circle.java`, and `Rectangle.java` files). In other words, the Java compiler (`javac`) acts a bit like the `make` utility in UNIX; `javac` determines the dependencies among classes and compiles all the necessary classes.

To run the `MakeShape` application, use the Java interpreter, as follows:

```
java MakeShape
```

Figure 23-8 shows the result of running the `MakeShape` program in an MS-DOS window under Windows 95.

Java program structure

A Java program consists of one or more classes. For stand-alone applications, you must have a class with a `public void static main` method. Applets require only a subclass of the Applet class.

The JDK expects the source files to have the same name as the class, but with a `.java` extension (thus, a class named `Circle` is defined in the file `Circle.java`). However, other Java development environments may have a different convention for naming files.

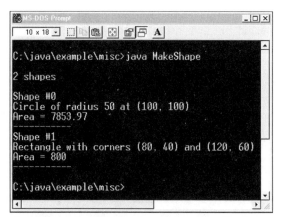

Figure 23-8: Running the `MakeShape` application in an MS-DOS window.

Within each source file, the parts of the program are organized as follows:

1. Comments at the start of the file describe the purpose of the class and provide other pertinent information such as the name of author and revision dates. Java supports both C- and C++-style comments. As in ANSI C, comments may start with /* and end after a */ pair. Or, you may begin a line of comment with a pair of slashes (//). A special type of comment, known as *doc comment*, begins with /** and ends with */. The doc comments can be extracted by the `javadoc` utility program to create online documentation for classes.

2. One or more `import` statements allow you to use abbreviated class names. For example, if you use the `java.applet.Applet` class, you can refer to that class by `Applet`, provided you include the following in the source file:

   ```
   import java.applet.*;
   ```

   Note that the import statement does not bring in any extra code into a class; it's simply a way to save typing so that you can refer to a class by a shorter name.

3. The class definition includes instance variables and methods. All variables and methods must be inside the class definition.

Primitive data types in Java

Java supports the standard C data types of `char`, `short`, `int`, `long`, `float`, and `double`. Additionally, Java introduces the `byte` and `boolean` types. Java also specifies the exact size of all primitive data types (in C, the size of the `int` type varies from one system to another). Table 23-1 summarizes Java's primitive types.

The following C-style usages are not allowed in Java:

✦ There is no `unsigned` keyword in Java; all integer values are signed.

✦ You cannot write `short int` or `long int` in Java.

	Table 23-1
	Java's Primitive Data Types

Type	Description
boolean	A 1-bit value that contains true or false. A boolean value is not an integer.
byte	An 8-bit signed integer with values between -128 and 127.
char	A 16-bit unsigned integer value representing a Unicode character. Unicode is a character encoding system designed to support storage and processing of written texts of many diverse languages. You can initialize a char variable with the notation \uxxxx where xxxx is a sequence of hexadecimal digits (for example, char c = \u00ff;).
double	A 64-bitdouble-precision floating-point value in the IEEE 754 format (a standard format that expresses a floating-point number in binary format).
float	A 32-bit single-precision floating-point value in IEEE 754 format.
int	A 32-bit signed integer with values between -2,147,483,648 and 2,147,483,647.
long	A 64-bit signed integer with values between -9,223,372,036,854,775,808 and 9,223,372,036,854,775,807.
short	A 16-bit signed integer with values between -32,768 and 32,767.

Non-primitive data types in Java

The non-primitive data types in Java are objects and arrays. All non-primitive types are handled by reference. This means that when you pass a non-primitive type to a method, the address of the object is passed to the method. The primitive types, however, are passed by value; that is, a copy of the data is passed to the method.

Webmaster Unlike C, Java does not have any pointer type. So, you cannot work with addresses of variables with the &, *, and -> operators. By eliminating pointers, Java gets rid of a common source of bugs and also prevents programmers from performing tricks with pointers that bypass Java's security mechanisms.

The fact that objects are handled through reference has the following implications:

✦ When you assign one object to another, Java does not copy the value of the object. All that happens is that you end up with two references to the same object. Consider the following example:

```
Circle c1 = new Circle(0., 0., 20.);
Circle c2 = new Circle(100.0, 60.0, 20.0);
c1 = c2; // c1 now refers to the same Circle as does c2
```

Here, both c1 and c2 end up referring to the same Circle object. The Circle object that c1 originally referred to is lost after you assign c2 to c1. (The Java garbage collector reclaims the memory allocated to the lost object.)

✦ To copy an object's value into another, call the `clone` method of the object (this assumes the object supports the `clone` method). Here is an example:

```
Vector x = new Vector();
Vector y = x.clone();  // Vector y is a copy of Vector x
```

✦ When you use the `==` operator, you check whether two variables refer to the same object. In other words, the `==` operator checks whether two objects are identical. To check whether two separate objects contain the same value, you must use a special method for that object type. For example, many Java classes provide an `equals` method to check for the equality of object values.

String **type**

Java includes a built-in `String` type; the compiler treats a `String` almost like primitive type. Java's `String` class is a part of the `java.lang` package, which the Java compiler uses by default.

The Java compiler automatically converts text placed within double quotes (`"..."`) into a `String`. Also, the + operator concatenates `String` objects. For example, you can write code such as the following:

```
String welcome = "Welcome to " + "Java.";
int numchars = welcome.length();
System.out.println("There are "+numchars+" characters in: "+welcome);
```

When executed, this code prints the following:

```
There are 16 characters in: Welcome to Java.
```

The `String` class supports a number of other methods that provide the functionality of C's string-manipulation functions (as defined in the `<string.h>` header file). Java includes two related classes for handling text strings:

✦ `String` to hold a string of characters that cannot be individually manipulated (in other words, you cannot insert or replace characters in the string).

✦ `StringBuffer` to represent a string of characters that may be manipulated. You can append, insert, and replace characters in a `StringBuffer` object.

Table 23-2 summarizes the methods of the `String` class.

Table 23-2
Methods of the String **Class**

HJMMethod	Description
`char charAt(int index);`	Returns a character at a specified index.
`int compareTo(String s);`	Compares this String with another String s.
`String concat(String s);`	Concatenates this String with another String s.
`String copyValueOf(char[] ca);`	Returns a String equivalent to the specified array of characters. This is a static method of the String class.
`boolean endsWith(String suffix);`	Returns true if String ends with suffix.
`boolean equals(String s);`	Returns true if this String matches another String s (case-sensitive comparison).
`boolean equalsIgnoreCase(String s);`	Returns true if this String matches another String s regardless of case (case-insensitive comparison).
`void getBytes(int srcBegin, int srcEnd, byte[] dest, int destBegin);`	Copies characters from a String into a byte array.
`void getChars(int srcBegin, int srcEnd, char[] dest, int destBegin);`	Copies characters from a String into a char array.
`int hashcode();`	Returns hash code for the String.
`int indexOf(int c);`	Returns index of the first occurrence of a character.
`int indexOf(String s);`	Returns index of the first occurrence of String s in the current String.
`String intern();`	Returns a unique instance of String from a global shared pool of String objects.

(continued)

Table 23-2 *(continued)*	
HJMMethod	*Description*
`int lastIndexOf(int c);`	Returns index of the last occurrence of a character.
`int lastIndexOf(String s);`	Returns index of the last occurrence of `String` s in the current `String`.
`int length();`	Returns the length of the `String` (the number of characters in the string).
`boolean regionMatches(int offset, String s, int soffset, int length);`	Returns `true` if a region of the `String` matches the specified region of another `String` s.
`String replace(char old, char new);`	Replaces all occurrences of an old character with a new character.
`boolean startsWith(String prefix);`	Returns `true` if `String` starts with specified prefix.
`String substring`	Returns a substring of this `String`. `(int begin, int end);`
`char[] toCharArray();`	Returns a character array from the `String`.
`String toLowerCase();`	Converts `String` to lowercase.
`String toString();`	Returns another `String` with the same contents.
`String toUpperCase();`	Converts `String` to uppercase.
`String trim();`	Removes any leading and trailing whitespace from `String`.
`String valueOf(type obj);`	Returns the `String` representation of an object's value (`type` may be any object of primitive type such as `boolean`, `char`, `int`, `long`, `float`, and `double`). This is a static method of the `String` class.

Webmaster The `String` class is defined with a `final` keyword. This means that you cannot subclass `String`. The Java compiler can optimize a final class so that the class can be used as efficiently as possible. To declare a class as final, use the following syntax:

```
public final class ClassName extends SuperClassName
{
// Body of class
}
```

Arrays

An array is an ordered collection of one or more elements. Java supports arrays of all primitive and non-primitive data types. As in C, you can declare an array variable by appending square brackets to the variable name, as follows:

```
byte buffer[] = new byte[256]; // Create an array for 256 byte variables
Shape shapes[] = new Shape[10];  // Create an array to hold 10 Shape
         objects
```

Webmaster Creating an array (for a specific type of object) does not create the objects that are stored in the array. All that Java creates is an array capable of holding references to objects of a specified type. All array elements are initialized with the value null (which is a Java keyword that means a variable that does not refer to any object). You must create the objects individually that you want to store in the array.

Here is how you might create and initialize an array of String objects:

```
String language[] = new String[4];
language[0] = "C";
language[1] = "C++";
language[2] = "Java";
// language[3] == null (the default value)
```

As this example illustrates, you access array elements the same way you use arrays in C — by putting an integer-values expression within square brackets after the array's name. The array indexes start at 0.

Tip You can always get the length of an array — the number of elements the array can hold — by accessing the length instance variable of the array. Here is an example:

```
String names[] = new String[5];
int len = names.length; // len = 5
```

Exception handling in Java

Exceptions refer to unusual conditions in a program. They can be outright errors that cause the program to fail, or conditions that can lead to errors. You can always detect when certain types of errors are about to occur. For instance, when indexing an array with the [] operator, you can detect if the index is beyond the range of valid values. But it's tedious to check for errors whenever you index into an array. Java's exception-handling mechanism allows you to place the exception-handling code in one place and avoid having to check for errors all over your program.

Java's exception-handling mechanism is similar to that in C++. The basic features are:

✦ When a block of code generates an error, it uses the `throw` keyword to throw an exception. When an exception is thrown, the Java interpreter stops executing that block of code and transfers control to a block that is designated as the handler for that exception (there are many types of exceptions).

✦ Enclose inside a `try` block any code that may throw an exception.

✦ Immediately following the `try` block, place one or more `catch` blocks that handle specific exceptions thrown by the code inside the `try` block.

✦ Place inside a `finally` block any code that should be executed to clean up before exiting the `try` block (regardless of whether there is an exception). In the `finally` block, you may include code to close files and network connections before the program exits.

The following code illustrates the syntax of `try`, `catch`, and `finally` blocks in Java:

```
try
{
    // Code that may generate exceptions of type AnException and
    // AnotherException
}
catch(AnException e1)
{
    // Handle exception of type AnException
}
catch(AnotherException e2)
{
    // Handle exception of type AnotherException
}
finally
{
    // This block of code is always executed after exiting the try block
    // regardless of how the try block exits
}
```

Interfaces

Java does not support multiple inheritance; each class can have only one superclass. However, sometimes you may want to inherit other types of behavior. For example, you may want to support a specific set of methods in a class (this is akin to saying that your class can do x, y, and z). Java provides the `interface` keyword, which allows a class to implement a specific set of capabilities.

An interface looks like an abstract class declaration. For example, the `run` method is used by the `Thread` class (see the "Threads" section) to start a thread of execution in a Java program. The `Runnable` interface specifies this capability through the following interface declaration:

```
public interface Runnable
{
    public void run();
}
```

If you implement all the methods of an interface, you can declare this fact by using the implements keyword in the class definition. For example, if a class defines the run method (which constitutes the Runnable interface), the class definition specifies this fact as follows:

```
import java.applet.*;
public class MyApplet extends Applet implements Runnable
{
// Must include the run() method
    public void run()
    {
// This can be the body of a thread
    }

// Other methods of the class
// ...
}
```

Threads

Java includes built-in support for threads. A *thread* refers to a single flow of control — a single sequence of Java byte codes being executed by the Java Virtual Machine. Just as an operating system can execute multiple processes by allocating short intervals of processor time to each process in turn, the Java Virtual Machine can execute multiple threads within a single application. You can think of threads as multitasking within a single process.

Threads can be very useful because you can turn individual threads loose on different sets of tasks. For example, one thread might monitor all user inputs to an applet while another thread periodically updates the display. A problem with threads is that they all share the same set of variables within the program. This means that each thread must be careful when accessing and updating any variable. As a thread changes parts of an object, it may lose its time slice and another may become active and use the partially updated object. Java includes the synchronized keyword that allows you to mark objects and methods that should not be accessed simultaneously by multiple threads. For example, you'd write the following code to ensure that a thread acquires a lock on myObject before executing the statements within the curly braces ({ . . . }):

```
synchronized(myObject)
{
// Some task that needs to be synchronized among threads
// ...
}
```

Using threads in an applet

The best way to understand threads is to go through a simple example. The following listing shows the `Clock` applet that uses a thread to display the current date and time:

```java
//------------------------------
// File: Clock.java
//
// Displays a digital clock using a thread.

import java.util.*;
import java.awt.*;
import java.applet.*;

public class Clock extends Applet implements Runnable
{
    private Thread clockThread;
    int interval = 1000;

// The run method is required by the Runnable interface

    public void run()
    {
        while(true)
        {
            try
            {
                Thread.sleep(interval);
            }
            catch(InterruptedException e) {}

// Repaint the clock face
            repaint();
        }
    }

    public void start()
    {
// Create and start the clock thread
        clockThread = new Thread(this);
        clockThread.start();
    }

    public void stop()
    {
// Stop the clock thread
        clockThread.stop();
    }

// The paint method draws the clock face
```

```
// It's a digital clock
    public void paint(Graphics gc)
    {
        Font helv = new Font("Helvetica", Font.ITALIC, 16);
        gc.setFont(helv);
        gc.drawString(new Date().toString(), 4, 20);
    }
}
```

Save this listing in the `Clock.java` file and compile the applet with the command:

```
javac Clock.java
```

Then create an HTML document, `Clock.html`, and embed the applet as follows:

```
<body>

<applet width=200 height=24 code=Clock>
A Java clock applet.
</applet>

</body>
```

Now type the following command to run the applet using `appletviewer`:

```
appletviewer Clock.html
```

Figure 23-9 shows the `appletviewer` window with output from the `Clock` applet.

As the applet runs, it should update the clock display every second.

Figure 23-9: Running the `Clock` applet in the `appletviewer`.

Understanding thread usage in an applet

After you have seen the `Clock` applet in action, go through the `Clock` applet's code to see how a thread works. Note the following:

✦ To create a thread, you need an instance of a class that implements the `Runnable` interface. Usually, you would implement the `Runnable` interface in your applet by providing a `run` method. Then you can create the `Thread` object by calling its constructor as follows:

```
myThread = Thread(this);
```

✦ The Java Virtual Machine (JVM) calls the applet's `start` method when the applet should run and calls the `stop` method when the applet should stop. Thus, the applet's `start` method is a good place to create the `Thread` object.

✦ After you create the `Thread` object, you must call that `Thread` object's start method (different from the applet's `start` method) to start running the thread.

✦ When started, the `Thread` executes the body of the `run` method. The `run` method should include code for the task you want the thread to perform.

✦ When you want to stop the thread, call its `stop` method.

Java applet API

The term API refers to Application Programming Interface — a collection of functions and variables that programmers use to develop applications. If you write applications in C, then the standard C run-time library serves as the API. The Java applet API is the set of classes and methods that you use to write applets. Because Java organizes classes into packages, the following packages constitute the Java applet API:

Package	Description
`java.lang`	Contains the classes central to the Java programming language. The `Object` class is the root class of the entire class hierarchy, and the `Class` is a class that describes a Java class (there is a `Class` object for each Java class). The `System` class provides a platform-independent interface to the system functions. The `String` and `StringBuffer` classes are for working with text strings. `Thread` class implements a thread of execution. The `Throwable` class serves as the root class of all exceptions.
`java.util`	Contains many useful classes such as `BitSet`, `Date`, `HashTable`, `Properties`, `Observable`, `Random`, `StringTokenizer`, `Vector`, and `Stack`.
`java.io`	Contains classes for input and output operations. Includes classes such as `DataInputStream`, `DataOutputStream`, `BufferedInputStream`, `BufferedOutputStream`, `StringBufferInputStream`, `PipedInputStream`, `PipedOutputStream`.

Package	Description
java.net	Contains classes that you need to access resources over the Net. The URL class lets you download an object from a specified URL by a single call. The Socket class allows you to connect to a specified port on an Internet host and read and write data using the InputStream and OutputStream classes (these are in the java.io package). The DatagramSocket class can be used to send and receive DatagramPacket objects.
java.awt	Contains classes that constitute Java's Abstract Windowing Toolkit (AWT) — a set of classes for creating graphical user interfaces (GUI) and rendering output within specific areas of the GUI. You'll use classes from this package in your applets because you often have to display graphics and images in an applet. The Graphics class defines the graphics and image output methods. To generate output and handle user's input, you'll use other graphics classes such as Color, Dimension, Event, Font, Image, Polygon, Point, MediaTracker, and Rectangle. To create the GUI and lay out the applet's work area, you'll use classes such as Button, Canvas, Checkbox, Choice, Dialog, Frame, FileDialog, Label, List, Scrollbar, TextArea, TextField, MenuBar, MenuItem, Menu, CheckboxMenuItem, BorderLayout, CardLayout, FlowLayout, GridBagLayout, and GridLayout.
java.awt.peers	Contains interface definitions that must be supported by the GUI components on any platform (that supports Java). Normal applications do not have to instantiate the peer classes directly.
java.awt.image	Contains classes for image manipulation. The ImageProducer interface represents an image source. FilteredImageSource applies a filter to a specified image source. CropImageFilter extracts a specified rectangle out of a larger image. MemoryImageSource can generate an image from an array of bytes or integers in memory. PixelGrabber can take pixels from an image source (ImageProducer) and store the pixels in an array.
java.applet	Contains the Applet class that serves as the superclass of all Java applets.

Note To become a proficient Java programmer, you have to become familiar with the classes and methods available in these packages. The best way to do so is to begin using some of these classes in your Java applets. Unfortunately, this chapter cannot cover all of the Java applet APIs in detail. It would require an entire book (maybe more) to cover Java programming in detail.

Because Java is very popular, there is no shortage of reference material on it. The problem is deciding which of the many Java books best suits your needs. Here are a few suggestions for reference books on Java programming and the Java applet API:

Ken Arnold and James Gosling, *The Java Programming Language* (Addison-Wesley, 1996). You may want a copy of this book for the very reason that C++ programmers want a copy of *The C++ Programming Language* by Bjarne Stroustrup — James Gosling is the originator of Java. This book provides a concise and precise presentation of how Java works and why.

James Gosling, Frank Yellin, and The Java Team, *The Java Application Programming, Volume 1: Core Packages* (Addison-Wesley, 1996). This is a reference guide to the Java libraries, written by the creators of Java. Volume 1 covers `java.lang`, `java.io`, `java.util`, and `java.net`.

James Gosling, Frank Yellin, and The Java Team, *The Java Application Programming, Volume 2: Window Toolkit and Applets* (Addison-Wesley, 1996). This reference volume covers the classes and methods you use to create applications and applets with graphical user interfaces. Volume 2 covers `java.awt`, `java.awt.image`, `java.awt.peer`, and `java.applet`.

URL
If you want to download the Java API documentation and print them, visit the Java documentation site at the following URL:

```
http://java.sun.com/products/JDK/CurrentRelease/ftp_docs.html
```

Follow the instructions at this site to download the API documentation in a compressed file (available in tar, ZIP, MacBinary, or Macintosh BinHex format).

Summary

Java provides a portable way to embed executable content in an HTML document. This means that you can provide small applications — called *applets* — that are downloaded and executed in any Java-capable Web browser. You can also use Java for stand-alone applications that can run outside a Web browser. This chapter provides you an overview of Java and gets you started with a few simple programming examples.

Where to go next . . .

✦ If you need a refresher course on HTML, read Chapters 10 and 11.

✦ For information on CGI applications, consult Chapter 19.

✦ To learn about JavaScript, turn to Chapter 24.

✦   ✦   ✦

Using JavaScript

◆ ◆ ◆ ◆

In This Chapter

Understanding
JavaScript

Writing your first
JavaScript script

Learning JavaScript
syntax

Using JavaScript
objects and arrays

Using the HTML
extensions for
JavaScript

◆ ◆ ◆ ◆

The previous chapter showed how to create applets using
Java and how to embed these applets in HTML documents.
This chapter turns to JavaScript, which provides an even simpler
way of embedding executable content in an HTML document.

JavaScript is an interpreted language that Netscape Navigator
(version 2.0 and later) supports. You can embed JavaScript
programs directly into an HTML document. There is no need to
compile the program; Netscape Navigator interprets and executes
the JavaScript program as it processes the HTML document.

Note You can use JavaScript to augment CGI programs that you might
use to handle user input entered in an HTML form. For example,
you can write JavaScript functions that validate the user's input
before the input is submitted to the CGI program residing at your
Web server. With JavaScript, you also can create dynamic forms
that change depending upon the checkboxes, radio buttons, and
input fields that the user fills in.

This chapter provides an overview of JavaScript and shows you
how to use JavaScript to interact with objects (such as forms
and buttons) in an HTML document.

Writing Your First Script in JavaScript

It's simple to write a script using JavaScript. As you prepare your
HTML document, add the JavaScript code within a pair of
`<script>` and `</script>` tags. For example, the following HTML
document includes a JavaScript script that displays Hello,
World! at the top of the page (the script is shown in boldface):

```
<html>
<head>
<title>Hello, World! in JavaScript</title>
</head>

<body>

<script language="JavaScript">
```

(continued)

```
<!- Hide script from "non-JavaScript" browsers

document.write("<h2>Hello, World!</h2>");

// This line appears as comment in JavaScript ->

</script>

This HTML document includes a JavaScript script.

</body>
</html>
```

To help you identify the script, the listing shows the entire `<script>` element in boldface. As you can see, the starting `<script>` tag has a `language` attribute that specifies the language of the script. In this case, the language is JavaScript. The actual body of the script follows the `<script>` tag and ends with the `</script>` tag.

Webmaster This simple example also illustrates a technique for ensuring that the script is not interpreted as part of the HTML document by browsers that do not support JavaScript. You embed the body of the script between two lines of text, as follows:

```
<!- Hide script from browsers that do not support JavaScript
...the body of the script goes here...
// This line appears as comment in JavaScript ->
```

To a Web browser, the first line appears as the beginning of an HTML comment and the last line as the end of that comment. Thus, the entire block of text is ignored by a browser that does not recognize JavaScript. However, a browser that expects JavaScript interprets the lines of text that follow the first line. The last line begins with a pair of slashes (//), which marks that line as a comment in JavaScript.

For the simple example above, the entire script consists of the following line:

```
document.write("<h2>Hello, World!</h2>");
```

This statement calls the `write` function of the `document` object (which refers to the current HTML document). That's what the syntax `document.write` means. The `write` function takes a string (within double quotes) as argument. In this case, the string is an HTML `<h2>` element. When Netscape Navigator executes this JavaScript statement, that HTML element gets inserted in the HTML document at the location where the `<script>` tag appears.

To see the result of this JavaScript, load the HTML file into Netscape Navigator (version 2.0 or later). As Figure 24-1 shows, the output of the JavaScript corresponds to the HTML tag generated by the JavaScript script followed by any other text in the HTML document. This example shows how you can add HTML content using a JavaScript script.

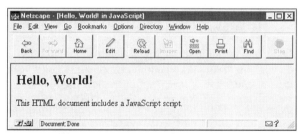

Figure 24-1: Netscape Navigator displaying an HTML document with a "Hello, World!" JavaScript script.

Learning JavaScript

If you know a programming language such as C, C++, or Java, you'll find JavaScript easy to learn. If you have never used a programming language, you'll need some practice to become familiar with JavaScript. In any case, the best approach is to start with a small subset of features, try them out in HTML documents, and view the results. With time, you will learn enough to make the most of JavaScript.

To learn JavaScript, become familiar with three types of information:

✦ **JavaScript syntax:** This category of information includes the reserved words, operators, data types, variables, and statements that you can use in JavaScript scripts. Learn the rules that the JavaScript interpreter follows.

✦ **JavaScript objects:** Learn about JavaScript's predefined objects to write powerful scripts. You cannot define new object types in JavaScript, as with Java, but there are predefined objects such as `document`, `form`, `string`, `text`, `textarea`, and `window`. Additionally, JavaScript includes utility objects such as `Date` for working with dates and `Math` for mathematical constants and functions.

✦ **HTML enhancements to support JavaScript:** You already may have seen the `<script>` tag that encloses a JavaScript script. Additionally, Netscape Navigator version 2 enhances some existing HTML tags (such as `<form>`, `<input>`, and `<textarea>`) to allow events such as mouse clicks and text entry to trigger the activation of JavaScript functions defined in that HTML document. These HTML extensions allow you to use JavaScript for tasks such as validating form input before sending the data to the Web server.

JavaScript information on the Net

This chapter provides an overview of JavaScript, highlights key points, and shows a few examples. There is not enough space in one chapter to provide all the information on JavaScript. Additionally, JavaScript is still evolving and some new details may emerge as the language definition matures. A few books are available that cover JavaScript. However, your best bet for detailed information is Netscape's JavaScript documentation, which you can find at the following URL:

```
http://home.netscape.com/eng/
mozilla/2.0/handbook/
javascript/index.html
```

On the Net, there are a quite a few Web sites with information on JavaScript as well as interesting JavaScript examples. The following site has a collection of links to JavaScript resources:

```
http://intergalactinet.com/
javascript/
```

Another good source of JavaScript information is the JavaScript FAQ (Frequently Asked Questions) at the following URL:

```
http://www.freqgrafx.com/411/
jsfaq.html
```

JavaScript syntax

JavaScript syntax is similar to that of C and C++. As in C, each statement ends with a semicolon (;).You can also define variables, write expressions using operators such as + and -, and define a block of statements as a function (which you can invoke by a single name). JavaScript comments may begin with two slashes (//) or may begin with /F and end with F/. In other words, JavaScript supports C- and C++ -style comments.

Because JavaScript is a scripting language, you can embed (inside <script> and </script> tags) one or more blocks of JavaScript statements in an HTML document. Although you can place large sequences of statements without any structure, it's customary to organize the script into functions. Organizing the script into functions also allows you to call those functions from other scripts, as necessary.

Webmaster You can place JavaScript scripts anywhere in an HTML document; indeed, a script that prints HTML text has to appear exactly at the location where you want that HTML text. However, you should embed all of your function definitions in the HTML document's <head>. That way, these functions are loaded, interpreted, and ready for use before the browser starts loading the body of the HTML document.

Data types and variables

JavaScript does not have strict variable types. As with many other scripting languages, such as Perl and Tcl, you can define a variable by assigning a value to a name. The following script defines a few variables and uses them in a statement:

```
<script language="JavaScript">
<!- hide from old browsers

title = "UNIX Webmaster Bible";   // a string
page_count = 800;                 // an integer
price = 44.95;                    // a floating-point number
this_doc = document;             // an object
purchase = true;                 // a boolean value

this_doc.writeln("Title = "+title
                 +", "+page_count+" pages"
                 +", $"+price);

// done hiding ->
</script>
```

If you embed this script in an HTML document and load that document in Netscape Navigator, the browser executes the script and displays:

```
Title = UNIX Webmaster Bible, 800 pages, $44.950000000000003
```

This line is the output of the `writeln` function call in the script.

You can also use the `var` keyword to define a variable. The following statement declares a string variable `message` and an uninitialized variable `i`:

```
var message = "Enter your name:", i;
```

Tip   The `var` keyword is commonly used in a function to declare local variables (especially to declare a variable with the same name as another variable declared outside the function). It is a useful practice to declare all variables with the `var` keyword.

You can initialize a JavaScript variable with four basic data types:

✦ *Object*: Any predefined JavaScript object (see the "JavaScript objects" section for a list of these objects).

✦ *String*: A set of characters enclosed within a pair of single or double quotes.

✦ *Number*: Integer or floating-point values.

✦ *Boolean*: `true` or `false`.

Note   Variable names must begin with an alphabetic character or an underscore. In the rest of the variable name, you can use only alphanumeric characters and underscores. JavaScript is case-sensitive.

Expressions

You can write expressions by combining variables with operators such as + (add), - (subtract), F (multiply), / (divide), and = (assign). Here are some examples:

```
count = 10;
x = count + 1;
price = 44.95;
total_price = ( count * price  )/ 2;
```

You can use numbers as well as variable names in expressions. You can use whitespace to enhance readability. Also, use parentheses to specify how you want expressions to be evaluated. Table 24-1 summarizes the JavaScript operators.

Table 24-1
JavaScript Operators

Operator	Description
+	Addition (+ also concatenates strings)
-	Subtraction or negation (for example, `-x`)
*	Multiplication
/	Division
%	Modulo (remainder after you divide one number by another)
—	Decrement (for example, `count—`)
++	Increment (for example, `count++`)
|	Bitwise-OR
&	Bitwise-AND
^	Bitwise-XOR (exclusive OR)
||	Boolean OR
&&	Boolean AND
!	Boolean NOT
<<	Shift bits to the left
>>	Shift bits to the right
<<<	Shift bits to the left and fill the right end with zeros (zero-fill left-shift operator)
>>>	Shift bits to the right and fill the left end with zeros (zero-fill right-shift operator)
==	Equal to
!=	Not equal to

Operator	Description
>	Greater than
<	Less than
>=	Greater than or equal to
<=	Less than or equal to
0=	Compound assignment (0 is one of the following operators: +, -, *, /, >>, <<, |, &, ^, and %)
[ ]	Subscript (for example, x[i] means i-th element of array x)
.	Object access (for example, document.writeln accesses the writeln function of the document object)
? :	Conditional (for example, z?x:y is x if z is true; otherwise it is y)

Note If you know C or C++, you'll recognize most of the JavaScript operators because they are the same as in C. The only two new operators in JavaScript are the zero-fill left-shift (<<<) and zero-fill right-shift (>>>) operators. C programmers should note that JavaScript does not have any -> operator because there are no pointers in JavaScript.

Statements

As in C, you use JavaScript statements to specify actions to be performed and to control the flow of execution of the script. A statement consists of JavaScript key-words, expressions, and other statements. Each statement ends with a semicolon.

You can enclose a group of statements in a pair of braces ({ . . . }). Such groups of statements are called compound statements. Also known as blocks, such compound statements can have local variables, declared with the var keyword. You'll typically use blocks of statements to define JavaScript functions.

Currently JavaScript uses the following reserved keywords:

break	continue	delete	else
eval	false	for	function
if	in	new	null
return	this	true	var
while	with		

Additionally, JavaScript reserves the following keywords (used in Java) for future use:

abstract	boolean	byte	byvalue
case	catch	char	class
const	default	do	double

(continued)

```
extends          final           finally         float
goto             implements      import          instanceof
int              interface       long            native
package          private         protected       public
short            static          super           switch
synchronized     threadsafe      throw           transient
try              void
```

The following sections alphabetically describe some JavaScript statements.

The break statement

Use the break statement to jump to the statement following the innermost for or while statement. Here is an example that uses break to exit a for loop:

```
var sum = 0;
for(i = 1; i > 0; i++)
{
    if(i > 10) break;
    sum += i;
}
document.writeln("Sum from 1...10 = "+sum);
```

This code prints the following result:

```
Sum from 1...10 = 55
```

The continue statement

The continue statement begins the next iteration of the innermost for or while statement in which it appears. You can use continue when you want to skip executing the loop. For example, to add the numbers from 1 to 10, excluding 5, you can use a for loop that skips the body when the loop index (i) is 5:

```
for(i=0, sum=0; i <= 10; i++)
{
    if(i == 5) continue;    // Exclude 5
    sum += i;
}
```

The delete statement

Use the delete statement to destroy an object that you have created with the new statement. In JavaScript, you can create a generic object by creating an instance of the predefined object class using the reserved keyword new. The following example creates a new object, initializes it with two properties (the variables of an object are called its properties), and then uses the delete statement to destroy the object:

```
// Create an object with the new statement
position = new Object;

// Initialize properties of the object (in JavaScript you can add
// properties on-the-fly)
position.x = 1.0;
position.y = -1.0;

// Print the object's properties
document.writeln("Position = ("+position.x+", "+position.y+")");

// Destroy the object
delete position;
```

The eval statement

The eval function is not really a statement; rather, eval is a built-in JavaScript function (that means a function that's already defined for use in your scripts). Use eval to evaluate a JavaScript expression stored in a string. In other words, you can create a JavaScript script in a string and call eval to execute that script. The following script illustrates how eval works:

```
// Parts of a JavaScript expression
obj = "document";
method = "writeln";
args = "\"Hello\"";

// Concatenate the parts to create an expression
expr = obj+"."+method+"("+args+")";

// Print the expression and then evaluate it
document.writeln("Next line shows the result of evaluating:<strong> "
                 +expr+"</strong><br>");
eval(expr);
```

Figure 24-2 shows the result of running this script. The "Hello" on the second line of output is generated by the eval statement.

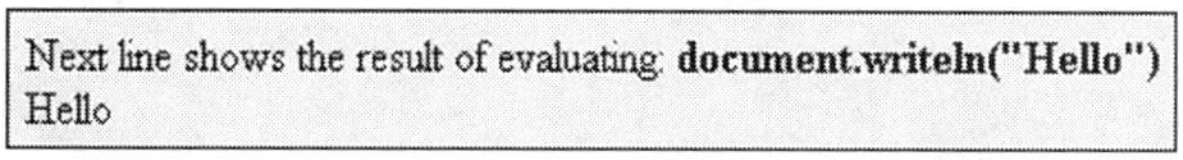

Next line shows the result of evaluating: **document.writeln("Hello")**
Hello

Figure 24-2: Result of evaluating a string that contains a JavaScript expression.

The `for` **statement**

Use the `for` statement to execute a statement zero or more times, based on the value of an expression. The syntax is as follows:

```
for (expr_1; expr_2; expr_3) statement
```

where `expr_1` is evaluated once at the beginning of the loop, and the `statement` is executed as long as the expression `expr_2` evaluates to `true`. The third expression, `expr_3`, is evaluated after each execution of the `statement`. Here is an example that uses a `for` loop to add the numbers from 1 to 10:

```
for(i=0, sum=0; i <= 10; sum += i, i++);
```

In this example, the work of adding the numbers is done in the third expression, and the statement controlled by the `for` loop is a null statement (the lone ; that follows the closing parenthesis of the `for` statement).

The `for...in` **statement**

Use the `for...in` construct to access all elements of an object. For example, the following script (embedded in the `<head>` element of an HTML document) uses the `for...in` statement to access and display all the properties of the `document` object:

```
<head>
<title>JavaScript sample</title>

<script language="JavaScript">
<!- hide from old browsers

document.writeln("<h3>Properties of this document:</h3><pre>");

// The following for loop prints the properties of the
// current document

for (count in document)
{
    document.writeln(count+" = "+document[count]);
}

// done hiding ->
</script>
</head>
```

To understand what this script does, load this HTML file into Netscape Navigator and see the output. Figure 24-3 shows the output when I loaded the file from a Web server on my local area network.

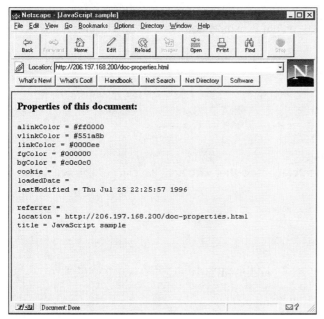

Figure 24-3: Output of a JavaScript script that displays the properties of the document object.

Tip

Figure 24-3 shows the name and value of the document object's properties — the variables that store the attributes of the document. The document object refers to the current HTML document (this is the document that contains the JavaScript script). The document object's properties include a number of colors as well as the document's URL and title. You can access these properties from any JavaScript script.

The function **statement**

Use the function statement to begin the definition of a function that you can call from other JavaScript scripts in the document. You do not have to declare the variable types. For example, here's a simple function to add two numbers:

```
function add(x, y)
{
    return x+y;
}
```

The if **statement**

Use the if statement to test an expression and execute a statement only when the expression is true. An if statement has the following form:

```
if (expression)  statement
```

The statement following the `if` is executed only if the expression in parentheses evaluates to `true`. That statement is usually compound. Here is an example:

```
// str is a string
var how_many = parseInt(str, 10); // convert string into an integer
if(how_many > 20)
{
    alert("Cannot create more than 20 items at a time!");
}
```

The `if...else` statement

This is a form of the `if` statement together with an `else` clause. The syntax is

```
if (expression)
    statement_1
else
    statement_2
```

where `statement_1` is executed if the expression within the parentheses is `true`. Otherwise, `statement_2` is executed. Here is an example that uses `if` and `else` to pick the smaller of two variables:

```
if ( a <= b)
    smaller = a;
else
    smaller = b;
```

The `new` statement

Use the statement to create an object by calling a constructor function (a function that returns an object). In the following example, `makeObject` is a simple constructor function and the variable `anItem` is created using the `new` operator:

```
function makeObject()
{
    return this;
}
anItem = new makeObject();
```

The `return` statement

The `return` statement stops executing the current function and returns control to the calling function. The syntax is

```
return expression;
```

where the value of the expression is returned as the value of the function.

The this **statement**

Use the this keyword in a function to refer to the object on which the function operates. The following example uses the this keyword in a constructor function that returns a new object:

```
function aThing()
{
    return this;
}
```

The var **statement**

Use var to declare variables, especially any variables you use locally in the body of a function. For example, you might use var to declare a local variable in a for loop:

```
sum = 0;    // this is a global variable
for(var i = 0; i < 10; i++)  // i is a local variable
{
    sum += i;
}
```

The while **statement**

The while statement has the following form:

```
while (expression) statement
```

where the statement is executed until the expression evaluates to false (in other words, the while loop runs as long as the expression is true). A while statement evaluates the expression before each execution of the statement. Thus, a while loop executes the statement zero or more times. Here is a while statement for copying one array to another:

```
var i = numItems;
while (i >= 0)  /* Copy one array to another */
{
    array2[i] = array1[i];
    i—;
}
```

The with **statement**

Use the with statement to indicate the default object for a block of statements enclosed within braces ({ . . . }). The general form of the with statement is as follows:

```
with (anObject)
{
    statements
}
```

This `with` statement specifies that `anObject` is the default object for the statements enclosed within the braces. This means that all property names and methods (functions) used in the statements refer to respective properties and methods of `anObject`. For example, if you have a block of statements that use mathematical functions from the `Math` object, you might enclose those statements in a `with` statement, as follows:

```
var radius = 10;
var theta = 30.0;
var area, x, y;

// Compute area and x, y coordinates
with(Math)
{
    area = PI * radius * radius;
    var theta_radians = theta * PI / 180.0;
    x = radius * cos(theta_radians);
    y = radius * sin(theta_radians);
}
```

In this way you do not have to write each method and property with a `Math.` prefix (such as `Math.PI` to refer to the `PI` property, which is the value of the constant "pi").

JavaScript objects

JavaScript uses a simple object model in which an object is a collection of properties and methods. The properties are JavaScript variables and the methods are the functions associated with the object.

JavaScript comes with a small set of built-in object types and predefined objects. You can also define your own object type by writing a constructor function that initializes the object's properties and returns this. Then, you can add functions that act as methods for the new object.

Using predefined objects

Predefined objects are objects that JavaScript defines for use in your scripts. Use predefined objects to access attributes of the Netscape Navigator browser. For example, `document` is a predefined object that refers to the HTML document containing the JavaScript script. The following list summarizes predefined objects:

Name	Description
anchor	An HTML-named anchor tag (`<a>` with `name` attribute) that marks some text as a possible target of a hyperlink.
anchors	An array containing all the `anchor` objects in a document.
button	An HTML `<input>` tag of type `button`. Refer to a `button` by the name you assign with the `name` attribute in the `<input>` tag.

Name	Description
checkbox	An HTML `<input>` tag of type `checkbox`. Refer to a `checkbox` by the name you assign with the `name` attribute in the `<input>` tag.
document	The current HTML document.
form	An HTML form defined with the `<form>` and `</form>` tags. Refer to a `form` object by the name you assign with the `name` attribute in the `<form>` tag.
forms	An array of all the `form` objects in a `document`.
frame	A frame defined by Netscape's `<frame>` tag. Refer to a `frame` object by the name you assign with the name attribute in the `<frame>` tag.
frames	An array of all the `frame` objects in a window.
history	Browser's history list (the list of URLs the browser has accessed).
link	An HTML anchor tag (`<a>` with a `href` attribute) that designates a hyperlink.
links	An array containing all the `link` objects in a document.
location	A URL such as `http://www.idgbooks.com/`.
navigator	An object containing information about the version of Netscape Navigator being used. Use this object to determine what version of Netscape Navigator your users are using.
password	An HTML `<input>` tag of type `password`. Refer to a `password` object by the name you assign with the `name` attribute in the `<input>` tag.
radio	An HTML `<input>` tag of type `radio`. Refer to a `radio` object by the name you assign with the `name` attribute in the `<input>` tag.
reset	An HTML `<input>` tag of type `reset`. Refer to a `reset` button by the name you assign with the `name` attribute in the `<textarea>` tag.
select	A scrolling list created by the HTML `<select>` tag. Refer to a `select` object by the name you assign with the `name` attribute in the `<select>` tag.
submit	An HTML `<input>` tag of type `submit`. Refer to a `submit` button by the name you assign with the `name` attribute in the `<input>` tag.
text	An HTML `<input>` tag of type `text`. Refer to a `text` object by the name you assign with the `name` attribute in the `<input>` tag.
textarea	An HTML `<textarea>` tag. Refer to a `textarea` object by the name you assign with the `name` attribute in the `<textarea>` tag.
window	A browser window. You can open new browser windows.

URL Each of these predefined objects contains a number of properties and methods. To use these objects effectively, become familiar with the properties and methods of the objects. You can view the details online by browsing Netscape's JavaScript documentation page at the following URL:

```
http://home.netscape.com/eng/mozilla/2.0/handbook/javascript/index.html
```

Using built-in object types

You can use built-in object types to create instances of new objects and access methods (such as the mathematical functions in the Math object type). JavaScript includes the following built-in object types:

Name	Description
Date	Use this object type to work with date and time. You can get the current date and time as well as convert a Date object to a string.
Math	This object type includes mathematical constants (such as PI) as properties and mathematical functions (such as abs, cos, sqrt) as methods.
string	Represents any string value (currently there is no explicit String class in JavaScript, but there may be such a class in the future).

Using the Date type

JavaScript provides a Date type, patterned after Java's Date class. JavaScript stores dates as the number of milliseconds since 00:00:00 hours of January 1, 1970. Currently, you cannot work with dates prior to January 1, 1970. To create a variable to hold a Date, use the new operator with the Date constructor function. To create a Date initialized with the current date and time, write

```
var curTime = new Date();
```

The Date constructor has several other forms that accept different arguments. The following examples illustrate the different Date constructors:

```
// Create new date specified by a string
newYear97 = new Date("January 1, 1997 00:00:00");

// Create new date specified by integer values for year, month, and day
// Note that month 0 is January, so month 7 = August
birthDay = new Date(84, 7, 16);

// Create new date with specific year, month, day, hour, minute, second
// The hours go from 0 to 23; seconds and minutes from 0 to 59
countDown = new Date(97, 8, 30, 9, 45, 0);
```

Print these dates by passing them directly to the document object's `writeln` method:

```
document.writeln("<p>"+newYear97+"<p>"+birthDay+"<p>"+countDown);
```

This statement prints the dates in the following format:

```
Wed Jan 01 00:00:00 EST 1997
Thu Aug 16 01:00:00 EDT 1984
Tue Sep 30 10:45:00 EDT 1997
```

The `document` object's `writeln` method calls the `toString` method of an object to obtain the string representation of an object. The `Date` object provides a `toString` method. If you need the string representation of a date, call `toString` explicitly:

```
var datestr = curTime.toString();
```

`Date` includes a number of other methods summarized in the following list.

Method	Description
getDate	Returns the day of the month of a `Date`. The day of the month goes from 1 to 31.
getDay	Returns the day of the week of a `Date`. The day of the week ranges from 0 to 6 (0 = Sunday, 1 = Monday, and so on).
getHours	Returns the hour of a `Date`. Hours range from 0 to 23.
getMinutes	Returns the minutes of a `Date`. Minutes range from 0 to 59.
getSeconds	Returns the second of a `Date`. Seconds range from 0 to 59.
getTime	Returns the number of milliseconds in a `Date` (the count begins at 00:00:00 on January 1, 1970).
getTimezoneOffset	Returns the time zone offset in minutes for the current location.
getYear	Returns the year (in terms of years since 1900) in a `Date`.
parse	Returns the number of milliseconds since January 1, 1970 00:00:00 corresponding to a date in string format (for example, `nxtBday = Date.parse("Aug 16, 1997");)`
setDate	Sets the day of the month in a `Date`. The day of the month ranges from 1 to 31.
setHours	Sets the hours in a `Date`. Hours range from 0 to 23.
setMinutes	Sets the minutes in a `Date`. Minutes range from 0 to 59.
setMonth	Sets the month in a `Date` (month 0 = January, 1 = February, and so on).

(continued)

Method	Description
setSeconds	Sets the seconds in a Date. Seconds range from 0 to 59.
setTime	Sets a Date to correspond to an integer representing the milliseconds elapsed since January 1, 1970 00:00:00 (for example, birthDay.setTime(Date.parse("Aug 16, 1997")); sets the Date birthDay to Aug 16, 1997).
setYear	Sets the year in a Date. Specify year in number of years since 1900.
toGMTString	Returns a string representation of a Date in GMT format (for example, Sat, 16 Aug 1997 05:00:00 GMT).
toLocaleString	Returns a string representation of a Date in the current locale's format (for example, this method returns 08/16/97 00:00:00 for Aug 16, 1997 00:00:00 in the USA).
toString	Returns a string representation of a Date (for example, Sat Aug 16, 00:00:00 EDT 1997).
UTC	Returns the number of milliseconds since January 1, 1970 00:00:00 corresponding to a date in comma-separated format (for example, nxtBday = Date.UTC(97, 7, 16); returns the number of milliseconds for Aug 16 1997).

Using the Math type

JavaScript's Math object type is similar to the Math class in Java. Unlike Date, you do not need to create an instance of the Math object with the new operator. Rather, the Math object contains a number of mathematical constants and mathematical functions that you access through the object. For example, you can use Math.PI to refer to the value of the constant "pi". Similarly, Math.cos is the function that returns the cosine of an angle. For example, to compute the sine of 30 degrees, you'd write

```
var x = Math.sin(30 * Math.PI / 180);
```

That multiplication by Math.PI and division by 180 is necessary to convert 30 degrees into radians (because Math.sin expects its argument to be in radians).

Tip You access the properties and methods by adding a Math. prefix to the name of the property or method. You can avoid typing Math. for each method by enclosing all math computations in a with block, as follows:

```
with (Math)
{
    area = PI * r * r;
    x = r * cos(theta);
    y = r * sin(theta);
}
```

where area, x, y, r, and theta are declared before the with block.

The `Math` properties are all constants. The following JavaScript code fragment lists these properties:

```
for (i in Math)
{
    document.writeln("Math."+i+" = "+Math[i]+"<br>");
}
```

The resulting output shows the names and values of the constants that constitute the properties of `Math`:

```
Math.SQRT1_2 = 0.70710678118654757
Math.SQRT2 = 1.4142135623730951
Math.PI = 3.1415926535897931
Math.LN10 = 2.3025850929940459
Math.LN2 = 0.69314718055994529
Math.LOG10E = 0.43429448190325182
Math.LOG2E = 1.4426950408889634
Math.E = 2.7182818284590451
```

The meanings of these `Math` properties are as follows:

Name	Description
SQRT1_2	Square root of one-half (1/2)
SQRT2	Square root of 2
PI	The constant "pi" (3.1415926535897931)
LN10	Natural logarithm of 10 (logarithm of 10 to the base e)
LN2	Natural logarithm of 2 (logarithm of 2 to the base e)
LOG10E	Logarithm of e to the base 10
LOG2E	Logarithm of e to the base 2
E	Euler's constant (e)

The `Math` methods include all common trigonometric functions and several other useful functions, as shown in the following list:

Method	Description
abs	Returns the absolute value of a number
acos	Returns the arc cosine of a number
asin	Returns the arc sine of a number
atan	Returns the arc tangent of a number
ceil	Returns the smallest integer that is greater than or equal to a number

(continued)

Method	Description
cos	Returns the cosine of a number (representing an angle in radians)
exp	Returns e (Euler's constant) to the power of a number
floor	Returns the largest integer that is less than or equal to a number
log	Returns the logarithm to the base e of a number
max	Returns the maximum of two numbers
min	Returns the minimum of two numbers
pow	Returns the first argument raised to the power of the second argument Thus, Math.pow(y,x) means y raised to the power x
round	Returns a number rounded to the nearest integer
sin	Returns the sine of a number (representing an angle in radians)
sqrt	Returns the square root of a number
tan	Returns the tangent of a number (representing an angle in radians)

Using the String type

JavaScript does not have a String object type (later versions of JavaScript may include a String type). Instead, JavaScript creates a string every time you assign a string value to a variable or a property. String literals — text within double quotes — are also stored as string objects. The following creates a string object named message:

```
message = "JavaScript is fun!";
```

A string object has only one property, named length. The length property defines the number of characters in the string. For example, you can refer to the number of characters in a string named message with the syntax message.length.

The string object allows many methods for working with strings. There are two categories of string methods:

✦ Methods that return parts or the whole of the original string with some changes to the characters (for example, convert to uppercase or extract a substring)

✦ Methods that return an HTML-formatted version of the string (for example, enclose the string in <B>...</B> to make it boldface)

Following is an example of the first method category. In this example, the toUpperCase method turns a string into uppercase:

```
message_u = message.toUpperCase(); // message_u = JAVASCRIPT IS FUN!
```

The next example illustrates the second method category where the bold method returns the original string embedded in <B>...</B> tags:

```
message_b = message.bold(); // message_b = <B>JavaScript is fun!</B>
```

The following list shows the string methods in JavaScript:

Method	Description
anchor	Returns the string in HTML format so that it can be the target of a hyperlink
big	Returns the string enclosed in `<BIG>...</BIG>` tags so that the text appears big when displayed
blink	Returns the string embedded in `<BLINK>...</BLINK>` tags so that the text blinks when displayed
bold	Returns the string embedded in `<BOLD>...</BOLD>` tags so that it appears bold when displayed
charAt	Returns the character at a specified index in the string (index 0 is the first character)
fixed	Returns the string embedded in `<TT>...</TT>` tags so that the text appears in a fixed-pitch font
fontcolor	Returns the string embedded in the `<FONT>...</FONT>` tags with the `COLOR` attribute set to a specified color name (that you provide as argument to `fontcolor`)
fontsize	Returns the string embedded in `<FONT>...</FONT>` tags with the `SIZE` attribute set to a value you specify as argument to the `fontsize` method
indexOf	Returns the location of the first occurrence of a specified character in the string
italics	Returns the string embedded in `<I>...</I>` tags so that the text appears in italics when displayed
lastIndexOf	Returns the location of the last occurrence of a specified character in the string
link	Returns the string embedded in `<a>...</a>` tags with the target of the hyperlink set to a string you provide as an argument to the link method (`message.link("http://home.netscape.com/");` sets up a hyperlink to Netscape's home page)
small	Returns the string enclosed in `<SMALL>...</SMALL>` tags so that the text appears small when displayed
strike	Returns the string embedded in `<STRIKE>...</STRIKE>` tags so that the text appears in strikeout mode when displayed
sub	Returns the string embedded in `<SUB>...</SUB>` tags so that the text appears in subscript when displayed

(continued)

Method	Description
`substring`	Returns a portion of the string between two specified indexes. For example, `message.substring(0,3)` returns the first three characters of message.
`sup`	Returns the string embedded in `<SUP>...</SUP>` tags so that the text appears in superscript when displayed.
`toLowerString`	Returns the string after converting it to all lowercase.
`toUpperString`	Returns the string after converting it to all uppercase.

Defining new object types

You can also define new object types in JavaScript as follows:

1. Define a constructor function that creates the object. The constructor function refers to the object by the `this` keyword and has `return this;` as the last statement.

2. Define one or more methods for the object. These are functions that refer to the object by the `this` keyword and perform whatever operations the method is expected to perform.

3. Associate the functions with the object. To make a function a method of an object, you must add each method to the object definition that you created in step 1 using the following syntax:

   ```
   this.method_name = method_name;
   ```

   where `method_name` is the name of the function that implements the method.

Creating a book object

As an example, suppose you want to define a book object. The first step is to write a function that creates an object and initializes its properties. Such a function would be the constructor for a book object.

Here is a simple book-object constructor that creates an object with two properties (`title` and `author`):

```
function makeBook(title, author)
{
    this.title = title;
    this.author = author;
    return this;
}
```

As this code shows, the `this` keyword inside the function refers to the object you are creating. To add properties, simply define them with the syntax:

```
this.property_name = property_value;
```

After you have initialized the properties, return `this` from the constructor function.

Writing methods for a book object

After you have defined the constructor function that creates the book object, you might want to write the methods that operate on that object. For example, suppose you want to write a show method to display a book object. To do this, write a function to display the book object's properties, as follows:

```
function show()
{
    document.writeln(this.title+" by "+this.author);
}
```

Functions representing an object's method use the this keyword to refer to the object to which the method belongs.

Now edit the book constructor makeBook, and add the following line before the return statement:

```
this.show = show;
```

The makeBook function now appears as follows:

```
function makeBook(title, author)
{
    this.title = title;
    this.author = author;
    this.show = show;
    return this;
}
```

Now you can call show as a method for any book object by using the following syntax:

```
bookname.show();
```

where bookname is the name of a book object.

Using the book object

Now you can also use the book constructor function to create one or more instances of books by calling the makeBook function with the title and author of each book. Here is an example that creates two books:

```
lxs = new makeBook("Linux SECRETS", "Naba Barkakati");
uwb = new makeBook("UNIX Webmaster Bible", "Naba Barkakati");
```

You can then refer to the title of these books with the syntax lxs.title and uwb.title. You can call the show method for any of these books as follows:

```
lxs.show();
```

This method produces the following output in the browser:

```
Linux SECRETS by Naba Barkakati
```

Checking a book object's properties

An interesting exercise is to check the properties of a book object. The following code uses a `for...in` statement to print the properties of the `lxs` book:

```
for (prop in lxs)
{
    document.writeln(prop+" = "+lxs[prop]);
}
```

This code extracts each property of the `lxs` object and prints out the name and value of the property. The output of this `for...in` statement is

```
show =
function show() {
    document.writeln(this.title + " by " + this.author);
}

author = Naba Barkakati
title = Linux SECRETS
```

Note that the `show` property is a method of the object and it's stored in the form of the JavaScript function that implements the method.

Creating an array in JavaScript

JavaScript does not have an explicit array data type, but you can create an array object type by writing your own array constructor function that creates and initializes an array. Following is a `makeArray` function that you can use to create and initialize an array with a specified number of elements:

```
function makeArray(numElem)
{
    this.length = numElem;
    for(var i=1; i <= numElem; i++)
    {
        this[i] = 0;
    }
    return this;
}
```

This function defines an array whose first property, `length`, represents the number of items in the array (`length` is also the item at index 0 of this object). The rest of the properties are the items in the array. You have to access them at indexes 1 or greater.

After defining the makeArray function, you can make an array by using the new keyword with the array name, as follows:

```
var books = new makeArray(20);
```

This creates an array with room for 20 elements and initializes all the elements to zero. You can then store items in the array by assigning values to the array elements (just remember to begin at index 1). Here is an example:

```
books[1] = "Linux SECRETS";
books[2] = "UNIX Webmaster Bible";
```

Webmaster Although you have initialized the array with 20 elements, you can add more elements at any time, even after you have stored 20 items in the array. JavaScript is very flexible about object properties, and the array is simply another object with properties that are integers (0, 1, 2, and so on) instead of textual names.

HTML extensions for JavaScript

Since JavaScript can be embedded in HTML documents, Netscape has added some new tags and some new attributes in existing tags to integrate JavaScript programs with the rest of the HTML document. There are two types of HTML extensions to support JavaScript (and, because these are extensions, only Netscape Navigator browser currently supports these extensions):

✦ The `<script>` tag to enclose JavaScript functions and statements

✦ New attributes in various HTML tags to associate JavaScript code as event handlers (that means JavaScript code gets executed when certain events occur, such as user clicks on a button in a form)

You already have seen a description of the `<script>` tag in " Writing Your First Script in JavaScript " section. The following sections summarize the event-handler attributes and how you can use event handlers to process a form's data.

Using event-handler attributes

Event-handler attributes are additions to HTML tags such as `<body>`, `<form>`, and `<input>`. These attributes allow you to specify JavaScript code as a handler for an event such as a document being loaded into a window, or a form being submitted by the user. By assigning handlers to specific events in a document, you can:

✦ Display a scrolling message in the status area of the browser window.

✦ Update fields in a form in response to the user's input (such as entering text in a field and then clicking a button).

✦ Validate the data entered by the user before the form can be submitted to the server (for processing by a CGI program on the server).

Typically, you'd write JavaScript functions to handle the events you are interested in and specify those functions as handlers for specific events. That association occurs when you set the event-handler attribute to a JavaScript function. Here's how you might specify the `compute` function as the `onClick` event handler for a form button:

```
<input type="button" value="Compute" name="cbutton" onClick="compute(this.form)">
```

The JavaScript code associated with the onClick event handler is called when the user clicks on the button. In this case, the JavaScript code is a function named compute. The this.form argument to the compute function refers to the form where the button resides. The this keyword refers to the current object, which in this case is the button. The form property of the button object indicates the form where the button resides. Hence, this.form is the form whose data is used in the compute function.

Tip If a JavaScript function expects a string literal and you need to use that function as an event handler, use single quotes to specify that literal string in the HTML tag:

```
<input type="button" value="OK" onClick="evtHandler('a string argument')">
```

There are nine event-handler attributes that support integration of JavaScript code with HTML. The following list summarizes these event handlers:

Event Handler	Called When
onBlur	User clicks to move away from one text-entry area to another (that means when the user clicks on another text-entry area).
onChange	User changes the value in a text, textarea, or select element. (You can use the onChange event handler to check if the input is valid.)
onClick	User clicks on a button, checkbox, link, or radio button.
onFocus	User clicks on a text-entry area, thus giving it input focus (the text-entry area with the input focus receives anything the user types).
onLoad	User loads a document into the browser (by accessing the link or by selecting Open from the browser's File menu). You can add this handler to the <body> and <form> tags only.
onMouseOver	User moves the mouse pointer over a link or an anchor (anchor means text that can be the target of a hyperlink).
onSelect	User selects text from a text-entry area such as a text or textarea.
onSubmit	User submits a form by clicking on a button (created by the <input> tag with the type attribute set to "submit").
onUnload	User exits the document by moving to another Web page.

Implementing an expression evaluator

As an example of how you might use an event handler, consider the problem of implementing a simple calculator in JavaScript. You want the user to enter an expression to evaluate and then click on a button to compute the result. You can implement such a simple expression evaluator by writing a JavaScript function as the onClick handler for the button. The following HTML source shows how this might be done:

```
<html>
<head>
<title>A simple JavaScript calculator</title>
```

```
<script language="JavaScript">

<!-- Begin JavaScript ------

function compute(form)
{
// Evaluate the expression and set result
    form.result.value = eval(form.expr.value);
}

// -- End of JavaScript ---->

</script>

</head>

<body>
<form>
<table cellspacing=10>

<tr>
<td>Enter an expression to evaluate:</td>
<td><input type=text name=expr size=50></td>
</tr>

<tr>
<td>Result:</td>
<td><input type=text name=result size=50></td>
</tr>

<tr>
<td></td>
<td><input type=button value="Compute"
    onClick="compute(this.form)">  <input type=reset></td>
</tr>

</table>
</body>
</html>
```

The <form> tag does not include the action or method attributes because this form works entirely inside the browser; it does not send data to the server. The form includes a text entry field where the user types in an expression and another text-entry area where the results are displayed.

The compute function, defined in the <head> element, does all the work. It takes the expression and calls the eval function to evaluate the expression. The compute function is assigned as the onClick handler for the button labeled Compute. That's how the user activates the compute function. Figure 24-4 shows the simple expression evaluator after the user has clicked on the Compute button to evaluate an expression.

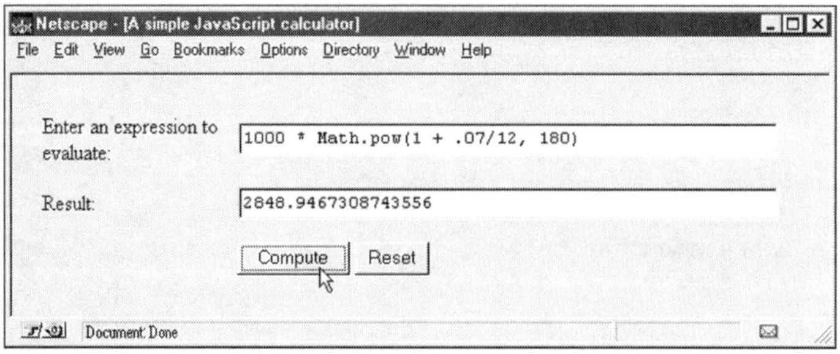

Figure 24-4: A simple JavaScript expression evaluator.

Displaying a scrolling message

A JavaScript event handler can display a scrolling message that appears in the status area of the Netscape Navigator browser. The best way to understand how to implement a scrolling status message is to see an example in action. The following HTML source shows the JavaScript function scroll_msg that implements the scrolling, and the <body> tag whose onLoad attribute turns on the scrolling message:

```
<html>
<head>
<title>Scrolling status message in JavaScript</title>

<script language="JavaScript">

<!-- beginning of JavaScript ---
// Message to be scrolled
    message = "This is a scrolling message implemented in JavaScript...";

// Width of the scroll region
    sbwidth = 100;

// Delay between status message updates
    delay = 200;

// In the following function, "start" denotes the starting location
// of the status message

function scroll_msg(start)
{
    var statmsg = " ";

    if (start > sbwidth)
    {
        // Starting position is to the right of scroll region
        // Just keep scrolling to the left

        start--;
        window.setTimeout("scroll_msg("+start+")", delay);
    }
```

```
    else if (start <= sbwidth && start > 0)
    {
        // Starting position is in the scrolling area
        // Add blank spaces to the front of message

        for(var i = 0; i < start ; i++)
        {
            statmsg += " ";
        }
        statmsg += message;
        start--;
        window.status = statmsg;
        window.setTimeout("scroll_msg("+start+")", delay);
    }
    else if (start <= 0)
    {
        if (-start < message.length)
        {
            // Starting position is to the left of window's edge,
            // but message is still visible. Display part of message.

            statmsg += message.substring(-start, message.length);
            start--;
            window.status = statmsg;
            window.setTimeout("scroll_msg("+start+")", delay);
        }
        else
        {
            // Starting position is to the left of window's edge
            // and message is not visible. Display blank spaces.

            window.status=" ";
            window.setTimeout("scroll_msg(sbwidth)", delay);
        }
    }
}
// -- end of JavaScript -->


</SCRIPT>
</head>

<body onLoad="window.setTimeout('scroll_msg(sbwidth)', delay);">

This page shows a scrolling message in the status bar at the
bottom of the browser window. You can use JavaScript to
implement such scrolling status messages.

</body>

</html>
```

Figure 24-5 shows the result of displaying this HTML file in Netscape Navigator.

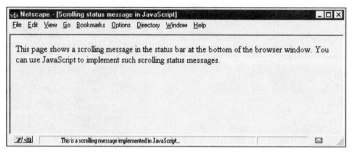

Figure 24-5: A scrolling status message implemented using JavaScript.

As you watch the browser window (shown in Figure 24-5), the status message scrolls from right to left. After the entire message scrolls to the left, the message reappears and the scrolling process starts all over again.

The `scroll_msg` function works by setting the `window.status` property. The browser displays this property in the status area of the window. The `scroll_msg` function also calls the `setTimeout` function to call itself again to reset the status message. The rest of the logic in `scroll_msg` has to do with constructing a status message depending on the current location of the message (as indicated by the `start` argument in `scroll_msg`). You can understand the logic by reading the comments inside each `if` statement in the `scroll_msg` function.

The initial call to `scroll_msg` is triggered by the `onLoad` event handler in the HTML document's `<body>` tag, which appears as follows:

```
<body onLoad="window.setTimeout('scroll_msg(sbwidth)', delay);">
```

The window object's `setTimeout` method requires two arguments:

✦ The first argument is a string containing the JavaScript statement to be executed after a specified delay.

✦ The second argument specifies the delay in milliseconds. In this example, `delay` is a JavaScript variable set to 200, which means a delay of 200 milliseconds.

Summary

Like Java, JavaScript provides a way to embed executable content in an HTML document, but JavaScript does it in a simpler way. You can embed JavaScript statements directly in an HTML document. A JavaScript-capable browser (such as Netscape Navigator, version 2.0 or later) interprets and executes the JavaScript statements. This chapter introduces you to JavaScript through some examples.

Where to go next . . .

✦ If you need a refresher course on HTML, read Chapters 10 and 11.

✦ For information on CGI applications, consult Chapter 19.

✦ To learn about Java programming, turn to Chapter 23.

✦   ✦   ✦

Appendixes

Webmaster Resources on the CD-ROM

URL

The companion CD-ROM is a customized version of the CD produced and marketed by SSC, Inc. (http://www.ssc.com/). In a nutshell, the CD-ROM contains everything you need to set up a Linux system and turn it into a World Wide Web site. All you need to provide is the network connectivity (which, of course, is easier said than done).

To begin with, you get Slackware Linux 3.1.0 with the Linux 2.0 kernel, which is the latest version of Linux available as of this writing (Fall 1996). Linux is a complete UNIX operating system for your 486 or Pentium PC. The Slackware Linux distribution includes over 300MB of source and binary files. By installing Linux on a PC, you can turn that PC into a full-fledged UNIX workstation.

Cross Ref

As long as the Linux PC is connected to the Internet, you can install a Web server and turn it into a Web site. If you don't have Internet connectivity, you should read Chapter 6 to learn about various networking options available to you.

Besides Linux, the rest of the CD-ROM contains various software that you can use to do your job as a Webmaster. This Appendix describes the contents of the CD-ROM, organized by top-level directories (excluding the directories that constitute the Slackware Linux 3.1.0 distribution; Linux is described in a separate section). You can read the contents of the CD-ROM from any MS-DOS, Windows 95, or UNIX system capable of accessing a CD-ROM.

Note Please note that the software contained in this CD-ROM is distributed under a variety of license agreements. Some of the software (such as Slackware Linux 3.1.0) is distributed in full source and binary format under the GNU General Public License. Many of the software packages are distributed as shareware and you are expected to pay a nominal fee if you decide to use the software in your work. In all cases, the software is copyrighted by the respective authors. In each directory, you should consult the README files (or files by the names such as COPYRIGHT, COPYING, and License) for information on the license terms for the software.

 Cross Ref For information on CD-ROM installation, see the "CD-ROM Installation Instructions" at the back of the book.

Slackware Linux 3.1.0

Much of the companion CD-ROM is devoted to Slackware Linux 3.1.0 (also known as Slackware 96), the latest Slackware release with the Linux 2.0 kernel (that's the core operating system). All of the files on the root of the CD-ROM are part of Slackware. Folders that are part of Slackware are bootdsks.12, bootdsks.144, contrib, docs, install, kernels, modules, rootdsks, slakware, source, and utils.

Installation can be one of the tricky steps in Linux, especially if you have a no-name IBM-compatible PC. You need some specific information about hardware, such as the disk controller, video card, and CD-ROM drive. Linux controls the hardware through drivers, so you need to make sure that the current release of Linux includes drivers for your hardware. Because Linux is free, you cannot really demand — or expect — support for some specific hardware. Linux is, however, continually growing through collaboration among programmers throughout the world. If your hardware is popular enough, there's a good chance that someone has developed a driver for it. In any case, the Slackware Linux on the companion CD-ROM already supports such a wide variety of hardware that all your PC's peripherals probably are supported.

 Tip Your best source of information on Linux installation, configuration, and use is one of the popular books on Linux such as *Linux SECRETS* by Naba Barkakati, IDG Books (1996). That book includes Linux on a CD-ROM and detailed instructions on how to install and use Linux.

Articles

 URL This directory contains the following text files with articles from the *Linux Journal* (http://www.ssc.com/lj/) and the *WEBsmith* magazine (http://www.ssc.com/websmith/):

```
README              cgi.security.txt    install.cern.server.txt
cgi-security        checklinks.txt      vrml.tech.talk.txt
cgi.column.1.txt    fix.overload.txt    world.wide.web.txt
```

Browsers

This directory contains the Linux version of VRWeb — a VRML (Virtual Reality Modeling Language) browser. Mosaic and Netscape Navigator browsers could not be included due to licensing restrictions. However, you can download and install the latest versions of Mosaic and Netscape Navigator by following the directions outlined in Chapter 4.

Another useful software program in the Browsers directory is `xpdf`, which is a viewer for Portable Document Format (PDF) files. (These files are also known as Acrobat files, named after the Adobe Acrobat PDF viewer sofware.)

CGI

This directory contains a number of sample CGI scripts. You'll also find the following subdirectories:

✦ `Ice` contains two Perl programs: `ice-idx.pl` and `ice-form.pl`. These Perl programs create an index of the documents served by your Web server and provide the CGI program so that users can look for documents by keyword. The HTML document `iceindex.html` contains information on how to set up and use `Ice` to index documents on your Web server.

✦ `vend-0.3.8` (version may be newer on the CD-ROM) contains a Web-based vending machine implemented in Perl 5. The software is distributed under the GNU General Public License. Look at the `setup` file for information on setting up `Vend`.

Conversion

This directory contains utility programs for converting various document types into HTML (and to convert HTML to PostScript). Here are some of the files and subdirectories:

✦ `PerlLib` subdirectory contains a number of useful Perl scripts. Consult the `CONTENTS` file for a description of the Perl files.

✦ `html-parser` subdirectory contains Perl scripts to parse HTML documents and generate ASCII versions of the HTML documents.

✦ `html2ps` subdirectory contains a Perl program (also named `html2ps`) that converts HTML to PostScript. Read the `manpage.txt` file for information on how to use `html2ps`.

✦ `ismap-editor.tcl` file contains a Tcl/Tk program to let you edit the clickable areas of an image map.

✦ `lsr2html` file is a Perl script that converts the contents of a directory tree into an HTML document. See the comments within the file for information on how to use `lsr2html`.

✦ `man2html` subdirectory contains the Perl program named `man2html` that converts UNIX man pages to HTML. You'll find documentation in the `doc` subdirectory.

✦ `troff2html` subdirectory contains the Perl program `troff2html` that converts `troff` documents (`troff` is a UNIX typesetting program) into HTML.

✦ `txt2html.pl` file is a Perl script that converts plain text files into HTML (Chapter 16 describes the `txt2html` utility).

DataBase

This directory contains a number of database programs that you can use at your Web site. Here are some of the subdirectories:

✦ `Harvest-1.4` subdirectory contains set of tools that let you gather, extract, and organize information from the Internet. You'll find further information on Harvest installation in the `INSTRUCTIONS.html` file in the `doc` subdirectory.

✦ `dbcgi` subdirectory contains the CorVu dbCGI software — a CGI gateway that lets users access any SQL databases (such as Sybase, Oracle, Informix, Ingres, Progress, and ODBC) through the Web. As a Webmaster, you write dbCGI files that are standard HTML files with an additional `<sql>` tag that lets you embed SQL commands in the file. For more information, consult the HTML files in the `doc` subdirectory.

✦ `glimpse` subdirectory contains the Glimpse indexing and query system that can search an entire file system. For more information, see the `README.install` file in the Glimpse source directory.

✦ `msql` subdirectory contains the popular MiniSQL relational database. For more information on mSQL, use a Web browser to view the `faq.html` file. Also, Chapter 22 describes mSQL in detail.

GraphicTools

This directory contains a number of well-known image manipulation programs for UNIX systems. Here are some of the useful subdirectories in this directory:

✦ `ImageMagick` subdirectory contains the versatile ImageMagick package for display and manipulation of images for the X Window System. To learn more about ImageMagick, use a Web browser to view the `ImageMagick.html` file. For a description of how to use ImageMagick to create GIF89a animations, consult Chapter 12.

✦ `Scanner` subdirectory contains Linux drivers for a number of popular scanners.

✦ `fiximg-1.4` subdirectory contains the `fiximg.pl` Perl script that you can use to add `width` and `height` attributes to all the `<img>` tags in an HTML document. If you use the `width` and `height` attributes, Netscape Navigator can load the document faster because the browser can set aside adequate space for all images (even before the images are completely downloaded).

✦ `gd` subdirectory contains the `gd` graphics library that you can use to create and write GIF images. See the `README` file for a note about where to find more information about `gd`.

✦ `gif-trans` subdirectory contains the `giftrans` program that converts any GIF image into GIF89a format. You can also set a transparent color, change colors, and add or remove comments embedded in the GIF file. The man page is in the file `giftrans.1`.

✦ `giftool` subdirectory contains the `giftool` program that you can use to convert a GIF image to a transparent GIF. See Chapter 12 for a description of `giftool`.

✦ `netpbm` subdirectory contains the Netpbm toolkit that provides utility programs to convert between a wide variety of image file formats (see the `FORMATS` file for a list of supported image formats). The `README` file describes the Netpbm toolkit.

✦ `urt-bin` subdirectory contains the Utah Raster Toolkit — a set of Linux binaries for converting images between various formats.

Httpd

This directory contains several Web servers — HTTP daemons (HTTPD). You'll find the following files in this directory:

✦ `Apache` subdirectory contains the latest release of the popular Web server. Consult Chapter 8 for detailed information on how to install and set up the Apache Web server.

✦ `CERN_W3` subdirectory contains the CERN Web server, also described in Chapter 8.

✦ `Jigsaw` subdirectory contains a new Web server, written entirely in Java. For more information about Jigsaw, use a Web browser to view the `Overview.html` file.

✦ `Plexus` subdirectory contains the Plexus HTTP server, which is written in Perl. Consult the `README` file for the Plexus HTTP server's installation instructions.

✦ `VirtualHosting.html` is a HTML document that describes how to set up a virtual Web site under Linux.

✦ `WN` subdirectory includes the WN Web server. For more information, use a Web browser to view the `wn-1.15.0/docs/index.html` file.

✦ `howtoSSL.txt` is a text file that describes how to set up a Secure Sockets Layer (SSL) compliant Web server using the NCSA HTTPD software.

Java

This directory contains the Java Developers Kit (JDK) for Linux. To learn more about the JDK for Linux, use a Web browser to view the `java/index.html` file.

You'll find the JDK for Windows 95 in the `UW_Bible` directory of the CD-ROM.

LIGS

This directory contains three versions (HTML, PostScript, and plain text) of the book, *Linux Installation and Getting Started* by Matt Welsh. The `README` file describes the contents. You can browse the HTML version of the book to learn how to install Linux.

Mail

This directory contains a number of utility programs that archive electronic mail messages and make them available via the Web server. The `mailarchive` subdirectory contains the Perl program MailArchive that converts a set of mail messages into an archive with an associated HTML index (that MailArchive generates). To learn more about MailArchive, use a Web browser to view the HTML document `MA.html`.

Sample

This directory contains a sample directory layout for a Web site. You can study the directory structure to see how a typical Web site is organized.

TextTools

This directory contains a number of HTML editors. Here are some of the files and subdirectories you'll find in this directory:

- ◆ `asWedit-2.5` subdirectory contains the `asWedit` HTML editor for Linux, statically linked with Motif (so you don't have to buy Motif). To install the program, consult the `README` file.

- ◆ `html-helper-mode` subdirectory contains the files you need to enable an HTML mode for the Emacs text editor. To learn more, use a Web browser to view the `index.html` file.

- ◆ `htmltext` subdirectory contains an HTML editing object for the Andrew ToolKit (ATK).

- ◆ `pico` is a popular, easy-to-use text editor.

✦ tkHTML-3.0 subdirectory contains the latest version of the tkHTML editor that uses Tcl/Tk for its graphical interface. See Chapter 17 for more information on tkHTML.

✦ webweave subdirectory contains the WebWeave macro language for developing HTML pages. For an overview of WebWeave, use a Web browser to view the HTML file README.html.

✦ xhtml subdirectory contains ASHE (A Simple HTML Editor). Turn to Chapter 17 to learn more about ASHE.

UW_Bible

This directory contains most of the source files from this book (*UNIX Webmaster Bible*). The directory is organized is as follows:

✦ html subdirectory contains some sample HTML files that were used in the book.

✦ java subdirectory contains sample Java code organized into three subdirectories. These Java source files were described in Chapter 23.

✦ cgi subdirectory contains C, C++, Perl, and Tcl samples (primarily CGI query parsing libraries). These source files were used in Chapters 20 and 21.

✦ msql subdirectory contains C and Perl interface programs to the MiniSQL database. Chapter 22 describes these programs. (You'll find the mSQL software in the DataBase directory of this CD.)

✦ JDKWin subdirectory contains the Java Developers Kit for Windows.

Usage

This directory contains a variety of Web server log-analysis tools and some tools to check hyperlinks in your HTML documents. This directory contains the following:

✦ Browsercounter subdirectory contains a Perl script that scans the agent_log file generated by NCSA or Apache Web servers and produces a table summarizing the types of Web browsers used to access the site.

✦ Count subdirectory contains the Count 2.3 CGI program (in the wwwcount2.3 subdirectory) that returns the time as well as the visit count as a GIF image. You'll find detailed descriptions and installation instructions in the wwwcount2.3/docs subdirectory.

✦ MOMspider-1.00 subdirectory contains the MOMspider Web roaming-robot program that can check all the hyperlinks in your Web site. To learn how to set up and run MOMspider, view the HTML documents in the docs subdirectory.

✦ analog subdirectory contains a fast Web server log-analysis tool that generates output in the form of an HTML document. The analog tool can handle NCSA and Apache Web server logs. Chapter 8 describes how to install and use analog.

✦ `cgiwrap-3.0` subdirectory contains the `cgiwrap` program that acts as a gateway to any CGI program and makes CGI somewhat more secure. You'll find installation instructions in the `docs` subdirectory.

✦ `checkl` subdirectory contains the `checklinks.pl` Perl script that can check all the hyperlinks in an HTML document. To learn more about `checklinks`, use a Web browser to look at the HTML document `checklinks.html`.

✦ `getstats-12` subdirectory contains the `getstats` Web server log-analysis tool written in C. View the HTML document `getstats.html` to learn more about `getstats`.

✦ `gwstat` subdirectory contains the `gwstat` program — an add-on to `wwwstat` (see below) — designed to generate the server usage statistics as a set of bar graphs in a GIF image. The man page is in the file `gwstat.1`.

✦ `libwww` subdirectory contains C source code that you can use to write Web servers and clients.

✦ `wusage3.2` subdirectory contains the `wusage` program that generates usage statistics for NCSA and Apache Web servers. See the `wusage.html` file for more information.

✦ `wwwstat-1.0` subdirectory contains the `wwwstat` program that analyzes NCSA and Apache Web server log files and generates usage statistics. The `README` file contains installation instructions. For a sample output of this program, view the HTML document `example.html`.

Validation

This directory contains `html-check`, a program that checks HTML documents for conformance to standards. The `html-check` program relies on the `sgmls` program to verify the syntax of the HTML document. The `sgmls` program, in turn, needs an SGML DTD (Document Type Definition) that defines the valid document syntax. You'll find DTDs for HTML 2.0 and HTML 3.2 (the latest HTML specification) in the `lib` subdirectory. The man page for `html-check` is in the `man/man1` subdirectory. To install `html-check`, you should run the `install.sh` shell script.

✦   ✦   ✦

Webmaster Resources on the Net

Throughout this book, I refer to many sources of information, programs, and utilities. Most of these resources are located on the Net, and you can access them from your Web browser. Most Net-based resources are updated frequently, so you can always get the latest information or the latest version of a program.

To use the Net-based resources, all you need is a starting point, a URL where you can begin your search. Once you have a good starting document, hyperlinks within that document should lead you to other relevant resources. This appendix provides that starting point by listing many useful URLs, organized by subject.

Cross Ref Many of the programs and utilities mentioned in this book are on this book's companion CD-ROM (see Appendix A).

Internet Basics

Internet Network Information Center (InterNIC) home page:

    http://rs.internic.net/

Templates for IP address application form:

    ftp://rs.internic.net/templates

Request for Comments (RFC) — the working papers of the Internet:

    ftp://rs.internic.net/rfc

Internet Engineering Task Force (IETF):

```
http://www.ietf.org/
```

World Wide Web Consortium (W3C):

```
http://www.w3.org/
```

Internet Information Services

Gopher server software:

```
ftp://boombox.micro.umn.edu//pub/gopher/Unix
```

Majordomo software to automate mailing lists:

```
ftp://ftp.greatcircle.com/pub/majordomo
```

`freeWAIS` software to implement Wide Area Information Servers (WAIS):

```
ftp://boombox.micro.umn.edu//pub/gopher/Unix
```

Introduction to the World Wide Web

HTTP and HTML

Hypertext Transfer Protocol (HTTP) standards news:

```
http://www.w3.org/pub/WWW/Protocols/
```

Hypertext Markup Language (HTML) news:

```
http://www.w3.org/pub/WWW/MarkUp/
```

Web browsers

List of available Web browsers:

```
http://www.w3.org/hypertext/WWW/Clients.html
http://www.yahoo.com/Computers_and_Internet/Internet/World_Wide_Web/
     Browsers/
```

Emacs W3 mode (text-mode Web browser for Emacs):

```
ftp://ftp.cs.indiana.edu/pub/elisp/w3/
```

Line mode Web browser:

```
ftp://ftp.w3.org/pub/linemode/www_src.tar.gz
```

Lynx, a popular text-based Web browser:

```
ftp://ftp2.cc.ukans.edu/pub/lynx
```

Tom Fine's perlWWW:

```
ftp://archive.cis.ohio-state.edu, in pub/w3browser/w3browser-0.1.shar
```

Cello (a Web browser for Microsoft Windows):

```
ftp://ftp.law.cornell.edu/pub/LII/Cello
```

Galahad for BIX (Microsoft Windows Web browser to access BIX):

```
http://www.mcs.com/~jvwater/main.html
```

GWHIS (a commercial Windows Web browser from Quadralay Corporation):

```
http://www.quadralay.com/products/products.html
```

Microsoft Internet Explorer (freely available Windows and Macintosh Web browsers from Microsoft):

```
http://www.microsoft.com/ie/
```

Mosaic for Windows:

```
ftp://ftp.ncsa.uiuc.edu/PC/Windows/Mosaic/
```

Mosaic In A Box for Windows 95 (a commercial version of Mosaic for Windows):

```
http://www.spry.com/about/products/mosaic.html
```

Netscape Navigator (a popular commercial Web browser; evaluation copy available):

```
ftp://ftp.netscape.com/
```

SlipKnot (Windows Web browser from MicroMind, Inc.):

```
ftp.netcom.com/pub/pb/pbrooks/slipknot/slnot150.zip
```

WinWeb (Windows Web browser from Tradewave Corporation):

```
http://galaxy.einet.net/EINet/WinWeb/WinWebHome.html
```

MacWeb (Web browser for Macintosh from Tradewave Corporation):

`http://galaxy.einet.net/EINet/MacWeb/MacWebHome.html`

Mosaic for Macintosh:

`http://www.ncsa.uiuc.edu/SDG/Software/MacMosaic/News/download.html`

Samba (Graphical Web browser for the Macintosh):

`ftp://info.cern.ch/ftp/pub/www/bin/mac`

IBM WebExplorer for OS/2:

`ftp://ftp.ibm.net/pub/WebExplorer/`

Arena (a freely available Web browser for UNIX systems):

`http://www.w3.org/pub/WWW/Arena/`

Chimera (X Windows based Web browser; does not require Motif):

`ftp://ftp.isri.unlv.edu/pub/chimera/`

Grail (Web browser written in Python and Tk):

`http://monty.cnri.reston.va.us/grail/`

MidasWWW Browser (X Windows based Web browser):

`ftp://ftp.slac.stanford.edu/software/midaswww/`

Mosaic for X:

`ftp://ftp.ncsa.uiuc.edu/Mosaic/Unix/binaries/`

tkWWW (a Web browser based on Tk):

`ftp://export.lcs.mit.edu:/contrib/tkWWW-0.7.tar.Z`

ViolaWWW (X Windows and Motif based Web browser):

`ftp://ftp.ora.com/pub/www/viola`

Web servers

List of available Web servers:

`http://www.w3.org/hypertext/WWW/Servers.html`

Apache (a popular UNIX Web server):

```
http://www.apache.org/dist/
```

CERN httpd (also known as W3C httpd, a freely available Web server):

```
http://www.w3.org/hypertext/Dist/httpd/httpd_src.tar.gz
```

GN (a UNIX Web server distributed under GNU General Public License):

```
ftp://ftp.acns.nwu.edu/pub/gn/gn.tar.gz
```

NCSA httpd (another popular UNIX Web server):

```
http://hoohoo.ncsa.uiuc.edu/docs/setup/OneStep.html
```

Netscape FastTrack Server (an entry-level commercial UNIX Web server):

```
http://home.netscape.com/
```

Netscape SuiteSpot (a commercial UNIX Web server with a set of tools):

```
http://home.netscape.com/
```

Plexus (a public domain HTTP server written in Perl):

```
http://www.earth.com/server/doc/plexus.html
```

Spinner (a Web server distributed under the GNU General Public License):

```
http://spinner.infovav.se/
```

WN (a freely available Web server distributed under the GNU General Public License):

```
http://hopf.math.nwu.edu/src.html
```

User's View of the Web

The White House home page:

```
http://www.whitehouse.gov
```

Netscape home page:

```
http://home.netscape.com/
```

YAHOO! home page:

```
http://www.yahoo.com/
```

AltaVista (a popular Web index) home page:

```
http://www.altavista.digital.com/
```

Open Text (a full-text search of the Web):

```
http://search.opentext.com/
```

Lycos (Web index):

```
http://www.lycos.com/
```

WebCrawler (Web index):

```
http://www.webcrawler.com/
```

DejaNews (a keyword search of Internet newsgroups):

```
http://www.dejanews.com/
```

Role of the Webmaster

List of Webmaster job openings:

```
http://techknowledge.com
```

Newsgroup for job openings (look for announcements for Webmaster positions):

```
news: misc.jobs.offered
```

Connectivity Options for a Web Site

Internet history

Final report of the NSFNET backbone project (1987-1995):

```
http://nic.merit.edu/nsfnet/final.report/
```

Internet network architecture:

```
http://nic.merit.edu/.internet.html
```

Network Access Points (NAPs)

Sprint Network Access Point (NAP):

```
http://nic.merit.edu/nsf.architecture/Sprint/
```

Ameritech Advanced Data Service (AADS) NAP:

```
http://www.ameritech.com/products/nap/
```

Pacific Bell NAP:

```
http://www.pacbell.com/Products/NAP/
```

MAE East and MAE West NAPs:

```
http://ext2.mfsdatanet.com/mfs-datanet/internet-services/
```

Routing Arbitrer (RA) peering agreement:

```
http://www.ra.net/nap_customer/
```

Organizations

Commercial Internet eXchange (CIX) Association:

```
http://www.cix.org/
```

North American Network Operators Group (NANOG):

```
http://nic.merit.edu/routing.arbiter/NANOG/NANOG.html
```

Frame Relay pricing information

Pacific Bell:

```
http://www.pacbell.com/Products/FR-RELAY/
```

Bell Atlantic:

```
http://www.bell-atl.com/internet/html/access.htm
```

Direct Network Access (an ISP in the San Francisco Bay Area):

```
http://www.dnai.com/services/frame.html
```

SprintLink:

```
http://www.sprintlink.net/
```

ISDN

Dan Kegel's ISDN page:

http://alumni.caltech.edu/~dank/isdn/

Livingston's PortMaster ISDN Office Router:

http://www.livingston.com/Marketing/Products/isdnor.html

Ascend Pipeline 50 ISDN router:

http://www.dfw.net/dfwnet/store/hardware/isdn/p50.html

Bell Atlantic's residential ISDN pricing information:

http://www.bell-atl.com/isdn/consumer/

Bell Atlantic's small business ISDN pricing information:

http://www.bell-atl.com/isdn/sbs/

Ameritech (ISDN pricing information and ordering details):

http://www.ameritech.com/products/data/

Pacific Bell (ISDN pricing information and ordering details):

http://www.pacbell.com/Products/SDS-ISDN/

US West (ISDN pricing information and ordering details):

http://www.uswest.com/ISDN.HTM

BellSouth (ISDN pricing information and ordering details):

http://www.smlbiz.bellsouth.com/bssbi.html

GTE (ISDN pricing information and ordering details):

http://www.gte.com/Cando/Business/Docs/Wired/isdn.html

Pacific Bell's Centrex ISDN from Direct Network Access:

http://www.dnai.com/services/centrex.html

T3

Pacific Bell (T3 connection to Pacific Bell's NAP):

```
http://www.pacbell.com/Products/NAP/nap2-3.html
```

Internet Service Providers (ISPs)

Mecklermedia's list of ISPs:

```
http://thelist.iworld.com/
```

YAHOO! ISP category:

```
http://www.yahoo.com/Business_and_Economy/Companies/Internet_Services/
        Internet_Access_Providers/
```

ANS CO+RE Systems Inc.:

```
http://www.ans.net
```

AT&T WorldNet:

```
http://www.att.com/worldnet
```

BBN Planet:

```
http://www.bbn.com
```

CERFNET, Inc.:

```
http://www.cerf.net
```

IBM Internet Connection:

```
http://www.ibm.com/globalnetwork
```

MCI Telecommunications, Inc.:

```
http://www.internetmci.com
```

Netcom Online Communications Services, Inc.:

```
http://www.netcom.com
```

PSINet, Inc.:

```
http://www.psi.net
```

Sprint:

```
http://www.sprintbiz.com
```

UUNet Technologies, Inc.:

```
http://www.uu.net
```

Web Server Installation

Popular Web servers

NCSA HTTP server and related documentation:

```
http://hoohoo.ncsa.uiuc.edu/
ftp://ftp.ncsa.uiuc.edu/Web/httpd/Unix/ncsa_httpd/current
```

Apache Web server:

```
http://www.apache.org/dist/
```

CERN W3 Web server:

```
http://www.w3.org/pub/WWW/Daemon/
```

Virtual hosts with Apache Web server:

```
http://www.apache.org/docs/virtual-host.html
```

Web server surveys

Web server surveys at YAHOO!:

```
http://www.yahoo.com/Computers_and_Internet/Internet/World_Wide_Web/HTTP/
      Servers/Surveys/
```

Netcraft Web Server Survey :

```
http://www.netcraft.co.uk/Survey/
```

Web server feature comparison:

```
http://www.webcompare.com/server-main.html
```

Secure Socket Layer (SSL) support in Apache server:

```
http://apachessl.c2.org/
```

Digital ID from VeriSign, Inc.:

```
http://www.verisign.com/apachessl-us/
```

GNU ZIP (Gzip):

```
ftp://prep.ai.mit.edu/pub/gnu/
```

Web server log analysis tools

List of Web server log analysis tools:

```
http://www.yahoo.com/Computers_and_Internet/Internet/World_Wide_Web/HTTP/
        Servers/Log_Analysis_Tools/
```

analog (a fast C program to analyze Web server log files):

```
http://www.statslab.cam.ac.uk/~sret1/analog/
```

getstats (a C program to analyze Web server logs):

```
http://www.eit.com/software/getstats/
```

wusage (a C program to analyze Web server logs):

```
http://www.boutell.com/wusage/
```

wwwstat (a Perl program to analyze Web server logs):

```
http://www.ics.uci.edu/WebSoft/wwwstat/
```

gwstat (a companion program for wwwstat):

```
http://dis.cs.umass.edu/stats/gwstat.html
```

Web Site Security

SOCKS (proxy server):

```
http://www.socks.nec.com/ftp/
ftp://ftp.nec.com/pub/security/socks.cstc/socks4
```

Internet Draft proposing SOCKS5 as an Internet standard for proxy services:

```
http://www.socks.nec.com/draft/
```

CERT summaries of known security problems:

```
http://www.cert.org/
```

Internet security and firewall information:

```
ftp://ftp.greatcircle.com/pub/firewalls/FAQ
http://www.netcraft.co.uk/security/http/
http://www.netcraft.co.uk/security/diary.html
ftp://info.cert.org/pub/cert_summaries/
```

Web server security:

```
http://hoohoo.ncsa.uiuc.edu/security/
```

The World Wide Web Security FAQ (Frequently Asked Questions):

```
http://www-genome.wi.mit.edu/WWW/faqs/www-security-faq.html
```

TIS Firewall Toolkit (a freely available firewall from Trusted Information Systems):

```
ftp:// ftp.tis.com/pub/firewalls/toolkit
```

Image Formats and Tools

JPEG Frequently Asked Questions (FAQ):

```
http://www.cis.ohio-state.edu/hypertext/faq/usenet/jpeg-faq/top.html
```

CompuServe's 1994 announcement about royalty payments for GIF:

```
http://www.lpf.org/Patents/Gif/origCompuServe.html
```

Clarification from Unisys on use of GIF:

```
http://www.lpf.org/Patents/Gif/unisys.html.
```

Portable Network Graphics (PNG, pronounced "ping"):

```
http://www.group42.com/png.htm
http://quest.jpl.nasa.gov/PNG/
```

Mu-law (`.au`) sound files:

```
http://sunsite.unc.edu/pub/multimedia/sun-sounds/
```

`giftool` (a tool to convert GIFs to transparent GIFs):

```
http://www.homepages.com/tools/
```

ImageMagick (image manipulation software for UNIX systems):

```
http://www.wizards.dupont.com/cristy/ImageMagick.html
ftp://ftp.wizards.dupont.com/pub/ImageMagick/
```

Imaging Machine Web site (interesting uses of ImageMagick):

```
http://www.vrl.com/Imaging/
```

Image Maps

Mapedit (a program to mark hot spots on an image map):

```
http://www.boutell.com/mapedit/
```

Webmap (a Macintosh shareware program to draw the hotspots on an image map):

```
http://www.city.net/cnx/software/webmap.html
```

Web Page Design

Collection of links to HTML style guides:

```
http://union.ncsa.uiuc.edu/HyperNews/get/www/html/guides.html
```

YAHOO! collection of HTML and Web support pages:

```
http://www.yahoo.com/Computers_and_Internet/Internet/World_Wide_Web
```

Yale WWW Style Manual:

```
http://info.med.yale.com/caim/StyleManual_Top.HTML
```

How Do They Do That With HTML?:

```
http://www.nashville.net/~carl/htmlguide/index.html
```

Document Conversion

List of HTML converters:

```
http://www.yahoo.com/Computers_and_Internet/Internet/World_Wide_Web/
        HTML_Converters/
```

`man2html` (a program to convert UNIX man pages to HTML):

```
http://www.oac.uci.edu/indiv/ehood/man2html.html
ftp://ftp.uci.edu/pub/dtd2html/man2html2.1.0.tar.gz
```

Information about Rich Text Format (RTF):

```
http://www.microsoft.com/KB/SoftLib/MSLFiles/Gc0165.EXE
http://www.sunpack.com/RTF/Webdocs/RTF-Spec/RTF1-4.htm
```

RTFtoHTML (a shareware program to convert RTF to HTML):

```
http://www.sunpack.com/RTF/rtftohtml_overview.html
```

Graphics Workshop (a shareware image manipulation program for Windows):

```
http://www.mindworkshop.com/alchemy/gww.html
```

Internet Assistant for Microsoft Word 95 (add-on to save Word files as HTML):

```
http://www.microsoft.com/msword/Internet/IA/
```

Internet Assistant for PowerPoint 95 (add-on to save PowerPoint files as HTML):

```
http://www.microsoft.com/mspowerpoint/Internet/ia/default.htm
```

EasyHelp/Web (a shareware add-on for Microsoft Word):

```
http://www.eon-solutions.com/easyhelp/easyhelp.htm
```

HTML Transit (a commercial HTML converter):

```
http://www.infoaccess.com/products/transit/httoc.htm
```

HyperMail (converts UNIX mailbox format into HTML):

```
http://www.eit.com/software/hypermail/hypermail.html
```

Internet Assistant for Microsoft Access for Windows 95:

```
http://www.microsoft.com/msaccess/internet/ia/default.htm
```

Internet Assistant for Microsoft Excel:

```
http://www.microsoft.com/msexcel/Internet/IA/default.htm
```

`txt2html` (a tool to convert text to HTML):

```
http://www.cs.wustl.edu/~seth/txt2html/
```

WebMaker (software that converts FrameMaker documents into HTML):

```
http://www.harlequin.com/webmaker/
```

WordPerfect Internet Publisher 6.1:

```
http://www.novell.com/corp/freesoft/wpip/
```

HTML Authoring Tools

List of HTML editors:

```
http://www.yahoo.com/Computers_and_Internet/Internet/World_Wide_Web/
       Authoring/
http://union.ncsa.uiuc.edu/HyperNews/get/www/html/editors.html
```

A Simple HTML Editor (ASHE) README file:

```
ftp://ftp.cs.rpi.edu/pub/puninj/ASHE/README.html
```

A Simple HTML Editor (ASHE) SunOS 4.1.3 binaries:

```
ftp://ftp.cs.rpi.edu/pub/puninj/ASHE/ASHE-1.3/bin/xhtml-1.3-SunOs-static-
       all-libraries.Z
```

A Simple HTML Editor (ASHE) source distribution:

```
ftp://ftp.cs.rpi.edu/pub/puninj/ASHE/ASHE-1.3/src/xhtml-1.3.tar.Z (137K)
ftp://ftp.cs.rpi.edu/pub/puninj/ASHE/ASHE-1.3/libcci/cci.tar.Z (22K)
ftp://ftp.cs.rpi.edu/pub/puninj/ASHE/ASHE-1.3/libhtmlw-2.7/libhtmlw.tar.Z
       (246K)
```

tkTHML (an HTML editor built using Tcl/Tk):

```
http://www.ssc.com/~roland/tkHTML/
```

HotDog 32-bit (an HTML editor for Windows 95 and Windows NT):

```
http://www.sausage.com/hotdog32.htm
ftp://ftp.sausage.com/pub/hd32supp.exe
ftp://ftp.sausage.com/pub/hd32inst.exe
```

HoTMetaL Free 2.0 (a freely available HTML editor from SoftQuad):

```
http://www.sq.com/products/hotmetal/hm-ftp.htm
```

Alpha (a shareware text editor for Macintosh that supports HTML editing):

```
http://www.cs.umd.edu/~keleher/alpha.html
```

BBEdit (a shareware text editor for Macintosh that allows HTML editing):

```
http://www.barebones.com/bbedit.html
```

GNNpress (a freely available Macintosh Web browser with HTML editing features):

```
http://www.tools.gnn.com/press/index.html
```

HoTMetaL (Macintosh version of a popular HTML editor):

```
http://www.sq.com/products/hotmetal/hm-ftp.htm
```

HTML Web Weaver (a shareware HTML editor for Macintosh):

```
http://webster.northnet.org/Web.Weaver/HTMLWW.html
```

HTML.edit (a freeware HTML editor for Macintosh):

```
http://www.stonehand.com/murray/htmledit.html
```

PageMill (a commercial HTML authoring tool from Adobe Systems, Inc.):

```
http://www.adobe.com/prodindex/pagemill/main.html
```

Web Site Promotion

"What's New?" page at NCSA:

```
http://www.ncsa.uiuc.edu/SDG/Software/Mosaic/Docs/whats-new.html
```

Open Market's Commercial Sites Index:

```
http://www.directory.net/
```

World Wide Web Consortium's Web site catalog:

```
http://www.w3.org/hypertext/DataSources/WWW/Geographical_generation/
    new.html
```

Virtual Tourist Web site:

```
http://www.vtourist.com/webmap/
```

Newsgroup for announcing non-commercial Web-related news:

```
comp.infosystems.www.announce
```

Newsgroup for announcing new sites, events, and publications on the Internet:

```
comp.internet.net-happenings
```

Net-happenings Web site:

```
http://www.mid.net/net/
```

Common Gateway Interface (CGI)

CGI specification:

```
http://hoohoo.ncsa.uiuc.edu/cgi/interface.hml
```

`cgi-lib.pl` (Perl library for CGI programming):

```
http://www.bio.cam.ac.uk/cgi-lib/
```

Latest information on Tcl/Tk:

```
http://www.sunlabs.com/research/tcl/
```

`cgi-lib.tcl` (Tcl procedures for CGI programming):

```
http://www.lnbsoft.com/code/tcl/
```

`cgi-lib.c` (C library for CGI programming):

```
http://www.lnbsoft.com/code/ccgi/
```

`CgiQuery` (C++ class for CGI programming):

```
http://www.lnbsoft.com/code/cppcgi/
```

Database Access through the Web

mSQL (MiniSQL database):

```
ftp://bond.edu.au/pub/Minerva/msql/
```

MiniSQL home page:

```
http://hughes.com.au/product/msql/
```

Database Interface (DBI) for Perl 5:

```
ftp://ftp.demon.co.uk/pub/perl/db/
```

`oraperl` (Perl extension to access Oracle databases):

http://sunsite.doc.ic.ac.uk/packages/perl/db/perl4/oraperl/

`sybperl` (Perl extension to access Sybase databases):

http://sunsite.doc.ic.ac.uk/packages/perl/db/perl4/sybperl/

Java

Java Developers Kit (JDK) information:

http://java.sun.com/products/JDK/CurrentRelease/

Java Developers Kit (JDK) download site:

ftp://ftp.javasoft.com/pub/

Java documentation:

http://java.sun.com/products/JDK/CurrentRelease/ftp_docs.html

JavaScript

Netscape's JavaScript documentation:

http://home.netscape.com/eng/mozilla/2.0/handbook/javascript/index.html

Collection of JavaScript resources:

http://intergalactinet.com/javascript/

JavaScript FAQ (Frequently Asked Questions):

http://www.freqgrafx.com/411/jsfaq.html

✦   ✦   ✦

HTML Reference

This appendix presents alphabetically arranged reference entries for HTML tags currently supported by popular Web browsers such as Netscape Navigator and Microsoft Internet Explorer. Each tag's reference entry shows whether the tag is part of HTML 2.0 and the recent HTML 3.2 specifications, and whether Netscape Navigator or Microsoft Internet Explorer supports the tag.

Each reference entry has a standard appearance with the following sections:

- ✦ *Purpose*: Tells you when to use the tag.

- ✦ *Syntax*: Shows the syntax of the tag with all possible attributes. Typical attribute values are also shown. If an attribute must have one of several specific values, these values are shown separated by vertical bars (see, for example, the rel attribute in the ⟨a⟩ tag).

- ✦ *Attributes*: Lists all attributes, along with a brief description of each attribute. Also tells you if an attribute is supported only in Netscape Navigator or Microsoft Internet Explorer.

- ✦ *Description*: Describes the tag and provides more details on how to use the tag.

URL Everything in the Web changes rapidly, including the specification of HTML. The World Wide Web Consortium (W3C) coordinates the release of new HTML specifications; the latest one being HTML 3.2, which was released in May 1996. To learn about the latest stable (as well as evolving) HTML specifications, you should periodically check the following URL:

    http://www.w3.org/hypertext/WWW/MarkUp/

`<!-- comment-->`	*HTML2.0* ✦	*HTML3.2* ✦	*Netscape* ✦	*Microsoft* ✦

Purpose	Enclose comments between the tags `<!--` and `-->`.

Syntax	`<!-- This is a comment -->`
	`<!-- This is a comment that`
	`    spans multiple lines`
	`-->`

Attributes	None
Description	Comments must appear between the `<!--` and `-->` tags. You cannot nest comments. Comments may span multiple lines.

`<a>`	*HTML2.0* ✦	*HTML3.2* ✦	*Netscape* ✦	*Microsoft* ✦

Purpose	Use `<a>` to create a hyperlink (with the `href` attribute) or a target of a link (with the `name` attribute).

Syntax	`<a`
	`    href="URL"`
	`    name="anchor_name"`
	`  rel="next"|"prev"|"head"|"toc"|"parent"|"child"|"index"|"glossary"`
	`  rev="next"|"prev"|"head"|"toc"|"parent"|"child"|"index"|"glossary"`
	`    title="Title of target of the link"`
	`    target="frame_name"> link text </a>`

Attributes	`href` specifies the target of the hyperlink `name` marks link text as a potential target of a link `rel` specifies the relationship from this document to the target of the link `rev` specifies the relationship from the target to this document `title` specifies the title of the target of this link `target` specifies the frame in which the target appears
Description	When used with the `href` attribute, the `<a>` tag marks the *link text* as a hyperlink. You can also use `<a>` with the `name` attribute to mark a portion of text as the target of a hyperlink. If you use frames in your document, use the target attribute to indicate the frame in which the browser should load the *target document* (the document specified by the `href` attribute).

<address>	*HTML2.0* ✦	*HTML3.2* ✦	*Netscape* ✦	*Microsoft* ✦

Purpose	Use the <address> tag to enclose an address.
Syntax	<address> An Address </address>
Attributes	None
Description	The <address> tag is a logical formatting tag that tells the Web browser that the text enclosed between <address> and </address> is an address. Typically, browsers format the address in italics. You can enclose a hyperlink within the <address> tag.

<applet>	*HTML2.0*	*HTML3.2* ✦	*Netscape* ✦	*Microsoft* ✦

Purpose	Use the <applet> tag to embed a Java applet (a small application) in an HTML document.

Syntax	<applet
	    codebase="URL"
	    code="classname"
	    name="appletname"
	    alt="alternate text"
	    align="top"|"middle"|"bottom"|"left"|"right"
	    width=wpixels
	    height=hpixels
	    hspace=hspixels
	    vspace=vspixels> Text or param elements
	</applet>

Attributes	codebase specifies an alternate URL for the applet code specifies the class name of the Java applet name specifies the name of the applet alt is alternate text to be displayed in place of the applet align specifies the alignment width specifies the width (in pixels) of the applet's output area height specifies the height (in pixels) of the applet's output area hspace specifies the amount of horizontal padding in pixels vspace specifies the amount of vertical padding in pixels
Description	The <applet> tag was previously supported by Netscape Navigator (Version 2.0 or later) only; it was also used to embed Java applets in an HTML document. The recent HTML 3.2 specification includes <applet> as a valid tag. The <applet> tag causes the browser to set aside an area for the applet's output and also load and execute the applet specified by *classname*.

`<area>`	*HTML2.0*	*HTML3.2*	*Netscape*	*Microsoft*
	✦	✦	✦	✦

Purpose	Use `<area>` (inside the `<map>` tag) to specify the hot spots in client-side image maps.
Syntax	```<area shape=rect|circle|poly|default coords="x1,y1,x2,y2,x3,y3,..." href="URL" nohref alt="Alternate Text" >```
Attributes	`shape` specifies the shape of the hot spot (circle, rectangle, polygon) `coords` lists the coordinates (in pixels) necessary to define the shape `href` is the URL activated when the user clicks on that hot spot `nohref` indicates that the hot spot is not active `alt` is the alternate text displayed if the browser cannot display image
Description	You use one or more `<area>` tags inside a `<map>` tag to define the mouse-sensitive regions of an inline image (an image embedded in an HTML document). You must place the image in the document with the `<img>` tag along with the `usemap` attribute.

`<b>`	*HTML2.0*	*HTML3.2*	*Netscape*	*Microsoft*
	✦	✦	✦	✦

Purpose	Use the `<b>` tag to enclose text that the browser should display in boldface font.
Syntax	`<b> text to be displayed in bold </b>`
Attributes	None
Description	The `<b>` tag is a font style tag; it tells the browser to use a boldface font for the text enclosed between `<b>` and `</b>`. If boldface font is not available, the browser may reverse video or underlining.

`<base>`	*HTML2.0* ✦	*HTML3.2* ✦	*Netscape* ✦	*Microsoft* ✦

Purpose	Use the `<base>` tag inside the `<head>` element to specify a base URL that should be used to interpret all relative URLs. These URLs do not include a complete host and pathname.

Syntax	`<base>`
	    `href="URL"`
	    `target="frame_name"`
	`</base>`

Attributes	`href` specifies the base URL used to resolve all relative URLs `target` specifies the frame in which hyperlinked documents appear (Netscape)
Description	The `<base>` tag tells the browser what URL should be used as the base when trying to resolve a relative URL. For example, when a URL specifies only the name of a document, the browser will use the host and pathname from the base URL. In Netscape Navigator, you can use the `<base>` tag with the `target` attribute to specify the frame in which the hyperlinked documents appear. You must use the `<base>` tag inside the `<head>` element only.

`<basefont>`	*HTML2.0*	*HTML3.2* ✦	*Netscape* ✦	*Microsoft* ✦

Purpose	Use the `<basefont>` tag to specify the font size to be used for the remainder of the document. Although the default size is 3, keep in mind that font sizes can range from 1 – 7.

Syntax	`<basefont`
	    `size="1"|"2"|"3"|"4"|"5"|"6"|"7"`
	`>`

Attributes	`size` specifies the base font size for the subsequent text
Description	The `<basefont>` tag tells the browser what font size to use for the remainder of the document. The font sizes can range from 1 – 7 and the initial base font is 3.

`<bgsound>`	**HTML2.0**	**HTML3.2**	**Netscape**	**Microsoft** ✦

Purpose	Use the `<bgsound>` tag with a sound file to be played as background sound (only in Microsoft Internet Explorer).
Syntax	```<bgsound src="URL" loop="aNumber"|"infinite" >```
Attributes	`src` specifies the sound file, usually a .WAV file (Microsoft) `loop` indicates how many times the sound is repeated (Microsoft)
Description	Adds a background sound to the document. Use the `src` attribute to specify the sound file and the `loop` attribute to control how Internet Explorer plays the sound. This tag works in Microsoft Internet Explorer only.

`<big>`	**HTML2.0**	**HTML3.2** ✦	**Netscape** ✦	**Microsoft** ✦

Purpose	Use the `<big>` tag to enclose text that the browser should display in a font one size larger than that used for the surrounding text.
Syntax	`<big> text to be displayed in bigger font </big>`
Attributes	None
Description	The `<big>` tag was originally a Netscape-only HTML extension that made it easy to display a portion of text in a bigger font than the surrounding text. The `<big>` tag is convenient because you don't have to understand exactly what font sizes are being used to display the text; simply place the text between the `<big>` and `</big>` tags. You can also nest `<big>` tags to successively enlarge the font size. The recent HTML 3.2 specification supports the `<big>` tag.

`<blink>`	**HTML2.0**	**HTML3.2**	**Netscape** ✦	**Microsoft**

Purpose	Use the `<blink>` tag to delimit text that the browser should blink on and off.
Syntax	`<blink> annoying message </blink>`
Attributes	None
Description	The `<blink>` tag is a Netscape-only HTML extension that blinks the enclosed text on and off.

`<blockquote>`	HTML2.0 ✦	HTML3.2 ✦	Netscape ✦	Microsoft ✦

Purpose	Use the `<blockquote>` tag to delimit text that the browser displays as a large quote.

Syntax	`<blockquote>`
	        `...text being quoted...`
	`</blockquote>`

Attributes	None
Description	Text enclosed inside the `<blockquote>` and `</blockquote>` tags is considered a large block of quoted text. Browsers typically display the entire block of text slightly indented from the left and right margins and sometimes in italics.

`<body>`	HTML2.0 ✦	HTML3.2 ✦	Netscape ✦	Microsoft ✦

Purpose	Use the `<body>` tag to enclose the HTML document's body.

Syntax	`<body`
	        `bgcolor=ColorName|#RRGGBB`
	        `text=ColorName|#RRGGBB`
	        `link=ColorName|#RRGGBB`
	        `vlink=ColorName|#RRGGBB`
	        `alink=ColorName|#RRGGBB`
	        `background="URL"`
	        `bgproperties="fixed"`
	        `leftmargin=Npixel`
	        `topmargin=Npixel`
	`>`
	        `...the HTML document's body...`
	`</body>`

Attributes	`bgcolor` specifies the color of the background `text` specifies the color of text `link` specifies the color of hyperlink text `vlink` specifies the color of links that user has already visited `alink` specifies the color of the currently active link `background` specifies the URL image to be used for background `bgproperties` freezes the background image in the window (Microsoft) `leftmargin` specifies the left margin in pixels (Microsoft) `topmargin` specifies the top margin in pixels (Microsoft)

(continued)

Description	The entire body of the HTML document is enclosed within the `<body>` and `</body>` tags. HTML 2.0 did not have any attributes for the `<body>` tag. Netscape Navigator and Microsoft Internet Explorer supports a number of attributes that control the appearance of the document (such as background color and text color). By now, HTML 3.2 has incorporated these extended attributes into the HTML specification.

` `	*HTML2.0* ✦	*HTML3.2* ✦	*Netscape* ✦	*Microsoft* ✦

Purpose	Use the ` ` tag to insert a line break into the text flow.

Syntax	`<br`
	`    clear=left|all|right|none`
	`>`

Attributes	`clear` lets you control the text flow in the presence of an image
Description	The ` ` tag breaks the line and stops the browser from automatically filling up the line. The `clear` attribute determines where the next line starts.

`<caption>`	*HTML2.0*	*HTML3.2* ✦	*Netscape* ✦	*Microsoft* ✦

Purpose	Use the `<caption>` tag inside a `<table>` tag to enclose the text that's used as the caption for the table.

Syntax	`<caption`
	`    align=top|bottom`
	`> Caption for a table </caption>`

Attributes	`align` specifies location of the caption with respect to the table
Description	The `<caption>` tag can be used inside a `<table>` to specify a caption for the table. You can use the `align` attribute to position the caption at the top or the bottom of the table. If you do not include the `align` attribute, the caption appears at the top of the table.

`<center>`	*HTML2.0* ✦	*HTML3.2* ✦	*Netscape* ✦	*Microsoft* ✦

Purpose	Use the `<center>` tag to enclose text that should be centered in the browser's window.

Syntax	`<center>`
	`...text to be centered...`
	`</center>`

Attributes	None
Description	You can center text by enclosing it within the `<center>` and `</center>` tags. You may enclose other HTML tags inside `<center>`. For example, to center an inline image, you'd place an `<img>` tag between the `<center>` and `</center>` tags.

`<cite>`	*HTML2.0* ✦	*HTML3.2* ✦	*Netscape* ✦	*Microsoft* ✦

Purpose	Use the `<cite>` tag to enclose a bibliographic citation.
Syntax	`<cite> a bibliographic citation such as UNIX Webmaster Bible </cite>`
Attributes	None
Description	The `<cite>` tag is a logical style tag; it tells the browser that the enclosed text is a bibliographic citation such as the name of a book or magazine. Then the browser uses an appropriate font style to render the citation.

`<code>`	*HTML2.0* ✦	*HTML3.2* ✦	*Netscape* ✦	*Microsoft* ✦

Purpose	Use the `<code>` tag to enclose computer source code in an HTML document. (This usage has nothing to do with executable content such as Java applet; the `<code>` tag is only for displaying source code.)
Syntax	`<code> some code such as import java.applet.*;` `</code>`
Attributes	None
Description	The `<code>` tag tells the browser that the enclosed text is computer source code. Then the browser uses an appropriate font style to display the source code.

`<dd>`	*HTML2.0* ✦	*HTML3.2* ✦	*Netscape* ✦	*Microsoft* ✦

Purpose	Use the `<dd>` tag (following a `<dt>` tag) to mark the definition portion of an item (enclosed between the `<dl>` and `</dl>` tags) in a definition list.
Syntax	`<dd> definition of a term </dd>`
Attributes	None
Description	The `<dd>` tag encloses the text that defines the term indicated by the preceding `<dt>` tag. Both `<dt>` and `<dd>` tags occur inside a `<dl>` tag. You can safely omit the `</dd>` tag that ends a definition (because a subsequent `<dt>` or `</dl>` tag unambiguously marks the end of the definition).

`<dfn>`	*HTML2.0*	*HTML3.2* ✦	*Netscape*	*Microsoft* ✦

Purpose	Use the `<dfn>` tag to enclose a definition.
Syntax	`<dfn> this is a definition </dfn>`
Attributes	None
Description	The `<dfn>` tag tells the browser that the enclosed text defines a particular term. This tag was previously used as an HTML extension supported by Microsoft Internet Explorer, but now it's part of HTML 3.2 specification.

`<dir>`	*HTML2.0* ✦	*HTML3.2* ✦	*Netscape* ✦	*Microsoft* ✦

Purpose	Use the `<dir>` tag to define a directory list where each item is defined by a `<li>` tag.

Syntax	`<dir`
	    `compact`
	    `type=circle|square|disc`
	`>`
	`...one or more <li> tags...`
	`</dir>`

Attributes	`compact` tells you to make the list as small as possible `type` specifies the style of the bullet in front of each list item (Netscape)

Description	The `<dir>` tag encloses a directory list, which is an unordered list meant to display filenames. The appearance of a `<dir>` list is typically the same as that of a `<ul>` list. Each item in a `<dir>` list is defined using an `<li>` tag.

`<div>`	**HTML2.0**	**HTML3.2** ✦	**Netscape** ✦	**Microsoft**

Purpose	Use the `<div>` tag to mark a division of a document and to assign an alignment for the enclosed text.
Syntax	```<div align=left|center|right > ...body of this division... </div>```
Attributes	`align` indicates the text alignment of this division
Description	The `<div>` tag delimits a division of a document and sets the alignment for the division. Note that the `<center>` tag is a synonym for `<div align=center>`.

`<dl>`	**HTML2.0** ✦	**HTML3.2** ✦	**Netscape** ✦	**Microsoft** ✦

Purpose	Use the `<dl>` tag to enclose a definition list consisting of pairs of `<dt>` and `<dd>` tags.
Syntax	```<dl compact > ...pairs of <dt> and <dd> tags... </dl>```
Attributes	`compact` tells you to make the list as small as possible
Description	The definition list is enclosed by the `<dl>` and `</dl>` tags. The items in a definition list consist of a term (indicated by a `<dt>` tag) followed by its definition (marked by a `<dd>` tag). Thus the definition list includes pairs of `<dt>` and `<dd>` tags. Typically the browser displays the term on a line and the definition in an indented paragraph that begins on the next line.

`<dt>`	HTML2.0 ✦	HTML3.2 ✦	Netscape ✦	Microsoft ✦

Purpose	Use the `<dt>` tag to mark the term being defined as an item in a definition list (which is enclosed between the `<dl>` and `</dl>` tags).
Syntax	`<dt>` term being defined `</dt>`
Attributes	None
Description	The `<dt>` tag specifies the term being defined in an item of a definition list. You must follow the term with its definition in a `<dd>` tag. Both `<dt>` and `<dd>` tags occur inside the `<dl>` tag. You can safely omit the `</dt>` tag that ends a term (because a subsequent `<dd>` tag unambiguously marks the end of the term).

`<em>`	HTML2.0 ✦	HTML3.2 ✦	Netscape ✦	Microsoft ✦

Purpose	Use the `<em>` tag to instruct the browser to display the enclosed text with emphasis.
Syntax	`<em>` some text to be emphasized `</em>`
Attributes	None
Description	The `<em>` tag tells the browser that the enclosed text should be emphasized. The browser then uses an appropriate font style (usually italic) to display the text.

`<font>`	HTML2.0	HTML3.2 ✦	Netscape ✦	Microsoft ✦

Purpose	Use the `<font>` tag to specify the size and typeface of the font to be used for the text enclosed within the `<font>` and `</font>` tags.

Syntax	`<font`
	`    size=+N|-N|N`
	`    color=color_name|#RRGGBB`
	`    face="typeface name">`
	`...text for which these settings are to be`
	`used...`
	`</font>`

Attributes	size specifies a new font size or change in font size color specifies a color by name or by RGB value face specifies the name of a font typeface (Microsoft)
Description	You can use the `<font>` tag to change the font size or color for a block of text. In Microsoft Internet Explorer, you can use the `<font>` tag with the face attribute to specify the typeface to be used. The new font settings apply to the text enclosed between the `<font>` and `</font>` tags. You can specify the font size as an absolute value or as an increment or decrement from the current size. For example, size=+2 means add 2 to the current font size whereas size=2 means use the absolute font size of 2. For the color attribute, you can use one of the standard names such as aqua, black, blue, fuchsia, gray, green, lime, maroon, navy, olive, purple, red, silver, teal, white, and yellow. You can also specify an arbitray color with the notation #RRGGBB where RR, GG, and BB denote hexadecimal digits that specify the intensity of the red (R), green (G), and blue (B) component of the color. Thus, #FF0000 denotes red and #FFFFFF denotes white.

`<form>`	HTML2.0	HTML3.2	Netscape	Microsoft
	✦	✦	✦	✦

Purpose	Use the `<form>` tag to enclose a form in an HTML document.

Syntax	`<form`
	`    action="URL referring to CGI program"`
	`    method=POST|GET`
	`    enctype="application/x-www-form-`
	`urlencoded"|"multipart/form-data"`
	`>`
	`...other tags such as <input>, <select>,`
	`<textarea>, ...`
	`</form>`

Attributes	action specifies the URL of a CGI program that processes form data method specifies how the form's data is sent to the server enctype specifies how the form's data is encoded
Description	You can place a form between the `<form>` and `</form>` tags. The form's body contains various HTML formatting tags and other form elements such as `<input>`, `<select>`, and `<textarea>`.

`<frame>`	*HTML2.0*	*HTML3.2*	*Netscape*	*Microsoft*
			✦	✦

Purpose	Use the `<frame>` tag (inside a `<frameset>` tag) to define a single frame — a part of the window capable of displaying an HTML document — that can be displayed by Netscape Navigator and Microsoft Internet Explorer.

Syntax
```
<frame
    name=NameOfFrame
    src="URL to display in frame"
    marginwidth=Npixels
    marginheight=Npixels
    noresize
    scrolling="yes"|"no"
>
```

Attributes

`name` is the name that identifies this frame
`src` is the URL of the document to be displayed in this frame
`marginwidth` is the horizontal margin (in pixels) around frame's content
`marginheight` is the vertical margin (in pixels) around frame's content
`noresize` tells you that the frame should not be resized
`scrolling` controls whether or not the contents of the frame scroll

Description

The `<frame>` tag is a Netscape-only HTML extension that allows you to define a frame. Each frame is a part of the Netscape Navigator window and each frame is capable of displaying an HTML document. With frames, you essentially get several Web browsers inside a single window. You use the `<frame>` tag inside the `<frameset>` tag to define a single frame.

`<frameset>`	*HTML2.0*	*HTML3.2*	*Netscape*	*Microsoft*
			✦	✦

Purpose	Use the `<frameset>` tag to enclose a collection of frames, each defined by a `<frame>` tag (frames are currently supported by Netscape Navigator and and Microsoft Internet Explorer only).

Syntax
```
<frameset
    cols="Numbers or percentages"
    rows="Numbers or percentages"
>
... two or more <frame> tags ...
</frameset>
```

Attributes	`cols` is the size and number of columns `rows` is the size and number of rows
Description	The `<frameset>` tag is a Netscape-only HTML extension that allows you to enclose a number of frames and treat them as a single set. You can nest `<frameset>` tags to create a complex layout of framesin which each frame provides a view into a different HTML document.

`<h1>`	***HTML2.0*** ✦	***HTML3.2*** ✦	***Netscape*** ✦	***Microsoft*** ✦

Purpose	Use the `<h1>` tag to enclose a first level heading in an HTML document.

Syntax	`<h1`
	    `align=left|center|right`
	`> heading text </h1>`

Attributes	`align` specifies the alignment of the heading
Description	The Web browser treats text between the `<h1>` and `</h1>` tags as a level 1 heading. Typically, you'd use an `<h1>` heading for the document's title.

`<h2>`	***HTML2.0*** ✦	***HTML3.2*** ✦	***Netscape*** ✦	***Microsoft*** ✦

Purpose	Use the `<h2>` tag to enclose a second level heading in an HTML document.

Syntax	`<h2`
	    `align=left|center|right`
	`> heading text </h2>`

Attributes	`align` specifies the alignment of the heading
Description	The Web browser treats the text between the `<h2>` and `</h2>` tags as a level 2 heading. Typically, you'd use `<h2>` headings as the section headings in an HTML document. The browser displays the `<h2>` heading with a font size somewhat smaller than that used for the `<h1>` tag.

`<h3>`	HTML2.0	HTML3.2	Netscape	Microsoft
	✦	✦	✦	✦

Purpose	Use the `<h3>` tag to enclose a second level heading in an HTML document.

Syntax	`<h3`
	      `align=left|center|right`
	`> heading text </h3>`

Attributes	`align` specifies the alignment of the heading
Description	The Web browser treats the text between the `<h3>` and `</h3>` tags as a level 3 heading. The browser displays the `<h3>` heading with a font size somewhat smaller than that used for the `<h2>` tag.

`<h4>`	HTML2.0	HTML3.2	Netscape	Microsoft
	✦	✦	✦	✦

Purpose	Use the `<h4>` tag to enclose a second level heading in an HTML document.

Syntax	`<h4`
	      `align=left|center|right`
	`> heading text </h4>`

Attributes	`align` specifies the alignment of the heading
Description	The Web browser treats the text between the `<h4>` and `</h4>` tags as a level 4 heading. The browser displays the `<h4>` heading with a font size somewhat smaller than that used for the `<h3>` tag.

`<h5>`	HTML2.0	HTML3.2	Netscape	Microsoft
	✦	✦	✦	✦

Purpose	Use the `<h5>` tag to enclose a second level heading in an HTML document.

Syntax	`<h5`
	      `align=left|center|right`
	`> heading text </h5>`

Attributes	`align` specifies the alignment of the heading

| *Description* | The Web browser treats the text between the `<h5>` and `</h5>` tags as a level 5 heading. The browser displays the `<h5>` heading with a font size somewhat smaller than that used for the `<h4>` tag. |

`<h6>`	***HTML2.0***	***HTML3.2***	***Netscape***	***Microsoft***
	✦	✦	✦	✦

Purpose	Use the `<h6>` tag to enclose a second level heading in an HTML document.

Syntax	`<h6`
	`    align=left|center|right`
	`> heading text </h6>`

Attributes	`align` specifies the alignment of the heading
Description	The Web browser treats the text between the `<h6>` and `</h6>` tags as a level 6 heading. The browser displays the `<h6>` heading with a font size somewhat smaller than that used for the `<h5>` tag.

`<head>`	***HTML2.0***	***HTML3.2***	***Netscape***	***Microsoft***
	✦	✦	✦	✦

Purpose	Use the `<head>` tag to enclose header elements (such as `<title>`, `<meta>`, `<link>`, `<base>`, `<isindex>`, `<script>`, and `<style>`) of the HTML document.

Syntax	`<head>`
	`...document header elements...`
	`</head>`

Attributes	None
Description	The Web browser treats everything between the `<head>` and `</head>` tags as the document header. You can place any of the following tags within the `<head>` tag: `<title>`, `<meta>`, `<link>`, `<base>`, `<isindex>`, `<script>`, and `<style>`. Of these, the `<style>` tag is not yet fully defined; it has been reserved in HTML 3.2 for future use.

`<hr>`	HTML2.0 ✦	HTML3.2 ✦	Netscape ✦	Microsoft ✦

Purpose	Use the `<hr>` tag to insert a horizontal rule in an HTML document.

Syntax	<pre><hr
	    align=left|right|center
	    noshade
	    size=Npixels
	    width=Npixels
	></pre>

Attributes	`align` specifies the alignment of the horizontal rule `noshade` turns off the three-dimensional shading `size` specifies the thickness (in pixels) of the horizontal rule `width` specifies the width (in pixels) of the rule
Description	The `<hr>` tag inserts a horizontal rule in the HTML document. In HTML 2.0, the `<hr>` tag did not accept any attributes. However, Netscape Navigator and Microsoft Internet Explorer supported a number of attributes that are now also in HTML 3.2. These attributes let you control the appearance of the horizontal rule.

`<html>`	HTML2.0 ✦	HTML3.2 ✦	Netscape ✦	Microsoft ✦

Purpose	Use `<html>` to enclose an entire HTML document.

Syntax	<pre><html version="-//W3C//DTD HTML 3.2//EN">
	...head and body of document...
	</html></pre>

Attributes	`version` describes the version of HTML
Description	You can enclose an HTML document between the `<html>` and `</html>` tags. However, this tag is optional and many browsers simply ignore the tag.

`<i>`	HTML2.0 ✦	HTML3.2 ✦	Netscape ✦	Microsoft ✦

Purpose	Use the `<i>` tag to enclose text that the browser should display in italic font.
Syntax	`<i> text to be displayed in italics </i>`
Attributes	None
Description	The `<i>` tag is a font style tag; it tells the browser to use an italic (or oblique) font for the text enclosed between the `<i>` and `</i>` tags.

<img>	*HTML2.0*	*HTML3.2*	*Netscape*	*Microsoft*
	✦	✦	✦	✦

Purpose	Use the <img> tag to specify an inline image that the browser displays embedded within a document's text.

Syntax

```
<img
    src="URL of image"
    alt="Alternate text"
    align=top|middle|bottom|left|right
    width=Npixels
    height=Npixels
    border=Npixels
    hspace=Npixels
    vspace=Npixels
    usemap="#MapName"
    ismap
    lowsrc="URL of low-resolution image"
    dynsrc="URL of AVI movie"
    controls="URL of movie controls image"
    start="fileopen"|"fileopen,mouseover"
    loop=Number|infinite
>
```

Attributes	src specifies the URL of the image file alt specifies the text to be displayed in lieu of image align specifies the image alignment with surrounding text width is the width of the image in pixels height is the height of the image in pixels border specifies the width in pixels of the border around image hspace is horizontal space (in pixels) between the image and text vspace is vertical space (in pixels) between the image and text usemap indicates a clickable image with a client-side map ismap indicates a clickable image with a server-side map lowsrc is a lower-resolution version of the image (Netscape) dynsrc specifies the URL of AVI movie to be loaded (Microsoft) controls specifies the URL of movie's controls (Microsoft) start specifies when to start running the movie (Microsoft) loop indicates how many times to play the movie (Microsoft)
Description	The <input> tag lets you embed inline images in an HTML document. The Web browser renders these images embedded in the document's text. You specify the image file's URL in the src attribute. If the image is a clickable image (that is, the image acts as a number of hyperlinks associated with various parts of the image), you'd use the ismap or the usemap attributes. Netscape and Microsoft support several new attributes. Netscape Navigator can load a low-resolution version of the image (the image that you

(continued)

specify through the `lowsrc` attribute) while the high-resolution image is being downloaded. Microsoft Internet Explorer uses the `<img>` tag with the `dynsrc` attribute to load a video in the Audio-Video Interleaved (AVI) format. You can control the video playback with the `controls`, `start`, and `loop` attributes.

`<input>`	HTML2.0 ✦	HTML3.2 ✦	Netscape ✦	Microsoft ✦

Purpose	Use the `<input>` tag (inside a `<form>` tag) to define a number of common input elements (such as text fields, multiple choice lists, and clickable images) as well as submit and reset buttons.

Syntax	`<input`
	`  type=text|password|checkbox|radio|submit|reset|file|hidden|image`
	`    name=FieldName`
	`    value=FieldValue`
	`    checked`
	`    size=Number`
	`    maxlength=Number`
	`    src="URL of image"`
	`    align=top|middle|bottom|left|right`
	`>`

Attributes	`type` specifies the type of input element `name` is the name of this input element `value` is the value of this input element `checked` means selected (for radio buttons and checkboxes only) `size` specifies the width of the text-entry field in number of characters `maxlength` specifies the maximum number of characters for a text field `src` specifies the URL of an image for a clickable image `align` specifies the image alignment
Description	The `<input>` tag is a multipurpose tag — depending on the value of the type attribute this single tag can create a text-entry field (`text`), a radio button (`radio`), a checkbox (`checkbox`), a submit button (`submit`), a reset button (`reset`), a hidden field (`hidden`) that does not appear in the display, a clickable image (`image`), and a file submission button (`file`). You use `<input>` tags inside a `<form>` tag to create data-entry forms through which the user submits information to the Web server.

`<isindex>`	*HTML2.0* ✦	*HTML3.2* ✦	*Netscape* ✦	*Microsoft* ✦

Purpose	Use the `<isindex>` tag (in the `<head>` tag) to indicate that a document is searchable.
Syntax	```<isindex prompt="text to be used as prompt" >```
Attributes	`prompt` specifies the text used to prompt the user for a keyword
Description	The `<isindex>` tag marks a document as searchable. The browser displays the document with a leading text-entry box and a prompt that asks the user for a keyword. When the user types the keyword and presses Enter, the keyword is sent to the server as a query appended to a URL. The server can then process the query and return the results in another HTML document.

`<kbd>`	*HTML2.0* ✦	*HTML3.2* ✦	*Netscape* ✦	*Microsoft* ✦

Purpose	Use the `<kbd>` tag to enclose text that is typed on a keyboard (in other words, to delimit text that the browser should display in a distinctive manner so the user can tell that it should be typed on a keyboard).
Syntax	`<kbd> text to be typed on keyboard </kbd>`
Attributes	None
Description	The `<kbd>` tag marks text that is typed on the keyboard. The browser typically displays this text in a monospace font. You could use the `<kbd>` tag in online documenation to show the commands that the user has to type on the keyboard.

`<li>`	*HTML2.0* ✦	*HTML3.2* ✦	*Netscape* ✦	*Microsoft* ✦

Purpose	Use `<html>` to enclose an entire HTML document.
Purpose	Use the `<li>` tag to mark items in an ordered, unordered, directory, or menu list.
Syntax	```<li type=disc|circle|square|1|a|A|i|I value=SequenceNumber > the list item```

(continued)

Attributes	`type` specifies the style of bullet or numbering for this list item `value` specifies the sequence number for this list item
Description	The `<li>` tag marks text that constitutes a list item. To add items, you can use the `<li>` tag inside `<ol>`, `<ul>`, `<menu>`, and `<dir>` tags.

`<link>`	*HTML2.0* ✦	*HTML3.2* ✦	*Netscape* ✦	*Microsoft* ✦
Purpose	Use the `<link>` tag (inside `<head>`) to define the relationship between the document containing the `<link>` tag and the document referenced by the `<link>` tag's `href` attribute.			

Syntax	<pre><link
	    href="URL"
	    id="SGML ID"
	    rel=next|prev|parent|stylesheet|script|print
	    rev=made|next|prev|parent
	></pre>			

Attributes	`href` specifies the URL of the target document `id` is an SGML ID (new in HTML 3.2) `rel` specifies the relationship between this document and the target `rev` indicates the relationship between the target and this document `title` is an advisory title (one that may be displayed by the browser)			
Description	Place the `<link>` tag in the document's `<head>` element to specify various relationships between this document and the document referenced by the `href` attribute (known as the *target*). Two types of relationships are allowed: the `rel` attribute specifies the forward relationship (from this document to the target) and the `rev` attribute specifies reverse relationship (from the target to this document). The `<link>` tag is not displayed on-screen; it's just stored as information. Note that values of the `rel` and `rev` attributes are not yet standardized.			

`<listing>`	*HTML2.0* ✦	*HTML3.2* ✦	*Netscape* ✦	*Microsoft* ✦

Purpose	Use the `<listing>` tag to enclose a computer code listing that the browser should display without any interpretation.
Syntax	```<listing>
...computer listing...
</listing>```
Attributes	None
Description	The `<listing>` tag marks a computer listing that the browser is supposed to display as is, without interpreting any HTML tags or special keywords that may appear in the text. This tag is a deprecated element of the HTML 3.2 specification.

`<map>`	*HTML2.0*	*HTML3.2* ✦	*Netscape* ✦	*Microsoft* ✦

Purpose	Use the `<map>` tag to enclose the definitions for a client-side image map that lets a browser determine which document to download when the user clicks on an image.
Syntax	```<map
name="mapName"
>
one or more <area> tags
</map>```
Attributes	`name` defines the name for this client-side image map
Description	Client-side image map lets the browser process mouse clicks and, in response to a click, jump to a new URL. The older server-side image map requires work at the server to determine what should happen when a user clicks on an image. The `<map>` tag encloses one or more `<area>` tags that define the client-side image map. To use a particular client-side image map, you must specify the map's name in the `usemap` attribute of the `<img>` tag that inserts the inline image.

`<marquee>`	*HTML2.0*	*HTML3.2*	*Netscape*	*Microsoft* ✦

Purpose	Use the `<marquee>` tag to enclose some text that Microsoft Internet Explorer scrolls horizontally across the window.

Syntax	<pre><marquee
	    align=top|middle|bottom
	    behavior=scroll|slide|alternate
	    bgcolor=ColorName|#RRGGBB
	    width=Npixels
	    height=Npixels
	    hspace=Npixels
	    vspace=Npixels
	    scrollamount=Npixels
	    scrolldelay=Nmilliseconds
	&gt;
	    message for the marquee
	</listing></pre>

Attributes	`align` specifiies the alignment of a message in the marquee area `behavior` indicates how the text should be moved `bgcolor` is the color of the marquee area `width` is the width (in pixels) of the marquee area `height` is the height (in pixels) of the marquee area `hspace` is the horizontal space between the marquee and other text `vspace` is the vertical space between the marquee and other text `scrollamount` is the amount (in pixels) by which to scroll `scrolldelay` is the delay (in milliseconds) between successive movement
Description	The `<marquee>` tag encloses text to be displayed as a marquee — scrolled in an area within the document. The `<marquee>` tag is supported in Microsoft Internet Explorer only.

`<menu>`	*HTML2.0* ✦	*HTML3.2* ✦	*Netscape* ✦	*Microsoft* ✦

Purpose	Use the `<menu>` tag to define a menu list where each item is defined by a `<li>` tag.

Syntax	<pre><menu
	    compact
	    type=circle|square|disc
	&gt;
	...one or more <li> tags...
	</menu></pre>

Attributes	compact tells you to make the list as small as possible type specifies the style of bullet in front of each list item (Netscape)			
Description	The <menu> tag encloses a menu list, which is a short list of items that may act as a menu of choices. For example, you might use a menu list to display a selection of hyperlinks. In practice, most browsers render a menu list as an unordered list.			

<meta>	*HTML2.0* ✦	*HTML3.2* ✦	*Netscape* ✦	*Microsoft* ✦
Purpose	Use the <meta> tag (in the <head> tag) to include additional information about the document.			

Syntax	<meta
	    content="item value"
	    http_equiv="MIME_header_name"
	    name="item_name"
	    url="URL"
	  >			

Attributes	content specifies the value of the meta-information http_equiv specifies the MIME header name to be used name specifies the name of the meta-information in the tag url specifies a URL used to automatically update the document (Netscape)			
Description	The <meta> tag provides meta-information — information about the document — to the Web browser. For example, you may provide a list of keywords that describes the document. Or, you may instruct the Web server to send a certain MIME header to the browser before sending the document. In fact, many Web indexing robot programs make use of information you embed in the document with the <meta> tag. In particular, some robots make use of keywords you provide with the name="keywords" and content="list of keywords" format in a <meta> tag. Netscape Navigator uses the http_equiv="refresh", content="numSeconds" and url="someURL" attributes in a <meta> tag to automatically update the current document (with the one specified by the url attribute) after the number of seconds specified in the content attribute.			

`<nobr>`	*HTML2.0*	*HTML3.2*	*Netscape*	*Microsoft*
			✦	✦

Purpose	Use the `<nobr>` tag to stop the Web browser from breaking up lines up to the next `</nobr>` tag.

Syntax	`<nobr>`
	`... text that should appear on a single line...`
	`</nobr>`

Attributes	None
Description	The `<nobr>` tag inhibits the browser from breaking up lines to fit the current browser window's width. To ensure that lines do not get too long, insert one or more `<wbr>` tags at appropriate locations.

`<noframes>`	*HTML2.0*	*HTML3.2*	*Netscape*	*Microsoft*
			✦	✦

Purpose	Use the `<noframes>` tag (inside the outermost `<frameset>` tag) to enclose HTML content that can be displayed by a browser that does not yet support frames (frames are currently supported by Netscape Navigator only).

Syntax	`<noframes>`
	`... HTML content for nonframe-capable browsers ...`
	`</noframes>`

Attributes	None
Description	The `<noframes>` tag is a Netscape-only HTML extension that allows you to provide some HTML content to be displayed by a browser that does not support frames. If you decide to use frames in your HTML document, include some information in the `<noframes>` tag for those accessing your Web page using browsers that do not yet support frames. For example, inside the `<noframes>` tag you might include a hyperlink to a version of your Web page that does not use frames.

`<ol>`	*HTML2.0*	*HTML3.2*	*Netscape*	*Microsoft*
	✦	✦	✦	✦

Purpose	Use the `<ol>` tag to define an ordered list where each item is defined by a `<li>` tag.

Syntax	`<ol`
	    `compact`
	    `type=1|a|A|i|I`
	    `start=Number`
	`>`
	`...one or more <li> tags...`
	`</ol>`

Attributes	`compact` tells you to make the list as small as possible `type` specifies the style of number in front of each list item `start` denotes the starting sequence number for the list
Description	The `<ol>` tag encloses an ordered list of items where each item is defined by a `<li>` tag. By default, each item is pefixed with a sequence number that begins with 1. You can change the starting sequence number by providing a numeric value for the `start` attribute. You can also change the style of numbering with the `type` attribute. Set `type` to `a` or `A` for an alphabetic sequencing (such as `a, b, c,...` or `A, B, C,...`). Use `type=i` for lowercase Roman numerals or `type=I` for uppercase Roman numerals.

`<option>`	*HTML2.0* ✦	*HTML3.2* ✦	*Netscape* ✦	*Microsoft* ✦
Purpose	Use the `<option>` tag (inside a `<select>` tag) to define menu items.			

Syntax	`<option`
	    `selected`
	    `value=ValueToBeSentToServer`
	`>`
	`Menu item text`			

Attributes	`selected` indicates that the item is selected by default `value` specifies the value to be sent to the server when form is submitted			
Description	The `<option>` tag defines an item in a `<select>` menu. Use `<option>` tags inside a `<select>` tag.			

`<p>`	HTML2.0	HTML3.2	Netscape	Microsoft
	♦	♦	♦	♦

Purpose	Use the `<p>` tag to mark the start of a paragraph.

Syntax	`<p`
	    `align=left|center|right`
	`>`

Attributes	`align` specifies the alignment of text in the following paragraph
Description	The `<p>` tag starts a new paragraph. The browser automatically leaves a bit of extra space when it encounters the start of a new paragraph.

`<param>`	HTML2.0	HTML3.2	Netscape	Microsoft
		♦	♦	♦

Purpose	Use the `<param>` tag (inside an `<applet>` tag) to supply a parameter to a Java applet (a small application) that has been embedded in an HTML document.

Syntax	`<param`
	    `name="ParamName"`
	    `value="ParamValue"`
	`>`

Attributes	`name` specifies the name of the parameter `value` is the value of the parameter
Description	The `<param>` tag was supported by Netscape Navigator (Version 2.0 or later) only; it was also used with `<applet>` to embed Java applets in an HTML document. The recent HTML 3.2 specification includes `<applet>` and `<param>` as valid tags. The `<param>` tag passes the value of a parameter (identified by the `name` attribute) to an applet.

`<plaintext>`	HTML2.0	HTML3.2	Netscape	Microsoft
	♦	♦	♦	♦

Purpose	Use the `<plaintext>` tag to turn off interpretation of HTML tags in the remainder of the document.
Syntax	`<plaintext>` `... no more HTML after this tag... there is no end tag.`
Attributes	None
Description	The `<plaintext>` tag causes the browser to render the remainder of the document as plain text. This tag is an archaic tag.

`<pre>`	HTML2.0	HTML3.2	Netscape	Microsoft
	✦	✦	✦	✦

Purpose	Use the `<pre>` tag to enclose text that should displayed as preformatted text.

Syntax	`<pre`
	    `width=numchar>`
	`...text to be displayed as is...`
	`</pre>`

Attributes	`width` indicates the number of characters to fit on a single line
Description	The `<pre>` tag indicates that the enclosed text should be displayed without any change to the character and line spacing (in other words, the normal word wrapping and paragraph filling is not done). However, HTML tags other than `<img>`, `<big>`, `<small>`, `<sub>`, `<sup>`, and `<font>` are recognized inside the `<pre>` element.

`<s>`	HTML2.0	HTML3.2	Netscape	Microsoft
				✦

Purpose	Use the `<s>` tag to enclose text that the browser should display in a strikethrough font (a line drawn through the text).
Syntax	`<s> text to be displayed in strike through font` `</s>`
Attributes	None
Description	The `<s>` tag is Microsoft Internet Explorer's abbreviated form of the `<strike>` tag.

`<samp>`	HTML2.0	HTML3.2	Netscape	Microsoft
	✦	✦	✦	✦

Purpose	Use the `<samp>` tag to enclose a sequence of literal characters.
Syntax	`<samp> literal character sequence </samp>`
Attributes	None
Description	The `<samp>` tag is meant for "sample text" — that is, a sequence of literal characters that should not have any special interpretation to the user. This tag is not used very often.

`<script>`	**HTML2.0**	**HTML3.2** ✦	**Netscape** ✦	**Microsoft**

Purpose	Use the `<script>` tag in Netscape Navigator to embed JavaScript statements in an HTML document (HTML 3.2 reserves the `<script>` tag, but does not define it).

Syntax	`<script`
	`    language="JavaScript"`
	`>`
	`... JavaScript statements ...`
	`</script>`

Attributes	`language` specifies the scripting language ("JavaScript" in Netscape)
Description	The `<script>` tag is meant for embedding a script in an HTML document. Netscape Navigator supports this tag for embedding JavaScript statements in a document. HTML 3.2 specification treats `<script>` as a reserved tag. In the future, the `<script>` tag may support other scripting languages besides JavaScript.

`<select>`	**HTML2.0** ✦	**HTML3.2** ✦	**Netscape** ✦	**Microsoft** ✦

Purpose	Use the `<select>` tag (inside a `<form>` tag) to create single- and multiple-choice menus where each menu item is defined by an `<option>` tag.

Syntax	`<select`
	`    name=MenuName`
	`    size=NumVisibleItems`
	`    multiple`
	`>`
	`.... one or more <option> tags...`
	`</select>`

Attributes	`name` is the name of the select menu `size` specifies how many items should be visible at a time `multiple` specifies that the menu is multiple-choice
Description	The `<select>` tag encloses a menu. Each menu item is defined by an `<option>` tag. By default, the menu is single-choice (that is, the user can only select one item at a time), but if you include the `multiple` attribute, the user will be able to select multiple items from the list. Use the `<select>` tag inside a `<form>` tag.

`<small>`	*HTML2.0*	*HTML3.2*	*Netscape*	*Microsoft*
		✦	✦	✦

Purpose	Use the `<small>` tag to enclose text that the browser should display in a font one size smaller than that used for the surrounding text.
Syntax	`<small>` text to be displayed in smaller font `</small>`
Attributes	None
Description	The `<small>` tag causes the browser to display the enclosed text in a smaller font than that used for the surrounding text. You can also nest `<small>` tags to successively reduce the font size. The `<small>` tag was originally a Netscape-only HTML extension, but it's now part of the HTML 3.2 specification.

`<strike>`	*HTML2.0*	*HTML3.2*	*Netscape*	*Microsoft*
	✦	✦	✦	✦

Purpose	Use the `<strike>` tag to enclose text that the browser should display in a strikethrough font (a line drawn through the text).
Syntax	`<strike>` text to be displayed in strike through font `</strike>`
Attributes	None
Description	The `<strike>` tag causes the browser to display the enclosed text with a line drawn through it, making it look crossed out. This tag can be used as an editing markup. On an online store, you might use `<strike>` to list items that have sold out or to cross out an old price and show a new (presumably lower) price.

`<strong>`	*HTML2.0*	*HTML3.2*	*Netscape*	*Microsoft*
	✦	✦	✦	✦

Purpose	Use the `<strong>` tag to enclose text that should be displayed with more emphasis than the `<em>` tag.
Syntax	`<strong>` text that needs strong emphasis `</strong>`
Attributes	None
Description	Use the `<strong>` tag to delimit text that needs strong emphasis. Typically, Web browsers render such text in boldface.

`<style>`	HTML2.0	HTML3.2 ✦	Netscape	Microsoft
Purpose	The `<style>` tag is reserved for future use. This tag will be used to associate a stylesheet with an HTML document — the purpose of the stylesheet is to specify the layout and appearance of the HTML document.			

`<sub>`	HTML2.0	HTML3.2 ✦	Netscape ✦	Microsoft ✦
Purpose	Use the `<sub>` tag to enclose text that the browser should display as a subscript.			
Syntax	`<sub> text to be displayed as a subscript </sub>`			
Attributes	None			
Description	The `<sub>` tag causes the browser to display the text enclosed between `<sub>` and `</sub>` as a subscript (half of a character lower than the rest of the text on that line). Use the `<sub>` tag for subscripts in mathematical equations or scientific notations.			

`<sup>`	HTML2.0	HTML3.2 ✦	Netscape ✦	Microsoft ✦
Purpose	Use the `<sup>` tag to enclose text that the browser should display as a superscript.			
Syntax	`<sup> text to be displayed as a superscript </sup>`			
Attributes	None			
Description	The `<sup>` tag causes the browser to display the text enclosed between `<sup>` and `</sup>` as a superscript (half of a character higher than the rest of the text on that line). Use the `<sup>` tag for superscripts in mathematical equations or scientific notations.			

`<table>`	*HTML2.0*	*HTML3.2* ✦	*Netscape* ✦	*Microsoft* ✦

Purpose	Use the `<table>` tag to enclose a table in an HTML document.
| *Syntax* | ```
<table
    align=left|center|right
    width=Npixels|Percentage
    border=Npixels
    cellspacing=Npixels
    cellpadding=Npixels
    bgcolor=ColorName|#RRGGBB
    bordercolor=ColorName|#RRGGBB
    bordercolorlight=ColorName|#RRGGBB
    bordercolordark=ColorName|#RRGGBB
    hspace=Npixels
    vspace=Npixels
>
... One or more rows of table in <tr> tags ...
</table>
``` |
| *Attributes* | `align` **specifies alignment of the table in the browser's window**
`width` **specifies the width of the table**
`border` **specifies the width (in pixels) of border around table**
`cellspacing` **is the spacing between cells**
`cellpadding` **is the space between a cell and its contents**
`bgcolor` **is the color of the table's background (Microsoft)**
`bordercolor` **is the color of the border (Microsoft)**
`bordercolorlight` **is the color for light shading around the border (Microsoft)**
`bordercolordark` **is the color for dark shading around the border (Microsoft)**
`hspace` **is horizontal space between the table and text (Netscape, Microsoft)**
`vspace` **is vertical space between the table and text (Netscape, Microsoft)** |
| *Description* | The `<table>` tag encloses a table that consists of one or more rows. Each row is defined by a `<tr>` tag. The `<table>` tag was previously used as an HTML extension supported by both Netscape Navigator and Microsoft Internet Explorer. The HTML 3.2 specification includes support for the `<table>` tag. Microsoft Internet Explorer supports additional color attributes for a table. |
```

`<td>`	HTML2.0	HTML3.2	Netscape	Microsoft
		✦	✦	✦

Purpose	Use the `<td>` tag (inside a `<tr>` tag) to define a data cell in a table row.

Syntax	<pre>`<td`
	`    align=left|center|right`
	`    valign=top|bottom|baseline`
	`    colspan=Number`
	`    rowspan=Number`
	`    nowrap`
	`    bgcolor=ColorName|#RRGGBB`
	`    bordercolor=ColorName|#RRGGBB`
	`    bordercolorlight=ColorName|#RRGGBB`
	`    bordercolordark=ColorName|#RRGGBB`
	`    width=Npixels`
	`>`
	`... Content of this cell ...`
	`</td>`</pre>

Attributes	`align` specifies the horizontal alignment of the cell's content `valign` specifies the vertical alignment of the cell's content `colspan` is the number of columns spanned by this cell `rowspan` is the number of rows spanned by this cell `nowrap` turns off text wrapping in this cell `bgcolor` is the color of the cell's background (Microsoft) `bordercolor` is the color of the cell's border (Microsoft) `bordercolorlight` is the color for light shading around the border (Microsoft) `bordercolordark` is the color for dark shading around the border (Microsoft) `width` is the width of this cell (Netscape, Microsoft)

Description	The `<td>` tag defines a data cell in a row. Use a number of `<td>` tags inside a `<tr>` tag to define all the data cells in a row.

`<textarea>`	HTML2.0	HTML3.2	Netscape	Microsoft
	✦	✦	✦	✦

Purpose	Use the `<textarea>` tag (inside a `<form>` tag) to create a multiline text-input area.

| *Syntax* | ```
<textarea
    name=FieldName
    rows=NumRows
    cols=NumCols
    wrap=physical|virtual|off
>
...default content of this field...
</textarea>
``` |

Attributes   `name` is the name of the text-entry area
`rows` specifies how many rows of text to display
`cols` specifies how many columns of text to display
`wrap` controls text wrapping

Description   The `<textarea>` tag displays a text-entry area in which the user can enter several lines of text. The text enclosed between the `<textarea>` and `</textarea>` tags is interpreted as the default value of the text area. By default, text wrapping is off. If you set `wrap=virtual`, the user sees text wrapped in the text-entry area, but the text is transmitted to the server without any wrapping. If you set `wrap=physical`, the text is sent to the server with the line breaks that appear on the display as the text wraps in the text-entry area.

`<th>`	*HTML2.0*	*HTML3.2*	*Netscape*	*Microsoft*
	✦	✦	✦	✦

Purpose   Use the `<th>` tag (inside a `<tr>` tag) to define a header cell in a row of a table.

Syntax
```
<th
    align=left|center|right
    valign=top|bottom|baseline
    colspan=Number
    rowspan=Number
    nowrap
    bgcolor=ColorName|#RRGGBB
    bordercolor=ColorName|#RRGGBB
    bordercolorlight=ColorName|#RRGGBB
    bordercolordark=ColorName|#RRGGBB
    width=Npixels
>
... Content of this cell ...
</th>
```

(continued)
```

Attributes	`align` specifies the horizontal alignment of the cell's content			

Attributes
`align` specifies the horizontal alignment of the cell's content
`valign` specifies the vertical alignment of the cell's content
`colspan` is the number of columns spanned by this cell
`rowspan` is the number of rows spanned by this cell
`nowrap` turns off text wrapping in this cell
`bgcolor` is the color of the cell's background (Microsoft)
`bordercolor` is the color of the cell's border (Microsoft)
`bordercolorlight` is the color for light shading around the border (Microsoft)
`bordercolordark` is the color for dark shading around the border (Microsoft)
`width` is the width of this cell (Netscape, Microsoft)

Description
The `<th>` tag defines a header cell in a row. Use a number of `<th>` tags inside a `<tr>` tag to define a row of header cells.

`<title>`	**HTML2.0** ✦	**HTML3.2** ✦	**Netscape** ✦	**Microsoft** ✦

Purpose
Use the `<title>` tag (inside the `<head>` tag) to enclose the document's title.

Syntax
`<title> The Document's Title </title>`

Attributes
None

Description
Place the document's title between the `<title>` and `</title>` tags within the document's header, which, in turn, is enclosed in the `<head>` and `</head>` tags. The browser typically displays the document's title in the window's title bar.

`<tr>`	**HTML2.0**	**HTML3.2** ✦	**Netscape** ✦	**Microsoft** ✦

Purpose
Use the `<tr>` tag (inside a `<table>` tag) to define a table row.

Syntax
```
<tr
    align=left|center|right
    valign=top|bottom|baseline
    bgcolor=ColorName|#RRGGBB
    bordercolor=ColorName|#RRGGBB
    bordercolorlight=ColorName|#RRGGBB
    bordercolordark=ColorName|#RRGGBB
>
... One or more <th> or <td> tags ...
</tr>
```

Attributes	align specifies the horizontal alignment of various cells in a row
	valign specifies vertical alignment of various cells in a row
	bgcolor is the color of the row's background (Microsoft)
	bordercolor is the color of the row's border (Microsoft)
	bordercolorlight is the color for light shading around the border (Microsoft)
	bordercolordark is the color for dark shading around the border (Microsoft)
Description	The \<tr\> tag encloses a table row. Use \<tr\> inside the \<table\> tag. Between the \<tr\> and \</tr\> tags, you'd place groups of \<th\> and \<td\> tags that define the cells in a row.

\<tt\>	*HTML2.0*	*HTML3.2*	*Netscape*	*Microsoft*
	✦	✦	✦	✦

Purpose	Use the \<tt\> tag to enclose text that the browser should display in a monospace font.
Syntax	\<tt\> text to be displayed in monospace \</tt\>
Attributes	None
Description	The \<tt\> tag is a font style tag; it tells the browser to use a monospace font for the text enclosed between \<tt\> and \</tt\>.

\<u\>	*HTML2.0*	*HTML3.2*	*Netscape*	*Microsoft*
		✦		✦

Purpose	Use the \<u\> tag to enclose text that the browser should display in an underlined font.
Syntax	\<u\> text to be underlined \</u\>
Attributes	None
Description	The \<u\> tag causes the browser to underline the text enclosed between \<u\> and \</u\>.

`<ul>`	HTML2.0 ✦	HTML3.2 ✦	Netscape ✦	Microsoft ✦

Purpose	Use the `<ul>` tag to define an unordered list where each item is defined by an `<li>` tag.

Syntax	`<ul`
	    `compact`
	    `type=circle|square|disc`
	`>`
	`...one or more <li> tags...`
	`</ul>`

Attributes	`compact` tells you to make the list as small as possible `type` specifies the style of bullet in front of each list item
Description	The `<ul>` tag encloses an unordered list of items where each item is defined by an `<li>` tag.

`<var>`	HTML2.0 ✦	HTML3.2 ✦	Netscape ✦	Microsoft ✦

Purpose	Use the `<var>` tag (usually inside `<pre>` or `<code>` tags) to enclose variable names (such as those that are part of some computer-documentation).
Syntax	`<var> a variable name </var>`
Attributes	None
Description	The `<var>` tag marks variable names in computer-documentation. Typically, you'd use `<var>` inside `<pre>` or `<code>` tags to variable names.

`<wbr>`	HTML2.0	HTML3.2 ✦	Netscape ✦	Microsoft

Purpose	Use the `<wbr>` tag inside a `<nobr>` tag to designate points where the browser may break the line of text.
Syntax	`<wbr>`
Attributes	None
Description	The `<wbr>` tag marks points where the browser may break a line. Use the `<wbr>` tag inside the `<nobr>` tag.

`<xmp>`	*HTML2.0*	*HTML3.2*	*Netscape*	*Microsoft*
	✦	✦	✦	✦

Purpose	Use the `<xmp>` tag to display preformatted text.

Syntax	`<xmp>`
	     `...Text to be displayed as is...`
	`</xmp>`

Attributes	None
Description	The `<xmp>` tag (which is supposed to stand for *example*) causes the browser to display the embedded text as preformatted text, as in `<pre>`. Unlike `<pre>`, no embedded tags are recognized. Do not use `<xmp>` anymore because its use is discouraged in the HTML 3.2 specification (`<xmp>` is marked as *deprecated*).

✦   ✦   ✦

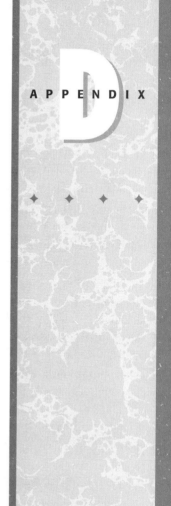

ISO Latin-1 Coded Character Set

HTML uses the International Organization For Standardization's ISO Latin-1 Coded Character Set (also referred to as ISO 8859-1) to represent alphanumeric characters and special symbols. The ISO Latin-1 character set is a superset of the well-known ASCII (American Standard Code for Information Interchange) character set. ISO Latin-1 adds 96 special characters to the 128 ASCII characters. The character codes — numeric values representing a character — range from 0 to 255; the codes in the range 0 to 127 correspond to the ASCII characters.

You can insert any of the ISO Latin-1 characters in an HTML document by referring to the character as a numeric entity with the following syntax:

&#*nnn*;

where *nnn* is the numeric code (between 000 and 255) for the character. When you insert such a numeric entity in an HTML document, the browser displays the actual character in its place. For example, if you use the numeric entity © the browser should display the copyright symbol (©). Because the user may select a different font in the browser and some browsers are not graphical, a browser may not always display all the characters from the ISO Latin-1 character set.

Figure D-1 shows (in tabular form) how Netscape Navigator renders the ISO Latin-1 numeric entities for the first 128 characters; Figure D-2 shows the last 128 characters of the ISO Latin-1 character set. Next to each numeric entity (with the format &#*nnn*;) you'll find the actual character displayed in boldface. Some of the numeric entities are not recognized in HTML. Figures D-1 and D-2 do not show anything next to these unrecognized numeric entities (for example, &#000;).

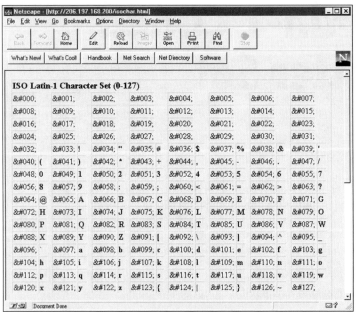

Figure D-1: The first 128 characters of the ISO Latin-1 character set as rendered by Netscape Navigator.

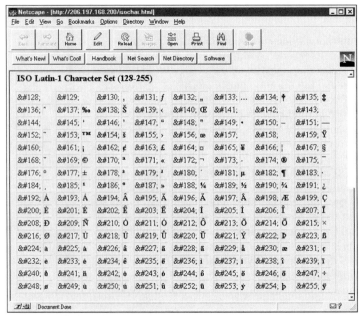

Figure D-2: The last 128 characters of the ISO Latin-1 character set as rendered by Netscape Navigator.

In addition to the numeric entities shown in Figures D-1 and D-2, you can also use named entities to refer to ISO Latin-1 characters in your HTML document. For example, to insert a copyright symbol (©) in a document, you could write the following:

```
&copy;
```

Figure D-3 shows the named entities in a tabular form. Note that the   entity refers to a non-breaking space — it's a blank space that the Web browser does not eliminate when filling a line (because it's a blank space, you don't see any character next to the entry for   in Figure D-3).

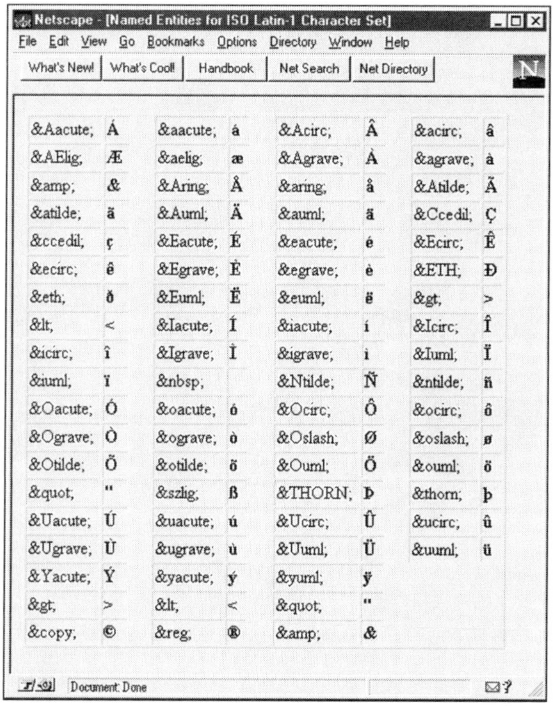

Figure D-3: Some of the named character entities as rendered by Netscape Navigator.

Index

(continued)

(continued)

G

Galahad for BIX browser, 94
garbage collection, Java, 659
gateways
   application, 253–255
   Common Interface. *See* CGI; CGI gateways to
     relational databases; CGI scripts
   PPP (Point-to-Point Protocol), 50, 51
   TCP/IP, 21–22
geometric shapes, Java, 655–659
GET command, HTTP, 86, 87–88
GET method, CGI scripts, 302, 520–522,
    528–529
getstats log analysis tool, 239
GIF89a animation loops, 362–364
   Netscape Application Extensions, 406–407
GIF graphics, 344–346
   converting to transparent GIFs, 359–362
   JPEG comparison, 346
   lossless compression, 344
   royalties for, 346
GN Web server, 99
GNNpress HTML authoring tool for Macintosh,
    475
GNU software, UNIX alternatives, 207
Gopher, 56–57, 73–79
   building programs, 77
   client, 77–78
   configuring servers, 78
   downloading software, 75–76
   extracting source files, 76–77
   protocol, 73–74
   selector strings, 73
   starting servers, 79
   type codes, 74, *75*
   URLs and, 335
goto statements, Perl programming, 548
government
   IRS page, 126–127
   THOMAS page, 125–126
Grail browser, 96
graphical browsers, downloading for X
    Window Systems, 108–115

graphics, 343–347
   centering, 389–390
   creating, 358–364
   embedded images, 294–296
   external images through links, 350–352
   GIF, 344–346
   image manipulation software, 362–363
   image maps, 296–298, *299*, 367–378
   inline images in Web pages, 355–357, *358*
   JPEG, 124, 343–344
   mastheads, 355
   painting and drawing programs, 358
   PNG, 347
   transparent GIF conversions, 359–362
graphics designers, Webmasters as, 139–140
graphics tools, Webmaster resources on the
    Net, 726–727
GraphicTools directory, Webmaster resources
    on companion CD-ROM, 710–711
grep command, Perl programming, 542
group files, CERN HTTP servers, 231
GWHIS browser, 94

H

<h1> tag, HTML reference, 747
<h2> tag, HTML reference, 747
<h3> tag, HTML reference, 748
<h4> tag, HTML reference, 748
<h5> tag, HTML reference, 748–749
<h6> tag, HTML reference, 749
Hawaii
   Lahaina, *124, 125*
   Maui, *123*
   Virtually Hawaii home page, *122*
HEAD command
   CERN HTTP servers, 226
   HTTP, 88
   Web servers, 174–175
<head> tag, HTML reference, 749
headers
   HTML, 312–314
   parsed and non-parsed in CGI scripts,
    529–531
heading elements, HTML, 318–319

(continued)

J

(continued)

T

(continued)

(continued)

X

Y

YAHOO! index, 131–133, 480–482
  Add URL link, *497*
  home page, *132*
  list of ISPs (Internet Service Providers), *172*
  results page, *133*
  Web site promotions, 497–498

Z

zcat command, unpacking Apache HTTP
      servers, 208

IDG BOOKS WORLDWIDE, INC.
END-USER LICENSE AGREEMENT

<u>Read This</u>.You should carefully read these terms and conditions before opening the software packet(s) included with this book ("Book"). This is a license agreement ("Agreement") between you and IDG Books Worldwide, Inc. ("IDGB"). By opening the accompanying software packet(s), you acknowledge that you have read and accept the following terms and conditions. If you do not agree and do not want to be bound by such terms and conditions, promptly return the Book and the unopened software packet(s) to the place you obtained them for a full refund.

1. <u>License Grant</u>. IDGB grants to you (either an individual or entity) a nonexclusive license to use one copy of the enclosed software program(s) (collectively, the "Software") solely for your own personal or business purposes on a single computer (whether a standard computer or a workstation component of a multiuser network). The Software is in use on a computer when it is loaded into temporary memory (i.e., RAM) or installed into permanent memory (e.g., hard disk, CD-ROM or other storage device). IDGB reserves all rights not expressly granted herein.

2. <u>Ownership</u>. IDGB is the owner of all rights, titles, and interests, including copyright, in and to the compilation of the Software recorded on the CD-ROM. Copyright to the individual programs on the CD-ROM is owned by the author or other authorized copyright owner of each program. Ownership of the Software and all proprietary rights relating thereto remain with IDGB and its licensors.

3. <u>Restrictions on Use and Transfer</u>.

    (a) You may only (i) make one copy of the Software for backup or archival purposes, or (ii) transfer the Software to a single hard disk, provided that you keep the original for backup or archival purposes. You may not (i) rent or lease the Software, (ii) copy or reproduce the Software through a LAN or other network system or through any computer subscriber system or bulletin-board system, or (iii) modify, adapt, or create derivative works based on the Software.

    (b) You may not reverse engineer, decompile, or disassemble the Software. You may transfer the Software and user documentation on a permanent basis, provided that the transferee agrees to accept the terms and conditions of this Agreement and you retain no copies. If the Software is an update or has been updated, any transfer must include the most recent update and all prior versions.

4. <u>Restrictions on Use of Individual Programs</u>. You must follow the individual requirements and restrictions detailed for each individual program in Appendix A of this Book. These limitations are contained in the individual license agreements recorded on the CD-ROM. These restrictions include a requirement that after using the program for the period of time specified in its text, the user must pay a registration fee or discontinue use. By opening the Software packet(s), you will be agreeing to abide by the licenses and restrictions for these individual programs. None of the material on this CD-ROM or listed in this Book may ever be distributed, in original or modified form, for commercial purposes.

5. Limited Warranty.

(a) IDGB warrants that the Software and CD-ROM are free from defects in materials and workmanship under normal use for a period of sixty (60) days from the date of purchase of this Book. If IDGB receives notification within the warranty period of defects in materials or workmanship, IDGB will replace the defective CD-ROM.

(b) IDGB AND THE AUTHOR OF THE BOOK DISCLAIM ALL OTHER WARRANTIES, EXPRESS OR IMPLIED, INCLUDING WITHOUT LIMITATION IMPLIED WARRANTIES OF MERCHANTABILITY AND FITNESS FOR A PARTICULAR PURPOSE, WITH RESPECT TO THE SOFTWARE, THE PROGRAMS, THE SOURCE CODE CONTAINED THEREIN, AND/OR THE TECHNIQUES DESCRIBED IN THIS BOOK. IDGB DOES NOT WARRANT THAT THE FUNCTIONS CONTAINED IN THE SOFTWARE WILL MEET YOUR REQUIREMENTS OR THAT THE OPERATION OF THE SOFTWARE WILL BE ERROR FREE.

(c) This limited warranty gives you specific legal rights, and you may have other rights that vary from jurisdiction to jurisdiction.

6. Remedies.

(a) IDGB's entire liability and your exclusive remedy for defects in materials and workmanship shall be limited to replacement of the Software, which is returned to IDGB at the address set forth below with a copy of your receipt. This Limited Warranty is void if failure of the Software has resulted from accident, abuse, or misapplication. Any replacement Software will be warranted for the remainder of the original warranty period or thirty (30) days, whichever is longer.

(b) In no event shall IDGB or the author be liable for any damages whatsoever (including without limitation damages for loss of business profits, business interruption, loss of business information, or any other pecuniary loss) arising out of the use of or inability to use the Book or the Software, even if IDGB has been advised of the possibility of such damages.

(c) Because some jurisdictions do not allow the exclusion or limitation of liability for consequential or incidental damages, the above limitation or exclusion may not apply to you.

7. U.S. Government Restricted Rights.
Use, duplication, or disclosure of the Software by the U.S. Government is subject to restrictions stated in paragraph (c) (1) (ii) of the Rights in Technical Data and Computer Software clause of DFARS 252.227-7013, and in subparagraphs (a) through (d) of the Commercial Computer—Restricted Rights clause at FAR 52.227-19, and in similar clauses in the NASA FAR supplement, when applicable.

8. General.
This Agreement constitutes the entire understanding of the parties, and revokes and supersedes all prior agreements, oral or written, between them and may not be modified or amended except in a writing signed by both parties hereto which specifically refers to this Agreement. This Agreement shall take precedence over any other documents that may be in conflict herewith. If any one or more provisions contained in this Agreement are held by any court or tribunal to be invalid, illegal or otherwise unenforceable, each and every other provision shall remain in full force and effect.

that Linux needs until you get the hard disk formatted and ready for Linux. You must select a boot floppy that supports the CD-ROM drive on your PC because you are going to install Linux from the CD-ROM that accompanies this book. The CD_inst.txt file on the CD-ROM provides instructions for making boot and root disks and installing Linux. Also, the CD-ROM comes with the view.exe program that allows a "floppyless" installation — just run the view program under MS-DOS and follow the instructions.

4. Boot with the Linux boot floppy. When Linux asks for it, insert the root floppy. This procedure gives you a minimal Linux system that you can use to further prepare the system and install the rest of the files from the companion CD-ROM.

5. Prepare the hard disk partitions where you plan to install Linux. Typically, you need at least two partitions: one for the Linux files and the other for use as the *swap partition*, which is a form of virtual memory. You have to run the Linux fdisk program to partition the hard disk. See the LIGS guide for a complete explanation of the hows and whys of partitioning.

6. Type setup to start the Slackware Linux setup program. From this setup program, you format the hard disk partitions, indicate where Slackware Linux is located (in the CD-ROM drive), and specify where to install Linux (usually, on a hard disk partition). You also select various *disk sets* (so called because Linux used to be distributed on sets of floppy disks). Each disk set represents a part of Linux, from the base operating system to components such as the emacs editor, programming tools, the Tcl/Tk scripting language, and the X Window System. As the setup program installs the disk sets, it may ask you to confirm your choices or make further selections within a disk set.

7. After the disk sets are installed, the setup program takes you through a configuration process. You get a chance to create a new boot floppy in this step. You also configure your network, modem, and mouse.

8. Use the boot floppy (created during installation) to reboot your PC. You will be able to log in with the user name root, with no password.

9. Run the xf86config program to configure XFree86, the X Window System server for Linux.

10. If you find that Linux does not work properly with one or more of your system components (such as the CD-ROM drive or sound card), you may have to reconfigure the Linux operating system to add support for those system components. This step requires you to compile the Linux operating system (which comes with complete source code on the companion CD-ROM).

CD-ROM Installation Instructions

You can read the contents of this CD-ROM from any MS-DOS, Windows 95, or UNIX system capable of accessing a CD-ROM. To learn more about the CD-ROM contents, read Appendix A.

If you do not have a UNIX system, you can install a complete copy of Slackware Linux 3.1.0 with the Linux 2.0 kernel from the CD-ROM. (Your PC must have a CD-ROM drive — one that is supported by Linux — to install Linux from this book's companion CD-ROM.)

The companion CD-ROM's LIGS directory contains three versions (HTML, PostScript, and plain text) of the book *Linux Installation and Getting Started* (LIGS) by Matt Welsh. Most of the instructions provided also apply to the version of Slackware on the CD-ROM. You can access the HTML version of LIGS by running a Web browser that allows you to open an HTML file from your system's disk. Open the file named GS.HTML located in the INSTALL-GUIDE-2.2 subdirectory of the CD-ROM's LIGS directory (note that the directory and file names appear in lowercase on UNIX systems). Browse the GS.HTML file and follow the links to access various parts of *Linux Installation and Getting Started.*

In addition to the information in LIGS, you can use the following general procedure to completely install and configure Linux and the X Window System, which is the graphical user interface (GUI) for Linux. Follow these steps:

1. Gather information about your PC's hardware before you install Linux. Linux accesses and uses various PC peripherals through software components called *drivers*. You have to make sure that the version of Linux that you are about to install has the necessary drivers for your system's hardware configuration. If you do not have a system yet, look at the list of hardware supported by Linux and buy a PC with components that Linux supports.

2. You may have to perform a process known as *partitioning* to allocate parts of your hard disk for use by Linux. If you are lucky enough to have a spare hard disk, you may decide to keep MS-DOS and Windows on the first hard disk and install Linux on the second hard disk. If you have only one hard disk, however, you may want to partition that disk into several parts. Use a part for DOS and Windows, and leave the rest for Linux. Note that partitioning the hard disk destroys all data on the disk. Back up your hard disk before partitioning it. (FIPS, provided on the CD-ROM and covered in the LIGS guide, allows you to non-destructively partition hard disks.)

3. Under DOS or Windows, create two floppy disks: the *Linux boot floppy* (or just *boot floppy*) and the *root floppy*. The boot floppy is used to boot your PC and start an initial version of the Linux operating system. The root floppy is the initial "disk" that contains some useful Linux files that you need to get the system ready for Linux. Basically, the root floppy provides the initial file system